THE GERMAN
FALLSCHIRMTRUPPE 1936-41

ITS GENESIS AND EMPLOYMENT IN THE FIRST CAMPAIGNS OF THE *WEHRMACHT*

Karl-Heinz Golla

Translated by the author
Edited by Duncan Rogers

Helion & Company Ltd

Published in cooperation with the Association of the United States Army

Helion & Company Limited
26 Willow Road
Solihull
West Midlands
B91 1UE
England
Tel. 0121 705 3393
Fax 0121 711 4075
Email: info@helion.co.uk
Website: www.helion.co.uk

Published by Helion & Company 2012, in cooperation with the Association of the United
States Army

Designed and typeset by Farr out Publications, Wokingham, Berkshire
Cover designed by Euan Carter, Leicester
Printed by Gutenberg Press Limited, Tarxien, Malta

Text and maps © Karl-Heinz Golla, 2012
Photographs © Archiv des Bundes Deutscher Fallschirmjäger, Bundesarchiv, A.M.A.
Goossens, Database Collection Australian War Memorial, Ernst Mößinger, *Brigadegeneral*
(ret.) Hans Teusen
Front cover image: *Fallschirmtruppe* on Crete, 1941. (Bundesarchiv, Bild 101I-166-0509-
36, photo: Franz Peter Weixler)
Rear cover image: *Fallschirmtruppe* and *Gebirgsjäger* stand before the burial place of a
group of their comrades, Crete, 1941. (Bundesarchiv, Bild 141-0848)

ISBN 978 1 908916 52 5

British Library Cataloguing-in-Publication Data.
A catalogue record for this book is available from the British Library.

For details of other military history titles published by Helion & Company Limited
contact the above address, or visit our website: http://www.helion.co.uk.

We always welcome receiving book proposals from prospective authors.

Contents

List of Photographs

around Modhion, from where the New Zealand artillery fired on the airfield at Maleme. (Courtesy of the Archiv des Bundes Deutscher Fallschirmjäger)

Crete 1941   View from the eastern slope of Hill 107 along the coastal strip toward the east. The built-up area in front is Pirgos. There, the remnants of the *5.* and *6.Kompanien* of *FschJgRgt.2* and of parts of *FschSanAbt.7* held out until relief, after they had been dropped as reinforcements to *Gruppe West* on 21 May. The unsuccessful counterattack of the New Zealand 5th Brigade was launched along the coastal strip on 22 May, the advance of *Gruppe Ramcke* commencing along it on 23 May. (Courtesy of the Archiv des Bundes Deutscher Fallschirmjäger)

Crete 1941   View of Cemetery Hill, located just south of Galatas, from the south. On 20 May it was defended by soldiers of the Greek 6th Regiment. The *Fallschirmtruppe* of *9.Kompanie* of *III./FschJgRgt.3* came down immediately in front of the hill. They launched their assault with the weapons they had carried on the jump, and despite suffering heavy losses, succeeded in seizing the hill and capturing more than a hundred of their opponents. In the afternoon, however, they were forced to give up their gains and to withdraw to the forward slope of the hill. (Photo courtesy of the author)

Crete 1941   View from Cemetery Hill just south of Galatas into the valley, which stretches to the south-west, to Alikianou. The regimental staff and the 1st and 2nd battalions of *FschJgRgt.3* were dropped around the prison, which can be seen in the center. Further to the rear runs a spur, where *FschPiBtl.7* landed as flank protection. The slopes to the left rear were occupied by the Greek 6th Regiment. (Courtesy of the Archiv des Bundes Deutscher Fallschirmjäger)

Crete 1941   View from the high ground just south-east of Galatas looking north-east, to where the Greek 6th Regiment occupied positions on 20 May. In the center, on the left side, is Karatsos. The slope further to the left formed part of the defensive positions of the New Zealand 19th Infantry Battalion. Behind this slope and further in the background are the suburbs of Chania, with the Akrotiri Peninsula rising behind them. In the background on the right is Perivolia. The terrain rises steeply in direction toward the White Mountains. After the area around Galatas had been cleared from its defenders, *FschJgRgt.3* advanced in the low ground toward Chania, with *GebJgRgt.100* on its left and *GebJgRgt.141* on its right. (Courtesy of the Archiv des Bundes Deutscher Fallschirmjäger)

Crete 1941   Typical terrain on the Akrotiri peninsula. A number of *Fallschirmtruppe* from *Sturmgruppe Altmann* were seriously injured when their gliders crashed into the rocks. Widely dispersed after the landing, the force was overcome by the Northumberland Hussars of CREFORCE, who were positioned on Akrotiri. (Courtesy of the Archiv des Bundes Deutscher Fallschirmjäger)

Crete 1941   View from the south-western tip of the Akrotiri Peninsula across the western end of Souda Bay. The bright green in the center is

Black and white photos

List of Maps

All appear in color section

Introduction and Acknowledgements

In early summer 2004 I was given the opportunity to write down the still outstanding first part of the history of the parachute force of the *Wehrmacht*. The offer came from the former director of the Office for Military Historical Research (MGFA) and *spiritus rector* for historical work about the German parachute troops in the Second World War, brigade-general Dr. Guenter Roth, in concert with the presidency of the Association of German Parachutists (BDF).

As I had started my military career in the parachute infantry and had remained a member of this "Band of Brothers" I found this offer a great honour. On the other hand, I was well aware of the tremendous workload ahead. I wanted this work to be different to the already existing German literature about the parachute force in the Second World War, much of which had been produced either for reasons of propaganda during the war or, in the years after, with the goal of providing the reader with 'the thrill of combat'. Fortunately, parachute soldiers of all ranks and arms had written down their experiences and impressions during and right after the war in many ways, so that incomplete official documentation occasionally could be supplemented with these personal memories. In a few cases, these memoirs helped rectify mistakes or omissions in official sources.

The official histories of the Second World War have proven very helpful. These were mostly published shortly after the war, and provide almost contemporary historical information from all combatant countries. The Internet also turned out to be an indispensable source of subject-related information, as institutions, concerned with military history, historians and military experts have commenced to use this device as an adjunct to more traditional research tools.

Another method of information gathering consisted of interviews and conversations with veterans of the parachute force of the *Wehrmacht*. Unfortunately the number of men who were able to pass on their memories to me had sadly become depleted by the time work on the book commenced, as most of the 'old eagles' had left us for good.

Thorough evaluation and cross-examination of these sources has allowed me to produce a manuscript which has met the demands of a military historical work. Maps, photographs and explanatory appendices supplement the text. In Spring 2006 the book was published in Germany. The positive reaction by its readers indicated that it had met its purpose. Quite unexpectedly for me, the publication of the book also triggered a renewed flow of sources, some of them of a corrective nature, others supplementary. Almost all of them related to those parts about Norway, Belgium and Holland for which I had sometimes been forced to rely on scarce and unsubstantiated sources. As the newly obtained material was of considerable weight, I decided to completely rewrite those parts for a second edition of the book, in order to bring them up to the quality standards of say, those parts dealing with the operations in Crete. Unfortunately, however, the German publisher, for commercial reasons, was unable to produce the desired second edition of this book.

As a stroke of luck, however, Roger Cirillo, Director of the Book Program of the Association of the U.S. Army (AUSA), well known to me from our times as officers in HQ CENTAG, became interested in the publication of my book for English-speaking readers. As, in the meantime, the German publisher had returned the rights of the book to me, Roger and I agreed on the publication of its intended second edition in the English language under the auspices of AUSA and Helion. I have mentioned all of the people, who generously and professionally supported me in the initial work in the foreword to the first (German) edition of that volume. However, I also wish to express my gratitude to those persons who have had an essential part in the genesis of this revised and expanded version:

Herr Guenter Schalich, a respected member of the Union of Interests in Fortifications of Both World Wars (IBA), who supported me with his profound knowledge about the events around Fort Eben-Emael and the bridges across the Albert Canal in its vicinity that enabled me to correct and supplement the previous account about assault-detachment Koch.

Brigade-General (ret.) Hans Teusen, who advised me firsthand about his combat experience as a lieutenant in the missions for "Fortress Holland", and the Corinth canal, and who provided me with instructive aerial photos about the airborne assault against the latter.

Colonel (ret.) Steffen Rhode, head of the research-service of the BDF, found some officially missing after-action reports regarding parachute infantry battalion Walther and its employment against "Fortress Holland", so that gaps from the first edition could be revised.

Herr Sven Jordan generously sent me the after-action report of another parachute infantry battalion and its employment in Holland, which had been regarded as lost.

Herr Ernst H. Simon, a veteran of the parachute force from 1940 to 1945 and after the war renowned and honoured as "the technical brain of Lufthansa", to whom I owe valuable insights about the training and equipment of parachute units, and an additional report about the fighting at Heraklion/Crete.

Herr Alexander Uhlig, a former non-commissioned officer in the parachute force from its very beginning and holder of the Knight's Cross, who not only provided me with his after-action report about the employment of his platoon near Dombås, but made me aware of some mistakes in other reports about the employment of parachute troops in Norway.

Herr Rudolf Mueller, a veteran of the fighting on Crete and former archivist of the BDF, who, has actively supported the search for documents about the parachute force in the military historical archive at Freiburg and has found answers to specific, detailed questions.

Herr Albert M.A. Goossens, who, as the leading Dutch expert about military events in Holland in May 1940, during a most fruitful dialogue over many years, has shared with me his professional knowledge, and the results of his meticulous researches in this field, and has granted me the use of numerous subject related photographs from his collection for my book. His generous and never-ending support has enabled me, to shape the part about the employment of the German parachute force in the battle for "Fortress Holland" to become probably the best military historical account of this kind in the existing literature.

Concluding, I should like to express my hope that, besides my aim to provide the best possible historical truth about the parachute force of the *Wehrmacht* from its creation to the period after the battle for Crete, I have also succeeded in raising the esteem for its men, which even their former adversaries have never denied them.

"... that, even when bad policy leads to crimes and suppression, the esteem that the brave extend to each other, is part of the ethical heritage of mankind." General de Gaulle, addressing the German people in 1962.

Glossary and List of Abbreviations

Abt	*Abteilung*	detachment/battalion
AMES		Air Ministry Experimental Station
Art	*Artillerie*	artillery
	Assistentarzt	lieutenant (medical service)
Aufkl	*Aufklärung*	reconnaissance
	Aufklärungsstaffel	reconnaissance squadron
Ausb.	*Ausbildung*	training
BA-MA	*Bundesarchiv-Militärarchiv*	Federal Archives (Military Archives)
Btl	*Bataillon*	battalion
DDF	*Der Deutsche Fallschirmjäger*	
DGT	*Die Grünen Teufel*	The Green Devils
DIM	Division d'Infanterie Motorisée	Motorized Infantry Division
Div	*Division*	division
DLM	Division Légère Motorisée	Light Motorized Division
	Eichenlaub	oak leaves
Fl.Div.	*Flieger Division*	aviation division
Fla/Flak	*Flugabwehr*	anti-aircraft
Fsch	*Fallschirm*	parachute
FschArtAbt	*Fallschirm-Artillerie-Abteilung*	parachute artillery battalion
FschFlaMGBtl	*Fallschirm-Flugabwehr-Maschinengewehr-Bataillon*	parachute anti-aircraft machine-gun battalion
FschJgErgäzungs-Btl	*Fallschirmjäger-Ergänzungs-Bataillon*	parachute replacement battalion
FschGeschBattr	*Fallschirm-Geschütz-Batterie*	parachute gun battery
Fsch NachrKp	*Fallschirm-Nachrichten-Kompanie*	parachute signals company
FschPiBtl	*Fallschirm-Pionier-Bataillon*	parachute engineer battalion
FschPzAbwKp	*Fallschirm-Panzer-Abwehr-Kompanie*	parachute anti-tank company
FschPzJgAbt	*Fallschirm-Panzerjäger-Abteilung*	parachute tank hunter battalion
FschPzJgKp	*Fallschirm-Panzerjäger-Kompanie*	parachute tank hunter company
FschSanAbt	*Fallschirm-Sanitäts-Abteilung*	parachute medical battalion
FschSanKp	*Fallschirm-Sanitäts-Kompanie*	parachute medical company
	Fallschirm-Artillerie Versuchskommando	parachute artillery test command
	Feldwebel	staff sergeant or technical sergeant
Geb	*Gebirgs*	mountain
Gefr	*Gefreiter*	private first class (US); lance-corporal (British)
	General der Artillery	general of artillery
	General der Flieger	general of aviation
	General der Infanterie	general of infantry
GenLt	*Generalleutnant*	lieutenant-general
	Generalquartiermeister	quartermaster-general

19

Gesch	Geschütz	gun
Geschw	Geschwader	wing (e.g. fighter wing)
GRCA	Groupe de Reconnaissance de Corps d'Armée	Corps-level Reconnaissance Group
GRDI	Groupe de Reconnaissance de Division d'Infanterie	Infantry Division Reconnaissance Group
GrWf	Granatwerfer	mortar
	Heer	German Army
HGr	Heeresgruppe	army group
Hptm.	Hauptmann	captain
Ia	1.Generalstabsoffizier	first staff officer
i.G.	im Generalstab	general staff officer
Inf.Rgt.	Infanterie-Regiment	infantry regiment
Jg	Jäger	light infantry
JG	Jagdgeschwader	fighter wing
KG	Kampfgeschwader	bomber wing
KGr z.b.V.	Kampfgruppe zur besonderen Verwendung	special-purpose battle group
KIA		killed in action
Kp	Kompanie	company
Krad	Kraftrad	motorcycle
KradSchtzZug	Kradschützenzug	motorcycle rifle section
	Kräftegruppe	task force
KTB	Kriegstagebuch	war diary
	Landespolizei	State Police
	Lastensegler-Kommando	glider command
LAA		Light Anti-Aircraft
LG	Lehrgeschwader	training/instruction wing
LAH	Leibstandarte Adolf Hitler	
	leichte Seetransportstaffel	light sea transport squadron
LL	Luftlande	air-landing
	Luftflotte	air fleet
LuftTrspStaffel	Lufttransportstaffel	air transport squadron
LnAbt	Luftnachrichten-Abteilung	Luftwaffe signals battalion
LNRgt	Luftnachrichten-Regiment	Luftwaffe signals regiment
MG	Maschinengewehr	machinegun
M.N.B.D.O.		Mobile Naval Base Defence Organization
Nachr	Nachrichten	signals
NSDAP	Nationalsozialistische Deutsche Arbeiterpartei	National Socialist Workers' Party (Nazi Party)
	Oberarzt	first lieutenant of the medical service
Ob.d.H.	Oberbefehlshaber des Heeres	commander-in-chief of the army
Ob.d.L.	Oberbefehlshaber des Luftwaffe	commander-in-chief of the air force
	Oberfeldwebel	master sergeant
	Oberjäger	corporal
Oblt.	Oberleutnant	first lieutenant

	Oberfeldarzt	lieutenant colonel of the medical service
OFW	*Oberfeldwebel*	master sergeant (US); sergeant-major (British)
OKH	*Oberkommando des Heeres*	Army High Command
OKL	*Oberkommando der Luftwaffe*	*Luftwaffe* High Command
OKW	*Oberkommando der Wehrmacht*	*Wehrmacht* High Command
	Oberst	colonel
	Oberstarzt	colonel of the medical service
OstArzt	*Oberstabsarzt*	major of the medical service
	Oberstleutnant	lieutenant-colonel
Pi	*Pionier*	engineer
PVK	*Panzerabwehr-Versuchskompanie*	anti-tank experimental company
Pz	*Panzer*	armor/tank
PzAbw	*Panzerabwehr*	anti-tank
PzJg	*Panzerjaeger*	tank hunter
R.A.F.		British Royal Air Force
RC	Régiment de Cuirassiers	Cuirassier Regiment
RDP	Régiment de Dragons Portés	Mechanized Dragoon [Cavalry] Regiment
Rgt	*Regiment*	regiment
	Regimentsarzt	regimental medical officer
RHM	*Regiment Huzaren Motorrijder*	Regiment of Hussars (Dutch)
	Ritterkreuz	Knight's Cross
	Rittmeister	captain (German cavalry)
San	*Sanitäts*	medical
San.Kp.	*Sanitäts-Kompanie*	medical company
Schtz	*Schütze*	rifleman/private
	Schwerte	swords
	Staffel	squadron
StG	*Sturzkampfgeschwader*	dive-bomber wing
	Truppenarzt	captain of the medical service
	Unterarzt	lieutenant of the medical service
WFSt	*Wehrmachtsführungsstab*	*Wehrmacht* Command Directorate
WIA		wounded in action
ZG	*Zerstörer-Geschwader*	heavy fighter wing

A note on unit designations

German unit designations appear in italics. Battalions or *Abteilungen* are designated with a Roman numeral, thus *II./FschJgRgt.3* is the 2nd Battalion of 3rd *Fallschirmjäger* Regiment. Companies or batteries are designated with an Arabic numeral, thus *3./FschJgRgt.3* is the 3rd Company of 3rd *Fallschirmjäger* Regiment. Within *Luftwaffe* aviation units, a Roman numeral denotes a *Gruppe*, thus *I./StG 2* is the 1st *Gruppe* of *Sturzkampfgeschwader 2*. An Arabic numeral denotes a *Staffel* or squadron, thus *3./JG 77* would be the 3rd Squadron of *Jagdgeschwader 77*.

Western Allied units (Dutch, Belgian etc) are not italicised. As with German units, battalions are designated by a Roman numeral prefix, thus III/12th Inf.Rgt. is the 3rd Battalion of the 12th Infantry Regiment (Dutch in this case).

Part I

The Genesis of the German
Fallschirmtruppe 1936–39

1

The use of the parachute for military means enters German strategic thinking

Progress in science and technology has always led soldiers to increase the efficiency of the armed forces of their countries to best accomplish their assigned tasks. This stands true for the employment of troops from the air.

In the course of the First World War the aircraft became the most important air vehicle available, its utilization reaching a scope hitherto unimaginable. The problem of reducing the growing losses among valuable pilots, from the ever increasing numbers of combat aircraft, together with the continuous improvement of weapons available to fight in the air and ground led to use of the parachute technology then available to save aircrew lives.

In 1495 Leonardo da Vinci had theoretically laid down the principle of the parachute. The idea had been picked up primarily by Joseph Montgolfier, who in 1797, convinced of the efficiency of his parachute, had jumped with it from the roof of his house and landed safely. The hot air balloon, which he had invented in 1783, had allowed for parachute-jumps from this type of platform. On 21 November 1785 Frenchman Jean Pierre Blanchard was saved by his self-constructed parachute, when his balloon was damaged in mid-air – probably the first person to be so saved. Problems, however, remained, as the strong swinging of parachutes with a round canopy allowed the air inside to exit only from its edges. This risk was lessened by Frenchman André Jacques Gamerin, who left a hole at the apex of the canopy. It had, however, still taken many calculations and trials well into the 20th Century, until a really satisfying solution for the stabilization of the parachute on its descent was found.

Around the end of 19th Century, parachute jumping had developed as an entertainment for the public, in which women also took part. After her first jump from a balloon in 1890, German Käthe Paulus had made parachuting widely known with daring actions during shows, such as, for example, with an intentional breakaway from a height of 1,200m, during which the first parachute was released and a second parachute was opened. Of more significance, however, was her idea to pack the parachute into a canvas bag, from which initially the suspension lines and then the canopy were pulled out. In the U.S.A, the first jumps from an aircraft had been conducted in 1911 or 1912, by Grant Morton or Captain Albert Berry. On 28 April 1914, the American Leslie L. Irvin had added another milestone to the history of parachuting, opening his parachute manually during a jump from a 500m height. Among many other things, Charles Lindbergh is known for the fact that he probably owed his life four times to manually released parachutes. In Germany in 1930, Richard Kohnke, who is still called the "father of German parachuting" conducted a free fall of 142 seconds after he jumped from a height of 7.800 meters.

By 1916, during the First World War, the German military command became seriously interested in the parachute due to losses amongst crews of captive observation balloons, and even more so, amongst the losses of valuable pilots of aircraft that had increased dramatically. From 1917 onward all German front-line pilots had been equipped with an automatically unfolding parachute as an air-rescue device.[1] In April 1917, parachutes had saved the lives of about twenty German observers after their balloons had been shot down over the front at Verdun. For the pilots of aircraft, the invention of the ripcord by Otto Heinecke had turned out to be particularly useful, as it prevented the parachute from becoming entangled with the aircraft during the opening-process. Heinecke had also constructed a harness, by which the parachute had to be fastened to the body of the pilot, thus enabling him to move his arms and legs unhindered during the descent and landing. Parachuting from unmanageable aircraft, however, had remained an exception during the First World War, as these pilots had often been hit in their lightly built aircraft, or whilst endeavoring to land them.

None of the warring parties of the First World War seriously attempted to make use of the parachute for dropping troops, despite the fact that this matter had intellectually been approached already in the 19th Century, for example by Benjamin Franklin. Only the U.S. Brigadier General William Mitchell,[2] who was tasked with the employment of almost 1,500 Allied aircraft during the pursuit of *Heeresgruppe* Gallwitz during its retreat from the area around St. Mihiel in September 1918 by the 1st U.S. Army, had picked up the subject. He had proposed to drop by parachute soldiers of the 1st U.S. Infantry Division behind the German-held fortress of Metz, thereby to conquer it in conjunction with a frontal thrust on the ground. However, as the end of the war was near, Mitchell's proposal had not been further discussed by the Allied high command.[3]

In the years after the end of the First World War, the victorious powers had neither conceptually, nor by planning, spent much thought on the employment of troops from the air. In the military environment of France, the main effort was directed toward the future protection of the country by defensive measures such as the Maginot Line. Military attention in Great Britain had turned toward securing her oversea possessions. Only in Italy did the armed forces commence with the creation of parachute troops during the 1920s, albeit on a modest level. [4]

In the United States, Mitchell's ideas had not totally been forgotten. Probably initiated by him, in 1928 a non-commissioned officer and ten other ranks had conducted the first mass jump from a transport aircraft. The immediate conversion of this successful action into military organizational measures, however, had not happened. As a sport, parachuting meanwhile had found many enthusiasts in the U.S.A.

---

1   The crews of dirigibles did not receive parachutes.

2   William Mitchell, 1879-1936. After his training as a pilot in 1916, he took over the aviation department in the U.S. Army. In 1917 he commenced in France with the organization and training of the U.S. Army Air Force. After the First World War, he remained involved in the organizational matters of this force. While demonstrating the efficiency of bombers particularly against warships, he became opposed to the views of the command of the U.S. Navy, and finally left the service. Today, he is regarded as one of the fathers of the U.S. Air Force.

3   For the deliberations of Mitchell in 1918 see http://homeusers.brutele.be/sgteagle/welcometothe alliedairborneheadquarters_usairborne.htm

4   The first jump of a stick of eleven Italian paratroopers had taken place on 6 November 1927. The leading Italian advocate for airborne operations, General Guitoni, was killed in a parachute jump in 1928. Nevertheless, at the outbreak of the Second World War, the Italian military forces had, after many trials, established a parachute unit of regiment strength.

In the Soviet Union, the creation of airborne troops was pursued to an ever-increasing extent from the end of the 1920s. In 1925 Stalin, at least to the outer world, had replaced Lenin's theories of 'world revolution' with his thesis of the co-existence of the social classes, and thereby had reduced the widely existing fear in the West about the spreading of socialism/communism with the support of the Red Army. However, as the latter, steered by the ideas of Tukhachevsky and Triandafillov,[5] had commenced to make deep penetration operations the doctrine for war, and adjusted its organization and equipment respectively, the employment of troops from the air had gained serious attention. Until the mid 1930s, hundreds of thousands of parachute-sportsmen had emerged from the stately institutions for paramilitary training.[6] In the Red Army the first parachute rigade was established in 1932. In impressive numbers parachute soldiers had jumped in entire plane loads during air shows in Moscow in 1933 and 1934. During maneuvres near Kiev in summer 1935, more than a thousand soldiers had been dropped by parachute, followed by an air-landing of about 2,500 troops and heavy weapons. After the tremendous blood-letting of the officer-corps of the Red Army during its 'cleansing', directed by Stalin in 1937, in which Tukhachevsky had become a victim, the further development of the parachute and air-landing forces ended, in conjunction with the renunciation of the deep penetration operations doctrine. Even already existing organizations partially had been disbanded.[7]

The Treaty of Versailles prohibited the German armed forces from acquiring and using modern war material. In spite of lacking essential material prerequisites, General Hans von Seeckt, in his function as the chief of the Army Office [*Truppenamt*], and then as the Chief of the Army Directorate [*Heeresleitung*], had orientated the principles of command and control as well as the training of the *Reichswehr* toward mobile warfare. Additionally, he had created the conditions for a later rapid increase of the German armed forces to numerically many times the size of the *Reichswehr*, including an air force. In order to circumvent the political restrictions on the *Reichswehr*, during the formation of the Soviet Union he had established contacts with the Red Army, aiming to set up with its support, testing and training facilities for a later German armor and air arm, and for chemical warfare testing in the Soviet Union.[8] Thinking ahead, he had also integrated a high proportion of former pilots into the relatively small officer corps of the *Reichswehr* masking it as a department for protection against air attacks, by establishing technical and tactical aviation offices in the *Truppenamt*. The sport of gliding, which had not been restricted by the Versailles treaty, was particularly strongly promoted by the *Reichswehr* ministry, as it was regarded as an elementary step toward the training of future military pilots. The withdrawal of the military

---

5   For the work of Tukhachevsky and Triandafillov and the doctrine of deep penetration operations see Simpkin, pp.37-39 and House, pp.65-66.

6   In 1936, there had been 559 towers for parachuting, and 115 parachute schools in the Soviet Union. During that year civilians completed nearly 1,600,000 jumps from towers, and about 30,000 from aircraft. See Thompson.

7   The still existing cadres and the rest of the units were employed in the Second World War in the winter 1941/42 and again with three parachute brigades with about 7,000 men in September 1943 at the Dnjepr bend north of Kanev. Badly planned and executed with insufficiently trained and equipped troops, both operations had failed.

8   It is little known that, in contravention of the Versailles treaty, there was an informal exchange of officers of the *Reichswehr* and the U.S. Army for many years after 1922. During this exchange, the former had tried to satisfy its interest in modern weapons, whereas the latter had sought to draw from the combat experience of the Germans. Research by Dr. Michael Wala, Sozialwissenschaftliches Institut of the Friedrich-Alexander-University Erlangen-Nürnberg, 1997.

missions of the victorious powers in 1927, which had supervised the disarmament and the observance of the military restrictions in Germany, had enabled the German authorities to create construction offices and testing-facilities for modern military technology at home.

The Germans had attentively observed the built-up of a parachute and air-landing arm in the Soviet Union. Reports about its development, which the German military *attaché* in Moscow, *Oberst* von Köstring, had sent to the *Truppenamt* from 1932, gained specific importance. The reports had been submitted to the chief of staff of the *Luftwaffe*, *Generalleutnant* Wever, who was assigned to this new position in March 1935. They also arrived on the desk of Göring, who in 1933 had been appointed as minister of aviation, and in March 1935 as commander-in-chief of the *Luftwaffe* [German abbreviation: *Ob.d.L.*]. Staff officers of the *Luftwaffe*, particularly some of its later generals, such as Student, Jeschonnek and Fiebig, had been given the opportunity to observe mass-jumps of Soviet soldiers with their own eyes after Hitler had come to power.

In the creation of the *Luftwaffe* in 1935, Göring had seen his chance to improve his position among the leadership of the National Socialist German Workers' Party [NSDAP]. As commissioner of the Prussian ministry of the interior, Göring had established a personal force within a few weeks of Hitler assuming power in Germany, using the provincial police group Berlin, or *Landespolizeigruppe Berlin*. It was organized as a military unit, and had been equipped with combat support weapons, soon reaching regimental size. After the neutralization of the leadership of the SA in 1934, in which he played a considerable part, he was able to compete with Himmler's SS in the struggle for internal party influence. After the reintroduction of compulsory military service with the national defence law on 21 May 1935, he succeeded in preventing his personal force, which had been renamed in September 1935 *Regiment General Göring*, from being integrated into the *Heer*, like all other provincial police groups, and adding it to his *Luftwaffe*. [9]

---

9   The step was formalized by him, effective 1 October 1935, with the order Der Reichsminister der Luftfahrt und Oberbefehlshaber der *Luftwaffe* L. A. Nr. 5450/35 g. Kdos., L. A. II A, dated 29 October 1935.

2

The formation of the German *Fallschirmtruppe*, their testing, and the search for a conception of their employment

In October 1935, Göring, probably upon a suggestion from *Generalleutnant* Wever, decided to form a parachute battalion and a parachute engineer company from volunteers of *Regiment General Göring*, although no groundwork for its organization, training and employment was yet available. Based on the ideas of *Major i.G.* Kammhuber, *Chef* of the *2.Abteilung (Ausbildung)* of the *Luftwaffe* General Staff, a table of organization and equipment was hastily developed. A field exercise by a battalion of *Regiment General Göring*, which had been put together according to this TOE, and for which a preceding parachute jump was simulated, confirmed the usefulness of Kammhuber's proposed organization. Thereupon, the high command of the *Luftwaffe* [*Oberkommando der Luftwaffe – OKL*], shortly prior to mid-November, issued the order for the re-organization of *Regiment General Göring*. Accordingly, on 18 November 1935, the first battalion of this regiment was transformed into a parachute battalion, and an engineer company, also made up of paratroopers, had to be formed additionally at the regimental level.[1] Both units had to consist exclusively of volunteers from the regiment.

As only very few of its soldiers had ever seen a parachute jump, the entire regiment was given the opportunity, at Jüterbog airfield, to observe the performance of a private who had already jumped once. Although this soldier hurt himself on landing, and had to be taken away in an ambulance, many members of the regiment volunteered for parachute training after the event, resulting in the formation of *I./Fallschirmschützen-Bataillon* and *15.(Pionier-)Kompanie*. *Major* Bräuer[2] was appointed as commander of the battalion. With the order Der Reichsminister der Luftfahrt, und Oberbefehlshaber der *Luftwaffe*, LA.

---

1   This order, which is mentioned in Student's memoirs by Götzel, unfortunately no longer exists. It has, however, to be regarded as the document by which the German parachute force was created. Götzel (p.26) points out that the soldiers of the newly formed battalion were designated as *Fallschirmjäger* for the first time in this order. Officially, however, the designation *Fallschirmschützen* remained valid for quite some time in the *Luftwaffe*.

2   Bruno Bräuer, born 1893. In the First World War non-commissioned officer in the infantry. Promoted to *Leutnant* in 1919. Served in the provincial *Polizeigruppe Berlin*. In October 1936, taken over by the *Luftwaffe* as *Major* and commander of *I./Regiment General Göring*. Thereafter commander of *I./FschJgRgt.1*. From 1 January 1939 on commander of *FschJgRgt 1* as *Oberst*. Commanded this regiment during its service in Holland, Crete and the East 1940-43. *Ritterkreuz* on 25 May 1940. 23 May 1943-1 June 1944 commandant of *Festung Kreta*. Captured by the British on 10 May 1945. Handed over to the Greeks. In a totally biased court-martial he was sentenced to death as a war criminal and was hanged on 20 May 1947. He now rests among his *Fallschirmjäger* in the German war cemetery in Crete.

262/36 g III 1 A, dated 29 January 1936, the following measures in preparation of the training for parachute jumping were directed:

- the forming of a first training cadre of 15 officers and non-commissioned officers after an examination of their qualifications;
- the duration of the parachute training;
- the provision of a transport aircraft of the type Ju 52;
- the designated airfield for jump training.

The instructors, who, beside *Major* Bräuer, included *Hauptmann* Reinberger and Kuhlo, *Oberleutnant* Kroh, *Leutnant* Kieß, Dunz, Rau and Moll as well as 14 non-commissioned officers and one private, were trained for four weeks as parachute cadets and for another four weeks as paratroopers, and thereby constituted the training cadre of *Regiment General Göring*. About the same time *Hauptmann* Immans, who had already gained experience in parachuting in his function as director of the air sport association of the SA, was tasked with the establishment of a training institution for paratroopers, as proposed by *Oberst* Pflugbeil, the inspector of combat aviation. Immans, who had been a combat pilot in the First World War, had let himself and twenty members of his association be trained as paratroopers by the jump-experienced *Polizei-Meister* Diete, from the air police department at Hamburg-Fuhlsbüttel airfield. In complete secrecy, the training command under *Hauptmann* Immans assembled at Stendal-Borstel airfield. At its core it consisted of *Hauptmann* Immans, *Polizei Meister* Diete as technical assistant and dispatcher, *Assistenzarzt* Dr. Greiling as medical attendant, and Dr. Brand as meteorological adviser. The supervision of the command was laid into the hands of *Oberst* Pflugbeil.

With great urgency technical research, development and experimentation took place, using the knowledge and experience of the German Parachute Society in Berlin, the technical office of the Master General of Ordnance [*Generalfeldzeugmeister*], the Ministry for Aviation in Berlin, and the testing office of the *Luftwaffe* at Rechlin (which took over the technical direction for all matters of parachuting and air transport for paratroopers). It was quickly discovered that for jumping from transport aircraft, only an automatically unfolding parachute could be used, as the paratroopers had to be dropped from a low altitude in order to reduce the time they were exposed to defensive fire from the ground during their descent. The solution to this requirement, after trials in the training command, was the RZ 1 parachute, which was developed from the already introduced and proven 27 II S 20 rescue parachute, and which was available at the beginning of jump training. Its canopy of white silk with 28 panels was semicircular, and it had a surface of 56 square meters. The canvas bag on the back of the paratrooper, into which the parachute as a whole was stowed, was fastened to the harness by D-rings. The deployment of the chute was triggered by a static line of 9 meters length, which was fastened by a snap-hook on a through-cable of steel wire in the aircraft. To allow for an unhindered deployment of the parachute, the paratrooper had to leave the aircraft by its door, in a dive with stretched body and arms and legs wide apart. For the jump, the aircraft reduced its speed to about 40 m/sec, in order to allow the paratrooper to maintain his position until the chute had unfolded, which took about 2.3 seconds.

The method of attachment of the parachute at the harness resulted in a position by the paratrooper whereby he was leaning forward during the descent. Because of strong wind buffeting during the descent, the RZ 1 tended to create strong oscillations. Moreover, the speed of the descent was rather high – jumping from 150m above the ground, it took a paratrooper with an average weight about 17 seconds until landing. There, if he succeeded in a forward landing, which was supported by his position on the chute, he had to conduct a neck-roll in order to reduce the impact of the fall. As a consequence rifles, or any other long pieces of equipment, could not be carried by the paratrooper.[3] The forward-leaning position of the paratrooper in conjunction with the rather high speed of impact on the ground, particularly in windy weather, often caused injuries.[4] To prevent these, protective pads for the knees and elbows soon were introduced.

To unstrap the harness after the landing – a chest belt of webbing with a sliding buckle to hold the shoulder straps in position, and a broad waistbelt of webbing on which the leg straps were fastened by snap-hooks in D-rings – took quite some time to complete.[5] As this process could be accomplished only in a kneeling or standing position, the paratrooper was particularly exposed to enemy fire. In the case that strong winds dragged the paratrooper over the ground, unstrapping could only begin after he had succeeded in running around his chute and thereby causing it to collapse.

As rifles and machine-guns could not be attached to the body of the paratrooper for the jump, specific weapon containers were developed. These were rectangular and had a shock absorber fixed on the bottom of their outside. Inside, the long weapons were stored safely to prevent movement. For a regular parachute infantry squad of 12 men, its rifles, two machine-guns, and the ammunition for these weapons, four weapon containers were required. With a parachute attached on each of the containers, they were dropped from shafts in the floor in the Ju 52 by members of the aircrew, either together with the jumping paratroopers, or separately in a new approach of the aircraft over the target area. Once on the ground, the containers could be carried by two men, for which handles were attached to their exterior. The containers had colour markings, and numbers for the sub-units of a company, so that they could find them on the ground.

Containers had also been developed to drop by parachute ammunition, rations, communication equipment, medical instruments and material. These containers could be distinguished, too, by their different colours. On the ground, they could be moved as provisional carts, by attaching a draw-beam and small wheels, which were stored in the interior of each of these containers. Initially, they were provided in three different sizes.

In order to prevent the suspension lines of the parachute from getting entangled with the uniform of the paratrooper or pieces of his equipment during its deployment, specific jump clothing had been created. Officially, it was designated as the paratroop rifleman's blouse, but was soon called by its wearers the 'bone-sack' or *Knochensack*.

Consisting of waterproof cloth, to put it on, the paratrooper first stepped into its legs, which reached down to the middle of the upper thighs. Then he pulled the upper part up, and slipped into the long sleeves. Finally the combination was closed on the chest with a

---

3   Bags for long weapons such as rifles or machine-guns, which were lowered by means of a rope shortly prior to the landing, were introduced only after the airborne attack on Crete.

4   Calculations and trials, directed by the meteorologist Dr. Brand, had demonstrated that at a horizont l wind of 8m/sec the diagonal speed of a landing paratrooper corresponded with an impact on the ground by a jump from 5m height. Dr. Brand's findings are stored under the signature BW 57/26 at the Bundesarchiv Militärarchiv in Freiburg, Germany.

5   The troops had been against the introduction of a central lock, by which the harness could be released with but one press, for reasons of security.

zipper, which was covered by a seam of cloth. Dyed in a green mix, occasionally also in grey-blue,[6] it had a number of pockets, opened and closed by press-studs or zippers, and on its back an integrated holster for a pistol. On the left side of its chest, the national military emblem was placed. From 1939 on specific rank insignia was attached to the upper sleeves – one to four white wings for *Feldwebel* to *Oberfeldwebel*, one to three white wings over a white bar for *Leutnant* to *Hauptmann*, one to three white wings over two white bars, for *Major* to *Oberst*, and gold-colored wings and bars for general officers.[7]

As the M1935 steel helmet which was introduced for the *Wehrmacht* was not suitable for parachuting because of its projecting neck protection and its broad rims at the front and sides, a new way had to be followed for the head protection of the paratrooper. Initially, the M1935 helmet with cut-off rims was used. Soon, however, a rimless helmet was developed. It had neck straps and was padded in its interior. In its specific form unchanged throughout the Second World War, it was to become the most visible outward feature of the German parachute force. At first issued in a shining blue-gray colour, it was soon delivered according to the prevailing terrain in the areas of employment in different dull colours.

Other items of the personal equipment of the soldier also had to be adjusted to the peculiarities of employment from the air. The respirator, for example, had to be packed into a canvas bag with a zipper, as the standard issue cylindrical metal container could cause injuries on landing. To enable the paratrooper to cut suspension lines after a tree landing or when the buckles for unstrapping the harness were jammed, a specific knife was introduced. Its blade was set free by holding its handle downward and pressing a release-lever. As the paratrooper could have to fight for some time without receiving supplies, an ammunition belt was constructed. It was made up of a 10-15cm broad strip of solid cloth, on which 12 pockets, each holding two cartridge clips of five rounds for the 98k rifle, were sewn. Thus a parachute rifleman could carry 120 rounds along for the jump. The belt was carried around the neck and fastened with both ends to the leather waistbelt of the soldier. For the MP38/40 sub-machine-gun, three to six pouches, each for a magazine with 32 rounds, were carried on the waistbelt.

The uniform, worn underneath the jump overalls, normally consisted of the short blue field blouse of the *Luftwaffe*, with customary rank insignia.[8] The trousers, which had been designed specifically for the parachute force, were of green woolen cloth, furnished with many buttoned up pockets, among them one for the knife.

The jump boots, too, were of specific design. They reached up to the middle of the shin and, as with the field footgear of the *Wehrmacht*, had soles of thick rubber. The first models were placed on the side and were in use into 1941. As this lacing had reduced the firm hold of the foot in the boot, which often led to injuries of the ankle, a new model with lacing on the front soon was introduced.

The main personal armament of the paratroopers was initially identical with that of the majority of the *Wehrmacht* – the 98k rifle, the MP 39/40 sub-machine-gun, the

---

6   From 1941 on the combinations were mainly dyed in camouflage colours and were improved in the numbers and sizes of the pockets and the chest clasp.

7   Prior to combat operations, these insignia often were removed.

8   On the transfer of *Regiment General Göring* to the *Luftwaffe*, its commander had succeeded in obtaining the white collar patches of the infantry for his unit. The patches of the soldiers of the parachute battalion additionally had green piping, the recognition colour of the Jäger (light infantry). After the separation of the parachute battalion from *Regiment General Göring* in 1938, its soldiers were issued the yellow collar patches of the *Luftwaffe*.

MG34 machine-gun and the anti-PAB 38/39 tank rifle model. The infantry heavy weapons consisted of mortars (*Granatwerfer – GrWf*) and anti-tank guns (*Panzerabwehr-Kanonen – Pak*). During the course of the war, heavy weapons specific for the employment of troops from the air were constructed and delivered.

During the process of selecting a suitable aircraft for the transport and drop of parachute troops, it turned out to be a stroke of luck that the designer and builder of aircraft, Hugo Junkers, had constructed the Ju 52 with three engines in 1932. Originally thought of as a passenger aircraft, it was designed to keep the Junkers works viable in the competition for the supply of commercial aircraft in the growing long distance air transport market. Characteristic of the Ju 52 was its planking of corrugated iron over a frame entirely of metal, which provided for stability and rigidity during flight, and in conjunction with its three engines made it highly reliable. With a maximum take-off weight of 10,500kg, the civil version was suited to transport a payload of up to 3,900kg. Beside the aircrew of three, it offered seating space for 15 to 17 passengers. For parachuting, 12-14 persons could be taken along. Its maximum speed in the air was 264 km/hour; its touchdown speed was around 100 km/hour. Under favorable flight conditions the range of the Ju 52 in its passenger version was up to 1,200 km. Of advantage for military utilization were the short distances of 340m, required for take-off, and of 245m for landing. The non-retractable undercarriage was solid, and allowed for take-offs and landings from non-hardened surfaces.

The production of the first military series of the aircraft, designated as Ju 52/3m g 3e, had commenced in 1934. It had been construed as a provisional bomber, although the first employment of this model as a military transport occurred during the Spanish Civil War, when 20 aircraft under the command of Lieutenant Colonel von Moreau conveyed about 13,000 of Franco's Nationalist troops, and 270 tons of war material, from Spanish Morocco to Andalusia in August 1936. Used as a bomber the aircraft had less success because of its low speed.

As a means to train and employ German parachute and air-landing troops, the Ju 52 became indispensable from the very beginning of its existence. The adjustment of the aircraft for this purpose, which included the strengthening of its floor for the transport of heavy loads, a more efficient protection for the fuel tanks in its wings, and the installation of a large loading door on its right side, however, had led to a reduction of its range to slightly below 900 km. Additionally, the number of paratroopers, including their weapon and equipment containers, had to be limited to twelve men. In the Ju 52/3m g 3e the containers were dropped from the four bomb doors. In the follow on model 3m g 4e, which was designed solely as a transport aircraft, the containers were dropped from shafts which had been built into the floor.[9] The armament of the Ju 52 comprised two machine-guns of 7.92mm caliber, which were fired from apertures on either side of the aircraft, and occasionally a machine-gun of 13mm caliber, in a revolving plexiglass cupola on the upper rearward part of the fuselage.

The majority of the aircraft of the originally existing Ju 52 bomber units had been organized for use in pilot schools and flight centres after the introduction of genuine bombers. Only *IV.Gruppe* of *Kampfgeschwader 152 Hindenburg* at Fürstenwalde was left over. It was placed directly subordinate to *Höherer Fliegerführer II* [Higher Aviation

9   See Morzik, p.35.

Commander II], for cooperation with the parachute force. Accordingly, the first aircraft of this group had been moved to Stendal-Borstel in May 1936. Thereafter the parachute school had formally opened in March 1936, the course for the instruction team from *I./ Regiment General Göring* under *Major* Bräuer, which had been summoned from Berlin-Charlottenburg, being conducted from 4 May to 3 July. The course was also thought to test the future training programme. This allowed for the paratroopers to acquire the skill of rigging and handling the parachute, to be physically thoroughly trained for the requirements needed during landing, and afterward to conduct five jumps during daylight, and one at night. Two of these were to be executed as solitary jumps, and the other four with a full stick of paratroopers from an aircraft, i.e. normally twelve men, at decreasing altitude.

On 11 May, shortly after the commencement of the training of the instruction team, *Major* Bräuer jumped for the first time from the wing of a sport aircraft, a Klemm KL 25. For all further parachuting, the Ju 52s from Fürstenwalde became available. All members of the instruction team met the objectives of the course. Thus, the planned sequence of training at the parachute school was proven to be suitable.

The successful accomplishment of the training course was to be confirmed by the receipt of the parachute rifleman's certificate or *Fallschirmschützen-Schein*. The first of these certificates bears the name of *Major* Bräuer.[10]

The demands for a future paratrooper were high. Only volunteers were accepted, and a thorough medical examination of the prospective trainee was the first hurdle. Strict rules of selection were also applied throughout training at the parachute school. Discharge from the course, and re-assignment to the volunteer's old unit, took place if the applicant could not cope with the physical and psychological requirements of the training, if a serious weakness of character was detected or if he refused to jump from an aircraft.

From 10 August to 26 September 1936 60 soldiers of various ranks from *I./Regiment General Göring* participated in the first parachute training course. Shortly after the completion of this course, the first mass jump for the eyes of the public took place – on 4 October 1936, 36 soldiers under *Oberleutnant* Kroh, were dropped from three Ju 52s flying aside of one another, during a demonstration of the *Wehrmacht* on the occasion of a harvest festival at the Bückeberg, south of Hamlin.

On 5 November 1936, the parachute rifleman's badge was first presented. With its gold-coloured diving eagle, surrounded by a silver-coloured wreath of oak and laurel leaves, it was to be the visible sign on the uniform of the successful completion of training as a *Fallschirmjäger* of the *Wehrmacht*.[11] From early 1937 onwards the training at the parachute school was conducted to an increased extent in three companies under *Hauptmann* Vogel, and *Leutnants* Becker and Moll. The training procedures, with six jumps at the end of the course, remain unchanged from those developed during the trial period. In addition a testing platoon, under *Leutnant* Schlichting, perfected methods for dropping weapons,

---

10   Student remembered that, in the case of the instruction team and the first parachute course, the certificate was handed out together with the parachute badge (Götzel, p.31). However, this is erroneous. The badge was introduced on 5 November 1936. The certificate for *Major* Bräuer, which exists in its original, shows 4 July 1936 as the date of receipt. It can therefore be assumed that the certificate was always handed out at the successful completion of the parachute course.

11   In a changed design, the diving eagle was also worn for some time by the paratroopers of the German *Bundeswehr*, and up to now has preserved its symbolic meaning for the German parachute force.

and for landing in water. In February 1937, *Major* Bassenge[12], a graduate engineer, took over command of the parachute school. On 1 April, he was promoted to *Oberstleutnant*.

During this time, another element for the employment of troops from the air was added to the tasks of the parachute school. During the early 1930s, trials with a large, wide-spanned glider had been conducted by the German Research Institute for Gliding [*Deutsche Forschungsanstalt für Segelflug* – DFS], at Datmstadt-Griesheim, following a proposal by Udet,[13] who at this time, as an *Oberst*, was the director of the technical department in the German Ministry of Aviation. *Generalleutnant* Kesselring, who had followed *Generalleutnant* Wever as the chief of the general staff of the *Luftwaffe* after the latter's unfortunate death, had decided to test the utility of gliders for the employment of troops from the air. After demonstrations for Udet, and *Oberst* Ritter von Greim[14], at this time the inspector general for aviation safety, the construction of a glider for the transport of a number of soldiers and their equipment was ordered by Udet. This task was accomplished by the engineer Hans Jacob, with the construction of the DFS 230 glider.

The fuselage of the DFS 230 consisted of steel tubes covered with linen, its wings being fabricated from plywood. The pilot was seated behind a removable cockpit, made of plexiglass. Behind him, there was space for nine soldiers and their equipment, sitting closely packed together in a row astride a beam. The armament of the DFS 230 consisted of a 7.92mm machine-gun, which projected from one side of the hull (later from the cockpit). The Ju 52 was to tow the glider.[15] For takeoff behind a towing aircraft, the DFS 230 had wheels attached, which were dropped once it was in the air. For landing, it was provided with a runner or skid, made from ash wood. In order to reduce the length of skidding on landing, barbed wire was wrapped around the runner as a provisional solution. At a later time parachutes and rockets were also used to reduce the length of the touch down. With a favorable wind from behind, the DFS 230 was able to glide up to 60 km if released from the towing-cable at an altitude of 3,000m above the ground.[16]

Leutnant Kieß from *I./Regiment General Göring*, who, together with a non-commissioned officer of this battalion, was trained from 11 January 1937 for two months as a pilot for the DFS 230 during testing, was immediately tasked with setting up a training command for gliding at the airfield at Darmstadt-Griesheim.

---

12   Wilehlm Bassenge. Proficient fighter pilot in the First World War. After his time as commandant of the parachute school, and several assignments on staffs of the *Luftwaffe*, he was appointed commanding officer of *19.Luftwaffenfelddivision*, in North Africa. He was captured by the Allies with the rank of *Generalmajor* and commandant of the fortress area Tunis-Bizerta on 10 May 1943.

13   Enst Udet. Popular because of his successes as a fighter pilot in the First World War, and as a daring aviation acrobat after it. He was recruited into the *Luftwaffe* by Göring in 1935. As inspector-general of dive bombers, he fostered the development of an air brake for this type of aircraft, with the famous aviatrix Hanna Reitsch doing most of the test flights. Decorated with the *Ritterkreuz* on 4 July 1940. Committed suicide on 17 November 1941, as *General der Flieger* and *Generallufzeugmeister*. Hitler, and then Göring, blamed him for the failure of the *Luftwaffe* in the air battle for England, and in the first months of the war against the Soviet Union.

14   Robert, Ritter von Greim. First inspector-general of fighters and ground-attack aircraft of the *Luftwaffe*, from 1 April 1935 to 9 February 1936. Committed suicide as *Generalfeldmarschall* and last commander-in-chief of the *Luftwaffe* on 24 May 1945 in U.S. captivity.

15   At a later date it was also towed by the He 111.

16   Technical data for the DFS 230: Length: 11.4m; span: 21.98m; height: 2.74m; weight empty: 860kg; maximum weight loaded: 2,100kg; maximum speed for towing: 210 km/hour; maximum speed for gliding or diving: 290 km/hour.

In October 1936 the *OKH* had also directed the establishment of a test unit for the employment of troops from the air. It was designated as a Parachute Infantry Company or *Fallschirminfanteriekompanie*. The company, commanded by *Oberleutnant* Zahn, and his deputy, *Oberleutnant* Pelz, was formed on 1 April 1937. A squad each of heavy machine-guns, light mortars and engineers, had been integrated into the unit. As the *Heer* had no training installations for parachuting, the company was quartered at Stendal, and had been trained at the parachute school of the *Luftwaffe* in accordance with the latter's regulations. It had, however, remained organic to the *Heer Infanterie-Lehrregiment*, as its *15.Kompanie*. Its members, after successful completion of jump training, had received the parachute badge of the *Heer*, which was designed specifically for them.[17]

The jump training for paratroopers of the *Luftwaffe* and the *Heer*, as well as the testing of equipment, was driven by the energy and the ideas of those directly involved. Soon *I./ Regiment General Göring*, the engineer company of this regiment and the parachute infantry company of the *Heer*, were filled up with fully trained paratroopers and the first glider pilots were also available for service, although clear thinking over the further expansion of the parachute force, and its utilization from the most senior levels of command, was still missing. Deliberations and proposals for the development of the new force were mainly brought about by the leaders of the force themselves, and by the few officials in higher staffs who were tasked with this subject. In the light of the small size of the new force, nobody, however, thought beyond the purely tactical level. No attention at all was received from Hitler, who at this time was primarily occupied with building up political stability in foreign affairs, and with increasing his power in the interior.

The fact that its school had obtained the position of a leading agency authorizing it to conclude binding arrangements with commands and offices of the *Luftwaffe* and the *Heer* was of great advantage to the parachute force. Consequently, deliberations and proposals pertaining to the future of the parachute force could be forwarded formally to Higher Command. This situation was exploited by *Oberstleutnant* Bassenge immediately after he took over the command of the school.[18] Based on the authorization to set up its own office for development, requests for the procurement of material for the parachute force were now placed directly from the school to industry, which considerably reduced lead times on production.

During the process of selecting employment capabilities for the parachute troops, the idea that finally won through in the general staff of the *Luftwaffe*, was to integrate them into the air attack concept. Targets which could not, partially or totally, be destroyed by bombing, were to be put out of action with demolition charges by small teams of paratroopers, after these had been dropped in their respective area(s). Afterward, the demolition teams were

---

17 This had also been the diving eagle. At the end of 1938, after the high command of the *Wehrmacht* had decided to place all parachute troops under the command of the *Luftwaffe*, the *Heer* badge ceased to be awarded. It continued to be worn, however, by its original recipients.

18 In his report about the formation of the German parachute force, provided for the Allies in August 1945 and registered under the signature ZA 3/69 at the BA-MA, Bassenge, however, points out, that most of his proposals to the *OKL* remained unanswered, owing to the increasing rivalry between the *Luftwaffe* and the *Heer* at that time.

to be picked up again by aircraft at suitable landing sites.[19] This concept, however, was little liked by the paratroopers, as, in the case of being captured during action, they had to expect to be treated as saboteurs. Moreover, the technical means of navigation for pinpoint landing, as well as radio bearing for pick-up points were not yet available. Nevertheless, the re-organization of *I./Regiment General Göring* to meet the requirements of the demolition concept commenced in the summer of 1937. As a part of it, the regimental engineer company was integrated into the battalion.

In the meantime, the re-organization of *Regiment General Göring* into an anti-aircraft unit was ordered. Its commanding officer, *Oberstleutnant* Jacoby, who had always fostered the parachute element of his battalion, was replaced in this process by *Oberstleutnant* Axthelm of the *Flaktruppe*. As a part of the re-organization of *Regiment General Göring*, which also included its expansion to the size of an anti-aircraft regiment, its parachute battalion was redesignated *IV.(Fallschirmschützen-) Bataillon* on 1 September 1937. It now became an outsider in the unit's new organization, and soon was treated as such.

The parachute infantry company, which was set up as a testing unit, had received little attention from the high command of the *Heer*, in spite of the fact that its extension to the size of a battalion had already been thought of at the departmental level. A concept for the employment of this force, possibly on the basis of deliberations by Bassenge, had not been exploited in depth, and was of a tactical nature only in view of its size. In support of offensive operations of ground forces, parachute troops, utilizing the high speed of approach by their transport aircraft, were to be employed against the flanks or the rear of the enemy, opposing the main attack force, or to seize key terrain or to keep defiles open.

Evidently following a proposal by Bassenge, the different employment concepts for parachute troops of the *Luftwaffe* and *Heer*, were tested during a large field exercise of the *Wehrmacht* in October 1937. Fourteen demolition teams from *IV./Regiment General Göring* were dropped in a night jump against railway networks in Pomerania and West Prussia, which served as the 'Eastern Party' for the deployment of its forces. The teams were able to accomplish their missions, i.e. to simulate the destruction of a number of medium-sized and small railway bridges, and thereby to delay the deployment of the troops of the 'Eastern Party'. At least on this occasion, the operational benefit of the destroyer concept had been proven. Because of the lack of technical capabilities for radio bearing, the pick up of the demolition teams after the accomplishment of their missions, however, had remained undone.

The parachuting of the infantry company of the *Heer* had taken place under the auspices of a tactical mission, to open a defile between two lakes for the advancing ground forces during a local combat scenario. For the first time, weapon and ammunition containers had been dropped together with the paratroopers from the bomb doors of the Ju 52. As the action had primarily to be thought of as a spectacle for high-ranking generals and Hitler the events was manipulated by the directing staff, so that findings of importance for the development of the *Heer* parachute concept were not examined.

In October 1937, *IV./KGr 152*, which up to that time had supported the training of the paratroopers with two squadrons of 12 Ju 52 each, was redesignated as *Kampfgruppe zur*

---

19   This concept had been examined in France at the end of the First World War. Only later had it been realized by the Allies in the form of commando actions. For the first time, Operation Colossus, February 1941, saw 38 British soldiers parachuted over southern Italy with the mission to blow up the Tragino aqueduct.

besonderen Verwendung 1 – KGr z.b.V. 1. Initially, the combat group remained subordinate to *Fliegerdivision 1*], formerly *Höherer Fliegerführer II.* The authority for its employment and its utilization for the training of paratroopers, however, was passed to *Luftwaffeninspektion 11* at the Ministry of Aviation, which was responsible for the development of the parachute force. At the same time, the combat group was brought up to four squadrons with 12 Ju 52s each, and a staff squadron with 5 aircraft of this type. This allowed for the air transport of the entire parachute battalion of the *Luftwaffe* for a parachute mission in one wave. The unit remained stationed in Fürstenwalde.

At the end of 1937, probably on the instigation of Udet and Jeschonnek, the director of the operations department on the general staff of the *Luftwaffe*, the tactical employment of the first three available gliders DFS 230 was tested at Darmstadt-Griesheim, and demonstrated for a larger group of generals from the *Luftwaffe* and the *Heer*.[20] The value of the glider, particularly for the *Fallschirmtruppe* of the *Heer*, had become plainly visible, as it allowed for the delivery of a number of infantrymen, with their organic weapons, combat-ready immediately onto an objective. Nevertheless, an application to introduce the DFS 230 into the inventory of the parachute force, and to commence its manufacturing in series, remained undecided by the *OKH*.

Resistance against this aerial vehicle also initially existed within the parachute force proper. The reason for this attitude was mainly emotional in nature. Some exponents of the force, and unquestionably also the public, regarded the training of paratroopers as exceptional, as it accentuated these soldiers' 'glamour' in peacetime, and emphasized them as being particularly brave and bold. Evidently there was some anxiety, that the glider could, to a great extent, supplant parachuting, and thereby would strip it of its kudos. It was probably for this reason that representatives of the parachute school declared the glider as unsuitable for the parachute force after they had seen a demonstration of its employment.

As a consequence of the transfer of *Regiment General Göring* to the *Flak-Artillerie* of the *Luftwaffe*, it was planned to remove its *IV.Battalion* from its organization. Before this occurred however, political events led to its first employment. As a part of the *Wehrmacht* which moved into Austria, on 13 March 1938 the battalion was flown by the Ju 52s of *KGr z.b.V. 1* to Graz, because the passes across the mountains in the south-east of the country were still blocked for motorized troops by snow. They landed on the airfield at Thalerhof and established contact with commands of the Austrian armed forces without incident. Transported back to Germany shortly thereafter, on 1 April 1938 the unit was released from the organization of *Regiment General Göring* and thereupon designated *I./Fallschirmjägerregiment* 1 or *I./FschJgRgt.1*, and was placed directly subordinate to the *OKL*.

It was quartered in Stendal, with Bräuer, now promoted to *Oberstleutnant*, remaining its commanding officer. In conjunction with change in command procedures, and the re-designation of rank insignia, the white collar patches with green piping on the uniform blouses of soldiers were replaced by the standard yellow of the *Luftwaffe*.

---

20   In his book *Hanna Reitsch – Ein deutsches Fliegerleben*, 1995, Armin Preuß reports that a number of these generals had let themselves be flown in a DFS 230 by Hanna Reitsch, after an infantry squad had been landed successfully.

3

The concept for the employment of Parachute and Air-landing Troops derives from Hitler's aim to form the *Wehrmacht* into an instrument for his aggressive politics

During a meeting with the minister of war, *Generaloberst* von Blomberg, the heads of the three services of the *Wehrmacht*, and the minister of foreign affairs on 5 November 1937, Hitler had secretly declared his intention to lead Germany into a war for "living space and economic independence" within a few years. As seen by him, the first preparatory step was the integration of Austria into Germany. As the next step, he planned to absorb the Sudetenland. As military resistance by Czechoslovakia had to be expected, and heavy losses had to be envisaged, the anticipated attack on the Czech border defences in the conventional way, was revised by the German high command, probably based on a proposal by Göring, for the use of a preemptive employment of parachute and air-landing forces. This was to be done at the weakest part of the Czech fortification line, in the valley of the Goldopa, north of Freudenstadt (today Bruntal), in the sector of the army of *Generaloberst* von Rundstedt, who was to attack from Silesia. As the prerequisites for a vertical envelopment were still lacking, they now had to be created with urgency.

After a conference on 29 May 1938[1] which had dealt with the military measures required for *Fall Grün*, i.e. the occupation of the Sudetenland, *Oberstleutnant* Bassenge from the parachute school was delegated to the *OKL*, where he received from *Generalleutnant* Stumpff, the chief of the general staff of the *Luftwaffe*, the following missions:

- To build up, until the autumn of 1938, the parachute troops of the *Luftwaffe* and the *Heer* to the highest possible strength.
- To immediately transform the *SA Standarte Feldherrnhalle*,[2] so that it is organized as a regular infantry regiment.

---

1   The conference was chaired by Hitler, who in February 1938, had also assumed the post as commander-in-chief of the *Wehrmacht*.
2   The participation of the *Standarte* was instigated by the SA leadership, calling upon Göring to grant it the chance of proving its value. Göring, who was interested in the formation of fighting units under his direct command, had gladly accepted the request.

The order to enlarge the parachute infantry company to a battalion had been issued by the high command of the *Heer* on 15 March 1938. Despite the urgency of this matter, the establishment of this unit, to be commanded by *Major* Heidrich,[3] took some time.

In summer 1938, an airborne battery for artillery support during parachute and air-landing operations was established. The battery was equipped with the 7.5cm 18 L/11 mountain infantry gun, which had already been used in the First World War. The gun weighed 440kg and could be transported in one piece in the Ju 52. Therefore it was quickly ready to fire after landing. With a well-trained crew, 8 to 12 shells could be delivered per minute. Its range, however, was but 3,550m. For movement after landing to a firing position or to alternate positions, the gun initially had to be drawn along by its crew or carried disassembled in 6 to 10 loads.

Consisting mostly of soldiers from *Regiment General Göring*, the battery was fully assembled on 1 October 1938, in Berlin-Reinickendorf, under the command of *Oberleutnant* Schram. In order to improve its mobility after an air-landing, trials were conducted initially with Rottweiler dogs as means to draw the guns. Finally, however, it was decided to use ponies for this purpose. They could be transported in the Ju 52 behind specifically fabricated wooden partitions.

For combat against armor by parachute and air-landing troops, the regular 3.7cm anti-tank gun was taken into consideration, and the establishment of a test unit was initiated.

During this time of developmental actions in the parachute environment, decisions about the composition of the force were made, resulting in the formation and designation of *Fliegerdivision 7* (*Fl.Div.7*).[4] The following units were assigned to it:

- *I./FschJgRgt.1* (*Oberstleutnant* Bräuer)[5]
- Parachute Infantry Battalion less two companies (*Major* Heidrich)
- *Luftlande Battalion General Göring* (*Major* Sydow)[6]
- *InfRgt.16* (*Oberst* Kreysing)[7]
- *SA Standarte Feldherrnhalle*, organized as an infantry regiment
- Medical Company (*Oberstabsarzt* Dr. Dieringshofen)
- Engineer Platoon (*Oberleutnant* Witzig)

---

3   Richard Heidrich. In the First World War officer in the infantry. Accomplished parachute training at 41 years as instructor for tactics at the war school. Returned to the *Heer* at the end of 1939 and commanded, as *Oberst*, *InfRgt.514* in the initial phase of the campaign in the West. Took over the command of the newly formed *FschJgRgt 3*, which he led in Crete and in the East. *Ritterkreuz* on 14 June 1941 for his performance in Crete. Commanded *Fl.Div.7/ 1.FschJgDiv* as *Generalmajor* from November 1942 to Fall 1944. *Eichenlaub und Schwerte* to the *Rittekreuz* for his service in southern Italy and particularly at the Cassino front, on 5 February 1944 and 25 March 1944, respectively. Captured with the rank of *General der Fallschirmtruppe* at the end of the war. Discharged from an accusation of being a war criminal. Seriously marked by the years of war and from his treatment by the victors, he died in 1947 aged 51 years.

4   This designation was chosen for reasons of deception, although it had deviated from that of the other aviation divisions of the *Luftwaffe*, because it had its numeral at the end. This was maintained in the official history of the *Wehrmacht*, until the renaming of the division to *1.FschJgDiv*.

5   The battalion was reformed from its organization as a "destroyer" unit into a parachute battalion with HQ and four companies, each with three platoons.

6   The battalion was formed *ad hoc* from the staff and two companies of the *Wach Bataillon General Göring* and two companies of the *Wach Bataillon* of the *Luftwaffe*.

7   This regiment, garrisoned in eastern Friesland, was released for the operation by the *OKH* after tenacious negotiations.

- Aviation Signals Company (*Oberleutnant* Schleicher)
- *Aufklärungsstaffel* (*Oberleutnant* Langguth)
- Five *Gruppe* of Ju 52 transport aircraft[8]
- *Schlachtgeschwader 100*[9]
- 1 *Jagdgeschwader*

The parachute school and the glider training command were also placed subordinate to *Fl.Div.7*. With the organic combination of ground forces, transport aircraft and a supporting component of combat aircraft, a hitherto unique major formation was created.

For the post of the commanding officer, the choice fell upon the 48-year old *Generalmajor* Student.[10] As *Oberst* and director of the test agency for aviation material, he had already been in constant contact with the parachute school and was now immediately set free from his position as commander of the *3.Fliegerdivision*, in *Luftwaffengruppenkommando 1* of *General der Flieger* Kesselring. On 4 July 1938, he took command of *Fl.Div.7*. As location for his headquarters, he selected Berlin-Tempelhof. *Oberstleutnant* Bassenge, was appointed as his chief of staff, *Major* Reinberger now took over the parachute school. While Bassenge with a few assistants in departments L and F (air-landing and parachute matters), of the *OKL* was mainly occupied with the allotment of forces for *Fl.Div.7*, *Generalmajor* Student initially saw his tasks primarily in the development of the employment plan of this force, and in the alignment of the units toward their mission through training and jointly conducted exercises.

As primary general staff officer/ Ia,[11] *Major i.G.* Erhard and as Ia Op 1, the 31-year old *Hauptmann i.G.* Trettner[12] were assigned to the staff of *Fl.Div.7*. Already after a very short time, the latter assumed the position of Ia.

---

8   The four squadrons of *KGr z.b.V.1*, which was under enlargement to a wing, designated as *Kampfgeschwader z.b.V.1* and *KGr z.b.V. 9*, altogether 265 Ju 52.

9   Most of the aircrew of this wing, which was equipped with the Henschel Hs 123, had served in Spain with the Legion Condor and therefore had abundant combat experience.

10 Kurt Student. Fighter pilot, at officer rank, in the First World War. After the war, was initially employed as captain in various agencies for aviation technology. Thereafter for short time periods company and battalion commander in *InfRgt.2*. As *Major*, transferred from the *Heer* to the *Luftwaffe* in 1933, becoming director of the training school of the *Luftwaffe*, of the test center for aviation equipment and of the school for aviation weapons. From 1 March to 30 September 1937, inspector general of the aviation schools. As *Generalmajor* from 1 September 1938 and subsequently as *Generalleutnant* until 31 May 1941, commander of *Fl.Div.7*, and at the same time inspector general of parachute and air-landing troops. *Ritterkreuz* on 12 May 1940. After convalescence from a serious head wound commanding as general of *XI.Flieger-Korps* from 1 January 1941 to 1 March 1944. From 1 June 1941 also commanding general of all parachute troops. *Eichenlaub* to the *Ritterkreuz* on 27 September 1943. Commander-in Chief of *1.Fallschirm-Armee*, and of *Heeresgruppe Student* from 1 March to 4 November 1944. During this time promotion to *Generaloberst*. CinC *Heeresgruppe H* from 7 November 1944 to 25 January 1945. From 25 January 1945 until the end of the war CinC of parachute troops. After three months in the *Führerreserve* of the *OKL* from 31 March 1945 and for short time periods CinC *Heeresgruppe Student* and *Heeresgruppe Vistula*. Entered British captivity on 8 May 1945. In May 1946 accused of offenses against the law during his command in Crete. Verdict – five years confinement. Released from confinement in 1948. Admired, respected and held in honor by the German parachute force until his death in 1978.

11 The primary general staff officer, abbreviated Ia, was assigned to each major formation from division-level upward. He was in charge of all matters within the staff pertaining to the conduct of operations.

12 Heinz Trettner. Transferred from the infantry to the *Luftwaffe* as *Oberleutnant* in 1932. Training as a pilot. Squadron commander in the Legion Condor from autumn 1937 to early 1938. After general staff training, he served as Ia in the staff of *Fl.Div.7* from 1 July 1938 to 14 December 1940. *Ritterkreuz* for

With great energy, the preparatory work for the planned employment of *Fl.Div.7* in *Fall Grün* began. Considerable effort was dedicated to the reorganization of the *SA Standarte Feldherrnhalle* into a unit capable of fighting as infantry, as its leaders, for the greater part, had not been selected for their military qualities, and only a minority of the lower ranks had gone through compulsory military service. On 1 August 1938 *KGr z.b.V.1* was also subject to organizational change. After additional personnel and material had been supplemented, *KGr z.b.V.2* commenced its formation. Initially, however, only the command of the new combat group was set up, with Brandenburg-Briest as its garrison. Following a decision by *Generalmajor* Student, the training command for gliding was moved from Darmstadt-Griesheim, to Prenzlau and was redesignated Glider Command or *Lastensegler-Kommando*. As passenger of a glider flight, piloted by *Leutnant* Kieß, the general had come to the conviction that the glider as a means of air transport was perfectly suited for surprise actions from the air. However, its employment during *Fall Grün* could be planned only on a very small scale – one infantry platoon in an advance attack, after landing with the DFS 230, was to seize the dominant Hill 698 south-east of Freudenthal. More use of the gliders had to be ruled out in view of the few which had become available for *Fl.Div.7*. Moreover their manufacturing in series still had not been authorized.

In an extended map exercise, with the chief of staff of the *OKL*, *Generalleutnant* Stumpff, the commander of *Luftwaffengruppenkommando 1*, *General der Flieger* Kesselring, and also with Göring attending, *Generalmajor* Student displayed the deployment of his division against the rear of the Czech border fortifications in the area around Freudenthal, and made his subordinate commanders familiar with their tasks. *General der Flieger* Kesselring, who was to support the operations of *Fl.Div.7* with his *Luftwaffengruppenkommando 1*, was able to draw his conclusions from the deployment of the parachute and air-landing troops.

After ongoing training of his troops, in mid-September Student directed a large field exercise near Jüterbog, whereby a company of paratroopers were dropped and a battalion was air-landed. The exercise also showed that the Ju 52 was capable of landing and taking off from hardened runways. In the final third of September 1938, the units of *Fl.Div.7*, foreseeing *Fall Grün*, moved to their deployment area, which stretched from Lower Silesia to the vicinity of the Czech border. The flying formations used the airfields located in this area. As the airborne operation was estimated to take no more than a few days only a small supply base was set up on the airfield at Breslau. The *SA Standarte* was deployed as the divisional reserve, more to the rear in the area around Jüterbog, where it continued its training. For the men of *Fl.Div.7*, down to the lower ranks, there were no doubts about the upcoming mission, as Hitler had announced it to the German public and the world in his speeches at the end of the congress of the National Socialist Party, *Reichsparteitag*, at Nuremberg on 12 September 1938 and in the sports palace in Berlin.

---

his performance in Holland on 25 May 1940. Ia on the staff of *XI.Flieger-Korps* until 6 April 1942. From 2 September 1942 to 30 October 1943 chief of staff of *XI.Flieger-Korps* as *Oberst*. On 4 October 1943 tasked with the build-up of *4.FschJgDiv*. Led this division at Anzio-Nettuno and became its commander from 1 June 1944 to 3 May 1945. *Eichenlaub* to the *Ritterkreuz* on 17 September 1944. In British captivity until 12 April 1948. Joined the German *Bundeswehr* in 1956 as *Generalmajor*. Ended service upon his own desire as inspector-general in 1966 because of his opposition to the so-called "union-enactment" or *Gewerkschafts-Erlass*. Continued to advocate for the honour of the German soldier until his death in September 2006. The author of this book is very much obliged to him for a great many facts about events concerning the German parachute force in the Second World War as a competent contemporary witness.

How near Germany was to a *coup d'état*[13] and possibly a civil war, had remained unnoticed by the command of the parachute and air-landing forces, as they had been regarded correctly as firmly loyal to Göring and therefore had received no information about the plans to overthrow Hitler that were planned, but never carried out.

The Munich Agreement of 30 September 1938 granted Germany the right to annex the Sudetenland and made combat action by *Fl.Div.7* unnecessary. The peaceful occupation commenced on 7 October. *Generalmajor* Student obtained permission to occupy the terrain for the planned operation of *Fl.Div.7* by way of an airborne field exercise. This turned out to be a great success. Ground forces were brought in by about 250 Ju 52, to all three originally planned landing sites. Göring, who was present during the air-landings, was so strongly impressed that he promised *Generalmajor* Student, on the spot, to further promote the concept for the employment of parachute and air-landing forces. Cleverly, Student had understood how to make use of Göring's striving for esteem, by the spectacular employment of a great number of transport aircraft in order to underline the value of airborne operations on a large scale and at the same time to stay in the centre as their front rank thinker and leader. As there was no parachuting and no glider action during the field exercise near Freudenthal, the role of paratroopers and gliders in surprise attacks against important objectives, and in the seizure and retention of landing sites had not been observed by foreign military attaches.

After the end of the peaceful occupation of the Sudetenland, however, the organization of *Fl.Div.7* for *Fall Grün* was dissolved. With the transfer of the units to their home garrisons, *Schlachtgeschwader 100* and *KGr z.b.V.9* were removed. The latter was now placed subordinate to the *Generalquartiermeister* of the *Luftwaffe* for temporary employment in the Memel operation. The fighter wing, which had only been detached for air escort, and air support during the airborne operation, returned to its superior command. *InfRgt.16* and the Parachute Infantry Battalion of *Major* Heidrich, were reassigned to the *Heer*. *Luftlande Bataillon Sydow*, which had been set up *ad hoc* from guard units of the *Luftwaffe*, retained its organization. The gun battery under *Oberleutnant* Schram was now assigned to this unit. The medical company was also removed from the organization of *Fl.Div.7*. The *SA Standarte Feldherrnhalle*, which only had imaginary status as a combat ready infantry regiment, was handed back to the SA leadership.

---

13   A group of influential men around the chief of the central department of the Office for Counter-Intelligence [*Abwehr*], *Oberstleutnant* Hans Oster, opposed Hitler's disastrous social and political goals and had, in vain, attempted to win over, in secret, England and France, for a policy of strength against Hitler's aggressive attitude toward Czechoslovakia. This group included the chief of staff of the *OKH*, *Generaloberst* Halder, his predecessor, *Generaloberst* (ret.) Beck, the head of the *Abwehr*, *Vizeadmiral* Canaris, the commander of the military district Berlin, *General* von Witzleben, the president of the police in Berlin, *Graf* Helldorf, secretary of state von Weizsäcker, the former lord mayor of Leipzig, Carl Goerdeler, judge of the Supreme Court von Dohnanyi, Professor Dr. Bonnhöfer from the Charité in Berlin and the leading social-democrats Wilhelm Leuschner and Julius Leber,. When the threat of war increased dramatically, because of Hitler's exacting demands during his meeting with the British Prime Minister Chamberlain on 22 September 1938, the group around Oster determined to overthrow Hitler and his regime by force, if war was declared against Germany. The killing of Hitler was regarded as desirable by some of the conspirators, and a shock group was kept ready for action. The Munich Agreement of 30 September, however, had deprived the conspirators of the prerequisites for action which they had given themselves. See Fest, pp.761-774, and Cartier, Vol 1, pp.19-20.

Generalmajor Student was nominally still the commander of *Fl.Div.7.* This, however, consisted of but one battalion, a few smaller units and sub-units, the assigned training installations and the air transport units to service these. In spite of Göring's promise to build a corps-sized parachute force, stated after the successful airborne exercise near Freudenthal, there was little hope for early expansion. In the *OKH* there was still considerable doubt about the practicality of operations for large formations by air, into the positions of a numerically strong and determined adversary. Little support could also be expected from the *OKL*, which was fully engaged in building up the flying combat formations, the anti-aircraft and the air signal organization, all the more as Göring obviously did not find the time to let his promises be followed by deeds. Moreover, the numerical enlargement of the parachute force was hampered by the lack of personnel, as recruits had already been distributed to the *Wehrmacht* services by the induction order for autumn 1938.

In spite of all these difficulties, *Generalmajor* Student set out with determination to bring the parachute and air-landing forces into his way of thinking. He forwarded a memorandum about the findings and experiences gathered during the planning, preparation and part execution of the airborne operation near Freudenthal. By means of numerous lectures and conferences, he acquainted various command agencies of the *Wehrmacht* with his views about the build up and organization of the airborne force, and its concept of employment. His activities evidently contributed to the publication of a decree by the *OKW* in early November 1938, whereby a fundamental decision was made in the form of a directive about the allotment of parachute and air-landing troops in peace, and their employment in war, in conjunction with operations of the *Heer*.[14] Issued as *OKW* Nr. 2676/38 g.Kdos. WFA/L II/I c, dated 8 November 1938, the directive read:

Concerning Air-landing and Parachute Troops.
According to the directives of the *Ob.d.H.* of the *Wehrmacht*, the following regulations become effective.

I. Air-landing Troops
Air-landing troops, which are foreseen for employment within the framework of ground operations, in peacetime are subordinate to the *Ob.d.H.* Initially, one division is to be provided for this purpose. The training for ground operations and the special equipment of this division as air-landing formation is to be arranged for in concert with the *Ob.d.L.* In war, the air-landing troops are placed subordinate to the *Ob.d.L.* for the preparation and execution of airborne operations

II. Parachute Troops
The parachute troops are subordinate to the *Ob.d.L.* in peace and war. *Ob.d.H.* is requested to arrange for the transfer of the parachute infantry battalion of the *Heer* to the *Luftwaffe*.

III. Principles of Employment
For the preparation and execution of airborne operations in conjunction with operations of the *Heer*, the following guiding principles are valid:

---

14   The statement in Götzel, p.49, that Student had a leading role in the development of this directive, must be doubted, as at that time *Oberstleutnant* Bassenge and his working staff were still active in the *OKL*.

As a rule, other elements of the *Luftwaffe* (ground-attack, fighter and possibly bomber formations) will be brought to bear besides air-landing and parachute troops. On the one hand, their employment must be in line with the operations of the *Heer*. On the other hand, they are highly dependent from the weather, the terrain and the defense by the enemy in the air and from the ground. It is therefore necessary, to generate the fundamentals for airborne operations by the exact cooperation between the *Heer* and the *Luftwaffe*, on the basis of the most extensive adjustment of mutual intentions. Particularly the commander of the airborne operation has to be instructed to provide for the closest possible cooperation with the respective command of the *Heer* (*Heeresgruppe*, *Armee*). From the time of contact on the ground until the extraction of the airborne troops, the local commander of the *Heer* regulates the tactical cooperation between airborne and *Heer* troops.[15]

On 1 January 1939, the *OKH* handed over its parachute infantry battalion to the *Luftwaffe* in accordance with the *OKW* directive. A short time later, an order by the *OKL* confirmed the continuance of *Fl.Div.7*, and *Generalmajor* Student as its commander. On 1 February the latter was also appointed as inspector general of the parachute and air-landing troops. The inspectorate was established in the *OKL*. *Oberstleutnant* Bassenge was appointed as its chief of staff. His staff personnel were provided by the headquarters of *Fl.Div.7* in a secondary function.

Fliegerdivision 7 at that time consisted of three parachute battalions – *I./FschJgRgt.1*, since October 1938 garrisoned in Stendal, *II./FschJgRgt.1*, the former parachute infantry battalion of the *Heer*, located at Braunschweig,[16] and *III./FschJgRgt.1*, which was building up from the Air-landing Battalion *General Göring*, in its new garrison Gardelegen. Additionally, there were a few smaller units, mostly still in an experimental stage. The gun battery was removed from *III./FschJgRgt.1*, and was renamed *Fallschirm-Artillerie Versuchskommando*, or Parachute Artillery Test Command. Gardelegen was planned as its new garrison.

During his endeavors to reduce the problem of personnel shortages in the first quarter of 1939 and to continue with the enlargement of the parachute force, *Generalmajor* Student, after tenacious and cleverly-led negotiations, succeeded in drawing on the potential of the *SA Standarte Feldherrnhalle*. As service in the *Standarte*, different to that in SS formations, did not clash with compulsory military service, he managed to bring about an order which offered the SA men the possibility to volunteer for service in the parachute force. About 1,200 of them did so as a result.

Upon the directive of the *OKW* from 8 November 1938, the dice finally were finally cast for the enlargement of the parachute force with the *OKL*. By an order of the *Generalquartiermeister* of the *Luftwaffe*, dated 7 March 1939, the following units were to be formed:

- on 1 June 1939: *I./FschJgRgt.2* and one-third of *San.Kp.7* in Gardelegen;

---

15   The directive in German language is registered under signature ZA 3/69-20 at the Bundesarchiv Militärarchiv in Freiburg. Apart from the fact that it obviously had been produced rather hastily, as can be seen by its style, it is interesting to note that it does not cover airborne operations conducted on the sole responsibility of the *Luftwaffe*.

16   The re-designation of the battalion was done by a directive of the *OKH*, dated 23 February 1939.

- on 1 August 1939: the staff of *FschJgRgt.2* and *II./FschJgRgt.2* in Magdeburg;
- on 1 October 1939: the staff of *KG z.b.V.1* in Gardelegen;
- on 1 April 1940: *III./FschJgRgt.2* in Magdeburg;
- Probably from 1 October 1940 on: *FschJgRgt.3.*

Luftflotte 2 was tasked with this reorganisation of parachute forces. The *Fallschirmtruppe* regiments and *KG z.b.V.1* were placed subordinate to *Fl.Div.7*. The creation of *III./KG z.b.V.1*, originally foreseen for 1 November 1939, was to be omitted for the time being.

However, before these enlargement measures could begin, *Fl.Div.7* was ordered to participate in the conquest of the remainder of Czechoslovakia, which Hitler had decided upon, thereby breaching the Munich Agreement.[17]

On 12 March 1939, *Fl.Div.7* was alerted and made ready for immediate deployment with its three parachute battalions, the gun battery and three groups of Ju 52. It received the mission to occupy by a *coup de main* the airfields at Kladno and Rudtyne, near Prague by an air-landing. Subsequently, one of the battalions was to advance into Prague and to seize the Hradschin, the seat of the Czech government.[18] Bad weather, with freezing rain on the night 14/15 March, however, prevented the airborne operation. Prague was occupied by troops of the *Heer* on 14 March. The preplanned forces of *Fl.Div.7* could not be flown to Prague until 16 March. As the Czechs rendered no armed resistance against the occupation of their country, after a short week the troops of *Fl.Div.7* were brought back to their home garrisons by rail.

The build-up of the parachute force now proceeded faster. In early April, the existing three parachute battalions were placed subordinate to the staff of *FschJgRgt.1*, located in Stendal. *Oberstleutnant* Bräuer was appointed as commander of the regiment. His battalion temporarily being taken over by *Major* Grazy, when, still in April, the parachute training was moved from Stendal, to the newly set up Parachute School II in Wittstock. This officer became its commander, *I./FschJgRgt.1* is then taken over by the 36-year old *Hauptmann* Walther.[19]

Hauptmann Ptager was appointed as commander of *II./FschJgRgt.1*. *Major* Sydow commanded *III./FschJgRgt.1*. In March 1939, the *Fallschirm-Artillerie Versuchskommando* in Gardelegen was rearmed with the 7.5cm 15 L/15 mountain gun, produced by the Skoda

---

17   On 13 March 1939 Hitler had urged Tiso, the leader of the Slovakian nationalist party, to declare independence from Prague. This happened the next day. On the night 13/14 March, Hitler had forced the Czech president of state Hacha, by an hitherto unheard of disregard of all principles of international law, to accept the submission of the Czech state under Germany, and to restrain the Czech people from rendering resistance against the occupation, which in fact had already began that night.

18   Whether this mission was provided offhand by the chief of staff of the *Luftwaffe* or was made up by Student remains uncertain. Unquestionably, however, it bears the handwriting of the latter, who was interested in furthering the reputation of the *Fallschirmtruppe* by spectacular actions.

19   Erich Walther. Commanded the battalion in Scandinavia in April 1940, and in Holland in May 1940. *Ritterkreuz* on 24 May 1940. Promoted to *Major* on 19 June 1940. Continued to command the battalion in Crete, and afterward in the East. Took over *FschJgRgt.4* in 1942. Commanded this regiment as an *Oberst* during the fighting in Sicily and Cassino 1943/44. *Eichenlaub* to the *Ritterkreuz* on 2 March 1944. Led *Divisionsgruppe Walther* during the fighting at Arnhem From winter 1944 commander of *FschPzGrenDiv 2 "Hermann Göring"*. *Schwerte* to the *Ritterkreuz* on 1 February 1945, as *Generalmajor*. Captured by the Soviets at the end of the war. Died in the Soviet prison camp Buchenwald in 1946.

works. With a weight of 630kg, it was somewhat heavier than the mountain infantry gun initially introduced, but had a maximum range of 6,650m. At this time, trials with ponies as draw horses were also completed successfully. One Ju 52 could transport one gun, one horse, an ammunition trailer and five men of the crew. The gun battery was equipped with four mountain guns. According to command directives, a parachute medical platoon was set up in Gardelegen already in May 1939. Thereby, *Fl.Div.7* for the first time had at its disposal organic medical troops.

On 26 July, the organization order of the *Generalquartiermeister* of the *Luftwaffe*, dated 7 March 1939, was changed. Accordingly the timetable for the establishment of the staff of *FschJgRgt.2* was moved to 1 October 1939, and Tangermünde was directed as a new garrison for it and for *II./FschJgRgt.2*.

The *Fallschirmtruppe* had their first appearance in front of the public at large when a battalion-sized formation of them, in jump overalls and harnesses, led the large parade of the *Wehrmacht* in Berlin on the occasion of Hitler's 50th birthday, and left behind an outstanding impression. Up to then, Hitler outwardly had paid little attention toward the new arm, and had visited none of its installations and barracks. However, he was well informed about its development and potential for employment.

In the course of June 1939, *I./FschJgRgt.2* under *Hauptmann* Noster was created. The available personnel initially sufficed only to build the staff, the signals platoon, two parachute infantry companies and the heavy weapons company. The supplementation of the battalion to its wartime strength, however, was secured, as from 1938 onwards a considerable number of fully trained paratroopers became available as reservists, after the end of their two years of service. At the end of July 1939, the jump training for all three battalions of *FschJgRgt.1* was completed. At this time the build-up of *II./FschJgRgt.2* under *Hauptmann* Pietzonka began, initially, however, only as an air-landing unit because of the training capacity at the parachute school.[20] In August 1939, the command of *Fl.Div.7* reported *I.* and *II./FschJgRgt.1*, the 11th and 12th companies of the regiment,[21] *I./FschJgRgt.2* and the battery of *Fallschirmartillerie* as fully combat ready.

On 3 August, a new organization order was issued.[22] Accordingly, from 1 August 1939 on, the following units would be established for *Fl.Div.7*:

- a parachute gun battery in Gardelegen;[23]
- a parachute transportation company in Gardelegen;
- a parachute construction company in Burg, near Magdeburg;

---

20 The majority of the soldiers of this battalion had not been jump trained at the beginning of the campaign in the West on 10 May 1940.

21 Consistent with the infantry regiments of the *Heer*, the companies in a *Fallschirmjäger* regiment were numbered continuously, so that they carried the numbers 1-12. The regimental units, i.e. the infantry, anti-tank and engineer companies, had follow on numbers, beginning with 13.

22 RLM und Ob. d. L. Generalquartiermeister, Generalstab, 2. Abt Az. 11 b 16 Nr. 2270/39 g. Kdos., registered under BW 57/26 BA-MA.

23 It is interesting to note that the *Fallschirm-Artillerie Versuchskommando* at that time still was subordinate to *Regiment General Göring*.

- a parachute anti-tank company (*14./FschJgRgt.1*)[24] in Stendal;
- a parachute anti-tank company (*14./FschJgRgt.2*) in Gardelegen.

After *Generalmajor* Student had succeeded in winning over some hundred volunteers among the recruits from the ground crews of the *Luftwaffe*, and the volunteers from the *SA Standarte* had been integrated into the parachute force, an organization order dated 3 August 1939 could also be executed for the build-up of:

- an anti-tank company as *14./FschJgRgt.1*;
- an anti-tank test company as cadre for a later planned anti-tank detachment;
- an air-landing transport company. [25]

In August 1939, the parachute medical platoon was enlarged to *Fallschirm-Sanitäts Kompanie 7*. It consisted of elements for parachuting and elements to be air-landed. *Oberstabsarzt* Dr. Neumann was appointed as its commander. The newly-built units, besides achieving the necessary state of combat readiness, were also ordered to find and test means which ensured the mobility of their weapons on the battlefield and, if possible, a method of how to drop them by parachute. This task applied particularly for the anti-tank test company [*Panzerabwehr-Versuchskompanie – P.V.K.*], which, since early July 1939, was commanded by the energetic *Hauptmann* Götzel. The two anti-tank companies were initially equipped with only six antitank-guns each, caliber 3.7cm, probably for reasons of the still limited number of transport aircraft for the parachute force. As tows for the guns after their landing, sidecar motorcycles with 750 cubic centimeters cylinder capacity had proven their value after some tests. For the transport of ammunition and other equipment of the anti-tank companies, uni-axial trailers with a load capacity of 500kg were constructed. These were also towed by sidecar motorcycles. For the time being, however, neither the anti-tank guns nor the means for towing them could be dropped by parachute. A motorcycle with a hydraulic chain-drive [Ketten-Kraftrad],[26]constructed by the NSU motor works and successfully tested in 1939, lent itself as a cross-country tractor for the mountain and anti-tank guns. The introduction of this vehicle into the parachute force, however, could not be expected before 1940.

In summer 1939, the staff of *KG z.b.V.1* and its third and fourth group had also been established, so that an entire parachute regiment could be transported and dropped in one wave. *Oberstleutnant* Morzik, was appointed as commander of this wing. Despite the build-up of *FschJgRgt.2*, no additional air transport wing was planned. Instead, in case of need, the large numbers of Ju 52s in the aviation schools, subordinate to the chief of the training organization of the *Luftwaffe*, could be utilized for air transport missions.

---

24   For easier reading, the term 'anti-tank' is used throughout the book, although it is worth noting that German military terminology up to summer 1940 used the term *Panzerabwehr (PzAbw)*, meaning tank defense and from then on the term *Panzerjäger (PzJg)*, meaning tank hunter, for the units and sub-units of this arm.

25   The company's task was to provide the parachuted or airlanded troops with supplies, dropped over the battlefield.

26   The Ketten-Kraftrad K 101 or *Kettenkrad* (Sonder-Kfz 1), with the motor of the Opel 'Olympia' had a displacement of 1,488 cubic centimeters. Its maximum speed initially was 62 km/hour. It could tow a load of 450kg (later 800kg). Its range on roads was about 250 km. The maximum number of passengers, including the driver, was three. Its own weight was 1,235kg.

In the meantime, the *OKH* determined *22.Infanterie-Division* as an air-landing force. In addition to its armament according to the table of equipment for a regular infantry division, this formation received heavy weapons which could be flown and landed by transport aircraft. A number of Ju 52s were detached for the training of its soldiers in the loading process. With *InfRgt.16*, the division had at its disposal a unit which had already gained practical experience as an air-landing force during the preparations for *Fall Grün*.

As for *Oberst* Bassenge, who was promoted to this rank on 1 May 1939, he felt unable to support *Generalmajor* Student's striving for a purely operational level role for the parachute force, and therefore asked for a new assignment at end of May. His request was granted and he was appointed as the chief of staff of *Luftgau XVII* of the *Luftwaffe* in Vienna. His successful work for the concerns of the parachute force in its early years, however, deserved recognition and respect.

It was evidently during this time of the fast growth of the parachute force, that *Generalmajor* Student had developed his specific relations, and his friendly orientation towards the soldiers of his arm, who, without interruption until the end of the Second World War, were to remain his subordinates. Although he had not undergone jump training (whether he had wanted to avoid a firm emotional tie toward the very being of a paratrooper in order to keep his head free for the development and command of the force, or whether his injuries from a crash as glider pilot in 1921 had prevented jump training, remained unsaid by him) he had recognized with a clear view the attitudes that had to be present for the training, education and command of the parachute soldiers. Later, he would state in writing:

> The mode of treatment must take account of the pride of the paratroopers and their membership of the parachute force. It must be more generous, more caring and more companionable than anywhere else. The education has to be built much more on strong mutual confidence than on discipline and obedience. I have endeavored to lead this way myself as an example. During the many visits to the troops, I have sought contact with my paratroopers particularly, often, have talked with them about their interests, their personal situation and worries, have asked them about their views and was glad to receive frank replies. By this manner, my company leaders, commanders and I have welded together the parachute force to an ever-growing family. For a paratrooper, it was a particularly harsh punishment, if he was expelled from this family and was assigned to another formation.[27]

Unquestionably, Student, ambitious as he was, also cared for his personal career. Both, his attitude toward the well-being of the parachute soldiers and the cohesion of the force, which could be called 'fatherly', and his striving for military acknowledgment, were the motives to retain at all costs his leading role in the parachute force. The second motive, as will be examined later, however, had not remained without comment on the effects on his soldiers during their combat operations, which occasionally also influenced his performance as commander.

The specific *esprit de corps* developing within the parachute force from the very beginning had also been grasped, and furthered, by the officers in direct command of the

---

27   Quoted in Kurowski, pp.21-22.

units. Richard Heidrich, who had commanded parachute soldiers as a battalion commander and up to the post of commanding general of a corps, stated this in writing as follows:

> None of us was a show boy. The thrill of the parachute jump created a particularly companionable relation between officer, non-commissioned officer and men. It differed decisively from that of other troops. The reason for it was that the parachute force lived under a high risk even in peacetime, requiring an engagement for life and death.[28]

With his directive, dated 3 April 1939, under the codename *Fall Weiss*, Hitler had instructed the *Wehrmacht* to take precautions for a war against Poland. Initially, he attempted to win over this country for an alliance against the Soviet Union, but was met with the firm refusal of the Polish government.[29]

The end of the policy of "appeasement", which had become obvious to the British and French governments, who were guarantors for Poland, caused Hitler to exclude any agreement with the Western powers pertaining to his demands against that country. In his political endeavors to tie the Soviet Union into a commitment for one side or the other, Hitler finally outwitted the West with the Non-Aggression Pact of 23 August 1939. In spite of his occasionally rising scruples about an immediate military intervention by the guarantor powers in the case of a German attack against Poland and in spite of various initiatives from the outside for a peaceful settlement of the potential conflict,[30] Hitler issued to the *Wehrmacht* the directive for offensive preparations against Poland, and ordered the completion of the deployment of its forces by 20 August 1939. After the conclusion of the Non-Aggression Pact with the Soviet Union, he regarded the security related prerequisites as achieved for his stroke against Poland.

Within the frame of the attack plans of the *Wehrmacht*, as late as 31 August *Fl.Div.7* received the mission, to deploy, reinforced with *InfRgt.16*, to the area around Liegnitz as operational reserve of the *OKW*. The late receipt of this order had led to the conclusion by the command of the division, that its employment at the beginning of the attack was not foreseen. The deployment took place on 1 September. The staff had taken its quarters in Wahlstatt, south-east of Liegnitz. The air transport formations – *KG z.b.V.1* of *Fl.Div.7* and *KG z.b.V.2*, which beforehand was formed from the aircraft inventory of the *Luftwaffe*'s training command, and had been placed directly subordinate to the commander-in-chief

---

28   Excerpt from Heidrich's report in the journal *Die Grünen* Teufel, November 1951, pp.4-6.

29   Most of all, it was the minister of foreign affairs, Josef Beck, who had attempted to achieve his goals of a territorial enlargement of Poland at the expense of Germany, and had nurtured the growth of political influence of his country and protection against the Soviet Union, with the help of Great Britain and France, and who therefore renounced any policy of agreement with Germany. In his scheme, he had been supported by the Polish highest military leadership, who, despising the true relations of military power, had demanded a policy of strength and, with the deployment of the Polish Army in spring 1939, had planned offensive operations into the area around Berlin and into East Prussia. The urgent appeal by the British and French governments to come to last minute negotiations with Hitler despite the latter's ultimatum, had been to no avail because of Beck's stubbornness.

30   So by Roosevelt on 14 April 1939 and Mussolini by the end of May 1939.

of the *Luftwaffe*, altogether nine groups were positioned at a number of provisional airfields around Liegnitz and Sagan on the evening of 1 September. The majority of the ground forces of *Fl.Div.7* were quartered in their vicinity. *II./FschJgRgt.2*, not yet jump trained, was immediately subordinated to the *OKL*, and was air-landed on the afternoon of 26 August, with two companies at the military airfield of Zipser-Neudorf (Spisska Nova Ves), in order to safeguard it as a base for fighters fighter bombers.

Probably at the request of the *OKW*, a first movement by parachute and air-landing troops of *Fl.Div.7* was planned into the area around Posen (Poznan) in support of a pincer movement of the *Heer* against strong Polish forces assembled there.[31] The operation, for which a part of the parachute units had already been seated in their transport aircraft, was then called off because of the exceedingly favorable development of the situation on the ground. Two more operations for the division which were planned in the course of the campaign were, to seize a bridge across the Vistula, at Pulawy, south-east of Deblin, and to establish a bridgehead across the San river near Jaroslaw – both were called off at the last minute, after all preparations had been completed. Instead, most of the parachute and air-landing units now were summoned for security and mop-up actions against the dissolving Polish armed forces. *Generalmajor* Student, for whom it was obviously of great importance to provide his paratroopers with the opportunity to gain combat experience even without prior parachuting, achieved the approval to move for this purpose *FschJgRgt.1*, *I./FschJgRgt.2*, the not yet committed 5th and 6th companies of *II./FschJgRgt.2*, both anti-tank companies and the gun battery, most of them by vehicle, into the area Pulawy/Deblin along the middle course of the Vistula.

On 11 September, *Generalleutnant* Freiherr von Richthofen, in his function as leader of the close combat formations of the *Luftwaffe* commanding the *VIII.Flieger-Korps*, requested the provision of a parachute battalion for the protection of his headquarters. For this purpose, during the early morning of 13 September, *III./FschJgRgt.1* was flown to Radom. The command post of *Generalleutnant* Freiherr von Richthofen was located north of this town, in the manor Sucha, close to the river Pilica. The parachute battalion was placed subordinate to *VIII.Flieger-Korps*, and moved forward abreast of the airfield at Kamien-Sucha to be initially deployed for security. Upon a report of the appearance of Polish cavalry in the vicinity of the airfield, the battalion was ordered to find out about the situation by reconnaissance on the morning of 14 September. As it had arrived without vehicles, it was provisionally motorized by *Kampfgeschwader 77* and supplied with weapons.[32] Additionally, it received four 2cm anti-aircraft guns from the airfield defence unit.

In the morning of 14 September, three patrols, consisting of a reinforced parachute platoon, were detached for reconnaissance. At the same time, probably upon urging by *Generalleutnant* von Richthofen, the 9th and 10th companies were ordered to clear a nearby wood. For this task, on the evening of 13 September, the battalion was reinforced with an airfield service company, a company made up from ground crews of *Kampfgeschwader 77*, a battery of 8.8cm anti-aircraft guns and an anti-tank company from *InfRgt.14* which

---

31   On the German side, it was the *8.Armee* from Silesia and the *4.Armee* from Pomerania; on the Polish side, the armies of generals Kutrzeba and Bortnowski, that had been deployed in the Posen bulge.

32   In his notes about the employment of the *Luftwaffe*, dated 9 October 1954 and registered under BW 57/26 at the BA-MA, the former general of the *Luftwaffe* Speidel reports that the battalion had arrived in a "desolate" condition almost without its main armament.

happened to be available. A short time after the beginning of the reconnaissance and mop-up action, parts of *III./FschJgRgt.1* were engaged in wood fighting against an enemy who was vastly superior in numbers. One of the reconnoitering platoons lost 7 killed and 5 wounded, of whom only 3 could be rescued. In the area around Jasionna, the enemy overran the positions of four platoons in the too widely dispersed perimeter of the 10th and 11th companies during the night 14/15 September, and broke out toward the south-east. Until 25 September the reinforced *III./FschJgRgt.1* remained engaged in combat in the unwieldy wooded terrain and lost altogether 13 killed and 25 wounded. As was found out later, the enemy had not consisted of scattered troops, as assessed by the command of *VIII.Flieger-Korps*, but of one and a half regiments of a combat effective Polish division. They left behind in the contested area about 150 killed and around 200 prisoners. The booty for the paratroopers was six heavy machine-guns, three mortars and one 3.7cm gun.

Upon pressure from the high command *III./FschJgRgt.1* was employed hastily, without thorough reconnaissance of an unknown terrain. Lacking combat experience and with an unfounded confidence in the assessment of the enemy situation by the superior command, led to an engagement for which neither the tactical leaders nor their soldiers had been trained. The consequences were unnecessary high losses, and a reduction in the confidence of the soldiers under their leadership.

On orders from *Fl.Div.7*, *II./FschJgRgt.1* was moved to the airfield at Ulez at the road Deblin-Brest, about 19 km east-north-east of Deblin on 22 September. The airfield was located about 9 km east of the security line, which the *Heer* had set up along the western bank of the Vistula. This area was occupied by *InfRgt.93*. The parachute battalion received orders to clear the surrounding woods of remnants of Polish forces, and to secure valuable war material. On 22 September, about 6-800 Polish soldiers with wagons were reported on the march toward the south-east, about 15 km north of the airfield at Ulez. At 1700 hrs the commander of *II./FschJgRgt.1* deployed part of his unit to interdict the Poles. In the meantime, however, these had moved on.

On 23 September, reports were received about a freight train of several kilometers length east of Okrzeja (about 15 km north of Ulez), and of Polish troops assembling there. As these were considered to be a threat because of their proximity to the airfield, in the early morning of 24 September the battalion commander deployed his entire unit, reinforced by *14./FschJgRgt.1*, as infantry against this force. During the action, the load of the reported freight train was also secured. Prior to this action, some truckloads of Polish war material had already been transported toward the west across the Vistula by a freight train, which had been found about 8 km north-east of Ryki, some 8 km north-east of Deblin.

The battalion commander then intended to surround the wooded area east of Okrzeja from three sides, and then to roll it up from the east. For this purpose, his 7th and 8th companies and the anti-tank company were deployed for blocking. Led by the battalion commander in person, the 5th and 6th companies and the assigned engineer platoon made ready for the attack 1.5 km south of the village of Wola Gulowska, about 9 km south-east of Okrzeja. A heavy machine-gun platoon and two mortar squads were to provide fire support. Also deployed for the attack were the parts of the parachute medical company, which was attached to the battalion. During the initial deployment, a detachment under *Oberleutnant* Böhmler – half of a heavy machine-gun platoon and two squads of paratroopers, were ambushed on entering Wola Gulowska. 3 soldiers were killed and 8 wounded, 2 of them mortally. Attracted by the noise of combat, the majority of the battalion (5th, 6th, 8th companies, staff and the engineer platoon) arrived in the village at 0925 hrs and joined the fighting. Now the enemy in Wola Gulowska, and in the immediate vicinity, were quickly overcome. At the end of the engagement, the commander of *FschJgRgt.1*, *Oberst* Bräuer, also appeared on the scene and reported the approach of *I./FschJgRgt.1*. After its arrival, the wooded terrain was cleared as originally planned in the direction toward Okrzeja. The last resistance of scattered elements of the enemy was broken. At the end of the fighting, *II./FschJgRgt.1* counted 8 of its men killed, and 13 wounded. *I./FschJgRgt.1* was spared losses on this day. The enemy left behind 58 killed, 35 wounded and 266 unwounded prisoners, most of them from a largely intact artillery regiment. The booty came to more than one hundred horses and some limbers and wagons.

Despite unclear information about the enemy, the deployment of *II./FschJgRgt.1*, like that of *III./FschJgRgt.1* in the area north of Radom, was planned with the troops widely dispersed. The situation, however, had not developed as unfavorably as that of its sister battalion, as elements of the battalion had encountered the enemy already during the deployment phase and the units were therefore still close together.

When it had become evident during the campaign in Poland that parachute and air-landing operations into enemy territory were unlikely, *InfRgt.16*, on direction by Göring, had been removed from its assignment to *Fl.Div.7* on 12 September, and was flown to *8.Armee* in the area of Lodz, because of the critical situation at Kutno. There, the regiment was placed subordinate to *30.Infanterie-Division*, and remained employed in the siege of Warsaw until the capitulation of Poland.

In early October 1939, the units of *Fl.Div.7* were moved back from Poland to their home garrisons. The special purpose combat groups of the training organization of the *Luftwaffe* to the greater part were dissolved, on the condition, however, that the staffs of the groups and the HQ sections of the squadrons were kept together at the aviation schools, to enable them to quickly take over their wartime functions again, if need be.

For the men of *Fl.Div.7*, the chance to prove themselves in combat after parachuting had not come. This had caused great disappointment, particularly in the parachute battalions and had led to a severe reverse in the morale of the entire parachute force. A number of soldiers had themselves transferred to the infantry, as this arm had better promise of the thrill of combat, because of the ongoing state of war with France and Great Britain. Some officers, too, forwarded requests for transfer immediately after the end of the campaign in Poland. How unfounded this disappointment and dissatisfaction was, however, would soon become evident in a drastic way. As the Western allies had not shown any indications of a willingness to negotiate about the situation which had developed after the dismemberment of Poland, Hitler was determined to wage the attack in the West despite opposition, particularly from the *OKH*.

The first course in parachute jumping, early 1936. In the front row, from left to right: Dunz, Greiling, Kroh, Bräuer, Immans (white jacket), Kuhno, Rau, Moll, and, probably, Schlichting.

Practising the roll backward, still on mats and with the assistance of an instructor.

Preliminary training for the neck-roll as part of the desired forward landing. The men need to learn to keep their heads out of harm's way when they hit the ground.

Learning how to jump in the correct attitude from a mock door of a Ju 52, so as to absorb the opening shock of the parachute.

A soldier learning how to deal with oscillations and wind directions for landings.

Practising jumping from a Ju 52 mock-up. The quicker the stick exits
from the aircraft the more concentrated the landing will be.

Using a wind machine (a *Windesel*), the troops learned how to get to their feet after landing in strong winds, and then how to collapse the canopy by turning it around.

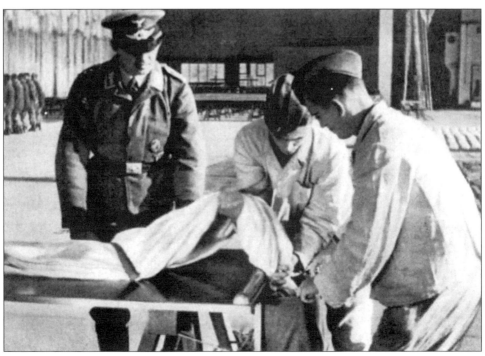

After the parachute has been spread out on the long packing table its canopy is folded into the inner canvas bag.

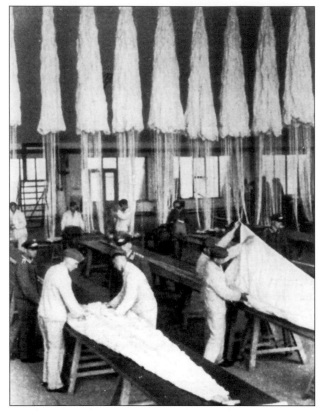

Two soldiers working together to pack away their parachutes.

Soldiers perform mutual checks prior to boarding the aircraft.

A mass jump from a Ju 52. The photo clearly shows how the outer canvas bag is pulled off by the ripcord.

The typical body position prior to the canopy unfolding.

Part II

The *Fallschirmtruppe* between the Campaign against Poland and the Offensive in the West

1

Preparations for *Fall Gelb*

Upon the outbreak of war on 1 September 1939 the *Wehrmacht* had attained a strictly defensive position against the Western powers. When Great Britain and France declared war on Germany on 3 September the German *Heer* had less than thirty divisions available for the defence of their borders in the West and less than half of this number could be considered fully combat ready. However while the majority of German ground and air forces had been tied up in the struggle against Poland, the thrust of French troops into Germany, which had been so feared by the *OKW* had not materialized.

As early as 27 September, the day of the capitulation of Warsaw, Hitler had summoned the commanders-in-chief of the three services of the *Wehrmacht* to his chancellery and informed them of his intention to launch an offensive in the West. He explained that this was in anticipation of an advance being launched by British and French forces into Germany, which could pose a threat to the industrial Ruhr region. Furthermore he argued that the *Wehrmacht's* head start in terms of its modern equipment could not last very much longer. As a result Hitler believed that the offensive in the West had to be conducted at the earliest possible time.

Subsequent to this conference Hitler published his Directive No. 6 for the conduct of the war on 9 October. The following day he read out a personal memorandum to *Generaloberst* von Brauchitsch, the Commander-in-Chief of the *Heer*, and to *General der Artillerie* Halder, Chief of the *Heer's* General Staff. In both documents he formulated the principal plan for the attack in the West, scheduled to commence on 25 November. To begin with the massed armored forces were to push forward between Luxemburg and southern Holland, excluding the fortified area around Liège. The speed and mobility of these forces meant the enemy would be assaulted whilst still deploying. This would avoid the build-up of a continuous front and would mean that the enemy could be beaten in parts. The *Luftwaffe* was to interrupt the enemy's lines of communication, thereby impeding and delaying any forward deployment for battle. In order to provide for an efficient base for a naval and air war against England, and to protect the Ruhr region, the largest possible portions of Holland, Belgium and northern France were to be brought under German occupation.

Unimpressed by the warnings made by the *OKH* regarding their lack of combat readiness, Hitler stuck to his decision. As a consequence the *OKH* hastily prepared an updated directive for deployment. Published on 19 October it stated that the main effort of the attack was to rest with *Heeresgruppe B* along the point of Liège/Brussels. A strong right wing was then to push forward to the Channel coast in Flanders. In the meantime the *Heer's* main forces would be concentrating in western Germany

This was despite the ongoing reports regarding the insufficient state of combat readiness in several formations. One problem was the low stocks of ammunition for heavy weapons and bombers which deteriorated as, Hitler, in his impatience to get the offensive under way, moved its initial phase to 12 November. On the same day the Chief of the *OKW*,

Generaloberst Keitel, and the Chief of the *Wehrmachtsführungsamt*, *Generalmajor* Jodl, met with the *OKH* it was revealed that the occupation of Holland was off the cards. During the same meeting, Keitel had also discussed Hitler's intention to seize bridges in Belgium which were close to the German border, to neutralize Fort Eben-Emael using commando troops of the *Luftwaffe* and employing airborne forces in the area around Ghent.

On 25 October Hitler met with the Commander-in-Chief of *Heeresgruppe B*, *Generaloberst* von Bock, and the commanders of that *Heeresgruppe's 6.* and *4.Armeen* and *Generaloberste* von Reichenau and von Kluge, in order to examine and develop operational plans. For the first time Hitler raised the question of whether the main thrust south of Liège could initially be aimed toward the west, and then later be redirected toward the north-west. Continuously studying the attack plans of the major formations he had obviously developed some doubts about the preparation of the mechanized forces in regard to the difficult terrain along the chosen axis for the main thrust. Furthermore he may have feared that the enemy could easily guess the area of the main effort and take respective precautions. However, in view of imminence of the scheduled date for *Fall Gelb*, any fundamental change of the operational plans was out of the question. Nevertheless, Hitler concluded the meeting directing the participants to further examine his new considerations.

On 28 October, in light of further consultations with the heads of the *OKW* and *OKH*, on 26 and 27 October, Hitler changed the attack plan in order to meet the new concept for his operations. The breakthrough was now to be forced north and south of Liège, with an armored group in each sector. He now recognised the importance of the early destruction of strong elements of the French and British ground forces as an aim of the operation. It was then decided that the seizure of the Belgian/French coast along the Channel would to follow, but only upon the completion of this primary aim.

On the 29 October the *OKH* had incorporated Hitler's new guidance in a second deployment directive. It also contained instructions for the deployment of *Heeresgruppe A*, which was to be generated by the order of 17 October and inserted left of *Heeresgruppe B. Generaloberst* von Rundstedt, who had arrived from Poland, assumed command of the new *Heeresgruppe* on 25 October. Despite the considerable shifting of ground forces which was required to apply to the new deployment directive, the date for the attack remained unchanged and was still scheduled for 11 November.

On 5 November *Generaloberst* von Brauchitsch, in his memorandum regarding the combat readiness of the German *Heer*, once more attempted to get Hitler's approval of a much later date for the attack in the West. He, however, failed. Hitler furiously rejected the reports about deficiencies in the morale and discipline among ground forces during the campaign in Poland as a generalization, and described them as an affront against the honour of the German soldier.

The parachute units of *Fliegerdivision 7* [*Fl.Div.7*] had returned from Poland to their peacetime garrisons. The first weeks were used to improve their internal organization and replace any losses of personnel. However, at this time a numerical increase of *Fl.Div.7* could not be achieved. This was as a result of the division's peace-meal employment in Poland where they acted solely as security forces for the *Luftwaffe* which had led to a considerable loss of attraction for this arm for potential recruits. The rush of volunteers had markedly dropped and quite a few soldiers in the division had requested their transfer to ground-units in order to get their share of future combat activities. Yet, despite this set back, the build-up of *II./FschJgRgt.2* was completed. The battalion, commanded by *Hauptmann* Pietzonka, received its garrison at Tangermünde and the first batch of its personnel was assigned to the jump training school. The command of *III./FschJgRgt.1* was handed over to *Hauptmann* Schulz.[1] In the meantime the battery of the division's artillery experimental command conducted intensive weapons training. The anti-tank experimental company [*Panzerabwehr-Versuchskompanie – PVK*], was increased to 12 anti-tank guns. To ensure mobility after landing with transport aircraft each of the anti-tank guns and one-axle ammunition trailers received a sidecar motorcycle as tractor. For normal movement on the ground the guns were pulled by Kübelwagen vehicles. The *14./FschJgRgt.1* (anti-tank) also received its complement of 12 guns, in line with those received by the experimental company. The glider command, under *Oberleutnant* Kieß, was also now furnished with DFS 230 gliders in growing numbers, as series manufacture had now commenced at the factory in Gotha.

In the past months the technical development of the parachute had also progressed. Originally the suspension lines had been laid into the pack-sack of the model RZ 1 as a bundle. This method sometimes caused one or more of the lines to be drawn over the canopy during the opening process. Consequently its full deployment was hindered and the speed of descent accelerated. Now a number of sleeves were to be sewn into the pack-sack, through which the suspension lines were drawn. By the weight of the paratrooper the suspension lines now were pulled successively out of the sleeves meaning they could straighten out before the canopy filled with air. This not only resulted in a correct opening process of the parachute, but also reduced the unpleasantly strong opening shock for the paratrooper. This improved parachute was designated RZ 16 and was introduced into the parachute force in 1940. The adjustment of the straps of the parachute to steel connection rings, sewn onto the harness remained unchanged. This meant that unhooking after the landing remained a cumbersome and time-consuming affair for the paratrooper, requiring him to stand or kneel. Initially the problem that the ripcord of 6m length, and a tensile strength of 500kg, could be cut by sharp edges on the lower fuselage of the Ju 52, if the paratrooper was pressed under the aircraft by the airstream after leaving the door, remained unresolved. This deficiency had caused a number of lethal accidents, but was removed some time later by introduction of a ripcord with 1100kg tensile strength.

On 27 October *Generalmajor* Student received the order to see Hitler for the first time. Hitler responded to Student's report about the decline in morale among the paratroopers, as a result of the lack of airborne operations in Poland, by explaining that the time for

---

1   Karl-Lothar Schulz, born 1907. He was transferred from the *Reichswehr* to the *Landespolizei*. When taken over by the *Luftwaffe* became a *Leutnant* in *Regiment General Göring* in October 1935. Volunteered for the parachute force and received jump training. In 1936 promoted to *Oberleutnant* and CO of *15.(Pionier-) Kompanie* in *Regiment General Göring*. Combat action in Holland in May 1940 as *Hauptmann* and CO of *III./FschJgRgt.1*. *Ritterkreuz* on 24 May 1940 for his service in Holland. CO of *III./FschJgRgt.1* with the rank of *Major* during the battle for Crete, and later on at the Eastern Front. CO of *FschJgRgt.1* in early 1942 during this unit's reconstitution in southern France. He saw combat action again as CO of this regiment in the East, after July 1943 in southern Italy, and subsequently at Cassino. He received a promotion to *Oberst* on 1 March 1944 and was decorated with the *Eichenlaub* to the *Ritterkreuz* on 20 April 1944. He was later entrusted with the command of *1.FschJgDiv* in October 1944 and decorated with the *Schwerte* to the *Ritterkreuz* on 18 November 1944. Schulz was promoted to *Generalmajor* on 1 January 1945 and taken prisoner by the British at the end of the war being released in 1946. He died in 1972.

worthwhile operations of this kind had now arrived. He claimed that the course of the war in Poland had not justified revealing the tactical potency with regard to this particular arm.[2] Subsequent to this explanation Hitler formulated the forthcoming tasks for the parachute and air-landing forces in *Fall Gelb*. They were:

a) To seize from the air and to hold until the arrival of ground forces at the Belgian *Réduit National* located west of Ghent.[3]

b) To seize the Belgian blocking fort, Fort Eben-Emael, the bridges across the Albert Canal north of the fort, and the bridges across the Meuse in Maastricht by a *coup de main* from the air.

By neutralization of the fort and the seizure of the bridges, the route to the west was to be opened for the *6.Armee* which was then to move through the Maastricht bulge speedily enough to forestall the arrival of French forces at both waterways.

Listening to Hitler, *Generalmajor* Student realized that the *Führer* must have occupied himself in great detail with the deployment options for the parachute and air-landing forces, as well as with the enemy situation in the sector of the main thrust across the border. Without hesitation Student understood the execution of an air assault against the *Réduit National* as feasible. The method foreseen by Hitler for the neutralization of Fort Eben-Emael, however, Student considered to be impracticable. He asked for some time to reflect on the strategic implications of such a risky operation. Yet, after Hitler had quickly stated the priorities regarded as mandatory for the accomplishment of the mission, Student, on 28 October delivered a far more favourable report.

Now, in view of the date for the attack, time became critical. After a thorough examination of the conditions required in order to transport the air assault forces to their objectives, the staff of *Fl.Div.7* concluded that the gliders could reach the target area if they were released by the towing aircraft at high altitude over the German/Dutch border. Flying over the Maastricht bulge the gliders could then be steered to the objectives at Fort Eben-Emael, the road bridges across the Albert Canal north of it at Kanne, Vroenhoven and Veldwezelt and the three traffic bridges across the Meuse in Maastricht.

The Albert Canal, constructed between 1930 and 1934, was 152 km in length and connected the Meuse with Antwerp. The southern part also served the Belgian border defence as it covered, in conjunction with the blocking fort, Fort Eben-Emael, the north-eastern flank of fortress Liège. The canal therefore presented a formidable barrier along the routes of advance leading from the area around Aachen through the Dutch province of Limburg towards Brussels. West of Maastricht the Dutch/Belgian border closely followed the east bank of the Albert Canal. A short distance after the location where the canal

---

2   Whether Hitler had just "constructed" this argument for Student can no longer be ascertained. However, as he had not interfered with the operations of the *Heer* and the *Luftwaffe*, other than insisting on artillery fire and bombing attacks on a large scale to enforce the quick capitulation of Warsaw, it can be assumed that it had been both high commands that had not seen the requirement to use the parachute force for its primary function.

3   In 1929 Belgium had planned to construct a heavily fortified 'national redoubt' along a 220 km long line from the Channel coast via Antwerp and Ghent back to the Channel coast. Political quarrels over the location of the forward defence, however, had prevented its realization. Only the modernization of the northern and eastern front of Fortress Antwerp, and the construction of a line of more than 200 small concrete bunkers on either side of Ghent had been accomplished.

branches off from the Meuse, about 6 km south of the southern suburbs of Maastricht, it penetrated the limestone mountain block of the Caster Plateau at a length of about 1.3 km. There it was cut up to 60m deep into the eastern slope of the plateau, with its sides rising almost vertically and smoothly to the top.

On the plateau, in a triangle formed by the Albert Canal and the Geer creek stood the blocking fort, Fort Eben-Emael. The fort was constructed between 1932 and 1935, and further improvements had been completed in the years thereafter. It was the most northern of four modern fortifications and rested like a shield in front of the 1914 fortress-belt around Liège. Eben-Emael covered the north-eastern flank of this belt. The Belgians had looked upon it as the most modern fortification work of its time and, with its 16 individual gun-emplacements, which had been inconspicuously embedded in the terrain it was the largest fully operational fort in the world.[4] The principal aim of the fort was to prevent the attacker advancing from the Aachen area to cross the Meuse over the bridge at Lanaye (about 1 km south of the location where the Albert Canal branches off from the Meuse) and then to the Albert Canal across the bridges at Kanne, Vroenhoven and Veldwezelt. Against direct assault by ground forces the fort was equipped with a large number of close defence weapons and obstacles which included ditches, moats and barbed wire entanglements. Formed as a wedge, its surface covered an area of about 40 hectares.[5] Its longest extension, north to south, was about 900m and from east to west was about 700m.[6] The main armament of the fort consisted of:

- 2 x 120mm guns in a heavily armored revolving cupola
- 2 x 75mm guns in each of the retractable steel turrets Cupola Nord and Cupola Sud;
- 3 x 75mm guns in each of the two concrete casemates, Maastricht I and Maastricht II, directed toward the North;
- 3 x 75mm guns in each of the two concrete casemates, Visé I and Visé II, directed toward the South.

For close defence of the fort, blocks I, II, IV, V, VI, Canal Nord and Canal Sud as well as the machine gun emplacements, Mi Nord and Mi Sud had been erected. All blocks had been made of strengthened concrete, had steel observation domes and were armed with 60mm anti-tank guns and machine guns. Most of them were also equipped with searchlights behind concrete loopholes. In summary the fort had 12 anti-tank guns, 25 heavy machine guns in pivot carriages, 40 light machine guns and 19 searchlights – at least one for each close-defence emplacement. For the defence of underground corridors and galleries a number of additional light machine guns were also stored. Of the eleven observation domes six were of the smaller type for infantry (in blocks I, II, IV, V, VI and Mi Sud). The two remaining infantry observation domes could be armed with a light machine gun (Canal Nord and Sud). Three domes were also constructed for artillery observation (in Mi Nord, Maastricht II and O I) and could also be armed with a light machine gun. Each

---

4   However there is no doubt that there were larger and more modern works in the Maginot Line.
5   One hectare is the equivalent of 24.711 acres.
6   The data about the fort and its garrison were provided by G. Schalich who has thoroughly evaluated the construction plans of the fort in the Belgian army archives, as well as the results of an examination of the Belgian Commission des Forts about the battle for the fort, conducted in the between 1946 and 1948.

emplacement was connected to the fort's centre by an underground corridor. Including those that linked the main communications of the command, housing and supply areas, the corridors totalled more than 3 km in length. Block O I, which sat outside the fort's perimeter and above the lock of the Meuse at Lanaye, was also connected with the fort by a long underground corridor. Based on experience of the First World War, the ventilation shafts of the fort were provided with special filters to act against poison gas and the gases which resulted from gunfire. The north-western arm of the fortified triangle was protected by a deep moat with vertical concrete sides filled with water. East of the moat a steep slope rose toward the fort's surface. Starting at block I, which contained the main entrance to the fort, another moat, with its inner side a wall of concrete, led past blocks VI, V and IV to the steep cliff which fell down to the Albert Canal. The counterscarp of this moat was formed from soil and piled up as a slope between the western end of the moat and block VI. On the northern part of the fort's surface two dummy cupolas, resembling that of the twin-gun revolving turret, were set up. They were made of 2cm-thick steel plate. In the south-east, just outside the fort area, another dummy cupola had also been erected. The access to the fort's surface from the south and the west up to block II was protected by barbed wire entanglements. The terrain between Mi Sud and Mi Nord had also been wired. Additionally a mound of soil was piled up along the whole length of the wire, and an artificial slope had been generated from Mi Nord via Visé I to cupola Nord. These two earth works were primarily thought to prevent observation from the Dutch territory east of the Meuse, but they also to provide for some cover for the defenders on the fort's surface, in the case of any attacks made by enemy infantry from the North or the East. No landmines had been laid out around the fort or on its surface.

The authorized strength of the fort's complement was 1,187 men, made up of 28 officers, 104 non-commissioned officers, and 1,055 lower ranks. The occupation of the adjoining terrain of the fort by units of the Belgian field army had been planned. The forces initially detailed for this mission had begun the construction of field fortifications.

The bridges at Kanne, Vroenhoven and Veldwezelt could be covered by the fire from the fort's guns. At the western exits of the bridges at Vroenhoven and Veldwezelt a concrete bunker was constructed. Each was armed with automatic firing gun and a heavy machine gun, which dominated the full length of the bridges, a searchlight had also been built into both bunkers. The bunkers also contained the devices for the firing of the demolition charges, which had prepared chambers in the structure to carry out this task. A similar concrete emplacement for the protection of the bridge at Kanne, designated O I, was built in about 200m distance from the western exit of the bridge. The firing device, however, was located at a scarp close to the bridge's western end. The demolition firing party provided from the fort's garrison were billeted in a small guard shack at the bridge.[7] The demolition chambers of this bridge were also loaded with charges. Demolition firing parties from the fort were also detailed to a bridge at Petit Lanaye (about 1.5 km south-east of Kanne) and to some pedestrian crossings over the locks of the Albert Canal situated about 3.5 km south-east of Lanaye. In essence no crossing site at the canal was to be left unattended at any time.

On either side of the bridges at Vroenhoven and Veldwezelt machine gun emplacements were incorporated into the concrete of the western bank of the Albert Canal, just above the water surface, at a distance of around 150m. From there the bridges and the canal banks

---

7   In some of the literature about Fort Eben-Emael it is stated that the demolition charges in the bridge at Kanne could also be fired remotely from the fort. However this statement is incorrect.

could be raked with fire. At the bridge at Kanne, two small concrete machine gun positions had been placed near its western ascent so as to provide for flanking fire along the canal.

The Germans had observed the construction of the fort carefully, so some information therefore may already have been gained during this period, particularly from workers of German origin. The majority of intelligence had, however, been gathered by high-altitude air reconnaissance and from photographs shot by ground agents. The exploitation of the available intelligence material had, for the most part, been undertaken by the Foreign Armies West [*Abteilung Fremde Heere West*] of the *OKH*. The intelligence that neither the fort nor bridges, which had been selected as objectives, were directly protected by anti-aircraft guns had helped to form the positive assessment of Student and his staff as to feasibility of an airborne assault.

Immediately after this assessment, but with only 10 days left until the date of attack, the forces and materiel were assembled. On 2 November, *Hauptmann* Koch, company commander of *1./FschJgRgt.1*, who was well known by *Generalmajor* Student for his initiative and daring, was ordered to transfer with his company, now directly subordinate to *Fl.Div.7*, to the airfield at Hildesheim. On 3 November the following elements arrived:

- The glider experimental command under *Oberleutnant* Kieß, with 2 officers and 97 other ranks, 11 Ju 52 transport aircraft and 4 DFS 230 gliders;
- The engineer platoon of the former *Heer* parachute infantry battalion under *Oberleutnant* Witzig, with 2 officers and 71 other ranks;
- Three beacon-parties, to be used for pathfinding along the flight route of the transport aircraft to the point of release of the gliders.

These elements were also placed under the command of *Hauptmann* Koch. On Hitler's order, his force was now designated as *Sturmabteilung Koch*.

Already on 3 November, *Hauptmann* Koch received the mission for his force:

- The bridges across the Albert Canal at Veldwezelt, Vroenhoven and Kanne were to be seized and held until arrival of ground forces.
- Fort Eben-Emael was to be neutralized by demolition of its artillery and close defence emplacements.
- For the time being the bridges across the Meuse in Maastricht also remained objectives for the assault detachment.

As the number of men in the actual assault force was still considered insufficient, it was to be reinforced by volunteers from other parachute units.[8]

On 4 November 31 additional gliders from the *Luftwaffe* depot at Anklam arrived by train and were hastily assembled. The *Heer*'s engineer instruction battalion at Rosslau

---

8   A copy of the war diary of *Sturmabteilung Koch* gives the personnel of *1./FschJgRgt.1* as 4 officers and 186 other ranks, and that of *Pionierzug Witzig* as 2 officers and 71 other ranks. 2 officers and 40 other ranks were tasked as glider pilots. As the overall strength of *Sturmabteilung Koch* for the actual assault is stated as 11 officers and 427 other ranks, it becomes evident that 3 officers and 130 other ranks came as volunteers from various parachute units. The overall number does not include the three heavy machine gun half-platoons, to be dropped by parachute as reinforcements at the Albert Canal bridge sites.

delivered the first batch of shaped charges 12.5, 25 and 50kg.[9] This unit also provided an officer to train the paratroopers in the technical aspects of the new demolition devices.

Hauptmann Koch used the few remaining days to familiarize the assault teams with the gliders and the shaped charges.

As all of the objectives of the assault detachment were located in the attack sector of the German *6.Armee* the newly-formed unit was now assigned to it. On 6 November *Generalmajor* Student, accompanied by *Hauptmann* Koch and *Oberleutnant* Kieß, flew to Düsseldorf for a conference with the *6.Armee's* chief of staff, *Generalmajor* Paulus. At the conclusion of this meeting the seizure of the three bridges across the Albert Canal, those across the Meuse in Maastricht and the neutralization of Fort Eben-Emael were finally confirmed by *6.Armee* to be the assault detachment's target. Paulus, as well as the commander-in-chief of *6.Armee*, *Generaloberst* von Reichenau, however, still considered the whole action as being far too adventurous.

On the same day another 10 gliders arrived from Eschwege at Hildesheim where 24 transport aircraft with 31 crews had been also been assembled and made combat ready. For deception purposes the aviation element of the assault detachment was designated *17./ Kampfgeschwader z.b.V.5* [*17./KG z.b.V.5*], so as it would appear as nothing more than an ordinary air transport unit.

The shift of the attack date, initially to 19 November and then later still, was primarily as a result of unfavourable weather conditions. Altogether there was to be twelve cancellations which prevented any long-term training plan on the part of the assault detachment. Consequently emphasis was placed on drills on the use of gliders and the new demolition charges. Meanwhile the staff of *Fl.Div.7* and the tactical leaders of the assault detachment were occupied with the development of detailed battle plans for the individual assault groups, and with the coordination of the operation with superior and supporting commands.

Improvements were also achieved in the organizational preparation for the mission. In order to ensure the secret move of the gliders to their jump-off airfields, a specific transport detachment, codenamed Kreuzotter, was formed under *Oberleutnant* Drosson. It was composed of 4 officers and 176 other ranks, and was equipped with 63 trucks, 4 moving vans with tractors and 2 tankers. 60 large and 7 small trailers were also used for the transport of the wings of the gliders. The men and the material for this detachment were assembled from 51 garrisons of the *Luftwaffe*.

The build-up of the assault detachment and its preparations for action were kept under the high degree of secrecy. Any release of information regarding the detachment and its mission was punishable by the death sentence.[10] Leave and short-term passes were also strictly controlled and kept to the utmost minimum. Concerned about the threat

---

9   The shaped charges of the types mentioned above had been designed specifically for use against heavily protected emplacements. The 50kg charge was provided in two parts. To move it to the targets on the ground normally required two soldiers for each part. Most of the charges used at Fort Eben-Emael, however, were made ready for use immediately after the landing of the gliders and then were hand-carried to the targets by two men. The 50kg charge could penetrate up to 25cm of armor plate. Its fuse was set for 12 seconds.

10   Three soldiers of a beacon-light platoon were sentenced to death by the field court of justice of VIII Air Corps for talking about their mission in a guesthouse. Another soldier of this platoon was sentenced to 10 years in prison for the same reason. After the victory over France, the four soldiers were paroled.

of espionage, *Hauptmann* Koch himself gave his detachment the initial cover-name *Versuchsabteilung Friedrichshafen*.

Probably following a proposal by *Vizeadmiral* Canaris, the head of the Foreign Countries/Counter-Intelligence department [*Amt Ausland/Abwehr*] in the *OKW*, on 18 November Hitler informed the commander of *Btl.z.b.V.100*[11] his adjutant and the intelligence officer of *6.Armee* of his intentions to seize the three bridges in Maastricht by a *coup de main* using the personnel of Canaris' troops, who were then to defend the bridges until the arrival of the forward troops of *4.PzDiv*. In order to approach the bridges undetected the advance party was to wear uniforms of the Dutch police. Planning for that action was to commence without delay.

During a conference at the Reich Chancellery on 20 November, in which the operations of *6.Armee* were examined, Hitler unexpectedly expressed his doubt about the likelihood of the German army succeeding in seizing the bridges on Belgian and Dutch territory with glider troops remaining undamaged. He based his doubt on the belief that these bridges were almost certainly prepared for demolition and therefore could be blown up in no time. The discussion was concluded with the decisions that the chief of staff of the *OKL* was to attempt the destruction of the ignition circuits leading to the bridges by the use of precision bombing with dive bombers. The probabilities of seizing the bridges by using tank raids ahead of the ground attack forces were deemed to be rather low.

In early December, Hitler issued a directive containing his new deliberations which were appropriate to the commando actions in and west of Maastricht, the forces which were under consideration for employment were as follows:

- The advance-party of *Btl.z.b.V.100* under *Leutnant* Hokke against the bridges in Maastricht;
- Glider forces of *Fl.Div.7* against Fort Eben-Emael and the bridge at Kanne;
- Dive bombers, glider forces and *Btl.z.b.V.100* against the bridges across the Albert Canal at Vroenhoven and Veldwezelt.

By this directive the mission of *Sturmabteilung Koch* was reduced to the achievement of just four objectives. Each of these targets was to be attacked by an autonomous assault group; three of these groups were to come down directly at the bridges and the fourth on top of Fort Eben-Emael. Each of the assault groups for the bridges was to be reinforced shortly after landing by a heavy machine gun half-platoon, dropped from a Ju 52. The airfields at Köln-Ostheim and Köln-Butzweilerhof were selected as jump-off locations for these assault detachments. The flight path for the glider-towing aircraft between jump-off and the point of release of the gliders was to be marked by directional searchlights and rotating beacons.

The timing for the assault was as follows:

---

11 *Btl.z.b.V.100*, commanded by *Hauptmann* Fleck, was the personal force of Canaris. The battalion was disbanded during the campaign in the west. Most of its personnel were then incorporated into *Bau-Lehrbataillon z.b.V.800*, the foundation unit of the 'Brandenburgers'.

- Touch-down of the gliders on top of the fort and close to the bridge at Kanne was to take place 15 minutes prior to sunrise;
- Dive-bomber attacks against Belgian field positions in the vicinity of the other two bridge-sites were to be immediately followed by glider landings;
- At the same time, the seizure of the bridges in Maastricht by the advance party of *Btl.z.b.V.100*, dressed in uniforms of the Dutch police, was to take place after they had crossed the German/Dutch border 45 minutes ahead of the general attack. It was hoped that the first tanks and anti-aircraft guns of *6.Armee* would quickly arrive at these bridges in order to bring them finally under control.
- A specific liaison team, attached to *6.Armee*, was to report the outcome of the surprise attack against the Maastricht bridges directly to Hitler's war headquarters, which would be set up for the initial phase of the attack in the west in the vicinity of Münstereifel.
- The attack operations of *6.Armee* further to the west would be influenced by the outcome of the actions in Maastricht.

On 7 December the *5.Flughafen-Betriebskompanie* of the *Luftwaffe*'s *Lehrgeschwader 1*, under *Hauptmann* Eisenkraemer, was assigned to the assault detachment. Its role was to be the maintenance and repair of the towing aircraft. After the arrival of 43 DFS 230 gliders and 34 Ju 52s from *17./KG z.b.V.5* on 12 December, the two beacon platoons were ready for employment.

Hitler visualized the execution of *Fall Gelb* sometime after Christmas,[12] therefore *Sturmabteilung Koch* had the time to conduct trial demolitions with the new shaped charges at former Polish fortifications east of Gleiwitz, and at former Czech bunker systems. The shift of the attack date allowed the forces a greater freedom of action as well as the opportunity to undertake improvements on the gliders, weapons and other military equipment. It also allowed them time to enhance glider drill and glider towing procedures. The actual assault on Fort Eben-Emael was rehearsed on models and sand tables. As such, its emplacements were assigned to individual assault teams and for this purpose they received Arabic numeral designations.

The mechanized forces of *6.Armee* had to cross the Meuse at Maastricht and the Albert Canal west of this city without delay. This would allow them to parry the expected thrust of French and British forces into Belgium as far to the west as possible. This required the reinforcement of the commando and parachute forces at the crossing sites quickly, before the enemy could retake and destroy them. The staff of *6.Armee* had commenced the planning for the relief of *Sturmabteilung Koch* in November. *InfRgt.151 (mot.)* of *61.Infanterie-Division*, commanded by *Oberstleutnant* Melzer, was tasked with the relief attack against Fort Eben-Emael. *Pi.Btl.51 (mot.)*, from *6.Armee* under *Oberstleutnant* Mikosch, and several other units and sub-units were placed under the command of *InfRgt.151*. The regiment received the following mission:

---

12   Hitler had made this decision after *Generalmajor* Jodl had delivered a very unfavourable report about the results of his examination of the German forward deployment areas in the west.

The regiment, with assigned special troops, particularly engineers, and in cooperation with air-landing and parachute forces will, after crossing of the Meuse take the Belgian fortification at Eben-Emael by assault.

For the accomplishment of this mission the regiment was placed under command of *4.Pz.Div.* and organized into three task groups. The most forward of these groups had to follow immediately behind the advance guard of *4.Pz.Div.*

On 20 November the troops tasked with the relief operations in and west of Maastricht conducted their first field exercise. The terrain chosen was a sector of the German West Wall. Resulting from the findings of this exercise, *II./InfRgt.151*, *14./InfRgt.151* (anti-tank), one platoon of multiple rocket launchers [*Nebelwerfer*], one platoon of *Pz.Abw. Abt.161* and elements of *Nachrichten-Abteilung 161* (these latter two from *61.Infanterie-Division*), were placed under direct command of task group A of *Pi.Btl.51*. *Oberstleutnant* Mikosch decided to lead this task group personally. In the case that the *coup de main* against Fort Eben-Emael failed, *6.Armee* planned to suppress its guns with heavy and super-heavy artillery.

Btl.z.b.V.100 (three rifle companies, one heavy infantry weapons company, and six motorized flamethrower teams) was ordered to lead the relief attack toward the bridges at Vroenhoven and Veldwezelt. Infantry of the *4.Pz.Div's Schützen-Brigade 4* was to close-up.

After 27 October the staff of *Fl.Div.7* also started planning for the airborne attack against the Belgian *Réduit National*, codenamed Operation 'G'. As all available gliders were needed for *Sturmabteilung Koch*, point landings at the objectives, however, had to be ruled out. The parachute infantry was faced with the problem of needing to rally quickly after landing so as to prevent the enemy from achieving his full defence readiness. Furthermore, suitable terrain for the landing, and the return of the aircraft bringing in the air-landing troops had to occur as close as possible to the objectives. The task to find and produce a report on the required terrain was laid into the hands of the office of *Vizeadmiral* Canaris.

The gaps in the units of the parachute force, resulting from the extraction of personnel for *Sturmabteilung Koch*, could be closed without difficulty mainly from *FschJg-Ergänzungsbataillon 1*, which was created after the outbreak of war in Stendal under *Hauptmann* von Kummer. The *1./FschJgRgt.1* was also rebuilt during this process.

One major weakness in the plan to employ *Fl.Div.7* and *22.Luftlande-Division* remained unresolved. The *OKH* raised doubt about the chances about the timely relief of the parachute and air-landing forces around Ghent. It argued that, if the desired quick breakthrough north of Liège was not achieved, or if the thrust toward the west did not gain the required depth, then there would be no military benefit in Operation ‚G' and the forces employed would ultimately be destroyed. As a result *General der Artillerie* Halder considered the whole undertaking as downright nonsense, Göring; the commander-in-chief of the *Luftwaffe*, also maintained a passive attitude.

Meanwhile the exclusion of Dutch territory from the strategic objectives of the attack in the west, which, on Hitler's guidance, had been set out in the *OKH*'s second deployment directive, was seriously questioned by the *Luftwaffe*. The *Luftwaffe* high command already raised its concerns during initial work on the new directive; stating that the exclusion of Holland from occupation by German troops would provide the British and French with the opportunity to utilize Dutch airfields and thereby to increase the threat against the Ruhr region. Hitler shared these concerns, with which he was briefed by the chief of staff of the *OKL*, *Generalmajor* Jeschonnek, on 30 October. He had, however, chosen not to change the directive. After granting the use of Dutch airspace by long-range reconnaissance aircraft upon commencement of the attack, Hitler still retained his position to restrict the utilization of Dutch territory to the Maastricht bulge, for which he intended to arrive at a political arrangement with Holland.

Ongoing pressure by the *OKL* regarding Holland soon led to a new directive by the *OKW*. The directive stated:

> The larger those parts of Dutch territory seized, the more effective the arrangements which can be made for the defence of the Ruhr area. The *Heer* therefore must be prepared to occupy Holland up to the Grebbe Line upon order. Whether the attack objectives have to be extended in depth later on will depend on the political and military attitude of the Dutch, and on the efficacy of the inundations expected as part of the Dutch defensive measures.

For the time being the Fortress Holland [*Festung Holland*] remained excluded as an operational objective. The fortress was the core area of Holland, which, according to the Dutch defence plans, had to be retained at all costs. In the north its boundaries were set by the coastline between the mouth of the Meuse at Hoek van Holland and Den Helder, in the east by the Amsterdam-Rhine-canal down to the Waal and Meuse rivers and in the south by the estuaries of the Waal and Merwede rivers – Hollandsch Diep and Haringsvliet.

The new Holland directive was also included in the *OKW* Directive No. 8, For the Conduct of the War in the West, dated 20 November. Although it confirmed the validity of the present deployment directive for *Fall Gelb* it also demanded that a shift of the main effort of attack from *Heeresgruppe B* to *Heeresgruppe A* must be considered.

For the parachute and air-landing forces the optional considerations of the later directives opened up a new spectrum of potential missions for them to undertake.

Hitler used the change of schedule for the offensive until after Christmas to allow an enhanced indoctrination of the military. On 23 November he ordered the heads of the *Wehrmacht* to his chancellery, making up his mind, once and for all, to overcome the ongoing reservation of his generals against an offensive war in the west. With the commanders-in-chief of the *Wehrmacht*'s three services, the army groups and the armies, the commanding generals of the *Flieger-Korps* of the *Luftwaffe*, the chiefs of staff of the *Luftflotte* and the chiefs of the general staff down to army corps level and corresponding commands in the *Luftwaffe* and the Navy as his audience, Hitler gave a lengthy speech which displayed his theories. He explained that the very centre of his reasoning was anchored in the firm belief that the war they were fighting could only be won by attack.

Immediately after his speech he opened his thoughts on the campaign in the west to several high-ranking commanding officers. He highlighted its difference from the plan of 1914 and requested that the time between warning and order be reduced and that the actual attack by moving the forces be closer to the borders.

Subsequently he summoned *Generaloberst* von Brauchitsch and *General der Artillerie* Halder. He strongly accused the *Heer* command of lacking the will to support his intentions without reservations; after this final act of coercion he withdrew to his office.

As the doubts about the feasibility of Operation 'G' had been accepted and as the attack-mission for *Heeresgruppe A*, should *Heeresgruppe B* fail to break through, had now clearly been noted, the *OKW* could now issue a new directive, which also took into account Hitler's guidance on his Holland directive. On 28 November the *OKW* issued a new directive, pertaining to the employment of the parachute and air-landing forces. It read:

> In the instance that that *6.Armee* cannot achieve a quick breakthrough north of Liège: Due to the destruction of the bridges across the Meuse and the Albert Canal, the plan to employ *Fl.Div.7* for Operation 'G' becomes invalid.
>
> The Führer's point of view is that *Fl.Div.7* must then be employed for another mission on the first day of the attack. He therefore requests to examine the following options:
> a) The seizure of the island of Walcheren including the port of Vlissingen or any other island in southern Holland which could be of particular value for the conduct of the naval and air war.
> b) Seizure of one or more bridge sites across the Meuse between Namur and Dinant, with the aim of keeping them open until the arrival of fast ground forces in the sector of *4.Armee*.
> c) Protection of the terrain north of Cardignan and north east of Sedan to enable fast ground forces from the sector of *4.Armee* to emerge from the wooded high ground south west and south east of Bouillon.

The exploitation of the potential new missions in combination with thorough terrain studies which were conducted by *Generalmajor* Student and the staff of *Fl.Div.7* upon receipt of this directive led to the following conclusions:

- The terrain of the Ardennes in the vicinity of Bouillon appears to be unsuitable for the landing of aircraft. Additionally, heavy snow drifts must be anticipated in winter time. An airborne operation in this area therefore is deemed inadvisable.
- Only minimal chances of success are envisgaed for an airborne operation against Walcheren or other islands in southern Holland.[13]
- An airborne operation to seize the Meuse crossings between Namur and Dinant lacks favourable conditions mainly because of the absence of airfields close to the river. Some open ground nearby, however, allows for the landing of troop-carrying transport aircraft.

---

13   Student never provided reasons for this assessment.

On 6 December the *OKH* was informed about Hitler's decision to cancel the airborne operations against Walcheren and in the area around Carignan. The employment of the majority of the parachute and air-landing forces now only had to be decided for either Ghent ('G') or Namur ('N').

In the case that French and British troops surprisingly moved into Belgium the *OKL* and the *Luftflotte* commands issued emergency directives by which the large-scale missions for *Fl.Div.7* could be cancelled.

Operation 'N' was subject to detailed discussions between the commander of *Luftflotte 2* (*General der Flieger* Sperrle), *Luftflotte 3* (then *General der Flieger* Felmy) and *Generalmajor* Jeschonnek in early January 1940. The key objective of 'N' was to prevent the destruction of the bridges across the Meuse at Annevoie, Yvoir and Houx to act as a prerequisite for a quick thrust of fast ground forces in a westerly direction. The chances of success for this operation, however, were assessed as being very low. The landing of troops by Ju 52 could only take place about 15 km west of the river. Furthermore parachuting would probably lead to a great many injuries among the paratroopers because of the stone hard frozen ground.

An unfavourable assessment for Operation 'N' was also submitted by the commander of *22.(LL)Inf.Div.*, *Generalmajor* Graf von Sponeck. On 7 January Sponeck has also raised doubts about the possibility of timely relief of his troops to the headquarters of *Heeresgruppe B*.

In spite of the perceived hazards of the directive of 28 November 1939, *Fl.Div.7* and the *OKL* now commenced planning for the airborne operation in the area around Namur, to be executed upon codename *Süd*. The airborne attack against the *Réduit National*, which was still a valid option, was also to be launched under codename *Nord*

On 10 January, during a meeting with the commanders-in-chief of the three services of the *Wehrmacht*, Hitler fixed the date for the attack in the west as 17 January as the weather forecast after 13 January was favourable for some time. A large-scale bomber campaign was to be flown against the airfields in northern France some days ahead of the ground attack.

On 11 January, a day with a minus 25 degrees centigrade ground temperature, Student, who had been promoted to *Generalleutnant* on 1 January, together with *General* Felmy from *Luftflotte 2* inspected *Sturmabteilung Koch* at the training area at Bergen. On the same day an *OKW* directive related to the new attack date was received. It contained the following orders for the parachute forces:

> A-day is 17 January 1940. *Fl.Div.7* is ordered to prepare, in addition to undertakings *Nord* and *Süd*, a third operation, codenamed *Festung* for the seizure of the core of Fortress Holland. The decision for the employment in Operation *Festung* will be taken latest in the morning of A minus 1. Operations *Nord* and *Süd* remain options only if a sufficiently thick snow covering on A-Day leads to an improvement of the conditions for parachuting and air-landings at Ghent and at the Meuse.

In the meantime, experience had shown that the ignition cables, which led to the demolition charges on bridges, could not be destroyed by air attack without risk to the target. As a consequence the time plan for *Sturmabteilung Koch* was altered so that all four assault groups would land simultaneously.

On 10 January, as the high commands of the *Heer* and the *Luftwaffe* were feverishly working to meet the new attack date, the *OKW* confronted an event that caused considerable confusion.

Major Reinberger, a parachute officer, but now assigned to *Fliegerführer 220* in Münster, was ordered to attend a conference at the location of *I.Flieger-Korps*. *Major* Hoenmanns, the commandant of the airfield at Münster-Loddenheide had offered to fly Reinberger to Köln-Ostheim, where the conference was to take place. As the subject of the conference was the cooperation between *I.Flieger-Korps* and *Fliegerführer 220*, *Major* Reinberger had, against strict orders, taken on the flight with him some top-secret documents which related to *Fall Gelb*. As a result of misty weather, Hoenmanns had missed Köln and had crossed the German/Belgian border. A mechanical problem then forced him to land his Me 108 aircraft in the vicinity of Maasmechelen (about 12 km north of Maastricht). Reinberger failed to burn the secret documents he carried and most of them, though scorched, were secured by Belgian policemen, who arrested the two German staff officers shortly after their forced landing. Within a few hours the documents were in the hands of the Belgian General Staff, who quickly recognized them as being genuine. King Leopold III had received a full report about the incident by the evening of 10 January. The following day he briefed General Gamelin, the commander-in-chief of the French army and Lord Gort, the commander-in-chief of the British Expeditionary Force in France, about the contents of the documents but chose not to release their origin. General Reynders, at this time commander-in-chief of the Dutch armed forces, was informed about the contents of the papers by the Belgian military *attaché* in The Hague. He had, however, remained sceptical and suspected that the plans were nothing more than a German act of deception.

The captured German documents had contained elements of Directive No. 5 for the defensive battle of *Luftflotte 2*, dated 11 December 1939. They had confirmed some previous indications about the planned occupation of Belgium and Luxemburg, as well as of Dutch territory, though they did not disclose the occupation of Fortress Holland. More revealing to the Allies had been remnants of several directives and orders from *Luftflotte 2*, and *Fl.Div.7*, which indicated the employment of *Fl.Div.7* around the area of Namur/Dinant. Moreover the mission for *VIII.Flieger-Korps* had also been captured; this included the suggestion of an airborne operation by *Fl.Div.7* in order to support of the thrust of *6.Armee* across the Meuse on the first day of the attack. However no intelligence had been detected regarding the organization of the attack forces or disclosing the main front of the attack. There was also no indication that the attack was imminent.

The *OKW* became aware of the Maasmechelen affair on the night of 10/11 January. On the morning of 11 January the German military *attaché* in Brussels was informed by the chief of the Belgian office for counter-intelligence of the arrest of the two staff officers and told that the incident had taken place in. Shortly afterwards he was ordered by the military *attaché* section of the *OKL* to establish contact with the officers so as to prevent any further disclosures of their attack plans. At the same time Hitler was told about the incident. He was angered by the careless handling of secret documents and he ordered the immediate dismissal of the commander-in-chief of *Luftflotte 2*, *General der Flieger* Felmy, and of *Oberst* Kammhuber, who had before been chief of staff of *Luftflotte 2*, but was assigned to a new post. *Generalfeldmarschall* Göring and *Generalleutnant* Student were also ordered to be reprimanded. Even though they lacked in-depth information about the potential consequences of the incident, or the exact information that had been obtained by the enemy, Hitler saw no reason to cancel the date of the attack. Therefore, on 11 January at 1845h, the *OKW* issued the order for the attack by all three services of the *Wehrmacht*. As such more than 60 German divisions began their movements into the jump-off areas, close to the borders.

The German military *attaché* in Brussels received permission to speak with *Majors* Reinberger and Hoenmanns on 12 January. The director of the German military *attaché* system for Belgium and Holland, *Oberstleutnant* Wenninger, arrived in Brussels from The Hague and participated in the hearing which started on 12 January at 1000h, which was doubtlessly overheard by the Belgians. During the hearing *Major* Reinberger, deviating from the truth, declared that he had been able to destroy almost all of the secret documents by burning them, leaving only small pieces the size of his palm. Three hours after the end of the hearing *Oberstleutnant* Wenninger reported Reinberger's statement to Berlin. As a consequence the initial tension dropped considerably, but Hitler demanded an additional report from the German embassy in Brussels.

In its assessment of the overall situation on the evening of 13 January the Belgian military high command came to the conclusion that the *Wehrmacht* could attack within a few hours. It based this assessment on specific reports pertaining to the attack date. In the first week of January they had received a warning from the Belgian ambassador in Berlin regarding the impending German attack on 15 January. The date had also been confirmed in a report to General Reynders by the Dutch military *attaché* in Berlin, Major Sas. The most alarming appraisal, however, was the report on the early evening of 13 January by the Belgian military *attaché* in Berlin, Lieutenant-Colonel Goethals, who passed on information freshly received from Major Sas. Goerhals reported that the new attack date was selected so as to advance ahead of any preventive measures by the Western European nations. This assumption was based on intelligence drawn from the documents captured after the forced landing of a German aircraft. The report of the military *attaché* was taken very seriously by the Belgian high command largely as a result of the fact that the reference to the aircraft incident could only have come from a high-ranking German source.

On the evening of 13 January all Belgian soldiers on leave were ordered back to their units. Simultaneously the highest level of mobilization was ordered and several divisions commenced their movement toward the eastern borders of Belgium. At around midnight the Belgian Prime Minister Paul Henri Spaak sent for the Dutch ambassador and instructed him that the Belgians anticipated the start of the German attack to be on 14 January at dawn.

In Holland the high command reacted less seriously to the warnings received on 13 January. General mobilization had been ordered by the end of August 1939, just prior to the outbreak of war. In conjunction with a number of improvements to the defensive installations, this measure was regarded as a sufficiently visible signal of the country's determination to defend its neutrality by force of arms, if required. Moreover many members of the country's political leadership could not imagine that the German attitude toward Holland could differ from that during the First World War. This would mean that in a war against France, Germany again could profit from the advantages drawn from strict regard to Holland's neutrality. Besides, the Dutch commander-in-chief had lost confidence in the truth of the reports received from Major Sas, who, since October 1939, had on several occasions transmitted dates for the German attack in the west, which all had turned out to be wrong. Even when Major Sas, in his latest report, indicated the absolute reliability of his source of information, the Dutch commander-in-chief retained his doubt.

Upon the receipt of a warning from Brussels General Gamelin ordered the execution of the Dijle plan. The plan was developed in coordination with the Belgian high command and had been laid down in Instruction No. 8 on 14 November 1939. It had planned for the movement of powerful French and British ground forces across the Belgian border to the line Antwerp-Leuven-Wavre-Namur, with the small river Dijle in its centre. There the French and British troops were to establish defensive positions in order to support the Belgian ground forces who were withdrawing from the Albert Canal and the area around Liège.

The French 1st Army Group under General Billotte commenced its movement toward the Belgian border where, by order of the chief of the Belgian General Staff, Lieutenant-Colonel van den Bergen, the border barriers were opened. However, this measure took place without the consent of King Leopold III, who on 14 January had ordered his troops to protect the nation's borders against foreign troops, sending a signal to the world that Belgium intended to preserve its neutrality. As a result of this order the barriers along the borders to France were closed again on 16 January, meaning the French were forced to halt their troops at the border, unable to proceed.

On 12 January Hitler still planned for the attack to commence on 17 January. However, the detection of military preparations in Belgium and Holland and the movement of powerful and mobile French ground forces to the Franco/Belgian border opposite of Tournai and Courtrai on 13 and 14 January made the German high command believe that the enemy had gained prior knowledge of the attack plans. On several occasions an intended date for attack had become known to the enemy, consequently a high-level leak was suspected but could not be proven. Nevertheless the weather, contrary to the forecasts, developed extremely unfavourable conditions and the offensive was postponed again, this time to 20 January, before being postponed until spring 1940. Hitler saw no risk in this decision, as the French, because of the harsh wintry weather, had moved their ground forces from the western Belgian border and back to their winter quarters. In the meantime, *General der Flieger* Kesselring had taken over the command of *Luftflotte 2*. Already on 18 January he inspected *Sturmabteilung Koch*, together with *Generalleutnant* Student. The detachment was now under operational command of *VIII.Flieger-Korps*, led by *General* Freiherr von Richthofen.

The was little doubt that the mission to prepare for a parachute and airborne operations against Fortress Holland had been included into the *OKW* directive of 11 January by insistence of Göring and the *OKL*. The *OKH* had not been consulted in the development of this directive.

On 13 January *Generalmajors* Jodl and Jeschonnek discussed details for implementation of *Festung*. Hitler approved the results and, in conjunction with his order to occupy all of Holland, ultimately decided on the overall deployment of the parachute and air-landing forces. He determined that operations 'G' and 'N' were to be dropped and only *Festung* and the airborne raids west of Maastricht were to be executed. This decision did away with the idea of the *OKH* being used to employ parachute and air-landing troops in support of the advance of *18.Armee* toward the Dutch Grebbe Line.[14]

The quick and unimpeded crossing of the water obstacles guarding the southern approaches into Fortress Holland was regarded as the most important prerequisite for its quick conquest. Therefore it was deemed that the few bridges across these obstacles had to be brought into German hands undamaged and at the same time their utilization by French and British troops moving forward from north-eastern France, had to be prevented.[15] For this task the early employment of sufficiently strong parachute and air-landing forces was considered mandatory.

Generalleutnant Student had gained knowledge about Göring's and Jeschonnek's concept of operations in good time. Based on Hitler's decision of 14 January he succeeded in securing the following missions for the parachute and air-landing forces for Operation *Festung*:

- Seizure of the bridges at Moerdijk, Dordrecht and Rotterdam for *18.Armee*, which was to advance with fast ground forces south of the Dutch main rivers.
- Simultaneous conquest of the capital The Hague, thereby neutralizing the highest Dutch political and military authorities.

Generaloberst von Bock, commander-in-chief of *Heeresgruppe B*, remained sceptical about the employment of parachute and air-landing forces in the Rotterdam area, as he had doubts about their being enough time for ground troops to bring relief.

---

14   The Dutch defences directed against Germany had rested on a number of lines, mainly behind terrain which could be flooded. The most important of these were:
- the Wons and Kornwederzand position, which barred access to the northern provinces across the 29 km long dike over Lake Ijssel into North Holland, together with fortress Den Helder;
- a line of defence positions along the Ijssel river;
- the Grebbe Line on both sides of the Grebbe hill west of Arnhem, which was the main line of resistance.

All of these lines had been strengthened by concrete bunkers and casemates. Against attacks from a south-westerly direction, the Meuse line and behind it the Peel-Raam Line had been prepared.

The Dutch high command intended to hold these lines successively, for as long as possible and to finally withdraw into Fortress Holland.

15   This move, indeed, was planned: General Gamelin had supplemented the Dijle plan by the Breda option with a new directive, dated March 1940. In this directive he had not only ordered the reinforcement of the forces foreseen for the advance into Belgium by additional armored and motorized formations, but had also instructed the French 7th Army under General Giraud, forming the left wing of the advancing troops, to move elements at the start of the German attack as quickly as possible through northern Belgium, to the area around Tilburg/Breda in Dutch Noord Brabant. There they were to establish contact with Dutch troops. The main purpose of the Breda option, however, was to protect the eastern approaches into the fortress area of Antwerp. After the French plan had become known at the Dutch high command, the southern areas of fortress Holland were regarded as sufficiently protected.

German signal reconnaissance had been able to pick up major portions of the French plans.

In the weeks of relative calm Hitler found the time to turn his thoughts towards a thrust from the left wing of the attack front, the idea of which had been on his mind since the submission of the first operational plan by the *OKH*. First, however, his directive to reduce the time frames required for the forward staging of the ground forces and his decision to take possession of all of Holland, were made known to the chiefs of the *Heeresgruppen* and *Armee* operational staffs on 22 January. This led to the publication of a third deployment directive. Although the main effort of the attack still rested with *Heeresgruppe B* more attention was to be given to a possible surprise attack of the enemy opposite *Heeresgruppe A* and the consequences thereof. Furthermore the demand to defeat as many elements of the French army and its allies for a quick and decisive victory would be more distinctly brought to fruition.

Far more extensive deliberations on a similar vein had also been taken up from another side. The chief of staff of *Heeresgruppe A*, *Generalleutnant* von Manstein, had seen the danger that a frontal attack with two wedges, as foreseen in directive No. 6, could be. In 1914 this had caused an attack to become stalled at a defensive front between Sedan and the lower Somme River. As such von Manstein concluded that a long war of attrition could not be withstood by Germany. At the core of his deliberations he emphasized that the main objective was to destroy the main forces of the enemy which were concentrated north of the Somme. Therefore the main attack had to be launched from an area south of Liège. From here the thrust had to be driven toward Arras and Boulogne. Consequently this would cause the French and British forces, who were positioned forward of this axis of advance, to be cut off. In order to induce the enemy into an instantaneous counter-attack into Belgium, with strong forces between the Moselle and Meuse rivers, he had to assess the German attack north of Liège as forming the main effort. Only then, by the forward move of the enemy's main ground forces into northern Belgium, could the desired effect of a 'revolving door' be achieved.

Von Manstein's initial memorandums in this matter, which were supported by *Generaloberst* von Rundstedt, had been ignored by the *OKH*, particularly by *General der Artillerie* Halder, the chief of the *Heer* general staff. He also prevented these memorandums from being passed to the *OKW*.

The assignment of fast ground forces of considerable strength to *Heeresgruppe A* by the *OKH* had met with Hitler's expectations and had created the option to shift, if necessary, the main effort of attack to *Heeresgruppe A* in direction of Sedan and thence across the Meuse. The execution of this option, however, would also increase the dependence of his own operations on the actions of the enemy. This risk had at several occasions been stressed by the *OKH*.

Wargames which had been conducted by *Heeresgruppen* A and B in early February 1940 had not led to an obvious solution for the main effort. Nevertheless the suitability of its shift to *Heeresgruppe A*, had begun to mellow in the *OKH*, too prior to the beginning of the attack.

On 13 February Hitler, probably after receipt of the first information about von Manstein's deliberations, had confirmed his own opinions about shifting the main attack to south of Namur to *Generalmajor* Jodl. Jodl immediately instructed the *OKH* on the subject of Hitler's position and requested the development of a respective operation plan.

The ultimate breakthrough for von Manstein's operational theories occurred on 17 February, after he had personally briefed Hitler. Von Manstein's proposal to shift the main effort of the attack to *Heeresgruppe A* on the left wing and to push forward with it to the lower Somme, while *Heeresgruppe B* would conducted a frontal attack, met with Hitler's unanimous approval. In order to reveal von Manstein's concept of operations, which he now claimed to be his own, Hitler summoned *Generaloberst* von Brauchitsch, and *General der Artillerie* Halder into his Chancellery on 18 February. As the examination of the changes required to shift the main effort to *Heeresgruppe A* had already commenced in the *OKH*, Hitler quickly agreed upon the respective measures proposed by the two generals.

On 24 February, in a truly masterful piece of staff work, the *OKH* produced a fourth deployment directive, in which the operational concept of von Manstein was made manifest. Churchill some time later would baptize this concept the "sickle cut" [*Sichelschnitt*].

The events between 10 and 24 January had been nerve-racking for the operational staffs and exhaustive for the troops moving back and forth. But they had confirmed, by the reaction of the allies, that the strongest French and British forces would try to meet the presumed German main thrust north of Liège and probably also in southern Holland. Thereby the conditions which were essential for the success of the "sickle cut" would actually be generated.

The activities in the German highest command levels had remained unknown to the parachute forces. The continuous raising and lowering of the alert status was a hindrance to long term training plans in *Sturmabteilung Koch*. Nevertheless its operational readiness had been improved step by step. In reaction to Hitler's decision to attack on 17 January, the first 30 gliders had been moved under difficult road conditions by transport detachment *Kreuzotter* from the airfield at Hildesheim to the jump-off sites near Köln.[16]

On 1 March *Generalfeldmarschall* Göring ordered *Hauptmann* Koch to personally brief Hitler about the deployment of his detachment. *Hauptmann* Koch and *Oberleutnant* Witzig travelled to Berlin on 5 March. On that very day they had to pre-brief *Generalmajors* Freiherr von Richthofen and Jeschonnek, with *Generalleutnant* Student also in attendance. In the early evening Hitler was briefed by the two parachute officers.

Intensified defensive preparations observed on the side of the enemy had, on the eve of the briefing, led to the decision to reinforce the assault groups for Fort Eben-Emael and the bridges at Vroenhoven and Veldwezelt, using the personnel of the assault group for the bridge at Kanne. During the briefing Hitler, however, insisted on the seizure of the bridge at Kanne as well, and so orders to re-form the respective assault group under its original commander were swiftly issued. To avoid a weakening of the combat power of the units of *Fl.Div.7* the *Heer* had to transfer 90 engineers for this task. After *Hauptmann* Koch and *Oberleutnant* Kieß had briefed the commander-in-chief *6.Armee* about this matter on 11 March, *6.Armee* provided for the required number of engineers and assault infantrymen – all of them volunteers. By 12 March they were airlifted to Hildesheim.

---

16   19 gliders were unloaded at Köln-Ostheim airfield and 11 at Köln-Butzweilerhof airfield under strict security provisions. There, they were assembled in hangars. On 12 January they were taken over by *Leutnant* Schacht, the officer in charge of the assault detachment's advance party.

While more conferences, inspections and communication exercises took place and advance parties arrived at Köln-Butzweilerhof, on 18 April *Sturmabteilung Koch* reached its final strength and its ultimate task organization. It now consisted of 33 officers and 1,127 other ranks. 11 officers and 427 other ranks, including the glider pilots, belonged to the actual assault element. The air transport crews for 44 towing aircraft and 4 in reserve, as well as for the 6 aircraft and one in reserve, ordered to drop paratroopers as reinforcements, counted 16 officers and 182 other ranks.

Since 31 March *17./KG z.b.V.5* had been organized as the 1st to 4th towing squadrons and the 5th glider squadron.

The task organization for the assault elements were as follows:

- Fort Eben-Emael: *Sturmgruppe Granit* – 2 officers and 84 other ranks with 11 gliders. Commander : *Oberleutnant* Witzig.
- Bridge at Kanne: *Sturmgruppe Eisen* – 2 officers and 88 other ranks with 10 gliders. Commander : *Leutnant* Schächter. Reinforcements: a heavy machine gun half-platoon with 25 paratroopers to be dropped from two Ju 52s shortly after the glider landings.
- Bridge at Vroenhoven: *Sturmgruppe Beton* – 1 officer and 80 other ranks with 10 gliders. Commander: *Leutnant* Schacht. Battle HQ, consisting of *Hauptmann* Koch, *Oberleutnant* Zierach, *Oberarzt* Dr. Jäger and 13 other ranks with 2 gliders. Reinforcements: a heavy machine gun half-platoon with 24 paratroopers to be dropped from two Ju 52s shortly after the gliders had landed.
- Bridge at Veldwezelt: *Sturmgruppe Stahl* – 1 officer and 91 other ranks with 10 gliders. Commander: *Oberleutnant* Altmann. Reinforcements: a heavy machine gun half-platoon with 24 paratroopers to be dropped from two Ju 52s shortly after the glider landings.

The orders of the *Heer* units which had been tasked to lead the attack across the Albert Canal, had seen them unable to provide artillery support for *Sturmabteilung Koch*. Therefore, on 17 March, a mixed anti-aircraft detachment under *Hauptmann* Aldinger was formed from elements of *II.Flak-Korps* of *Luftflotte 2* and placed under direct command of *VIII.Flieger-Korps*. It consisted of 3 batteries with 8.8cm heavy anti-aircraft guns, and 2 platoons of quadruple 2cm anti-aircraft guns. Its mission was to provide support at the earliest possible time for the actions of the paratroopers from the eastern bank of the Meuse. For the advance to its firing positions the detachment was to be incorporated into the march column of *4.Pz.Div.* Target acquisition for the heavy batteries was to be arranged for via the radios provided for each assault group.

During these hectic months nobody found the time to think about a substantial enlargement of *Fl.Div.7* which was still incomplete and entirely unsuitable for combined arms warfare. On 1 April the division consisted of the staff, *FschJgRgt.1*, with three parachute infantry battalions and an anti-tank company, two parachute infantry battalions of *FschJgRgt.2*, *Sturmabteilung Koch*, *FschGeschBttr.7*, *PzAbwKp.7* (the former experimental unit), *leichte FlaBttr 106* (assigned), *LuftNachrKp.7*, *FschSanKp.7*, *LuftTrspStaffel*, *AufklStaffel*,

KradSchtzZug and *Lastensegler-Kommando. KG z.b.V.1* at present remained organic to the division.

Endeavours were made to better integrate heavy weapons into the division structure. To implement this elements of the former anti-tank experimental company had been moved to the factory at Gotha with the aim to develop and test, together with technicians from the works, the possibility of loading anti-tank guns and their towing devices into the DFS 230 glider. After some technical changes to both the guns and the gliders, this was successful in such a way that a dismantled gun and its towing sidecar motorcycle, including the crew, could be loaded and flown in two gliders. For this method of air transport three guns and their towing motor-bicycles together with six gliders had been made ready.

The trials were terminated in early March 1940 and the experimental team returned to its unit. Meanwhile *PzAbwKp.7* was tasked with employment in the airborne attack against Fortress Holland. However, no gliders could be provided for this mission as all of those which had been produced up to this date were required for the air transport of *Sturmabteilung Koch*. Lack of gliders had also been the reason why the three technically revised anti-tank guns could not be assigned to the assault detachment to increase its firepower.

While the preparations of the *Wehrmacht* for the offensive in the west were carried out with maximum effort, a situation had developed in another geographical area. This required attention and action from all of the war's participants.

2

The employment of the *Fallschirmtruppe* in Operation *Weserübung*

During the increasing political tensions in Central Europe and after the outbreak of armed conflict within them, the Scandinavian states of Norway, Denmark and Sweden had undertaken policy strict neutrality, as in the First World War. This neutrality was much to the liking of Hitler and the *OKW*, as it had made the sea-lanes along the Norwegian coast safe for unarmed German ships[1] and had shut off the Baltic Sea for British and French naval forces. But in September 1939 Churchill, at that time First Lord of the British Admiralty, had proposed that the governments of the Western Allies and their general staffs cut Germany off from Swedish iron ore stocks and from the nickel mines at Petsamo in Finland, both of which were vital for the German war industry.[2] However, his proposals were not accepted by the Chamberlain government because they could only be achieved by violating the neutrality of the Scandinavian states. Nevertheless, Churchill doggedly pursued his aims. In a memorandum dated 16 December 1939, he stressed the need to temporarily lift the protocols of the League of Nations during the struggle against Germany, and in particular the violation of the Scandinavian states' neutrality by the Allies. The British cabinet again turned down any military action in Scandinavia, but did instruct its chiefs of staff to develop contingency plans for a potential occupation of Norway.

In Germany *Großadmiral* Raeder, commander-in-chief of the Navy, for the first time laid down his opinions in writing. He argued that that for naval-strategic reasons the coast of Norway must not come under the control of the enemy and therefore any such attempt by the Allies must be forestalled. His concerns that Great Britain could quickly interrupt German imports from Norwegian/Swedish territory and seal off the German Navy's access into the Atlantic Ocean had not been shared by Hitler or by the high commands of the *Wehrmacht*. Apparently upon request by Raeder the Navy Directorate for Naval Warfare [*Seekriegsleitung*] had commenced to examine how bases for the Navy could be established in Denmark and Norway.

Shortly after the Soviet Union invaded Finland on 30 November 1939, the *OKW* had concluded that the Western allies could use military support for Finland as pretence to occupy the Norwegian port of Narvik and the Swedish ore deposits.

---

1   On 2 September 1939 Germany had formally declared that it would respect Norway's neutrality, as long as it would not be violated by a third power.
2   Churchill had proposed to enter the Baltic Sea with the Navy (Plan Catherine) and to mine the north Norwegian coastal waters.

As a result of his conversations with the Norwegian politician, Quisling, on 16 and 18 December 1939[3] but also on the insistence of Raeder, Hitler had ordered the development of a study to examine options for military actions against the Western powers regarding to Norway. After it had become known that the British had tried to gain the approval of Norway and Sweden for the operation of British naval forces within Norwegian territorial waters in January 1940, the study had been passed to the high commands of the *Wehrmacht* services. The *OKH* and the *OKL*, who were fully occupied with the planning for the campaign in the west, paid little attention to the study, yet the OKM had looked at it in more detail and arrived at two important conclusions:

1) Surprise would have to be a prerequisite for success of the operations in Norway:
2) Elements of the initial occupation forces of the *Heer* would have to be transported to their objectives by fast warships.

On 23 January Hitler ordered the withdrawal of the study and tasked the *OKW* with the supervision of all future planning. This planning was to be conducted under the code name *Weserübung*. On 5 February the planning staff for *Weserübung* was formed and consisted of representatives of all three services of the *Wehrmacht* under direction of *Kapitän zur See* Krancke.

For the development of the operation plan speed had become necessary for the following reasons:

- On 29 January the Finish Marshal Mannerheim urgently had asked the Western allies for military intervention and had received a positive reply.
- With the attack against the German tender *Altmark* on 16 February the British high command had indicated that it was willing to close the sea lanes along the coast of Norway for German merchant ships even under violation of this country's neutrality.[4]

In spite of the difficulties in planning an operation which involved all three services of the *Wehrmacht* first time, Krancke's staff succeeded in solving this task within three weeks. The plan would involve the simultaneous landing of troops in Oslo, Kristiansand, Årendal, Stavanger, Bergen and Trondheim, which were considered the economic hubs of Norway and the home to the majority of the country's population. The plan was built upon the necessity to take control of these areas without the resistance of the Norwegian

---

3   Vidkun Quisling had founded the party of 'national congregation' [*Nasjonal Samling*], with anti-Jewish and pro-German Norwegians, some of them in prominent political positions. He had explained to Hitler that entry of the *Wehrmacht* into Norway as early as possible would be necessary in the light of the intentions of the Western allies. Hitler and his political advisers had counted little on the active support offered by Quisling, but saw him as a welcome follower after the assumption of control over Norway.

4   The *Altmark*, with 303 British sailors from ships brought up by the battle cruiser *Graf Spee*, had been detected on its way home by British naval forces close to Norwegian territorial waters. Thereupon the tender, under escort by two Norwegian patrol boats, had taken refuge in the Tossing Fjord. Despite Norwegian protests the British destroyer *Cossack* followed her into the fjord and boarded her. Controversially, the boarding team fired on the unarmed German sailors when some attempted to escape, killing six, and wounding a great number. With the British sailors rescued from the *Altmark*, the *Cossack* then left for Great Britain.

armed forces. This would mean convincing the Norwegian government beforehand of the preventative nature of the occupation. The task force organization had planned for the assignment of five parachute battalions of *Fl.Div.7* as part of the first wave of troops. Within the first three days *22.(LL)Inf.Div.* was to follow by airlift.

The commanding general of *XXI.Armee-Korps*, *General der Infanterie* von Falkenhorst, was designated commander-in-chief for Operation *Weserübung* after being proposed by *Generalmajor* Jodl.[5] Von Falkenhorst had accepted the assignment and already on 22 February had approved Krancke's work.

Concerning Denmark, Krancke had assumed that the bases required at the northern tip of Jutland could be obtained by diplomatic pressure, or by the threat of military actions. Von Falkenhorst's study group which was called together in Berlin on 26 February, however, had assessed the inherent risk as too high. Therefore on 28 February *General* von Falkenhorst submitted a draft plan to the chief of the *OKW*, which pre-empted the military occupation of Denmark as well.

Prior to further planning, however, a solution had to be found to avoid complications regarding the prioritization of resources for the forces assigned to *Fall Gelb* and to *Weserübung*.

The issues surrounding the prioritization of resources were particularly relevant for the aviation formations of the *Luftwaffe* and the parachute and air-landing troops, which altogether had already been assigned to the campaign in the west. A proposal by *Generalmajor* Jodl, approved by Hitler on 28 February, had solved these issues and from thereon had formed the basis for all on-going preparations. Jodl suggested preparing both operations in such a manner that they could be conducted independent from each other.

In the light of the responsibilities of the parachute and air-landing forces at the beginning of the campaign in the west, the *OKW* had also recommended the use of just four parachute companies in *Weserübung* and to retain a single regiment of *22.(LL)Inf.Div.* as reserves. On 29 February Hitler had approved von Falkenhorst's plan, after the changes suggested by the *OKW* had been integrated. On 1 March he had enacted the directive for Operation *Weserübung*. Although the forces assigned to undertake the offensive were strong enough to enforce the occupation of both Norway and Denmark, the basic aim was still for the "peaceful occupation of both countries in order to safeguard their neutrality with arms."

Denmark and Norway were to be occupied simultaneously by *Weserübung Süd* and *Weserübung Nord*. For this purpose General von Falkenhorst was placed directly subordinate to Hitler.

The uncertainty in planning this operation was as a result of the sequence of events in the west and in Scandinavia. The *OKL*, in particular, was heavily burdened as a result. However, on 3 March this was somewhat reduced as Hitler declared that *Weserübung* was to take place first. Nevertheless Hitler pointed out that the period of time between both attacks had to be minimal so as to prevent counter-attacks by the enemy. *Weserübung* was intended to be a preventive measure, and, as such, its execution prior to the campaign in the west would also remove the risk of the Western allies using the violation of Holland's neutrality as a reason to occupy Narvik.

---

5   Von Falkenhorst had gained some experience in amphibious operations during the German intervention in Finland in 1918.

The objections that were raised against *Weserübung* by the *Heer* and the *Luftwaffe*, whose commanders-in-chief had almost completely been left out of the planning process, had been ignored by Hitler. Instead he argued the anticipated intervention of the Western powers in Finland created the need for *Weserübung* forces to be operation ready by 13 March, ready for their potential deployment in Norway around 17 March.

The original operational command of the formations of the *Luftwaffe* by the chief command for *Weserübung*, which was designated as *Gruppe XXI*, had been omitted after vehement protests by Göring. Instead they were placed under the command of *X.Flieger-Korps*, which was provided by *Luftflotte 2* for the operations in Denmark and Norway. Thereby the intention to generate a joint command structure for the first time had failed.

On 5 March Operation Order No. 1 for the occupation of Norway was published by *Gruppe XXI*. Section 9a stated that the *Luftwaffe*, who had been assigned on the basis of cooperation [*auf Zusammenarbeit angewiesen*], was to assume responsibility for the air transport of paratroopers to Oslo, Kristiansand, Stavanger and Bergen as well as for parachuting at these locations.

The order did not contain a date for the start of operations. For the Navy the original plan had remained unchanged, as a result, its larger warships continued to be committed to *Weserübung*.

The start of armistice negotiations between the Soviet Union and Finland on 12 March had surprised both the Allied and the German governments. In reaction the Western powers attempted a last minute change of events in northern Europe in order to bring to mount pressure upon Germany.[6]

A telephone conversation between the Finish ambassador in Paris and his Minister of Foreign Affairs on 12 March was picked up by Göring's signal reconnaissance. This conversation, combined with intelligence gathered through the signal reconnaissance of the *Seekriegsleitung*, left no doubt as to the advanced state of preparations of the Western powers for the occupation of ports in middle and northern Norway.

The peace treaty signed on 13 March between the Soviet Union and Finland deprived the Western allies of an explanation for the deployment of troops in Scandinavia. For the German side too, the reason for military action in Norway had lost its urgency. Nevertheless Hitler remained convinced that his plan was the necessary course of action and insisted on the implementation of *Weserübung*. This was an assumption which proved to be correct as the British did not abandon their plan to interrupt German imports from Sweden. The command relations, and thus the bounds of compliance between the services of the *Wehrmacht* had principally been settled in a directive dated 14 March. The decision that *X.Flieger-Korps General der Flieger* Geissler, who was based at his HQ in Hamburg, was

---

6   On 5 February the British and French councils of war had decided to send an expeditionary corps of 3/4 divisions via Narvik to Finland and to utilize that move by taking over the Swedish iron ore deposits. The temporary landing of troops at Trondheim and Narvik had also been conceived. The assembly of the expeditionary forces had to be completed by 20 March. No cooperation in this matter had been considered with Norway and Sweden, after both countries had turned down a request for the transit of Allied troops to Finland.

to be in command of all air operations during *Weserübung* was also obligatory. This also included the transportation of troops and material by air.[7]

The command of the operations of the *Wehrmacht* in Denmark was delegated to *General der Flieger* Kaupisch. It was directly subordinate to *Gruppe XXI*.

Due to the geographical situation of the countries to be occupied, and because of the need for surprise, the air transport forces allocated had to be considerable in strength. So as to prevent a reduction of the air transport formations appropriated for the operations in the West, combat groups for special purposes were formed – *Kampfgruppen z.b.V.* – *KGr z.b.V. 101–107*. Each of these was made up of a staff and four squadrons with 53 Ju 52; they were formed of personnel and aircraft from the aviation schools and were run by the chief of training of the *Luftwaffe*. Additionally *KGr z.b.V.108* had long-range aircraft including Ju 90, Fw 200 and G 38. All of these combat groups as well as *I.* and *II./KG z.b.V.1*, were placed for deployment under the command of an 'air transport ground chief' [*Lufttransportchef Land*]. Those aircraft which were suitable for landing on water (the He 59, some Ju 52 and the sea planes of the Navy) were concentrated in three groups under an 'air transport chief sea'. Both of the newly created air transport chiefs were made directly subordinate for employment in *Weserübung* under *X.Flieger-Korps*. The *KG z.b.V.1* (*Oberstleutnant* Morzik) and the still-forming *KG z.b.V.2* (*Oberst* Conrad) remained independent from *Fl.Div.7*.

The operation Order No. 1 of *Gruppe XXI* for the occupation of Denmark was published on 20 March. It stated that the airfields and the Lagerak crossings at Ålborg had to be seized at the earliest possible time by paratroopers and by the air-landed *III./InfRgt.159*. In Operation Order 8cc it was stated that for this mission the air transport units for *III./InfRgt.159* and the parachute company were to be subordinate to *X.Flieger-Korps*.

On the same day *X.Flieger-Korps* also published its operation order for the initial phase of *Weserübung*. Under section 5d it stated that the paratroopers must secure the airfields at Oslo-Fornebu, Stavanger and Ålborg prior to the landing of troops by transport aircraft. As a result *X.Flieger-Korps* changed the operation Order No. 1 of *Gruppe XXI*, instead stating that the parachute insertions at Bergen and Kristiansand must to be abandoned. This measure became a necessity as a result of a shortage of parachute units and had probably been coordinated in advance with *Gruppe XXI*.

Hitler remained hesitant to fix a date for *Weserübung*. He intended to justify the launch of military actions in Norway and Denmark as being enforced by the enemy, thereby hoping to avoid being accused as a usurper by world opinion. On 26 March he was urged again by *Großadmiral* Raeder to get ahead of the Western powers by immediately occupying Norway. Raeder had reasoned that dark nights were mandatory for the operations of his naval forces due to the overwhelming strength of the enemy's fleets. In view of the meteorological

---

7   See also the study German Air Force Airlift Operations written in 1961 by the former air transport chief of the *Luftwaffe*, *Generalmajor* (ret.) Fritz Morzik, placed online by the Air Force Historical Research Agency, Maxwell AFB, Alabama under No. 157.

conditions in the northern part of Norway, and the adjoining sea, he believed that 7 April was the latest possible date for naval transport operations under cover of darkness.

Hitler received the report stating the preparations for *Weserübung* were complete on 1 April. So, after one more conference with Göring, Keitel, Raeder and von Falkenhorst, he had finally ordered the occupation of Norway and Denmark to begin on 9 April (,Weser day') at 0515 hrs (,Weser time'). Fast merchant ships with heavy materials and logistic goods had left the jump-off ports heading for Norway on 3 April. At midnight on 6 April the warships, most of them with troops aboard, set sail.

In spite of the valid intelligence regarding the preparations of the British navy for actions directed toward northern Norway, the German side remained convinced that it could steal a march upon the enemy.[8] As a result of this positive assessment precautions for the case of Allied landings ahead of friendly forces had not been laid down in any of the directives and operation orders for *Weserübung*.

However there is no doubt that Raeder was fully aware of the risk posed to his warships for the return to home stations after the landing of troops at the ports of central and northern Norway. At the same time he had to anticipate the appearance of the vastly superior British Home Fleet in the sea region close to the Norwegian coast.

On 8 April several groups of British destroyers, covered by a task force around the battle cruiser *Renown*, arrived for mining operations in the West Fjord between the Lofoten islands, the Norwegian mainland and the sea region south of it. The movements of German warships, which were reported by British reconnaissance aircraft in the Skagerrak toward Norway, were initially assessed by the British Admiralty as an attempted breakthrough of the Shetland-Norway passage into the Atlantic Ocean.[8]

On 6 April the first battalion of *I./FschJgRgt.1*, under *Hauptmann* Walther was released from its assignment to *Fl.Div.7* and was placed under command of *X.Flieger-Korps*. The order to achieve full combat readiness within four hours indicated that it was to be used for parachute operations at short notice. The battalion was alerted on 8 April 0500 hrs while at its peacetime garrison of Stendal. At 0930 hrs the Ju 52 of *II./KG z.b.V.1* with the men of *I./FschJgRgt.1* aboard took off from Stendal-Borstel to their designated jump-off airfields in three groupings:

- HQ, 1st Company (*Oberleutnant* Schmidt), and 2nd Company (*Oberleutnant* Groetschke) to Schleswig;
- 3rd Company (*Oberleutnant* von Brandis) to Ütersen;
- 4th Company (*Hauptmann* Gericke) to Ütersen.

Upon arrival the units received their missions:

- *I./FschJgRgt.1*, less two companies, were to be dropped over the Oslo-Fornebu airfield to seize it for the air-landing of follow-on troops of the *Heer*;

---

8   Churchill, in his works about the Second World War, points out that on 7 April the British Admiralty had strongly doubted that the German naval force sighted on a northerly course could have Narvik as its objective.

- 3rd Company was to seize the airfield at Stavanger-Sola by parachute assault and keep it open for the air-landing of follow-on forces;
- 4th Company, less one platoon, was to be dropped on the island of Masnedø, which they were to seize and retain undamaged until the arrival of *Heer* forces the Storstrømmen Bridge which connects, via Masnedø, the two large islands Falster and Seeland.[9] The remaining platoon of the company was to seize the important airfields Ålborg-East and Ålborg-West by parachute and to defend them alongside the air-landed infantry battalion until relief ground forces arrived.

Each of the groupings was to be accompanied by some heavy fighters – Me 110 from the first group of *I./ZG 76*, for protection during parachuting and for close air support during the assault.

On 9 April the German military actions for the occupation of Denmark and Norway were initiated according to the operation orders. Yet, for the troops on the way to their objectives, the position of the Danish and Norwegian armed forces remained unknown.[10]

As a result of unfavourable weather conditions the 9 Ju 52 of *8./KG z.b.V.1* arrived over Masnedø around 20 minutes behind schedule. There, close to the Storstrømmen bridge, they dropped *4./FschJgRgt.1*, less one platoon, at 0635 hrs.[11] A part of the parachute force came down close to the coastal fort which covered the southern approaches to Masnedø and was equipped with 8 heavy guns and a searchlight battery. Without picking up their main individual arms from the weapon containers these paratroopers immediately entered the fort and captured the two Danish naval soldiers and a civilian forestry official who were present there.[12]

On stolen bicycles a few of the paratroopers rode onto the bridge in a southerly direction and captured the astounded soldier who was guarding the bridge. While they examined the bridge for explosive charges they met the advance party of reinforced *III./ InfRgt.305*. This battalion was approaching from Gjedser at the southern tip of Falster, to where it was ferried over from Warnemünde.

At the same time another parachute platoon moved over the bridge in a northerly direction and entered the small town of Vordingborg at the northern bank of the Storstrømmen. There it took possession of the railway station and the post office. Steamers and boats attempting to flee from the town's harbour were stopped with a few shots in the front of their bows. The small garrison of Vordingborg, the staff of 5th Infantry Regiment and soldiers from the still assembling 19th Infantry Battalion surrendered without

---

9   The parachute assault on Masnedø had not been scheduled in any of the operations orders by *Gruppe XXI* and *Höheren Kommando XXXI. Hauptmann* Gericke had received this mission directly from *Höheren Kommando XXXI* on 7 April. The original mission and jump-off airfield were omitted.

10   The German ambassadors in Oslo and Copenhagen had been instructed to hand over the German demands to the governments exactly at the time of the entry of German troops into the territory of both countries.

11   It is quite certain that *4./FschJgRgt.1*, being a heavy weapons company, had left the greater part of its heavy machine guns and mortars behind and was employed as infantry.

12   German propaganda reports, based on the report of *Hauptmann* Gericke, conveyed the impression of a much stronger garrison at the Fort, but were definitively refuted by reliable Danish sources after the war.

resistance, but not before the regimental commander had reported the landing of German *Fallschirmtruppe* on Masnedø by telephone to the Danish high command in Copenhagen.

Later in the morning *Hauptmann* Güricke's troops were relieved by ground forces. They were brought to Gjedser on confiscated vessels and ferried over to Warnemünde. There transport aircraft were already waiting, to carry the paratroopers back to Stendal. The mission has been accomplished without losses.

The third platoon of *4./FschJgRgt.1*, which was dropped from the remaining 3 Ju 52 of *8./KG z.b.V.1* on 9 April at 0700 hrs near Ålborg, seized the two airfields as well as the bridge across the Limfjorden to the northern tip of Jutland without losses. Shortly afterward the first group of *I./KG z.b.V.1* landed *II./InfRgt.159* on the airfields Ålborg-East and Ålborg-West. From the south, *11.Schützen-Brigade*, which was formed specifically for the relief of the parachute and air-landing forces at Ålborg, was approaching. Fortunately for the air transport of troops to the Ålborg area the order of the Danish high command, early in the morning of 9 April, to move all combat aircraft of the Army from Copenhagen-Vaerloese to Ålborg could no longer be executed as a result of an air-raid by *I./ZG 1*, against Vaerloese at 0545 hrs.[13]

Late in the morning of 9 April, the forward elements of *11.Schützen-Brigade* reached Ålborg. During its advance through the western part of Jutland the brigade was able to quickly overcome the little resistance the Danish forces offered.

Around noon the airfields at Ålborg were ready for operational use by the *Luftwaffe* against Norway. By 10 April they were also protected against possible British air attacks by an anti-aircraft detachment. The platoon of *4./FschJgRgt.1* left the Ålborg area by train on 9 April to return to its home garrison.

King Christian X of Denmark directed his armed forces on 9 April at 0720 hrs to cease all further resistance, after the citadel of Copenhagen was occupied by a reinforced battalion of *InfRgt.308* without a shot being fired. As the Danish government had so quickly bent to the German demands the losses in personnel on both sides were only light.[14] *4./FschJgRgt.1*, the only parachute unit involved in *Weserübung Süd*, had not been forced to prove its value in combat.

The first phase of *Weserübung Nord* began as the *7./KG z.b.V.1*, with *3./FschJgRgt.1* aboard took off from Stade on 9 April at 0530 hrs heading for the airfield at Stavanger-Sola 590 km away. A Ju 52 with specific long-range radios, designated a 'signals Ju', was also assigned to the squadron. The transport aircraft with the company's 8th squad aboard was held back due to technical difficulties. The Ju 52 with the 3rd squad was forced to conduct an emergency landing in Denmark and was as a result separated from the squadron. Finally the aircraft carrying 9th squad returned to Schleswig because of dense fog.

Following closely behind the two escorting fighters[15] which strafed the airfield with their machine guns, the air transport squadron, approaching from the east, dropped the

---

13   During this air raid 11 of 48 Danish combat aircraft had been destroyed and 14 were badly damaged.

14   The Danish army and the army air force had lost 13 KIA and 21 WIA.

15   Two of the Me 110s from the original escort had crashed on the way and others had turned back because of the weather. The remaining two Me 110s, however, had succeeded in shooting down two of the Norwegian

parachute infantry company from 70m height at 0845 hrs. The sequence of the parachuting was HQ section – heavy weapons platoon – first to third platoon, the latter just with the HQ section, and one squad.[16]

The preceding air raid was ineffective but had alerted the defenders of the airfield. Consequently during their descent the paratroopers came under machine gun fire from two bunkers which had not been detected beforehand; one at the eastern edge of the airfield and the other at its south-eastern edge. Nevertheless the 7th squad succeeded in quickly neutralizing the heavy machine gun emplacement at the south-eastern edge of the airfield where it captured eight Norwegian soldiers. Covered by the fire of two machine guns which were directed by the leader of third platoon, who had hurt himself on landing, the squad-leader and one of his men subsequently assaulted a nearby house and took an officer and 24 soldiers as prisoners.

The 1st Platoon, which came down on the runway, attacked, under fire, the airfield HQ. During its advance the platoon was erroneously strafed by one of the Me 110s, as a consequence one paratrooper was killed and five others were wounded. After seizing three machine gun positions and capturing the deputy commandant of the airfield, the platoon took possession of the departure building.

The 5th squad came down directly in front of the bunker at the eastern edge of the airfield, two men were killed and three wounded by fire from its defenders. The remainder of this squad, and some men of the 4th squad, under the command of the squad-leader of the 5th squad, attacked the bunker with hand grenades and pistols. This was because there had been no time to pick up their main arms from the weapon containers. Nevertheless they quickly overcame the resistance of the bunker crew.

In the meantime the HQ section had cleared the runway of barbed wire rolls and the canopies of parachutes were laid out as recognition flags and landing crosses. At the same time the reinforced 5th squad seized a large house about 500m from the airfield from which it was fired upon. The 6th squad occupied a beach hotel which had been abandoned by the enemy.

50 minutes after the start of the parachute assault, the first transport aircraft of *KGr z.b.V.104*, with soldiers of *I./InfRgt.193* aboard, landed on the runway which had survived the preceding air raid intact. During these initial air-landings another German soldier, a *Stabsfeldwebel* of a radio team, was killed by fire from a Me 110.

3./FschJgRgt.1 had paid for its successful *coup de main* against the airfield at Stavanger-Sola with three killed and eight wounded. About half of these losses were as a result of friendly fire. Of the Norwegian forces located on or near the airfield, 57 soldiers, among them 4 officers, were made prisoners of war. By noon the killed and wounded men of *3./FschJgRgt.1* were being flown out to Germany and around 1300 hrs the missing 8th squad arrived from Stade.

---

reconnaissance aircraft which had taken off from Stavanger-Sola.

16 According to the war establishment [*Kriegsgliederung*] the parachute infantry companies of *I./FschJgRgt.1* consisted of the HQ section with 12 men, the first to third platoons with 36 men each, and the heavy weapons platoon with 24 men. The latter was equipped with two heavy machine guns, one mortar and two anti-tank rifles. For the mission at Stavanger-Sola the two anti-tank rifle-teams had been assigned to 2nd Platoon.

By the evening of 9 April the headquarters of *InfRgt.193*, *I.* and *II./InfRgt.193*, 2 fighters, 6 dive bombers of *I./StG 1*, a squadron of He 111 bombers and an air transport squadron with aviation fuel has been landed at the airfield.[17]

An airfield service company and elements of *Luftgau-Stab 200*, which was air-landed by *KGr z.b.V.105*, were able to render the airfield fully operational by the afternoon of 9 April.

On 10 April at 0800 hrs, *3./FschJgRgt.1* handed over the security of the airfield to *I./InfRgt.193* and at 1300 hrs were airlifted back to Stade. They arrived at 1650 hrs and were transported by rail to Stendal-Borstel, arriving on 11 April.

On 9 April 0530 hrs. the HQ of the 5th and 6th squadrons and an assigned *Nachrichten-Ju*, of 9 Ju 52s took off from Schleswig with *I./FschJgRgt.1*, less its 3rd and 4th companies, bound for the airfield at Fornebu situated about 6 km west of Oslo. In the operation order of *Gruppe XXI* for the occupation of Oslo, dated 14 March 1940, section 8c stated that the mission for this battalion was the securing and air-landing of the first air transport squadron with follow-on forces provided by the *Heer*. This would gain a start position for the occupation of Oslo from the west. The sole responsibility for the seizure of the airfield was assigned to the commanding officer of *I./FschJgRgt.1*, *Hauptmann* Walther.[18] In number 8, the operation order also contained a subsequent mission for *I./FschJgRgt.1*. This was the seizure of the airfield at Kjeller, which lay about 17 km north-east of Oslo, in order to accelerate the air-landings.

Dense and low cloud over the Skagerrak made it necessary, for security reasons, to break up the flight formation of the two squadrons of *II./KG z.b.V.1* into individual flights of three aircraft each. When some of the aircraft lost visual contact within the formation its commanding officer, *Oberstleutnant* Drews, against the heavy protest of *Hauptmann* Walther, ordered his formation to return to Schleswig.[19] Drews reported his decision via radio to the air transport ground chief but received confirmation directly from the command of *X.Flieger-Korps*. All aircraft of the formation were now on their way back, except the flight of two Ju 52, with the battalion staff aboard, and the *Nachrichten-Ju*.

The air movement toward Fornebu was continued by 8 Me 110 fighters of *I./ZG 26* under *Oberleutnant* Hansen, which were detailed for close air support during the parachute assault and for protection against enemy fighters.

About 60 km west of the airfield the cloud cover began to break up. The aircraft were now visible and so received anti-aircraft fire from Fornebu airfield. Consequently the *Nachrichten-Ju* now turned away. The Me 110s which were flying ahead were engaged in a lengthy aerial combat with nine Norwegian Gloucester Gladiator biplane fighters which had taken off from the airfield. The fighters succeeded in shooting down one of their agile opponents and in destroying two more on the ground after these had landed on the airfield

---

17   The Me 110 and the Ju 87 B were unable to reach the Trondheim area in a non-stop flight from their jump-off airfields in Germany and therefore had to be refuelled underway.

18   It is interesting to note that the order of *Gruppe XXI* had foreseen that the *163.Infanterie-Division*, after landing in the port of Oslo and the occupation of the city, would have to secure it for the arrival of the parachute and air-landing forces at Fornebu. The mission for *I./FschJgRgt.1* therefore seems to have been valid only in case *163.Infanterie-Division* had not yet taken possession of the airfield.

19   The decision of *Oberstleutnant* Drews was probably influenced by the fact that not all of his crews had received training for flying by instruments.

to refuel. Two of the Me 110s were also lost. After the remaining Gladiators had withdrawn the Me 110s began to suppress the anti-aircraft weapons on the ground. The crews of two anti-aircraft machine guns at the northern edge of the airfield quickly abandoned their positions, whereas the three anti-aircraft guns in the emplacements at the eastern edge continued to fire heroically.

At 0933 hrs the two Ju 52 carrying the staff of *I./FschJgRgt.1*, *Oberleutnant* Götte, a medical officer, nine non-commissioned officers and five other ranks touched down on the airfield. The landing was successful, as the anti-aircraft guns had no view over its western part. Quickly the soldiers, who had got rid of their parachutes and picked up their arms from the weapon containers during the approach flight, occupied the buildings with the direction finder and the switchboard, after they had overcame the weak resistance of the Norwegians of a searchlight platoon west of the runway.

About this time the first of 53 Ju 52 of *KGr z.b.V.103*, with *II./InfRgt.324* aboard, which was following 20 minutes behind *I./FschJgRgt.1*, arrived at the airfield. The commanding officer of this group, *Hauptmann* Wagner, had also received an order to return to base from the command of *X.Flieger-Korps*. As this order was not submitted by the "air transport ground chief", as arranged beforehand, *Hauptmann* Wagner suspected a ruse by the enemy and carried on with his original mission.

The first Ju 52, piloted by *Hauptmann* Wagner, was hit by anti-aircraft fire during the descent. In this attack Wagner and four of the plane's passengers were killed. As a result this Ju 52 left formation, but the aircraft right behind it had managed to land undamaged and unloaded its infantrymen. In short intervals more and more transport aircraft followed.

In the meantime the first of the Me 110s, which were running out of fuel, also landed. Their crews joined in the combat on the ground, firing the rear machine guns of their aircraft at the anti-aircraft guns. These stopped firing at 1000 hrs because their crews withdrew about 3 km along the road leading to the north. Here, in positions more favourable for defence, they waited for reinforcements.[20]

By 1100hrs the majority of *II./InfRgt.324* was on the ground. The battalion took over the protection of the airfield from the paratroopers. In this brief engagement they captured six Norwegian soldiers and seized two anti-aircraft guns and two anti-aircraft machine guns as well as destroying two searchlights.

As ordered by the chief of staff of *Gruppe XXI*, *Hauptmann* Spiller, the *Luftwaffe attaché* at the German embassy in Oslo, arrived and temporarily took over the function of the airfield commandant.[21] At this time Spiller had no telephone or radio communication with the embassy and therefore was not informed of the costly failure of the Navy's *coup de main* in the Oslo Fjord. Here, the cruiser *Blücher*, which was leading *Gruppe 9* into the fjord, capsized after heavy bombardment from coastal guns and torpedo batteries of the Norwegian coastal command. It sank in the Døbrak defile. Around 1,500 of the 2,500 soldiers and naval personnel aboard the cruiser perished in this catastrophe. Among the

---

20 A company of the Norwegian Life Guard battalion from Oslo arrived too late, as the anti-aircraft crews had given up their positions in the face of approaching German infantry from the airfield.

21 *Oberstleutnant i.G.* Pohlmann arrived in Oslo on 8 April in civilian attire with directives for the German ambassador Dr. Bräuer. He also had been tasked by *General* von Falkenkorst to coordinate the German military actions around Oslo.

troops embarked had been elements of the staffs of *Gruppe XXI* and *163.Inf.Div.* as well as the SD members who were supposed to arrest the Norwegian king and government.[22]

Utilizing the considerable confusion on the Norwegian side, Götte and his men, riding in confiscated motor vehicles, managed to reach the German embassy around noon.[23] After he had reported the seizure of the airfield at Fornebu, the embassy's naval *attaché* guided his group to a Norwegian anti-aircraft position at the edge of Oslo in order to seize it. However the position had already been abandoned by its crew. Two heavy anti-aircraft guns, two anti-aircraft machine guns, a radio transmitter and a range finder were captured undamaged. On the way back to Oslo *Gruppe Götte* met with German infantry approaching from Fornebu and was informed about the capitulation of the Norwegian garrison of Oslo.[24]

The first shock troop, under *Oberleutnant* Götte, was tasked with the pursuit of the Norwegian king and government. For the mission the troop was reinforced with a heavy machine gun half-platoon of an infantry battalion and received marching orders for Hamar. Its task was to arrest the political leadership and to bring them back to Oslo.

About 30 km north of Oslo the shock troop came up against a Norwegian cavalry unit. An officer and 22 cavalrymen were taken prisoner and later two motorcycle dispatch-riders were also captured. However when superior Norwegian forces were detected, *Oberleutnant* Götte decided to withdraw his forces. During the ride back he quite unexpectedly met *2./ FschJgRgt.1* accompanied by *Hauptmann*s Walther and Spiller. *Hauptmann* Walther, who received the same mission as *Oberleutnant* Götte, ordered the latter to turn around and to take the point of the detachment with his shock troop. Quickly the question about the sudden appearance of *Hauptmann* Walther and his 2nd Company was answered.

After the commanding officer of *II./KG z.b.V.1* had ordered the two squadrons of his command with him to return to Schleswig his own aircraft, and those with the majority of *2./FschJgRgt.1* aboard had landed on one of the airfields at Ålborg around 1030 hrs. Upon hearing the news that Fornebu was in German hands these aircraft were refuelled.[25] At 1300 hrs they had taken off for Fornebu with *Hauptmann* Walther and his paratroopers who had left their jump gear and picked up their arms from the weapon containers. Together with the aircraft transporting *III./InfRgt.307,* Walther's detachment landed on Fornebu at 1500 hrs. *2./FschJgRgt.1* was made up less four squads, as their Ju 52 had joined the aircraft of *1./FschJgRgt.1* and taken the battalion's signals platoon back to Germany and finally to Stendal.[26] On this flight one Ju 52 with a squad of *1./FschJgRgt.1* aboard collided

---

22   Even after the seizure of the naval port Horten and Ranøy Island in the Oslo Fjord, the Norwegian resistance continued, meaning that the remainder of the warship group had not been able to enter the harbour of Oslo earlier than 1200 hrs.

23   After rejecting the German demand to accept the occupation of the country without military resistance, King Haakon VIII of Norway, his entourage and the majority of the Norwegian government left Oslo by train on 9 April at 0930 hrs and moved to Hamar, which lay about 110 km further to the north. In Oslo, Quisling had attempted to rescind the partly-called mobilization of the Norwegian armed forces, which added to the confusion.

24   The capitulation was arranged between the Norwegian military commandant of Oslo and the commanding officer of *InfRgt.324* in the fortress of Akershus. It was valid for all Norwegian troops and training installations within the city, but not for the 2nd Infantry Regiment, of which elements had been detailed for the protection of the airfield at Kjeller.

25   *III.* and *IV./KG z.b.V.1* delivered aviation fuel from Hagenow immediately after the seizure of the airfields at Ålborg.

26   This is the reason why the reports by *Hauptmann* Walther regarding the actions on 9 and 10 April against Hamar and Elverum speak of a strength of 80-100 men in his detachment.

with another Ju 52 and crashed into the sea. Its crew and all 12 paratroopers aboard were killed. With confiscated vehicles *Hauptmann* Walther and the reduced *2./FschJgRgt.1*, accompanied by *Hauptmann* Spiller, drove from Fornebu to Oslo and took billets in the city hall. Shortly afterwards *Hauptmann* Spiller had given the mission to *Hauptmann* Walther to bring back to Oslo the Norwegian king and government, who were presumed to be still in Hamar. *Hauptmann* Spiller then stayed with the detachment.

Due to the priority of the new mission, but probably also in view of the weak personnel strength of *2./FschJgRgt.1*, *Gruppe XXI* avoided undertaking the originally planned deployment of *I./FschJgRgt.1* against the airfield at Kjeller. The two battalions of *InfRgt.324*, parts of which were still on the move to Oslo, were considered indispensable for the occupation of the Norwegian capital and for the protection of Fornebu. At this time they were the only fully available units of combat troops after the failure of the *coup de main* from the sea. After all, elements of the Norwegian 1st and 2nd divisions were known to be positioned in the vicinity of Oslo and could well attempt actions to retake the city.

After some vehicles had been confiscated, the majority of *2./FschJgRgt.1* had to ride on two buses, *Abteilung Walther* moved out at 1700 hrs in the evening darkness and after a while picked up *Stoßtrupp Götte*.

Just before midnight on 9 April the point of Walther's column was stopped at a barricaded bridge at the southern entrance to Hamar and was fired on by infantry. Half an hour later the obstacle was removed after the Norwegian pickets had withdrawn. One squad of paratroopers remained in Hamar, tasked with the mission to occupy the public buildings and to interrupt telephone communications from the town to the outside. On 10 April 0045 hrs the detachment moved on in the direction of Elverum on receipt of information that the Norwegian king and government had settled down there for the night.

At around 0110 hrs the detachment came up against a road barrier at the farmstead at Midtskogen, about 4 km south of Elverum. From there it was fired at with machine guns and rifles.[27] During the advance of *2./FschJgRgt.1* upon the road barrier one paratrooper was killed and *Hauptmann* Spiller was mortally wounded. The heavily defended farmstead was taken after half an hour of combat and two Norwegians were captured. Due to the growing resistance in front of Elverum, *Hauptmann* Walther decided to break off the engagement and to return to Oslo. After picking up the squad left back in Hamar the march continued under sporadic rifle fire from the surrounding terrain.

About 30 km south of Hamar the detachment encountered a large column of motor vehicles manned by Norwegian soldiers and approaching from the opposite direction. By bold and resolute action the paratroopers succeeded in disarming a few hundred of their surprised opponents, among them were 30 officers and a colonel.[28] The seized Norwegian unit was the 1st Regiment of Dragoons. Its equipment comprised some field guns but the officers were taken prisoner and the vehicles were integrated into the column. The hundreds of Norwegian other ranks were sent away into the adjoining terrain with some shots fired in the air, after they had shown some signs of resistance in the face of the few Germans.

---

27   The road had been barred and occupied by some mobilized soldiers of the Norwegian 15th Infantry Regiment and probably also by soldiers of the 1st Company of the Life Guard battalion, who had been on a field exercise near Elverum with its three machine gun platoons and its mortar platoon.

28   German after-action reports differ about the number of Norwegian soldiers in the column -between 400 and 900. Norwegian sources, stating about 400-500 men, are probably correct.

Walther's column was now considerably larger, and with many of the captured vehicles now being driven by inexperienced paratroopers, moved on.

Shortly after a Norwegian anti-aircraft position was taken out, at about 1100hrs the point of the detachment came up against another column of Norwegian troops in front of a bridge some 30 km south of Minnesund. However, this time the Norwegians were combat ready. The German leading vehicles were stopped from crossing the bridge by only a few shots in front of them. The commanding officer of the Norwegian force seemed to be well informed about the low strength of Walther's detachment and so he dispatched an officer with a flag of truce. He referred to three infantry regiments and artillery following close behind the Norwegian column and requested Walther to surrender. However the German commander refused to believe this ruse. He called a bluff on his part, making the negotiator believe that three parachute infantry regiments had been dropped right behind his detachment and was poised for attack if the case that the road was not cleared of the Norwegians. As a consequence he requested their capitulation. Eventually a mutual ceasefire was agreed upon and Walther's detachment, made up of about 50 vehicles, including the captured officers, passed the Norwegian column without incident. At around 1700 hrs it arrived at a German outpost on the edge of Oslo. Beside the captured prisoners and the vehicles, the booty comprised 3 field guns, 7 heavy and 21 light machine guns, 600 rifles and 220,000 rounds for infantry weapons. On the way into the city, *Hauptmann* Walther stopped at the fortress of Akershus in order to report to the commander of the *162.Inf. Div.*, *Generalmajor* Engelbrecht, who in the meantime was placed in charge of all troops of the *Heer* around Oslo. For the first time *Generalmajor* Engelbrecht received regarding the operations of Walther's soldiers, who had not slept for the past 48 hours and lived under conditions of continuous strain, they now spent the night 10/11 April resting in their quarters in Oslo City Hall.

In the course of the morning of 10 April the remainder of the troops, who had originally been allocated for the occupation of Oslo from the sea, had been landed in the city's port. Some of them were immediately employed against Norwegian forces identified north and south of the capital. *Abteilung Walther* was also drawn upon for reconnaissance. *2./FschJgRgt.1* received a mission early in the morning of 11 April; together with two companies of infantry it was to advance into the hinterland of Oslo to the North and East.

The company moved out at 0730 hrs in the direction of Lillestrøm-Fedsund. At a destroyed bridge across the Vorma River west of Mes the point platoon, under *Leutnant* Zuber, met with its first resistance. The balance of *2./FschJgRgt.1* bypassed the contested area, moved on in a northerly direction and crossed the Vorma over an undefended bridge at Swanfossen and advanced along the river. The new point platoon under *Leutnant* Graf von Blücher, consisting of two squads, soon encountered an abatis in front of Bastuolen and was fired at from a nearby hill by riflemen in civilian clothes. A shock troop, ordered forward by the company commander stormed the hill, consequently most of its defenders were killed in the firefight.[29] In the meantime, other sub-units of the company had overcome the weak

---

29   It remains unclear whether Norwegian civilians who fought were members of the territorial force who had just been called up and had not found time to change into their uniforms. It cannot be excluded that the volunteers were from Sweden and, coming to the aid of the Norwegians, had crossed the nearby border. The event id not receive the attention of German higher commands. It may even have remained unknown

resistance in Bastuolen. The two infantry companies which had been transported in buses took almost no part in the engagement at Bastuolen. Their transports had continuously broken down and therefore had not caught up with the paratroopers.

On 11 April *2./FschJgRgt.1* returned to Oslo. During the mission one soldier was seriously wounded. It brought back 20 Norwegians as prisoners, two of whom wore civilian clothing. A heavy machine gun with 3,000 cartridges, 10 rifles and various entrenching tools had also been captured.

Leutnant Zuber and 11 other ranks from *2./FschJgRgt.1* were detailed to an infantry battalion on 12 April, in order to instruct its personnel about the experience gained so far in combat against the Norwegians. The infantry battalion was to conduct a reconnaissance in force into the area of Spyderberg, where elements of a Norwegian division were suspected of being based. When the infantry was engaged, Zuber's men were ordered to outflank an enemy force which had tied down an infantry platoon. The mission was undertaken successfully but on their way back the paratroopers were hit by concentrated machine gun and artillery fire. The fire caused a *Feldwebel* and another paratrooper to be seriously wounded. The latter died during his evacuation.

With the reconnaissance mission accomplished Zuber's detachment reported back to the company at 1600 hrs.

The following day *2./FschJgRgt.1* was again employed. It was to reconnoitre via Dammen and Titusberg against Porsgrunn, about 40 km south-west of Oslo, and to destroy a broadcasting station there. For the mission the company was reinforced with the three captured 8.5cm field guns and with 25 artillerymen as crews. The inexperience of the driver caused a truck to overturn near Dammen, causing two soldiers to be seriously hurt and five others lightly. So far the company had come up against a road guard only once. In this event six Norwegians, who had been captured, reached Porsgrunn and destroyed the broadcasting station, as ordered. In spite of the fatigue of the drivers, the road march back through partly mountainous terrain was accomplished without further incidents. The detachment arrived in Oslo on 14 April 0100 hrs. Here the soldiers had a well-deserved rest.

1./FschJgRgt.1, together with the battalion's signals platoon and four squads of *2./FschJgRgt.1*, was flown back to Schleswig as ordered by *Oberstleutnant* Drews. On order of *X.Flieger-Korps* these paratroopers was airlifted to Stendal on 12 April and arrived about 1300 hrs. On the same day at 1530 hrs *X.Flieger-Korps* was ordered to convey *1./FschJgRgt.1* and the signals platoon to Oslo. The squad of the company which was lost over the North Sea had been replaced by one of the four squads of *2./FschJgRgt.1* which were also to be returned to Stendal. After a stop-over in Schleswig, *1./FschJgRgt.1* and the signals platoon were airlifted to Oslo-Fornebu, where they arrived on 13 April at 1900 hrs and took billets near the airfield.

On this evening a meeting was convened at the headquarters of *Gruppe XXI* in a hotel in Oslo, to which *Hauptmann* Walther had also been ordered to attend. The subject of the meeting was a parachute operation in the area of Dombås. Some time earlier, the *OKW* had conducted deliberations about the employment of parachute forces in central Norway.

to them, as Hitler, in his order to *General* von Falkenhorst on 9 May 1940 to release all captured mobilized Norwegian soldiers, had explicitly stated that no Norwegian civilians had participated in combat against German troops.

These deliberations were probably triggered by intelligence about preparations for the landing of troops of the Western allies at Trondheim and Bergen which had been gathered by German signal and air reconnaissance.[30]

On the morning of 14 April consultations about parachute operations in central Norway were continued, but now under the direction of the liaison staff of the *Luftwaffe* at *Gruppe XXI* under *Oberst* Knaus. The basis for a decision was a directive from the *OKW*, which arrived at *Gruppe XXI* headquarters in the morning and contained an order for the employment of *Fallschirmtruppe* in the area of Dombås. This town, halfway between Oslo and Trondheim at the northern exit of the Gudbrandsdal and about 250 km north-west of Oslo, constituted an important traffic hub. Here the railway and the road from Oslo merged in a westerly direction toward the coast at Åndalsnes, and in a northerly direction toward Trondheim. Whoever wanted to exercise control over central Norway therefore had to be in possession of Dombås.

The conference was attended by the commanding officer of *II./KG z.b.V.1*, *Oberstleutnant* Drews, responsible for the transport of the paratroopers to the drop zone; *Hauptmann* Walther; *Oberleutnant* Schmidt, the commanding officer of *1./FschJgRgt.1*; *Oberleutnant* Diley from *3./StG 1*, which was to fly interdiction against the railway from Åndalsnes and *Hauptmann* Flakowski, the commandant of the airfield at Fornebu.

Shortly after noon, the operation order for the liaison staff was ready. It stated:[31]

- That British naval forces had landed troops at Åndalsnes in the course of 13 April.
- Friendly motorized forces had advanced to Dombås via Lillehammer. Bombing attacks from Stavanger against British naval forces and troops around Åndalsnes could be counted upon.
- In order to prevent the advance of the British landing force from Åndalsnes to Dombås

  > *I./FschJgRgt.1* (two companies)
  > *II./KG z.b.V.1*
  > *3./StG 1*

will be employed and placed under command of *Gruppe XXI*.

Execution:

a)   *3./StG 1* is to destroy the railway Åndalsnes-Dombås at vulnerable points as far to the north-west as possible;

b)   *I./FschJgRgt.1* is to seize the traffic hub at Dombås;

c)   *II./KG z.b.V.1* is to reconnoitre, together with *I./FschJgRgt.1*, suitable terrain for the parachuting near Dombås; drops elements of *I./FschJgRgt.1*, and is to prepare to supply the dropped parachute units from the air.

More precise information about the situation was not available to the liaison staff. The Germans, however, had also recognized the landing of British troops at Namsos about 220

---

30   Shortly after the loss of Trondheim, and more urgently on 12 April, the Norwegian high command urgently requested that efforts be made to retake the town by a coordinated action of Allied amphibious forces and Norwegian troops. The Allied supreme war council shared the view of the Norwegians that the possession of Trondheim was the prime prerequisite for the retention of central Norway and had initiated measures for the taking of the town.

31   The order has been translated into English as closely as possible to the German text.

km north of Trondheim, during the night of 13/14 April and probably had also detected the approach of naval convoys with additional troops toward the Norwegian coast.

As was found out later, the Allied supreme war council, after some deliberation, had decided to cancel a direct attack against Trondheim. Instead, Operation Maurice, the British 146th Brigade (2 bns) and the 5e demi-brigade of the French 5th Light Division were to be landed at Namsos. It had been the advance-party of these forces, some 350 British marines and armed sailors, whose landing in Namsos on the night of 13/14 April was detected by the Germans. At Åndalsnes, about 350 km south-west of Trondheim, the British 15th and 148th brigades (3 bns each) were to be landed shortly in Operation Sickle. In cooperation with Norwegian troops Maurice Force and Sickle Force subsequently were to seize Trondheim from two sides.

The command of *Gruppe XXI* was now aware of the threat to the garrison at Trondheim. For the time being the town could only be reinforced and resupplied from the air and possibly by submarine because of the appearance of strong British and French naval forces along the coast of central and northern Norway and of the resulting closure of the land lines of communication. Therefore it ordered *163.Inf.Div.* to advance along the Gudbrandsdal via Lillehammer to Dombås and from there along the Romsdal Valley to Åndalsnes. Simultaneously *196.Inf.Div.* was to advance along the Østerdal Valley east of the Gudbrandsdal and then through the Glomma Valley directly toward Trondheim. It was intended to crush the Norwegian troops in central Norway, so as to prevent Allied forces from establishing themselves there and to open the land lines of communication to Trondheim. The employment of parachute forces with the aim of delaying the advance of Allied troops into central Norway and their union with the Norwegians, had obviously been part of the plan which in its principal feature was developed by the *OKW*.

Upon agreement of all parties participating in the conference on 14 April in the morning, *1./FschJgRgt.1* and the signals platoon of *I./FschJgRgt.1* were designated to conduct the parachute operation at Dombås, [32] altogether 4 officers and 173 other ranks.[33]

This allocation had constituted not only a divergence from the directive of the *OKW*, which, in its operation order 3c, had stated that Dombås was to be seized and held by all available *Fallschirmtruppe*. It had also deviated from the operation order of *Gruppe XXI*, which had foreseen the employment of both companies of *I./FschJgRgt.1*.[34]

Two serious restrictions stopped the execution of this mission on 14 April;

---

32   The assignment of the signals platoon, despite its restricted combat value, can only be explained by a desire to maintain communication with the commands in Oslo. The radios of the signals platoon were not technically suited for ground-to-air communication with supporting aircraft.

33   Conveyed to the author in 2006 by Alexander Uhlig, who participated in the mission at Dombås as commander of the heavy weapons platoon of *1./FschJgRgt.1*, who recorded the events in a personal diary during the deployment. The force comprised 12 men in the HQ section, 36 men in the signals platoon and 36 men each in the 2nd and 3rd Platoons. 1st Platoon was lacking one man and the heavy weapons platoon had left behind two of its 24 men and the 5cm mortar because of a lack of capacity in the assigned 15 Ju 52s.

34   An explanation for these deviations could be that *2./FschJgRgt.1* had returned from its mission at Porsgrunn as late as 14 April 0100 hrs totally exhausted, and was still without its jump equipment, which had been left back in Ålborg. Quite obviously *Gruppe XXI* had been surprised.

First there were extremely unfavourable weather conditions. Dense fog came down to less than 100m over the Fornebu airfield and at times icy sleet rained down. Additionally, for the flight route from Fornebu to Dombås, the weather service reported that the mountains were shrouded in low cloud and that there was a risk of icing-up of aircraft in heights over 1,000m. Secondly there was still a total lack of information about the situation in the operational area around Dombås.

Therefore at 1300 hrs *Oberst* Knaus decided that the following requirements had to be fulfilled by aerial reconnaissance prior to the execution of the mission:

There was to be a clear picture about the weather conditions over and in the area of operation, the location of suitable drop zones was to be noted and the options for the enemy to interfere with the operation to be recorded

None of these requirements, however, would be met. At 1430 hrs *Oberstleutnant* Drews reported to *Oberst* Knaus that the reconnaissance aircraft were unable to take off because of the weather. At 1500 hrs *Generalmajor* Süßmann appeared at the airfield. He introduced himself as the chief-of-staff of *General der Flieger* Kitzinger, the designated territorial commander of the *Luftwaffe* for Norway, who had arrived with his staff in Oslo just a few hours earlier.

Generalmajor Süßmann took over command for the execution of the parachute mission after the liaison staff had been disbanded on short notice. He exerted considerable pressure on the commanders of the aviation elements, who had been hesitant to execute their missions because of the weather conditions and the lack of ground intelligence from the operational area. Eventually they had to comply with Süßmann's order for immediate take-off, lest that they were accused of insubordination. No objections against the immediate execution of the mission had been brought forward by *Oberleutnant* Schmidt and *Hauptmann* Walther took no further part in the decision making process that afternoon.

The paratroopers of *1./FschJgRgt.1* and the signals platoon arrived at the airfield at 1630 hrs. They had only been marginally instructed regarding their mission by the platoon leaders and *Oberstleutnant* Drews was now pressing for take-off, in view of the approaching darkness and the lack of appropriate maps of the operational area. The paratroopers mounted the 15 Ju 52s. The aircraft took off in flights of three aircraft in the sequence, HQ section and heavy weapons platoon – signals platoon – 3rd, 2nd, 1st Platoon took off between 1700 and 1730 hrs.

The first two flights flew in cloud using instruments only. In the airspace over Lillehammer one of the Ju 52s, which carried men of the signals platoon, was shot down by Norwegian anti-aircraft weapons but managed to conduct an emergency landing. All passengers and crew survived. In the ensuing firefight with investigating Norwegian infantry the dispatcher was killed. The other soldiers, some of them wounded or injured, were taken prisoner.[35]

At about 1830 hrs the Ju 52 of *Oberstleutnant* Drews descended from the cloud cover over Dombås. As the aircraft received fire from this direction, *Oberleutnant* Schmidt and his HQ section were dropped about 8 km south of the town. Advancing toward Dombås in terrain covered in deep snow the section was engaged by a Norwegian outpost. First *Oberleutnant* Schmidt was seriously wounded and a *Feldwebel* was slightly wounded. The

---

35   At the time of this event the high command of the Norwegian Army was located in Lillehammer. The captured airmen and paratroopers were liberated on 24 April by German forces advancing along the Gudbrandsdal.

men now withdrew again to the South, carrying the company commander along. At some distance from Dombås an all-round defence position was set up in the snow. The original arrangements, to lay out signal panels and to fire very lights as identification for the other aircraft, were not carried out.

The two other Ju 52 of the first flight, with a heavy weapons platoon aboard, lost contact with the leading aircraft. They dropped their passengers about 25 km east of Dombås close to the hamlet of Lora along the railway and road leading to Åndalsnes. The platoon leader, *Feldwebel* Uhlig, ordered the occupation of Lora and placed outposts around the hamlet. At 2100 hrs the machine gun outpost at the eastern entrance to Lora was engaged in a firefight with a Norwegian reconnaissance patrol. They succeeded in driving off the Norwegians but one of his soldiers was killed. The platoon's position had now been detected by the enemy and consequently was far too exposed. Uhlig decided to withdraw his men to a farmstead away from the road and set up a position at this location.

The two Ju 52s which carried 24 soldiers of the signals platoon, among them the platoon leader, *Oberleutnant* Gerhold, dropped their passengers just below the peak of an almost 1,600m high mountain which was about 10 km east of Dombås. With great efforts in the deep snow on the slope and in a continuing snow storm, the men managed to assemble and to recover their equipment. As everybody was exhausted and orienteering was impossible in the darkness, *Oberleutnant* Gerhold ordered the building of snow caves for the men to spend the night in.

After the two aircraft which carried members of the 1st Platoon had crossed the Dovre-Fjlell mountains, the 23 paratroopers and their platoon leader, *Leutnant* Becker, jumped into the basin of Dombås, close to a railway. In the snow storm seven of the soldiers were dragged over the ground by their parachutes, causing some of them to be seriously injured. As a result the assembly of men took considerable time. Moreover, some of the weapon containers remained undiscovered due to the drifting snow. As adequate maps were unavailable, it was only after searching some huts close to the railway, that the location of the drop zone could eventually be found. It was at Fostua, which lay about 10 km east of Dombås. Due to the inclement weather and the bad condition of some of his men, *Leutnant* Becker decided to spend the night in the available huts. The missing squad of 1st Platoon jumped south east of Dombås. After they had recovered their weapon containers, the 12 men started moving in order to establish contact with other elements of the company.

The two rear flights of Ju 52s, with the 2nd Platoon led by *Leutnant* Mößinger and the 3rd Platoon under *Feldwebel* Bobrowski, had approached Dombås, in low level flight, along the railway from Oslo. Over Hamar the aircraft which carried 2nd Platoon received heavy anti-aircraft fire which slightly wounded the platoon leader.

Two of the Ju 52s, with *Leutnant* Mößinger and 23 paratroopers of the 2nd Platoon aboard, dropped their passengers about 2 km south of Dombås. Only some of their weapon containers could be found. As they advanced in the direction of Dombås, the platoon came up against a column of Norwegian soldiers about 400m in front of the town. In the ensuing fight one paratrooper was killed. A *Feldwebel* who was missing after the encounter was captured by the Norwegians. The platoon disengaged and made its way in a southerly direction to make contact with the HQ section. Led by *Leutnant* Mößinger, both sub-units in the darkness continued the withdrawal to the farmstead at Hagevoll, about 3 km south of Dombås, located by the road leading to Dovre.

The missing squad of 2nd Platoon, a *Stabsfeldwebel* and 11 other ranks, conducted an emergency jump about one kilometre southeast of Dombås, when their Ju 52 began to go down after it was hit by anti-aircraft fire. The pilot and the observer of the aircraft were killed in the resulting crash, the other two members of the crew were injured. The squad which had escaped the crash by its emergency jump was completely on its own. Its men tried in vain to recover their weapon containers from the wreck of the Ju 52.

The last flight, with the 3rd Platoon aboard, dropped the paratroopers of the second aircraft and five of the third, on a hill about 5 km east of Dombås. Their assembly in the deep snow took quite some time and was very strenuous and, as with elsewhere, some of the weapon containers remained lost. Advancing toward Dombås, Bobrowski's men came up against superior numbers of Norwegian soldiers approaching from the town. After a short contact they managed to disengage, but one paratrooper was killed and a *Feldwebel* was recorded missing. A reconnaissance patrol was now dispatched in order to avoid being surprised again and to establish contact with the balance of the company. After some time the patrol met a few men from 2nd Platoon, returning from a demolition mission at the railway north of Dombås. These guided the 3rd Platoon to the farmstead at Hagevoll.

The missing paratroopers from the third aircraft, a *Stabsfeldwebel* and 6 other ranks, had jumped too soon right over Dombås and were attacked while landing. During their desperate resistance with only pistols and hand grenades, the *Stabsfeldwebel* and one man were killed, and two other paratroopers were wounded. All five survivors of the firefight were subsequently captured.

By nightfall of 14 April the reinforced *1./FschJgRgt.1* was split up into five isolated groups over an area of 30 by 15 km. Of the 15 Ju 52s which had flown the unit to its operational area two had been shot down. Three others, including the aircraft of the group commander, had been forced to conduct emergency landings on the way back.[36] Three Ju 52s had reached the airfield at Trondheim-Stjørdal, which was by now in German hands. The remaining seven aircraft, some of them damaged, made it back to Fornebu.

The Norwegian troops around Dombås had arrived prior to the German parachute operation.[37] They were by now fully alerted and combat ready to a high degree. Reports about German paratroopers had quite certainly been sent to the military command in Dombås by inhabitants of the settlements around this town, as the telephone net had still been operational. This enabled it to direct counter-measures quickly and effectively.

Early in the morning of 15 April the commanders and men of reinforced *1./FschJgRgt.1* set out to accomplish their mission, despite the unfortunate start of the operation. Dombås was to be the primary objective.

---

36   One had landed in Swedish territory. The Swedes interned the crew and the battered aircraft was returned to the Germans a year later.

37   As the Norwegian high command was conscious of the importance of Dombås for the operations of both sides in central Norway, it must be assumed that strong elements of two line and one territorial battalions of 11th Infantry Regiment, as well as of three anti-aircraft platoons, all of which had their garrison and mobilization points in Åndalsnes/Setnesmoen, had been ordered to the traffic hub at Dombås.

The 12 paratroopers of 2nd Platoon, who had managed to jump from a falling aircraft 12 km south-east of Dombås and were armed only with pistols and hand grenades, were confronted at first light by vastly superior Norwegian troops. After a short engagement they were forced to surrender.

Leaving the injured soldiers behind in one of the huts, 1st Platoon moved out from Fokstua at about 0500 hrs. On the railway the paratroopers discovered four small drays which they rode on the track toward Dombås. As there was no contact with enemy forces up to now, they were unaware of the presence of Norwegian troops in considerable strength in and around the town. Accordingly they were far from cautious on the ride. About 2 km north of Dombås the paratroopers took fire from both sides of the track. From the drays, which had collided with each other, they returned fire but were, from the very first moment of the ambush, in a hopeless situation. Increasingly surrounded by the Norwegians, *Leutnant* Becker ordered his men to give up the fight and to surrender. Shortly afterwards the Norwegians took the injured paratroopers left behind at Fokstua prisoner.

After a little rest in the snow caves and at an altitude of 1,500m, early in the morning the signals platoon moved out in the direction of the sound of some explosions, which were thought to originate from an eastward direction. The platoon was joined by the squad of 1st Platoon, which had been dropped and isolated south-west of Dombås but had reached the location of the signals platoon. The troops were heavily burdened with the communication equipment and so moved downhill in the deep snow with great difficulty. Turning northward, and after several hours, they reached a few huts. Stopping for a rest and totally exhausted, they observed a column of Norwegian trucks halting on the road from Dombås to Åndalsnes about 5 km away. During the further move, the *Stabsfeldwebel*, who was reconnoitring some distance ahead, was nowhere to be found. Nevertheless the platoon struggled along until at 1800 hrs. Still about 1.5 km south of the hamlet at Bølia and 3 km away from the road leading to Åndalsnes, it was fired at by machine guns. When these stopped firing, a *Feldwebel* of the 1st Platoon and Norwegian soldiers approached under a flag of truce. The *Feldwebel* reported that he was to demand the surrender of the platoon, as it was surrounded by Norwegian ski-troops. After a Norwegian officer declared that the paratroopers would remain in Norwegian custody and not be turned over to the British, *Oberleutnant* Gerhold ordered his men to destroy their radios and weapons and give themselves up.

The elements of *1./FschJgRgt.1* assembled in the farmstead at Hagevoll on the morning of 15 April totalled 2 officers and 61 other ranks. *Oberleutnant* Schmidt, who was unable to move and was being taken care of by a medical *Feldwebel* in the farm's cow-shed, decided to stay at the present location for the time being. From here, the railway tracks were to be demolished. The telephone lines and the circuits in the vicinity of the farm were to be destroyed. The tactical commander, *Oberleutnant* Schmidt, ceded command to the two platoon leaders.

Around the farmstead, field positions were built. The road through Hagevoll was barred in both directions. The demolition of the railway immediately north-east of Hagevoll was successful. However, it remained impossible to establish communications with Oslo from the radio which had been taken along by the HQ section. Therefore the paratroopers wrote into the snow in large letters 'Ammunition! Food! We hold out!' for friendly aircraft to see. Nevertheless very little tine remained to prepare for the defence at Hagevoll. On 15 April, at about 1100 hrs, Norwegian soldiers on skis and in snow-camouflage clothing appeared in front of the farmstead. As they were just a reconnaissance party they were easily driven off but the position of the paratroopers had now been detected. Around noon a single Ju 52 appeared over Hagevoll. It was heavily assaulted from the surrounding terrain as it dropped containers with ammunition. As these come down without parachutes they became badly dented on impact with the ground, meaning that most of the ammunition was unusable.

At about 1300 hrs the Norwegians again advanced toward Hagevoll, this time in trucks along the road from Dovre. After the Norwegian recognized the situation at Hagevoll, they dismounted and continued the advance on foot. From their forward positions, the paratroopers opened fire at close range. The Norwegian captain in charge and six of his men were killed. All others, about 30 soldiers, some of them wounded, were taken prisoner by the paratroopers.[38]

At about 1700 hrs, the defenders of Hagevoll defeated another attack by the Norwegians, this time supported by heavy machine guns and mortars. After a reconnaissance patrol reported the arrival of a trainload of troops from Åndalsnes in Dombås, a demolition party was sent out at 2200 hrs in order to block the railway west of Dombås. The party returned around midnight with nothing achieved. It reported that Hagevoll was completely encircled by Norwegian troops.

During the night of 15/16 April the positions held by the paratroopers were under continuous fire from the surrounding terrain. At dawn another demolition party moved out against the railway west of Dombås and a small reconnaissance patrol was tasked with gaining a picture of the situation in the area near the town. Both teams failed to return and it was later discovered that one of the soldiers of the demolition party was killed and both teams had been captured.

At some point during a counter-thrust of paratroopers against closely advancing Norwegians, on the morning of 16 April, more prisoners were taken, increasing their overall number to almost forty. Shortly after some motor cars, which were approaching on the road from Dombås, were ambushed by fire from an outpost of the paratroopers. Leaving behind the dead, the wounded and the vehicles, the survivors fled. A shock troop, led by *Leutnant* Mößinger, which investigated the vehicles, discovered that one of them was filled with bundles of money totalling around two millions of Norwegian Crowns. More important for the shock troop, however, were the rucksacks full of food which had been left behind – the hunger of the defenders and their prisoners had become an increasing issue. In addition the medical treatment of the many wounded became increasingly difficult, as, against orders, no medical officer was assigned to the company's HQ section and the medical *Feldwebel*, though accomplishing his tasks to the best of his ability, was clearly overworked.

---

38   The event is well covered by Norwegian sources. The captain and 37 soldiers had been detailed as an escort for the king, his family and members of the government on their journey along the Gudbrandsdal to Åndalsnes, where they were to embark for northern Norway. Whereas the king, who had travelled by rail, had spent the night 14/15 April in Otta, about 40 km away from Dombås, the members of the government had already moved on by car to Dovre together with the escort. Here two of the ministers, one of them being Trygve Lie (who after the war was appointed secretary general of the UN), had called upon the captain to drive ahead of them to Dombås, as they were of the opinion that only a few survivors of downed German aircraft were blocking the road at Hagevoll.

At about 1400 hrs the Norwegian troops attacked again. This time they also employed light artillery.[39] Hagevoll now became untenable and the commanders of the paratroopers agreed to move to another position after nightfall. In order to lengthen the time until then, and to keep the surrounding enemy busy, one of the Norwegian prisoners was sent to their commanding officer with a demand for surrender. After a short while, a captured parachute *Feldwebel* appeared at Hagevoll, with a demand from the local Norwegian commander to give up further resistance. The latter's announcement, to have all captured paratroopers shot if his demand was not accepted, was regarded as an empty threat. The request therefore was refused by *Oberleutnant* Schmidt.

The bombardment of Hagevoll commenced at 2100 hrs, but was interrupted and the evacuation of the position commenced at 2230 hrs. The wounded and the prisoners were transported in captured vehicles along the road to the south. About 1 km away the point group of the paratroopers came up against a road block south of the hamlet of Arnkleiv, from which it received machine gun and rifle fire. In a lightning action the barricade was stormed and about 20 Norwegians were taken prisoner. A short distance to the south, the company settled down for the night in some buildings along the road, protected by strong security elements. The rearguard, which was using the captured Norwegian machine guns, soon caught up with the rest of the company. During the various engagements in the course of 16 April, two more paratroopers had been killed and four wounded, among them, for the second time, *Leutnant* Mößinger.

On this day the commitment of the heavy weapons platoon came to an end. It had left its billets in the early hours of 16 April and had moved along the valley of a brook south of the railway in the direction toward Dombås. After a march of 13 km, for which the 21 soldiers were loaded with heavy machine guns, anti-tank rifles and ammunition cases, marched for six hours in deep snow, before being surrounded by Norwegian ski-patrols. As it was impossible to set up firing positions for the two heavy machine guns and resistance consisted of just four rifles, *Feldwebel* Uhlig decided to surrender his platoon at 1500 hrs after the men had made their weapons unusable.

In the early morning hours of 17 April the paratroopers around *Oberleutnant* Schmidt and their prisoners continued their movement and set up a new position about 3 km to the east in the farmsteads at Lindsø. From here the railway and the road which led from Dombås to Dovre could be dominated by fire. The railway close to the new position was once more blown up. Outposts did manage to capture some Norwegian soldiers who attempted to bypass Lindsø in a northward direction, among them a staff officer.

Soon the enemy was moving forward against this new position. During contacts with patrols a paratrooper was killed, another was wounded, as were several of the prisoners. The defenders had also run out of field dressing material. During the night of 17/18 April a

---

39   Although none of the available sources confirms the origin of this artillery, the light field guns employed against Hagevoll could have come from the two batteries of 3rd Artillery Regiment, which had been garrisoned at Trondheim and probably had been partly mobilized before the town had fallen into German hands.

Norwegian attack was warded off, similarly an attack by stronger forces at first light on 18 April was also repelled.

At around 1100 hrs a Ju 52 appeared over the contested area. Probably attracted by the lights of the paratroopers, it dropped a container with machine gun ammunition, warm clothing, rations and medical material. Also dropped was information about the frequency by which radio communication with the aircraft could be established from the ground. Fortunately, this method worked.[40] Now the crew of the Ju 52 could be informed about the situation at Lindsø and was asked about the arrival of relief forces. After the question about landing sites for aircraft with infantry aboard was not answered from the ground, it bid farewell, announcing that relief by ground forces could be expected in one or two days.

However the resupply drop had alerted the Norwegians. In the afternoon they commenced another attack and for the first time a heavy gun was employed.[41] The defenders of Lindsø were forced back to their original positions. After another paratrooper was killed and more wounded the number of combat effectives was reduced to about forty. As a result the prisoners had to be guarded by the less seriously wounded men. There was also the problem of about 50 inhabitants from the farmsteads who were still living in the defended buildings.

At 1700 hrs a Norwegian officer delivered a demand for surrender under a flag of truce. When this was turned down again the commanding officer of the Norwegians let *Oberleutnant* Schmidt know that the Norwegians would from now on shell the position without regard for the prisoners and the civilians. During the negotiations a Norwegian medical doctor, who had arrived together with the officer, treated the most seriously wounded of both sides.

The shelling was maintained through the night of 18/19 April and in the morning the Norwegians, supported by artillery and mortars, attacked Lindsø from three sides. Yet again, ultimate success was denied to them. A new demand for surrender was again refused by *Oberleutnant* Schmidt, who gambled for time by the announcement that a German bombing attack was underway.

In the course of the renewed battle, a Ju 52 with resupply stores once more approached Lindsø. However, the aircraft was directed by a radio on the ground to turn away, as the ring of enemy around the position was considered too tight to allow for the recovery of dropped material.

After two more paratroopers were killed and three wounded by the increasingly precise fire of the enemy, their ammunition running out and a successful breakout considered impossible, *Oberleutnant* Schmidt, in agreement with his two platoon leaders, around noon

---

40   The fact that radio communication between the paratroopers on the ground at Lindsø and a Ju 52 was made on 18 April and again on 20 April (confirmed in the after action-report for Norway by *I./FschJgRgt.1*) requires an explanation. Several trustworthy sources, among them members of the signals branch of the German parachute force and the officer who had piloted the Ju 52 of the commander of the air transport group involved in the operation at Dombås, have stated that the radio sets of the parachute units and those in the transport and combat aircraft of the *Luftwaffe* were technically incompatible for ground-to-air communications and vice versa in the parachute assaults of 1940 in the west and 1941 in Crete. The solution to this problem found for Dombås was probably that a radio set, as used by the paratroopers on the ground, had hastily been built into the Ju 52 which had twice been detailed for a resupply mission. For unknown reasons this method was not repeated for the parachute operations in the west or against the island of Crete.

41   It was a 4-inch howitzer. Two guns of this type had been brought ashore by the advance party of Sickle Force at Åndalsnes. One was transported together with its crew by rail to Dombås.

decided to end the fight. After the remaining ammunition was used up, the radio and the weapons were destroyed and the position was handed over to the Norwegians at 1400 hrs.

The paratroopers at Lindsø were taken prisoners. Initially they were taken to Dombås, where they were also interrogated by British officers.[42] In the evening the men who were considered fit for transport were brought to Åndalsnes. There they joined the previously captured paratroopers. During the transport to Åndalsnes, a *Feldwebel* and a private managed to escape, however they were caught by British soldiers and were later sent to Canada under British custody.

The 3 officers and 126 other ranks of reinforced *1./FschJgRgt.1* deemed fit for transport were then loaded on a trawler and brought to Kristiansund, an island about 60 km north of Åndalsnes. There they were confined in a school building under strong guard. When Kristiansund was completely destroyed by a German bombing attack on 28 April, the paratroopers were moved to a heavily guarded prison camp on the isle of Averøy, not far from the previous location. There one of the men was shot in the camp, without any reason, by a soldier of the guard from outside the camp. His was the twenty-fourth death since the start of the company's deployment.

On 5 May a detachment of motorcycle infantry from *Regiment General Göring* reached Averøy and liberated their fellow soldiers. The paratroopers, who by this action had been saved from being shipped to Great Britain, were brought back to Oslo, where they arrived on 9 May. Still marked by the past combat and captivity they were ordered, quite incomprehensibly to them, to remain there. A few days earlier the seriously wounded of the company had arrived by means of a medical transport, but had immediately been moved to military hospitals in Germany. They had been taken care of by Norwegians in a medical installation in Alesund (about 80 km west of Åndalsnes) until the arrival of German troops.

Abteilung Walther was airlifted back to its home garrison at Stendal on 18 April, after *Gruppe XXI* had launched the offensive into central Norway, and the operations against remaining Norwegian forces in north-eastern Norway.

Upon the return of *Abteilung Walther* to Stendal the employment of *I./FschJgRgt.1* in the initial phase of *Weserübung* had officially been terminated. The 3rd and 4th companies of the battalion had accomplished their tasks as had been planned. Their role in the operation was totally unexpected by the enemy. Therefore, almost no defensive measures had been prepared at their objectives. The losses in personnel of the staff and of 2nd and 3rd companies were replaced and all units which returned to Stendal were refitted as required. Immediately upon notice of the fate of reinforced *I./FschJgRgt.1* the rebuild of the company and the signals platoon was initiated.

The parachute assault foreseen for the 1st and 2nd companies of *I./FschJgRgt.1* at Fornebu, should have been as successful as those of its sister units. However it had failed

---

42   The British 148th Brigade was landed in Åndalsnes on the evening of 18 April. As the situation around Lillehammer became critical, the brigade was ordered to move to the location along the Gudbrandsdal without delay. In order to deal with the paratroopers at Lindsø who still blocked the railway, two companies of the brigade had been moved to Dombås by rail on the night of 18/19 April. Their commitment had turned out to be unnecessary. Already on 19 April the first elements of 148th Brigade had passed through Dombås by rail in the direction of Lillehammer.

because of the weather or, to be more precise, due to lack of preparation in allowing the air transport to the approach objective independent of weather conditions.

To the same degree as Operation *Weserübung* as a whole, the successful employment of parachute troops had been a matter of achieving surprise as well as trust in the lack of enemy aggression and in his irresoluteness in waging war. With reference to Denmark, the risks for airborne actions had been rather low as relief forces of the *Heer* had already been close to the objectives at the time of their execution. These objectives could probably have been taken from the ground anyway. Organized resistance by Danish troops or the interference of British air forces could, however, have threatened the quick success of the airborne operations against the airfields at Ålborg, the early utilization of which was necessary for initial air operations against Norway.

The seizure of the airfield at Stavanger-Sola by parachute assault had allowed for the unhindered air-landing of combat and service support troops, following close up with the initial units. These had been required for two highly important reasons:

- The fast occupation of the seaport of Stavanger and its hinterland, as fast warships of the Navy for the transport of troops had not been available;
- The build-up of the spacious airfield as a main base for the interdiction of the *Luftwaffe* against British and French naval forces operating in the sea regions along the coast of southern and central Norway, and as a stopover for short-range combat and transport aircraft destined to operate over and from Trondheim.

3./FschJgRgt.1 had accomplished its mission with relatively low losses as the enemy had not been prepared to counter a parachute assault. Nevertheless, by the high standard of their training and vigour these men had fully confirmed the confidence placed in them.

Fornebu, too, had been more of an example of incomplete and belated defensive preparations, in conjunction with a Norwegian lack of equipment for modern warfare, than of a well thought of contingency plan on the German side. A single unit the size of a battalion, equipped with adequate numbers of automatic weapons, fighting resolutely, could have defeated the improvised initial air-landing of German troops. Thereby, as the *coup de main* of German naval forces in the Oslo Fjord had failed, an extremely unfavourable situation for southern Norway could have developed for *Gruppe XXI*.

The parachute attack at Dombås was ordered by the *OKW* as the intention of the Allies to land troops on the coast of central Norway had been detected. This measure had to be regarded as expedient, as, under the prevailing circumstances, it was the only one promising to delay the anticipated (and then executed) thrust of Allied troops into central Norway and their uniting with Norwegian forces sufficiently long to allow for the interference of German divisions from Oslo. In the light of the *OKW*'s intention, the question needs to be answered as to why *X.Flieger-Korps*, upon receipt of the *OKW* directive, dated 14 April, had not moved the 3rd and 4th companies of *I./FschJgRgt.1* to Norway for commitment in Dombås, thereby complying with number 3c of the directive? One reason may have been that, by the time the directive was received, exploited and reinforced *1./FschJgRgt.1* had already been underway to Dombås or, possibly, had even jumped there. The principal reason for denying the commitment of these companies at Dombås, however, must be seen in the fact that about this time the start of the offensive in the west was ordered for 13 May.[43] Every man was now required to accomplish the tasks planned for the parachute force in Holland. This was also true for the aircraft of *I.* and *II./KG z.b.V.1*. Moreover *X.Flieger-Korps* may not have felt competent enough for the commitment of *Fallschirmtruppe* in the Norwegian area of operations, as it had been placed under command of *Luftflotte 5*. In the meantime the *Flotte* had been created in order to direct all air operations in Norway, in cooperation with the likewise formed *Luftwaffe* territorial command for Norway.

The reason why the *Luftwaffe* liaison staff with *Gruppe XXI* had bent its own order as to the number of parachute units to be committed at Dombås, has already been mentioned. That *Generalmajor* Süßmann had insisted on the execution of the operation on 14 April may have been based on additional information about the enemy and the operational intentions of *Gruppe XXI* which he may have brought along from Oslo. In view of the approaching darkness, he had obviously seen no more opportunity to meet the missing objectives of the operation and therefore had taken the risk to neglect them. His attitude, as the events had shown, had decisively contributed to the failure of the mission. On the other hand, the fact that all transport aircraft had managed to take off safely from Fornebu despite the inclement weather had spoken for the *General*, who had based his order to fly on his experience as commander of an aviation formation in his previous position.

The narrow time frame between the order to conduct a parachute attack at Dombås and its execution clearly indicates that the higher command involved still lacked experience about the lead time which was required for operations of this kind. *Generalleutnant* Student, too, seems to have been ignorant about the importance of the requirements of successful airborne operations and even more so about the inevitable head-start in time for the technical and logistical preparations of such operations. This had become visible during the course of the prosecution against *Generalmajor* Süßmann, who was suspected of a dereliction of the duties of a superior after the operation at Dombås. When called up, Student, as an expert witness, had stated that mission and time pressure could make it necessary to conduct a parachute attack without prior complete intelligence-gathering, and reconnaissance of the drop zone.[44]

The views of the staff of *Fl.Div.7* differed from those of Student; they had raised a warning about the operational shortcomings during the commitment of parachute and air-landing troops in Norway, with a view on the future commitment of forces of this kind. Its secret report about the experiences of the deployment in Scandinavia, dated 23 April 1940, had requested binding orders by the highest command involved and had stated verbatim that it was impossible to place the responsibility for the take-off of transport aircraft or its cancellation into the hands of individual commanders by phrases such as "according to

---

43   When this date was shifted, primarily because of the unexpectedly long struggle in Norway, the *OKW* directive pertaining to Dombås had been overcome by events.

44   The prosecution against *Generalmajor* Süßmann by a military court, with Göring presiding, had been dropped mainly because of Student's expertise. Grave neglect of thorough reconnaissance prior to the parachute operations in Holland and Crete indicated that Student himself actually lacked the understanding for this vital part of operational planning.

the weather conditions." In subsequent copies of this report the warnings were even more drastic, pointing out that the employment of parachute troops in unknown terrain without preceding reconnaissance would result in failure and in high losses. It had also requested that jumps in the immediate vicinity of an enemy airfield had to be the exception.

As to what extent the commander of the parachute force and his superiors paid attention to these statements in future operations will be examined later.

The first performance of the German parachute force in its very own mode of employment during the initial phase of Operation *Weserübung* had shown that the aims intended for it had been achieved. All of them had been operational-level in nature. The Norwegian and Danish armed forces had been totally unprepared for the dimensions of the use of air power on the German side as well as for parachute attacks and air-landings of ground forces. After *Weserübung*, however, the secret about the parachute force, which had still been guarded during the campaign in Poland, was lifted with the exception of that of the glider. The principal opponents of Germany and the military commands of Holland and Belgium had been provided with the opportunity to take precautions against this kind of warfare. Whether this opportunity was used will also be examined later.

The actions of the paratroopers in Denmark, at Stavanger and around Oslo but also the dogged endurance of the still combat ready elements of *1./FschJgRgt.1* after the unfortunate start of the operation at Dombås, gave proof to the superior military commands, that the newly created troops had confidence in themselves to master the tasks presented. There had been no lack in resoluteness, ingenuity and will to fight among both commanders and men. Therefore the high command could confidently look forward to more missions for the parachute force.

The risky employment of almost all of the surface craft of the German Navy and the airborne operations at Stavanger, Fornebu and Trondheim had resulted in the desired surprise success, but had not ended the fighting in Norway. Only after the lines of communication into central Norway had been opened against Norwegian and British troops, forcing the latter to hastily embark again, did the German command consider its gains in the Norwegian theatre of war safe. However, the situation in northern Norway, where a task force of about 2,000 soldiers from the *3.Gebirgs-Div.* under *Generalmajor* Dietl had been landed by ten destroyers at Narvik, remained critical. After successful actions by British naval forces against the German destroyers in the fjords at Narvik,[45] the loss of most of the vessels with supplies and heavy weapons on the way to Narvik and the closure of the sea lanes around the Lofoten and Vesterålen islands by the British Home Fleet, Dietl stood isolated and inadequately supplied. Units of the Norwegian 6th Division[46] moved toward Narvik from two sides through the mountainous terrain. Moreover, since 16 April strong Allied ground

---

45   For details see the chapter about Narvik. The loss of destroyers during the initial phase of the campaign in Norway had been so great that their support to the *Heer* and the *Luftwaffe* against Belgian and Dutch ports and waterways, as ordered in the directives for the conduct of the war No. 6 and 8, had not been possible.

46   This division, commanded by General Fleischer, was organized in two brigades, each consisting of two infantry battalions, a reserve company, an artillery battery, an engineer platoon and some combat service support troops.

forces[47] were landing at the port of Harstad, on the northern tip of the Hinnoya islands, about 60 km north-west of Narvik. Preliminary operations of both Norwegian and Allied troops aiming to retake Narvik and to eliminate *Kräftegruppe Dietl* were launched on 24 April. Allied warships entered the fjords and fired in support of the ground forces, thereby considerably hampering the movements of the defenders.

After 13 April Hitler saw the operation against Narvik as a failure and looked for possibilities to rescue *Kräftegruppe Dietl*. The resolute attitude of *Generalmajor* Jodl and the confidence displayed by *Generalmajor* Dietl, however, had won over Hitler's fears, so that the operation had been carried on despite tremendous difficulties.

After the end of April it became possible to resupply Dietl from the air and to provide air support, although to a very limited extent due to the distance of more than 600 km between Trondheim and Narvik, the adverse weather, the air threat from the airfield at Bardufoss and from British carrier groups, which were most obstructive.

For relief operations on the ground, elements of *2.Gebirgs-Div.*, under *Generalmajor* Feurstein, were brought to Trondheim. However for the relief to become effective several weeks of waiting first had to be reckoned with.

Of the air transport formations, only *KGr z.b.V.107* and *108* remained in Norway, primarily for the support of the garrison at Narvik. *KG z.b.V.1* and *2* were speedily refitted in Germany for the campaign in the west. Two of the special purpose air transport combat groups were returned to the *Luftwaffe* in order to again enlarge the training capacity for pilots and aircrews.

After his strongest doubts about Narvik had been dispersed, Hitler turned his attention fully back to *Fall Gelb*. British documents, dated early April 1940, which had been captured in Norway, were considered extremely useful for political action. They clearly laid open the planning of the Allies to occupy ports in Norway, to get ahead of similar German actions. These documents were now widely used for propaganda purposes and Ribbentrop, the German minister of foreign affairs, published a white paper in order to convince the German people and the world at large that the Allies were unwilling to respect the neutrality of smaller European countries. The deeper idea behind this step obviously had been to make the impending military actions against the Benelux states appear to be preventive measures upon their execution.[48]

---

47   Rupert Force consisted of the British 24th (Guards) Brigade (3 btns), the 27e Demi-Brigade of the French mountain troops (3 btns), the 13e Demi-Brigade of the French Foreign Legion (2 btns), a Polish brigade (4 btns), two companies of light tanks and numerous combat support and logistic troops. The British brigade and the French mountain infantry had been landed in the timeframe 16-24 April. The 13e Demi-Brigade had followed on 6 May, the Polish brigade on 9 May.

48   An even more far-reaching disclosure of the war plans of the Allies which indicated their intentions to make Norway, Sweden and the Balkans theatres of war and to conduct military actions even against the oil fields in the Soviet Union occurred when a train with most secret documents of the French General Staff and of the Allied commission of the general staffs of Great Britain and France had been captured on 16 June 1940 at the rail station of La Charité, France. The contents of these documents had been used by Hitler in his speech to the Reichstag on 19 July 1940 and had also been sent to the Soviet Union.

On 27 April Hitler disclosed his intention to begin *Fall Gelb* between 1 and 7 May. He passed the command of the Norwegian area of operations to *Gruppe XXI*, *Luftflotte 5* and the Office for Naval Warfare. On 29 April he determined that the *Luftwaffe* had to be ready for *Fall Gelb* on 5 May. The following day he ordered that from the 4 May the *Wehrmacht*, as a whole, most be able to commence the attack on 24 hours' notice.

The decisive factor for the beginning of the offensive in the west now became the weather. It remained unfavourable for the employment of the *Luftwaffe*, which was regarded as the key to success in the initial phase of *Fall Gelb*; consequently the date for the attack was moved back on a day-to-day basis. As the weather forecast was more favourable on 9 May, and Holland, because of serious warnings, had commenced with measures for civil defence, Hitler decided to fix the ultimate date for the attack as 10 May. Announced to the public on a visit to Oslo, on the evening of 9 May he and his personal staff travelled in his special train to the command post for the campaign in the west, which was prepared near Münstereifel.

The attack forces of all three services of the *Wehrmacht* had, like in the preceding days, again received two code words for 10 May, one for the beginning of the attack and the other for its cancellation. *Sturmabteilung Koch* and the *Luftlande-Korps* stood ready at their jump-off airfields with the highest degree of readiness.

Part II Photographs

The Danish coastal fort on the island of Masnedø near Vordingborg, which was seized by *4./FschJgRgt.1* without fighting, on 9 April 1940. As can be seen by the photo, it was soon reactivated by the *Wehrmacht*.

Fallschirmtruppe of *4./FschJgRgt.1* who have been relieved by forces from the *Heer* on the island of Masnedø and at Vordingborg await their transport back to Germany.

Part of the airfield at Fornebu, near Oslo, during the ongoing invasion of Norway by the *Wehrmacht*. At this time it was used as a stop-over base for transport aircraft, delivering troops and supplies to the northern part of the country, where fighting was continuing.

Men from *FschJgRgt.1* at the airfield of Fornebu near Oslo, Norway, April 1940. (Bundesarchiv, Bild 101I-757-0023-32, photo: Ruge)

Dombås. The Dovrefjell, about 15 km north-east of Dombås, a few weeks after the end of the fighting in this area, by which time the snow was already beginning to melt. The 1st Platoon of the reinforced *1./FschJgRgt.1* landed in the open area to the left of the middle of the photo, near Fokstua.

Dombås. A view of Dombås from the south, some weeks after the end of the fighting. The view is from the roughly where the 2nd Platoon of the reinforced *1./FschJgRgt.1* landed. At the time of the combat the snow was deeper. In the foreground is the railway leading from Dovre to Dombås. In the valley behind Dombås a road and railway lead to Trondheim.

Part III

The employment of the *Fallschirmtruppe* during the Campaign in the West

1

Sturmabteilung Koch paves the way across the Albert Canal for the *Heer*

L ike all forces of the *Wehrmacht* who were preparing for *Fall Gelb*, *Sturmabteilung Koch* had little time for rest in the first days of May 1940. There was an alert almost every day before each was called off. The detachment was isolated for months for reasons of security. Additionally the soldiers' morale was greatly affected as they began to realize that their baptism of fire was fast approaching.

At 1420 hrs on 9 May *Hauptmann* Koch received the code name *Vernichtung* ['annihilation'], from the command of *VIII.Flieger-Korps*. As had been laid down in advance, he passed the specific instruction "1500 Uhr – Rumänien" to all elements of his detachment. This triggered the final phase of the plan to assume full combat readiness. Almost immediately the *Sturmgruppen* and the battle HQ were transferred to their jump-off airfields; the Ju 52 of *17./KGr z.b.V.5*, with *Sturmgruppen Stahl*, *Eisen* and *Beton* aboard, arrived from Hildesheim and touched down on the airfields at Köln-Ostheim and Köln-Butzweilerhof between 1800 and 1830 hrs. *Sturmgruppe Granit* arrived by truck from the anti-aircraft barracks at Hilden (near Düsseldorf) at 1830 hrs.[1] The gliders stood ready for flight and were loaded with the equipment of the detachment in hangars at the jump-off airfields. At 2000 hrs, the tow aircraft were refueled and placed on their start positions. Behind each of them, the appointed glider was brought into position by hand. After one final check they were connected to the Ju 52s by a towing cable.

At 2100 hrs, after a short address and some final instructions, *Hauptmann* Koch allowed the men of the assault force a rest period. On the airfields the preparations for the take-off of the air components were continued into the first hours of 10 May. This included the preparation of three six Ju 52 of *I./KG z.b.V.172* carrying the three heavy machine-gun half-platoons, to be dropped as reinforcements, of the five He 111 bombers from *I./KG 4* for aerial resupply and of the Ju 87 dive bombers of *I./StG 2*, tasked with close air support missions.

The assault force was roused on 10 May at 0245 hrs and at 0330 hrs the men moved to their gliders and boarded them. At 0415 hrs the leaders of the *Sturmgruppen* reported readiness for take-off. At 0430 hrs a green flare was fired as the signal for take off for the transport group.

After 10 minutes all of the towing craft were in the air; 31 with *Sturmgruppen Granit*, *Beton* and *Stahl* (less one team) from Köln-Ostheim, 11 with *Sturmgruppe Eisen*, and one team from *Sturmgruppe Stahl* from Köln-Butzweilerhof. The towing craft from Butzweilerhof filed in behind those from Ostheim. Since the gliders were loaded to the

---

1   It remains unknown why this assault group was moved to Hilden.

limits of their capacity,[2] the tow aircraft were initially slow during their ascent. The gliders therefore had to be flown in curves to gain speed and to prevent them from crashing. During this initial phase of the flight, the close order of the transport formation was lost for a while and the aircraft were only slowly able to gain height.

The flight route to the point of release for the gliders was 73km. It was marked on the ground with five rotating beacons and two searchlights. The latter, emitting their rays to the east at an angle of 45 degrees, were switched off for a short period every 10 seconds. The point of release at the Vetschauer Berg, close to the German/Dutch border north-west of Aachen, was marked by three searchlights whose beams were continuously directed to the east. There, the glider pilots were to detach the towing cables at a height of 2,600m. The flight path to the landing areas had also been determined in great detail – for the direction to the objectives in grades, for the descent, based on a gliding speed of 125-130km per hour, in flight minutes for every 500m. Only for the last leg of the glide-in, at a height of 500m and a distance to the objectives between 26.5km for *Granit*, and 29.5km for *Stahl*, were the glider pilots to steer to the ground using their own field of vision. In order to stay on the flight route to the point of release, darkness was required so as the beacons were recognizable from above. Equally important, however, was that the glider pilots got their bearings from the ground for the final run-in to the objectives in the first light of dawn. At 0525hrs, five minutes prior to the attack of the ground forces across the borders in the west, all four *Sturmgruppen* were to land at their objectives simultaneously.

Most of the tow aircraft had to accomplish an additional task after releasing the gliders. They had to drop the towing cables over the jump-off airfields, turn around to cross the Albert Canal and penetrate on a broad front about 40km deep into Belgian airspace. There they had to drop 120 paratroop dummies. It was intended to confuse the enemy with regards to the extent of the deployment of German troops from the air by this action and confuse their counter-measures.[3]

In spite of the exemplary preparation of the air transport for *Sturmabteilung Koch*, things did not progress according to plan. To begin with, the towing cable of the glider with *Oberleutnant* Witzig, the commander of *Sturmgruppe Granit* aboard, snapped shortly after taking off. The glider was forced to land in a field south of Köln. Near Düren, another glider of *Sturmgruppe Granit* had to land, after its pilot had detached the towing cable on a signal from the tow aircraft.

The other 40 towing craft continued their flight. With increasing height the passengers of the gliders had to cope with the ice-cold draught whilst remaining almost motionless. Close to the German/Dutch border another deviation from the plan had to be accepted, as the tow aircraft had not yet reached the required ceiling of 2,600m for the point of release. Consequently they continued the climb across the border and the towing craft

---

2   This applied in particular to the gliders of *Sturmgruppe Granit*. In addition to its 86 soldiers with their personal gear, the following equipment was loaded: 2,401kg demolition munitions, 825kg hand grenades of all kinds, 30,040 rounds (7.92 and 9mm) for 6 machine guns, 18 machine pistols, 54 rifles and 65 pistols, 1 radio set, 4 flame throwers, 7 rope ladders, 71 entrenching tools and 13 signal panels.

3   This deception measure was highly efficient. The reports about dropped German parachute- troops during the first days of the attack had generated so much unrest among the armed forces and the population that the French minister-president Reynaud had issued an instruction whereby all captured German paratroopers were to be shot on the spot.

of *Sturmabteilung Beton* flew deep into Dutch airspace, before the tow cables could be detached.

At 0510hrs the six Ju 52s, carrying the three heavy machine-gun half-platoons which were to be dropped as reinforcements for the *Sturmgruppen* at the bridges of the Albert Canal, took off from Köln-Ostheim.

The approach of the air transport formation from the east had not gone unnoticed by the Dutch, if only because of the great noise produced by the engines of the Ju 52s as they laboriously climbed. It is also possible that the towing craft were also sighted from the ground at daybreak. In any case the Dutch anti-aircraft gunners were soon at work. The gliders of *Sturmgruppe Eisen*, approaching the bridge across the Albert Canal at Kanne, received anti-aircraft fire from south of Maastricht. Evasive flying prevented losses but brought the group behind its time schedule. The gliders of *Sturmabteilung Beton* were also fired at from the area near Maastricht on their way to the bridge at Veldwezelt. The Dutch anti-aircraft fire was heard by Belgian guards on the western bank of the Albert Canal, but did not trigger an alert.[4] However, a few minutes after 0500hrs Major Jottrand, who was inspecting the fort's surface, recognized gliders approaching from the east. Quickly moving to a telephone inside the fort he ordered the immediate demolition of the bridge at Kanne.

As part of the national defence plan, but also on the basis of agreements achieved with the French, the Belgian high command had planned to meet an initial German attack in a forward position behind the Meuse River and the Albert Canal, leaning on the fortified areas of Namur and Liège.[5] This position would have to be held for 48 hours so as to enable the French and British allies to occupy the 'Dijle position', which was backed up by the fortress area of Antwerp to the north and by Namur in the south. The Belgian divisions were to withdraw from their forward positions to the 'Dijle position'.[6] The Belgian General Staff had decided to hold the Albert Canal line north of Liège for only a limited time after an enquiry in March 1940 as to whether it could count on French advance forces of about 6 divisions arriving at the Albert Canal within 4 days of the move to the 'Dijle position', was answered non-committally by General Gamelin.

The strongest of the Belgian ground forces had been deployed on the left flank of the defensive position, between Hasselt and Antwerp. Some of the divisions to the south had stretched defences which considerably exceeded normal tactical doctrine. This also applied to the 7th Infantry Division under Major General Vantrooyen, which had to defend the sector

4   Obviously there was no direct telephone link between the Dutch troops around Maastricht and the Belgians west of the Albert Canal.

5   The forts, located in a semi-circle around the belt-fortifications of Liège and Namur, had been rearmed after the First World War. In the 1930s bunker-lines had been constructed between these forts. Since September 1939 these lines had been occupied by troops from the Belgian III Army Corps. Another position in the rear of the bunker lines had been occupied by units of the Belgian 2nd and 3rd divisions.

6   Belgian sources mainly speak of the line Koningshooikt-Wavre, to which the Belgian divisions were to withdraw. There, obstacles like anti-tank ditches, inundations and an extensive iron lattice (the so-called "iron wall") had been prepared, but no bunkers for the troops.

between the bend of the Albert Canal south of Lanaken and the Meuse, a few kilometers north-east of Liège. Its width of 20km was twice that indicated by tactical norms, but was justified by superior command with the argument that the division could lean its right flank on the fortress at Liège and had the Albert Canal in front, which was difficult to cross and was protected by Fort Eben-Emael and fortifications at the permanent bridges.

For its defensive mission the 7th Infantry Division was composed of three infantry regiments, with ten infantry battalions, a detachment of bicycle infantry, an artillery regiment, an anti-tank detachment and an engineer battalion. Moreover it was still hoped by the Belgian high command that French troops would advance from the 'Dijle position' to the Albert Canal line, as it offered much better possibilities for defence than the terrain of the former.

The 7th Infantry Division had taken over the sector opposite Maastricht on 30 April 1940 from the 5th Infantry Division. This division was deployed here for several months but had failed to complete the planned field fortifications along the Albert Canal. Nevertheless, high command foresaw a good chance for a temporary defence of the sector. This confidence obviously had blurred their view against its manifold deficiencies. Possibly some of these had even not been realized. For example, generous leave regulations had generated a situation whereby about 15 percent of the personnel of 7th Infantry Division were not present for duty in the first days of May 1940. The garrison of Fort Eben-Emael, too, was somewhat short of its complement of 1,187 soldiers as some of them were still on leave and not all of the replacements for the men who had been dismissed at the end of their regular military service had arrived.[7]

The garrison was organized into two 'divisions,' each consisting of an active garrison in the fort and a reserve garrison element with billets in the village at Wonck, about 4km south-west of the fort. In its full complement 1st Battery, who manned the artillery emplacements, consisted of 318 men and 234 reserves. The 2nd Battery, manning the close-defence emplacements, had 234 soldiers in the fort and 228 as reserves in the billets. Additionally, 30 soldiers were assigned to operate the anti-aircraft machine-guns on the fort's surface and to man emplacement 'O' outside of the fort. Their reserve consisted of 18 soldiers. The 1st Battery had an additional 20 soldiers for observation and guard duties on the surface of the fort. Included in the overall number were about 300 soldiers for technical and logistical support and for communications in the underground facilities. Taking into account the absentees, there were probably 600-650 soldiers present in the fort and on its surface at the time of the landing of *Sturmgruppe Granit*.

The reconstruction work in the fort, which was still being undertaken in early May, proved to be troublesome for telephone communications between the fire control centre and some of the artillery emplacements, and also for the ventilation of the command posts.

---

7   Research in official Belgian sources, undertaken by G. Schalich and passed to the author in 2008, reveals that on 10 May 1940, the fort's garrison was short of 4 officers, 10-15 non-commissioned officers and some dozens of other ranks.

The morale of the garrison was suffering. It had been low from the very beginning of their deployment due to the poor quality of personnel and the monotony of garrison duty and the high level of readiness which was maintained over many months.[8]

Little attention was paid to cooperation between the various forces employed in the sector opposite of Maastricht. The garrisons of the bunkers at the bridges near Vroenhoven and Veldwezelt were provided by the *Cyclistes frontière*,[9] who were known as crack troops. The responsibility for the demolition of these bridges had been given to Major Giddeloo. He was the company commander of the *cyclistes* employed opposite Maastricht and had his command post at Lanaken. Major Jottrand, the commandant of Fort Eben-Emael, was responsible for the demolition of the bridge at Kanne. Both officers and their troops, however, were not in any way subordinate to 7th Infantry Division, despite the fact that their defensive installations were located in that division's sector. 7th Infantry Division, like the garrison of Fort Eben-Emael, received its orders from I Army Corps, although the latter actually was a part of Fortress Regiment Liège (Colonel Modard). For administrative and technical matters, Fort Eben-Emael was subordinate to the command of the fortress area for Liège. This area, however, was within the defence sector of III Army Corps, in which the 2nd Infantry Division was deployed.

On 10 May at 0030hrs, after receipt of an urgent warning by the Belgian military *attaché* in Berlin, the Belgian armed forces were placed on general alert. The alert message arrived at III Army Corps at 0125hrs and at I Army Corps at 0155hrs.[10] Due to the training and many false alarms the combat readiness in the sector of 7th Infantry Division was rapid.[11] Its troops were about ready for action from between 0400 and 0500hrs.

In Fort Eben-Emael itself most of the emplacements were manned by about 0230hrs; the anti-aircraft machine-guns on the surface were prepared by 0415hrs. Soon, however, many of the soldiers were withdrawn from their fighting positions in order to accomplish tasks outside the fort, such as for the construction of additional obstacles or the clearing of the peacetime barracks in front of the fort's entrance area. Consequently in two of the four gun casemates only a few men remained posted, Mi Sud was completely abandoned and Mi Nord abandoned with the exception of a few soldiers. No permission had yet been given to unpack the artillery shells, which were enclosed in paraffin, in sealed cases. Furthermore the alert for the reserve garrison in Wonck was totally forgotten. They were finally alerted between 0300 and 0400hrs but needed considerable time in order to be ready for action.

---

8   Based on his research of the post-war examination of the Belgian Commission des Forts, in an unpublished study by van Daele/Depasse about the 7th Infantry Division at the Albert Canal and in a dissertation about the rapid loss of Fort Eben-Emael by André Bikar, G. Schalich gives the reasons for the low morale of the fort's garrison as follows:
   - no cohesion among the officers who had partly been selected from less qualified graduates of the officers' school;
   - only a few qualified non-commissioned officers; diverse disciplinary cases among them;
   - many disciplinary proceedings among the other ranks, as Eben-Emael was considered a prison;
   - no improvement of the defence state of the fort by Major Jottrand, who had been its commandant since July 1939.

9   The *Cyclistes frontière* had been formed in 1934. Its personnel were made up from professional soldiers and long-serving volunteers. Its rifle companies were equipped with bicycles. At the regimental level there were also some lightly armored type T 13 tracked vehicles, armed with a 47mm anti-tank gun and a machine-gun in a revolving turret.

10   The reason for this late receipt was attributed to a lack of telex equipment.

11   A reason for that may have been that the division was warned of another training alert for 10 May.

Shortly before dawn all troops in the Belgian sector opposite of Maastricht were to some extent prepared for their defence missions. In view of the distance of the positions to the German border, the Dutch territory in front of them and the perceived protection of the fortifications, the commands responsible for the defence of the sector were not overly perturbed. The hours to come, however, would display that the Dutch forces were neither composed nor prepared for the kind of attack the Germans had chosen.

At daylight on 10 May, the Friday prior to Whit Sunday, three of the four *Sturmgruppen* of *Sturmabteilung Koch* landed almost simultaneously at their objectives.

At 0515hrs the ten gliders[12] of *Sturmabteilung Beton* and the battle HQ of the assault detachment came down west of the Albert Canal,[13] most of them close to the bridge at Vroenhoven and a few in the rear of the reinforced 1st Company of the Belgian 18th Infantry Regiment, which was entrenched there. The Belgian guards commenced firing with machine guns and rifles during the descent of the gliders. One glider was badly hit, having to crash-land from a height of 15m although astonishingly only three of its crew was seriously hurt. The other soldiers, although lightly injured, immediately went into action. The gilder with the HQ section of the assault detachment aboard touched down about 150m west of the bridge. Together with *Oberleutnant* Kieß, who had piloted the glider and a *Feldwebel, Hauptmann* Koch captured a length of occupied trench toward the bridge, and ordered *Oberleutnant* Zierach and five soldiers of his glider crew to establish a protective position in a westerly direction against the village of Vroenhoven. The glider with the assault group's radio team aboard came down between the villages of Vroenhoven and Kesselt, about 500m north-west of the bridge. Its crew, led by *Oberarzt* Dr. Jäger, was hit by machine-gun fire, which killed a radio operator and seriously wounded another one.

Team 4, led by *Oberfeldwebel* Hoffmann, landed about 120m west of the road bunker at the western approach to the bridge and immediately assaulted it. A *Gefreiter* gained access through the door, which had remained open, and ripped out the already burning fuse, thereby preventing the explosion of the charges built into the bridge structure.[14] Almost simultaneously with the bunker on the western approach to the bridge the emplacements, which were built into the concrete slope of the western canal-bank on either side of the bridge, were attacked with incendiaries and concentric charges. However, the defenders held out. At about 0600hrs the two platoons of the 1st Company of the Belgian 18th Infantry Regiment close to the bridge were overwhelmed. Most of these soldiers were killed or taken prisoner. Although the fighting in the vicinity of the bridge was not yet over the

---

12   The glider with the assault group's engineer squad aboard had to conduct a landing at Hottdorf, still on German territory, after its towing cable had broken.

13   A statement made in a Belgian source, and some German ones, that 3 of the gliders had landed east of the Albert Canal, is incorrect.

14   This description deviates from the German after-action report and is based on more correct Belgian sources. According to these the commandant of the bunker had ignited the fuse after he had been unable to reach Major Giddeloo in Lanaken. Then he had vacated the bunker together with his garrison. In some doubt about his action he had returned to the bunker with the intention of extinguishing the fuse. However, a detonating shaped charge killed him, and the two soldiers who had accompanied him. Major Giddeloo was killed during an air attack against the barracks in Lanaken. The execution of demolitions of the bridges in the greater area of Liége by electrical ignition was dismissed some months earlier, after a railway bridge in Liége, prepared for demolition by this method, had been blown up in August 1939 by a lightning strike.

assault detachment's radio team, which had set up its equipment since 0520hrs, reported the seizure of the bridge in an undamaged state.[15] At 0615hrs, *Oberleutnant* Zierach set up the detachment command post about 80m west of the bridge. At 0630hrs, the heavy machine-gun half-platoon was dropped into the small air bridgehead as planned. About 0700hrs the reserve platoon of the Belgian close-defence company had also been put out of action. Shortly afterward Ju 87 of *StG 2*, and ground attack aircraft of *Lehrgeschwader 2*, attacked, as planned, disrupting elements of 18th Infantry Regiment with telling effect.

Led by *Oberleutnant* Altmann, the ten gliders of *Sturmgruppe Stahl*, which had been allocated for the seizure of the bridge at Veldwezelt, swooped down for a landing under heavy machine-gun and rifle-fire at 0520hrs. Some landed as far as 400-1,000m away from the objective. Hit by defensive fire, one of the gliders crashed from 10m height, its crew escaped with only light bruising. Fortunately, the glider of *Oberjäger* Ellersiek landed exactly alongside the road bunker which guarded the western approach to the bridge. As its door had not been shut it was quickly put out of action with hand grenades, a flame-thrower and a concentric charge. All of the occupants were killed, with the exception of one seriously wounded soldier. A soldiers' mess located close to the bunker was blown up with two containers of mortar rounds, the bunker was filled with explosives, putting the soldiers out of action. The 15 man crew of the concrete emplacement built into the western foot of the bridge initially held out. This was despite the two doors at the sides of the bunker, from which stairs led upward on the concrete slope, being blocked by explosives. This led the two machine-guns in the bunker became unusable. After a short while its garrison, including three injured men, surrendered. For the time being they were left locked up in the bunker by the paratroopers.

The crews of the flanking emplacements in the concrete slope of the western bank of the canal on either side of the bridge provided stubborn resistance throughout the day. Yet, as they could direct their fire only alongside the canal, the men of the assault group were only slightly hampered. One task was the removal of the explosives on the bridge by the team of *Oberfeldwebel* Arpke, which had also neutralized the bunker at the foot of the bridge. The balance of the group had to fight through the trenches of the defenders west of the bridge. Thus two platoons of the 6th Company of the *2nd Carabiniers* Regiment were, to a great extent, put out of action. Quickly the paratroopers used the captured machine-guns against their former owners. A short while later the reinforcing machine-gun half-platoon of *Leutnant* Ringler was dropped. It had taken some losses during landing, as the fighting was not yet over. Nevertheless, at 0630hrs *Sturmgruppe Stahl* reported the accomplishment of its mission by radio.

At about 0900hrs a counter-attack by the Belgians took place. German dive bombers appeared just in time but particularly the ground attack fighters of *Hauptmann* Galland, and the concentrated defensive fire of the assault group, caused the counter-attack to collapse during its build-up stage. The supporting aircraft were directed against the staging

---

15   It remains unclear whether this report was ever picked up and by whom. The war diary of *Sturmabteilung Koch* gives the radio contact with *VIII.Flieger-Korps* not earlier than 1132hrs. How the *OKW* had received information about the situation at the Albert Canal earlier than that time remains unknown.

areas of the Belgians by means of signal panels.[16] After the defeat of the attempted first counter-attack the enemy remained quiet for some time. This allowed the assault group to form up for a renewed defence of the air bridgehead.

At about 0520hrs the remaining nine gliders of *Sturmgruppe Granit*, descending from several directions, landed on the surface of Fort Eben-Emael, little harassed by defensive fire. As they were flying too high during the final phase of the approach, they had to make a nose-dive landing.

The individual emplacements of the fort had received numeric designations in the models that had been used for training purposes based on the most recent aerial photos.[17] This had led to the allocation of emplacements as objectives to be neutralized by each of the assault teams in the initial phase of the *coup de main*, even though pin-point landings of the gliders close to the allocated emplacements could not be guaranteed. Furthermore the loss of one or more of the assault teams during the approach flight or the landing could not be excluded. The low overall strength of the assault group due to many emplacements, however, had not permitted more than one assault team as a reserve for such an eventuality.

The allocation of objectives, together with the distribution of all kinds of explosives for each of the assault teams prior to the start, now allowed for immediate action without having to wait for orders. The fact that two of the emplacements were not assaulted in the initial phase of the *coup de main*, as their allocated assault tems were absent, was probably realised by only a few men of the assault group in the first minutes after landing.

The first glider, with team 5 under *Feldwebel* Haug, came down so close to the position of the anti-aircraft machine-guns, designated as Emplacement 29, that a wing tore one of the weapons from its mounting and dragged it along. Like lightning the team left the glider and attacked the anti-aircraft position. After a burst from the submachine-gun of Haug and several hand grenades, its crew of 20 men under Adjutant Longdoz surrendered. Three soldiers of team 5 immediately advanced against Gun Cupola 23 (Belgian designation: Coupole Sud/Block V), at the southern edge of the fort. The observation dome of Block IV was also assaulted from where the entire surface of the fort could be overlooked. It was blasted open by a 50kg shaped charge, which killed the observer.

In the meantime the other eight gliders also landed and their crews, including the pilots, despite being heavily burdened with equipment and explosives, rushed forward to the initial objectives. Team 4, led by *Feldwebel* Wenzel, came down about 100m away from Emplacement 19 (Belgian designation: Mi Nord). The work, being a concrete casemate, armed with three heavy machine-guns in embrasures directed to the north and south and equipped with two searchlights under armor protection. *Feldwebel* Wenzel arrived ahead of his team and threw a charge into the opening of the observation periscope. Men of his team attached one of the 50kg shaped charges on top of the artillery observation dome and detonated it. The explosion did not penetrate the protective steel because of its thickness,

---

16 Because of the lack of ground-to-air radio communications, signal panels with directional arrows and signal flares were the most common means to draw the attention of combat aircraft toward the locations of the enemy, observed from the ground.

17 The German aerial photo evaluation initially had overrated the artillery armament of the fort. This had, in particular, applied to the type of guns, of which four had been rated as 22cm and one even as 28cm. Furthermore a number of the observation domes had wrongly been seen as weapon emplacements. Most of the initial mistakes were only corrected after additional aerial reconnaissance.

but killed the two observers inside the dome. Thereafter the embrasure of the machine-gun directed to the north was blasted open with a 12.5kg shaped charge. During the entire action of team 4 and also afterward, not one shot was fired from the emplacement.[18]

The other teams that landed in the centre of the fort's surface operated similarly. Team 1 under *Feldwebel* Niedermeyer assaulted Emplacement 18 (Belgian designation: Maastricht 2), team 3 under *Feldwebel* Arent Emplacement 12 (Belgian designation: Maastricht 1). At both concrete casemates, each of which was armed with three 75mm guns, a shaped charge was detonated at the embrasure of each gun.

A 50kg shaped charge was ignited on top of the artillery observation dome of Emplacement 18. Here, too, the charge did not penetrate the armor but both observers inside were mangled by the effects of the pressure and the fragments which split off from the inside of the dome. Due to the explosion of the 12.5kg shaped charge one of the guns of this emplacement was hurled into the interior of the casemate. Two of its crew was killed and one mortally wounded. The remaining gun crews descended to the lower part of the casemate and blocked the entry to the underground gallery with a girder obstacle, prepared for that purpose, and with sand. In Emplacement 12 the explosion of the charge made all three guns unusable and killed one soldier. At both emplacements the demolitions created an opening through which paratroopers of both teams could slip through into the interior, hurling small explosive charges after the withdrawing Belgian soldiers. For the time being, however, the attackers were content to occupy the casemates at ground level and to defend against attempts by the Belgians to again ascend from the underground corridors.

The teams that came down in the central area of the fort faced unexpected resistance from a shed, designated Emplacement 25, which was located about 100m south-east of the large revolving turret. A few men of the fort's garrison, who had taken refuge there, fired machine guns in every direction. At once paratroopers from two teams advanced against this point of resistance, and eventually took it out with some concentric charges, but not without the cost of two killed and several wounded.

With some men of his team 8 not engaged in the fighting at Emplacement 25, *Feldwebel* Unger attacked Emplacement 31 (Belgian designation: Coupole Nord). At this time, its armored turret with its two 75mm guns was retracted.[19] After the detonation of a first shaped charge of 50kg had no effect another one was exploded on the same spot. It jammed the turret putting it out of action. A 12.5kg shaped charge destroyed the iron lattice the steel door and the machine-gun for the defence of the entrance area of Emplacement 31, and killed one Belgian soldier. The paratroopers, however, were prevented from entering the emplacement, as the explosion of the charge filled up the entrance area with earth. During the assault against this emplacement, *Feldwebel* Unger was killed by a shot to the head.

The glider with team 9 under *Feldwebel* Neuhaus had landed in the middle of an extended wire obstacle surrounding Emplacement 13 (Belgian designation: Mi Sud) a machine-gun casemate. The team had to cut its way through the barbed wire and initially used a flame-thrower against the casemate. Subsequently, one of the machine-gun

---

18   According to the research of G. Schalich, the few soldiers who had been present in the casemate had left it after the destruction of the embrasure.

19   The turret was retracted because its guns, from lack of care during the time prior to the airborne assault, had been left unattended, and the ammunition elevator was blocked.

embrasures was breached with a 12.5kg shaped charge. During the entire action not one shot was fired from the emplacement.[20]

The most powerful installation of the fort, Emplacement 24 (Belgian designation: Coupole 120), the large revolving turret in the south of the fort, armed with a 12cm-twin gun, was also attacked at the beginning of the assault: The glider pilot of team 5, observing that the turret was not yet dealt with by his fellow soldiers, dragged a 50kg shaped charge to it and ignited it. However, the charge failed to penetrate the thick armor of the casemate. During the whole time from the start of the assault, the guns of the turret had not fired once.[21] The approaching paratroopers from teams 5 and 8 were fired at with rifles from the opening of the panoramic telescope sight. Nevertheless, they managed to push 1kg charges into the barrels of the guns. The resulting explosions damaged both guns.

The employment of forces against the northern part of the fort was the result of an intelligence mistake. Teams 6 (*Oberjäger* Harlos) and 7 (*Oberjäger* Heinemann) had been ordered to destroy the large steel cupolas detected there by air reconnaissance. Both teams had landed close to their objectives and had immediately attacked them. Only after 50kg shaped charges had shattered the cupolas to bits did the teams found out that these were dummies made of 2cm thick steel plate. Evidently inadequate reconnaissance had led to the waste of scarce forces during the first minutes of the assault.

In spite of the inefficient initial allocation of teams 6 and 7, and the absence of teams 2 (*Oberjäger* Maier), and 11 (*Oberleutnant* Witzig), in the initial 10-15 minutes following the landing of the first glider the 55 paratroopers of *Sturmgruppe Granit* succeeded in attacking eight emplacements. Six 75mm guns were put out of action with certainty, as well as the 12cm guns.

It was only now that the teams found the time to look around and to establish contact with each other. The senior non-commissioned officer, *Feldwebel* Wenzel, probably only now understood that *Oberleutnant* Witzig and his team had not arrived, and that the other officer of the group, *Leutnant* Delica, had remained at his radio set, brought along by team 1, in order to direct supporting fire of *FlakAbt Aldinger*, as planned. At 0542hrs the radio team sent a first short message about the situation at the fort, and the initial achievements to the command post of the assault detachment at Vroenhoven.

Feldwebel Wenzel now assumed command of the assault group. He directed team 10, which hitherto was retained as reserve, against the enemy-held Emplacement 26 (Belgian designation: Visé 1,) in the eastern part of the fort, with its guns trained to the south-east. *Feldwebel* Arent, with some men from his team 3, was ordered to attack Emplacement 14 (Belgian designation: Block III), the work enfilading the moat at the north-western edge of the fort. While team 7 remained as a security cordon in the northern tip of the fort, team 6 was ordered to neutralize Emplacement 17 (Belgian designation: Canal Nord), the northern of the two enfilading weapon platforms embedded into the upper part of the precipice down to the Albert Canal. *Feldwebel* Wenzel advanced against Coupole 120 with some of his men. After another 50kg-shaped charge did not penetrate the 59cm thick steel of the turret and one of the 12cm guns evidently was still serviceable, more 1kg charges

---

20   It was unoccupied during the assault. Only later had Belgian soldiers ascended into the casemate.
21   The turret had not been ready for action. The crew was unable to execute the order to commence firing at 0530hrs because parts of the machine to set the fuse had disappeared, the recoil weights of the guns could not be lowered and the turret's elevator was jammed.

were pushed into the gun barrels. Their explosions caused the jamming of the gun breeches inside the turret, whereby the guns were finally put out of action.[22]

As team 10 proved unable to cope with the resistance from Emplacement 26, *Feldwebel* Wenzel reinforced it with two men of his team. Now, one of the three 75mm guns was destroyed by demolition, whereupon the gun crews retreated into the fort's interior. *Feldwebel* Arent and his men managed to blow open the observation dome of Block II by means of a 50kg-shaped charge. Here the observer was killed. No attack, however, could be launched against the weapons of this emplacement because of the increasingly heavy artillery fire on the fort's surface. This fire had commenced about ten minutes after the landing by the guns of Coupole Sud. From 0557hrs on, artillery from positions about 8-10km west of the fort had joined in.[23] Consequently a number of paratroopers sought cover behind the northern side of the earthen mound between Emplacements 13 and 19. There they were also protected against observation from the west by the trees at the north-western edge of the fort. Other paratroopers found protection inside of casemate Maastricht 2.

To the surprise of the men of *Sturmgruppe Granit*, the glider with *Oberleutnant* Witzig and the six soldiers of his team 11 landed on the fort at 0915hrs. After the glider landed in a field south of Köln, Witzig had ordered his team to remove fences and shrubs and prepare the ground for the landing and takeoff of a Ju 52 rescue lift. He had confiscated a bicycle, informed the airfield command at Köln-Ostheim about the incident from a telephone booth and driven to the airfield. Sometime later, he landed in the field in a Ju 52, which had been summoned from Gütersloh. The takeoff of the Ju 52, with the glider connected to it by a towing-cable, had also succeeded. After detaching the cable at sufficient height, the glider pilot, without any difficulty, was able to approach the fort in plain daylight. After a short situation report by *Feldwebel* Wenzel, *Oberleutnant* Witzig resumed command over his assault group.

The coup of *Sturmgruppe Eisen* to seize the bridge at Kanne undamaged failed. When its ten gliders commenced landing at 0535hrs, ten minutes behind schedule because of time lost through evasive flying against Dutch anti-aircraft fire, the bridge blew up before the eyes of the crews and plunged into the Albert Canal.[24] Due to the lack of landing space at the canal-banks, the gliders could not be brought down immediately beside the bridge.

---

22   One of the guns, indeed, was made operational by its crew. However, it was put out of action again before firing instructions from the fort's command post had arrived.

23   It had initially been delivered by Detachment V of the 14th Artillery Regiment of the Belgian III Army Corps. The artillery fire on top of the fort from several detachments of this regiment and of 7th Infantry Division's 20th Artillery Regiment as well as that from the adjacent forts Pontisse, Barchon and Evegnée was requested by the commandant of Fort Eben-Emael by means of the still operational underground telephone net of Fortress Regiment Liège.

24   The firing party at the bridge had carried out the demolition immediately upon the receipt of the order from Major Jottrand without regard to soldiers of 2nd Grenadier Regiment, of whom a number were still on the opposite bank of the canal. It is highly questionable whether the demolition could have been prevented if *Sturmgruppe Eisen* had landed in time.

On general alert for least half an hour, and alarmed by explosions on the nearby fort at Eben-Emael and the sound of combat in Maastricht, the demolition guard at the bridge and soldiers of the 2nd Battalion of 2nd Grenadier Regiment, which was positioned immediately west of the bridge, commenced firing on the approaching gliders. Several of the crew were wounded in the air. Some of them landed within the positions of the 2nd Grenadier Battalion. One glider came down burning, as the explosives carried on board had been set alight by anti-aircraft fire. Another glider, which had not gained sufficient height before it was disconnected from the towing aircraft, landed on the high ground east of Kanne. Yet another landed about 2km too far to the south at the village of Eben-Emael itself.

Nevertheless the assault group, initially with one team, succeeded in putting out of action the two small concrete machine-gun-bunkers at the western approach to the bridge. After bitter close combat the field fortifications extending west of the bridge were wrested from the enemy. At 0540hrs the group's radio team reported to *Sturmabteilung Koch* the destruction of the bridge, but added to the report that it could still be used after the deployment of engineers.

The reinforcing heavy machine-gun half-platoon was dropped at 0630hrs, albeit 500m too far to the west. It was almost completely destroyed during the landing by defensive fire which caused 14 to be killed and 8 wounded. Only three of the paratroopers, among them the commander, *Oberjäger* Nollau, managed to break through to the positions of the assault group around the western approach to the bridge. At this time the commander of the group, *Leutnant* Schächter, was already out of action after being seriously wounded, and his deputy, *Leutnant* Meissner, assumed command in his place.

Probably through reports from reconnaissance aircraft *VIII.Flieger-Korps* was aware of the destruction of the bridge at Kanne. At 0726hrs, the command of *XXVII.Armee-Korps*, in the attack sector which the bridge and Fort Eben-Emael were located, and informed of the situation. This also applied to *IV.Armee-Korps*, adjacent to the right of *XXVII. Armee-Korps*. However, neither command passed this information on to the command of *4.Panzer-Division* (*Generalmajor* Stever), so that it continued to plan for the relief of *Sturmgruppe Granit* and the final taking of Fort Eben-Emael based on the use of the bridge at Kanne. Even without this requirement to adjust the planning due to an unfavourable development of the situation, *4.Panzer-Division*, one of the spearheads of *6.Armee's* envisaged thrust toward Brussels, still had its fill of problems. The Maastricht bulge was protected by weak Dutch forces,[25] narrow, curved roads, a few carefully selected and partly mined roadblocks and blown up bridges in the valley of the Geul River[26] and had delayed the *4.Panzer-Division*, which had advanced in three march-columns abreast. Its forward elements therefore had not arrived at the eastern outskirts of Maastricht until 0730hrs. *Gefechtsgruppe Mikosch* was integrated well forward into the southern march column. In

---

25   According to the comprehensive and careful research of Dutch military historian A.M.A. Goossens, only the 3rd Battalion of 37th Infantry Regiment and 4 companies of border guards had been deployed along the three delaying lines in the Maastricht bulge.

26   Resistance along the Geul Valley was met primarily at Gulpen, Wijle and Schin op Geul. It was overcome everywhere by 0740hrs.

Maastricht, the advance of the division had ended at the eastern bank of the Meuse, as all three bridges crossing it had been blown up.

This unfavorable situation had developed as follows. *Sonderverband Hocke*, consisting of soldiers of *Btl.z.b.V.100* and some Dutch collaborators, moving slightly ahead of the main attacking force, was ordered to seize the three bridges by surprise attacks. By 0510hrs, all of the sabotage teams, disguised as Dutch workers, who were to render the ignition cables on the bridges unusable, had been arrested by attentive Dutch border guards. Neither the main group of the special unit, nor *Btl.z.b.V.100*, following on its heels, had been able to seize the bridges. After armored cars of the battalion overcame the last of the Dutch rearguards in the city, they approached the St. Servatius Bridge, which was blown up at 0740hrs. At 0755hrs the Wilhelmina Bridge had followed. The railway bridge to the north, which was protected by a Dutch infantry platoon, some machine-guns and a few anti-tank rifles, was also attacked by elements of *Sonderverband Hocke*, among them its commander. When Dutch resistance began to slacken and the first Germans had crossed the bridge, it was blown up at 0800hrs. The explosion killed the Germans on the bridge and with them *Leutnant* Hocke. At about the same time, however, a party of the *Sonderverband*, after considerable losses, succeeded in crossing the Meuse over the lock at Borgharen, just north of Maastricht. Thus, the entry into the part of the city west of the Meuse had been achieved. In the meantime, German troops had occupied the eastern bank of the Meuse at Maastricht along its entire length. The troops who advanced from Borgharen along the western bank of the Meuse to the south, had contributed in breaking the last resistance of the Dutch within the built-up area of Maastricht itself. Only a detachment, located on the St. Pietersberg, about 2km south of the city, was able to hold out for some time, and to inflict some losses to a column of the *4.Panzer-Division* approaching the eastern bank of the Meuse.

The Dutch territorial commander of the province of Limburg, who was present in Maastricht during the fighting, over the course of the morning had made up his mind to hand over the city to the Germans. He believed that further resistance was hopeless and feared for the preservation of the city's cultural heritage in the case of ongoing combat. He therefore arranged for a meeting with the attackers at the Wilhelmina Bridge. At 1110hrs[27] the capitulation of all Dutch troops in and around Maastricht took place. During the fighting in the Maastricht bulge 47 Dutch soldiers had been killed. The losses on the German side had been between 130 and 190 killed and wounded. Nine German vehicles, mostly reconnaissance vehicles, had been put out of action.

The destruction of the bridges in Maastricht caused considerable delay to the advance of the German *6.Armee* in the direction of its main thrust. Moreover, plans for the relief of *Sturmabteilung Koch* needed to be modified. The flexibility of the German command and control system was able to prevent the worst. The forward movements of two *Panzergrenadier* regiments of the *4.Panzer-Division* and of *Gefechtsgruppe Mikosch* were accelerated. First elements of the infantry and the engineers could be brought across the Meuse without difficulties by means of their organic rubber boats and of ferry materials

27   Here, as later, German time is used, if not specifically mentioned otherwise. German time was 1 hour and 40 minutes behind Dutch time.

found at the river. For the construction of pontoon bridges and the repair of the blown-up permanent crossing sites, however, the arrival of bridging columns had to be awaited. At about 1000hrs the commander-in-chief of *Heeresgruppe B*, *Generaloberst* von Bock, arrived in Maastricht true to German principles that commanders should lead from the front. He had discussed the continuation of the operation with the commander of the *4.Panzer-Division*. As a result, the staff of *Pionier Rgt.601* and six bridging columns were put under the command of *4.Panzer-Division*. These forces, however, were still far behind.

In the meantime, the struggle of *Sturmabteilung Koch* for its objectives had continued.

At 0900hrs Belgian infantry launched a counter-attack from the village of Veldwezelt. It was quickly parried by air attacks and the concentrated defensive fire of *Sturmgruppe Stahl*. From 0940hrs on the assault group was also supported by *FlakAbt Aldinger*, which had positioned guns on the eastern bank of the Meuse and delivered indirect fire particularly against Belgian machine-guns south-west of the air bridgehead. The artillery of the enemy which had been firing into the area from 1000hrs on was silenced around noon by dive bombers. About this time the 6th Company of *Schützen-Rgt.12* and the 7th Company of *Schützen-Rgt.33*, both motorcycle units, arrived at the air bridgehead. Since 1300hrs, *ArtRgt.103* of the *4.Panzer-Division* had sent a forward observer into the air bridgehead to provide support.

Due to the attentive nature of the *Luftwaffe* the Belgians abandoned their plan to retake the air bridgehead by counter-attack after the first attempt. Alternatively they tried to destroy the bridge using heavy artillery. However, this method also failed.

In the course of the afternoon increasing numbers German infantry were ferried across the Meuse in Maastricht and advanced toward the Albert Canal. At 1930hrs a reinforced infantry battalion from *Schützen-Rgt.33* arrived at the air bridgehead at Veldwezelt. Its commanding officer assumed command over the forces here; he extended their boundary and ordered the relief of *Sturmgruppe Stahl*. Up to this point 8 soldiers of the group had been killed and 30 wounded. The very same evening, *Oberleutnant* Altmann led his men into Maastricht.

The Belgian *Cyclistes frontière*, manning the enfilading emplacements on the western bank of the Albert Canal on either side of the bridge, held out until 11 May, before being forced to surrender. About the same time, the garrison, blocked in the bunker at the western foot of the bridge, was released into captivity.

On the Belgian side, 115 soldiers had been killed and around 200 had been taken prisoner in the fighting for the bridge at Veldwezelt. A considerable amount of weapons and ammunition had also fallen into German hands. Deplorably, the civilian population in the contested area also suffered, with 35 dead and 45 injured.

Sturmabteilung Beton at Vroenhoven had received efficient support from dive bombers and ground-attack planes throughout the morning. These had frustrated all intentions of the enemy to launch counter-attacks during the process of staging. Soon the guns of *FlakAbt Aldinger* had also joined the fighting, expending large amounts of ammunition, so that the battle HQ of *Hauptmann* Koch and the paratroopers of *Leutnant* Schacht had to disengage. As the chance to regain the bridge at Vroenhoven by counter-attack was considered hopeless by the Belgians, their heavy artillery, including 21cm mortars, directed fire against the bridge with the aim of destroying it from 1030hrs on. However, these efforts were unsuccessful.

Shortly after 1200hrs, the 7th Company of *Schützen-Rgt.12* and some troops of *Btl.z.b.V.100* arrived at the air bridgehead. They were accompanied by the assault group's engineer squad, which had managed to find transport by vehicle from ground forces, after its glider had gone down at Hottdorf.

At 1300hrs the command of *VIII.Flieger-Korps* passed the information by radio that *Hauptmann* Koch was awarded the *Ritterkreuz* for his performance as commander of the assault detachment. At 2000hrs, the 1st Battalion of *Schützen-Rgt.12* crossed the Albert Canal over the bridge at Vroenhoven. After a short fight it had took the village of Kesselt, north-west of the bridge and took over the protection of the air bridgehead. Already by 2140hrs, the assault detachment's battle HQ and *Sturmabteilung Beton* had moved off to Maastricht. Of the 134 paratroopers engaged in the area around Vroenhoven, 7 had been killed and 24 had been wounded. Among the latter was *Leutnant* Schacht. The Belgian defenders had lost almost 150 men and about 300 had been taken prisoner.

At Fort Eben-Emael the situation gradually developed into stalemate. *Sturmgruppe Granit* succeeded in putting the artillery which could have threatened the bridges across the Meuse in Maastricht and across the Albert Canal west of that city out of action. However it was unable to take Emplacements 17 and 35, which were the two enfilading bunkers which dominated the Albert Canal below the fort. Emplacement 4, at the southern end of the moat at the north-western edge of the fort and Emplacement 3, covering the main entrance into the fort, also remained unconquered. The assault team which was directed against the latter by *Oberleutnant* Witzig as well as the men of other teams, positioned at Emplacements 12 and 13, were tied down for the whole day in continuous firefights with Belgian infantry, advancing on the densely covered slope between Emplacements 3 and 4.[28] The paratroopers lost one *Feldwebel* and two other ranks killed and several wounded.

Coupole Sud turned out to be unexpectedly troublesome, as its guns had not been destroyed during the first onslaught. With one of its 75mm guns the turret fired throughout the day into the area around Eijsden, at the eastern bank of the Meuse, about 7km south of Maastricht. [29] Here, in the attack-sector of the *269.Infanterie-Division*, a pontoon-bridge was under construction. The guns of casemate Visé 2 had not yet been attacked as they had not posed a threat to the bridges in and west of Maastricht, joined the fire of Coupole

---

28   A synopsis of Belgian sources reveals the following picture of these events: At 0920hrs the 7th Infantry Division had ordered a counterattack to regain the fort's surface. Thereupon 2nd Grenadier Regiment had detailed a platoon of 40 men of its 1st Company for this task. The platoon had advanced to the fort's main entrance, but was denied access into the fort. From 1130hrs on it had attempted to advance along the slope, but had failed to reach the fort's surface. After it had lost one killed and several wounded and had expended most of its ammunition, it had withdrawn at about 2100hrs. As only its wounded had been granted access into the fort, the platoon had returned to its company. The defending paratroopers had been lucky in that the Belgians had not been able to make use of their light mortars, as the fuses for the mortar rounds had been left behind.

29   Until the capitulation of the fort on 11 May this gun had fired about 2,000 rounds. As all observation domes on the fort had been destroyed the gun crew had to rely on target acquisition from Emplacement 'O' 1 outside of the fort.

Sud and directed it against the area around Lanaye. The artillery fire on the fort's surface, delivered from the adjacent forts Pontisse, Barchon and Evegnée, temporarily hampered the movements of the assault group considerably. This is probably explains why the several attempts of team 1 failed to get at Coupole Sud/Block V from Emplacement 18.

Throughout the course of the morning two He 111s appeared over the fort and dropped parachute containers with additional supplies of explosives and ammunition. Despite the artillery fire they were recovered by soldiers of the assault group and by Belgian prisoners summoned for this task. Around noon *Oberleutnant* Witzig observed a concentration of enemy forces on the high ground west of the fort. Suspecting preparations for a counterattack, he requested the support of dive bombers by radio.[30] The dive bombers actually attacked the entrance area of the fort causing the peacetime barracks to be destroyed. Bombs also hit the village of Eben-Emael, causing casualties among its population. About the time of this bomb attack, *Oberleutnant* Witzig was informed by a message dropped from an aircraft that he was awarded the *Ritterkreuz*.

At 1700hrs, between 120 and 150 Belgian soldiers launched a sortie against the fort's surface from its entrance area.[31] They managed to advance almost to a line between Emplacements 4 and 12, before they were driven back by the fire of the machine-guns and submachine-guns of the paratroopers. At arounf 1900hrs all attackers again had withdrawn into the fort. A short time later *Feldwebel* Arent and some men of his team succeed in destroying the anti-tank gun in Emplacement 4, which had fired toward Kanne.

As *Oberleutnant* Witzig anticipated a resolute counterattack from the north-west during the hours of night, the assault group now established itself in defensive positions in Emplacements 12 and 13, and in field fortifications built by the Belgians between Emplacement 12 and the northern tip of the fort. Prior to this the staircase and the elevator in Emplacement 12, leading down to the fort's interior, were destroyed with concentric charges and a 50kg-shaped charge was detonated at the foot of the stair well in Emplacement 19, to prevent attacks of the fort's garrison from below. Attempts to silence the rapid-fire guns and machine-guns of Emplacement 17 by charges, lowered with ropes and by filling up the weapon embrasures with earth from above, proved abortive. This emplacement into the night continued to direct its fire against relief forces, attempting to cross the Albert Canal in rubber boats.

Contrary to their anxiety, the men of *Sturmgruppe Granit* were only disturbed by occasional sporadic fire by Belgian artillery and enjoyed a quiet night.

---

30   The layout for the wireless traffic of the assault detachment shows that *Sturmgruppe Granit* had no direct radio communication with the command post of *VIII.Flieger-Korps*. Therefore the request must have gone out via the radio set in the battle HQ of *Hauptmann* Koch.

31   A part of these attackers probably had come from the reserve contingent at Wonck. At 1230hrs, Major Jottrand had ordered a counterattack by 200 soldiers from Wonck. From 1300hrs on, 233 men from there, summoned by Lieutenant Levaque, had commenced to move in groups of 20 toward the fort. Repeatedly attacked from the air, 40 soldiers under Lieutenant Levaque had finally made it to the fort. By evening, this number had grown to about 100 men. The rest of the counterattack force had taken refuge in caves on the way. A few men had reached the fort on 11 May. During the night 10/11 May the others had moved to the rail marshaling area in Liège, which had been determined as a collection point for the reserve personnel of all forts around Liège.

In the air bridgehead at Kanne *Sturmgruppe Eisen*, despite considerable losses and several counterattacks by the infantry of 2nd Grenadier Regiment, supported by artillery, not only managed to hold out but to even occupy around noon the settlement of Opkanne. Ahead of relief forces, team 2 of *Sturmgruppe Granit*, led by *Oberjäger* Maier, arrived at the air bridgehead late in the morning and immediately joined the fight. After its emergency landing near Düren, and with its original objective in mind, the team had reached the Meuse on vehicles of the spearhead of the main attack force. Completely on its own, it had crossed the Meuse and had moved to Kanne.

Gefechtsgruppe Mikosch, which was to act as relief for the *Sturmgruppen Eisen* and *Granit*, arrived in Maastricht at 1330hrs, five hours later than ordered because of traffic-congestion. As the original plans for crossing the Meuse had turned into a shambles because of the destruction of the bridges in Maastricht, *Oberstleutnant* Mikosch was ordered by *Generalmajor* Stever to get his force across the Meuse on his own. This was to relieve the paratroopers fighting at Kanne and Fort Eben-Emael as quickly as possible and to complete the taking of the fort. Stever did not mention the destruction of the bridge at Kanne, probably because he had not yet been informed himself about this event. Early in the afternoon *Gefechtsgruppe Mikosch* commenced their crossing of the Meuse near the St. Servatius Bridge in Maastricht on inflated rubber-bags and a quickly constructed pedestrian causeway. At about 1500hrs some of the first troops across the river, mainly the motorcycle squad of *PiBtl.51* under *Leutnant* Ohm, were sent off for reconnaissance toward the bridge at Kanne. The fact that the bridges at Veldwezelt and Vroenhoven at this time were already firmly in German hands, remained hidden from *Gefechtsgruppe Mikosch*.

The commanding officer of *InfRgt.151*, *Oberstleutnant* Melzer, had also driven forward into the area north of Kanne and had assessed the situation as such, that the advance into the air bridgehead and further to Fort Eben-Emael would require a deliberate attack. After he was provided with a report, stating that the bridge at Kanne could be repaired rather quickly,[32] he returned to Maastricht in order to accelerate the movements of his troops to this crossing-site. He arrived again at Kanne at 1815hrs where he discovered that the bridge there could not be made functional within a short time; about half of his regiment was already close behind him.

Around the same time a first attempt by the forward troops of *Gefechtsgruppe Mikosch* to cross the Albert Canal near Kanne, using rubber boats, was beaten off by enfilading fire from the bunkers which had been built into the precipice from the fort down to the canal. The losses in men and boats were considerable. Another attempt, this time under the cover of darkness at 2100hrs, was also broken off as the movements of the crossing forces toward the eastern bank of the canal were observed in the light of flares and searchlights from above. Some paratroopers, who had crossed the canal from the air bridgehead by swimming, finally guided troops of the crossing force safely to the eastern bank. At 2230hrs after more rubber bags had arrived a number of engineers and infantrymen succeeded in crossing the canal and in reinforcing *Sturmgruppe Eisen*. In the meantime the initial attack forces were organized into three crossing groups; each consisting of an engineer company and a

---

32   Melzer mentions in his book about the history of *InfRgt.151*, that this information had come from *Oberstleutnant* Mikosch. This must, however, be doubted, unless Mikosch had relied on the rather vague report from *Sturmgruppe Eisen*.

reinforced infantry company. To suppress the enfilading fire, heavy weapons, among them the quadruple anti-aircraft guns of detachment Aldinger, were brought into position.

On 11 May at about 0100hrs, the relief troops of *Gefechtsgruppe Mikosch*, which included two platoons armed with 3.7cm anti-tank guns from *14./InfRgt.151* (*Hauptmann* Haubold), covered by the fire of supporting weapons managed to cross the Albert Canal on either side of Kanne almost unmolested. At 0300hrs, the air bridgehead was relieved by parts of *Gefechtsgruppe Mikosch*. At 0400hrs it was extended, so that it ceased to come under observed fire. The remainder of the reinforced battalion of 2nd Grenadier Regiment which was positioned west of Kanne now withdrew further to the west. Since the morning of 10 May it had lost about 400 men. [33]

Shock troops of *Gefechtsgruppe Mikosch* and of *14./InfRgt.151* advanced toward Fort Eben-Emael without delay. *Sturmgruppe Eisen* was relieved of its position and assembled for transfer to Maastricht which was planned for the afternoon. From its number of 115 men, 22 had been killed, one missing and 26 wounded. Among the killed was *Oberjäger* Maier, the commander of team 2 of *Sturmgruppe Granit*.

Exhausted, but confident as the situation was now in their favour, the men of *Sturmgruppe Granit* in the first hours of 11 May remained positioned in the emplacements and field fortifications occupied the evening before. At about 0700hrs, an engineer shock troop, led by *Feldwebel* Portsteffen, succeededs in crossing the moat at the north-western edge of the fort with two damaged rubber boats, dragged along from the Albert Canal. Immediately, Portsteffen established contact with some of Witzig's parachute-engineers. In cooperation with these and some anti-tank guns, which had also been brought forward and positioned opposite of Emplacements 3, 4 and 6, Emplacement 4 was finally overcome. It turned out that this casemate had been abandoned by the crew already, after the demolition of the embrasures for its quick-fire guns.

At 0930hrs, *Inf.Rgt.151*, supported by *III./Art.Rgt.161* of *61.Inf.Div.*, attacked from the bridgehead opposite Kanne toward the west and south. Its 1st and 2nd battalions dealt with Belgian troops still holding out opposite the bridgehead and the 3rd battalion turned to the south against the village of Eben-Emael. After its northern part was occupied, Emplacement 6 (Belgian designation: Block VI), after heavy fighting, was also overcome. Emplacement 3, protecting the fort's main entrance, thereupon ceased firing. It took until noon for the anti-tank guns of *14./InfRgt.151* to destroy the weapons of Emplacements 17 and 35, which finally put an end to their enfilading fire along the Albert Canal. Soldiers of *PiBtl.51* also succeeded in demolishing Emplacements 26 (Belgian designation: Visé 1), and 31 (Belgian designation: Coupole Nord). Men of *Sturmgruppe Granit* detonated a 50kg-charge at the locked steel door at the entrance to the underground gallery at the bottom of Emplacement 12 (Belgian designation: Maastricht 1). This caused the collapse of the stairs and the elevator, so that an entry into the fort's interior from this emplacement became impossible. The explosion killed 6 Belgian soldiers who had positioned themselves behind the steel door.

Around noon Major Jottrand came to the conclusion that Fort Eben-Emael had lost its value for the defence of the Albert Canal-sector immediately north of Liège. So, in order to

---

33   The majority of 2nd Grenadier Regiment, three infantry battalions deployed south-west of Lanaye and at Heulekom, was withdrawn toward Brussels in the course of 12 May.

spare the demoralized garrison further losses, after consultation with some of his officers he decided, to take up negotiations with the Germans regarding the surrender of the fort. Prior to this he had tried, in vain, to get hold of the commander of the 7th Infantry Division and the commanding general of I Army Corps, to obtain their approval for handing over the fort. He was able to contact the commanding general of III Army Corps, who simply stated that he saw the responsibility for the fort's fate solely in the hands of its commandant.[34]

After he had administered instructions for the destruction of the still operational installations of the fort,[35] Major Jottrand, at 1215hrs, dispatched an officer under a flag of truce and a trumpeter in order to offer surrender terms to the Germans. This measure, however, came too late: When the draw bridge at the main entrance of the fort was lowered by the crew of Emplacement 3 upon request by a German non-commissioned officer, about 200 Belgian soldiers rushed outside with their hands up. There was now nothing else left for Major Jottrand than to capitulate. Since the beginning of the airborne assault, the fort's garrison had lost 23 men; among them were 3 of the exchange personnel from Wonck, and 63 had been wounded. Between 600 and 700 men were now taken prisoner.

The disarming of the garrison and occupation of the fort, which also led to the end of the resistance from Emplacement 35, took place without the participation of *Sturmgruppe Granit*. *Oberleutnant* Witzig assembled his men and directed them to prepare for departure. Prior to this the 5 paratroopers killed in combat on the fort's surface, were buried north of Emplacement 15 and *Oberjäger* Maier found his grave at the north-western ramp of the bridge at Kanne. The 20 of the *Sturmgruppe* who had been wounded had to take care of themselves or were helped by fellow soldiers, as there had been no space for a medical officer and his equipment on any of the gliders. The serious cases were now moved onto rubber boats along the Albert Canal to Maastricht for professional medical treatment. The other soldiers of the group also left the fort. On their way to Maastricht, they crossed the Meuse over a pontoon-bridge, which had been constructed in the meantime.

Although *Sturmgruppen Stahl* and *Eisen* were transferred to Köln-Butzweilerhof on 11 May, *Beton* and *Granit* remained in Maastricht until the morning of 12 May. There they witnessed the heavy air attacks by the Allies against the first pontoon bridges across the Meuse and particularly against the permanent bridges across the Albert Canal at Vroenhoven and Veldwezelt as the Allies attempted to interrupt the flow of movements of *6.Armee* which were now in full swing.[36]

On 12 May the soldiers of *Sturmabteilung Koch*, who had actually participated in the fighting in marching formation behind a playing band, arrived at the airfield of

---

34 Based on his evaluation of the documents of the Belgian Commission des Forts, pertaining to the fall of Fort Eben-Emael, G. Schalich points out that Major Jottrand had tried to persuade the fort's garrison to carry out a sortie toward friendly positions, but had failed to carry his intention through.

35 As far as these had been executed at all, they had been confined to mere obstructions, as measures for demolitions inside the fort, except one in the underground corridor leading to Emplacement O I, had not been prepared.

36 These attacks had mainly been carried out by the Royal Air Force with Blenheim and Fairey Battle bombers. The German fighter and anti-aircraft forces protecting the bridges had claimed more than 60 enemy aircraft as total losses. The only positive result of the air attacks was the damage of the bridge at Vroenhoven in an attack by five Battles from No. 12 Squadron, escorted by eight Hurricanes from No. 1 Squadron on 12 May, whereby all five Battle and six Hurricane aircraft had been shot down.

Köln-Ostheim. There, *Hauptmann* Koch reported their return to *Generalmajor* Frh. von Richthofen.

There is no doubt that the paratroopers of *Sturmabteilung Koch* had accomplished their tasks. They had succeeded in the undamaged seizure of the two most important bridges across the Albert Canal on the routes from Maastricht to Brussels and had retained them until the arrival of the *Heer*. They had quickly put out of action most of the artillery of Fort Eben-Emael so that only three of its guns had remained to deliver fire against the German troops which advanced toward the Meuse south of Maastricht. The unsuccessful *coup de main* against the bridge at Kanne was a disadvantage for the attack of the *6.Armee* only in as much that it had delayed the relief of the paratroopers at Kanne and Fort Eben-Emael, and had caused additional losses in personnel. The latter could have been avoided to some degree if the reports about the early seizure of the bridges at Vroenhoven and Veldwezelt had become available in time for the troops posed for the relief of the air bridgeheads at Kanne and Fort Eben-Emael. [37]

The failure of the surprise attacks against the bridges in Maastricht, and the resulting delay of reinforcements for the paratroopers at Vroenhoven and Veldwezelt fortunately had not led to a serious threat for the bridges there. This was largely as a result of the Belgian ignorance regarding the German potential for airborne attacks and therefore had missed the chance to prepare resolute counter-attacks at short notice.

The surprise of the enemy deployed along the Albert Canal, west of Maastricht, was mostly derived from the German use of gliders. Their potential for the landing of combat ready troop's right on top of objectives had not been recognized by the *attaché* and secret services of the enemy. This was despite the fact that gliders had more or less become known publicly by their occasional appearance in military exercises and during tests. It was only after they had been decided upon as the means to convey airborne troops to the Albert Canal that their planned utilization had been kept secret with utmost care, ingenuity and rigor. Primarily for that reason, they had also not appeared in *Weserübung*, although some of the tasks assigned to paratroopers in this operation could have been accomplished quite well by the employment of gliders.

For the destruction of the emplacements in Fort Eben-Emael the availability of shaped charges was essential. Their penetration potential surmounted that of the armor-piercing munitions of even the heaviest of artillery which up to then, had been the only means to overcome armor-protected fortifications. Moreover the guns of this type of artillery first had to be brought into position and ranged, which, as was experienced during the First World War, could take days. However, Fort Eben-Emael would have served its purpose, i.e. to gain time.

Both technical elements, gliders and shaped charges, however, had obtained the desired effects only because they had been joined by a third element: They had been brought to bear by men who had been trained in their utilization. Moreover these men

---

37   The reason for the obvious gap in the flow of information about the situation at the Albert Canal was probably the absence of adequate and timely communications between *VIII.Flieger-Korps* and the staffs of the troops planned for the thrust across the Albert Canal, but also among the latter.

approached their tasks highly motivated and with the will to make sacrifices. The seizure of the bridges at Veldwezelt and Vroenhoven, as well as the destruction of the essential artillery emplacements of Fort Eben-Emael within a few minutes has to be attributed to the successful combination of these three elements.

The fact that the attackers had been able to retain their objectives until the arrival of relief forces was the fault of the Belgian high command. Void of a clear view of military necessities it had chosen a sector, favorable for a lasting defence, only as a temporary forward position and later-on lacked the determination to attack and subsequently annihilate a numerical weak enemy who had been deployed in isolation. It was only in conjunction with the intention of the Belgian high command to have the permanent bridges across the Albert Canal blown up by the advance of the German ground attack forces and their ignorance about the threat by airborne forces, which meant anti-aircraft defence of the canal crossings had been disregarded – discounting a few anti-aircraft machine-guns.[38] In spite of some knowledge about the German parachute arm, the Belgians had not anticipated airborne operations against the fortress area of Liège probably based on conclusions which had been drawn from the German documents captured in January 1940. Unlike Holland, they had made no effort to reduce their weakness in ground based anti-aircraft weapons during the time that remained between the outbreak of war and the German attack in the West.

As the airborne surprise attacks against Fort Eben-Emael and the bridges across the Albert Canal opposite Maastricht were clearly Hitler's idea, he had been particularly generous vis-à-vis *Sturmabteilung Koch* after the successful completion of its mission: *Hauptmann* Koch and *Oberleutnant* Witzig had been awarded the *Ritterkreuz* on the morning of 10 May. All other officers who had participated in the actual airborne assault, including the senior medical officer, Dr. Jäger, were decorated with it a short time later, as well as *Oberfeldwebel* Arpke.[39] All officers received the Iron Cross 1st or 2nd Class, if they had not already been decorated with it during the campaign in Poland. All other ranks who had been members of the *Sturmgruppen* and the battle HQ were also awarded the Iron Cross, excluding the few who had not performed as required.

It should not remain unmentioned that even a complete failure of the airborne operations at the Albert Canal would not have created a risk for the realization of the *Sichelschnitt*, as on 10 May at 0700hrs the Allies had commenced to activate the ‚Dijle-Breda plan' and thereby reacted in the way that was expected in the operational plan of the *OKH*. In the worst case the French 1st Army and the nine divisions of the British expeditionary corps would have gained one or two more days for the build-up of their defences between Leuven

---

38   Of the two anti-aircraft batteries deployed in the sector of I Army Corps, the one at Riemst, more than 5km west of Fort Eben-Emael, had only partly covered the airspace over the Albert Canal. The other battery, in position about 9km south-west of Tongeren, had been unable to cover even the artillery west of the canal.

39   *Oberstleutnant* Mikosch and *Feldwebel* Portsteffen, the latter with simultaneous promotion to *Oberfeldwebel*, had also been awarded the *Ritterkreuz*.

and Gembloux. Under this reasoning the German *6.Armee* would have paid heavily for the assault crossing of the Albert Canal in a clash with the better prepared Allies, with considerable higher losses.

The way in which the airborne operation at the Albert Canal had been executed provided Hitler with the opportunity to demonstrate his competence in rating the potential of the new airborne arm with more foresight than the high command of the *Heer* and some of his conservatively-oriented commanders-in-chief. Once more after *Weserübung* he had shown his talent for achieving success by bold ventures and unconventional ideas. After *Sichelschnitt*, for which he also claimed credit, it was only a small step for him to slip into the fatal role of military master.

2

Parachute and Air-landing Troops force entry into Fortress Holland

During the planning process for *Fall Gelb* Hitler had dedicated specific attention to the deployment of parachute and air-landing troops against Fortress Holland. His decision on 14 January 1940 to occupy Holland as a whole, primarily met the demand of the *Luftwaffe* command, which had seen the possession of the coast of the North Sea for its entire length as an inevitable prerequisite for the air war against England. As it could not be excluded that the Dutch had arranged for military assistance from the Allies in the case of a German attack against their country,[1] it could not be ruled out that the latter would rely on Fortress Holland. The core of Dutch national defence was protected in the south by formidable watercourses and lines of fortified positions in the east. Consequently just attacking from the east was assessed as being too slow an option to prevent the Allies from arriving in time to support the Dutch and from building up a continuous front toward the south, relying on Fortress Holland. The solution for this problem had been seen by the early deployment of parachute and air-landing forces. This measure had already been ordered on 14 January in conjunction with Hitler's directive to occupy all of Holland.

Hitler's preparation for *Sichelschnitt* had been made without planning for the use of parachute and air-landing troops against Fortress Holland. On the contrary, it would serve, in addition to the operational purpose, as a means to further deceive the Allies about the main effort of the attack and lure them into the intended trap with the strongest possible forces. The most important measure for the airborne mission was to keep it absolutely secret until its execution[1] and organize the relief and reinforcement of the troops employed from the air in such time that they could take place before they and their objectives would fall victims to counter-measures by the enemy.

The mission to occupy Holland had specifically been allocated to the *18.Armee* under *General der Artillerie* von Küchler, which, using its 10 divisions, was to attack the Dutch defensive lines from the east, on a broad front between Venlo and Groningen. Thus, the relief of the parachute and air-landing troops was allocated to this command. As it was considered highly important to forestall the anticipated thrust of Allied forces via the area around Antwerp into the Dutch province of Noord Brabant, the main effort of the *18.Armee*'s attack was assigned to *XXVI.Armee-Korps*, to be employed south of the large rivers. *9.Panzer-Division*, under *Generalleutnant* Ritter von Hubicki, and with the *SS-Verfügungsdivision* following close-up, were to speedily enter Fortress Holland from the south via Hertogenbosch and Breda. This was to be completed using the bridges across the Hollandsch Diep at Moerdijk which had been seized by elements of *Fl.Div.7*, after infantry divisions and prior to the thrust of the *9.Panzer-Division*, had punched a hole into the Peel-

---

1   A Dutch-French exchange of views had only begun end of March/early April 1940, though unofficial. It had remained unsatisfactory for both sides.

Raam defensive line. Subsequently these spearhead divisions, in cooperation with airborne forces, were to smash the Dutch defences around Rotterdam.

The relief of *22.(LL)Inf.Div.*, which was employed to take possession of Den Haag, would primarily be the task of *X.Armee-Korps* positioned to the right of *XXVI.Armee-Korps*, but also of the *1.Kavallerie-Division*, which was to attack across Lake Ijssel and to form a bridgehead in the province of North Holland.

The Germans did not rate the combat value of the Dutch ground forces highly, mostly because they had not been involved in a European war for more than a hundred years. Greater problems had been observed in the Dutch terrain due to its numerous water obstacles, which, by a sophisticated system of locks and dams, could additionally be used for flooding areas of land. There was no doubt in the German high command that the Dutch would not hesitate to strengthen the defence of their country by this method.

The High Command operational plan for the *18.Armee* stated that: *18.Armee*, by fast occupation of all of Holland, is to prevent forces of the enemy from establishing themselves in the Dutch coastal region. Simultaneously with the advance of forces north of the Waal against the eastern front of Fortress Holland, the coast between Hollandsch Diep and Westerschelde is to be reached by the thrust of fast troops south of the Waal. The unification of British/Belgian with Dutch forces is to be prevented and the prerequisite for the surprise break-in into the southern front of Fortress Holland is to be generated.

On 2 May, Hitler summoned *Generalleutnant* Student and *Generalleutnant* Graf von Sponeck to his Chancellery and revealed to them that he would set the date for the attack in the West for 8 May. The combat missions for the troops ready to attack Fortress Holland from the air, which hitherto had been kept strictly secret,[214] could now be released to them on the basis of a time-table which Hitler himself had laid down. Moreover he had issued a specific guidance for the treatment of Queen Wilhelmina of the Netherlands, assuming that she would stay in her country after its occupation – she was to be approached with great respectfulness.

After *22.(LL)Inf.Div.* was moved to a concentration area around Paderborn in March, the units of *Fl.Div.7* were now deployed from their peacetime garrisons into the vicinity of their planned jump-off airfields in north-western Germany. Here the *Luftwaffe* formations which were to be used for the air transport of the troops and for their support equipment had been assembled.

The fundamental organizational preparations had taken place shortly after the decision for an airborne attack against Fortress Holland. They had been executed under the command of *General der Flieger* Kesselring. As his *Luftflotte 2* was tasked with the air war over, and forward of, the entire right flank of the attack front, *IX Flieger-Korps z.b.V.*, under *Generalmajor* Putzier, was formed for the specific air support of the parachute and air-landing forces. Subordinate to *Luftflotte 2*, it consisted of *Jagdgeschwader 26* and *51* (with Me 109s) under *Jagdfliegerführer 2*, commanded by *Generalmajor* von Döring, of *Kampfgeschwader 4* and *54* (He 111s), of two groups of *Zerstörer-Geschwader 26*, and of *Fern-Aufklärungsgruppe 122*. *Kampfgeschwader 30* (including one group with Ju 88) and *Sturzkampfgeschwader 77* were temporarily assigned. The missions for this aviation group, with a permanently assigned strength of about 240 aircraft, included the protection of the air transport formations, preceding air attacks against the enemy, at and near the objectives, and the neutralization of the air forces of the enemy prior to and during operations on the ground. *Oberst* Bassenge, who was familiar with airborne operations and the proficiency of the *Fallschirmtruppe*, was assigned to *Generalmajor* Putzier as his chief of staff.

Kampfgeschwader z.b.V. 1 and *2*, each consisting of four groups with four squadrons (twelve Ju 52 in each), plus five Ju 52s in the staff squadron of each group, was tasked with the parachuting and the air-landings. *KG z.b.V.2* was made up from the newly-formed *Kampfgruppen z.b.V. 9, 11, 12* and *I/172*. The Ju 52s which had been employed for *Sturmabteilung Koch* was now earmarked for Holland, after completion of their missions in Belgium.

KG z.b.V.1 (*Oberstleutnant* Morzik), in the first wave of air transport movements, was to bring along *Fl.Div.7*, while *KG z.b.V.2* (*Oberst* Conrad) was tasked with the execution of the air-landings of the *22.(LL)Inf.Div.* from the very beginning. The air-landing troops were to be transported to their landing sites in up to three waves. The arrival of the second wave in the area of operations was planned to occur 5-8 hours after that of the first wave. The air transport of the third wave of troops had to take place on the second day.

The provision of the large number of transport aircraft had not proceeded without difficulties. The course of the war in Norway had made it necessary to leave some units of the air transport arm there. The additionally required aircraft for the airborne operation against Fortress Holland, for the greater part had been made available from ongoing production increases. The gap in trained aircrews, however, had to be closed by again reverting to pilots from the *Luftwaffe* aviation schools, thereby reducing their training capacity considerably.

The overall command of the airborne operation was laid into the hands of *General der Flieger* Kesselring. The lower command relations, however, had shown some weaknesses: *Generalleutnant* Student had received the command of the *Luftlande-Korps*, which was made up of of *Fl.Div.7* and the *22.(LL)Inf.Div.* In order to ensure the unity of command, *Generalfeldmarschall* Göring had placed the *22.(LL)Inf.Div.* subordinate to *Fl.Div.7*. However, for his role as commanding general Student neither had received a specific staff nor additional units for command and control, consequently the staff and the few divisional troops of *Fl.Div.7* had to perform a twofold function. The form of cooperation between *18.Armee* and *Fl.Div.7* was laid down as "guidance-oriented connection" or "*weisungsgemässe Koppelung*". [2] Thereby, *18.Armee* was provided with the opportunity to align the actions of the *Luftlande-Korps* with the operations of its own forces in the field of common missions, if required and possible. The subordination of *Fl.Div.7* to *Luftflotte 2* was to cease upon the unification of the former with ground forces advancing through Noord Brabant.

---

2   Seen from this perspective, it is rather incomprehensible why *Sturmabteilung Koch* had received a head-start of 30 minutes over the airborne attack in Holland. Quite obviously, however, this time had been seen as too short to allow for reactions in Holland.

Generalleutnant Student, whose staff had moved to Wiedenbrück, near Gütersloh, assumed overall responsibility for planning pertaining to the use of parachute troops, and the selection of the drop zones and the air-landing sites. For an appreciation of the actual enemy situation and the terrain conditions in the area of operations of the *Luftlande-Korps*, he had to rely mainly on the results of reconnaissance and the inquiries of the German military *attaché* staff in Den Haag. The latter had only been provided after the decision in January 1940 to attack Holland, and on a few aerial photos taken from great height in the months preceding the attack.[3] For more information, it was necessary to draw upon the archives of the intelligence services, which were not up to date. However Student had not been overly perturbed by this insufficient intelligence. [4]

Considerable problems in the planning process also developed from the divergent aims of the airborne attack – the opening of the entries into Fortress Holland from the south, and the neutralization of the Dutch government in Den Haag. In order to interrupt the defensive measures of the Dutch against the seizure of the bridges along the traffic arteries from the south, across formidable watercourses, and against the landings of troops on airfields, surprise attacks by paratroopers were considered as indispensable. Their number, due to the incomplete organization of *Fl.Div.7*, was limited. *Generalleutnant* Student's plan for the airborne attack, developed in concert with *Luftflotte 2* and the other aviation units, the *22.(LL)Inf.Div.*, and the two air transport wings paid attention to this problem: The mingling of both divisions of the *Luftlande-Korps* had been foreseen straight away. Because of the mandatory assignment of parachute infantry for the seizure of the landing sites of the *22.(LL)Inf.Div.*, *Fl.Div.7* lacked the strength to retain the entry points into Fortress Holland for three days – the time assessed until the arrival of relief forces on the ground. It would be reinforced with *InfRgt.16* from the *22.(LL)Inf.Div.* Mission objectives of *Fl.Div.7* would be:

To keep open the southern entries into Fortress Holland for ground assault troops via Tilburg/Breda and therefore to firmly seize by surprise attack with *Fallschirmtruppe* the bridges at Moerdijk and Dordrecht.

To simultaneously take possession of the bridges in the southern part of Rotterdam and the airfield at Waalhaven, and to protect the latter until the arrival of air-landing troops, the individual missions and the task plans of the parachute and air-landing troops of the first wave had been laid down as follows: [5]

---

3   Whether this wording was actually used in writing must be doubted. It was used by the former operations officer (Ia) of the *22.(LL)Inf.Div.* after the war to explain a specific command relation hitherto unparalleled in the *Wehrmacht*.

4   W. Pissin, in his report about a briefing of the former *Luftwaffe* generals Putzier, von Döring and Bassenge about the campaign in the West on 8 February 1955, has summarized their statements as follows: "Air reconnaissance over Holland prior to 10 May 1940 was prohibited by pain of death". It had only been flown by the high-altitude squadron of the commander-in-chief of the *Luftwaffe* during periods of clear weather in 8-10,000m height. This had not permitted the spotting of the terrain conditions and the details of the defence on the Dutch airfields. Furthermore, the German military *attaché* in Den Haag, in his findings dated 9 April 1940, had primarily reported about the locations of the Dutch commander-in-chief and the successors to the throne and the dispositions of Dutch troops in the area of Katwijk."

5   This incomprehensible neglect of an essential element of command and control had already become visible in his attitude toward the lacking of intelligence for the mission against Dombås, which was in striking contradiction to the requests, formulated by the staff of *Fl.Div.7* after the end of *Weserübung*. It is a clear

- *Gruppe Süd* – reinforced *FschJgRgt.1*, commander: *Oberst* Bräuer, with 1st and 2nd battalions and 14th (anti-tank) company *FschJgRgt.1* (*I.* and *II./FschJgRgt.1* and *14. (PzAbw)/FschJgRgt 1*), divisional gun battery (*GeschBttr*), *FschSan-Halbkompanie*, parts of *LuftNachrKp.7*, one platoon of *leFlaBttr.106* and *1./ PiBtl.22*, after preceding air attacks, would take possession of both bridges at Moerdijk, which had to be retained at all costs until the arrival of advance troops of the *Heer*. Simultaneously, one company was to be employed for the seizure of the bridges at Dordrecht, to be relieved later by elements of *InfRgt.16* and thereafter to become available for Moerdijk.

- *III./FschJgRgt.1*, directly subordinate to *Fl.Div.7*, after preceding air attacks, would seize the airfield at Waalhaven and protect it for subsequent air-landings. At the same time, the bridges in Rotterdam were to be occupied by one company, which would revert to the regiment after relief by elements of *InfRgt.16*. The bridge across the Meuse [6] at Hoogvliet (7 km south-west of Waalhaven) was to be blocked.

- *Gruppe Nord* – reinforced *InfRgt.16*, commander: *Oberst* Kreysing, with *InfRgt.16*, *2./PiBtl.22* and *4./Art.Rgt.22* – upon arrival, would occupy the area of Dordrecht – at the southern part of Rotterdam and protect it toward the east and the north. Utilizing the basin of the harbour of Rotterdam, a bridgehead was to be established immediately north of the bridge across the Meuse.

It was also important to:

- Protect the crossing sites at the road connecting Dordrecht with Rotterdam;
- Block the bridges across the Merwede and the Wantij east of Dordrecht as well as the ferry-point east of Ridderkerk.

II./FschJgRgt.2 (less 6th Company) after its landing[7] was to reach Barendrecht (about 5 km south-east of Waalhaven). There it should remain available for the Division, using all means to become motorized.

The divisional anti-tank company,[8] *1./PzAbwAbt.22*, and the divisional transportation company would receive their orders on the airfield at Waalhaven on day A + 1.

Luftwaffen-Sanitätskompanie 7, less its parachute half-company, was to establish the main medical treatment facility in the southern part of Rotterdam.

To clearly define the operational areas of his two divisions *Generalleutnant* Student had determined a line of separation leading from Maassluis (about 10km south-east of the

---

indication of Student's willingness to disregard principles of command and control, thereby accepting high risks for his troops and trusting their ability, to overcome these risks by their performance in battle.

6   According to the order for the employment of the *Luftlande-Korps* for Operation *Festung*, dated 23 February 1940.

7   The mission outlined above unfortunately had not distinguished between the branches of the Meuse. It should have read correctly Old Meuse (Oude Maas), the branch passing the isle of Ijsselmonde in the South. In the mission for *Gruppe Nord*, it should have read New Meuse (Nieuwe Maas), which is the branch of the river passing through Rotterdam and along the North of Ijsselmonde.

8   As the majority of the soldiers of *II./FschJgRgt.2* had not yet been jump trained, they had to be brought along with transport aircraft. The *6./FschJgRgt.2* planned to parachute into the operational area of the *22.(LL)Inf.Div*.

mouth of the Oude Maas) via the northern edge of Rotterdam at Kethel, Overschie and Terbregge to Nieuwerkerk (about 6km south-east of Gouda).

During the planning for these missions, it became apparent that the many watercourses and drainage ditches in the operational area of *Fl.Div.7* would offer no opportunity for transport aircraft to land in open terrain. Therefore the surprise attack and retention of the airfield at the Waalhaven, designated as landing site IV – the only one in the entire operational area – received paramount importance.

To increase the effect of surprise, a squadron of He 59 hydroplanes was made available, probably from a proposal by Göring, with which the balance of a company of *InfRgt.16* was to be landed on the Nieuwe Maas and at the harbour of Rotterdam, close to the bridges connecting both parts of the city. It was to quickly occupy these bridges undamaged and to form a bridgehead immediately north of them.

Based on the evaluation of aerial photos and of reports from the German military *attaché* staff in Den Haag, three sites for the landing and takeoff of transport aircraft, located in a semi-circle around the Dutch capital, were assessed as suitable to support the mission of the *22.(LL)Inf.Div.*:

- In the south the airfield at Ypenburg to be used by the Dutch air force;
- In the west a small airfield for sports aircraft near Ockenburg-Loosduinen;
- In the east an airfield near Katwijk and Valkenburg identified as still being under construction but already as serviceable.

Moreover, sections of the auto-route from Rotterdam via Delft toward Den Haag had been planned as possible runways for Ju 52, after respective tests by the air transport squadron of *Fl.Div.7* on the Autobahn near Gütersloh had been successful.

As *InfRgt.72* was assigned to *22.(LL)Inf.Div.* as reinforcement,[9] *Generalleutnant* Graf von Sponeck, in spite of the dispatch of *InfRgt.16* to *Fl.Div.7*, had nine infantry battalions at his disposal. His attack plan was to land elements of *Inf.Rgts.47* and 65, as well as the first divisional troops, and his battle HQ, simultaneously on all three airfields. This would allow the encirclement of Den Haag to be accomplished. Preceding the air-landings, the assigned parachute infantry – *I./FschJgRgt.2* under *Hauptmann* Noster and *6./FschJgRgt.2*, commanded by *Oberleutnant* Schirmer, were to clear the airfields of defending enemy troops. *I./FschJgRgt.2*, to be dropped with the battle HQ and three companies (1st, 2nd and 4th) was to seize the airfield at Ypenburg, measuring 800 x 750m, as a preliminary mission for the air-landing of the first wave of troops, which were to be reinforced *InfRgt.65* (less its 2nd Battalion), under *Oberst* Friemel. This airfield, designated as landing site III, had been considered due to its size and location, as the most important for the *22.(LL)Inf. Div.* Therefore the division commander and his battle HQ, the balance of *NachrAbt.22*, and some other units required for command and control functions, were to follow close up. The paratroopers were to protect the airfield along a wide defensive area. Afterwards they were to advance north to the Hoorn Bridge forming the south-western entry into Den Haag and toward Delft in the south. *3./FschJgRgt.2*, under *Oberleutnant* von Roon, was tasked with the seizure of the airfield at Ockenburg, designated as landing site II. The size

---

9   The former anti-tank experimental unit.

of this airfield was relatively small, measuring only 650 x 250m. Its advantage, however, was that two roads, not intersected by watercourses, led directly into the centre of Den Haag. The parachute company, besides protecting the airfield was also to expel enemy troops from the dunes around Kijkduin, about 1km to the north-east, if required.

6./FschJgRgt.2 was tasked with the seizure of the airfield at Valkenburg, designated as landing site I, planned for the landing of *InfRgt.47*. After the arrival of sufficiently strong combat troops of this regiment, the paratroopers were also to prevent the advance of Dutch forces across the Oude Rijn south-west of Leiden.

The actual occupation of Den Haag was planned in the aftermath of the arrival of the balance of *Inf.Rgts.47* and 65, and was to be by concentric attack from all three airfields. On the basis of a declaration, containing the justification for the military occupation of Holland, to be handed over by the German ambassador in Den Haag, Count Zech von Burkersroda, at the beginning of the German attack against Holland,[10] the Dutch royal family were to be taken into custody. This would hopefully lead to political and military collapse in the country.

During the German attack against Poland and the declaration of war against Germany by France and Great Britain, Holland had maintained its neutrality and had hoped to stay out of armed conflict. From 1936 on it had finally devoted more attention toward matters of its defence which had been neglected since the Great War. This included the procurement of modern equipment for its armed forces which strongly depended on mobilization. About 280,000 men in the Army and the Air Arm, which was integrated into it, were kept under arms in the motherland in early May 1940.

Up to early 1940 about 80 modern combat aircraft[11] had been acquired for the Army Air Arm.

However, the lack of armored vehicles had not been overcome by early 1940. Of the 12 light DAF M39 armored cars, equipped with a 37mm gun and three machine guns, ordered for the Army, only 6 were combat ready.[12] For the Dutch Light Division, 12 M36 Landsverk L 181 and 14 M38 Landsverk 180 had been bought from Sweden. Both types, except two command vehicles, were equipped with a 37mm gun and three 7.9mm machine-guns. Beside the armored cars, the Army also had 5 Carden Lloyd machine-gun-carriers, so that in May 1940 the total inventory was 43 armored vehicles, of which only 37 were combat ready.

The main anti-tank weapon of the Dutch Army, organized in companies and platoons in the regiments and battalions of the infantry, were 368 47mm Boehler anti-tank guns.

---

10   *InfRgt.72* had not been trained for air-landings and therefore was planned as divisional reserve by *Generalleutnant* Graf von Sponeck. The regiment then received some instruction for its planned role in its concentration area.

11   This declaration was handed over to the Dutch minister for foreign affairs, van Kleffens, on 10 May at 0600hrs. It stated the imminent invasion of Belgium, Holland and Luxemburg by British and French troops. The Dutch government had rejected the German accusation and then declared Holland as being in a state of war with Germany.

12   29 Fokker D-XXI single-seat fighters, 23 Fokker G-1 twin-seat fighter-bombers, 11 Douglas 8 A bombers and long-range reconnaissance aircraft, 9 Fokker T-V bombers, and 10 Fokker C-X light bombers/ long-range reconnaissance aircraft. The Fokker D-XXI was considerably slower than the Me 109, but was rated equal because of its excellent flying performance.

In addition, there were about 60 20mm anti-tank rifles. The light guns[13] had also been provided with armor-piercing munitions. 47mm anti-tank guns had also been built into a number of bunkers in fortified defence sectors.

Considerable efforts had been undertaken to improve the ground-based anti-aircraft defence. In early May 1940 81 of the highly effective 75mm Vickers anti-aircraft guns and 9 Skoda guns of the same type were also in use. From licensed production of the British 40mm anti-aircraft gun in Poland and Hungary 45 weapons, mounted on trailers, had been acquired. While only a few 37mm anti-aircraft guns had become available, the number of 20mm guns was increased to about 150. Less favorable, however, was the situation for the 45 platoons equipped with MG 08 type machine-guns of First World War German vintage. These had been found increasingly unreliable for technical reasons. A number of obsolete large caliber anti-aircraft guns were also still in service.

The artillery, consisting of about 1,000 guns, was also, for the greater part, obsolete.

By 2 September 1939 the Dutch Army was deployed in considerable strength for its defensive missions. However, the overall mobilization had not been completed. Only the contingents 40-I and 40-II of men liable for military service had been called up to the depots, which had to train and distribute the field replacements. Furthermore not all of the mobilization slots could be filled with fully trained personnel because of changes in the military service system.

The Field Army was organized in four corps commands (I-IV Army Corps), with two divisions each. In addition there was the Light Division of three independent brigades, as well as combat, combat support, logistical and medical troops at the corps level. The territorial commands had at their disposal a considerable number of infantry and border battalions. The former were generally combined in regiments. The mobilization procedures were conducted in depots which had been established for each branch of the Army and spread throughout the centre and the west of the country. The depots were also ordered to train recruits and soldiers for internal security duties.

The Dutch high command did not lack knowledge about a possible German attack. First indications that Germany might not honour the neutrality of the Netherlands in its struggle against the Allies had already been received in November 1939. A report, submitted in the second half of November by the Dutch military *attaché* in Berlin, stated that the German attack in the West was imminent. This news had triggered further mobilization measures in the Dutch armed forces and led to the opening of the locks in front of the Grebbe Line. The information about German attack plans passed to the Dutch government by the Belgians as a result of the Maasmechelen affair in January 1940 had furnished indications that Holland would be drawn into the war. Although the German attack did not materialize and the warning by Major Sas had proved wrong, the Dutch armed forces remained on an enhanced level of readiness. They had also gone ahead with the improvement of the delaying and defence positions in front of Fortress Holland, and had increased their manning.

As early as 1 December 1939 the Dutch government had officially declared that it would ask France and Great Britain for military support in the case of a German invasion.

---

13   Two were not yet armed and four were undergoing technical transitions.

Prior to this the Dutch military *attaché* in Paris had been in touch with the Allies so as to gain clarity about their plans, pertaining to Holland, in the case of a German attack. At the end of March/early April the Dutch military high command understood that the Allies, within the framework of their Dijle-Breda plan, did plan to advance with the French 7th Army into the western part of the province of Noord Brabant at the beginning of a German attack, in order to protect Antwerp. However they had shown no intentions of moving forward to the Dutch Peel-Raam position east of Eindhoven, which was prepared to cover the south of Holland. Instead, the French commander-in-chief had expressed his view expecting the participation of Dutch ground forces in the protection of the approaches toward Antwerp in the area Tilburg-Breda. The desire of the Dutch high command, to see the French join the defence along the extension of the Peel-Raam-position to the south, however, had come to nothing.

It had not been possible to form an arrangement with the Belgians for a defensive position to cover the Peel-Raam position. Instead they aimed for a more substantial retention of the line Maastricht-Venlo by the Dutch, obviously thought to serve as a buffer for their own Meuse-Albert Canal line. Additionally they had considered a stable common defence as not feasible forward of a line between Turnhout and Tilburg. The Dutch had seen themselves unable, if only for lack of forces, to meet the Belgian desire for a stronger retention of the line Maastricht-Venlo. Similarly the Belgians had not been willing to extend their forward line of defence to the Peel-Raam-position, thus a gap of about 40km width of unoccupied terrain was left between the Dutch Peel-Raam-position and the Belgian Albert Canal-line. The Dutch high command had seen little chance for a successful common defence further to the west, mainly because no positions had been prepared in the western part of Noord Brabant. General Winkelman was appointed as commander-in-chief of the Dutch armed forces on 10 February 1940. Upon his appointment he decided to engage the attack on the right flank of the Dutch defensive front with weak forces already on the western bank of the Meuse, in order to gain time for further improvements of the main defence. Due to the unprotected southern flank the Peel-Raam Line could be retained only for a limited period, the forces which originally had been planned for its protection– the majority of III Army Corps and the Light Division – were to withdraw into Fortress Holland on the second day of a German attack. Then they were designated to protect the Fortress toward the south, along the northern bank of the Waal River. In the Peel-Raam-position, a force of one division was to fight for time, and then to withdraw along successive delaying positions toward the French in western Noord Brabant.

In the centre of the defensive front, where II and IV Army Corps were deployed, General Winkelman had planned to prevent the attacker from entering Fortress Holland from the east along the Grebbe Line. This line, extending from Lake Ijssel via Amersfoort to the Waal,[14] consisted of three successive positions, the most forward of these was strengthened by numerous concrete bunkers and weapon casemates. The so-called New Waterline was determined as the final protective position behind the Grebbe Line along the eastern edge of Fortress Holland. In northern Holland a lasting defence was prepared on both ends of the heavily fortified dam, shutting off Lake Ijssel from the shallows of the North Sea. The provinces east of Lake Ijssel were considered indefensible and were to be given up in the case of a German attack there.

---

14   These were the six 57mm infantry guns and the seven 75mm field guns.

I Army Corps (Major General Carstens), consisting of the 1st and 3rd Infantry Divisions, was deployed inside of Fortress Holland, initially as reserve of the Field Army. The 1st Infantry Division (Colonel Bischoff van Helmskerk) was concentrated on either side of Den Haag,[15] the 3rd Infantry Division around Haarlem.

The defence of Holland was given to Lieutenant General van Andel. The combat troops of his command consisted of several independent infantry regiments or battalions, which had been formed on 28 August 1939 from cadres of the field divisions, from reservists and from recruits. Lieutenant General van Andel organized his forces into three task groups:

- East Front, outside of the areas of operation of the German parachute and air-landing forces (therefore not listed here).
- West Front, with troops at Alkmaar, Haarlem, Leiden and the naval base Ijmuiden and with II/39th Inf.Rgt., a reserve border infantry company and coastal defence forces of the Navy around Hoek van Holland and on the island of Rozenburg.
- South Front, on the large islands between Oude Maas/Nieuwe Waterweg, Kil and Hollandsch Diep/Haringvliet with:
   ♦ Group Spui: I/39th Inf.Rgt., 39th Reserve Border Infantry Company, 13th Engineer Company and I and II/14th Art.Rgt., 26th Art.Rgt. in the western part of the island of Hoekse Waard, and on the island of Putten. One company of I/39th Inf.Rgt., half a platoon of the Battalion's machine-gun company and a detail of Engineer's for lock control in the disarmed and obsolete fortress of Willemstad. Not subordinate was a coastal artillery battery at Numansdorp, on the northern bank of Hollandsch Diep, opposite Willemstad.
   ♦ Group Kil: II/28th Inf.Rgt., some elements of III/28th Inf.Rgt., parts of the sub units of 28th Inf.Rgt., III/34th Inf.Rgt., I and III/23rd Art.Rgt. and 25th Art.Rgt. in the eastern part of the island of Hoekse Waard. Also positioned there, but subordinate to the Air Defense Command was the 6th Anti-Aircraft Battery in the Moerdijk bridgehead. 3 companies of III/28th Inf.Rgt., 12th Machine-gun-Company, 2 platoons of I/41st Inf. Rgt., one section of 28th Infantry Gun Company, a detail of police troops and machine-gun crews for the manning of the large casemates covering the bridges. (82nd and 83rd Anti-Aircraft Machine-Gun Platoons (subordinate to the Air Defense Command).
   ♦ In the west and south of the island of Dordrecht: 2 reinforced companies of I/28th Inf.Rgt., I/17th Art.Rgt.

The forces of the Fortress command also included the Lake Ijssel flotilla (the gunboat *Friso*, river gunboat *Hefring*, and eight armed motorboats) as well as some more units of the Navy who would man a few armed tugs, small steamers and motorboats in support of the task groups.

Intelligence gathered in conjunction with the Maasmechelen affair of January 1940 led to the assessment that German air attacks against the core of the Dutch national defence must be anticipated from the outset of an invasion of Holland. Consequently

---

15   Actually the line had ended at the Nederrhijn. The positions extending from there about 6 km to the Waal had been designated the Betuwe-line.

considerable ground anti-aircraft forces had been positioned in Fortress Holland. In the area of Rotterdam-Den Haag-Delft, 36 75mm anti-aircraft guns, 6 40mm anti-aircraft guns, 38 20mm anti-aircraft guns, 108 anti-aircraft machine-guns and 70 searchlights had been concentrated, subordinate to the Air Defense Command under Major General Best.

By early May 1940, the Dutch depot battalions had partly been filled with recruits and with reservists, who were not yet needed in the Field Army. After a state of increased readiness was been declared from February 1940 onwards, the 10th Depot Battalion from Ede and the 15th Depot Battalion from Breda was moved to Leiden to join the 22nd Depot Battalion, which had arrived earlier. Moreover, a recruit depot of artillery and an instruction battery, altogether about 2,000 men was located in Oegstgeest, a suburb of Leiden just to its north. In so doing Leiden was strongly garrisoned.

Troops from the reserves, or still in basic training, were also stationed in Delft, including seven light anti-aircraft platoons, elements of the 6th, 3rd and 14th Depot Battalions of the infantry and a company formed from students of the Delft technical high school.

For the protection of the royal family the governmental institutions, the high command of the armed forces, elements of the elite Grenadier Regiment (including its border infantry battalion), a number of depot troops and some anti-aircraft units were garrisoned in Den Haag proper.

Dordrecht, a town with about 60,000 inhabitants and located on the southern banks of the Oude Maas and the Merwede in the north-western part of the island, had a garrison of about 1,600 soldiers. Made up of the depot for specialized engineers – a staff and four companies with 1,040 bridge engineers, and 308 torpedo/mine operators[16] – a platoon of railway engineers (61 men) and a few soldiers in the town's military hospital, armory and in a depot for anti-tank munitions. The garrison's commander was *Oberstleutnant* Mussert[17] who was assisted by a small staff. Included in the overall number of soldiers, but not subordinate to the garrison commandant, were the 14th Engineer Company (120 men) of Group Kil and two platoons of anti-aircraft machine-guns tasked with the protection of two bridges across the Oude Maas.

Rotterdam had a population of more than 600,000 and was the second largest city in Holland and the largest port in the country, and was garrisoned by nearly 7,000 soldiers. However, almost 6,000 of them were non-combat troops – about 2,000 in the engineer depot, 900 of the ordnance services, about 600 in a depot for the Navy, more than 1,000 in a depot for the Naval Air Arm, and a number of soldiers in staffs, guard details and medical installations. Among the 1,100 combat troops was a detachment of 300 marines (Dutch designation: *mariniers*), all of them professional soldiers, of whom about 200 were fully trained. Of III/39th Inf.Rgt. (800 men) one company was located in the part of Rotterdam south of the Niewe Maas, one more to the west of the island of Ijsselmonde, tasked with the protection of the petroleum installation at Pernis, and one on the northern bank of the Nieuwe Maas. At the latter's location, the battalion staff and its machine-gun company were also quartered. I/10th Art.Rgt., belonging to I Army Corps and equipped with 12 modern 10.5cm howitzers, was quartered in Hillegersberg, a suburb in the north of Rotterdam.

---

16   Some units of this division had already been deployed to Rotterdam, Den Haag and in the fortress at Den Helder. Its engineer company was assigned to the task *Gruppe Ost* of the fortress.

17   The torpedo/mine operators were part of the naval garrison, and were to be used for the mining of watercourses.

Of the eight platoons of the 13th Anti-Aircraft Machine-gun Company deployed in greater Rotterdam three were positioned for the protection of the petroleum installation at Pernis. One was placed on the northern bank of the Nieuwe Waterweg opposite Pernis and another on the northern bank of the Nieuwe Maas opposite the basin of the Waalhaven. Three platoons were deployed on the airfield at Waalhaven.[18]

Three batteries of anti-aircraft guns covered a large portion of the airspace over Rotterdam from positions north-west of Vlaardingen, at Smitshoek and on pier 7 at the western end of the Waalhaven. The Dutch volunteer militia for air defense was still in training. Three platoons with three anti-aircraft guns each, however, were operational by 10 May.

In the sector of Hoek van Holland, at the western tip of the Fortress, a detachment of the Navy, with 60 marines and 140 sailors, were selected for coastal protection. This was in addition to the fully trained II/39th Inf.Rgt. and the anti-tank, mortar and infantry gun companies of 39th Inf.Rgt. For the coastal defence of this sector, which also included the island of Rozenburg, a brigade group of the Navy was formed. At its disposal were three 15cm guns, two 7cm guns in concrete casemates, two 24cm guns and two 15cm guns in revolving steel cupolas. On the coast of Westland, just north of the sector Hoek van Holland, two battalions of the Jager Regiment[19] from the 1st Inf.Div. were quartered in Gravenzande and Monster.

South of the Hollandsch Diep the 3rd and 6th Border Infantry Battalions were deployed for protection tasks along the Dutch/Belgian frontier on the general line Bergen op Zoom (at the coast of the Oosterschelde)-Roosendal-Breda-Gilze (9km east of Breda). These units, under the command of III Army Corps, prepared a number of obstacles and demolitions. The 6th Border Battalion was tasked with the occupation of the Moerdijk bridgehead upon the approach of German forces through Noord Brabant.

In early 1940 the Dutch had not seen any threat by German *Fallschirmtruppe* to Fortress Holland. The Dutch high command obviously appeared to associate itself with the opinion of Major General Alting von Geusau, who had considered such a threat as insubstantial.[20]

Information about the employment of German parachute and air-landing troops, in particular regarding the seizure of Fornebu from the air,[21] had become available in Holland after the German invasion of Denmark and Norway. The Dutch high command drew the conclusion that a stronger coverage of the Fornebu airfield by ground fire would probably have led to the failure of the air-landings. The actions of German paratroopers at Stavanger-Sola and on the island of Masnedø, if information had been received at all, had not been examined seriously. The German parachute action at Dombås, about which the Dutch had quite certainly gained information of from the Allies, in fact had contributed to the theories of von Geusau. Anyhow, on 20 April General Winkelman, with regard to the

---

18   He was the brother of the leader of the pro-German national-socialist collective movement of Holland, the NSB.

19   The Anti-Aircraft Machine-Gun Platoons (German designation: *FlaMG-Zug*), were equipped with four machine-guns MG 08 each, some of them additionally with two 20mm anti-aircraft guns.

20   The term Jager was used for light infantry. It is identical with the same German term.

21   Von Geusau, the former commanding officer of I Army Corps, in his book *Nederland is Paraat* published in early 1940, stressed the point that paratroopers could be decimated in the air by machine-gun-fire and, after the landing, could be encircled and cut off from their logistical support. Thereupon they could be neutralized quickly.

events at Fornebu, in addition to the already positioned anti-aircraft assets, had ordered the deployment of troops for the protection of the airfields in Fortress Holland as follows:

- On the airfield Ypenburg III/Grenadier Regiment from 1st Inf.Div.
- On the airfield Waalhaven III/JagerRgt, also from 1st Inf.Div.
- On the airfield Valkenburg two companies and a machine-gun platoon from III/4th Inf.Rgt. from 1st Inf.Div.
- On the airfield Amsterdam-Schiphol an infantry battalion from 3rd Inf.Div.

Probably drawing on the events at Fornebu, the field positions of the infantry around the airfields had been designed such that weapons were primarily directed toward the runways, in order to engage landing aircraft. Preceding parachute assaults from outside the airfields, however, had not been considered a likely initial attack option for commands tasked with the protection of airfields. As landings of German troop carrying planes on the auto-routes Den Haag-Rotterdam, Den Haag-Utrecht, Rotterdam-Gouda and Rotterdam-Breda could not be excluded, these were blocked by parked motor vehicles and concrete tubes filled with sand every 100-150m. In addition the motorized 1st Hussar Regiment from the Light Division had been moved to Wassenaar (about 6km north-east of Den Haag). It had detailed half a squadron of light armored cars each for the protection of the airfields at Schiphol and Ypenburg, and two light machine-gun carriers to Waalhaven. Furthermore it was warned to assume the surveillance of the blocked auto-routes. When the order arrived on 8 May the Regiment dispatched two motorcycle-companies and two heavy machine-gun platoons on sidecar motorcycles for patrolling duties.

The warning by Major Sas from Berlin about an imminent German attack resulted in the ordering of a high state of readiness for all airfields in Fortress Holland on 7 May. On the same day the protection of the airfield at Ockenburg[22] by combat troops had also been ordered, but a weak company of 22nd Depot Battalion was moved to this location. However, elements of the 1st and 2nd battalions of the Grenadier Regiment and its machine-gun company were quartered only 2km away.

On the evening of 9 May Major Sas telephoned and stated with absolute certainty that the German attack in the West would begin on the next morning. The Dutch supreme political and military authorities were convinced that they had undertaken all necessary measures for the defence of their country. Nevertheless they remained sceptical about the veracity of the warning, remembering the many false alarms in the past. The commandant of Fortress Holland abstained from placing his troops on alert, because he did not see a threat by parachute troops against the Fortress, and rightfully excluded an imminent attack by enemy ground forces against his area of operation. It was only early on the morning of 10 May that he called for the highest state of alert.

---

22   The pilot of a Dutch DC-3 passenger plane, who had witnessed the air-landings at Fornebu during a stopover on this airfield, had reported the events to the Dutch high command upon his return on 16 April 1940.

10 May

At 0535hrs on 10 May the German forces along the entire Western Front moved into Holland, Belgium, Luxemburg and France. At the same time air transport units of the *Luftwaffe* with parachute infantry of *Fl.Div.7* aboard flew across the German/Dutch border, following behind the air attack forces. About 30 minutes prior to the planned arrival of the transport aircraft over the airfields to be seized, bombers, escorted by fighters, launched the first air attacks. In some cases the deception to initially fly out over the North Sea in a direction toward England and then to turn around and attack the Dutch airfields unexpectedly from the north-west, succeeded. Due to this, most of the Dutch military aircraft stationed at Bergen and Gilze-Rijen were destroyed on the ground. However, as the Dutch Air Arm had been on a high level of readiness since 7 May, the deception was only partially successful against the airfields at Schiphol, Ypenburg and Waalhaven and against the naval airbase at de Kooy (near Den Helder). In these locations most of the modern Dutch combat aircraft managed to take off just prior to the air attacks or even during the initial phases. The fighters were immediately engaged in aerial combat with German Me 109 and Me 110s that were escorting bombers and transport planes. They succeeded in inflicting some losses among the German air armada, but paid dearly for it. Thereafter, the remaining Dutch combat aircraft were forced to yield airspace over the area of operations of the *Luftlande-Korps* due to the vastly superior numbers of their enemy. On the reserve airfield at Ruigenhoek, which had passed the attention of the *Luftwaffe*, the few Dutch aircraft still in flying condition were made ready for further sorties. The airfields at Schiphol and de Kooy, which had not been not intensively attacked during the first German air onslaught, were soon operational again.

A few minutes after 0530hrs He 111 and Ju 88s of *KG 4*[23] attacked identified Dutch ground positions around the bridges at Moerdijk. These bridges were formidable steel constructions on huge stone pillars, separated by about 300m, stretched across the Hollandsch Diep to a length of about 1.5km over the water – the traffic bridge in the west, and the railway bridge in the east.[24] They were the two most important thoroughfares leading from the west of Noord Brabant to Rotterdam.

So as to protect the approach toward the bridges from an enemy advancing from the south-east and against landings of troop carrying aircraft in the open terrain south of the bridges, the 3rd Company of III/28th Inf.Rgt. was deployed at the bridgehead. The field positions of its four platoons were set up in a semi-circle around the southern ramps of the bridges south of them – in the village at Lochtenburg (about 3 km south-west of Moerdijk, in the hamlet of Versluis, at the railway station Lage Zwaluwe, and at the western edge of the village Lage Zwaluwe). The 12th Machine-gun Company moved three of its four platoons forward in support of the infantry company and had positioned its fourth platoon at the road about 250m south of the traffic bridge. Two 57mm guns of the infantry gun company from 28th Inf.Rgt. were located in the vicinity of Versluis. In the hamlet the command post

---

23   Contrary to German intelligence, the airfield at Ockenburg in May 1940 had also be used by the Dutch air force. 5 Douglas 8 As and 2 Fokker G-1s, all of them unfit for flying, had been parked there. Furthermore service support and guard personnel of the air force had been stationed there permanently and a searchlight-squad during the hours of darkness.

24   This wing had belonged to *IV.Flieger-Korps* of *Luftflotte 2*.

of the commandant of the bridgehead was established. The 82nd and 83rd Anti-Aircraft Machine-Gun Platoons, with four MG 08 each, were in positions immediately south of the southern bridge ramps. At the north-eastern edge of the small harbour-town of Moerdijk, at the southern bank of the Hollandsch Diep, two serviceable 75mm guns of the 19th Anti-Aircraft Battery were set up. A squad of engineers from the ferry service was on duty in the small harbour of Moerdijk. It had its quarters on the ship *Mathida* which, together with a few other small ships, was anchored in the harbour.

The artillery, deployed in the southern part of the island of Dordrecht – I/10th Art. Rgt. with two batteries of 75mm guns in the Beerpolder and III/14th Art.Rgt. with three batteries of obsolete 12cm guns further to the north-east, along the Zeedijk – was able to deliver fire into the area around the bridges. This also applied to the artillery of Group Kil, positioned in the south-east of the island of Hoekse Waard.

Wieldrecht sector, which included all of the island of Dordrecht except the town proper, was under command of the commanding officer of I/28th Inf.Rgt., whose command post was located in the villa Amstelwijk, about 2km south-west of Dordrecht. The sub-sector Wieldrecht-West stretched from the area around Willemsdorp, where the bridges reached the northern bank of the Hollandsch Diep to Prinsenheuvel, located at a side-branch of the Nieuwe Merwede, about 4km north-east of Willemsdorp. The principal mission of the forces deployed in this sub-sector was to protect the bridges from the northern bank of the Hollandsch Diep. For this purpose the 1st Company of I/28th Inf.Rgt. prepared field positions toward the south along the entire width of the sub-sector. The covering detachment 'Willemsdorp' was tasked with the close protection of the bridges. It included two platoons of I/41st Inf.Rgt., two platoons of the machine-gun company of I/28th Inf. Rgt., one platoon of 11th Machine-gun Company, armed military police[25] and a machine-gun platoon from the 3rd Border Battalion, manning large bunkers at the northern ends of the bridges. Bunker Willemsdorp II was located on the northern ramp of the traffic bridge; bunker Willhelmsdorp I, about 250m north of the end of the railway bridge, was located on the railway embankment. Both bunkers had several floors and were armed with a 47mm quick-fire gun and a heavy machine-gun behind embrasures directed toward the bridges. In the abutment of the northern part of the traffic bridge two small machine-gun-casemates were embedded. A large machine-gun-bunker, designated Hollandsch Diep I, was located on the western bank of the Kil where the river connects with the Hollandsch Diep. From here the traffic bridge could be enfiladed by fire. Another bunker of this type, Hollandsch Diep II, protected the southern approach toward the railway bridge and was located immediately east of the railway embankment on the northern bank of Hollandsch Diep. Both bridges had been provided with a barrier made of steel plates, which could be lowered from the superstructure to the passageways. Close to the northern end of the traffic bridge, a double-T beam-barrier was installed in the roadway.

Both bridges were prepared for destruction by demolition. At three locations in their framework steel boxes, filled with explosives, were placed in order to create span collapses. The ignition of the explosives was to be triggered from the two large bunkers. However, as a

---

25   The length of the bridges was often understated in the relevant German literature. The railway bridge, completed in 1872, with its 14 arches of 100m each, had an overall length of 2,536m. For quite a while, it had been the largest bridge of this kind in Europe.

safety measure against undesired premature explosion – the bridges were to be used for the passage of the Light Division during its return from Noord Brabant and possibly for French forces, coming to the support of the Dutch – the fuses were not connected with quick-firing charges. An electrical ignition system was not yet available the final preparation of the bridges for demolition and its execution required the order of the Fortress commander.

For guard duty on the Hollandsch Diep on either side of the bridges, two small boats, armed with a machine-gun each had also been made available.

The command relations of the forces around the Moerdijk bridges were complex and caused confusion from the very beginning: Whereas the troops in Willemsdorp were subordinate to the command of sector Wieldrecht, those in the bridgehead were directly subordinate to the command of Group Kil.

A number of small bunkers had been constructed along the northern bank of the Nieuwe Merwede, facing to the south, at the western bank of the Kil opposite the bridges, close to the barracks, about 500m north of Willemsdorp, along the railway to the north on the island of Dordrecht, and in the park at Amstelwijk. The artillery positioned in the eastern part of Hoekse Waard – 25th Art.Rgt. with three batteries of 75mm guns and I/23rd Art.Rgt. with two batteries of 15cm guns – was able to deliver fire across the Hollandsch Diep into the southern part of the bridge head.

In the sub-sectors Wieldrecht-Centre and Wieldrecht-East, on the island of Dordrecht, the reinforced 2nd Company of I/28th Inf.Rgt. was deployed in field positions close to the northern bank of the Nieuwe Merwede, facing toward the south, whereas the 3rd Company of this battalion, reinforced by a mortar and a machine-gun section, was positioned south of Dubbeldam. There was no physical contact between the forces on the island of Dordrecht and the troops of Group Merwede, deployed east of the Nieuwe Merwede. This group planned to occupy the swampy area of the Biesbosch with a detachment of the 3rd Company of torpedo/mine operators.[26]

On the evening of 9/10 May the commandant of Fortress Holland had not yet ordered the highest level of readiness for the troops under his command and so those in the bridgehead at Moerdijk and in the sub-sector Wieldrecht-West, except a few outposts and guards, spent the night in their quarters. Only the 19th Anti-Aircraft Battery in Moerdijk and the Anti-Aircraft Machine-Gun Platoons at the bridges assumed a high level of readiness, as ordered by the Anti-Aircraft Command. Therefore they were able to commence firing against the German reconnaissance aircraft, appearing in the airspace over Moerdijk at about 0545hrs and against the bombers of *KG 4*, which attacked between 0555 and 0610hrs. They shot down a He 111 of 5./*KG 4*. A Ju 88 also from *KG 4* was probably the victim of a Fokker G-1 which had strayed from the airspace over the airfield at Waalhaven.

During the air attack, most of the soldiers on duty on and around the bridges abandoned their posts to seek cover. A few, however, remained at their positions. The two guard boats, which had anchored under the bridges during the hours of darkness, departed downstream for safety.

---

26   The armed military police was formed at the end of the First World War, in order to crush revolts that had broken out in the Dutch Army. Afterward, they were kept in service. These carefully selected soldiers had as a main task the manning of the armed bunkers, which had been constructed in the 1930s. They had the status of combatants.

Into the ebbing air attack, *IV./KG z.b.V.1*, with *II./FschJgRgt.1* aboard, coming from Werl, arrived in the airspace over the bridges at Moerdijk. The battalion arriving under the command of *Hauptmann* Prager[27] consisted of 5th Company, 6th Company, the battle HQ and signals platoon of 7th Company and 8th Company. From a height of 100m the 5th Company was dropped north of the traffic bridge, the 6th Company north of the railway bridge, the 7th Company near the southern ramps of both bridges, the battle HQ between the southern ends of the bridges, the two heavy machine-gun platoons of the 8th Company in the polder at Oostgors, south-east of the railway bridge, and the mortar platoon of 8th Company, which was to be used as infantry without its heavy equipment, in the polder just east of Moerdijk. Only a few anti-aircraft machine-guns delivered return fire against the transport aircraft which approached in groups of three Ju 52s. The last serviceable gun of 19th Anti-Aircraft Battery was abandoned by its crew after a few shots after the position had been attacked from the air. Nevertheless the defensive fire was not totally in vain. In one of the Ju 52s a paratrooper was killed and seven others wounded. Consequently the pilot decided to turn back without dropping his unwounded passengers. Another Ju 52, which was also hit, conducted an emergency landing east of Zevenbergschen Hoek, about 5 km south of the bridges. Three of the paratroopers managed to jump before the plane went down. The other nine, together with the aircrew, were taken prisoner by the Dutch. One group of Ju 52s erroneously joined the air transport group which was carrying *I./FschJgRgt.1*. It dropped the platoon of *6./FschJgRgt.1* aboard in the area near Tweede Tol.

Immediately after the paratroopers of *7./FschJgRgt.1* (*Oberleutnant* Pagels) had landed, formed up and picked up their main arms from weapon containers, the 1st Platoon, under *Leutnant* Tietjen, attacked the traffic bridge. Simultaneously the 2nd Platoon, led by *Leutnant* Lehmann, against the railway bridge. The 3rd Platoon initially remained in reserve.[28] When the Dutch soldiers, who sought cover against the air attacks, attempted to get back to their weapons they found their positions already occupied by the paratroopers. Almost all of them were now taken prisoner. Without losses on the German side the guards at the southern ramp of the traffic bridge were also quickly overwhelmed. In spite of the defensive fire now commencing along the whole length of the traffic bridge, some soldiers of the 1st Platoon, led by *Leutnant* Tietjen, managed to move forward and put out of action the machine-gun casemate, embedded in the southern abutment of the bridge. During the further assault a *Feldwebel* of Tietjen's platoon was killed, and another one wounded. The attempt of some more soldiers of the 1st Platoon to join their commander and the few men with him failed, causing additional losses in wounded, primarily by the fire of the anti-tank gun and the heavy machine gun from the large bunker north of the traffic bridge. While *Leutnant* Tietjen and a machine-gun-team of his platoon, who had reached the northern end of the bridge, set up for the defence, paratroopers from *5./FschJgRgt.1* (*Oberleutnant* Straehler-Pohl) advanced from the north and turned against bunker Willemsdorp II, which was firing incessantly. Its commandant, a sergeant-major of the military police, rejected a

---

27 The detachment was equipped with 26 boats of several types, which were mostly armed with heavy machine-guns. A part of it, about 80 men, with some heavy machine-guns, later on 10 May was sent to Dordrecht as reinforcement on order of the commandant of *Gruppe Ost* of Fortress Holland.

28 The fate of this officer is mentioned here with respect. In spite of being incurably ill with cancer of the intestine, *Hauptmann* Prager had managed to remain in command of his battalion for the airborne operation against Fortress Holland. Shot through both legs early during the fighting at the bridges he continued to command his unit until the capitulation of Holland. For his and his battalion's merits during the battle he was awarded the *Ritterkreuz* on 24 May 1940. A few weeks later he died in Germany.

call to surrender. Impeded by smoke grenades thrown into the bunker through loopholes its crew operated the weapons wearing gas masks. The order by the Germans to blow up the bunker evoked fear among its defenders as they were aware of the 1,200kg of explosives being stored in the basement. However, this had no influence on their will to resist. Only after the paratroopers had managed to blast open the steel door in the rear wall of the bunker and began to throw hand grenades into it, did the crew finally surrender. Shortly prior to noon, *Leutnant* Tietjen was able to examine the bridge thoroughly for explosive charges, and to remove those in the superstructure. He and his men now also found the time to establish firm contact with the soldiers of the 6th Company north of the bridge.

Simultaneously with the assault of the 1st Platoon of 7th Company against the traffic bridge, the squad of *Oberjäger* Gajewski from the company's 2nd Platoon, after it had eliminated the crew of the anti-aircraft platoon just south of the railway bridge and a few guards at its southern ramp, stormed toward its northern end. The squad was initially engaged by the crew of the machine-gun-bunker Hollandsch Diep II which had left its cover and positioned themselves with its heavy machine-gun on the railway embankment. Gajewski's men quickly dealt with this resistance, reaching the northern end of the railway bridge and advancing further to the north. After about 400m they met fellow soldiers of the *6./FschJgRgt.1* (*Oberleutnant* Spangenberg) approaching from the north-east. While Gajewski's squad examined the bridge for explosive charges and removed those found, some paratroopers of 6th Company attacked bunker Willemsdorp I on the railway embankment. Like its counterpart, this emplacement was occupied by a crew of five policemen and a machine-gun-team. From fire against the embrasures, they were forced to take cover and thus remain unharmed, when hand grenades were thrown into the bunker. After a short while, unable to operate their weapons, they answered the call for surrender.

Close examination of the railway bridge after this event revealed that it had also been planned for the crossing of vehicles, as stacks of sleepers to cover the rails were placed near both of its ramps.

The measure to train one squad of each rifle company of the battalion as assault engineers during the preparation phase of the parachute assault had almost paid off. The removal of the explosive charges on the bridges and for the attack against the bunkers had protected them.

The platoon of 6th Company, which had landed north of the farmstead of Den Engel, about 2.5km north of Willemsdorp, at once attacked toward the south and captured three platoons of the 1st Company of I/28th Inf.Rgt., quartered in Den Engel and a farm nearby, before the Dutch soldiers could get ready for combat. Some men of the platoon were overwhelmed by surprise, including the few outposts and guards in the firing positions of I/17th Art.Rgt., about 500m north of Den Engel. Two platoons of *2./FschJgRgt.1*, which had been incorrectly dropped between Willemsdorp and Den Engel obviously had no part in these actions but moved toward the drop zone of their company near Tweede Tol.

Paratroopers of the 5th Company advanced along the railway embankment north of the rail bridge with the aim of clearing this terrain of the enemy who had escaped the first onslaught. In the meantime they had established two areas of resistance: 20-30 soldiers, mainly from a platoon of the 1st Company of I/28th Inf.Rgt. and their company commander, who managed to get away from the barracks were based at the railway underpass just north of the camp. A smaller group, mostly members of the naval ferry service had established themselves with two machine-guns in their quarters, the hotel Waterloo, on the eastern bank of the Kil, about 250m south of the barracks. The Dutch soldiers at the underpass were able to ward off a first probe by paratroopers of the 5th Company from the direction of the barracks. The unexpected arrival of paratroopers by bus from the opposite direction created a new situation. The bus was confiscated along with its driver by the platoon of the 6th Company after it was dropped wrongly near Tweede Tol. The bus was stopped by a hand grenade, which exploded inside it, wounding some of its passengers and causing a few others to come out with their hands up. However, most of the paratroopers, after dismounting, joined the fight. Under fire from two directions, the Dutch soldiers at the underpass now surrendered. A short time later, the resistance from the hotel Waterloo also ended after the defenders had been called up to surrender by a Dutch officer sent by the Germans under a flag of truce.

About noon the struggle for the northern approaches to the bridges at Moerdijk came to an end. But now Dutch artillery, positioned in the south-eastern part of Hoekse Waard, opened fire against the bridges and into the area around Willemsdorp. This fire hampered the ongoing removal of the explosive charges from the bridges and caused some causalties, among them *Leutnant* Tietjen. Much more effective was the hitting by friendly fire of Dutch soldiers in the barracks. Three of these men were killed and two more so seriously wounded that they died on the way to the hospital at Dordrecht.

The fighting north of the bridges had cost *II./FschJgRgt.1* 13 dead, 10 of whom were from the 5th Company, which had borne the brunt of the engagement. On the Dutch side, 20 soldiers had been killed on and near the bridges, eight of them from the two infantry platoons of I/41st Inf.Rgt.

The battalion's 8th Company, commanded by *Oberleutnant* Böhmler, which included a HQ section and two heavy machine-gun platoons, was dropped correctly in the Oostgor polder. Here they quickly succeeded in seizing the field positions immediately south and south-west of its drop zone and in capturing numerous Dutch soldiers before these had recovered from the surprise. Along these positions the heavy machine-gun platoons set up combat outposts. A reconnaissance patrol which was sent to Zevenbergschen Hoek reported that the village was unoccupied by the enemy. Elements of 7th Company's 1st and 2nd Platoons, not involved in the fighting for the bridges, supported by parts of 8th Company were organized in several combat teams and moved against identified or assumed Dutch positions further to the south. One of these teams attacked the positions of two platoons of the 3rd Company of III/28th Inf.Rgt., who were still facing toward the south, from the rear. While one of the Dutch platoons was overwhelmed on the spot, the other was overtaken during its retreat to the west and was overcome in cooperation with another combat team. In this engagement the Dutch company commander was killed. The two 57mm infantry guns, which had been moved a short distance to the west and had set up a firing position along the road from Moerdijk to Zevenbergschen Hoek, were silenced by rifle and machine-gun-fire after a few rounds. Here the battery commander was mortally wounded. Immediately thereafter, the guns were captured by the paratroopers. The gun crews, who retreated toward the command post of the commandant of the bridgehead at Versluis, were encircled together with about 20 soldiers of 12th Machine-gun Company. All of them were captured after a short firefight. The Dutch heavy machine-guns positioned behind a dam to the south-west were ignored by the paratroopers, due to belief that an advance across the open polder was considered too wasteful in potential losses.

The heavy mortar platoon of 8th Company, commanded by *Oberleutnant* Schwarzmann,[29] was dropped without its mortars. Their mission was to attack the reserves of the enemy, assumed to be in Moerdijk, and to prevent them from interfering in the assault against the bridges. Advancing toward the town the platoon, however, was forced to ground by defensive fire from its eastern edge. A combat team from 7th Company, under *Leutnant* Lemm, made up of the company's command group, the HQ sections of its 1st and 2nd Platoons and the light mortar teams of these platoons, which had also been tasked with the seizure of Moerdijk, was dropped widely scattered. Nevertheless it advanced at once, and small groups of it joined together. A reconnaissance patrol sent ahead estimated the town's garrison at 60-80 men. The paratroopers now forced their way into the eastern part of Moerdijk and captured about 20 Dutch soldiers. Among them was the company commander of the 3rd Company of III/28th Inf.Rgt., who was also the commandant of the bridgehead, the commander of the 12th Machine-gun Company and an officer of the 19th Anti-Aircraft Battery. Moving toward the town centre, now with men of the heavy mortar platoon joining them, the paratroopers again met resistance from Dutch soldiers and two officers of the regular police (Dutch designation: *Marechaussee*)[30] *Oberleutnant* Lemm was mortally wounded by a pistol shot from one of these policemen.

Before the resistance was finally broken, two Dutch soldiers, who had been previously captured, were killed and all three Dutch officers were wounded in the crossfire.[31] Advancing further toward the harbour, combat team Lemm again was engaged in a firefight with a number of Dutch soldiers. A *Feldwebel* was killed and the *Oberfeldwebel* of 7th Company and *Oberleutnant* Schwarzmann, who had just before joined Lemm's team with some soldiers of his platoon, were seriously injured.

In the meantime, *Oberleutnant* Pagels became aware of the situation in Moerdijk. He dispatched his 3rd Platoon, which up to now had been the company reserve. This platoon advanced toward the harbour via the position of the Dutch anti-aircraft battery and the barracks of its crew. On the way they captured a number of the anti-aircraft soldiers.

At the same time, another group of paratroopers approached the harbour from the west. Now the commander of the forces defending[32] the harbor decided to embark his men on the ships anchored in the harbour and retreat across the Hollandsch Diep. His plan succeeded thanks to the dogged resistance of a rearguard of five naval engineers. Three of these brave men were killed during this action and the other two taken prisoner.

While a growing number of paratroopers were fighting for the possession of the harbour, elements of 8th Company's heavy mortar platoon built up protection against Dutch soldiers who still held out in the southern part of Moerdijk. These were now attacked by parts of the 7th Company's 2nd Platoon who were no longer required at the bridges. They quickly managed to dislodge the enemy and to take additional prisoners.

---

29   As the heavy weapons platoons of all three companies are not specifically mentioned in the after-action reports, it is assumed that their men had been distributed among the other platoons.

30   As a member of the German gymnastic team during the Olympic Games of 1936, Schwarzmann had won three gold and two bronze medals and therefore was well known throughout Germany.

31   According to the rules of war these policemen were not combatants and therefore not entitled to participate in the fighting.

32   Some Dutch sources claim that the Dutch prisoners had been used as a shield in front of the attacking paratroopers. More likely is that the prisoners had been taken along by the paratroopers, because they lacked personnel for guard duties.

At about 1100hrs, all of Moerdijk was in the hands of the paratroopers of 7th Company. While 3rd Platoon, with the heavy mortar platoon now subordinate to it, set up the defence at the western and north-western edge of the town, parts of 2nd Platoon established positions at its southern and south-western edge. More than one hundred prisoners had been taken during the fight for the town. Amongst the numerous pieces of equipment captured were two anti-aircraft guns and six heavy machine-guns. A shock troop of 1st Platoon, commanded by *Leutnant* Lehmann, pursued the enemy retreating from Moerdijk to the village of Lochtenburg. As this locality turned out to be occupied by considerable Dutch forces, the pursuit was called off and only a standing patrol was left behind for observation.

In the meantime, *Oberleutnant* Pagels requisitioned the monastery in Moerdijk. There, all inhabitants who had been found in the town were lodged and a dressing station was established. The wounded of both sides received treatment from the two medical officers of the battalion. Paratroopers of 1st Platoon were tasked with the protection of the monastery and the guard of prisoners of war kept in the barracks of the anti-aircraft battery and in the church. At the western and south-western edge of Moerdijk the 2nd and 3rd Platoons commenced to dig in and to create gun pits along the possible approaches. They were being fired at with heavy machine-guns from Lochtenburg until late afternoon.

A combat team of 7th Company also moved against the village at Lage Zwaluwe about 3km east of the southern ramps of the bridges. Advancing along the southern bank of the small river Amer the team managed to get into the rear of a Dutch infantry platoon moving to the west and south-west. In the ambush, the Dutch lost two soldiers and two more were wounded. At 1140hrs they surrendered. The paratroopers moved back to their main position with their prisoners and left only an outpost at Lage Zwaluwe.

In the early afternoon of 10 May the parts of II./*FschJgRgt.1* which were deployed south of the Hollandsch Diep, set up a main line of resistance of about 3km length between Moerdijk and the Oostgors-polder. The 6th Company was also transferred into this line and took over its eastern flank. The battalion's command post was established about 300m south of the southern ramp of the traffic bridge. Radio teams, which jumped simultaneously with their companies, maintained permanent communication with the battle HQ. In spite of his wounds in both legs, *Hauptmann* Prager remained in command of his battalion. He was assisted by *Hauptmann* Pelz, a paratrooper, who had been assigned to the staff prior to the airborne operation against Holland.

The surprise fire by Dutch artillery were mainly directed into the area north of the bridges and into the harbour area of Moerdijk. They hampered movement but did not cause losses in personnel.

Shortly after, a patrol which had reconnoitered south of Zevenbergschen Hoek in requisitioned motor cars, reported Dutch infantry approaching from the south. Over the course of the afternoon these troops appeared in front of the German positions south of the bridges.[33] The security elements of the paratroopers in Zevenbergschen Hoek, Blauwe Sluis

---

33   It was a squad of 12 naval engineers, about 20 men of the crews manning the ships in the harbour and about 25 air defense soldiers, who had managed to escape from their former position.

and Lage Zwaluwe were forced back to the battle line by the numerically superior Dutch infantry, supported by anti-tank guns.[34] At about 1830hrs three Dutch Fokker C-X aircraft attacked the bridgehead with bombs and machine-guns. After they left a fourth Fokker C-X continued the attack.[35] This causing an armorer of the battalion staff to be killed as the Dutch artillery on Hoekse Waard intensified its fire. However, its fire was inaccurate and hit the Dutch infantry, thereby hampering its own movements.

The platoons of *7./FschJgRgt.1* that were deployed south-west of Moerdijk remained detached from any action. A reconnaissance patrol, sent toward Lochtenburg in the early evening, reported Dutch soldiers leaving the village on trucks in a westerly direction.[36]

As the anticipated attack against the bridgehead south of Hollandsch Diep had failed to materialize, the men of *II./FschJgRgt.1* spent a relatively quiet night uninterrupted by artillery fire and used the time to improve their positions. In the area around Willemsdorp their attention was directed to the protection of the eastern bank of the Kil against possible enemy landings from Hoekse Waard and at the build-up of the enemy toward the north. The barracks north of Willemsdorp was chosen as prisoner collection point for all of *Gruppe Süd*. The regimental commander, who had briefly visited the battalion's command post in the evening, told *Hauptmann* Prager about the critical situation at the bridges in Dordrecht and Rotterdam. He also stated his unease regarding the detected movements of strong French forces into the area east of Antwerp, which could lead to attacks by them against the bridgehead at Moerdijk.[37]

During the planning phase for the parachute assaults in the area of operation of *Gruppe Süd*, *Oberst* Bräuer tasked *3./FschJgRgt.1*, commanded by *Oberleutnant* von Brandis, with seizure of the two bridges across the Oude Maas between Dordrecht and Zwijndrecht on the island of Ijsselmonde. These bridges were of particular importance for the success of *Generalleutnant* Student's operational plan as they constituted the only permanent solid connection between the islands of Dordrecht and Ijsselmonde. Consequently they were required to quickly move reinforcements from the airfield at Waalhaven to the south and later would allow for the unhindered advance of mechanized ground forces from the south into the region around Rotterdam. However, intelligence about the strength and

---

34   At 0740hrs the 6th Border Battalion was ordered by III Army Corps to attack the paratroopers who had landed near the bridges at Moerdijk. This mission had somewhat been in line with the original intention by III Army Corps, to have 6th Border Battalion take over the responsibility for the bridges in the case of a German attack. From Terheijden the 1st Company of the battalion was directed toward Blauwe Sluis, the 2nd Company toward Zevenbergschen Hoek, the 3rd Company toward Lage Zwaluwe and a platoon of this company to Lochtenburg.

35   Dutch sources state that the two anti-tank platoons of 6th Border Battalion (altogether four guns) had received only armor-piercing ammunition, which had little effect against infantry.

36   The air reconnaissance detachment, stationed in Bergen, at 1730hrs had received the mission to support the attack of 6th Border Battalion. Of the five aircraft made available, four had taken off with eight bombs of 50kg each. They crossed the airspace, dominated by the *Luftwaffe*, in very low level flight.

37   Probably the 1st Platoon of the 3rd Company of III/26th Inf.Rgt. and a platoon from 12th Machine-gun Company, that was positioned in Lochtenburg throughout 10 May. They left the village shortly prior to the arrival of elements of the 6th Border Battalion.

dispositions of Dutch forces in and around Dordrecht was almost zero, which posed a veritable risk to the current planning.

The operational plan of *3./FschJgRgt.1* had foreseen that as the entire company could not be dropped in the immediate vicinity of the bridges, due to the terrain on either side of Oude Maas being densely covered with buildings and being intersected by several harbour basins, only the 3rd Platoon could parachute in on the west bank of the river between the two bridges. Consequently it was to take possession of the bridges and retain them undamaged until the arrival of the main body of the company. They were to be dropped into the polder terrain at the southern edge of Dordrecht, between the residential area of Krispijn and the cemetery. After its assembly it was to reach the bridges along the railway, which passed through the southern part of Dordrecht to the west.

Carried without incident by a squadron of *II./KG z.b.V.1* from Dortmund, at 0630hrs the majority of *3./FschJgRgt.1* parachuted from nine Ju 52s into the polder immediately east of Krispijn in the sequence of 1st Platoon – command group/ 4th (heavy weapons) platoon – 2nd Platoon. The last group of the squadron, consisting of three Ju 52s with the 3rd Platoon aboard, flew on to the bridges across the Oude Maas.

During the landing at Dordrecht the paratroopers were fired at by machine-guns and rifles from the park, which stretched south of the railway. Here 40-45 men of the platoon of railway engineers manned prepared field positions along the southern edge of the park at the start of the parachute drop.[38] Two machine-gun teams of the 1st Platoon of *3./FschJgRgt.1* positioned themselves on the street which passed along the eastern edge of Krispijn and provided protection toward the south and west. *Oberleutnant* von Brandis, without waiting for the assembly of his company, attacked with a hastily scratched together group of paratroopers from 2nd and 4th Platoons against the south-western corner of the park. He was killed in this assault, alongside others who were wounded.[39] *Leutnant* Schmelz, the commander of 1st Platoon, now assumed command and ordered an assault on a wide front against the railway by 1st and 2nd Platoons, covered by the heavy weapons platoon. Only 2nd Platoon, moving around the eastern edge of the park, managed to reach the railway crossing about 200m east of the station of Dordrecht. Then, the pressure from Dutch troops brought forward through the town, became so strong that the platoon was forced to retreat toward its landing site, hotly pursued by the attackers. The 1st Platoon broke into the south-western part of the park after the defenders had withdrawn a short distance in the direction of the railway station of Dordrecht. Here, however, the assault was stalled by enemy fire.

In the meantime the 1st and 2nd depot companies of the Dutch naval engineers, quartered in Krispijn, occupied all of the eastern edge of this residential area. They now joined in the combat from buildings there by first putting out of action the security screen of paratroopers along the street to the south and then by thwarting the attempt of a number

---

38   Information about the actual movements of French forces into the area east of Antwerp, though anticipated by the German high command, was not available for *Fl.Div.7* until the evening of 10 May. Obviously they had been passed on to *Gruppe Süd*. The critical situation in the northern part of the operational area of *Fl.Div.7* and the lack of forces, however, had prevented strong reactive measures, directed toward the Moerdijk area.

39   There is no doubt that these railway engineers were the first Dutch troops in Dordrecht in contact with the paratroopers and hindered these considerably in the accomplishment of their planned movement.

of men of *3./FschJgRgt.1*, to mount two captured trucks with the aim of breaking through to the bridges. Unable to move away from their positions near the church at the eastern edge of Krispijn and south of the south-western corner of the park, split up into several small groups, encircled and running out of ammunition the remaining paratroopers had to give themselves up shortly after 1300 hrs. Only 10 soldiers of 1st and 2nd Platoons, led by *Feldwebel* Görtz and *Oberjäger* Januschowski, who became separated from the company during the fighting, managed to escape the disaster and fight their way through to the bridges.

During the fighting south of the railway in Dordrecht 13 paratroopers had been killed. The 12 who were seriously wounded, among them *Leutnant* Schmelz, were moved into a hospital in Dordrecht. The other almost 80 captured men of *3./FschJgRgt.1* initially were confined in a school in Dordrecht, then on 11 May transferred to ships at Gorinchem and then brought via Wijk bij Duurstede and Den Haag to Ijmuiden. From there they were, together with other German prisoners of war, shipped to England on 14 May.

The 3rd Platoon of *3./FschJgRgt.1*, commanded by *Oberfeldwebel* Hoffmann, was dropped at 0635hrs precisely into the small open ground on the western bank of the Oude Maas between the two bridges connecting Dordrecht with Zwijndrecht on the island of Ijsselmonde. Air reconnaissance had identified an anti-aircraft machine-gun position on the western bank of the Oude Maas, just north of the railway bridge and another one on the eastern bank of the river, a short distance south of the traffic bridge.[40] Guards on both bridges had to be reckoned with.

Immediately after picking up their main arms, *Oberfeldwebel* Hoffmann and seven soldiers of the 7th squad (the squad commander and the rest of the squad were still looking for their weapon-container) advanced toward the traffic bridge. The 9th squad was on its way to the railway bridge with the 8th squad initially being kept in reserve. After effective fire from *Oberfeldwebel* Hoffmann and his men, the four Dutch soldiers guarding the traffic bridge were forced to abandon their posts and withdraw toward Dordrecht, one of them was killed. During this action the rest of 7th squad also arrived on the bridge. As the paratroopers on the bridge were receiving fire from the anti-aircraft position south of them *Oberfeldwebel* Hoffmann dispatched a shock troop of five men to deal with it. Advancing unobserved, the shock troop succeeded in ambushing the position with hand grenades and submachine-guns. In the short fight, two Dutch soldiers were killed. The other 21 who were manning the position and the wounded officer were forced to surrender, after they rendered their machine-guns unusable.

On its way to the railway bridge the 9th squad unexpectedly found itself faced with a number of Dutch soldiers positioned on the railway embankment and in nearby houses. They turned out to be the members of the anti-aircraft machine-gun platoon, located north of the railway bridge, who had left their position in order to protect the approach to the bridge from the west. With the Dutch officer who was in command of both anti-aircraft

---

40   *Oberleutnant* von Brandis, whose family was well known in Germany because of the merits of one of its members during the conquest of Fort Douaumont in the First World War, had proven himself as reckless and daring in peacetime, when he had let himself be dropped from a Ju 52 over Hamburg for a weekend furlough. He displayed these characteristics again during the seizure of Stavanger-Sola. At Dordrecht, they cost him his life.

platoons offering himself as the negotiator, the 12 Dutch soldiers were persuaded to give themselves up. Led by *Oberjäger* Hissen the 8th and 9th squads now occupied the railway bridge after it was abandoned by its two guards. During the firefight with Dutch soldiers established in buildings around the eastern end of the bridge, *Oberjäger* Hissen was killed. His death remained the only fatal loss in 3rd Platoon. Additionally, only one of its soldiers was wounded on 10 May.

At 0830hrs both bridges across the Oude Maas were in the possession of Hoffmann's platoon.[41] However instead of the desperately awaited relief by its company, only *Oberjäger* Januschowski with four men from 2nd Platoon arrived at about 0840hrs; shortly afterwards *Feldwebel* Görtz, with six soldiers from 1st Platoon also arrived. Their reports about the situation of the company at the southern edge of Dordrecht led *Oberfeldwebel* Hoffmann to decide to retain both bridges with the forces available to him. He ordered *Feldwebel* Görtz to defend the bridges against the enemy in Dordrecht alongside the arrivals from 1st and 2nd Platoons, which he reinforced with a few men from his own platoon. The paratroopers under *Feldwebel* Görtz managed to establish defence positions in spite of the almost continuous fire from buildings along the eastern bank of the Oude Maas. The greater part of 3rd Platoon was then ordered to prepare positions in a semi-circle around the western ramps of the bridges.

Simultaneously with *II./FschJgRgt.1* and *3./FschJgRgt.1*, *I./FschJgRgt.1* (less two companies), commanded by *Hauptmann* Walther, the battle HQ of *FschJgRgt.1* and the regimental signals platoon were dropped south and south-west of Dordrecht by *II./KG z.b.V.1*. *I./FschJgRgt.1* consisted of the staff, the signals platoon and 2nd and 4th companies. The new 1st Company was still under training in Germany.[42] The initial objective for *I./FschJgRgt.1* and the command element of the regiment was the area around Tweede Tol. The operational plan for the battalion had originally anticipated a drop by 2nd Company (under *Hauptmann* Gröschke) into the polder, south-east of Wieldrecht and east of the railway at Breda-Dordrecht. Advancing south-west the company was then to capture identified bunkers and troop quarters of the Dutch. *Hauptmann* Gericke's 4th Company was to be dropped immediately east of 2nd Company and to assemble on the road between Tweede Tol and Kop van't Land, which ran on the Zeedijk and was to stay available as the reserve of *Gruppe Süd* about 3km east of Tweede Tol. The command post of *Oberst* Bräuer was to be set up at Tweede Tol. Based on intelligence received the heavy fighting on the island of Dordrecht had not been expected.[43] According to the operational plan and the available intelligence *Oberst* Bräuer would have had a small but efficient force with which he would have been able to intervene at the bridges at Moerdijk or at those at Dordrecht if required by the evolving situation, even prior to the arrival of the reinforcements planned

---

41   The positions were manned by the 86th respectively 85th Anti-Aircraft Machine-Gun Platoons. Each was equipped with four MG 08s. 40 soldiers, commanded by a lieutenant, were assigned as crews.

42   The neglect of adequate protection for the bridges at Dordrecht against attacks on the ground, quite obviously had been the result of a lacking awareness of the German conception for the use of parachute troops. Group Kil viewed the bridges as outside of its area of operations, with their western ends located on Ijsselmonde and eastern ends in the urban area of Dordrecht.

43   The original 1st Company, after its liberation from Norwegian captivity, had remained in Norway for employment at Narvik. This also applied to the original signals platoon of the battalion. However, this sub-unit had been replaced for Holland.

for *Gruppe Süd. FschSan-Halbkompanie 7*, which was to parachute at Tweede Tol as part of the second wave of the air transport operation could then be used in its medical function from the very beginning of its employment.[44]

In spite of the experience *II./KG z.b.V.1* had already gained by working together with parachute forces, the landing of *I./FschJgRgt.1* (less two companies) was not executed according to plan. The 1st and 2nd Platoons of 2nd Company alongside *Hauptmann* Walther and a plane load of his staff, were dropped too far to the south and landed in the polder about 1.5km north of Willemsdorp. Furthermore one squad of 1st Platoon was missing as its Ju 52 had turned back to Germany due to motor damage.[45] On their way to Tweede Tol the wrongly dropped paratroopers encountered hasty resistance from a barracks located south of the Zeedijk, between the auto-route and the railway to Dordrecht. By a determined thrust, the enemy, soldiers of I/17th Art.Rgt., were quickly overcome. The Dutch lost some killed and wounded and one officer and 20 men was take prisoner. On the German side one NCO was killed and another wounded. Near Tweede Tol the two platoons joined the other parts of 2nd Company. These had been dropped correctly north-east of the junction of the auto-route and the Zeedijk. Here they assembled and immediately attacked Tweede Tol and the barracks which lay south-east of the village. After short but bitter fighting, which cost two killed and six wounded on the German side, the defenders, mainly soldiers from I/17th Art.Rgt., were overwhelmed having lost some killed and wounded and more than 60 prisoners. Only a few Dutch soldiers had escaped the onslaught.

The platoon of *6./FschJgRgt.1*, which landed in the drop zone of *2./FschJgRgt.1*, did not participate in the engagements around Tweede Tol but travelled south in a confiscated bus.

A HQ section of *I./FschJgRgt.1*, under the command of *Oberleutnant* Götte, had parachuted into the polder about 2km north-east of Tweede Tol. It assembled undisturbed by the enemy and set up a provisional battalion command post. When a new mission arrived from *Oberst* Bräuer, a part of the staff section occupied a secure position toward the east, as protection for the regimental headquarters, while the other part, led by *Oberleutnant* Götte, moved to the west, bypassing Tweede Tol in the north. On its way the latter was engaged in a fight with a large number of Dutch soldiers, mainly from I/17th Art.Rgt., who were withdrawing from the area of Tweede Tol toward the north. *Oberleutnant* Götte, reinforced by a group of men from the regimental signals platoon who had come down nearby, beat off the Dutch. They now retreated to the west into a large farmstead. There,

---

44   The picture of the enemy's strength and dispositions on the island of Dordrecht north of the Willemsdorp area, resulting mainly from high-level air reconnaissance, had been incomplete. Identified were the firing positions of two artillery units, the bunkers along the eastern bank of the Kil, along the northern bank of the Nieuwe Merwede and at Amstelwijk, the barracks near Tweede Tol and the two anti-aircraft positions at the bridges across the Oude Maas at Dordecht. No intelligence was received about the considerable strength of the Dutch troops located in Dordrecht, the existence of a command post at Amstelwijk, and the presence of two reinforced infantry companies in the South and the east of the island.

45   For the employment of the medical personnel, a solution was developed with regard to the peculiarities of combat in the German parachute force: the medical personnel were dropped or air-landed initially without the specific markings of their principal function, i.e. a Red Cross. Therefore they were able to participate in combat actions, for which they were fully trained and equipped as parachute infantry. Only after sufficient space had been gained, so that the medical functions could be executed sufficiently far away from the actual combat to provide for the safety of the wounded, were the medical personnel to deploy the Red Cross markings on themselves and their installations. From that time on, the use of weapons by medical soldiers was strictly forbidden other than in protection of the wounded in the case of a direct attack against them.

they were attacked by the combined groups of staff and signals soldiers. After bitter fighting the farm, which had been used as quarters for troops, horses and equipment of the Dutch artillery, was in German hands. Beside some killed and wounded, 20 Dutch men were captured. On the German side, three soldiers of the signals platoon were killed during the assault and the commander of the platoon, *Oberleutnant* Schuller, was mortally wounded.

The staff personnel under *Oberleutnant* Götte now advanced toward the eastern bank of the Kil where the commander who was sent ahead of the patrol was killed. At about 1600hrs Götte's men took up positions along the eastern bank of the Kil north of Tweede Tol. From here they engaged machine-gun and mortar-crews which they observed on the opposite bank of the canal. A light mortar which had been dispatched in support from the regimental headquarters shortly after 1815hrs, set ablaze a building south of Gravendeel. Heavy explosions indicated that large amounts of ammunition had been stored there. During the course of the evening artillery fire from the opposite side of the Kil became stronger and movements of troops were observed, an attempt by the enemy to cross the canal during the night was suspected. In anticipation of this Götte's men therefore departed from their position, although this movement was quickly countermanded. At about 2300hrs they re-occupied the line along the Kil.

4./FschJgRgt.1 was dropped too far to the east in the polder between the Zuidendijk and the Zeedijk, about 4km north-east of Tweede Tol. Here it became separated from *2./FschJgRgt.1*. Moreover 3rd Platoon, under *Oberleutnant* Eckleben, had not arrived;[46] reducing the strength of the company to 3 officers and 109 other ranks.[47] The deviation from the planned drop zone was of advantage as a number of paratroopers came down in, and immediately behind, the firing positions of the Dutch III/14th Art.Rgt. The few startled artillerymen on guard opened fire as the paratroopers began to land, killing one. Afterwards they were quickly overwhelmed. After *4./FschJgRgt.1* had assembled and rendered eight of the guns useless by running them into nearby ditches, it then marched off toward Tweede Tol. Here it would form the reserve of *Gruppe Süd*, east of the village. A heavy machine-gun squad, reinforced by two anti-tank rifle teams, commanded by *Feldwebel* Niedermeyer, remained on watch in the Dutch firing position. It soon came under pressure as the artillerymen of III/14th Art.Rgt. from their quarters around the cemetery at the Zuidendijk commenced to advance along the Schenkeldijk, with the aim of retaking their guns. During the now developing firefight one of Niedermeyer's men was killed.

In the meantime *Oberst* Bräuer's staff became aware of the threat developing from the east as well as of the need to safeguard the impending drop of *FschSan-Halbkompanie 7*. Therefore *Oberleutnant* Richter, with several men from the regimental staff, was dispatched to reinforce the security element of *4./FschJgRgt.1* at the Zeedijk. Under the command of *Oberleutnant* Richter, the Dutch artillerymen got threateningly close to the Zeedijk and were repulsed to the north-west, so that an acceptable defence position could be established at the junction of the Zeedijk and the Schenkeldijk. During this action, two paratroopers were wounded.

---

46   The squad was air-landed at Waalhaven on 11 May and had joined its company on the same day.

47   The group of Ju 52s with this platoon aboard had erroneously joined *I./KG z.b.V.1*, which had transported *I./FschJgRgt.1* to the area south of Den Haag. It then had dropped its passengers at the western edge of Delft.

At 1120hrs, while the engagement of Richter's security detachment was still in progress, *FschSan-Halbkompanie 7* was dropped by a squadron from *II./KG z.b.V.1* along the Zeedijk and north-east of it. The half-company consisted of four officers, 16 non-commissioned officers and 86 other ranks. All of them belonged to the medical service but were also fully trained and equipped as parachute infantry. The half-company was organized in a staff group and three platoons and commanded by *Stabsarzt* Dr. Lange. On landing they established contact with the regimental staff and with their two machine-guns and set up a security position at a farm east of Berkenhof. From here they engaged Dutch soldiers positioned about 400m further to the north-east, who fired with machine-guns at soldiers of the half-company along the Zeedijk. They succeed in driving the enemy back, but lost a *Feldwebel* killed, and another man seriously wounded. The paratroopers who landed at the Zeedijk in the vicinity of the security position – the missing squad of 1st Platoon and five men from the staff-group – made use of the temporary withdrawal of the Dutch to reach Berkenhof.

The majority of the staff group and 2nd and 3rd Platoons were widely scattered and were positioned more to the north-east of the Zeedijk. Heavy machine-gun and rifle fire, and soon mortar fire, forced the soldiers of these sub-units to the ground, so that regrouping was impossible. Furthermore a number of containers with weapons and medical equipment could not be recovered. In engagements with Dutch troops advancing from the north and east,[48] which lasted throughout the day and into the night, a number of the medical paratroopers were wounded or captured. The members of the staff group, among them all three medical officers, the majority of 3rd Platoon and a few men of 2nd Platoon finally succeed in fighting through to Berkenhof during the night 10/11 May.

From their initial position, the men under *Oberleutnant* Richter and *Feldwebel* Niedermeyer were able to pick up seven soldiers of *FschSan-Halbkompanie 7* who had landed nearby; this helped to prevent encirclement by the Dutch forces. During these engagements the enemy, beside some killed and wounded, had lost nine prisoners, among those captured was a wounded artillery officer. In the late afternoon, however, the security position became untenable as it came under pin-point fire from mortars, causing one of the prisoners to be killed, one wounded and five paratroopers also wounded. A light mortar, which was brought forward for support, remained ineffective because of its inadequate range. Consequently at 1800hrs the wounded *Oberleutnant* Richter decided withdraw his men to Berkenhof. Here he was relieved by *Oberleutnant* Platow from the regimental staff.

The intention to replace the present medical aid station at Tweede Tol by a dressing station of the FschSan-Halbkompanie could not be realized, as the greater part of the unit's medical equipment had not yet been recovered. The overriding reason for this was the departure of almost all of *I./FschJgRgt.1* for the defence of the bridges at Dordrecht. This, in conjunction with the imminent threat against the area around Tweede Tol from the east, demanded the employment of the newly arrived medical paratroopers as infantry. As a first step, the line of outposts established east of Berkenhof under the command of *Oberleutnant* Platow, was extended to a group of twelve men with two machine-guns from the half-company. The situation north-east of Tweede Tol however, remained tense. As the enemy resumed advancing to the west in the first hours of 11 May, all the men of the

---

48   According to the war establishment, a heavy weapons parachute infantry company at that time consisted of a command group, two heavy machine-gun platoons (four heavy machine-guns each and probably two anti-tank rifle teams), a heavy mortar platoon (four mortars) and a small rifle platoon.

half-company, as far as they could, joined their own lines, and were now deployed for the defence. Also deployed at this time were all the men of the battle HQ of *FschJgRgt.1*, the second staff section of *I./FschJgRgt.1* and the signals platoons of these two commands.

On the receipt of news from *3./FschJgRgt.1* that it was unable to accomplish its mission, at 0730hrs on 10 May *Oberst* Bräuer ordered *Hauptmann* Walther of *I./FschJgRgt.1* to push through with his 2nd and 4th companies to the bridges at Dordrecht and to safeguard these at all costs.

After they had assembled and their commanders had been instructed about the new mission, the companies moved out toward the north. 4th Company moved along the auto-route, 2nd Company was positioned to the left of it, along the parallel concrete road, with the HQ group in front, followed by 2nd Platoon under *Leutnant* Graf von Blücher. A short distance south of the farmstead at Gravenstein von Blücher received machine-gun and rifle fire from approaching Dutch infantry.[49] A spontaneous thrust by von Blücher's men forced the Dutch back. Both sides suffered some losses. About 150m further to the north the enemy, now reinforced, rallied for the defence. *Hauptmann* Gröschke deployed his 3rd Platoon for a flanking movement to the right. By close cooperation with the 3rd and 2nd Platoons the enemy was totally defeated and lost a number of dead and wounded. The remaining 100 men were taken prisoner. *2./FschJgRgt.1* suffered two killed and five wounded.

In the meantime 4th Company deployed for combat. Side by side the two companies advanced against the park at Amstelwijk. 4th Company, in particular, suffered flanking fire from a few Dutch heavy machine-guns during its advance. *Leutnant* Graf von Blücher, whose platoon formed the point of *2./FschJgRgt.1*, managed to swim across a moat of about 10m width with a few of his men and penetrated into the park. It was only now that he detected several small bunkers, hidden between the brushwood and containing a considerable number of Dutch soldiers. However the bunkers had not been constructed as battle stations and they lacked loopholes except at the doors, looking toward the north. Still unnoticed by the Dutch, von Blücher summoned a few more of his men and a machine-gun across the moat by means of a skiff. He then set up a covering party and moved forward with five of his soldiers as an assault team and attacked the Dutch with total surprise. Screened by smoke grenades and covered by the fire of the group's machine-gun, the *Leutnant*, with three of his men firing their weapons, assaulted the bunkers. Before they reached the first one, the *Feldwebel* at his heels was seriously wounded by the scattered defensive fire. Then, the *Leutnant*, who was also slightly wounded, quickly silenced four of the bunkers by throwing hand grenades into them through the loopholes in the doors. During the action against the bunkers 12 Dutch soldiers were killed and about 25 wounded. Another 50 uninjured surrendered to the assault group.

---

49 The Dutch forces consisted of several groupings of soldiers from III/14th Art.Rgt. and of elements from the 3rd Company of I/28th Inf.Rgt., moving forward from the east of the island of Dordrecht along the Zuidendijk. They had succeeded in re-occupying the firing positions of III/14th Art.Rgt. and recovered the guns which had not been ditched by the Germans. Elements of the 2nd Company of I/28th Inf.Rgt. had also advanced against the security position of *Oberleutnant* Richter from the southern edge of the island of Dordrecht.

Simultaneously *4./FschJgRgt.1* attacked Amstelwijk from the east and by 1240hrs all resistance at this location was subdued. Primarily as a result of the determined fight of a few Dutch heavy machine-gun crews 4th Company lost four killed and five wounded soldiers around Amstelwijk.[50]

On the Dutch side about 80 soldiers had been killed and approximately 150 had been captured in the engagements with *I./FschJgRgt.1* during the morning. Among the prisoners was the commandant of the Wieldrecht-sector and the commander of Artillery Group Prinsenheuvel. Immediately after the end of the fighting in Amstelwijk, the medical officer, assigned to *2./FschJgRgt.1*, assisted by two captured Dutch military physicians, set up a field hospital in the villa at Amstelwijk.

After a short time for reorganization and leaving back only a few men for the operation and protection of the field hospital, the two companies of *I./FschJgRgt.1*, now accompanied by the 4th Company, pushed on in the direction of their objective. Crossing a bridge on the auto-route east of the Zeehaven, the company was fired at from a school building and some adjacent houses at the north-western edge of the residential area of Krispijn.[51] Fire from heavy mortars of the company forced the Dutch soldiers to abandon the houses close to the school. Now other elements of the company began breaking into the school and overwhelmed its defenders after heavy fighting.[52] The losses of the company were again severe: three dead and two wounded.

On the last part of the route toward the bridges, both companies were continuously fired at from the built-up area along the western edge of Dordrecht, fortunately for them, to little effect.[53] A few enemy positions along the way were quickly silenced, adding to the number of prisoners. The paratroopers who had to be detailed to guard the growing number of captured Dutch soldiers weakened the combat effectiveness of both companies, which was paricuarly notable due to the high nuber of fatal losses, although slightly wounded men were being used for guard duties.

Shortly before 1600 hrs the two companies reached the bridges across the Oude Maas. Here, in spite of the growing presence of the enemy along the western edge of Dordrecht and a few attempts to gain access to the bridges,[54] *Feldwebel* Görtz from *3./FschJgRgt.1* and his few men succeeded in firmly retaining the eastern ramps.

---

50   It was the advance platoon of the 2nd Company of III/34th Inf.Rgt. This company, with two platoons and an assigned heavy machine-gun, was ferried across the Kil to Wieldrecht in the early morning upon request of the commandant of sector Wieldrecht as reinforcement for his command post. A misunderstanding during the briefing of the company commander had led to his decision to move his company to the south along the concrete road.

51   The main resistance had come from the crews of two heavy machine-guns of the machine-gun company of I/28th Inf.Rgt. They had initially been positioned along the auto-route, and then had retreated into the park at Amstelwijk. A heavy machine-gun of 12th Machine-gun Company had also participated actively in the fight. The soldiers of the staffs of the Wieldrecht sector-command, and of the command of Artillery Group Prinsenheuvel, as well as stragglers from I/17th Art.Rgt. took little part in the fighting.

52   The school was defensively prepared by 14th Engineer Company (less one platoon). A platoon of the 1st Depot Company of the naval engineers had occupied the adjacent houses prior to the approaching Germans. Three heavy machine-gun teams from the torpedo/mine unit, who was sent to reinforce the garrison of Dordrecht, had joined the defenders of the school.

53   The after-action report of *4./FschJgRgt.1* mentions 250 prisoners. In light of the actual strength of 14th Engineer Company, and the three heavy machine-gun teams in the school, this number is by far exaggerated and could have been reached only if a great number of naval engineers had also been captured.

54   The fire came mainly from the naval engineers of 3rd Depot Company, who had moved opposite the bridges from their nearby quarters. Other elements of the garrison had commenced to join them after the

Immediately after its arrival, *2./FschJgRgt.1*, under fire, but without losses, crossed the traffic bridge and established itself in field positions forward of the western ramps of both bridges. *Hauptmann* Gröschke placed under his command the 3rd Platoon of *3./FschJgRgt.1*, which up to now had safeguarded the bridges toward the west. *4./FschJgRgt.1* formed a bridgehead around the traffic bridge on the eastern bank of the Oude Maas and engaged the enemy positioned in the buildings and harbour facilities opposite the bridges. A few persistent Dutch heavy machine-gun teams[55] who tried to advance along the railway embankment were finally beaten off with losses.

The elements of *1/PiBtl.22*,[56] that arrived at the bridges from the airfield at Waalhaven in the course of the afternoon, were of little help to *4./FschJgRgt.1* as they had lost a number of wounded from an artillery barrage during the crossing of the Oude Maas and were preparing to move on further to the south as ordered.

The situation at the bridges improved around 1745hrs, when the greater part of *7./InfRgt.16*, provisionally motorized, arrived from the airfield at Waalhaven and was deployed by *Hauptmann* Walther on the Zwijndrecht side, thereby allowing for the defence of the eastern bank of the Oude Maas with all of *I./FschJgRgt.1*.

The fast seizure of the airfield at Waalhaven was not only important for the retention of the bridges heading from the southern part of Rotterdam across the Nieuwe Maas, but also had significance with regard to the operational extent of the entire operation against Fortress Holland. Due to the troops to be landed there, the lines of communication between the Hollandsch Diep and the northern bank of the Nieuwe Maas in Rotterdam, including the three pairs of bridges, had, in cooperation with the parachuted units of *Fl.Div.7*, to be kept open until the arrival of mechanized forces of the *Heer*, which it was hoped would occur after three days. In case of a failure of the airborne attack against the Waalhaven airfield the reinforcement of *Fl.Div.7* with units initially employed in the area around Den Haag had to be ruled out. The vast urban area of Rotterdam, strongly garrisoned and with its two significant river systems, prevented this option in an acceptable time-frame. The air-landings of sizeable bodies of troops on the partly blocked auto-route or on the terrain of the island of Dordrecht or the island of Ijsselmonde, covered by innumerable drainage ditches and densely inhabited, had to be regarded as a last emergency measure, as it could lead to the loss of a large number of transport aircraft, and probably also to high losses in personnel.

Waalhaven airfield, located in the northern part of the island of Ijsselmonde and immediately south-east of Rotterdam's suburb of Feijenoord, and named after the large basin north of it, was constructed in 1920 as a base for aircraft production, and servicing, by the firm of Koolhoven. Its size of about 1,000 x 800m meant it was also used for civilian

---

defeat of *3./FschJgRgt.1*.

55   The most daring attempt was undertaken by a number of Dutch soldiers on a truck, who had tried to rush the traffic bridge. However the attempt failed, whereby 10 Dutch soldiers, including the commanding lieutenant, were captured.

56   Of the 10 machine-gun teams of the reinforcing units, three had been employed against the bridges. Four had been detached to protect the railway station of Dordrecht and the command post of the garrison-commander.

long-distance air traffic. For both reasons, it had an abundance of hangars and service buildings. A considerable number of completed Koolhoven aircraft, planned for delivery to the Dutch Air Arm, were parked in the hangars.

Since 20 April, III/Jager Regiment of the Dutch 1st Infantry Division had assumed protection of the airfield against ground attack. Its 2nd Company positioned all four platoons in field positions along the eastern edge of the airfield. The 3rd Company had a security mission with three platoons along the road leading from the east of the Waalhaven toward Rotterdam. Here it was to prevent the approach of potential Dutch supporters of the Germans coming to their aid. The 1st Company was located with three platoons along the railway embankment between the Waalhaven and the airfield. It was, however, separated from the latter by a large steep mound. Seven heavy machine-guns of the battalion's heavy machine-gun company were distributed in field positions along the southern edge of the airfield. Two more were assigned to 2nd Company, and two were in positions in the north-eastern corner of the airfield, close to its main entrance. Probably based on evaluation of information obtained about the German airborne attacks in Norway, the line of fire of the weapons of 2nd Company and of all heavy machine-guns was directed toward the runway, in order to engage troop-carrying aircraft. This also applied to the two machine-guns situated in a concrete bunker at the eastern edge of the airfield. Two lightly armed machine-gun-carriers (Carden-Lloyd type) were parked near the main entrance. The battalion reserve, a Jager platoon from 1st Company and one from 3rd Company, were billeted in a guardhouse at the main entrance. Nearby the commanding officer of the Jagers, Major de Vos, set up his command post in a fortified communication trench. Only the 2nd Company received its full complement of ammunition. All the other units of III/Jager Rgt had been supplied with a small amount of ammunition. The bulk of their supplies, ammunition included, were stored in one of the hangars.

An anti-aircraft machine-gun platoon was positioned in the vicinity of the south-western corner of the airfield, another one at the north-western corner, a third near the main entrance at the north-eastern corner. Each platoon was equipped with four MG 08 Spandau machine-guns. The platoon at the south-western corner and that at the north-eastern corner additionally possessed two 2cm-machine-guns. For nighttime air defense four searchlight teams were also placed around the airfield.

The two heavy anti-aircraft batteries in the vicinity of the airfield were able to almost completely cover the airspace over the eastern part of the island at Ijsselmonde. The 77th Battery had four 75mm guns in an open firing position on a pier just west of the Waalhaven. 4th Battery, had its 75mm guns in field positions in the Charlois polder near Smitshoek, about 3km south-east of the airfield.

The 3rd Fighter Squadron (3e JaVA) of the Dutch Air Arm was stationed on the airfield. It had 11 Fokker G-1 Mercury fighters, of which 10 were ready for aerial operations. Outside the runway a squadron of Fokker G-1 Wasp fighters were parked together with some obsolete military aircraft. The Wasps originally had been planned for export. Now, they were awaiting technical alterations so that they could be employed by the Dutch Air Arm. They were not ready for take-off. The parked aircrafts were guarded by a company made up of ground crews.

The airfield command, under Major of the Reserve Thomas, was billeted in the dispatch office of the airfield. Thomas was in command of all personnel belonging to the Dutch Air Arm.

At 0525hrs the aircrews of 3e JaVA were alerted by the noise of many approaching aircraft and rushed to their fighters, which had already been prepared for take-off. At 0540hrs two He 111 bombers of the staff squadron of *KG 4*, one of them piloted by its commander, *Oberst* Fiebig, flew a first attack run. It was mainly aimed against the south-western part of the airfield and the anti-aircraft and heavy machine-guns positioned there. Following immediately behind, 28 He 111 of *II./KG 4*, escorted by Bf 109 fighters, joined the attack. Nevertheless eight of the Dutch fighters managed to take off. One of them, ablaze, crashed into the Nieuwe Waterweg near Vlaardingen. The remaining seven engaged the attackers, who now appeared in ever growing numbers. The Dutch were quite successful and managed to shoot down at least ten German aircrafts – six He 111, among them that with *Oberst* Fiebig aboard, and one Ju 52, Ju 87 B, Do 17 Z and Bf 109 each. Most of these were forced to conduct emergency landings in terrain still under Dutch control.[57] However after this day 3e JaVA ceased to exist. Six of their Mercury aircraft, which had participated in the aerial combat, went down heavily damaged or out of fuel in open terrain. Only one fighter of 3e JaVA was able to reach the airfield at Bergen, where it joined 4e JaVA. On the way to Bergen it had probably shot down the Ju 88 which was lost during the air attack of *KG 4* in the airspace south of the bridges at Moerdijk.

During the air attack a number of bombs hit and set ablaze a number of the hangars, production sheds and service buildings, destroying all of the stored ammunition. The two platoons forming the reserve of III/JgRgt and the platoon of 2nd Company near the main entrance lost 21 dead and many wounded. The survivors fled in panic towards Rotterdam. The heavy machine-gun, positioned close to the main entrance, was destroyed by a direct hit, which killed four of its crew. The two machine-gun-carriers on either side of the road leading into the airfield were hit by numerous bomb fragments. One was put out of action, the other, although damaged, could be made ready for use by its crew, but retreated after a few bursts from its machine-gun. The officer in command of both vehicles moved into the polder toward the south-east, taking the machine-gun of the damaged carrier along with him. There he participated in the fighting until he was captured. Behind the mound along the northern edge of the airfield 1st Company remained unscathed. The troops deployed along its southern edge suffered only minor losses in their weapon-pits. 3rd Company, north-east of the Waalhaven, were not attacked from the air.

At 0640hrs in the final phase of the bombing attack and while the aerial combat over Ijsselmonde was still ongoing, *III./FschJgRgt.1*, commanded by *Hauptmann* Karl-Lothar Schulz, parachuted into a semi-circle around the airfield. *II./KG z.b.V.1*, which brought the parachute battalion along, managed to drop three of its companies and the staff elements correctly and in close order, despite the defensive fire; 11th Company under *Oberleutnant*

---

57   The company had arrived incomplete on the airfield at Waalhaven, as one of its Ju 52s had been shot down over Zaltbommel, during the approach from Germany, 13 engineers being killed. Small details of the company had also remained on the island at Ijsselmonde for engineering tasks.

Karl-Heinz Becker in the South-west,[58] 9th Company commanded by *Oberleutnant* Gessner, in the east and 12th Company under *Hauptmann* Herbert Schmidt, north-east of 9th Company.[59] Only 10th Company, commanded by *Oberleutnant* Dunz, came down some distance too far to the south-east. While most of its soldiers quickly gained the south-eastern edge of the airfield after they picked up their main armament, taking over their original mission there from 11th Company, elements of one platoon initially were drawn into firefights against patrols of the Dutch 4th Anti-Aircraft Battery before they could join their unit.[60]

Immediately after *III./FschJgRgt.1* had jumped some of the Ju 52s of *II./KG z.b.V.1* dropped a number of dummy paratroopers over the airfield. This deception was successful as it drew the attention of some of the defenders and their fire away from the landing battalion.[61]

9th Company and the battle HQ attacked against the area behind the main entrance, and the field positions stretching along the eastern edge of the airfield. 11th Company, less one platoon, broke into the Dutch positions at its south-western corner. Soldiers of this company, who had landed immediately in front of these positions, did not have time to pick up their main arms. Covered by the Reedijk along the southern edge of the airfield, they assaulted the weapon- pits of 49th Anti-Aircraft Platoon and those of the heavy weapons to the west of them using pistols and hand grenades. The Dutch crews, being completely surprised and still shocked from the preceding bombing, surrendered after a few pistol shots and hand grenades. Therefore, they suffered only a few losses. Until 10th Company arrived at the scene of the fighting, elements of 11th Company dealt with the former's initial objective and put some of the Dutch positions there out of action.

The defence positions of 2nd Company and the assigned heavy machine-guns were attacked from the rear. Only the few soldiers who had been positioned to protect these positions against attack from the east initially rendered some resistance. They were quickly overcome although they did inflict some losses to the approaching paratroopers. Able to utilize the cover of trees and small houses, the attackers succeeded in quickly crossing the railway embankment just east of the Dutch position-line and overwhelmed most of its defenders before they could turn around to meet the threat. The concrete casemate, which had commenced firing at the first groups of transport aircraft during landing approach,

58   The surviving aircrews were captured by the Dutch. Some of them, however, were liberated later, among them *Oberst* Fiebig. All the others forced to land in terrain controlled by the Dutch during the five-day struggle, were shipped to England and thence to Canada.

59   It had probably been elements of this company, which was observed by the reinforced platoon from III./34th Inf.Rgt., guarding the bridge across the Oude Maas south of Barendrecht and by the staff of 3rd Searchlight Detachment in Rhoon. Group Kil thereupon had additionally dispatched two reinforced platoons from III./28th Inf.Rgt. to the southern end of the bridge south of Barendrecht. At 0840hrs, Group Spui had sent a reinforced platoon from II./34th Inf.Rgt. to the bridge at Spijkenisse, which hitherto was unprotected. This platoon crossed the Oude Maas and had moved to Hoogvliet, where, at 0940hrs, it encountered a patrol from the paratroopers approaching from the east. Around noon, a force the size of a mixed company had additionally been tasked by Group Spui with the defense of the bridge at Spijkenisse.

60   There is little information about 12th (heavy weapons) Company for 10 May. It had probably taken over the protection of the battalion toward Rotterdam, north-east of the airfield. As the company only lost one man killed on 10 May, it may not have seen a great deal of combat action.

61   There is no confirmation of Dutch reports by German sources that some of these paratroopers had been captured during these engagements.

was yet to be taken. For a short period of time guns of the 51st Anti-Aircraft Machine-gun Platoon in the north-eastern part of the airfield also fired at the landing aircraft until their crews could be taken out by paratroopers in close-combat. With its three platoons still stretched out behind the entire length of the mound north of the airfield, 1st Company of III/JgRgt was given no time to join in the fighting. After its small guardposts south of the mound were eliminated in the first onslaught, the company was assaulted by paratroopers simultaneously from the east and west. A few bursts of submachine-gun fire and a few hand grenades sufficed for its surrender. The soldiers from 3rd Company of III/JgRgt, with the exception of its hard-hit platoon of the battalion reserved, became eyewitnesses to the initial fighting for the airfield. Nevertheless quite a few of them chose to use the general confusion to retire on their own toward Rotterdam. The company, who were placed far away from the actual fighting, remained isolated, whilst the company commander had not yet arrived from his quarters. Therefore, one of its platoon leaders assumed command, and at around 0710hrs ordered the still available elements to move off to the south-east in the direction of the village Charlois. There, the company commander, who in the meantime had arrived, quite incomprehensibly ordered the company to move toward the south at the southern edge of Charlois. However, before this order could be put into effect, the commanding officer of III/JgRgt arrived from the airfield and ordered 3rd Company to follow him back to Rotterdam.

At 0725hrs six Ju 52s with two infantry platoons of *9./InfRgt.16* aboard, touched down on the runway, whilst the final resistance continued on and around the airfield. The commanding officer of *III./InfRgt.16*, *Oberstleutnant* von Choltitz,[62] determined that these two platoons should be the first reinforcements for the bridges in Rotterdam. During the landing run the Ju 52s were hit by fire from isolated Dutch automatic weapons that had not yet been put out of action by the paratroopers. Although some of them were badly damaged, their passengers dismounted with few losses and immediately joined the fighting. With their support *Hauptmann* Schulz, leading the action in person, succeeded in breaking the last resistance around the main entrance of the airfield. At 0740hrs he entered the command post of the airfield commandant, Reserve-Major Thomas, and took him and his small staff prisoner. Schulz now decided to take advantage of the captured commandant in order to bring the last resistance from the eastern edge of the airfield to an end. Reserve-Major Thomas agreed to the demands of *Hauptmann* Schulz to act as negotiator.[63] Thomas persuaded the few remaining defenders at the eastern edge of the airfield to surrender. The crew of the machine-gun casemate, however, only ceased fighting after their previously captured platoon leader, pressed by *Hauptmann* Schulz, convinced them that further resistance was hopeless. Immediately, Schulz set about achieving the surrender of 77th Anti-Aircraft Battery on the pier west of Waalhaven, again with the help of Reserve-Major Thomas. Technical problems with the fire-control gear and unprepared ammunition prevented the battery from opening fire at the beginning of the German attack and later had allowed only for a slow rate of fire. When paratroopers moved against the battery's firing position part of its crew and the organic two anti-aircraft machine-guns had

---

62   Statements in several Dutch sources that a number of the German paratroopers had fallen into burning buildings and were drowned in the basin of the Waalhaven, are incorrect. They had been dummies. The loss report of *III./FschJgRgt.1* for 10 May does not mention any paratroopers burnt to death or drowned.

63   As commandant of Paris, the then *General der Infanterie* Dietrich von Choltitz in August 1944 was to save the city from the total destruction which Hitler had ordered.

been deployed as infantry for its protection. Thereby the loss of this position was prevented for the time being, although a German fighter plane had joined the combat by strafing the anti-aircraft guns.

The ensuing firefight between paratroopers and the anti-aircraft soldiers was interrupted when *Hauptmann* Schulz and Reserve-Major Thomas arrived in front of the battery position in a motor vehicle marked by a white flag of truce. After some negotiations Thomas negotiated the surrender of the majority of the gun crews. Shortly afterwards the paratroopers stormed the pier, overwhelming the Dutch soldiers still showing signs of resistance, only a few of them evaded capture.

The last resistance in the eastern part of the airfield was overcome as the 77th Anti-Aircraft Battery was neutralized. *Oberstleutnant* von Choltitz, his battle HQ, the rest of *9./InfRgt.16*, *2./PiBtl.22* (less one platoon and one squad) and an anti-tank gun of *FschPzAbwKp.7* landed.[64] Following right behind, the two advance platoons of *9./InfRgt.16* landed. *Oberstleutnant* von Choltitz immediately set about executing his mission: the reinforcement and extension of the bridgehead on the northern bank of the Nieuwe Maas which was established by the advance forces. He was also charged with the protection of the traffic and railway bridges which led from the south of Rotterdam across the Koningshaven to the densely populated island of Noordereiland and from there to the northern bank of the Nieuwe Maas.

The conquest of these formidable bridges was a prerequisite to the planned thrust of mechanised forces into the core of Fortress Holland and caused the commands of Luftflotte 2 and *Fl.Div.7* considerable problems during the planning of the airborne operation. Parachuting or glider-landings close to the bridges was out of the question because of the densely built-up urban area and the numerous canals and basins around them. Deliberations to anchor ships with troops hidden on them ahead of the operation in the harbour area in the vicinity of the bridges had not been further pursued because of the risk of discovery and the the evident breach of international law. Eventually, probably following a suggestion by *Generalfeldmarschall* Göring, the plan was developed to land an advance force by means of hydroplanes beside the bridges and take possession of them until the arrival of air-landed reinforcements from the airfield at Waalhaven. Prior to the landing of the hydroplanes a platoon of paratroopers was to be dropped into the stadium of Feyenoord and push through to the bridges in a supporting role.

To facilitate the raid against the bridges a squadron of 15 hydroplanes (He 59s), was formed from *KGr z.b.V.108* employed in Norway. Designated *Sonderstaffel Schwilden* after its commander, *Hauptmann* Schwilden, it was to take from the Zwischenahner Meer (a large lake near Oldenburg) with two platoons of *11./InfRgt.16*, the company's HQ, two heavy machine-gun teams and an engineer team from *2./PiBtl.22* aboard and to land immediately below the bridges in Rotterdam. For the air transport of this advance force additional seating-space was created aboard the He 59.[65]

---

64   Dutch authorities, examining the event after the war found that Major Thomas had not energetically resisted the demand of Schulz, although it had constituted a clear offense against the Hague Convention for Land Warfare.

65   The assignment of this gun to the advance elements of *III./InfRgt.16* had been arranged between the company commander of *FschPzAbwKp.7*, *Hauptmann* Götzel, and *Oberstleutnant* von Choltitz at a beer-hall prior to the beginning of the operation.

The approach to the destination area passed without incident and the first 12 He 59s, approaching in low-level flight along the Nieuwe Maas, touched down on the water either side of the Willems Bridge and the railway bridge next to it, leading from Noordereiland to the northern bank of the river. Shortly after three more He 59s arrived using their engine-power to get to the quay along the northern bank of the Nieuwe Maas close to the bridges. Some propelled themselves into the Koningshaven and there to the southern ends of the Koninginnen Bridge and the railway bridge next to it, which connected Noordereiland with the southern part of Rotterdam. By means of some rapidly-inflated rubber boats the soldiers of the advance force paddled to the quays. A part of its western group landed at the riverside street at Boompjes, which led from the west to the Willems Bridge, and positioned machine-guns along the street. Another group occupied the northern ramps of the Willems Bridge and the railway bridge, as well as the buildings of the National Insurance Bank and the Maas Hotel, located just north of the bridge rampart. Security teams were also posted at the Vierleeuwen Bridge, which crossed a harbor basin immediately east of the rampart and at the railway station at Beurse, north of the railway bridge. Soldiers of the advance force's eastern group landed at the Oosterkade, east of the railway bridge, and advanced toward the adjoining Maas station. The four engineers who had been assigned to *11./ InfRgt.16* examined the bridges for demolition charges, but none were found. The elements of the company which landed in the Koningshaven occupied its southern quay and took over the protection of the Koninginnen Bridge and the railway bridge just next to it. The commanding officer of *11./InfRgt.16*, *Hauptmann* Schrader, coordinated the tasks of his platoons.

The appearance of *Sonderstaffel Schwilden* at the bridges, and the disembarkation of its passengers was observed by hundreds of Dutch citizens on their journey to work. As news about the outbreak of the war had not yet been disseminated most people around the bridges regarded the events as an exercise of the Dutch armed forces[66] and nothing more than a welcome distraction from the daily routine.

However this situation changed rapidly. On Noordereiland a Dutch policeman was shot dead as he attempted to prevent the occupation of the island by soldiers of *11./InfRgt.16* with his pistol drawn. On the northern bank of the Nieuwe Maas another policeman was also killed. The first military resistance was met from a security post of about 20 men of the Rotterdam Citizen Guard, led by a captain, which had been established in the Maas station. The German soldiers returned fire and drove the Dutch back into the city. The Germans now seized the station and a Dutch guard was captured. A police inspector, who was taken together with another policeman, was killed during an attempt to overwhelm his three German guards on the way to the Maas Hotel, which now served as a prisoner holding area. The other policeman was wounded as he tried to flee.

---

66 As no information about the actual strength of the advance force is available, it is written here based on assumptions. The basic assumption is that the number of He 59s was 15 (confirmed by two sources, one of which is a report by the Rotterdam Air Warning Service, dated 10 May 1940), and that each He 59 had space for 5-6 passengers in addition to the aircrew of 3-4.

In order to not exceed the seating-space, which was slightly below 90 and of which at least two were required for the two heavy machine-guns and their ammunition supply, the strength of the sub-units of the task force had to be kept somewhat below their authorized war-time strength. Therefore it may have been 35 for each infantry platoon (three squads with one leader and 10 men each and a platoon leader with a runner), four for the company's command group (by far under normal strength), four (instead of six) for each heavy machine-gun-team and the 4 men of the engineer team i.e. altogether 86 men.

In the meantime, the hydroplanes which were still fit to fly had taken off from their base. Four of the He 59s remained behind due to the damage they had received. Their aircrews joined the landed infantry, taking along some of the machine-guns from the aircraft. The He 59 with *Hauptmann* Schwilden aboard was hit by the fire of 56th Anti-Aircraft Machine-gun Platoon, in position on the northern bank of the Nieuwe Maas shortly after its take-off, opposite the Waalhaven. It landed on the river but during the action *Hauptmann* Schwilden was killed and the three non-commissioned officers of his crew were taken prisoner.

At 0740hrs, the 3rd Platoon of *11./FschJgRgt.1*, commanded by *Oberleutnant* Kerfin, established contact with the pickets of *11./InfRgt.16* at the Koninginnen Bridge. There, *Hauptmann* Schrader initially sent the platoon to the Noordereiland as his reserve. Kerfin's platoon was dropped between 0635 and 0645hrs over the stadium at Feyenoord according to plan, constituting the first reinforcement for the advance force at the bridges in Rotterdam. During the approach flight one of the paratroopers was seriously wounded by anti-aircraft fire. The drop was executed without resistance from the ground but two paratroopers hurt themselves during landing. At 0715hrs, after the platoon had picked up its principal weapons and organized itself for departure, it moved out on confiscated vehicles along the railway. On the approach to the objective two paratroopers had been wounded seriously and another slightly during firefights with small groups of Dutch soldiers who were retreating from the airfield at Waalhaven.

On the airfield *Oberstleutnant* von Choltitz assembled the troops of his task force who had already been landed and moved them in a direction toward the bridges in Rotterdam. The arriving elements of his task group – *12(schw.)/InfRgt.16* and the platoons of *13./*, and *14./InfRgt.16* (infantry gun and anti-tank respectively) received orders to follow. *10./InfRgt.16* was still missing. The troops under *Oberstleutnant* von Choltitz were to use a different route through Rotterdam-South compared to *Oberleutnant* Kerfin's platoon. There, two units of the garrison of Rotterdam were billeted following the mobilization of the Dutch military.

As impacts from bombs and other combat noise was heard from the airfield at Waalhaven and the commander of the reserve company had seen the occupation of the traffic bridges in Rotterdam while crossing them from his quarters in a taxi, both companies initiated defensive measures. These, however, were uncoordinated and varied from one another. From 2nd Reserve Company only the soldiers of the infantry guard-detachment were deployed. They set up provisional security positions south of the company billets. The majority of the company, owing to its insufficient armament and military training, remained in the school building. A group of soldiers had arrived from the airfield, including 28 engineers with two machine-guns, and these remained for local protection.

At 0710hrs the commander of the 2nd Company of III/39th Inf.Rgt. was ordered to set up defensive positions at the Afrikaander-Plein. At 0740hrs a patrol sent out toward the bridges across the Nieuwe Maas returned and reported their occupation by the Germans. The company commander was able to relay his information about the enemy unhindered by telephone to the staff of the city commandant of Rotterdam, as the Germans, as in Dordrecht, had neglected to cut the telephone cables leading across the bridges.[67]

---

67   The He 59 had not been marked with a swastika but with a large Iron Cross.

Shortly after their arrival south of the school building, the security elements of the reserve company were attacked by the task group of *Oberstleutnant* von Choltitz. After a short encounter with the passengers of a motor car in which a Dutch soldier was killed, engineers of *2./PiBtl.22* on motorcycles with sidecars, followed by *9./InfRgt.16*, advanced firing against the defensive position. They were supported by the anti-tank gun of *FschPzAbwKp.7*, assigned to *III./InfRgt.16*. After about ten minutes of fighting, in which another Dutch soldier was killed and one wounded, the Dutch company commander, watching from the school-building, came to the conclusion that further resistance was hopeless and would only threaten the groups of civilians who were observing the fight. At 0900hrs he stepped into the street with a white flag and surrendered the troops under his command. On the German side, there was neither the time to remove the more than 200 captured Dutch soldiers, nor the possibility to leave behind guards to watch over them. Upon the word of honour of the Dutch company commander, they were therefore left in their quarters but only after they handed over their weapons. The company commander was taken along by the Germans as a kind of hostage. Later he was brought to Noordereiland.

During the fighting, a tragic accident had occurred. Thinking that the attacking German engineers had been fired at from a building forward of the quarters of the reserve troops, into which a number of persons had retreated, one of the engineers threw a hand-grenade into its basement. The retreating people, who had been taken as Dutch soldiers because of their uniform clothing, had in fact had been friars from a nearby religious institution. The explosion from the hand-grenade killed one of them and had wounded another. The tragic error only became evident after the friars had left the basement. Notwithstanding the disaster which had struck, the friars, together with some more people from the institution, offered their services as medical assistants to take care of German wounded in the street. But in the crossfire, three more were killed.[68]

Continuing its advance a short distance, the German task force received fire from the Dutch positions around the Afrikaander-Plein. There, the commander of III/JgRgt, Major de Vos, who had arrived from the airfield at Waalhaven with some officers, about a platoon of infantry, and some men from 3rd Searchlight Platoon, assumed command over all troops deployed around the Afrikaander-Plein. A first German attack against their positions came to a halt. During the attempt to renew the thrust with a few men, *Oberleutnant* Grave, the adjutant of *Oberstleutnant* von Choltitz, together with a *Feldwebel* of his staff, was killed. Again supported by the anti-tank gun of the paratroopers, von Choltitz managed to suppress the defenders, so that he, his staff and *9./InfRgt.16*, could bypass the Dutch positions on a route between the Maashaven and the Afrikaander-Plein and reach Noordereiland at about 1030hrs. Ahead of them *12./InfRgt.16*, with its heavy machine-guns and mortars, as well as the infantry guns and anti-tank guns of the assigned platoons from *13.* and *14./InfRgt.16*, which had moved on the direct route along the street and the railway leading to the bridges, also reached Noordereiland. Kerfin's platoon had to be deployed in teams and squads as reinforcements into the bridgehead north of the Nieuwe Maas between 0800 and 0900hrs, after the c.40 soldiers of *11./InfRgt.16* and the aircrews of the four damaged hydroplanes,

---

68   The telephone cables across the bridges in Dordrecht, among them one for long-distance calls and for teletype-communication from Den Haag and Rotterdam to London, were disconnected by the Germans not earlier than 12 May. This is an indication of how poorly the German parachute force was prepared for the execution of such an important task.

occupying an area of about 1,000m wide and up to 500m deep, had found themselves exposed to numerically-superior Dutch forces approaching from several directions.

Opposite the Dutch positions around the Afrikaander-Plein, only the soldiers of *2./ PiBtl.22* remained in position for the time being. Their mission was to tie down the enemy until additional forces could be air-landed and brought forward. The Dutch defenders used the opportunity of the combat activity of the German forces to improve their positions. No attempt, however, was undertaken to overrun the few troops opposing them, or to break out toward the west.

The soldiers of 2nd Searchlight Platoon, who had set up defensive positions in the Zuidersee Hospital in Feyenoord, ceased their resistance against a German infantry patrol for lack of ammunition, when the Germans moved up an anti-tank gun. A number of these men managed to flee after putting on civilian clothing.

Upon the receipt of reports about the occupation of the Nieuwe Maas bridges by Germans and about the fighting at the airfield at Waalhaven, the first counter-measures were initiated by the Dutch commands located in Rotterdam by their duty officers. Each command acted on its own, as it had not been possible in the time preceding the German attack to achieve unity of command for the troops garrisoned in Rotterdam, let alone for a methodical preparation for the defence of the urban area. An early appearance of German ground forces had not been contemplated seriously and Lieutenant General van Andel, the commandant of Fortress Holland, had strengthened this negative approach. Nevertheless the military commandant of Rotterdam, Colonel Scharroo, had requested additional combat troops on several occassions. However, his requests were continually refused. Even when, on 9 May, the 1st Infantry Division which was deployed along the coast between The Hook of Holland and Haarlem, had been placed under the command of Lieutenant General van Andel and the Light Division had been earmarked for him upon its arrival in the Fortress, he had saw no requirement to reinforce the troops in and around Rotterdam.

Command relations had remained unchanged in spite of the ever-growing threat of a German attack against Holland. Increased readiness, as throughout Holland, was ordered some time earlier, however only for the anti-aircraft forces around Rotterdam.[69] These, however, like the depot of the Dutch Air Arm in Rotterdam, were under the command of the commander-in-chief of Air Defense, Major General Best.

The commander of the Dutch marines viewed himself and his troops in Rotterdam as directly subordinate to the high command in Den Haag and had not offered any kind of cooperation to Colonel Scharroo.

The depots of the Dutch Navy in Rotterdam had remained subordinate to their commander-in-chief, Vice-Admiral Furstner.

Colonel Scharroo, therefore, had command authority only over III/39th Inf.Rgt., which constituted the infantry garrison for Rotterdam.

In spite of the warning about the imminent German attack against Holland, including the use of airborne forces, which was passed to him on the evening of 9 May from the Dutch military *attaché* in Berlin, Colonel Scharroo abstained from immediately bringing

---

69   After the war, some Dutch sources had declared the hand-grenade attack as deliberate, and the medical aid by the friars as enforced by the Germans. These accusations in the meantime have been disproved by Dutch historians, particularly by A.M.A. Goossens.

Rotterdam into a pre-attack state of alert. Obviously disregarding the possibility of German airborne attacks, he was still content with protective measures mainly against action by the so called 'Fifth Column'[70] – some time earlier the railway stations at the entrances into the city, the buildings, housing the commands, and some important municipal installations had been provided with guard-details.

Unprepared for short notice combat actions and with most of their soldiers not trained for them, the staffs of the depot troops and the training installations which were dispersed all over the city needed some time to adjust to the unexpected situation. This was all the more difficult as the commanding officers first had to arrive from their lodgings and the painfully correct distribution of weapons and ammunition was proving cumbersome. Moreover, as first reports about the presence of German soldiers north of the Nieuwe Maas had been rather sketchy, the actual situation needed to be clarified before plans could be developed. Nevertheless the first detachments of the depot battalions sent out for this task, mostly around 40-70 men, succeeded in sealing off the streets leading from the bridges into the centre of the city and in occupying the Beurse and Maas stations after German security posts had been withdrawn. They also put out of action the German machine-gun-team at the Vierleeuwen Bridge.

A detachment of Dutch marines who were billeted in barracks at the Oostplein, near the Maas bridges, was combat-ready from an early hour, as they had been alerted at 0545hrs. The commanding officer, who had arrived at 0710hrs, ordered the barracks to be prepared against attack and reconnaissance patrols sent out. At 0740hrs a half-platoon of the marines blocked the bridge across the Haringsvliet, east of Beurse station, and subsequently received orders to occupy this station as well as the Maas one. Both tasks were accomplished with no losses and slightly ahead of the depot troops. These had erroneously fired at marines who had already advanced from Beurse station further to the South.

At 0910hrs Lieutenant General van Andel placed I/10th Art.Rgt., located in Hillegersberg, in the north-east of Rotterdam under the command of Colonel Scharroo. This detachment, the only corps-level artillery of I Army Corps, was composed of three batteries with 12 modern guns which had a range of up to 16,500m. As Colonel Scharroo obtained reports that the airfield at Waalhaven was in the hands of the Germans and transport aircraft landing there could be observed from locations north of the Nieuwe Maas, he ordered the artillery detachment to direct its fire primarily against this target. However one of the batteries was ordered to support the attack against the German bridgehead from positions in the area of Zalmhaven/Veehaven.

The combat teams of *11./InfRgt.16* and those of Kerfin's platoon were hard pressed by the increasing number of Dutch troops who were able to utilize the cover of the densely built-up terrain. A few German outposts had been put out of action and others pushed back toward the bridges. Furthermore the commanding officer of *11./InfRgt.16* was nowhere to be found. Fire support by heavy weapons from Noordereiland was not yet available, as *12./InfRgt.16* and the two platoons from the regimental units of *InfRgt.16* were still in the process of setting up their positions. *Oberstleutnant* von Choltitz now arrived on the island

---

70   These forces had been assigned to the air-defence sector Rotterdam's Gravenhage, which had at its disposal 36 anti-aircraft guns 75mm, six 40mm and 38 of 20mm as well as 108 anti-aircraft machine-guns and 70 searchlights.

with parts of his task group and established his command post there. As a first measure, the anti-tank gun from *FschPzAbwKp.7* was placed on the Willems Bridge, which would allow the best possible support of forces in the bridgehead. The reinforcement by *9./InfRgt.16*, however, met almost insurmountable difficulties for a number of reasons.

On the Dutch side, the machine-gun company of III/39th Inf.Rgt. which was located downstream of the bridges, received orders to engage with the enemy.[71] After a through reconnaissance two of its four platoons, each equipped with two heavy machine-guns, advanced toward the Boompjes between 0810 and 0940hrs. The other two platoons set up firing positions at the northern bank of the Nieuwe Maas, just west of the south-western tip of Noordereiland, called the Prinsenhoofd. The platoons advancing along the Boompjes engaged the German machine-gun teams positioned there. They were supported by a small detachment of marines who moved forward entering buildings and climbing onto their roofs. The platoon's south-west of the Prinsenhoofd directed their fire primarily against the Willems Bridge, the north-western part of Noordereiland and the southern ramps of the bridges leading across the Koningshaven. Only a few soldiers of *9./InfRgt.16* succeed in crossing the Willems Bridge.

Shortly prior to 1000hrs, another formidable adversary made its appearance on the Dutch side. Along the Nieuwe Maas, coming from its berth on the Nieuwe Waterweg, the torpedo-boat Z 5 (263 tons), arrived and opened fire on the Willems Bridge and the buildings in the bridgehead which were occupied by the Germans from a distance of about 400m with its 7.5cm bow gun and its two 12.7mm machine-guns. The four German hydroplanes which had to be left behind because of damage were now destroyed for good. However, when three members of the torpedo boat were wounded on its bridge, its commandant decided to break off the action for the time being, and to return the wounded to safety. Accompanied by the motor torpedo boat TM 51 (32 tons, a crew of 10 and armed with two 2cm guns), Z 5 shortly after 1010hrs again approached the bridges firing. But this time fire was returned by the anti-tank gun on the Willems Bridge.[72] The anti-tank gunfire particularly endangered the motor torpedo boat with its thin hull. It was also attacked from the air and damaged by a near-miss from a bomb which killed one of its crew. It then withdrew. For a short time Z 5 continued to fight and then moved back to its berth, only slightly damaged.[73]

Even after the end of the bombardment from the river it was almost impossible for the Germans to get reinforcements across the Nieuwe Maas, let alone to evacuate wounded from the bridgehead, as the bridges were continuously kept under fire by the heavy machine-guns of III/39th Inf.Rgt. and the machine-guns and snipers of the marines and depot troops,

---

71   The fear of actions by agents and supporting pro-German elements, particularly by members of Anton Mussert's National Collective Movement (NSB) was widely spread in the Dutch military and civilian environment. It was well known that the NSB had followers among officers of the Dutch armed forces, and in the state authorities.

72   The 3rd Company of III/39th Inf.Rgt., which was co-located with the machine-gun company, had not been deployed against the bridges, but had been used for guard-duties in some squares in the interior of Rotterdam.

73   The gun was served solely by its wounded crew-chief, as all other members of the crew had been put out of action while positioning it.

who came dangerously close to the bridge-ramps. Attempts to move infantrymen across the Willems Bridge by means of fast moving sidecar motorcycles were quickly abandoned as the losses were too high. Less than 10 soldiers got into the bridgehead unscathed by this method.

At 1330hrs the Germans gave up the majority of their forward positions and withdrew into buildings close to the bridge ramparts. The Dutch followed up and occupied the ‚Witte Huis' [White House].[74] Located near the north of the bridge ramps, the 43m high building was of particular advantage to the attackers, as it offered unhindered fields of observation and fire onto the bridges and the terrain still held by the Germans north-east of the bridge ramps, from its roof and the upper stories. Additionally, its thick walls provided protection fire from flat-trajectory infantry weapons.

At the bridgehead the Germans were able to retain a few buildings along the Boompjes and forward of the bridge ramps. To the north-east of these a row of houses toward the Haringsvlet on the Oosterkade was also still controlled by them. *Oberleutnant* Kerfin withdrew the paratroopers of his platoon, (as far as he was able to account for them, a *Feldwebel* and nine other ranks), into the building at the corner of the row of houses on the Oosterkade. During the fighting in the morning, two *Feldwebels* and four other ranks of his platoon were killed and a *Feldwebel* and three men had also been seriously wounded. The rest of his platoon had not been found by him at this location. In his search *Oberleutnant* Kerfin came across a few soldiers from *9./InfRgt.16*. As he was the sole officer available at present, he organized the defence east of the bridge ramps. He was now assisted by the heavy machine-guns, anti-tank guns, infantry guns and mortars which were in position on Noordereiland. This led to one of the Dutch heavy machine-guns which was delivering flanking fire from the Boompjes being put out of action. This enabled the soldiers of *11./ InfRgt.16*, who still held out in the eastern part of the Boompjes, to slow down the advance of the Dutch from the west, although three men of a machine-gun-team were killed in the ensuing firefight.

Later in the afternoon, pressure against the bridgehead increased again as Dutch marines began to close in from both sides.[75] The Maas Hotel was again occupied; however it was abandoned again due to heavy damage from mortar fire which caused some losses in personnel. At about 1700hrs, Dutch marines advanced along the railway from the Beurse station toward the bridges. Their commander was killed by defensive fire and so they withdrew again into the protection of buildings. The firefight continued on until the evening, resulting in a soldier of *InfRgt.16* being killed and three others being wounded.

The enemy now ceased attacks, but continued with undiminished intensity to deliver fire at the German positions north of the Nieuwe Maas using machine-guns and high-angle weapons.[75] The buildings forward of the bridge ramparts which were still occupied by German soldiers were heavily damaged and set ablaze as a result.

---

74   The reason for its withdrawal, given by some Dutch sources, was that Z 5 had run out of ammunition, is doubted by other Dutch sources. On the way back a crew member of Z 5 had been killed during an air attack. A few days after its action, the boat escaped to England.

75   Erected in 1898 in the style of Art Nouveau, this formidable building had 10 floors. It received its name from the white tiles, which covered the entire façade.

At 2000hrs the commanding officer of *9./InfRgt.16*, *Oberleutnant* Schreiber-Voltening, who had managed to get across the bridges with a few men of his unit, assumed command of the bridgehead. When he was reported missing around midnight, *Oberleutnant* Kerfin took over command. As the houses still occupied along the railway forward of the bridge ramparts could collapse under the bombardment Kerfin withdrew all his soldiers into the solid building of the Dutch National Life Insurance Bank. It was the last building in German hands forward of the bridge ramparts and had therefore to be retained at all costs.

At the end of 10 May, the situation in contested Rotterdam was as follows:
No contingency plans had been developed to ward off an early counter-attack by enemy troops against the bridges across the Nieuwe Maas, nevertheless the German *coup de main* was successful and lasting.

Lacking unity of command the Dutch troops present in Rotterdam could only apply an uncoordinated deployment of their first line forces. These had seen as an initial task the blocking of the Germans into the city north of the bridges. The chance to conduct a decisive counter-attack in the late morning of 10 May, by concentrating all available depot troops and the marines under determined commanders, had not been utilized, although the arrival of German reinforcements was delayed by the dogged resistance at the Afrikaander-Plein.

In the light of the ongoing build-up in strength of the Germans on Noordereiland and the air superiority of the *Luftwaffe* over Rotterdam, in the early afternoon of 10 May Colonel Scharroo came to the conclusion that the German bridgehead could not be eliminated and the north of Rotterdam could not be retained for a longer period with the forces he had at hand. He therefore urgently requested reinforcement from the Dutch high command. However neither he nor the commander of the marines had undertaken any steps to unite the actions of their troops with a common plan.

The German commanders had been conscious of the critical situation which had developed at the bridgehead during the course of 10 May. As long as the enemy's fire blocked the passage across the bridges, the retention of the bridgehead would depend on the skill and bravery of its few defenders, on the support by heavy weapons from Noordereiland and on air support. However the latter two would be almost nil during the hours of darkness. It had to be hoped therefore that the enemy would not attack again in that time. The main effort in the coming day would be placed on the attempt to silence the weapons blocking the bridges by concentrated fire, in order to move fresh troops across the river before the worn-down and decimated defenders in the bridgehead were overcome. The only chance to neutralize the Dutch long-range artillery rested with a timely and massive employment of the *Luftwaffe*.

While *Kräftegruppe von Choltitz* was still involved in action with Dutch forces, blocking the access route to the bridges in the south of Rotterdam and the elements of the advance force made first contact during their attempts to extend the bridgehead north of the Nieuwe Maas, the air transport formations were reorganized for the second wave of ground forces of the *Luftlande-Korps* on airfields in Germany. [76]

---

76   At noon the commander-in-chief of the Dutch marines, Colonel Freytag Drabbe, had formed a company-sized unit with marines and naval personnel and ordered it to attack the bridgehead.

At around 0800hrs *III./FschJgRgt.1* had full control of the airfield at Waalhaven and security positions were established in all directions. As early as 0840hrs *Generalleutnant* Student and a small battle HQ of *Fl.Div.7* had arrived at the airfield aboard two Ju 52s equipped with radio sets (*Nachrichten-Ju*). Student had supervised the launch of *III./FschJgRgt.1* from the airfield at Gütersloh, and departed about 30 minutes later. The low-frequency radios in the *Nachrichten-Ju* were to maintain communication with *Luftflotte 2* and with the liaison staff of the *Luftlande-Korps* established in Wiedenbrück, near Gütersloh. The mission of the liaison staff, directed by *Oberst* von Fichte, was to supervise the air transport movement timetables for the *Luftlande-Korps* and adjust them as required. Moreover, they had to pass requests for air support to the directing commands of the *Luftwaffe* and initiate the air resupply mission. For this purpose a specific depot was set up at the airfield at Gütersloh.

During the approach flight *Generalleutnant* Student observed that the pairs of bridges at Moerdijk and Dordrecht had been captured and were apparently undamaged. After landing he received a situation report from *Hauptmann* Schulz and then moved to a provisional command post of *Fl.Div.7* about 1,500m south of the airfield. Student's decision to fly into the air bridgehead of *Fl.Div.7*, had been based on his attempt to establish unity of command for his widely dispersed forces as fast as possible. His desire to be present well forward corresponded with the ethos of command and control in the German *Heer*, which was applicable to the deployment of the parachute and air-landing troops.

The first batches of transport aircraft of the second wave landed at Waalhaven late in the morning. It had not been possible to maintain the original aircraft loading-plans for this wave because of the unexpected high losses and serious damage to the Ju 52 fleet. The allotment of air transport forces to ground units therefore had to be re-arranged in most cases, resulting in prolonged times for takeoff. The Dutch air defense along the approach routes was still intact and highly active for the greater part. Therefore a number of Ju 52s were so heavily damaged that they had to conduct emergency landings on the way, or were forced to turn back to German airfields. For this reason, only seven of the 23 Ju 52s, carrying approximatly 100 men of *I./InfRgt.16* aboard, initially landed at Waalhaven late in the morning. The Ju 52 transporting a platoon from *2./PiBtl.22*, which was assigned to *I./InfRgt.16*, had to land near Delft after being hit by ground fire. The platoon managed to report its situation by radio to the command post of *Fl.Div.7*. Then, it became silent.[77]

II./InfRgt.16, which was planned as the reserve of *InfRgt.16*, was landed around midday. *leFlakBttr.106* was also unloaded at this time and immediately assumed protection for the airfield against air attacks with its five 2cm guns.

At 1140hrs *Oberst* Kreysing, the commander of *InfRgt.16*, arrived at the airfield with his battle HQ and the regimental signals platoon. His command post was then set up in the village of Hordijk, south of the airfield. After Kreysing obtained a picture of the situation, he realized that the original deployment plan for his regiment could not be adhered to. He therefore decided, after consultation with *Generalleutnant* Student, that *I./InfRgt.16*, which up to now had been landed with parts of three companies, was not to be sent to the bridges at Dordrecht for the relief of the paratroopers there, rather it was to be kept in an assembly area near Hordijk for the time being. Additionally, he directed this battalion to

---

77   A platoon of the 2nd Battery of I/10th Art.Rgt. had commenced firing at the buildings on the Oostkade at 1710hrs from a position near the Zalmhaven.

dispatch security forces to the northern bank of the Oude Maas, in particular to the bridge south of Barendrecht. On their way, these elements encountered the medical aid station of 4th Anti-Aircraft Battery in Barendrecht. Its personnel were made prisoners, but allowed to continue their tasks. Approaching the bridge south of Barendrecht they then came up against a detachment of Dutch soldiers who had crossed the Oude Maas over the bridge. These men withdrew to the opposite bank of the river after a short firefight.[78] The cantilever part of the bridge, however, remained undamaged.

Patrols from *I./InfRgt.16* reconnoitering from Barendrecht further to the west, detected enemy forces on the southern bank of the Oude Maas. The presence of Dutch troops in the south-western part of Ijsselmonde was reported by a patrol from *11./FschJgRgt.1*, which returned from a reconnaissance mission in which it lost one paratrooper who went missing during an engagement in Rhoon.[79]

Shortly after midday, in the Charlois polder, the attempt by a platoon of the paratroopers failed to take the security post of 4th Anti-Aircraft Battery. Forty minutes later *Hauptmann* Schulz and a few of his men appeared in front of this post in a motor car marked with a white flag of truce. Reserve-Major Thomas was again to act as negotiator to achieve the surrender of the soldiers of the anti-aircraft battery. However the negotiation failed and in the ensuing firefight Thomas and one of the paratroopers were killed.[80] *Hauptmann* Schulz and the rest of his men managed to get away unharmed.

With the action in the Charlois polder the struggle of *III./FschJgRgt.1* for the possession of the airfield at Waalhaven came to an end. The battalion had paid for its success with 13 dead; six from 9th Company, three from 10th Company, two from the battle HQ and one each from 11th and 12th companies.[81]

On the Dutch side the number of killed, on and near the airfield, totalled 30 from III/JgRgt, 13 from the Air Arm, five from anti-aircraft units, three from the guard company of depot troops of the engineers and three from the voluntary air observation militia. Additionally, more than 400 Dutch soldiers had been captured.

---

78   The flight-time of the Ju 52s, dropping the paratroopers into the area of operations of *Fl.Div.7* on average had been 1 hour and 40 minutes. That for the Ju 52 dropping paratroopers into the area of operations of *22.(LL)Inf.Div.* had been about 15 minutes shorter. One assumes about the same time for the flight back, and at least one hour for refueling, loading troops and material and small repairs, the earliest time for the take-off of the second wave would have been around 0930hrs. Thereby, it becomes evident, that the forces arriving on the airfield at Waalhaven in the first hours after the parachuting of *III./FschJgRgt.1* must have been transported in the first wave.

79   The 40 men including the engineer squad, who had been planned for a security task at the Noord River, had been able to fight through to a larger group of Germans south of Delft, which had formed from the passengers and crews of emergency-landed Ju 52.

80   After the appearance of German troops close to the northern bank of the Oude Maas Group Kil reinforced the platoon of III/39th Inf.Rgt. who were tasked with the protection of the bridge alongside two platoons and two heavy machine-guns from III/28th Inf.Rgt. Some of these probably had conducted the reconnaissance-in-force to the northern bank of the Oude Maas toward Barendrecht.

81   There the command post of III Searchlight Detachment was set up. However, it was relocated after the clash with the paratroopers.

After the parachute platoon failed to deal with the Dutch anti-aircraft battery in the Charlois polder and *Hauptmann* Schulz's platoon failing to achieve surrender by negotiation, *II./ InfRgt.16* received its first mission. *Oberst* Kreysing ordered its 7th and the majority of its 6th Company, to attack the position of the anti-aircraft battery. Its commanding officer, however, meanwhile decided to make the guns and the fire-control gear unusable, and to withdraw his personnel to Hoekse Waard. This action was accomplished almost unobserved by the Germans, as they had not yet reached the bridge south of Barendrecht over which the withdrawal would take place.

When the two companies of *II./InfRgt.16* reported the position of the Dutch near Smitshoek vacated, *Oberst* Kreysing ordered them back to Hordijk. Instead of the still incomplete *I./InfRgt.16*, he now sent the *7./InfRgt.16* to relieve the paratroopers at the bridges at Dordrecht. In the evening *Oberst* Kreysing dispatched a platoon of *6./InfRgt.16*, reinforced by an anti-tank gun, to the ferry site on the western bank of the Noord, near Ridderkerk. There it was to execute the surveillance mission instead of the engineer squad from *2./PiBtl.22*, which had not yet arrived.

A little after midday the air transport units arriving on the airfield at Waalhaven managed to land and leave again without major difficulties. A few of the Ju 52s, which had been damaged by anti-aircraft fire during the approach flight and were unfit for flying, had to be left behind. Like the Fokker G-1s which had been destroyed during the air attack in the early morning, they were also moved from the runways to the edges of the airfield. For the time being only a Dutch anti-aircraft battery, positioned near Vlaardingen east of Rotterdam, was troublesome as it shot down one aircraft and damaged several others.[82]

Among the troops incoming at this time was the first half of *FschGeschBttr 7* under the battery commander, *Oberleutnant* Schram. Arriving with the battalion were two mountain guns and their crews, two ammunition carts, the draught horses and some personnel for fire control and target acquisition.[83]

By this time the Dutch high command was clearly aware of the threat, largely as a result of the unimpeded use of Waalhaven by the Germans for the entire area of Fortress Holland south of Rotterdam, and the development of plans to counter this threat commenced. Consequntly the forces which were available on short notice had already received orders for immediate action.

---

82   The employment of Reserve-Major Thomas as negotiator by *Hauptmann* Schulz has gained particular attention from Dutch historians. The latter, rightfully, has been accused of repeated offenses against the rules of war for this attitude. Moreover, the death of Thomas has been seen as a deliberate act by the Germans during the firefight with the anti-aircraft soldiers. In the meantime, most Dutch historians have moved away from the view that Thomas, under threat of his life, was forced to act as negotiator.

83   However it should be noted that on 10 May 11th Company had also lost six killed in the bridgehead and one more in Rhoon.

Prior to this, the British Royal Air Force made its appearance.[84] Six Blenheim 1 F bombers from 600 Squadron, that had taken off in England with a mission to strafe landed troops and transport aircraft, were engaged by Bf 110s of *3./ZG 1* over Pernis at about 1230hrs. The German fighters had escorted bomber and dive-bomber formations into the airspace west of Rotterdam[85] and managed to ambush their opponents from above. Four of these were shot down immediately. The other two flew on, pursued by some Bf 110s. One of them crashed before it could reach the airfield. The remaining aircraft flew one strafing attack, the pilot further succeeded in escaping his pursuers and returned home. However the aircraft was beyond repair and had to be scrapped.

A short time after midday the landings on the airfield at Waalhaven suddenly ceased as the aircrews returning from Waalhaven erroneously reported obstructions. The reports were overrated by the liaison staff of *Fl.Div.7* in Wiedenbrück, causing them to not only cancel all further operations, but to also recall air transport units already in the air. As the radio communication between the liaison staff and Student's command post was, from time to time, interrupted for technical reasons and inquiries by the latter had gone out belatedly, it took almost three valuable hours before the mistake was rectified.

Just prior to the interruption of the air-landing activities *10./InfRgt.16* was unloaded on the airfield. As the route to the bridges through the center of Rotterdam-South was still blocked by Dutch infantry *Oberst* Kreysing ordered the employment of *10./InfRgt.16* against the block. Upon their arrival, and after having been briefed by the commander of the engineers, the company commander deployed his unit for an attack against the Dutch position at the Afrikaander-Plein. He assessed the strength of the defence correctly and requested support from the mortars of *12./InfRgt.16* from Noordereiland. The precisely directed fire forced the defenders back step by step and when they were finally enclosed onto a very small piece of ground and running out of ammunition Major de Vos decided to end the hopeless resistance. At 1740hrs, after eight hours of fighting, he surrendered the forces under his command. He and the other officers were subsequently brought to Noordereiland. Under its last remaining officer, *2./PiBtl.22* was now also moved onto this island. For the time being *10./InfRgt.16* remained behind for mop-up actions and for the protection of Rotterdam-South.

In the early afternoon, Dutch aircraft attacked Waalhaven for the first time. Five Fokker C-Xs[86] which approached from Bergen, managed to drop their 50kg bombs on the south-

84   It was equipped with three 75mm guns and some anti-aircraft machine-guns. Throughout the five days of fighting against Holland the Germans had been unable to neutralize this battery. During this time it had probably brought down ten German aircraft of various types.

85   For the air transport of one mountain gun, its ammunition cart, the draught-horse and a crew of five, two Ju 52s had been required.

86   The British high command had directed its main attention toward Belgium and Northern France. But little opportunity was seen in London for a successful defence by the Dutch. Nevertheless their request for support could not be ignored. Moreover, it had also been in Britain's own interest, to deny the *Luftwaffe* the airfields in north-western Holland as a springboard for the air war against Britain for as long as

western part of the airfield. By these means a few of the Ju 52s parked there were damaged. Turning back to Bergen, they were attacked by German fighters which were guarding the airspace over Waalhaven. Two Fokkers were forced to conduct emergency landings. The other three, although damaged, managed to land again in Bergen.

At 1410hrs, Dutch artillery positioned in the north of Rotterdam fired for about 30 minutes onto the airfield, destroying one (of the two) *Nachrichten-Ju* with a direct hit, a few other transport aircraft were damaged by splinters. Four soldiers of *LuftNachrKp.7* who were manning communication equipment were killed. The cratering effect of the shells, which for this purpose had been fitted with delay-action fuses, remained negligible and did not fulfil the hopes of the Dutch.

The smoke from the impacts of the artillery had scarcely dispersed when again Dutch aircraft, at an altitude of about 1,000m, approached the airfield (the three bombers were Fokker T-Vs, with six Fokker D-XXI fighters).[87] However this time Bf 109s from *6./JG 27* and *1./JG 1*, flying protection over Ijsselmonde, were also present. They engaged the Dutch fighters in aerial combat and managed to shoot one of them down. The three bombers dropped their load of 400kg of bombs almost undisturbed on the eastern part of the airfield. Only one D-XXI was able to disengage from the aerial combat and to follow behind the bombers, strafing the airfield with its machine-guns. The German fighters, which in the meantime had driven off their opponents, now succeeded in catching up with the bombers and shot down two of them. As these had attempted to escape by low-level flight their aircrews could not use their parachutes. Seven airmen perished in the crashes. Only one was saved, seriously wounded. The D XXI which had joined the attack with the bombers was heavily damaged by pursuing German fighters, but, like the other four Dutch fighters, was able to get back to Schiphol. On the German side the physical effects of the attack had been minimal. Some losses among personnel fell mainly upon aircrews of Ju 52s who had remained at their aircraft during the attack.

Considerably more efficient than the Dutch action was the subsequent action by the R.A.F. At about 1600 hrs eight Blenheim IVs skilfully conducted a low-level attack against the airfield.[88] They were engaged by the 2cm guns of *leFlakBttr.106* as no German fighters were present over Ijsselmonde. Although each of the Blenheims dropped only 90kg of bombs most of these burst among Ju 52s which were in the process of unloading. Of the 32 transport aircraft parked on the airfield eight were destroyed.[89] Of the arriving half of *FschPzAbwKp.7* two anti-tank guns, which had not yet been unloaded, were destroyed and an entire gun-crew wounded. A direct hit killed the crew of a 2cm flak gun and destroyed the weapon. Following this successful surprise attack all of the R.A.F attackers returned

---

possible. Therefore, after the British embassy in Den Haag early in the morning of 10 May had reported the loss of the airfields at Waalhaven and Ypenburg, the decision was taken to release parts of bomber-command for employment over Holland.

87   There, some dive bombers of *IV./LG 1* had attacked the Dutch destroyer *Van Galen* on its way from Hoek van Holland to the bridges in Rotterdam. Near-misses had damaged the ship below the waterline so seriously, that it had to enter the Merwede port, where it sank.

88   These aircraft, assigned to the Strategic Reconnaissance Detachment, had been used as light bombers. After a first attack of 9 Fokker C-Xs against the airfield near Valkenburg, Five remained for use against Waalhaven. Each had carried 8 bombs of 50kg.

89   The aircraft had taken off from Amsterdam-Schiphol at 1355hrs. At 0910hrs, they had already flown an attack against the airfield at Ockenburg.

home undamaged as there was no German fighter protection over Waalhaven present at the time.

In the morning patrols from *III./FschJgRgt.1* advanced to the western bank of the Noord but withdrew again as no enemy had been observed in this area. The reinforced platoon from *6./InfRgt.16*, which was tasked with the protection of the ferry site east of Ridderkerk, reached its destination early in the evening. At 2000hrs, during the reconnaissance of a suitable position for his platoon, *Oberleutnant* Brückner discovered a traffic bridge spanning the Noord to a length of 183m, just south of the town of Alblasserdam and on the eastern bank of the river,[90] its swing-section close to its eastern end remained open.[91] *Oberleutnant* Brückner reported the results of his observations to the command post of *InfRgt.16* and deployed a part of his forces for the surveillance of the bridge at its western ramp, the other part at the ferry site east of Ridderkerk. However the Germans had failed to notice that Dutch troops had already entered Alblasserdam from the east in the late afternoon. It was only at around midnight, when the noise of many motor vehicles approaching from the east toward the eastern bank of the Noord could be heard, that Brückner urgently requested reinforcements.

In the course of the late afternoon the second half of *FschGeschBttr.7*, commanded by *Oberleutnant* Loesch arrived at Waalhaven. It remained on Ijsselmonde under the command of *Fl.Div.7*. In the meantime the first half of the battery was ordered to support *Gruppe Süd*. After it had crossed the traffic bridge at Dordrecht, where some of its soldiers were wounded by fire from the western edge of the town, it engaged a Dutch artillery observation post. Afterwards it moved on to Tweede Tol with its horse-drawn guns; there it received the mission to support *II./FschJgRgt.1* from a position just north of the Moerdijk bridges. Late in the evening the half-battery arrived, established its firing position and set up an observation post south of the bridges. On the way to the half-battery and in total darkness the sidecar motorcycle carrying *Oberleutnant* Schram hit a truck which the Dutch had placed across the auto-route to prevent the landing of transport aircraft. The *Feldwebel* with Schram was killed and the officer injured.

In the early evening *II./FschJgRgt.2* under *Hauptmann* Pietzonka landed at Waalhaven with its battle HQ and three incomplete companies.[92] As was planned, the battalion immediately moved off to the area around Barendrecht. There, it established contact with security elements near the northern end of the bridge across the Oude Maas and, upon request by *Oberst* Kreysing, the battalion was placed under his command. *Hauptmann* Pietzonka now was tasked with the protection of the northern bank of the Oude Maas

---

90   These aircraft, assigned to 15 Squadron, had taken off from Alconbury, England at 1500hrs.

91   The Blenheim crews had claimed 16 Ju 52s destroyed. This appears to be exaggerated, although it is possible that some Ju 52s, parked unfit for flying at the edges of the airfield had again been hit.

92   As part of the new auto-route Gorinchem-Rotterdam, the bridge was opened for traffic in November 1939. It had almost certainly been detected by reconnaissance planes of the *Luftwaffe* in the weeks preceding the attack against Holland. Information, however had neither found an entry into the German standard map for Holland, nor had it been passed to the command of the *Luftlande-Korps*.

south of Barendrecht. Actions beyond this mission, such as an energetic thrust against the bridge at Spijkenisse, which was reported occupied at both ends by Dutch infantry, were not yet initiated. The elements of *I./InfRgt.16* which had initially been tasked with surveillance south of Barendrecht, remained deployed there for the time being.

Later in the evening the air-landing element of *FschSanKp.7* with the personnel and equipment for the establishment of a field hospital was unloaded at Waalhaven. Commanded by *Oberstabsarzt* Dr.Neumann,[93] the company was to set up its hospital in Feyenoord. Just before dark at around 2200 hrs most of the still missing parts of *I./InfRgt.16* arrived on the airfield so that the battalion was now available for employment as a whole. Although it had arrived, *1./InfRgt.72* was not without losses during the approach flight. Nevertheless, the company was ordered to advance into the western part of Ijsselmonde during the first light of the next morning.[94]

Unexpectedly *4./InfRgt.65* and parts of *7./InfRgt.65*[95] had also arrived at Waalhaven late in the morning. The confusing development of the situation around Den Haag had prevented these units, which were planned to be elements of the second wave for *22.(LL) Inf.Div.*, from being landed on the originally designated airfields. As a consequence the transport aircraft with *I./InfRgt.65* aboard had been forced to look for alternate landing sites causing their close order to disintegrate and only *4./InfRgt.65* was brought to Waalhaven as a whole. The whereabouts of the other units of *I./InfRgt.65* remained unknown to the command of *Fl.Div.7*. In order to support the troops which were fighting for Rotterdam with whatever infantry could be made available on short notice, the liaison staff at Wiedenbrück ordered the air transport of *6./InfRgt.72* to Waalhaven. Immediately after its arrival this company dispatched to the hard-pressed *III./InfRgt.16*.

As a result of the troublesome situation at the airfields around Den Haag four Ju 52s, each with an anti-tank gun of *14./InfRgt.65* aboard, at 1600hrs had also flown to Waalhaven. As one of them was shot down by Dutch anti-aircraft fire during the landing approach, only three anti-tank guns and their crews had been unloaded.

According to the report of *Oberstleutnant* de Boer, the commanding officer of *Art. Rgt.22*, who had arrived with a few men of his staff at Waalhaven in the afternoon after the airfields in the operational area of *22.(LL)Inf.Div.* had become unusable, for the first time *Generalleutnant* Student received a coherent picture of the critical situation in the

---

93   This measure was taken upon the request of the mayor of Alblasserdam, who had observed and reported the German attack against the airfield at Waalhaven.

94   The battalion had to be brought along by transport aircraft as its personnel, except that of 6th Company, had not yet been jump trained. The strength of each of the three companies was 60-80 men as a maximum.

95   Dr. Heinrich Neumann, born in 1908 and entered military service in 1932 after studying medicine. He transferred to the *Luftwaffe* in 1934, was promoted to *Oberstabsarzt* and passed pilot training. In 1936 he was made *Truppenarzt* in the Legion Condor in Spain. In 1938 he moved to the parachute force and was company commander of *FschSanKp.7*, as of May 1939. From there he was promoted to *Regimentsarzt*. He saw combat action in Holland in May 1940 and was made commander of *FschSanAbt.7* in June 1940. He then moved to the *Luftlande-Sturmregiment* as *Regimentsarzt* and saw combat action on Crete in May 1941. On 21 August 1941 he was decorated with the *Ritterkreuz* for his service in the struggle for Crete. In 1942-43 he completed assignements as medical officer in the east, outside of the parachute force. Subsequently he was promoted to *Oberfeldarzt*. Returned to the parachute force in 1944 as chief medical officer in *II.Fallschirm-Korps*. At the end of the war he was *Oberstarzt* in a hospital. After the war Dr. Neumann became a physician.

command area of *Generalleutnant* Graf von Sponeck. Up to that time only a few garbled radio messages from the staff of *22.(LL)Inf.Div.* had been picked up. However it was only from a situation report by radio from *Luftflotte 2*, sent at 2010hrs, that the command of *Fl.Div.7* realized that *22.(LL)Inf.Div.* had in fact failed to accomplish its mission.[96]

Until late into the night the staffs of *Generalleutnant* Student and *Oberst* Kreysing had remained ignorant of the arrival of first Dutch forces in the vicinity of Alblasserdam, let alone about their identity, although this area had received some more attention after the still vague reports from the security elements at the western bank of the Noord. Reports from air reconnaissance assets could not be expected until after first light on 11 May.

The decision of the Dutch high command to eliminate the German air bridgehead on the island of Ijsselmonde had been taken in the late afternoon. According to the plans for the defence of Holland III Army Corps and the Light Division (Colonel van der Bijl) had already been directed to move from their assembly areas Hertogenbosch-Eindhoven-Tilburg across the Maas and Waal rivers into the southern part of Fortress Holland. Subsequently the Light Division was to come under the command of the commandant of the Fortress in order to cover the Merwede front between Dordrecht and Gorinchem. However at around 1740 hrs, when its divisional headquarters had arrived in Alblasserdam, this mission had become obsolete as the order to seize Waalhaven by an attack across the Noord had just arrived. Up to this point the division command were completely unaware of the events in the south of Fortress Holland. Further inquiries by Colonel van der Bijl around 1840hrs revealed that the attack had to commence immediately after the end of the bombing of the airfield by the R.A.F., scheduled for the time-frame between midnight and 0400 hrs. The staff of the Light Division finalized the attack-order at 1925hrs. Accordingly, after the crossing of the Noord, the 1st Bicycle Infantry Regiment, which was reinforced by an artillery detachment, was to advance on the right, the equally reinforced 2nd Bicycle Infantry Regiment on the left. The actual attack was to be launched forward of the line at Bolnes–Barendrecht (about 3km north of Hordijk). Both bicycle infantry regiments were to cross the Noord over the bridge at Alblasserdam. On the way to the line of departure, the 2nd Bicycle Infantry Regiment was to detach one of its battalions via Zwijndrecht, as reinforcement for the garrison of Dordrecht.[97]

By early afternoon the most forward units of the Light Division had crossed the Bergsche Maas using the bridges at Keizersveer and Drongelen, which lay about 10-15km east of the bridges at Moerdijk. The *Luftwaffe* had only appeared over this area once and in the ensuing air attack eight soldiers of a machine-gun company were killed and 10 wounded.[98] At the

---

96   During the planning of the airborne operation against Fortress Holland *InfRgt.72* and *1/PiBtl.88* from *47.Inf.Div.* was planned for *22.(LL)Inf.Div.* as a substitute for *InfRgt.16*, which was assigned to *Fl.Div.7*. The unfortunate development of the situation in the operational area of *22.(LL)Inf.Div.* had led to the decision to also employ the units of *InfRgt.72* with *Fl.Div.7*.

97   Other parts of this company had been landed at Valkenburg. Still others had come down near Hoek van Holland after emergency landings of their Ju 52.

98   The development of the situation of *22.(LL)Inf.Div.* will be dealt with later in the text. It is interesting to note here that the situation report did not contain any information about the initial movements of strong Dutch forces from Noord Brabant into the Fortress Holland, and about the appearance of formidable mechanized French forces on their way into the area east of Antwerp. At least the movements of the latter had already been detected by the *Luftwaffe*.

time that the attack order was issued for the Light Division, the two forward battalions of the 2nd Bicycle Infantry Regiment, which had formed the point of the Division's marching columns, had been ferried across the Waal and were about 20km east of Alblasserdam.

A German operation, which was planned from Hoekse Waard against Waalhaven remained undetected. On the orders of III Army Corps the 3rd Border Infantry Battalion were released from a security mission along the Belgian-Dutch border, in order to be able to take over the defence of the bridgehead around the former fortress at Willemstad (at the mouth of Hollandsch Diep, about 14km west of Moerdijk). The battalion had just arrived at its new destination when it had received an order by Group Spui to assemble without delay at Numansdorp, on the northern bank of Hollandsch Diep. However, it remained totally unknown to the battalion commander that Lieutenant General van Andel had issued an order at 1335hrs to Group Kil, commanding them to employ the unit for an attack against Waalhaven via Barendrecht.

Supported by the ferry service, Haringsvliet Oost, the ferrying of the battalion to Numansdorp commenced in the early afternoon and was completed by about 2040hrs. The *Luftwaffe* had appeared only once and an aircraft dropped magnetic mines between the two ferry points. This forced part of the battalion's heavy equipment to stay behind, as the danger to ferries was considered too high. At 2140hrs the battalion commander received orders for the attack against Waalhaven at the command post of Group Kil.[99] There he was informed about the attack of the Light Division from the east, as the timing for the attack was scheduled for the end of the British bombing of the airfield previously.

The commanding officer of 3rd Border Infantry Battalion had planned the crossing of the Oude Maas so that two of his companies were to cross with boats at the ferry site at Goidschalxsoord and another one, also with boats, at Puttershoek. They were given the mission to clear the area north of the lift-bridge south of Barendrecht from the enemy. The fourth company, who were reinforced by heavy machine-guns, anti-tank guns and a mortar, was to move across the bridge. From the area around Barendrecht all four companies were to advance in unison.

There was no coordination of the attack plans between the commands of Group Kil and the Light Division, so that the attacking forces had no knowledge of the other unit's actions. The command of Group Kil had assumed that German security elements on the northern bank of the Oude Maas were weak and no artillery support had been foreseen for the attack of 3rd Border Infantry Battalion.

However the Dutch artillery on Hoekse Waard had not remained idle and it was ordered by Group Kil to support the action initiated for the taking of the bridges at Dordrecht on 11 May. For this aim at 1310hrs II/28th Inf.Rgt. had received the order to cross the Kil at Gravendeel after the onset of darkness and to advance via Amstelwijk toward the bridges.[100]

With the cover of darkness and by artillery fire on suspected German positions north and south of Wieldrecht, the attacking force – two companies and the staff of II/28th Inf.Rgt., one company of I/34th Inf.Rgt. and half a machine-gun company, led by the

---

99 This plan for the attack makes it plain that Colonel van der Bijl, in his telephone inquiry, had not been informed by Lieutenant General van Andel about the actual situation on the bridges at Dordrecht and on Ijsselmonde. Therefore the plan had been doomed from the beginning.

100 The air defense forces in the operational area of Group Merwede – two heavy air-defence batteries and two anti-aircraft machine-gun platoons – had been concentrated in the area of Gorinchem around midday. From there the 114th Anti-Aircraft Battery had shot down a He 111 and probably also a Ju 52.

commander of II/28th Inf.Rgt., Major Ravelli – succeeded in crossing the Kil undetected by the Germans. At about 2125hrs the force was assembled in Wieldrecht. Up to this time it had not met with any resistance. After the companies received their further orders the attack force moved on to Amstelwijk, which was bombarded for 30 minutes by artillery from Hoekse Waard.[101] When Battalion Ravelli arrived in Amstelwijk shortly after 2200hrs it encountered only a provisional field hospital which was being run by German and Dutch medical officers.[102] Major Ravelli now allowed his troops to eat and rest as he intended to launch the attack against the bridges before first light on 11 May.

The decision by the Dutch high command to substantially strengthen the defence of the northern part of Rotterdam and of the northern bank of the Nieuwe Maas was suspected by the command of *Fl.Div.7*. However no signs of respective actions had yet been detected. Indeed the commander-in-chief of the Dutch Field Army, at around 1410hrs, was ordered to make infantry to the strength of a regiment available and also some artillery from the army corps tasked with the protection of the eastern front of Fortress Holland and to dispatch these troops to Rotterdam on 11 May.

Generalleutnant Student had largely remained in the dark about the enemy situation south of his area of operation for a number of reasons. Firstly the situation report by *Luftflotte 2* at 2010hrs had not covered the area south of the line Hollandsch Diep-Merwede-Waal and reconnaissance in depth by their own forces south of the Moerdijk bridges had not been possible because of the tight containment of the bridgehead by Dutch troops. Thus Student remained ignorant of the fact that Noord Brabant had already become the arena for far-reaching events. The hope of the Dutch high command to prevent the outflanking of the heavily fortified Peel-Raam position by a solid front of French divisions south of it had been shattered already some time prior to the German attack because of the refusal of the French to move that far forward. General Winkelman thereupon decided to concentrate the defence of Holland on its core area – the provinces of Noord Holland, Zuid Holland and a part of the province of Utrecht – with the aim of retaining these regions to the utmost and waiting for the counter-strike of the Allies. According to the respective planning the transfer into Fortress Holland of III Army Corps from its assembly area in the rear of the Peel-Raam Line and of the Light Division who were kept available in the area around Tilburg, was initiated a few hours after the start of the German attack. For a time sensitive defence of the thinned-out Peel-Raam-position and to cover the departure of the formations, the Peel Division was formed from a number of infantry battalions from various regiments and by an artillery detachment. The command of the Peel Division was given to Colonel. L. J. Schmidt. In conjunction with the extraction of III Army Corps he had also been assigned the function of territorial commander in the province of Noord

101 On the morning of 10 May, Group Kil had under its command: 28th Inf.Rgt., III/34th Inf.Rgt., 12th Machine-gun Company, one platoon of 11th Machine-gun Company, 14th Engineer Company, Detachment Willemsdorp with 2 platoons from I/41st Inf.Rgt. and a heavy machine-gun platoon of 3rd Border Infantry Battalion, III/14th Art.Rgt., I/17th Art.Rgt., I/ and II/25th Art.Rgt. .

102 As the attack-order for the Light Division had not yet been issued, the employment of II/28th Inf.Rgt. has to be seen as a stand-alone decision within the command of Group Kil.

Brabant. As the speedy arrival of the first French forces in Noord Brabant, announced by General Gamelin to General Winkelman in a telephone conversation in the morning of 10 May, could be reckoned with, the role of liaison officer on the Dutch side had also been assigned to Colonel Schmidt. However he had not received any instructions from his superiors.

As a result of the unfolding critical situation at Mill,[103] where German troops had appeared after they had crossed the Maas over the bridge at Gennep, at 2210hrs Colonel Schmidt was ordered to surrender all of the Peel-Raam Line. He had feared being cut off with the majority of the Peel Division if the Germans were able to break through at Mill. As a replacement defensive position he selected the western bank of the canal at Zuid-Willemsvaart, stretching from Hertogenbosch through the area east of Eindhoven and to the area north of Weert, where it constituted the forward edge of the Peel-Raam position. Throughout the day he had very little influence on the actions of his division as he spent his time changing the location of his command post four times before finally settling down in the evening in Tilburg. At midnight he was informed about the arrival of a French detachment in the area around Breda.[104] It was a reconnaissance-group, designated Groupement Lestoquoi and dispatched by 1st Light Mechanized Division (1er DLM) to cover its deployment.[105]

In the early hours of 11 May its commander, Lieutenant Colonel Lesoquoi, arrived in Tilburg and reported to Colonel Schmidt. He explained that his unit was to be the spearhead of the forces from the French 7th Army (General Giraud) who were approaching from Antwerp. He stated that his mission was to cover the advance of the first units of the main force and provide the safe conduct of General Mittelhauser to the Dutch high command in Den Haag.[106] According to his instructions from the command of 7th Army he was to employ his group in a covering position between Oosterhout (about 18km south-east of the Moerdijk bridges) and Tilburg behind the Wilhelmina Canal. The forces of Colonel Schmidt were to deploy into positions between Tilburg and the area around Turnhout, just south of the Dutch-Belgian border and establish contact there with the Belgian 18th Inf. Div. Furthermore, he indicated that the French high command would not consider the deployment of French forces forward of the Wilhelmina Canal.[107]

Until the evening of 10 May little intelligence was available for the command of *Fl.Div.7* regarding the enemy situation in the western part of the island of Ijsselmonde. Intelligence reports had not been obtained from aerial reconnaissance assets or by patrols

---

103 It is interesting to note that Group Kil obviously had not foreseen the participation in the blocking of the German line of communication between Tweede Tol and the Dordrecht bridges by the two companies of I/28th Inf.Rgt., positioned in the south-eastern part of the island of Dordrecht. These could easily have established contact with the Battalion Ravelli via Dordrecht. Their additional employment would probably have increased the chances of success considerably.

104 Most wounded from the fighting in the late morning had already been transferred to hospitals in Dordecht.

105 However an immediate breakthrough was prevented for a short time by the employment of a squadron of hussars on order of III Army Corps.

106 In his memoirs Student mentions French forces in Noord Brabant for the first time on 11 May. As he had sent anti-tank guns to the south already in the night 10/11 May, it could be that he had received some information about the French at that time.

107 The Group was composed of 2e GRCA (a corps-level recce detachment) and of 5e GRDI (a division level recce detachment). It was equipped with a considerable number of Panhard AMD 178 armored cars, a platoon of Hotchkiss H-35 light tanks, several motorcycle infantry platoons, a platoon of anti-tank guns and some mortars.

sent forward from the area around Barendrecht. This left the command ignorant about the relatively strong protection of the petroleum installation by a company from 29th Inf. Rgt. and four anti-aircraft machine-gun platoons in a position, covered from three sides by water. The picture of the enemy on either side of the lift-bridge across the Oude Maas at Spijkenisse also remained unclear, after a patrol on the way to this objective had been repulsed around 0940hrs at Hoogvliet, 1.5km north-east of the bridge.[108]

By the evening of 10 May the situation in the operational area of *Fl.Div.7* represented itself as follows:

The Division was able to accomplish its initial missions by parachute assaults, which had taken the Dutch by surprise. The three parachute infantry battalions had suffered only small losses except for the unfortunate action of *3./FschJgRgt.1* at the southern edge of Dordrecht. Where the landed troops had been engaged in combat they had shown the aggression fostered during their training. They had quickly decided most of the engagements in their favour owing mostly to the initiative of the tactical leaders on all levels and the physical fitness and combative spirit of all soldiers. Led from the front by their officers and non-commissioned officers the men of *III./InfRgt.16* who had been employed against the bridges in Rotterdam, had equaled the deeds of the paratroopers. While it had been possible, although under increasing difficulties, to reinforce the troops in the area around Rotterdam after the airfield at Waalhaven was seized, until the late afternoon *Gruppe Süd* had to get along with the parachute units dropped in the early morning.

Disturbances in the air transport plan, mainly caused by the Dutch air defenses, but also the initial reactions of the enemy against the air bridgeheads, however, had made it necessary to alter the original operational plan already in the late afternoon:

- *I./InfRgt.16*, planned for the relief of the paratroopers at the bridges at Dordrecht, had initially arrived incomplete. Instead, one company from *II./InfRgt.16* was sent to the south.
- *II./InfRgt.16* (less 7th Company), and the only available artillery battery unexpectedly had to be deployed for the defense at the Noord.
- *II./FschJgRgt.2* had been tied down on the northern bank of the Oude Maas opposite Dutch forces on Hoekse Waard, and therefore released as a reserve for the Division command.
- *Kräftegruppe von Choltitz* had come under the utmost strain at the bridges in Rotterdam. Renewed efforts by the Dutch after the arrival of reinforcements could even lead to its destruction.

Generalleutnant Student soon decided that he was not willing to accept the situation which had developed through the day. He recognized the first reactions of the enemy against all three pairs of bridges even though these had been conducted with insufficient forces and without appropriate coordination. His perceived attitude stood true all the more as after the results of his operations around Den Haag, his adversary now had the opportunity

---

108 General Mittelhauser had been assigned the function as liaison officer in order to coordinate the operations between the French and the Dutch forces.

to concentrate on the recapture of Waalhaven. Only an early success at the airfield would deprive *Fl.Div.7* of further reinforcements. In this case the air bridgeheads would have to be held with the troops to hand, with particular attention to those around the bridges at Dordrecht and Moerdijk, in order to safeguard the entry of mechanized forces into the south of Fortress Holland.

The commands of *Fl.Div.7* and of the subordinate *InfRgt.16* were clearly conscious of this threat. Consequently plans for 11 May to prevent forces of the enemy from advancing toward the airfield gained high priority beside the ongoing task, to retain the bridges at Moerdijk and Dordrecht at all costs.

In the light of the current situation, *Generalleutnant* Student contemplated abandoning the hard-pressed bridgehead in Rotterdam-North and in the worst case retaining only the southern bank of the Nieuwe Maas.[109] He had made up his mind to counter the threat against the bridges at Dordrecht and the line of communication from there to Tweede Tol without delay. He regarded their possession, together with that of the Moerdijk bridges, as an indispensable prerequisite for the entry of mechanized ground forces into Fortress Holland from the south. Therefore at around midnight he decided to return *III./FschJgRgt.1* to *Oberst* Bräuer for employment in the operational area of *Gruppe Süd*.[110] In spite of the suspected attack of Dutch forces across the Noord on 11 May he assessed the situation on Ijsselmonde as being sufficiently stable, as he could count on the reserve elements of *InfRgt.16* and additional air-landing forces, now diverted to him after the failure of the mission of *22.(LL)Inf.Div.*

The release of *III./FschJgRgt.1* left the command of *Fl.Div.7*, excluding its command and control elements, with only three anti-tank guns of the half *FschPzAbwKp.7*, which had been landed in the afternoon. The division's fourth gun had been assigned to *III./InfRgt.16* already in Germany.

Even late in the evening *Oberst* Kreysing did not feel compelled to reinforce *Kräftegruppe von Choltitz*. He kept *I./InfRgt.16*, except the elements on guard at the northern bank of the Oude Maas, at his disposal for later operations in the west of the island of Ijsselmonde. When more of *3./InfRgt.16* was landed around 2200hrs he intensified the reconnaissance in the area. *4./InfRgt.65* were kept as infantry reserve after they arrived unexpectedly.

The first reports about the unfavorable conduct of the operations of *22.(LL)Inf.Div.*, which were then confirmed by radio from *Luftflotte 2*, made *Generalleutnant* Student realize that the gravest hours were still before him. It was now essential to organize the forces which had already arrived and to bring the troops that were still waiting in Germany for deployment

---

109 It had become known to the Dutch that the French high command with the employment of elements of 7th Army into the area around Breda had primarily aimed for the protection of Antwerp and the approaches toward the mouth of the Scheldt River. The Breda variant of the Dijle plan mainly had served this aim.

110 Shortly prior to 0900hrs, after German troops had been observed on the northern bank of the Oude Maas near Rhoon, Group Spui had dispatched a reinforced platoon from II/34th Inf.Rgt. to the western end of the bridge at Spijkenisse. About 1210hrs, two platoons of I/39th Inf.Rgt. and one from 39th Border Infantry Company had additionally arrived there. The platoon from II/34th Inf.Rgt. had advanced to the eastern edge of Hoogvliet. It had repulsed the German patrol and subsequently had withdrawn to the bridge.

to the anticipated focal points of the battle for Fortress Holland, and to safeguard the movement of the relief forces of the *Heer*.

The radio message from *Luftflotte 2* in the evening contained no details about the situation in the operational area of *22.(LL)Inf.Div*. The instruction to this division to assemble its landed forces in the area south of Delft indicated that these were to be concentrated for a thrust against Rotterdam from the north, although no respective mission had yet been planned. To support such an action by *Fl.Div.7* was out of the question for the time being, as, in the light of the developing enemy situation, its units had taken up a defensive poisition. In order to move its forces into an assembly area south of Delft *22.(LL)Inf. Div*. would have to rely strongly on the support of *Flieger-Korps Putzier*. Beside ongoing air support in the struggle for the bridges in Rotterdam, massive employment of the *Luftwaffe* for *Fl.Div.7* would become necessary on 11 May to successfully defend against the anticipated strong attack of Dutch forces across the Noord. Respective requests were sent out during the night hours. The assignment of additional air assets from the main areas of operation of the *Wehrmacht* could only be counted upon in the case of utmost emergency, as the vast majority of the *Luftwaffe* was tied up in support of the German armored wedges and in counter operations against the formidable French and British air forces. Unknown to *Generalleutnant* Student, the *Luftwaffe* nevertheless had become active south of the operation area of *Fl.Div.7*. When the advance of French mechanized forces into the area around Antwerp had been detected in the afternoon, dive bombers were sent forward to destroy the tunnels underneath the Scheldt river in this city, in order to delay the movements of the enemy into Noord Brabant. However the dive bombers had been unsuccessful.

On first day of the attack the Ju 52s and the paratroopers that were tasked with the seizure of the three airfields around Den Haag had taken off 30 minutes ahead of the first wave of the air-landing troops of *22.(LL)Inf.Div*. A few minutes prior to their arrival over the drop zones, aircraft of *Flieger-Korps Putzier* had attacked the airfields at Valkenburg and Ypenburg and Dutch troops identified in the area around Den Haag. A preceding air campaign against the heavy and medium Dutch anti-aircraft guns around at Den Haag and Delft and along the Waal river, in spite of the high threat which these posed for the approaching air transport formations, had been ruled out, as it would have led to the loss of surprise. Moreover dive bombers, which were best suited to attack point-targets such as anti-aircraft sites, had not been made available for *Flieger-Korps Putzier*.

The airfield at Ypenburg was rated the most important for the operations of *22.(LL)Inf.Div*. It was located about 2.5km away from the southern edge of Den Haag and as such lent itself as the starting point for a quick thrust into the city, in order to eliminate the highest Dutch governmental and military authorities. Moreover, its size and technical infrastructure would allow for the landing of complete units. The de Vliet Canal, which passed from Delft to Den Haag immediately west of the airfield, would provide some protection against conceivable counter-attacks by the Dutch. Sufficiently strong forces had to be planned for the occupation of the area between the airfield at Delft as the interference of the garrison of Delft had to be reckoned with, and the auto-route leading from Rotterdam to Den Haag via Delft could be used as an alternate landing site for transport aircraft.

The operation plan of *22.(LL)Inf.Div.* for the airfield at Ypenburg had taken account of these conditions:

- The preceding air attacks to destroy the airfield command positions.
- Parachuting of *I./FschJgRgt.2* (less its 3rd Company) immediately west, south and north of the airfield. Seizure of the airfield by the paratroopers and subsequent establishment of security positions in the direction toward Delft and at the Hoorn Bridge across the de Vliet Canal, located at the south-western edge of Den Haag.
- Landing on the airfield by *KGr z.b.V.12* of the staff and the signals platoon of *InfRgt.65* under *Oberst* Friemel, together with this regiment's 6th and 8th companies.
- Landing with *KGr z.b.V.12* of the staff, the motorcycle messenger platoon and the military police section of *22.(LL)Inf.Div.*, as well as the staff and the 2nd Company of *NachrAbt.22*, the reconnaissance platoon of *InfRgt.65*, one platoon of *3./PiBtl.22* and *13./InfRgt.47* (infantry guns).

The second wave of troops with the majority of *InfRgt.65* and other units of *22.(LL) Inf.Div.*, was to follow between four and seven hours after the start of the airborne attack. A third wave was planned for the next day.

Within the framework of the measures for the defence of Holland against German attack, because of its proximity to the capital, the airfield at Ypenburg had gained an especially important role. Of the Dutch Air Arm, 9 Fokker D-XXIs (eight of them combat ready) from 1st Fighter Detachment (1e JaVA) and 12 Douglas 8A-3N light bombers (11 of them combat-ready), had been stationed there. Moreover, five Koolhoven FK 51s and 7 Fokker C-Vs from the 2nd Reconnaissance Detachment had been moved to Ypenburg from the airfield at Utrecht-Soesterberg, although these had initially been parked at the edges of the airfield. Based on information about the German attack against Oslo the Dutch high command had not excluded a similar airborne operation aimed at the occupation of Den Haag, and thus it had also directed a considerable number of ground forces and weapons for the defence of Ypenburg. The 3rd battalion of the Grenadier Regiment was tasked with the defence of the airfield. One of its infantry companies, together with the machine-gun company, occupied field positions along the western and northern edge of the airfield. The 12 light and nine heavy machine-guns of this force and the light machine-gun of the airfield's police guard, were set up in such a way that they could cover the airfield in its entirety. Another infantry company was established with a security mission in factories and farmsteads along the de Vliet Canal and north of the airfield. The third infantry company was divided into platoons for the protection of the Hoorn bridge and the area north of Delft. It also served as the quick-reaction force of the battalion. Six Landsverk light armored cars from one of the squadrons of the Light Division were positioned between the office buildings and hangars in the northern part of the airfield. At the southern, western and north-eastern edges of the airfield three anti-aircraft machine-gun platoons (numbers 59-

61) with four guns each had been positioned in such a manner that they could fire against low approaching and landing transport aircraft. Two heavy anti-aircraft batteries with three 75mm guns were set up just south of Den Haag; the 13th at the south-eastern edge of the city, near the Leeuvenbergh park and the 76th in the open terrain about 2.5km north-west of the airfield. From there they also covered the airspace over the airfield. A light anti-aircraft platoon of the garrison of Delft, positioned north of the town, was able to direct the fire of its modern 2cm guns over the southern part of the airfield at Ypenburg.

For the local protection of Den Haag two battalions and the independent companies of the Grenadier Regiment, the border infantry battalion of this regiment and elements of the Jager Regiment were garrisoned in the city. Five companies of the 14th Depot Battalion were billeted in Rijswijk, a suburb of Den Haag just west of the Hoorn Bridge. The capital was also the garrison for the headquarters of 1st Inf.Div., some command and control and logistic troops, and the depots of the cavalry, the Grenadiers and the Jagers. The 57th and 58th platoons of 14th Anti-Aircraft Machine-gun Company, which also commanded the 59th-61st Platoons on the airfield, were deployed in the city specifically for the protection of government buildings. Additionally, the 164th Heavy Anti-Aircraft Battery was positioned in a sports stadium in Den Haag. The I Army Corps, which had been placed under the commandant of Fortress Holland in the morning, with the exception of its troops on the airfields at Ypenburg and Valkenburg and some units in Den Haag, was currently deployed for the protection of the coastal strip between Gravenzande and Haarlem, and had the potential to move some of its forces quickly further inland if required. For movements across the Oude Rijn however it was dependent on the possession of the undamaged bridges along the lower course of this river.

Delft, the home of the famous porcelain and only 4km south of Ypenburg, was, like Leiden, not garrisoned by units of the Field Army. Nevertheless the troops which were present in the town were of considerable numerical strength. Of the three battalions, formed from the VI Depot of the Infantry, some companies of the 3rd and 6th Depot Battalions were filled up almost to their authorized strength. With the exception of the cadres, their personnel, for the greater part, were made up of new recruits.[111] A unit to the strength of a company was formed from members of the faculty and students of the Delft Technical High School. The town's light air-defence consisted of the 64th and 65th anti-aircraft machine-gun platoons. Another asset, however, was far more formidable. From modern 2cm anti-aircraft guns which had been procured from the state-owned Artillerie Inrichtingen armaments plant in Delft, five platoons with two or three guns each were formed and manned by reservists. Except the platoon north of Delft, they were positioned at the four corners of the old town. As the 2cm guns were also very effective against ground targets they were placed to dominate the most important routes leading into the centre of the town.

In order to prevent any landings of transport aircraft on the auto-route which went around the west of the town from Rotterdam and towards Den Haag, trucks were parked on its surface every 100-150m. Some of them were manned by men with a machine-gun each, moreover the auto-route was constantly patrolled by motorcycle teams from the 1st Regiment of Hussars, with heavy machine-guns mounted on their sidecars.

---

111 Student has laid down these thoughts in his memoirs, pointing out that he had not shared them with anybody else at that time.

Lastly, some protection for the area around Den Haag against German aircraft, approaching from the south-east could also be reckoned with from the blocking position along the Waal and the Bergsche Maas.

From 0540hrs German He 111 bombers in several waves of three aircraft each escorted by Bf 110s and Bf 109s attacked Ypenburg and targets in the surrounding areas. In spite of the considerable number of attacking bombers, neither the Dutch infantry along the edges of the airfield, nor the anti-aircraft machine-gun platoons positioned there, had losses worth mentioning.[112] The 13th Anti-Aircraft Battery east of Voorburg received a direct hit causing losses among its crew and destroyed the fire-control device for its 75mm guns. On the northern part of the airfield, one of the light cars was put out of action by machine-gun-fire from the air.

Shocked by the initial air attacks many of the Dutch soldiers who were deployed along the western edge of the airfield abandoned their positions and retreated toward Den Haag. Their officers, however, quickly quelled the panic so that most of the positions had been reoccupied when the parachuting began.

As the personnel of the two air squadrons which were stationed on the airfield had been alerted a short time prior to the attack, they had found the time to warm up the aircraft. All eight combat-ready Fokker D-XXI fighters and eight of the light bombers (Douglas-Northrop 8A-3N), took off unharmed just in time. The other three Douglas aircraft which had been damaged at the start of the air attack also managed to get into the air. Still in the airspace over the airfield, seven of the unwieldy bombers were quickly shot down by the German fighter escorts. Two others were so heavily damaged that they had to conduct emergency landings on the island of Rozenburg. Of the Fokker D-XXIs which were immediately drawn into aerial combat only one was shot down and two more were damaged beyond repair due to emergency landings. Two fighters and two light bombers managed to get away from the aerial combat and land with very little fuel on the airfield at Ockenburg. As there were no fuel stocks on this airfield they were left and later destroyed during its occupation by the Germans.

During their presence in the contested airspace over Ypenburg, which had probably lasted until the arrival of the first German air transport formations, the D-XXIs had turned out quite troublesome opponents because of their flight performance. According to Dutch reports, they had shot down or forced into emergency landings a Bf 109, a He 111, a Do 17 and a Ju 52.[113]

At 0502hrs three squadrons and the staff group of *IV./KG z.b.V.1* with the battle HQ and three companies of *I./FschJgRgt.2* aboard, had commenced their take-off from Münster-Loddenheide. In order to avoid the Dutch anti-aircraft fire, the transport formation crossed the airspace over Dutch territory in low-level flight. A short distance east of Delft the aircraft climbed to an altitude of about 150m and at 0620hrs reduced their speed for parachuting. This left them initially exposed to the anti-aircraft fire from Delft

---

112 *General* Trettner, who was the operations officer on the staff of *Fl.Div.7* during the operations in Holland, in a personal letter to the author, dated. 3 June 2005, describes this decision as one of Student's typical intuitive acts, which afterward had turned out to be right.

113 As five companies of 14th Depot Battalion had their billets in Rijswijk the remaining 1st Company was placed under the command of 3rd Depot Battalion.

and shortly later to that from around Ypenburg. Evasive moves by the transport aircraft and navigational errors by the pilots and the dispatchers caused the transport formation to break cohesion and the paratroopers were mostly dropped in the wrong drop zones and were left widely dispersed.[114]

Hauptmann Merten's 1st Company was dropped with its three rifle platoons and the assigned heavy machine-gun-squad immediately west of the airfield. They were tasked with the clearance of the auto-route from the enemy and the seizure of the north-western and northern edge of the airfield, but came down without its 2nd Platoon west of Delft. The battalion commander *Hauptmann* Noster, a part of his battle HQ and the signals platoon had parachuted with 1st Company. One Ju 52, with another part of the battle HQ aboard, was badly damaged by anti-aircraft fire and had to conduct an emergency landing quite some distance south of Delft.[115] The aircraft with the 2nd Platoon of 1st Company had been delayed at take-off at Münster-Loddenheide for about 15 minutes and so had not been able to close up and remained missing.[116] A platoon of *4./FschJgRgt.1* under *Oberleutnant* Eckleben was dropped immediately west of the town centre of Delft. Its transport aircraft had erroneously joined *IV./KG z.b.V.1* during the approach flight from Germany.

Oberleutnant Schlichting's 2nd Company was tasked with parachuting its three rifle platoons immediately south of the airfield, seizing its southern part and clearing the runways for the aircraft with the air-landing troops aboard. The company was dropped west of the airfield in the vicinity of the chemical factory at Hopax. There, a company of III/Gren.Rgt. occupied a security zone which stretched toward the south between the auto-route and the de Vliet Canal. Its soldiers were established in field positions and buildings. In the last phase of the approach flight to the drop zone two Ju 52s were hit by anti-aircraft fire and went down ablaze. The paratroopers in one of these aircraft managed to leave it by undertaking an emergency jump. However their weapon containers were lost. In another Ju 52 which was transporting men of 2nd Company paratroopers were wounded by machine-gun fire.

Hauptmann Morawetz's 4th Company contained an HQ section, two rifle platoons each reinforced by a heavy machine-gun-squad, a heavy machine-gun platoon and one 8cm mortar and its crew. It was to parachute north of the airfield as close as possible to the de Vliet Canal and seize the bridges at Rijswijk and Voorburg. This was in preparation for the subsequent thrust of air-landing forces into Den Haag. Furthermore it was to block the road leading from Leiden to Voorburg and to support the attack of 1st Company against the northern part of the airfield by fire from heavy machine-guns. The company was dropped, as planned, between the de Vliet Canal and the airfield. However one part was dropped too far to the east and the other part too far away from the Hoorn Bridge, which had been assigned as the most important initial objective. Furthermore this made any coherent assault impossible. One of the heavy machine-gun squads did not arrive at all, as its late-arriving Ju 52 dropped it together with *6./FschJgRgt.2* on the airfield at Valkenburg.

---

114   In order to avoid damage on the runway, most bombs had been dropped outside of the airfield.

115   There was no confirmation of these losses by the German side. This stands particularly true for the Ju 52, which had probably been forced to an emergency landing after hits by an anti-aircraft gun.

116   *Fl.Div.7*, after the airborne operation in Holland had reported the insufficient mission training of the lately formed air transport wings and particularly of the dispatchers. The reason was seen in the restrictions on training and exercises.

The assembly of 1st Company was taking considerable time, as the continuous defensive fire forced the paratroopers to move mainly in the drainage ditches, which were only to 1.5m deep and 1.5-3m wide. Of the widely dispersed weapon containers only a few could be found and picked up. Their actions were further impeded by the resistance of a reinforced motorcycle platoon of the hussars which was positioned at the auto-route east of the drop zone. However, before long it was attacked and thrown back by the assembled first parts of 1st Company, led by the battalion commander. During this assault 16 of the hussars were taken prisoner, and some of their motorcycles captured.

At 0700hrs the assembly was completed to the best extent possible. Up to that time there had been losses of four killed, 10 wounded and about 20 missing. Shortly after the assembly was complete and the company and the elements of the battle HQ – altogether four officers and 79 other ranks – commenced their advance toward the north along the auto-route. On the way seven trucks, all of which were fully operational and some with heavy machine-guns, which had been placed across the auto-route as obstacles, were captured. While a rearguard of 12 men under *Oberfeldwebel* Weiland remained behind, the advance now continued in the trucks. Several times the column met with machine-gun nests on either side of the auto-route which had to be neutralized. At 0820hrs the paratroopers, having lost another four wounded, arrived at the original drop zone of 1st Company and at 0900hrs deployed for the assault toward the northern part of the airfield.

By that time and certainly observed by the paratroopers closing for the attack, the first landing of troops on the airfield had already failed with disastrous results. Additional landing attempts shortly later had been discontinued after more of the transport aircraft and their passengers had been lost.

What had happened?

At 0650hrs 32 Ju 52s of *KGr z.b.V.12* in four groups of eight aircraft each had commenced landing on the airfield, which they assumed to be in the hands of the paratroopers. Aboard this formation had been the battle HQ and the signals platoon of *InfRgt.65* with its commanding officer, *Oberst* Friemel, together with the 6th and 8th companies of *II./InfRgt.65*. The first group had just touched down in perfect order when all of a sudden the weapons of the Dutch began to open fire. Within seconds, all aircraft of this group had been riddled with bullets and had exploded under fire from the 37mm guns of the armored cars. Only a few of the passengers managed to get out of the planes. As the second group had already touched down close up to the first one six of its Ju 52s had crashed into the burning wrecks on the runway and another two had been brought to a stop just behind. A great number of the passengers and aircrews of the second group had also been hit in the ongoing firestorm of the defenders, while disembarking. This disaster left 200 soldiers of the regimental staff, the signals platoon and the 6th Company of *InfRgt.65* and most of the aircrews of the two landed groups killed or wounded within minutes. Among the men who had escaped the inferno were *Oberst* Friemel and the commander of *KGr z.b.V.12*, *Hauptmann* Frh. von Hornstein. During their descent the third group had just enough time to gain speed again and to turn away under fire. Almost all of its aircraft then landed along the auto-route south of Delft. As this had also been barred by trucks most of the planes were wrecked in the ditches alongside the road. The fourth group was able to turn around before it had reached the airfield and flew back in the direction of the German border.

One of the Ju 52s of *KGr z.b.V.12* was shot down during its approach flight by the 164th Heavy Anti-Aircraft Battery and crashed with all of its passengers aboard on Adelheid Street in Den Haag. Beside the corpse of an officer a briefcase was found containing the partly-scorched operational orders and the air transport plans for *22.(LL)Inf.Div.* These documents were immediately sent to the Dutch high command for evaluation.

At about 0745hrs the 2nd and 4th squadrons and the HQ group of *KGr z.b.V.9* coming from Lippspringe approached the airspace over Delft/Ypenburg. During the attempt to land on the airfield which was now covered with burning and destroyed aircraft, two Ju 52s of the HQ group and one of 2nd Squadron were hit by anti-aircraft fire. Another Ju 52 of 2nd Squadron crashed, probably after also being hit, as it searched for a suitable landing site. Six aircraft of *KGr z.b.V.9* and the aircraft of the commander of the 2nd Squadron landed on the auto-route south of Delft, causing five of the planes to be written off. After the passengers of these six planes, most of which belonged to the command troops and the logistics and medical services, had been unloaded, the Ju 52s of the squadron leader managed to take off again. Of the ten aircraft of the 4th Squadron, five landed in open terrain south-east of the airfield, near the village of Pijnacker. Four others had come down on the auto-route about 2km south of Delft. One Ju 52 turned back to Germany with its passengers aboard. The Ju 52 of 4th Squadron had brought along mainly personnel from the headquarters of *22.(LL)Inf.Div.*, from *NachrAbt.22* and from the staff of *FlakAbt.22*. Among the pilots who had brought down their aircraft on or beside the auto-route south of Delft was the commander of *KG z.b.V.2*, *Oberst* Conrad. He had managed to take off again with the three remaining serviceable aircraft, and to take back to Germany a number of the crews of stranded aircraft. The passengers who disembarked from the transport aircraft along the auto-route immediately came under fire from Dutch troops and their light anti-aircraft guns which were positioned at the southern edge of Delft. As most men, with the exclusion of a few soldiers from *8./InfRgt.65*, had not been trained for infantry combat and lacked experienced tactical leaders, their initial action was uncoordinated and at first they looked for cover.

Around midday the highest-ranking officer present, *Oberfeldarzt* Dr. Wischhusen, the chief medical officer on the staff of *22.(LL)Inf.Div.*, assumed command of the parties strewn out along the auto-route. With the support of the few officers and NCOs on hand, he established order. After the attempt to penetrate into the south of Delft failed, he set up a perimeter opposite the Dutch positions with about one hundred men. When another group of soldiers from aircraft which lay to the south was detected, he deployed them in a defensive position along the auto-route toward Rotterdam. The arms of his scratch force, beside small arms, consisted of machine-guns extracted from aircraft, an infantry gun with forty rounds of ammunition which had been found in one of the planes, and a mortar from *8./InfRgt.65*.

The strip of terrain along the auto-route being held by *Gruppe Wischhusen* was about 2km long. The continuous fire from Dutch light anti-aircraft guns and heavy machine-guns prevented any contact with the passengers of the aircraft which had gone down to the east, in the area around Pijnacker, and which were also engaged in heavy fighting.

The radio team of the command group of *22.(LL)Inf.Div.* had also been unloaded south of Delft; Wischhusen was able to establish radio communication with the command post of *Fl.Div.7* and to send a first situation report. Radio communication was also achieved with the staff of *InfRgt.47* in Valkenburg. No radio contact could be made with the staff elements of *22.(LL)Inf.Div.* at Ockenburg or with the division commander there.

Late in the afternoon a platoon from *4./FschJgRgt.1*, under *Oberleutnant* Eckleben, was south-west of the old part of Delft. The platoon had managed to take possession of the factory of the world-famous Delft porcelain immediately after its landing. A counter-attack by parts of the Dutch 3rd Depot Battalion had forced *Oberleutnant* Eckleben, whose men had been reinforced by the troops left behind by *1./FschJgRgt.2*, to abandon the factory and to withdraw in a southerly direction. There the attempt had failed to seize the ammunition storage site at Kruithuis, which lay immediately west of the auto-route. Wischhusen now assumed command over the force under *Oberleutnant* Eckleben and instructed him to set up his platoon along the auto-route so as to protect against enemy attacks from the west and north-west. The troops under *Oberfeldwebel* Weiland were ordered to reinforce Wischhusen's main force.

During the night under continuous fire from the southern edge of Delft and from the terrain east of the auto-route, *Gruppe Wischhusen* improved its positions. Sporadic probing attacks by the Dutch from Delft were repulsed due to their lack of drive. Nevertheless Dr. Wischhusen continually strengthened the morale of his inexperienced and discouraged men. Even with the onset of darkness it was not possible to establish physical contact with the passengers of the aircraft stranded in the area around Pijnacker and Nootdorp, all the more since most of them had already been overwhelmed by the Dutch.

In spite of the disaster for the first wave of the air-landing troops which was witnessed by the paratroopers of *I./FschJgRgt.1*, they tried with unbroken morale to change the situation to the better and to accomplish their missions.

Shortly after 0900hrs shock troops from 1st Company succeed in neutralizing the Dutch machine-gun positions along the north-western edge of the airfield and, taking the previously captured Dutch soldiers along with them,[117] to storm the guard building and the adjoining commissary. Among the German losses were *Hauptmann* Noster and the commander of 1st Platoon, *Leutnant* Tappen, who were both seriously wounded. During the fighting for the control of the buildings between 70 and 80 Dutch soldiers, including the commandant of the airfield, were taken prisoner. Those elements of 1st Company which had not participated in the actual assault were now summoned forward. The captured buildings were provisionally prepared to repel any attack. A few air-landing soldiers who escaped the slaughter on the airfield joined the paratroopers. They now attempted to gain ground toward the north and the east but failed due to the fire of Dutch heavy machine-guns. The two shock troops which were dispatched against particularly troublesome machine-gun nests failed to return. At 1000hrs the Dutch launched a counter-attack from the north-eastern part of the airfield which was repulsed by aggressive action. As a result some of the light armored cars which accompanied the attackers were damaged by anti-tank rifle fire. Nevertheless, three of them managed to retreat to the north-west. *Hauptmann* Noster, who was fully aware of the importance of the Hoorn Bridge for the planned attack of the air-landing forces into Den Haag, now dispatched some men of the 1st Company for a *coup de main* against this objective. Mounted on captured vehicles – a motor car and two motorcycles – a squad of paratroopers attempted to reach the bridge at

---

117 The passengers of this Ju 52, among them *Hauptmann* Noster's adjutant and the medical officer, had managed to reach the force under *Generalleutnant* Graf von Sponeck at Overschie, after two days of isolated fighting.

high speed. Heavy defensive fire ended the undertaking and all of the soldiers assaulting in it became casualties. A short time later, a counter-attack by the Dutch for the retaking of the north-western part of the airfield commenced. An attack from the north by infantry to the strength of a company was thwarted by defensive fire about 250m in front of the north-western corner of the airfield. Soon it became evident that the 1st Company was almost completely surrounded by superior enemy forces. In the meantime the defenders, who were running out of ammunition, had to increasingly revert to captured Dutch machine-guns. At 1130hrs *Hauptmann* Merten arranged for a short ceasefire to allow for the evacuation of the seriously wounded. *Leutnant* Tappen who was taken moved to a medical facility in Den Haag by Dutch ambulance. At 1200hrs the fighting renewed and the Dutch attacked again after receiving reinforcements. Until shortly after 1500hrs the paratroopers were able to keep the attackers away from the occupied buildings. However they could not stop the Dutch from retaking all other parts of the airfield.[118] After an attack by twelve British Blenheim bombers on the airfield at 1650hrs,[119] Dutch artillery fire[120] set ablaze the buildings being occupied by the Germans, forcing them to withdraw into open terrain nearby. There, almost without ammunition, they were quickly overwhelmed. Just before their resistance had ended, the seriously wounded *Hauptmann* Noster was handed over to the Dutch medical services.[121]

Already weakened by the loss of two plane-loads during the drop *2./FschJgRgt.2* now suffered further casualties during the landing west of the airfield by fire from the Dutch grenadier company which was positioned in a defensive zone and also from machine-guns at the western edge of the airfield. The fire from the chemical factory at Hopax, located north-west of the drop zone on the bank of the de Vliet Canal, hindered the assembly of the paratroopers and the collection of their weapon containers; as such *Oberleutnant* Schlichting ordered the instant seizure of this installation. The assault was successful but only with considerable losses of the parachute forces; *Oberleutnant* Schlichting was among those killed. The remainder of 2nd Company now assembled in the factory. Some machine-guns were brought into position, a guard was located toward the south at the auto-route and the wounded were brought into the factory. At 0930hrs *Oberleutnant* Massalski, who assumed command of the company after the death of *Oberleutnant* Schlichting, ordered 1st Platoon to neutralize some of the Dutch machine-guns along the western edge of the airfield and establish contact with 1st Company. In addition a shock troop of 11 men and two machine-guns crossed the de Vliet Canal by boat to its western bank with the mission to destroy some machine-gun nests firing at the factory. The shock troop succeeded in silencing some of the machine-guns but then disappeared.[122] The 1st Platoon failed to push

---

118   The platoon had probably been dropped in the area of Wateringen. According to Dutch reports, about 40 German soldiers were captured there on 11 May in a mill.

119   Dutch sources later accused the paratroopers of using the prisoners as human shields in front of them.

120   On the Dutch side, a depot company had led the attack against the north-western corner of the airfield, whereas a company of II/Gren.Rgt. on its left had established contact with the Dutch troops still holding out at the north-eastern edge of the airfield. A short time later another company of II/Gren.Rgt. had attacked from the Hoorn Bridge toward the South west of the auto-route. The attacks was directed by the commander of II/Gren.Rgt.

121   The attack was requested by the Dutch high command at the start of the German assault against Ypenburg. As it could not be canceled the Dutch infantry had temporarily withdrawn from the airfield and later had re-occupied it.

122   The fire was delivered by II/2nd Art.Rgt., which, with its three batteries of 75mm guns was brought forward from Den Haag in positions southwest of Rijswijk.

through to the north-western corner of the airfield and was forced to retreat in a southerly direction. *Oberleutnant* Massalski, who now intended to clear the southern part of the airfield for another landing attempt, followed 1st Platoon with most of the men left over in the factory, leaving behind a small guard force. The advance of 2nd Company toward the south was soon broken up by heavy defensive fire from the northern outskirts of Delft, causing considerable losses. In the late afternoon, Dutch infantry, moving forward from the north and west managed to overwhelm the outpost of the paratroopers in the factory and the many wounded who were left there were captured. At 1910hrs the Dutch also succeeded in breaking the resistance of the nearby farmstead at Loos and in the surrounding terrain. The prisoners captured were mostly air-landing soldiers who had been able to get out of the destroyed aircraft, including *Oberst* Friemel, *Hauptmann* Frh. von Hornstein and the two chaplains of *22.(LL)Inf.Div.*[123] At around 2300hrs the remaining paratroopers of 2nd Company were overwhelmed by Dutch depot troops who were advancing from Delft, after a last-ditch defence south of the airfield

The elements of 4th Company that were dropped farthest to the east during the landing had received fire from the position north of them and from the north-eastern corner of the airfield. *Hauptmann* Morawetz was wounded but continued to lead his unit. Some machine-guns now directed their fire against the anti-aircraft battery. As its crew had taken casualties during the preceding air attack and a number had run away, the fighting quickly turned in favour of the Germans. Those defenders that could still fight, an officer and seven men, surrendered to the paratroopers. In the battery position the attackers discovered a number of dead and seriously wounded and four anti-aircraft guns. At 0830hrs, with his HQ section and some paratroopers who had landed with them, *Hauptmann* Morawetz advanced from the battery position to the settlement of Zuiderberg. Here he was able to drive away the security guard established there and seize the bridge across the de Vliet Canal which lay about 800m south-west of Voorburg. Here the attack was stopped by fire from Dutch infantry that were entrenched on the northern bank of the canal. *Hauptmann* Morawetz and his men then retreated to the anti-aircraft position and made the guns ineffectual. After an attack by pursuing Dutch infantry had been beaten off Morawetz and his walking wounded attempted to establish contact with the parts of 4th Company who were engaged in fighting to the west. However, only Morawetz and two of his soldiers managed to reach the farmstead at Johannahoeve, about 500m north of the north-eastern corner of the airfield. Here the remainder of a heavy machine-gun-squad being led by *Leutnant* Hasseldiek set up a defensive position. The squad originally acted as a rearguard for 3rd Platoon, which had attempted to attack across the de Vliet Canal. With only one of its two machine-guns still operational, the squad occupied Johannahoeve, when the attack of 3rd Platoon had failed to accomplish its task. Until 2000hrs, *Hauptmann* Morawetz, *Leutnant* Hasseldiek, 11 paratroopers and a number of air-landing soldiers managed to hold off several assaults by Dutch infantry. This caused the attackers some painful losses. Despite the continuous machine-gun fire the resistance from Johannahoeve remained unbroken and the Dutch moved forward two 75mm field guns and at 2015hrs commenced fire at point-blank range. Their well-aimed shots caused losses not only among

---

123 In spite of his wounds *Hauptmann* Noster, was shipped to England. In November 1943 he was exchanged as permanently disabled for active military service. As *Oberst* and commander of the II parachute officers' school he was seriously wounded during the final fighting in Berlin in 1945 and thereupon committed suicide.

the defenders, but also among the residents of the farmhouse who had been quartered in its basement.[124] After 20 rounds the guns ceased fire and a company of the border battalion of the Grenadier Regiment stormed the farm and about 30 Germans surrendered. Four more had been killed and six wounded. *Hauptmann* Morawetz and three *Feldwebels* of the paratroopers initially managed to escape but at 2300hrs they were captured by Dutch search teams.

At 0930hrs 1st Platoon of 4th Company led by *Oberleutnant* Lüdke, advanced north of the airfield for an attack against the Hoorn Bridge and forced its way into a small wood, about 200m east of the objective. During the fight against Dutch infantry that were entrenched there, the platoon leader and one squad-leader were killed and two other squad-leaders were wounded. Defensive fire from the north and the west prevented any further advance; this caused two-thirds of the platoon to become casualties. By 1230hrs the remainder, surrounded by vastly superior Dutch forces, was overwhelmed. A short time earlier two Bf 109s that had strafed the Dutch positions at the Hoorn Bridge in support of the paratroopers were shot down by anti-aircraft fire.

Oberleutnant Wolf's 3rd Platoon was intended to block the road from Den Haag via Voorburg to Leiden. However they were only able to pick up four of their weapon containers; the others had fallen into the de Vliet Canal or landed between the buildings on its northern bank. Furthermore one of its squads had wrongly been dropped north of the canal and had been quickly neutralized. Thus, from the very beginning of the action, Wolf's platoon established itself in some buildings along the road to Voorburg-Leiden, level with the underpass of the railway which ran from Gouda to Den Haag. Several dashes toward the canal were repulsed with losses. Subsequent attempts, one at 1400hrs and one more at 1700hrs, to fight through to Johannahoeve were also stopped. The few men of the platoon who were still effective held out in some houses but were later overwhelmed by Dutch troops as they advanced across the de Vliet Canal.[125]

The seizure of the farmstead Johannahoeve at about 2130hrs marked the end of the last organized resistance of *I./FschJgRgt.2* in the area around Ypenburg came to an end. Except for the twelve members of the battle HQ who came down south of Delft, the twelve men of the security guard under *Oberfeldwebel* Weiland who had joined *Gruppe Wischhusen*, and the twelve paratroopers of the heavy machine-gun-squad, who had been dropped together with *6./FschJgRgt.2*, three companies and half the battle HQ of a parachute infantry battalion had been put out of action to no avail.

Initial reports undertaken after the capitulation of Holland among members of *I./FschJgRgt.2*, freed from captivity, of wounded found in Dutch medical installations and of men who had joined *Gruppe Wischhusen* indicated reported losses of 58 killed, 135 wounded and 356 missing.[126] The Dutch reported the overall number of German soldiers

---

124 The shock troop had picked up some stragglers of 2nd Company and two weapon containers west of the de Vliet Canal. Mounted on two captured trucks this group was forced to withdraw further to the west, where some time later it was overwhelmed.

125 Dutch sources state that the Germans had occupied mainly the principal houses at Dorrepal and Zeerust, close to the southern bank of the canal. The high number of 90 prisoners indicated that a great number of air-landing troops had also found refuge in this area.

126 However this compilation is not reliable as regards the missing. The maximum number of paratroopers who were dropped around Ypenburg could not have exceeded 470-480 men. If the number of 135

captured in the immediate vicinity of the airfield at 720 and soldiers captured additionally in the areas around Pijnacker, Nootdorp and Delft were 571.[127] Grave registrations later indicated that 59 soldiers from *22.(LL)Inf.Div.* had been killed on and around the airfield. The Dutch reported their losses as 51 killed around the airfield and 43 in its environments.

The air-landing of *I./InfRgt.65* with the battle HQ and three companies, scheduled as a part of the second wave for the airfield at Ypenburg, was cancelled. The Ju 52s of *KG z.b.V.1*, which had been ordered to deliver this force from Münster-Loddenheide, upon observing the situation on this airfield, had either searched for alternate landing sites or had returned to Germany.[128] As they searched for a suitable landing site a formation of eleven Ju 52s was forced to the west by Dutch anti-aircraft fire. Between 1130 and 1150hrs nine of them touched down at three different locations south and east of the Staalduinse wood, near Hoek van Holland. After they unloaded their passengers – soldiers from *2./* and *3./InfRgt.65*, and from *AufklAbt.22* – six of them were able to take off again, but three remained damaged on the ground. The 125-strong force was able to assemble unnoticed and, led by the company commander of *3./InfRgt.65*, *Oberleutnant* Martin, they were able to establish itself in the south-eastern part of the Staalduinse wood. The Dutch troops around Hoek van Holland were alerted by the flight activities of the German transport aircraft. A patrol which was dispatched from Hoek van Holland did not detect any enemy.[129] It was not until 1700hrs that part of a company of II/39rh Inf.Rgt. with a mission to clear the Staalduinse wood, came across *Gruppe Martin*. However they were repulsed, causing two Dutch soldiers to be killed and the commander to be wounded. Breaking contact, they now withdrew to their start point. A company of II/JgRgt from Gravenzande was not much better off. It had destroyed the three stranded Ju 52s and was engaged in a longer firefight with the German air-landing soldiers. It lost two killed and at 1740hrs retreated toward the north. From this time on, *Gruppe Martin* was left peacefully in its positions at the south-western corner of the Staalduinse wood, until the end of the fighting in Holland. However, it thus avoided any offensive action, or any attempt to fight through to the main forces of the *Luftlande-Korps*.

Shortly prior to 1300hrs the remaining two Ju 52s in the formation touched down on the western part of Rozenburg, located south of the Nieuwe Waterweg. There they unloaded their passengers – soldiers of *2./InfRgt.65*. Thereafter, one of them managed to take off. A patrol from 3rd Company, II/39th Inf.Rgt., deployed on the island for coastguard duties and for the protection of two coastal gun batteries, first captured the aircrew of the Ju 52 who were stranded in the polder and then advanced against the

wounded, found in Dutch medical establishments is correct, the number of soldiers who had joined *Gruppe Wischhusen* and *6./FschJgRgt.2* was about 30 and the number of paratroopers who had been killed in action or had later died of their wounds was, as was later found by the grave registration, 76, then 250-260 unwounded must have been taken prisoners by the Dutch around Ypenburg. This calculation is also a corrective of the Dutch numbers, reported immediately after the end of the fighting around the airfield, with 150 captured and more than 130 dead paratroopers.

127 These numbers could be slightly exaggerated. Nevertheless, the high number of prisoners around the airfield allows for the conclusion, that many more air-landing soldiers must have managed to get out of destroyed aircraft than originally were reported by the Dutch.

128 Two Ju 52s with soldiers from *2./InfRgt.65* aboard were shot down over the Waal river during the approach-flight, the passengers either perished or were captured. At least the whole of *I./InfRgt.65* was flown back to Germany. Even later, this unit had not participated in the fighting for Fortress Holland.

129 The parts of *3./FschJgRgt.2* which had been dropped near the Staalduinse wood shortly prior to the air-landing of *Kräftegruppe Martin*, had in the meantime moved away in the direction of Ockenburg.

landed German infantrymen.[130] The Germans had occupied a farmhouse and engaged the advancing patrol. After a short firefight which killed the patrol-leader and wounded two of his men, 21 Germans surrendered.

In opposition to the airfield at Waalhaven, where half of the Dutch infantry deployed had not been involved in the fighting against the assaulting paratroopers, the defence of Ypenburg was prepared with professional care and adjusted to the anticipated plans of the attackers. The establishment of three security areas was of paramount importance, these were designated as 'screens', around the airfield; one in the north around the Hoorn Bridge, one in the west between the de Vliet Canal and the auto-route Delft-Den Haag and one in the south, north of the town of Delft. Furthermore the settlements and farms east of the airfield had been occupied by troops. In addition to these measures, field fortifications had been prepared along the northern bank of the 15m wide and more than 2m deep de Vliet Canal between Rijswijk and Voorburg. The canal crossings were manned by security elements from the garrison of Den Haag who had been kept in a high state of readiness. Infantry battalions brought forward from 3rd Infantry Division had intervened in the fighting south of the capital by the afternoon of 10 May.

The remarkably strong Dutch anti-aircraft defence between Den Haag and Delft had broken up the formation flight of the transport aircraft carrying *I./FschJgRgt.2* during the last phase of their approach to the drop zones. This caused the paratroopers to not be dropped according to plan, in fact the majority came down in the security-screen areas. Evidently their existence and formation had not been detected beforehand; this not only constituted a considerable hindrance during the assembly and the collection of the weapon containers, but had also cost valuable time in the ensuing fighting. Thrusts against the Dutch security forces at the Hoorn Bridge and against the permanent crossings of the de Vliet Canal had failed from the very beginning of these actions. The clearing of the area between the de Vliet Canal and the auto-route had been so time-consuming that the Dutch positions along the northern part of the airfield were still fully intact when the first parts of *22.(LL)Inf.Div.* had attempted to land. Radio communication between the staff of *I./FschJgRgt.2* and the approaching *KGr z.b.V.12* did not exist due to technical problems so that instructions from the ground for a delay of the air-landing until the seizure of the airfield had not been possible.

The Dutch military authorities that were commanding the troops in the area Den Haag, upon perceiving the German airborne assault, had not hesitated to immediately release II/Gren.Rgt., the companies from 4th Depot Battalion, and parts of the border infantry battalion of the Gren.Rgt. for the blocking of the approaches toward Den Haag from the south, and for the support of the troops fighting for the airfield.

The evaluation of the operation order of *22.(LL)Inf.Div.*, captured from a Ju 52 which had crashed in the Adelheit-Straat in Den Haag, provided evidence that besides

---

130   Fearing pro-German actions the command of Fortress Holland had demobilized all Dutch soldiers who had worked in Germany prior to the outbreak of the war. Therefore, 3rd Company from II/39th Inf. Rgt. numbered only 90 men. The two coastal batteries with their 12cm guns numbered 115 men each. Additionally, a mobile searchlight-team was stationed on Rozenburg. On the morning of 10 May a squad of marines had arrived from Hoek van Holland as reinforcement. In the evening, an infantry squad of 11 men and a mixed squad of marines and naval militiamen had also been dispatched from Hoek van Holland.

the airfields already attacked, no further air-landings were planned for other locations in Fortress Holland. This knowledge considerably increased the freedom of action of the Dutch high command. Despite the fact that the flood of incoming and partly confusing reports had not yet allowed for a clear picture of the overall situation, it became possible to identify priorities for the employment of troops that were still available for commitment. Consequently, the recapture and subsequent firm retention of Ypenburg and the area around Delft were the main considerations. Despite the developing success there a threat to the capital was yet to be soon. III/9th Inf.Rgt., reinforced by an anti-tank platoon, was ordered to move to Voorburg late in the morning in addition to the forces already involved in the fighting. This unit had arrived shortly after midday and assumed an important role in the consolidation of the situation at the de Vliet Canal and north-east of the airfield. At 1340hrs II and III/12th Inf.Rgt. had additionally been ordered to Den Haag, of this regiment, only its first battalion had remained in Haarlem.

Although Valkenburg was reported as being unusable for any further air-landings, the German troops there, and in the dunes to the west, had also been assessed as an immediate threat to Den Haag. Therefore 3rd Inf.Div., which until then had remained uncommitted, without its 12th Inf.Rgt. but with 1st Inf.Rgt. from 1st Inf.Div. assigned to it, was released for the counterattack into the area around Valkenburg and into the coastal strip, stretching from there to Den Haag. The commanding officer of 3rd Inf.Div. organized his forces into three task groups.

- On the right: 4th Inf.Rgt., reinforced by I/1st Inf.Rgt., III/2nd Art.Rgt. and III/6th Art.Rgt. for the area around Katwijk.
- On the left: 1st Inf.Rgt, with 15th Machine-gun Company and I/6th Art.Rgt. assigned, for the area around Wassenaar.
- In reserve: 9th Inf.Rgt. (less III/9th Inf.Rgt.), 3rd Machine-gun Company, one anti-tank company and II/6th Art.Rgt. in the area around Rijnsberg.

After receiving reports throughout the course of the afternoon the Dutch authorities were sure that substantial German reinforcements by air could be expected to arrive only at Waalhaven. They also understood that the German commanders in charge of the airborne operation had adjusted their plans respectively. Consequently Lieutenant General van Andel issued orders for the elimination of the German air bridgehead on Ijsselmonde. In the light of the transfer of III Army Corps and the Light Division to the north across the Waal and the employment of the majority of I Army Corps for a sweeping of the coastal strip between Katwijk and Den Haag, he assessed those forces remaining as insufficiently strong for the retaking of the bridges at Moerdijk. However the Dutch high command firmly relied on the advance of the French 7th Army into the area around Tilburg and in conjunction with it, on actions by the French against the southern air bridgehead of the German parachute forces.

The airfield at Valkenburg, named after the village about 1.5km to its north-east and located between the townships of Den Haag and Leiden, had not been constructed until 1939. It had been planned as the largest military airbase in Holland. Yet by May 1940 it had to be used by the Dutch Air Arm. Its soft and partly swampy ground first had to be covered with tarmacked runways for heavy aircraft. The German intelligence services were not aware of this situation. This was primarily the fault of the German military *attaché* in Den Haag, who had not been aware of the importance of information about the state of landing sites.[131]

In spite of the unfinished state of the airfield, the Dutch high command had not excluded the possibility of air-landing-attempts by the Germans. Therefore, on 20 April 1940, two companies and a heavy machine-gun platoon from III/4th Inf.Rgt. had been dispatched for its protection. Incomprehensibly, the positions of these troops – altogether about 450 men with 24 light and three heavy machine-guns – had been placed on all four sides of the airfields and with their lines of fire toward its interior. Should the defence against air-landings on the airfield become necessary all positions were threatened by friendly fire from the opposite side.

On the morning of 10 May a third of the protective force occupied field positions, another third was deployed some distance around the airfield and the last third rested in the hangars on its northern edge. Numerous Dutch troops were quartered or deployed close to the airfield. In Katwijk aan den Rijn, about 1.5km north of the airfield, the remainder of III/4th Inf.Rgt. which included staff, 2nd Company and the majority of the heavy machine-gun company were all were available as a quick reaction force. The town of Leiden, a good 4km south-east of the airfield, was the garrison for the II Depot of the Infantry and contained the headquarters and 10th, 15th and 22nd Depot Battalions, each consisting of four companies, an anti-tank platoon and a mortar platoon.[132] Leiden was also the Depot of the 5th Horse Artillery – like those of the II Depot of the Infantry these were dispatched to settlements along the lower course of the Oude Rijn and to Wassenaar. In the area near Katwijk aan Zee, located at the mouth of the Oude Rijn, two batteries with 12cm howitzers of III/2nd Art.Rgt. from 1st Inf.Div. set up firing positions, the third battery was located about 3km more to the north-east, at the beach near Noordwijk. Quartered here were I and II/4th Inf.Rgt. and the regimental headquarters. The 3rd Inf.Div., 1st Inf. Rgt. and I/6th Art.Rgt., had their quarters around Sassenheim and Lisse, around 9km north of Leiden. A detachment of the Depot of the Horse Artillery was dispatched to Oegstgeest, the north-western suburb of Leiden. 7th Training Battery, from this depot, with its two 75mm field guns, was quartered in Katwijk aan Zee. Of some disadvantage for the movement of troops in a north-south direction and vice-versa was that only one bridge strong enough to support the traffic of heavy vehicles existed between Leiden and the mouth of the Oude Rijn. Located at the inn Haagse Schouw, it was here that the road and the tram-line from Leiden to Wassenaar and further to Den Haag crossed the river. Crossing-sites with less weight-bearing capacity and a smaller width spanned the Oude Rijn between Rijnsburg and Katwijk aan den Rijn, where two arms of the river formed an island of some length. The flood-gates near the mouth of the river offered another crossing for infantry and small vehicles.

---

131 The intelligence services of the higher commands of the *Luftwaffe*, including the *OKL*, should also be blamed, as they obviously had not asked questions, perhaps because they had relied on the excellent landing and take-off capabilities of the Ju 52.

132 The enlisted men in the depot companies mainly had been recently called-up recruits. In some companies, only the cadres had been present.

The area south-west of the airfield in the direction toward Den Haag was also occupied by Dutch troops. In Wassenaar, a village of some size 2km south-west of the airfield, the 1st Regiment of Hussars (RHM – *Regiment Huzaren Motorrijders*) from the Light Division was stationed. Quartered in this location was the regiment staff, a reconnaissance platoon, two squadrons of motorcycle infantry, a heavy machine-gun-squadron on motorcycles with sidecars, an anti-tank platoon and a mortar platoon. A reinforced motorcycle squadron was tasked with surveillance of the auto-route, leading from Leiden to Amsterdam. The important central telephone office in Wassenaar was protected by a platoon from the II Depot of the Infantry. In the dunes, along the Wassenaarse Slag, leading from Wassenaar to the beach, elements of 4th Reserve Border Company were deployed in outposts. Immediately west and south of Wassenaar and at Voorschooten, were three batteries with 75mm anti-aircraft guns and one with 40mm guns, all subordinate to Anti-Aircraft Command. The three heavy batteries were able to cover the airspace over Valkenburg and located in Wassenaar was an anti-aircraft machine-gun platoon.

The plan for the seizure of the airfield at Valkenburg, designated by the Germans as airfield Katwijk or Landing Site I, was, in principle, identical with the method of attack chosen for the other airfields in the operational area of the *Luftlande-Korps*. It was based on the surprise and speed of operations against an enemy of inferior fighting efficiency and flexibility of their own command and control system. The forces planned for the airborne attack were 6./FschJgRgt.2, commanded by *Oberleutnant* Schirmer,[133] and the majority of *InfRgt.47* under *Oberst* Heyser. During the planning phase for the operation in Holland, *Oberleutnant* Schirmer had discovered how to carry the sub-machine guns with the paratroopers, so that the landing troops had considerable firepower prior to the location and unpacking of the weapon containers.

At 0530hrs three German He 111 bombers conducted an attack against the airfield. Their targets were the hangars at its northern edge where command installations, troops and ammunition stores were assumed to be. As the airfield was required for the landing of transport aircraft, no bombs were dropped on the Dutch field positions along its edges. Therefore the occupants suffered no losses. Nevertheless the air attack delivered a highly welcome effect in the area around the hangars. Here, a number of soldiers from the field

---

133 Gerhard Schirmer, born 1913. Joined the *Luftwaffe* from the police in 1935, he undertook pilot training before being made squadron commander in 1936 and receiving a promotion to *Oberleutnant* in 1937. He joined the parachute force in May 1939 from 9/39 as CO of 6./FschJgRgt.2. He participated in the campaigns against Poland and Holland, the parachute attack against the Corinth Canal in April 1941, and the airborne assault against Crete in May 1941. For this he was decorated with the *Ritterkreuz* on 14 June 1941. Later he participated in the campaign in the East from November 1941 to February 1943, before being assigned, in November 1943, to the staff of FschJgRgt.5 and tasked with the temporary command of the regiment in February 1943. He returned to Germany in March 1943 and was made CO of II./FschJgRgt.5 before receiving a promotion to *Major* in June 1943. He was subsequently transferred to Italy with his battalion and then to the Eastern Front with 2.FschJgDiv in November 1943. In January 1944 he returned to Germany and was promoted to *Oberstleutnant* and made CO of FschJgRgt 16. He was employed on the Channel coast in France in May 1944 and transfered to the Eastern Front in July 1944. He saw combat action in Lithuania for which he was decorated with the *Eichenlaub* to the *Ritterkreuz*. In February 1945 he became operations staff officer of FschJgAusbDiv 1 in Berlin. He was taken as a British prisoner of war in May 1945, then handed over to the Soviets. In Soviet imprisonment he undertook forced labour in Workuta until 1956. He joined the *Bundeswehr* immediately upon return from imprisonment in December 1956. Between 1957 and 1962 he was CO FschJgBrig 25, then CO Army Aviation Command 2 (*HFlgKdo 2*), then CO Territorial District Command 1 (*VBK 1*). He retired in March 1971 before dying in September 2004.

positions had assembled to be relieved by those, resting in the hangars. The hits had destroyed the hangar, containing the ammunitionstores, but had caused little losses among the men in and around the other buildings. Most of these, however, fled in panic toward the north, hiding behind a dam. When they were also attacked with bombs and machine-gun fire, they retreated even further north to seek cover in the dunes. During this attack the cohesion among these troops vanished. Thus almost two-thirds of the defenders on the airfield vacated the focal point of combat as the parachute assault began. Obviously this turned out to be of considerable advantage to the attackers. Although the type of Dutch troops and their dispositions at some distance to the airfield had correctly been identified by the German intelligence services, based on reports by the permanent German military *attaché* in Den Haag, they had been unable to gather reliable information about the strength of the defenders of the airfield at Valkenburg.

Transported by 4th Squadron of *I./KG z.b.V.172* from Paderborn, at 0610hrs *6./FschJgRgt.2* parachuted with the HQ section and one squad of 2nd Platoon directly on the airfield, with 1st Platoon led by *Leutnant* von Plessen and reinforced by the heavy machine-gun squad of 3rd Platoon, into the dunes immediately north-west of it and with 3rd Platoon under *Leutnant* Teusen, between the southern edge of the airfield and the road between Amsterdam-Den Haag.[134] The 2nd Platoon (less one squad) under *Oberleutnant* Gunkelmann was dropped in the vicinity of Delft about 15km south-west of the airfield. However *Oberleutnant* Gunkelmann died from a neck fracture as his parachute became caught on the chimney of a foundry. A heavy machine-gun squad from *4./FschJgRgt.2* was also unexpectedly dropped at Valkenburg, as its Ju 52 had joined the formation transporting Schirmer's company.

While Schirmer and the paratroopers around him advanced against the hangars under the fire of a few defenders who were still holding out, elements of 1st Platoon attacked the Dutch soldiers who had retreated into the dunes and captured a number of them. Other parts of the platoon advanced in a direction toward the village of Valkenburg.

Immediately after 3rd Platoon assembled, *Leutnant* Teusen positioned one squad along the road Den Haag-Amsterdam with its line of fire directed toward the west. Another squad moved on this road to the east and, without contact with the enemy, reached the large road and tram bridge across the Oude Rijn at the nearby restaurant. Here it positioned itself on the western bank of the river, so that it could dominate the bridge and its approaches from the east by fire. With the remaining soldiers of his platoon, *Leutnant* Teusen occupied the bridge across the drainage ditch about 500m north-west of the hamlet of Maaldrift and the estate at Landlust, at the road between Leiden-Den Haag, 500m east of Maaldrift. The blocking of the bridge at Haagse Schouw, which was important for Dutch supply traffic, and which enabled fast connection between the regions around Amsterdam, Leiden and Den Haag, turned out to be to the utmost annoyance to the enemy. An officer of the 1st Regiment of Hussars was captured while crossing the bridge and the senior logistics officer of the commandant of Fortress Holland was shot dead as he attempted to cross the bridge by motor car.

At 0630hrs Teusen's platoon engaged in combat at Maaldrift and Landlust against hussar motor-cyclists, to the strength of about a company, who were advanceing from Wassenaar toward Haagse Schouw. Soon the hussars were reinforced by two anti-tank

---

134 As was frequently done in the parachute operations in Holland, the elements of the heavy weapons platoon had been distributed among the rifle platoons.

guns. As the enemy slowly attacked, the paratroopers, with great effort and some losses, managed to hold on. Maaldrift, however, was lost. After his heavy machine-gun-squad arrived and some support was delivered by air, *Leutnant* Teusen's men repulsed all further attacks by the hussars. At 0930hrs a Ju 52 made an emergency landing west of Maaldrift, the infantry men from this aircraft advanced against the rear of the hussars, causing them to terminate the fighting at about 1110hrs and withdrew in a westerly direction. At this point they had lost eight killed, 15 wounded and 9 captured. On the orders of *Oberleutnant* Schirmer Teusen's platoon abandoned its position at Maaldrift and Landlust, retiring to Valkenburg, where it established itself south-west of the village. In the preceding fighting, some of Teusen's paratroopers had also been killed, among them *Assistenzarzt* Dr. Kuhlo, who had been assigned to 3rd Platoon. In the previous area of deployment, only the squad near the bridge at Haagse Schouw was left behind as a rearguard.

Before the paratroopers of 1st Platoon were able to end the fighting in the dunes and join *Oberleutnant* Schirmer on the airfield, at 0700hrs the squadrons of *KGr z.b.V.11* began landing. The operational commanding officer, *Oberst* Heyser, arrived, as did parts of the battle HQ of *II./InfRgt.47*. A Dutch Fokker D-XXI fighter which appeared during this landing was shot down by three escorting Bf 110s and crashed near Maaldrift.[135] Of the landing Ju 52s, only one was set ablaze by heavy machine-gun fire.

Immediately after landing, the troops advanced against the Dutch soldiers who were still holding the edges of the airfield. As these were now also attacked from the rear by combat teams from von Plessen's platoon they surrendered after a short fight. At about 0800hrs, the airfield was firmly in German hands. The losses during the fighting had been moderate. The passengers of one Ju 52, however, were missing.[136] On the side of the Dutch defenders, 29 soldiers from III/4th Inf.Rgt. had been killed, and 39 wounded. Additionally, more than 150 of the men present on the airfield during the attack were captured unwounded.

In spite of his injuries *Oberst* Heyser immediately assumed command over his forces, ordering mop-up actions in the vicinity of the airfield and the establishment of guard posts. Elements of *9./InfRgt.47* occupied some farmsteads and production facilities near the western bank of the Oude Rijn in the direction of Haagse Schouw. At the same time a small detail of air-landing soldiers occupied and prepared for defence the hotel-restaurant at Albertushoeve, to the west of the airfield. Paratroopers who came down north of the airfield entered the village of Valkenburg and drove away the few Dutch soldiers there.

Probably unnoticed by Schirmer's men during their drop, the 3rd Platoon from *3./FschJgRgt.2* was dropped at about the same time north of Wassenaar.[137] Twice during the morning these paratroopers had attempted to seize the central telephone office in Wassenaar, but had been repulsed, with losses, by the platoon from 22nd Depot Battalion that was guarding this installation.[138]

---

135 Its injured pilot had hidden in the aircraft until he had been rescued by Dutch civilians and had been brought to a hospital in Leiden.

136 Their aircraft was damaged by Dutch fire and had crashed into the sea near Katwijk aan Zee. Of its passengers and the crew, 14 men had managed to reach the shore, there they had been captured.

137 The dispatcher and the pilots of the group of Ju 52s with this platoon aboard probably had mistaken the airfield at Valkenburg for the airfield at Ockenburg, which was the objective for *3./FschJgRgt.2*.

138 It is quite certain that the remainder of this platoon had managed to fight through to Valkenburg in the course of the day and had joined the fighting there, as seven of its soldiers had been reported killed in action on 10 May in the area around Valkenburg. Regrettably, no further information about this platoon is available.

To some extent owing to the effects of the preceding air attack the seizure of the airfield was extremely fast and more than 500 men had been unloaded in less than half an hour. The further air transport movements which had been planned were interrupted, however, when the airfield at Valkenburg became unuseable – almost all of the Ju 52s of *KGr z.b.V.11* sank into the soft ground of the airfield up to the wheel axles of their undercarriage during their final landings. This obviously prevented them taking off again. As, like in all air-landings, it was the aim to deliver the air-landing units in their entirety to their commanders as quickly as possible, the aircraft had touched down in their flight formation with the groups close behind each other. The adverse conditions of the landing ground had been ignored by the leading group, or had not been recognized. Within 30 minutes after the start of the landing, the airfield was crammed with more than 50 transport aircraft, including five Ju 52s with parts of the 6th and 8th companies of *InfRgt.65*, which had been unable to deliver their passengers elswhere. The last two aircraft of the first wave of *InfRgt.47* had found no more space on the airfield and came down in open terrain; one in the dunes south of Katwijk, the other in the vicinity of Ockenburg. The paratroopers dropped on the airfield had not had time to examine the state of the runway and had not been tasked with this mission anyway. As alternate options for the landing of troops in the area around Valkenburg had not been looked at such a mission would have been to no avail anyway.

Heavy salvage equipment was not available and so the state of Valkenburg could not be improved within a measurable time. Consequently the crews of the stranded aircraft, with machine-guns taken from the Ju 52s and captured weapons, were deployed for the defence of the airfield under the command of the commander of *KGr z.b.V.11*, *Oberstleutnant* Wilke.[139] This allowed the number of soldiers available for action to be increased to about 700, but the aircrews lacked experience in ground combat.

At about 0900hrs an aircraft from the Dutch III Reconnaissance Group at Ruigenhoek[140] returned to report that Valkenburg was crowded with up to 50 German transport planes, and the commander-in-chief of the Dutch Air Arm immediately ordered its commander to launch an attack. Shortly before 1000hrs five Fokker C-Vs from Ruigenhoek dropped four 25kg-bombs each on the airfield and managed to fly back unhindered. Some of the stranded Ju 52s were destroyed or damaged. Ten minutes later Dutch artillery, positioned in the area around Katwijk, opened up with observed fire on the airfield. Direct hits destroyed about 20 of the transport aircraft and caused losses among the troops still present. The hangars where the seriously wounded of both sides were accommodated – most of the prisoners and the transportable wounded had been moved to Valkenburg at the start of the range-finding fire of the artillery – were also hit several times. Fortunately for the German side, the greater part of the paratroopers and air-landing troops had also left the airfield prior to the bombardment due to the combat missions they were scheduled to undertake. The majority of *III./InfRgt.47*, the unexpected elements of *II./InfRgt.65* and the staff of *InfRgt.47* had moved away to the east, in order to establish a defensive line along the western bank of the Oude Rijn between Katwijk aan Zee and the bridge at Haagse Schouw. While most of these forces initially remained in Valkenburg, details pushed forward to the north and occupied a seminary and a limestone factory on the island between the two arms of the Oude Rijn,

139 Wilke, on 24 May 1940, was to receive the *Ritterkreuz* for his participation in the fighting for Fortress Holland.
140 The airfield, located north of Hordijk, obviously had not been detected by the *Luftwaffe* and therefore had not been attacked.

south-east of Katwijk aan den Rijn. From there, they dominated the three narrow bridges leading across the river from Rijnsburg to Katwijk. A patrol at 1040hrs even advanced to a Shell petrol station south of Katwijk aan den Rijn.

In the meantime the outskirts of Valkenburg and the buildings along the dike road to the north and south of the village were occupied. The prisoners from the previous fighting were gathered in a meadow near the church. The wounded of both sides were lodged in a school building, which was clearly marked as a medical installation with Red Cross panels. On the airfield and in field positions just north of it, except for a few paratroopers and the medical personnel, caring for the wounded, only a number of the aircrews stayed behind for its protection.

At 1055hrs the second wave of troops planned for deployment in the area around Valkenburg – the three rifle companies, and some HQ staff from *II./InfRgt.47* – arrived in the airspace south-west of Leiden with 39 Ju 52s. As the airfield was unusable 26 of these aircraft landed on the beach between Katwijk and Scheveningen and unloaded their passengers there, only six of these managed to take off again. The 320 soldiers of the 5th, 6th and 7th companies, and the staff from *II./InfRgt.47* and about 60 airmen of the stranded Ju 52s retired into the dunes south of the beach in four separate groups. There, they settled down as a radio link with the forces at Valkenburg and east of it could not be achieved. The largest group attempted to reach the airfield, but were repulsed by the fire of Dutch troops positioned south of Katwijk aan Zee. The highest-ranking officer present was the commander of *5./InfRgt.47*, *Oberleutnant* Voigt.

Of the 20 Ju 52s left stranded along the beach some had been damaged by fire from the Dutch heavy anti-aircraft batteries, positioned near Wassenaar and Voorschooten. A short time after landing they had been bombarded by the 75mm guns of 7th Training Battery, which had caused further damage. In the course of the day they were time and again attacked by small groups of Fokker C-X and C-Vs with machine-guns. By the evening, most of them had been destroyed.

Three more aircraft with soldiers from *II./InfRgt.47* aboard came down in a field south of Valkenburg. After a short time, their passengers managed to join the force under *Oberst* Heyser. One Ju 52 conducted an emergency landing near Maaldrift.[141] All other transport aircraft of the second wave for the area at Valkenburg turned back without unloading.[142]

In the early afternoon a patrol from the forces of *II./InfRgt.47* situated in the dunes entered Wassenaar from the north-west. It was surprised by security elements from the 1st Regiment of Hussars and driven back with losses to the watertower at the northern edge of the village. There it joined another group of German soldiers. When these were also engaged by Dutch reinforcements and an anti-tank gun they again withdrew into the dunes. There, on either side of the Wassenaarse Slag, the separately landed groups of *II./InfRgt.47* linked up and established an all-round defence. Wassenaar remained firmly in Dutch hands, although no determined attack was launched from here. The main reason for this lack of initiative was that the majority of the 1st Regiment of Hussars had been ordered

---

141 The action of its passengers in support of the paratroopers of platoon Teusen has already been described.

142 The number of 14 Ju 52s, which had turned back, as reported by a Dutch source, indicates that aircraft with reinforcements other than *II./InfRgt.47* must also have approached Valkenburg at this time. The air transport plan of *22.(LL)Inf.Div.* had planned for Valkenburg the landing of the motorcycle company from *AufklAbt.22* and parts of an anti-aircraft machine-gun company at 1230hrs, of *I./InfRgt.47* with its three rifle companies and *11./InfRgt.47* at 1515hrs and of *8./InfRgt.47* at 1900hrs. None of these units afterward were employed again in air-landings.

to move to Den Haag, as reserve for the Dutch high command. Of the left task group of 3rd Inf.Div., II/1st Inf.Rgt. had reached the area around Maaldrift in the afternoon. III/1st Inf.Rgt. had arrived in Wassenaar only in the evening. At this time 6th Company from the Depot of Grenadiers and a platoon from the Depot of the Jagers had been moved from Den Haag to Wassenaar, but required time to become familiar with the situation. Reconnaissance patrols from the right task force of 3rd Inf.Div., which had cautiously moved forward, had easily been repulsed by German outposts east of the Wassenaarse Slag. Thus, as 3rd Inf.Div. had not yet completed its deployment for the clearing of the dunes north-west of Wassenaar, its attack was postponed until 11 May.

Like the attack by parts of the 1st Regiment of Hussars at Maaldrift and Landlust, the actions of depot troops from Leiden against the blocking of the bridge at Haagse Schouw had been initiated *ad hoc* by their local commanders. Elements of 22nd Depot Battalion succeed in regaining the bridge by a *coup de main* against the squad of paratroopers, positioned around its southern ramp. These were driven back some distance with two men killed and one captured. At 0930hrs between eight and 10 platoons from 22nd and 15th Depot Battalions and the Depot of the Horse Artillery moved to the banks on either side of the Oude Rijn, between the traffic bridge at Haagse Schouw and a railway bridge, located somewhat further to the south. However they were unable to gain more ground in a westerly direction, as soldiers from *9./InfRgt.47*, together with elements from *Leutnant* Teusen's squad, had set up several machine-gun nests north of Haagse Schouw. This allowed them to dominate the bridge and the open terrain west of the dike of the Oude Rijn by accurate fire. Nine Dutch soldiers who attempted to charge across the bridge in spite of this fire, paid for their bravery with their lives.

Coordinated Dutch countermeasures for the area around Valkenburg were accomplished slowly as the situation reports regarding the German landings were initially inaccurate and confusing. Although the first order for a counter-attack in the area around Den Haag was issued by the command of Fortress Holland at 0630hrs, it had to be modified several times over the course of the day as more conclusive pictures of the situation had been obtained. Incomplete reports about the strength of German troops in the areas around Valkenburg and north of Wassenaar and the blockage of the airfield there, as well as uncertainty about the next operational steps of the Germans, were the reasons why the command of Fortress Holland initially had tasked only 4th Inf.Rgt. with the consolidation of the situation around Valkenburg, although Lieutenant General van Andel had already received most of I Army Corps under his command.

When 3rd Inf.Div. was released for employment around Den Haag at 1000hrs, 4th Inf. Rgt. was placed subordinate to the division. Its original mission remained unchanged and the commanding officer of 4th Inf.Rgt. planed to attack Valkenburg from the north with his three battalions abreast. The commanders of 3rd Inf.Div. and of 4th Inf.Rgt. were in disagreement about the follow-on mission for the regiment. Neither of them knew that the island in the Oude Rijn, at the eastern edge of Katwijk aan den Rijn, had been occupied by the Germans.

Over the course of the morning I/4th Inf.Rgt. (less one company) marched from Noordwijk via Katwijk aan Zee toward its concentration area for the attack. During its advance through the dunes south-west of Katwijk the battalion was time and again involved in firefights with German machine-gun-outposts which caused a number of losses. It was not until 1700 hrs that it could be deployed to its start-position for the attack. On its left III/4th Inf.Rgt. had attempted to retake the airfield with its still complete 2nd Company, the remaining three machine-gun platoons and the remainder from 1st and 3rd companies in the morning, but had failed. It advancing again in the early afternoon and was forced to ground by flanking fire from German machine-guns. Only after 1600hrs, when the mortars had silenced a particularly troublesome machine-gun nest, did the battalion, which in the meantime had been joined by two recruit platoons from 10th Depot Battalion, struggle forward to about 200m distance to the northern edge of the airfield.

Delayed by an air attack, II/4th Inf.Rgt. (less one company), following behind I/4th Inf.Rgt., and late in the morning arrived in the area immediately north and west of Katwijk aan den Rijn. During its further advance to its attack position, the battalion was unexpectedly fired on by Germans, who had set up positions on the Oude Rijn island in a seminary, a limestone factory, and some adjoining houses.[143] As directed by Colonel Buurman, the commander of 4th Inf.Rgt., who had set up his command post south-west of Katwijk, II/4th Inf.Rgt., reinforced by a platoon from I/4th Inf.Rgt. and supported by heavy machine-guns and some artillery, set out to eliminate the Germans on the island. In the ensuing firefight, both sides suffered losses of killed and wounded but the attackers were unable to gain much ground. It was only after elements succeeded in crossing the western arm of the Oude Rijn by boat and getting close to the buildings occupied by the Germans from several sides, that these first abandoned the limestone factory and shortly thereafter the seminary and withdrew in the direction toward Valkenburg, leaving behind their dead, wounded and some men as prisoners. At 1440hrs, the island was again in the possession of the Dutch. Now, these were able to attack the German guard at the Shell petrol station from two sides and drive it off.

In the early afternoon the depot troops who had been brought forward from Leiden in order to open the road to Wassenaar, commenced a thrust toward the north along both banks of the Oude Rijn. The commander of Group Leiden, Colonel Siperda, assumed command over these forces, which consisted of elements of all four depot battalions. The primary objective of this thrust was to neutralize the last German strongpoint which was able to dominate the traffic bridge at Haagse Schouw with its machine gun fire. This strongpoint was located in a farmhouse with a barn at the dike on the left bank of the river, north of the bridge. It was occupied by about a dozen air-landing soldiers and the remainder of the parachute squad which had been driven away from Haagse Schouw. The plan to cross the river by boat from a stone-cutting works on the right bank and get behind the strong point, had to be abandoned as German heavy machine-gun-fire from the left bank prevented the occupation of this work. The attempt to ferry a storming party of 14 men across the river from the cemetery at Rijnvliet also failed under fire from the defenders of the strongpoint. However by the late afternoon the shock troop succeeded in crossing the river. Its fire into the farmhouse from short range wounded some of its occupants. This

143 German after-action reports do not cover the fighting for the island in any detail. From the abundance of respective Dutch reports, it becomes evident that elements of von Plessen's platoon and some elements from *InfRgt.47* fought on the island and near the Shell petrol station. Right after their arrival these had shot up a motor car with an officer and a non-commissioned officer of the artillery approaching one of the bridges, and afterward had captured a truck-load of 15 recruits from IV Depot of the Horse Artillery, along with the non-commissioned officer in command and the truck-driver. Subsequently, they occupied these buildings.

caused nine German paratroopers to retire toward the north and surrender. In the barn four seriously wounded Germans were detected and near the farmhouse an officer and a non-commissioned officer, who had probably been killed by the preceding machine-gun, fire were found.

After taking the last German strongpoint and blocking the bridge at Haagse Schouw, II/1st Inf.Rgt. from 3rd Inf.Div., which in the meantime had arrived from Haarlem, could now get across the Oude Rijn unhindered. Its reinforced advance company quickly overcame some resistance at Maaldrift and thereby put twelve Germans out of action. Now the route to Wassenaar and further to Den Haag was finally secure for the Dutch.

After the German strongpoint at the dike-road north of Haages Schouw was removed, elements from 22nd Depot Battalion advanced to this location. For the night they positioned themselves along a nearby drainage ditch, behind them heavy machine-guns and mortars were also placed. On the right bank of the Oude Rijn elements of 15th Depot Battalion, on their way forward from Leiden, were hit by a German air attack and lost two killed and three wounded. Pressing on at about 1650hrs they managed to occupy the stone-cutting works north of the cemetery at Rijnvliet. Fire from a German position in the farm at Rijnvliet, located on the left bank of the river, halfway between Haagse Schouw and Valkenburg, prevented their further advance along the river toward the north.

In Valkenburg and its immediate surroundings preparations to repel attack were intensified and the 300 Dutch prisoners were moved into the church. From the command post of *Oberst* Heyser in the townhall, telephone communication to Katwijk was still possible. As a preventive measure against any trouble by the population, around 190 male inhabitants of Valkenburg between 18 and 60 years of age had been confined under guard in a guesthouse. However in the evening all of them, except 12 kept as hostages, were released to their families. For the night, *Oberst* Heyser ordered a curfew.

However, in the meantime the Dutch had not remained inactive. Shortly before 1700hrs infantry (to the strength of about a company), accompanied by heavy machine-guns and anti-tank guns, were observed advancing from Katwijk toward Valkenburg. After a short firefight, the German guard post in a brick-yard, about 600m north of the village, retired. After an artillery bombardment of three minutes the Dutch attack force entered the brick-yard at 1740hrs, it then pushed further forward and succeeded in occupying some of the foremost houses in the northern part of Valkenburg with its advance elements. For about one hour, intensive artillery fire hit the northern part of the village. This caused some losses among the defenders, Dutch prisoners and the inhabitants. The German fire was increasing, meaning the few intruders were unable to gain any more ground. As they were not reinforced they retired again toward the north and were soon joined by the entire attack force; only a rearguard was left near the brick-yard.

After a short artillery bombardment of Valkenburg, and after the last German machine-gun nest north of it was overrun and its crew captured, the soldiers of the depleted III/4th Inf.Rgt., joined by the two platoons of recruits from 22nd Depot Battalion, stormed its entrance at about 1740hrs. The few defenders who were still resisting – some paratroopers on the roofs of hangars and some aircrews behind stranded aircraft – were either put out of action or were forced to withdraw. At 1940hrs the airfield was retaken by the Dutch. Near the end of the fighting, more Dutch infantry made it to the airfield; a company from

I/4th Inf.Rgt. and a company of II/4th Inf.Rgt., which conducted a flanking attack against the village of Valkenburg. The latter was retained by the commanding officer of III/4th Inf.Rgt. and therefore could not accomplish its original mission. The wounded of both sides and the mostly German medical personnel found in one of the hangars were brought by ambulances to hospitals in Leiden via Katwijk. During the fighting for the airfield the Dutch had lost ten killed and eight wounded and 25 German soldiers had been captured. The almost continuous fire from German heavy machine-guns and mortars from the western edge of Valkenburg and two farmsteads caused the majority of the attack forces to retire from the airfield into the dunes north of it. While this movement was still underway three British Blenheim bombers attacked the airfield with bombs and machine-gun fire. Fortunately the retiring Dutch remained unscathed. At nightfall quiet returned over the contested areas around Valkenburg and north of Wassenaar which was only once in a while interrupted by short firefights between patrols and guard posts.

With some uneasiness the commanders of the isolated German forces anticipated the coming morning. Reports had been received from aerial reconnaissance and returning transport aircraft, and also by radio communication through *Gruppe Wischhusen*, which had at least temporarily been in radio contact with *Oberst* Heyser's force. This meant that, on the evening of 10 May, the command of *Luftflotte 2* was roughly aware of the situation of the troops around Valkenburg and west of it. As their lines of communication toward the south-west had been blocked since around midday by increasing numbers of Dutch troops arriving there, their breakthrough to *Fl.Div.7* was out of the question. Therefore their holding of position was considered the best option in order to support the overall operations in the area of the *Luftlande-Korps*. Here it could tie down strong Dutch forces between the lower course of the Oude Rijn and Den Haag, thereby preventing these from being committed against *Fl.Div.7*.

The small flying sports airfield at Ockenburg, named after an estate at the edge of a wood of just south of it, was located about 500m south the North Sea and close to the western outskirts of Den Haag. Due to its small size it was utilized by the Dutch Air Arm for the technical rigging of aircraft that were not yet combat ready and as a storage area for material. On the morning of 10 May, five Douglas-Northrop 8A-3Ns and two G-1 Wasp fighters were parked at its north-western edge. Since 9 May, it was protected against ground attack by two platoons and the HQ section of a company from 22nd Depot Battalion totalling 96 men with three light machine-guns. Additionally some personnel for aircraft-rigging and logistics support were stationed there and a searchlight platoon was on duty at night. Parts of the 1st and 2nd battalions of the Grenadier Regiment and its 13th Machine-gun Company were quartered in Loosduinen, 2 km south-east of the airfield. At the eastern edge of the village the command post of the Grenadier Regiment was set up. About 2km to the north-east 23rd Anti-Aircraft Battery with three 75mm guns and some anti-aircraft machine-guns was positioned. The similarly equipped 76th Anti-Aircraft Battery was located about 2km south-west of Rijswijk. Near Poeldijk, 3km south of the airfield, an artillery unit with three units of 12cm howitzers had also set up its firing positions. From Monster at the coast, about 4km south-west of the airfield, a battalion of the Jager Regiment conducted coastal surveillance.

At 0600hrs two D-XXI fighters and two Douglas-Northrop 8A-3Ns from Ypenburg touched down on the airfield for refueling and rearming. As supplies of this kind were unavailable the aircraft were parked near the hangars, when a squadron of German Bf 110 fighter-bombers attacked the airfield. In the course of this attack, the buildings and the parked aircraft were destroyed.

The German mission for the airfield at Ockenburg had planned to initially drop *3./ FschJgRgt.2* under *Oberleutnant* von Roon in its immediate surroundings with the object of quickly seizing the airfield. Shortly afterwards *II./InfRgt.65*, reinforced by *13./InfRgt.65* (infantry guns), and two platoons of the bicycle squadron from *AufklAbt.22* were also to be airlanded. Subsequent to the seizure of the airfield the paratroopers were to clear the dunes around Kijkduin, on the coast about 1km to the north-east. Meanwhile the air-landing-troops, beside the protection of the airfield, were ordered to block the roads leading from Den Haag to the south-west, and to reconnoiter in the direction toward Monster and Den Haag. Only a few additional combat-support troops had been planned as reinforcements for the area around Ockenburg and were to arrive as parts of the second and third waves of the air transport operation.

Evasive manouvres by the transport aircraft as a result of the intensive anti-aircraft fire around Den Haag, coupled with the inexperience of the dispatchers, resulted in most of the Ju 52s with *3./FschJgRgt.2* aboard missing the planned drop zones. The greater part of the company, consisting of 71 men and their company commander, were dropped in two separate groups far away from the objective – the group with *Oberleutnant* von Roon about 2km east of Hoek van Holland, the other near Naaldwijk, about 5km more to the north-east. As the pilots had mistaken the airfield at Valkenburg as the objective, 3rd Platoon was dropped north of Wassenaar. This caused the platoon leader's *Feldwebel* to become separated from his men, and he was instantly killed.

Oberleutnant Genz[144] and his 1st Platoon were dropped correctly but came under fire from machine-guns on two approaches north of the airfield, close to the beach near Kijkduin.[145] Consequently two paratroopers drifted out to sea and were drowned. A Dutch patrol that was approaching the drop zone was taken prisoner after a short firefight. Thereafter, Genz's platoon moved off in a direction toward the airfield.[146] They were fired

---

144 Alfred Genz, born in 1916. Transferred from the police to the parachute force in 1935 and participated as *Leutnant* in the campaign against Poland and as *Oberleutnant* in the parachute operation in Holland. He fought as company commander in the *Luftlande-Sturmregiment* in May 1941 on Crete. For his service in this assault he was awarded the *Ritterkreuz* on 14 June 1941. Both his brothers were killed as paratroopers on Crete, and so, according to the decree about the preservation of families, he was withdrawn from combat and as a *Hauptmann* served as instructor for ground combat in the *Luftwaffe*, and as member of the staff of *General* Student until end of 1943. From January 1944 on, returned to combat action as commander of *III./FschJgRgt.12* at Anzio-Nettuno and in northern Italy. From October 1944 until January 1945 he served as *Major*, commander of *II/FschJgRgt 10* in northern Italy. His last combat action in was in March 1945 as commander of *FschJgRgt 29* in Austria. After the end of the war he was handed over by the U.S. to the Soviets. He returned from captivity in the Soviet Union in 1949 and joined the German *Bundeswehr* in 1956 as *Oberstleutnant* and commander of the first parachute infantry battalion of the new German Army. After receiving promotion to *Oberst* in March 1968 he was made commander of the German Airborne and Air transport School. He retired in 1974 and died in April 2000.

145 Genz later had reported that the dispatcher in his aircraft was killed by anti-aircraft fire during the first approach and that he therefore had jumped alone.

146 The organization and armament of the platoon – platoon leader and runner, a 5cm mortar section with 4 men, an anti-tank rifle-team with two men and two parachute squads with 12 men and two light machine-

at by the defenders of the airfield. 5th and parts of 7th companies from *II./InfRgt.65* had already been landed at 0645hrs and immediately had engaged in the ongoing fighting. Thirteen Ju 52s from *1./KGr z.b.V.9* touched down at 0745hrs with two platoons and the HQ section from the bicycle squadron of *22.(LL)Inf.Div.*, commanded by *Rittmeister* Pollay. By 0830hrs the air-landing troops and particularly the incomplete *InfRgt.65* had cleared the airfield of its defenders. These attempted to continue the fight from behind an earthen wall at its southern edge but were quickly dispersed by the fire of paratroopers from Genz's platoon, who in the meantime got behind them. Here the commander of the Dutch depot company was killed and a number of his soldiers captured. The remainder managed to escape into a park about 1.5km north-east of the airfield. During the air attack and the ensuing ground combat the depot company lost 28 killed and 18 wounded. The personnel of the Dutch Air Arm, quartered in barracks at the southern edge of the airfield, had been able to retire in time and therefore had lost only 4 killed.

A formation of five Ju 52s, with soldiers of *II./InfRgt.65* aboard, had not landed on the airfield at Ockenburg probably because this was already full, and instead looked for alternate landing sites. One of them, which had been damaged by ground fire, had come down south of Monster; here its passengers and the aircrew had been captured. Another of these aircraft, after it was damaged by machine-gun-fire, had conducted an emergency landing at Hilwoning at the beach near Hoek van Holland after it was set ablaze by mortar fire during unloading. When a Dutch patrol arrived shortly afterwards at the crash-site, the passengers, some of them wounded, surrendered. In the wreck of the aircraft were two killed and one mortally wounded from *7./InfRgt.65*, as well as about 20 burnt bicycles. At around 1140 hrs a third Ju 52 of this formation had come down on the island of Rozenburg, south-west of the village with the same name. Of its passengers, 14 soldiers were hiding in a barn in the polder and surrendered without a fight in the evening after being surrounded by a Dutch detachment formed from civilian citizen guards, men from the searchlight team and a squad each of infantrymen and marines. The remaining two Ju 52s of the group landed on the airfield at Waalhaven, where they unloaded soldiers from *7./InfRgt.65*.

Shortly after the seizure of the airfield at Ockenburg it became evident that this site was blocked for further air-landings by stranded Ju 52s and destroyed Dutch aircraft. Shortly after 0830hrs, four Ju 52s from *3./KGr z.b.V.9* with *Generalleutnant* Graf von Sponeck, a part of his battle HQ and other elements for command and control functions, approached Ockenburg after the failure of the air-landings at Ypenburg. They were forced to touch down for unloading in a field south-west of it. Only two of these aircraft, both of them damaged, were able to take off again. Four more Ju 52s from *3./KGr z.b.V.9* which were also transporting troops for the command and control of *22.(LL)Inf.Div.*, landed on the auto-route south of Delft and at the beach near Kijkduin. A number of other transport aircraft, which originally had been planned for landings on the airfields at Ypenburg and Valkenburg, due to the chaotic situation there changed plan and selected the area around Ockenburg as a landing site.[147] Among the newly arrived troops was also a platoon from

---

guns each, indicates again that the war establishment for the parachute infantry companies often was modified to meet the tactical requirements according to the mission.

147 Altogether, 47 Ju 52s had come down on and around Ockenburg on 10 May. Some of them had unloaded their passengers in the dunes near the beach. 18 Ju 52s had landed directly on the airfield. Of these, only five from *1./KGr z.b.V.9* had managed to take off again. They had, however, taken along 37 aircrew from stranded aircraft.

3./PiBtl.22. The presence of the commander of *II./InfRgt.65*, *Major* Zuern, turned out to be of high value for the command and control of the landed forces, as his competence and combat experience radiated confidence among the men.

At 0910hrs, three Dutch Fokker T-V bombers attacked the airfield and dropped 30 light bombs, causing a few of the air-landing soldiers to be killed and four of the Ju 52s, still parked on the site, to be destroyed. One of the bombers was shot down over the North Sea by pursuing German fighters during its flight back.

In the meantime *7./InfRgt.65* occupied positions along the northern and eastern edges of the airfield. Elements from *5./InfRgt.65* advanced to a road-junction east of it and set up defensive positions in a nearby farmstead and small factory. Other elements of this company moved forward against Loosduinen. Here they succeeded in overrunning a heavy machine-gun platoon, but were stopped in their tracks by the fire of more machine-guns, brought to bear by the Dutch. After the delivery of its prisoners at the airfield, Genz and his men had set out again toward the north in order to establish contact with the majority of *3./FschJgRgt.2*, which were assumed to be there. It was, however, stopped by Dutch security posts on the western outskirts of Den Haag and thereafter restricted its activity to reconnaissance and surveillance only.

At 0800hrs the command post of the Dutch Grenadier Regiment in Loosduinen alerted all troops in the vicinity after the fall of Ockenburg. These were now deployed to build up a continuous front between Loosduinen and the western edge of Den Haag. II/Gren.Rgt. was unavailable for action around Ockenburg and was involved in the fighting around Ypenburg. For the counter-attack, the Dutch command dispatched I/Gren.Rgt. west of Den Haag and I/JgRgt from Monster. At the northern edge of Loosduinen, the machine-gun, anti-tank and infantry gun companies from the Grenadier Regiment set up blocking positions. The three batteries of the artillery detachment near Poeldijk had been shelling the airfield since 1000hrs. Fire directed from the watertower in Monster caused the destruction of 12 more of the German transport aircraft still stranded on the airfield. A German air attack against the artillery positions had no effect at all; its bombs fell into the wood north-east of the airfield.

Into this wood, *Generalleutnant* Graf von Sponeck and the 300 soldiers, who had been unloaded with him retreated and established a command post. Protected by men forward of the edges of the wood and based in the estate house at Ockenburg, *Major* Zuern[148] directed the construction of field positions around the small hill at Belvedere. After *Oberleutnant* Genz saw no further possibilities for active measures in the dunes and a patrol dispatched by him in the direction toward Monster, in order to liaise with the majority of *3./FschJgRgt.2*, had not reappeared,[149] he joined *Gruppe von Sponeck* around midday with the remainder of his platoon. While entrenching at the edge of the wood one more of his men were killed by artillery fire.

---

148   For his performance in the fighting around Ockenburg and later in the defence of Overschie, *Major* Zuern, together with the commander of his 5th Company, *Oberleutnant* Lingner, was awarded the *Ritterkreuz* on 16 June 1940.

149   The patrol, a *Feldwebel* and three men, had been captured near Monster and later had been taken to England together with numerous other paratroopers.

Late in the morning I/Gren.Rgt., two of its organic companies and an assigned company of recruits, formed up to attack against the airfield in the park at Meer en Bosch, about 1km north of Loosduinen. At the western edge of the park anti-tank guns, heavy machine-guns and infantry guns had been positioned. When the artillery from Poeldijk ceased firing at 1230hrs,[150] the infantry, supported by its organic heavy weapons, commenced its attack. The German security screens around the road junction and along the eastern edge of the airfield were quickly overrun and 55 Germans were taken prisoners. Some of the defenders managed to withdraw into the airfield where they continued to fight from positions behind wrecked aircraft. The last resistance from this area was broken at around 1630 hrs and the entire airfield returned to Dutch hands again. Here 30 fellow-soldiers, who had been captured during the German assault in the morning, were liberated. About 100 Germans, mainly wounded crews from the stranded transport aircraft who had been left on the airfield, and medical personnel caring for them, were captured. Some of the German soldiers who had been killed on the airfield had unlawfully been shot after they had surrendered.[151]

While the companies of I/Gren.Rgt. were content with the retaking of the airfield and the mopping-up of German stragglers – the Dutch had lost 17 killed during the attack – I/JgRgt, engaged with small groups of German soldiers. By the afternoon it had reached the Ockenburg wood on foot from Monster. One of its companies quickly overcame the machine-gun outposts from *Gruppe von Sponeck* in front of the northern edge of the wood. The other two companies halted in front of the estate house at Ockenburg, from where a German outpost dominated the clearing north of it by fire. By outflanking the house one of these companies finally forced the Germans to withdraw. It then continued to advance almost 1km to the south, before it came across German positions at Belvedere. There it was involved in fierce close-combat. In the meantime I/JgRgt was, for unknown reasons, ordered to Loosduinen and so the company discontinued the fight and moved off to Loosduinen with 15 German prisoners. The struggle in the wood had cost the Jagers 22 killed.

The 50 men from *3./FschJgRgt.2* who had parachuted with *Oberleutnant* von Roon into a polder about 2km east of Hoek van Holland had collected their weapons and assembled undisturbed in the nearby Staalduinse wood. A Dutch patrol of 25 soldiers which was sent out from Hoek van Holland had actually observed the paratroopers in the western part of the wood at about 0930hrs. However it had decided not to engage them and returned to its base.

Later when the Staalduinse Wood was shelled by artillery from the island of Rozenburg, *Oberleutnant* von Roon and his force retired to the east into the village of Maasdijk. There he confiscated two small trucks, a service vehicle for canal-cleaning and two other vehicles. Lacking a precise map, he decided to drive north and follow the coast to Ockenburg. Some of his men moved ahead of the column on foot. North-west of Maasdijk, they surprised a reinforced platoon of the Dutch II/JgRgt from Gravenzande. In the close-combat that developed the Dutch lost three killed and one captured, before they were able to withdraw.

---

150 The attempt to send a radio team from the artillery to the grenadiers, in order to provide fire-support during the attack, had failed, as the team had been captured by German troops.

151 This offence against the rules of war is reported in a Dutch source. It may have happened because German soldiers in the vicinity of those signaling their surrender had continued to fight.

Oberleutnant von Roon let his advance party mount the vehicles and then moved on toward Gravenzande via Naaldwijk. In front of this village, the column ran up against another platoon from II/JgRgt and was forced to dismount. In the short firefight two of the Dutch, and one paratrooper were killed, before von Roon's force retired in a south-easterly direction. The vehicles and a number of weapons on them remained in the hands of the Jagers.

Near Naaldwijk, the paratroopers from *3./FschJgRgt.2*, who had been dropped from two Ju 52s south of Monster, joined their company commander. Von Roon's party was now 70 strong. Provisionally motorized, it moved on toward the north-east. Driving past Monster, the paratroopers again were engaged in a short firefight with a number of soldiers from the Jager Regiment, who were still present after the departure of I/JgRgt. These were captured, confined in a building, or driven off. A few more paratroopers were also wounded.

In the evening *Oberleutnant* von Roon and the men with him reached the Ockenburg Wood. As the Dutch Jagers who had attacked during the afternoon had been drawn away, liaison with *Gruppe von Sponeck* could be established unhindered. Immediately thereafter, *Oberleutnant* von Roon assumed responsibility for the protection of the wood toward the west.

After the arrival of the majority of *3./FschJgRgt.2* and with some stragglers from the airfield *Gruppe von Sponeck* achieved a strength of about 400 men. Radio communication with *Generalleutnant* Student and the staff of *Fl.Div.7* was not made, that with the command of *Luftflotte 2* was firmly established. It was the report about the situation at the air bridgehead of *22.(LL)Inf.Div.*, submitted by *Generalleutnant* Graf von Sponeck, in conjunction with the situation reports received from *Flieger-Korps z.b.V.* and from the various air transport formations, which let General Kesselring come to the conclusion in the evening that the mission of *22.(LL)Inf.Div.* had failed. He therefore prohibited all further planned air-landings in the area around Den Haag. At 2000hrs he directed *Generalleutnant* Graf von Sponeck to fight through with as many of his forces as possible, to the air bridgehead of *Fl.Div.7*.[152] Preceding the transmission of this decision, the liaison staff of the *Luftlande-Korps* in Wiedenbrück had already stopped the move of the third wave of the air transport formations planned for 11 May and instead had issued orders for the delivery of additional troops and supplies into the operation area of *Fl.Div.7*.

The *Flieger-Korps z.b.V.* which was formed to provide air support for the *Luftlande-Korps*, had been unable to neutralize the Dutch forces around Den Haag. This was largely due to their forces having little time between their initial attacks and the arrival of the air transport formations. Furthermore it had been keen to neutralize the air forces of the enemy as a first priority as they threatened their own bombers and transport aircraft. Furthermore they had to split up over many target areas. Almost no time was left prior to the start of the parachute and air-landing assaults to plan in depth for a targeted campaign against the

---

152 *General* (ret.) Trettner, who had been the chief of staff of *Fl.Div.7* during the airborne operation against Fortress Holland, in a letter to the author, 3 June 2005 pointed out, that Kesselring had made the decision to give up the operation of *22.(LL)Inf.Div.* all by himself, as Hitler had not interfered in the operations of the *Luftlande-Korps*, and there had been no time to coordinate with the *OKW*. The time of Kesselring's decision is laid down in a report of the liaison officer from *Luftflotte 2* at *Heeresgruppe B* on 10 May 2020hrs stating that *22.(LL)Inf.Div.* just had received the order to withdraw from Katwijk and Kijkfuin to the site south of Delft.

Dutch anti-aircraft batteries. Last, but not least, the anticipated effects against the well dispersed anti-aircraft weapons may have been over-estimated.[153] This had also proved true for air attacks by low level bombers against Dutch ground forces in prepared field fortifications or bunkers. Dive bombers, with their capability to hit targets, would have greatly assisted in overcoming particularly troublesome anti-aircraft positions, but please had not been made available permanently or only in inadequate numbers.

One of the particularly negative consequences of the lack of effectve air attacks against Dutch anti-aircraft defence was that many of parachute forces assigned to *22.(LL)Inf. Div.* were often dropped wrongly or too far away from their objectives as a result of the evasive manouvres of their transport aircraft. This meant that none of the airfields in the operational area of *22.(LL)Inf.Div.* had been seized and secured by the paratroopers prior to the arrival of the first wave of the air-landing troops. Freedom of action for the tactical leaders of the parachute units, allowing them to stop or delay the air-landings until the airfields had been seized, had not been understood, as ground-to-air radio communications had not existed. Other methods of communication, such as flares or signal panels, had not been given consideration. Most of all, full reliance was placed in the capability of the paratroopers to accomplish their task within the given time-frame, this proved to be a major mistake. The weak units of the parachute force who were assigned to seize the large airfield at Ypenburg had a high risk of failure from the outset, as it remained unknown that the airfield's location, near the towns of Den Haag and Delft, would provide the Dutch with the opportunity to quickly and effectively reinforce the positions there. The question whether *II./TschJgRgt.2*, lf lts three landed companies had been jump-trained,[154] could have improved the situation for *22.(LL)Inf.Div.* at Ypenburg decisively, is a hypothetical one.

At Ypenburg the lack of adequate organic heavy weapons for the parachute force had become clearly visible. This deficiency had little negative impact on the operations of *Fl.Div.7*, as heavy weapons were landed on Waalhaven airfield early and the forces of *FschJgRgt.1* had not yet been subjected to a combined arms attack during 10 May. For the paratroopers fighting for Ypenburg the situation had been quite different. Once they had failed to overcome the defenders of the airfield and the air-landing of troops and heavy weapons from *22.(LL)Inf.Div.* had ended in a catastrophe, they had to depend on the machine-guns and the few anti-tank rifles and short-range mortars which had been dropped with them. These, however, were out-ranged by highly effective 3.7 and 2cm guns and also by mortars and artillery with observed fire. The heavy infantry weapons of the paratroopers soon ran out of ammunition, as the fighting was longer than expected and resupply from the air had been neither foreseen nor feasible. Against the well-led Dutch infantry, the dispersed and surrounded men stood no chance after hours of fierce fighting.

---

153   After this deficiency was recognized, the *Luftwaffe* attempted to achieve the desired effects by repeated massive air attacks, The results, as experienced against a well dug-in and disciplined enemy, as for example on Crete, was modest. This result was repeated later in the war by the Allies, in spite of their tremendous airpower. Only after precision-guided and/or highly efficient scatterable munitions had become available for air forces 30 years later in the Vietnam War, and perfected another 20 years later in the conflicts in the Near- and Middle East, had air attacks against ground forces and installations achieved most of the desired results.

154   Why *II./FschJgRgt.2* had not yet been jump-trained probably has to do with the transfer of the jump-school from Stendal to Wittstock which caused a temporary interruption of the jump-training. Another reason may have been the removal of Ju 52s from jump-training to the air transport formations required for the airborne operations in Norway and in the West.

For the first time it became evident that the bravery of the paratroopers alone could hardly turn the tide against a better equipped and determined fighting opponent.

As the tactical cooperation on the battlefield between *Fl.Div.7* and *22.(LL)Inf.Div.* had not been planned the assignment of even a minimum of corps-level troops for the airborne mission had been neglected. For the same reason there was no exchange of liaison staffs and related means for radio communications. When the landing plan of *22.(LL)Inf.Div.* had failed to come to fruition and the division's internal communications net had failed to function, the staff of *Fl.Div.7* had received information about the situation around Den Haag only through runners.

Command relations between the *Luftlande-Korps* and *Flieger-Korps z.b.V.* had been unsatisfactory from the very beginning. The latter remained directly subordinate to *Luftflotte 2* and had only been ordered to cooperate with the *Luftlande-Korps*. This meant that the requests for air support had to be submitted to the command of *Luftflotte 2* before they were passed to the *Flieger-Korps* if considered appropriate, often leading to a considerable loss of time.

Luftflotte 2 was responsible for air operations over the entire attack-sector of *18.Armee* and in the initial phase it had acted restrictively regarding information given to the *Luftlande-Korps* about the enemy situation in regions adjoining its area of operations. Consequently no reports were received about the movements of the Dutch 3rd Inf.Div. from the area around Haarlem/Noordwijk, in a south-westerly direction across the Oude Rijn. *Flieger-Korps z.b.V.* clearly lacked resources for an efficient interdiction from the air, which could have reduced the pressure on those German ground forces still holding out north-east of Den Haag. This was mainly due to its many support missions and too few combat aircraft.

The command of the *Luftlande-Korps* was also ignorant about the operations of the *Luftwaffe* over the areas near the Dutch coast and over the mouths of the large rivers. Due to the lack of any German naval forces worth mentioning and the under-resourced air forces assigned for operations over Holland, these areas were dominated by ships of the Dutch and their Allies.

Although no landings of British or French combat troops as reinforcements for the Dutch had been observed on 10 May, the possibility could not be ruled out, as the initial phase of the campaign against Norway had shown. Intelligence about the sea regions close to the Dutch coast and about potential embarkation sites in England would have been of importance to the command of the *Luftlande-Korps*. To what extent this was not considered by the German highest commands is indicated by the following two examples: German intelligence was aware of the huge Dutch oil stores in the western part of the Ijsselmonde, yet no instructions from high command had been issued for their quick seizure during the planning of the airborne operation against Fortress Holland.

Despite the ample indications from the events prior and during the initial phase of the campaign against Norway with regards to the capability and willingness of the British to cause as much damage as possible to the German war economy, the threat was still not taken sufficiently seriously. German aerial reconnaissance, probably lacking clear tasks for an ongoing surveillance of the sea approaches toward the Dutch ports, had either missed the landing of British troops from destroyers on 10 May[155] or had seen no need to pass this information on to the command of the *Luftlande-Korps*.

There was aso a gap in the flow of information regarding events in the Dutch province of Noord Brabant, through which the relief forces for *Fl.Div.7* were to advance and from which a threat for the air bridgehead at the bridges at Moerdijk had developed.

11 May

On the evening of 10 May the Dutch high command acknowledged that the German airborne attack of Den Haag had failed. The troops who were employed to eliminate of the isolated German forces in Valkenburg, the dunes north of Wassenaar, Ockenburg Wood and south of Delft were assessed of adequate strength to accomplish their missions. Although the situation immediately east of Hoek van Holland was not yet completely clear their own forces at the tip of Westland were also considered to be of sufficient strength to withstand attack by German parachute and air-landing-forces which had been observed there. For the east of Holland, the intent was to fight for time and preserve the combat effectiveness of the troops from IV and II Army Corps, for the battle in the so-called New Waterline between Lake Ijssel and the Waal river; an area which was to be retained at all costs. Extending to the west along the Waal and the Bergsche Maas, the positions of III Army Corps were to connect with the New Waterline. The Dutch high command firmly relied on the deployment of the French 7th Army for Noord Brabant. The army consisted of five infantry divisions (two of them mechanized), a reinforced tank division and mechanized reconnaissance forces of about a brigade strength, and was located at least as far to the east as abreast of Tilburg.[156] The most forward of its units had reached Dutch territory in the area around Breda by the evening of 10 May. The deployment of the main forces of 7th Army was to be along the canal at Zuid-Willemsvaart by units of the Dutch Peel Division, which on the night 10/11 May was retiring from the Peel-Raam position because of the start of the German breakthrough along the axis Mill-Gennep. Supported by French forces, as had been agreed by General Gamelin during a telephone conversation with General Winkelman in the morning of 10 May, the bridges at Moerdijk were to be retaken as soon as possible.

During the morning of 11 May the Dutch high command had little knowledge about the consequences of the crisis which was developing in the northern part of the Peel-Raam position, as the territorial commander for Noord Brabant was left in sole responsibility for this province. With his small staff and lacking adequate means for command, control and communications, Colonel Schmidt, was overburdened in his role of commanding the Peel Division in difficult combat actions and to arrange for coordinating with the

---

155 Without coordination with Dutch military authorities or the Dutch government the British, under the codename XD Ops, had landed troops, made up of specialized engineers and marines, in Hoek van Holland, Ijmuiden and Vlissingen. There, they were to destroy the Dutch oil supplies, so that they would not fall into the hands of the Germans. Additional missions had been, to support the Dutch in the transport of their gold and jewel reserves to England, and to prepare for the landing of troops for the protection of a possible evacuation of the Dutch royal family and government.

156 In execution of the Breda variant of the Dijle plan which had been ordered by the French high command at 0700hrs on 10 May, 7th Army had commenced to move in the direction of the western part of Noord Brabant with some of its formations.

approaching French. The first reports about the withdrawal of the Peel Division from the northern part of the Peel-Raam Line and about strong German forces pushing ahead there had led the Dutch high command to conclude that the window for the desired build-up of a solid continuous line by the French abreast of Tilburg had become narrower. North of the large rivers the enemy had not yet advanced to the fortified lines – the Grebbe Line west of Arnhem, and the Wons position in front of the locking-dike – it appeared that the approaches toward Fortress Holland from the east were still safe.

By the afternoon of 10 May considerable reinforcements had been made available for Rotterdam.[157] No instructions for their deployment or their cooperation with the command of Fortress Holland, however, were issued. The primary attention of the command of Fortress Holland was directed toward the retaking of the German occupied parts of the islands of Ijsselmonde and Dordrecht. The thrust of a battalion against the bridges at Dordrecht was unknown to Lieutenant General van Andel, as was the state of planning of the territorial commander for Noord Brabant for cooperation with French troops. His ignorance about the initiated action of Group Kil against the bridges at Dordrecht may have been the reason why he had not delegated his direct command over the garrison of Dordrecht to Group Kil and why he had not issued instructions to the garrison commander, Lieutenant Colonel Mussert, regarding how to cooperate with the attacking force from Group Kil.

In the operation area of *22.(LL)Inf.Div.* maintaining a unity of command over the isolated groups of the division and the provision of instructions for the coordination of their actions became impossible due to the failure of the airborne attack against Den Haag. Only *Gruppe von Sponeck* in the Ockenburg Wood received orders to fight through to *Fl.Div.7*. The troops in Valkenburg and in the dunes north of Wassenaar, according to Kesselring, were to tie down as many Dutch forces as possible and prevent them from intervening elsewhere. The exsistence of the company-sized force under *Oberleutnant* Martin in the Staalduinse Wood, east of Hoek van Holland, seemed to remain unknown to the commands of *Luftflotte 2* and the *Luftlande-Korps*.

With first light on 11 May machine-gun and light artillery fire on the southern edge of Delft commenced and became almost continuous, preventing any attempt by the Germans to enter the town. Soon artillery fire was also delivered as the Dutch tried to destroy the stranded transport aircraft. Unfortunately for the Dutch, the artillery shells either fell far off or too short. However, the artillery fire did succeed in significantly disturbing the inexperienced soldiers of Wischhusen's force.

---

157   Reinforcements as follows had to be moved to Rotterdam in the evening of 10 May:
- headquarters 11th Inf.Rgt., I/11th Inf.Rgt., IV/10th Inf.Rgt. (less MG company), IV/15th Inf.Rgt. (less MG company and the anti-tank and mortar companies of 11th Inf.Rgt. from II Army Corps.
- III/21st Inf.Rgt. from IV Army Corps:
- II/25th Inf.Rgt. from Group Lek.
- II/32nd Inf.Rgt. from Group Utrecht.

Altogether, these numbered 3,500 combat troops. Additionally a battery with modern 10.5cm howitzers was ordered to Rotterdam.

Around midday, two Dutch light aircraft strafed the German positions. At about the same time, it became evident that Dutch infantry were working around the eastern flank of the group along the road at Delfgau-Ruiven.[158] Worried about the increasing enemy pressure, Dr. Wischhusen[159] requested air attacks against the particularly troublesome Dutch forces in the south-eastern corner of Delft. The requested air attacks were executed twice during the course of 11 May. However they were directed against the south-western corner of Delft, rather than the area requested by Wischhusen. What little relief they gave to the hardpressed soldiers on the ground was paid for by the loss of one of the attacking Ju 88 bombers.

Late in the morning, a task force of Dutch hussars launched a surprise attack on the auto-route. About 30 German soldiers were captured and the unity of the entire position was threatened. By a determined counter-thrust the situation was able to be reconsolidated. As his force was running out of ammunition and because of the undisciplined continuous firing of his inexperienced soldiers, Dr. Wischhusen requested re-supply from the air. In the afternoon the request was met but the supplies were dropped on the meadows west of the auto-route between Rotterdam-Den Haag, which was dominated by the fire from the Dutch. They mistook the dropping of supplies as the parachuting of troops and shelled the drop zone intensively for almost two hours with artillery. When, late in the afternoon, *Oberleutnant* Eckleben reported outflanking movements by the enemy in the west and after the location of the command post of *Fl.Div.7* finally had been made by radio, Dr. Wischhusen decided to discontinue the defence of his present positions and retire his force in a direction toward Rotterdam. There he hoped to join *Fl.Div.7*.

While the preparations for this move were underway a Dutch officer, accompanied by a German *Feldwebel*, arrived at 1800hrs from Rotterdam under a flag of truce. He informed Dr. Wischhusen about a ceasefire and his task to pick up German wounded in the two ambulances which followed behind him. After all but two of the wounded had been loaded, Wischhusen let the officer and the ambulances move on toward Delft. As soon as the ambulances withdrew, the Dutch reopened fire with unabated force. Later, under the cover of darkness, Wischhusen's men were able to salvage the ammunition which had been dropped in the afternoon. As the Dutch remained astonishingly quiet the picket posts were drawn back unnoticed. Around midnight, *Gruppe Wischhusen* joined by Eckleben's platoon and moved off toward the south. The Dutch soldiers who had been captured in the previous engagements and some civilians, who had been arrested because of suspicious behavior, were taken along. After a march of about 4km, Dr. Wischhusen let his force rest for two hours in a farmstead by the road protected by pickets.

Gruppe von Sponeck set up an all-round defence in the Ockenburg Wood. During the morning of 11 May he had almost no contact with the enemy, who were content to shell the wood from time to time with artillery. An emissary who was sent to Den Haag in order

---

158 Elements from two battalions of 3rd Inf.Div., which on 10 May was ordered to join the fighting east of Ypenburg – III/9th Inf.Rgt. and II/12th Inf.Rgt. – had advanced further to the south and had established contact with the depot and air-defence troops in the southern part of Delft. Elements of II/Gren.Rgt. had also arrived there.

159 A radio team, which originally had been planned for the battle HQ of *Generalleutnant* Graf von Sponeck, had come down in an emergency landing together with other parts of *Gruppe Wischhusen*. It was able to establish radio communication with the command post of *Fl.Div.7* and to maintain it almost continuously.

to negotiate the admittance of the wounded of *Gruppe von Sponeck* to Dutch hospitals, returned without having accomplished his goal, as the commanding officer of the Dutch 1st Inf.Div. rejected the request. His ultimatum to the Germans to surrender at 1200hrs was rejected by *Generalleutnant* Graf von Sponeck.

Shortly after midday the Dutch began their advance towards the German positions. About the same time, supplies which had been requested by radio for the impending break-out of *Gruppe von Sponeck* were delivered. However yet again most of them came down on terrain which was in the hands of the Dutch. Reconnaissance patrols sent out toward the south by *3./FschJgRgt.2* soon came across the enemy. Nevertheless *Generalleutnant* Graf von Sponeck decided to break-out in a direction toward the operational area of *Fl.Div.7* in the coming night, as he anticipated a massive Dutch counter-attack against his present positions within the next few hours. Yet, the commands of the Dutch 1st Inf.Div. and the Grenadier Regiment lost valuable time in preparing the attacking forces. A preliminary thrust of two grenadier platoons against the Belvedere hill failed, when one of these platoons was caught in a German ambush, with considerable losses in killed and wounded. It took until 2100hrs for both platoons were able to withdraw.

At 2200hrs *Gruppe von Sponeck* left behind the wounded not fit for marching and a few medical staff for their care and moved out past Loosduinen toward Wateringen. The rearguard, *3./FschJgRgt.2*, was also able to retire unnoticed and soon joined the main body. The Dutch grenadiers and jagers were to commence their attack no earlier than 0400hrs on 12 May. In the Ockenburg Wood, they found only the few German wounded and medics left behind. At about the same time *Gruppe von Sponeck*, still undetected, approached the village of Wateringen, about 4km south-west of the Ockenburg Wood.

A group of 26 paratroopers and air-landing soldiers who, after the disaster at Ypenburg, had found refuge in a steam-powered mill south of Wateringen. They had found no opportunity to join other German forces and had been captured by Dutch depot troops after a short firefight during the evening of 11 May during mop-up operations.

The German forces which moved to Valkenburg and its surroundings included elements of the staff and the command elements of *InfRgt.47*, the battle HQ and the majority of three companies from *III./InfRgt.47*, small elements from two companies from *II./InfRgt.65*, around 100 members from the aircrews of stranded aircraft and the HQ section with the remainder of two platoons from *6./FschJgRgt.2*. After the loss of Valkenburg and the road across the Oude Rijn toward Wassenaar these troops had been able to improve their positions undisturbed during the night of 10/11 May. Solid strongpoints had also been set up in the farmsteads at Rijnvliet, Zonneveld and Torenvliet south of Valkenburg. After the loss of the stone-cutting works on 10 May surveillance of the ground toward Katwijk aan den Rijn had become difficult as the ground was now dominated by observed fire from across the Oude Rijn.

At 0910hrs Dutch artillery commenced fire. Initially it was directed onto the terrain around the stone cutting works. Under cover of the artillery the Dutch infantry advanced to the drainage ditch abreast the stone-cutting work. The attack force, as ordered by the commanding officer of 4th Inf.Rgt., consisted of II/4th Inf.Rgt., the depleted III/4th Inf. Rgt. and a platoon each of mortars, infantry guns and anti-tank-guns from regimental-level companies. Artillery support was to be provided by III/2nd Art.Rgt. from around Katwijk aan Zee and by II/6th Art.Rgt. and was to be reinforced by a heavy battery from the area south of Rijnsburg. From there anti-tank guns and heavy machine-guns commenced firing at German positions at the northern edge of Valkenburg. III/2nd Art.Rgt. were extremely well directed from an observation post on the steeple of the church in Katwijk aan den Rijn and provided a creeping barrage in front of the attack force. II/6th Art.Rgt. hit the town heavily and its fire caused heavy losses among the civil population. The church, which was clearly marked as an installation of the Red Cross, received three hits. Five of the Dutch prisoners were killed and ten others wounded. In a telephone call, the mayor of Valkenburg begged the commander of 4th Inf.Rgt. in Katwijk to spare the church and the school in accordance with the Geneva Convention as protected installations. The commander ignored this appeal on account of the observed or assumed presence of German soldiers near these buildings.

In the meantime a few of the attacking Dutch infantrymen penetrated the village. The attack force behind them was hit by artillery fire which prevented them from following up, the advance detail was thus forced to withdraw from the occupied buildings. As a result the attack was halted and the force retired behind the drainage ditch.

Consequently the German troops in Valkenburg were able to enjoy a relatively quiet afternoon, which allowed them to improve their positions in the village and reinforce areas north of it. The mayor of the village put forward a petition to allow for the evacuation of the population of Valkenburg. Although it was agreed upon by colonel Heyser, it was rejected by the commander of the 4th Inf.Rgt.

Throughout the afternoon the German strongpoint at the farmstead of Rhijnvliet was time and again subject to artillery, mortar, and heavy machine-gun-fire from across the Oude Rijn. At 1910hrs, when the Dutch artillery again directed its fire into the area just north of Valkenburg and infantry of considerable strength were observed from Katwijk from 2040hrs, there was no doubt that another attack against the village was imminent.[160] German defensive fire commenced before the attack force had gained the drainage ditch and the stone-cutting works. At about the same time four He 111s dropped supplies in so-called 'supply bombs' just south of Valkenburg by parachute and then flew off in a north-easterly direction over Katwijk. The resupply action caused serious confusion on the Dutch side. The attack force had initially assumed the landing of additional paratroopers and the anti-aircraft fire from Katwijk against the disappearing German aircraft was interpreted due to German fire in its rear. These incorrect interpretations contributed to the failure of the attack as the hesitantly advancing infantry could not be urged further forward past the drainage ditch. At nightfall offensive movements from the north were ended, having cost the Dutch two killed and several wounded. South of Valkenburg the Dutch infantry, positioned along the drainage ditch at Wassenaarse Watering,[161] took possession of an unoccupied house south of the farmstead of Rijnvliet. In a surprise move two Landsverk armored cars approached along the dike road. However they stopped at the Wassenaarse Watering and seemed content to fire from there at recognized, or assumed, German

160 The Dutch had brought forward from Noordwijk I/9th Inf.Rgt. from 3rd Inf.Div. As about one-third of its infantry had been detailed for security and guard duties and two of its heavy machine-gun platoons had been ordered to support the attack from positions on the eastern bank of the Oude Rijn, only two companies and two heavy machine-gun platoons had been mustered for the attack.

161 The mission to attack Valkenburg from the south fell to parts of 6th Company from 22nd Depot Battalion, reinforced with a platoon each from I and II/1st Inf.Rgt.

positions south of Valkenburg. As nigh tfell, they retired again and the Dutch infantry, positioned opposite Rijnvliet, also ceased combat actions.

In the dunes south-west of Valkenburg the Dutch operation to clear the area between the Oude Rijn and Den Haag had been initiated in the evening of 10 May. Here they sustained a reverse caused by the German forces and were able to hold out north of Wassenaar. Directed by Colonel Buurman, the commander of 4th Inf.Rgt., II/9th Inf.Rgt., I/4th Inf.Rgt. and I/1st Inf.Rgt. had planned to attack abreast on a front of about 3km against German positions, which were assumed to be along the Wassenaarse Slag/Rijksdorp road and the coast. The attack was to be launched on the morning of 11 May. Due to the postponed movement of II/9th Inf.Rgt. across the Oude Rijn, Buurman halted I/4th Inf.Rgt. halfway to its line of departure. I/1st Inf.Rgt., reinforced by anti-tank and infantry guns, served as the left task force and, after a fatiguing march through the dunes, in the early hours of 11 May reached the terrain around Belvedere, about 2km north-west of Wassenaar. As no enemy had been met up to this point and contact with the task force on the right could not be established, the battalion commander decided to let his exhausted troops bivouac there, but adequate security measures were disregarded. Nevertheless the arrival of the Dutch battalion had not gone unobserved and was reported by German sentries west of Belvedere and at Rijksdorp. *Oberleutnant* Voigt quickly alerted and concentrated his forces positioned west and south of the Dutch encampment for a counter-attack. Around 0530hrs, 200-300 German soldiers raided the bivouac from two sides. The few sentries were put out of action without trouble and the attackers stormed the camp. Most of the Dutch soldiers were still sleeping, causing the battalion commander and about 20 of his men to be killed and numerous others wounded. Only parts of a company and some heavy machine-guns, which were bivouacked some distance away, managed to escape toward the northern edge of Wassenaar where they quickly set up a blocking position. The majority of the battalion was forced to surrender – nine officers, two ensigns and about 300 other ranks all capitulated. Over the next few hours another 50 Dutch soldiers, who initially had managed to escape, were caught in the surrounding area and taken to a nearby farm where prisoners were being confined under guard. During the attack the Germans lost two killed. Taking possession of the highly welcome haul of heavy machine-guns, anti-tank guns and two infantry guns, the Germans then settled down in the hotel restaurant at Albertushoeve.

I/4th Inf.Rgt. arrived on the dunes about 1000m east of the Wassenaarse Slag at 0840hrs, entirely unaware of the fate of its sister battalion to the left. It was fired at from the south and from Albertushoeve and initially went to ground to avoid attack. It was unable to establish contact with II/9th Inf.Rgt., which was advancing on the right, before 1240hrs. The battalion commander was informed that the time of attack was set for 1540hrs. However the plan was soon frustrated. The forward elements of II/9th Inf. Rgt. approached the hotel at Duinoord at 1320hrs; they assumed the hotel was unoccupied but were quickly fired upon by well-hidden German troops. In a subsequent counter thrust, the Germans drove back the Dutch advance guard, capturing the equipment of an entire anti-tank platoon. With their booty and numerous Dutch prisoners, they then retired back to their original positions. After recovering from the surprise II/9th Inf.Rgt. engaged the assumed German positions in and around the Hotel Duinoord with heavy machine-guns and the remaining anti-tank guns. After several German air attacks into the dunes east of the Wassenaarse Slag between 1440hrs and 1540hrs, and after the Dutch mistook the arrival of additional German paratroopers in the area around Valkenburg,[162] II/9th Inf.Rgt. hastily retired into the area south of Katwijk aan Zee. I/4th Inf.Rgt. now stood isolated in the dunes at Groot Berkeheide and at 1840hrs retired about 1km to the north. At 2140hrs it was ordered back into the area south of Katwijk by the commander of 4th Inf.Rgt. The plan to defeat the German troops north of Wassenaar by an attack of vastly superior forces had failed completely. This can largely be explained by poor communication between the attacking units, of time and terrain, and the fact that the Germans began to seize the initiative when the opportunity arose.

After its successful aggressive defence *Oberleutnant* Voigt's force set up an additional defence line between Duinrell, north-west of Wassenaar and Albertushoeve, marking it with signal panels for the supporting *Luftwaffe*. Shortly afterwards a resupply partly came down in Dutch-controlled terrain. The rich booty of heavy weapons and ammunition compensated for most of the unit's shortcomings. However the adequate care for the increasing number of wounded in spite of the captured Dutch medical personnel remained unresolved and food for the many prisoners became scarce.

Due to the lack of suitable and protected landing sites for transport aircraft around Den Haag, *Luftflotte 2* saw itself obliged to resupply the four isolated groups of *22.(LL)Inf.Div.* exclusively by air drops. This task not only extracted a number of He 111s from their main function as bombers, but also ran the risk of decreasing the number of supply containers, which were only available in restricted numbers.[163] Fighters and bombers had to be provided almost continuously to make up for the lack of heavy weapons in the isolated landing groups and for the escort of the resupply flights. This limited their air combat potential over the operation area of *Fl.Div.7*. Throughout 11 May the Dutch had been unable to carry on with the achievements they had gained against *22.(LL)Inf.Div.* the previous day. They did succeed in moving a number of additional troops from areas not under attack, to and across the Oude Rijn and into Den Haag. However these were mainly individual battalions extracted from the command structure of their regiments and, employed in terrain unfamiliar to them, they had been unable to accomplish their missions. At no time during this day had the commandant of Fortress Holland or the command of I Army Corps and the territorial command in Leiden been given a clear picture of the situation. This was reflected in the actions of the troops – the confusion that ensued can be seen in Leiden. Around 1730hrs depot troops fired into a bus with captured German officers inside after mistaking them for an attacking force, causing the death of a German prisoner and numerous wounded.

On the night of 10/11 May, in the operational area of *Fl.Div.7*, neither Student and his staff, nor his subordinate commanders, had any doubt that the coming day would bring severe trials for the troops. In the east the arrival of Dutch forces at the Noord, though in still unknown strength, had been detected. It was assumed that these would attempt

---

162 It was the same supply drop, which had frustrated the attack of II and III/4th Inf.Rgt.
163 A He 111 was capable of carrying between five and nine containers of 250kg each, dependent on the distance to the drop zone.

to cross the river and pose an immediate threat to Waalhaven as the firm retention of its western bank was of particular importance. It was equally important to bring the whole of Dordrecht Island, including the town, quickly into their own hands so as to prevent the enemy from moving troops onto the island from the north, across the Merwede, or from Hoekse Waard. For this sufficiently strong forces were still lacking. The situation was even worse, as the western part of the Ijsselmonde Island had not yet been seized. Offensive actions by the enemy from across the Oude Maas or the Nieuwe Waterweg could not be ruled out. Therefore, the retention of strong security elements in the areas around Barendrecht and Rhoon was thought mandatory for the time being.

The situation in the southern part of the air bridgehead of *Gruppe Süd* was only temporarily eased; as almost no troops could be set free by *Oberst* Bräuer after the dispatch of the majority of *I./FschJgRgt.1* to the bridges at Dordrecht, and as Dutch troops were still present south of Dordrecht, causing concerns about an enemy attack with superior forces against *II./FschJgRgt.1* at the Moerdijk bridges. Student was therefore forced to rely primarily on the steadfastness of the troops at hand. He could however be confident that the air-landing forces still available at the assembly areas in Germany would provide him with a quick and complete reinforcement. After the neutralization of the majority of the Dutch Air Arm, adequate air support could also be anticipated. No help was expected from the isolated groups of *22.(LL)Inf.Div.* other than them tying down as many Dutch troops as possible. However, at the time it was out of the question to come to their aid.

The few German soldiers who had remained at Waalhaven and in its immediate vicinity, mainly security-details, signal personnel and aircrews repairing damaged aircraft, had spent a restless night. From midnight until shortly before dawn British Wellington bombers had attacked in waves of three aircraft each almost continuously.[164] The Germans had neither nightfighters nor heavy anti-aircraft guns available to them, meaning the bombing had continued unmolested, although it had resulted in astonishingly little damage among the stranded aircraft and on the runways. However the losses in personnel had also been minor, *LuftNachrKp.7* was forced to interrupt its telecommunication activities from time to time, but had not sustained further losses.

During the ongoing bombing of the airfield at 0330hrs *III./FschJgRgt.1*, mounted on requisitioned trucks, assembled on the road which led from Rotterdam-South to Dordrecht and then commenced its move further to the south. Shortly prior to 0700hrs the column arrived at the positions of *7./InfRgt.16*, about 500m in front of the western ramps of the Dordrecht bridges. There, the paratroopers dismounted, crossed the traffic bridge and advanced toward the command post of *I./FschJgRgt.1* which was set up in a school south-east of the traffic bridge. On the way, 11th Company, which was in the lead, was hit by accurate Dutch artillery from Hoekse Waard. In the attack the company lost 11 wounded, 10 of which were noted as walking wounded.

---

164   These attacks had been arranged between the British embassy in Den Haag and the Dutch high command, and had been intended to make the airfield unusable for the landings of German reinforcements during the attacks of the Light Division and 3rd Border Infantry Battalion. The Wellingtons had been provided by 3 Group of Bomber Command from 7 different squadrons. They had attacked in 36 waves, whereby each bomber had flown twice with a load of 18 bombs of 200 lbs. Altogether 58 tons of bombs was dropped. All aircraft safely returned to England.

After the platoon from *6./InfRgt.16*, which was on guard along the western bank of the Noord, reported the concentration of considerable Dutch forces on the eastern bank of the river near the bridge at Alblasserdam, *Oberst* Kreysing dispatched all of *II./InfRgt.16* (less its 7th Company) at 0415hrs and assigned *4./ArtRgt.22* to its western bank. The battalion immediately moved off in trucks, arriving at the Noord around 0540hrs and had set up its positions by about 0900hrs. Some time earlier, the security platoon from *6./InfRgt.16* observed some Dutch infantry who had taken the western bank of the Noord just north of the bridge. It was one of two units containing 20 men each. They had been able to cross the Noord undetected under the cover of darkness, on either side of the bridge. The unit south of the bridge remained unobserved for the time being but that north of the bridge was engaged and lost three killed and five wounded.

At 1000hrs Dutch infantry under cover of heavy machine-guns fire stormed across the bridge, and succeeded in gaining ground in the direction of Hendrik Ambacht, located about 2km south-west of the bridge site.[165] When the Dutch infantrymen were fired at by machine-guns, they retreated back across the bridge again under the cover of Dutch mortars positioned on the eastern bank of the Noord. *6./InfRgt.16* was now deployed around Hendrik Ambacht and had lost two killed and one wounded. The Dutch unit which had crossed the Noord in two large rubber boats about 500m south of the bridge, succeeded in taking out a small German security post but was now detected during the withdrawal of their fellow soldiers across the bridge and like the other troops, retired across the river.

After another attempt to cross the bridge was abandoned due to German defensive fire, the Dutch succeeded in landing parts of an infantry company on the western bank of the Noord by means of a motor barge. The infantrymen managed to gain some ground toward Hendrik Ambacht and occupy a number of buildings. As the barge ran aground at the landing site reinforcements could not be moved easily. The renewed use of large rubber boats also failed, as they were shot by German machine-guns while being carried to the riverbank, the attack causing some soldiers to be wounded.

Early in the morning Student had obtained a picture of the situation at the Noord with his own eyes. Probably on his initiative, between 1150 and 1210hrs, the *Luftwaffe* made the first attack against the area around Alblasserdam using dive bombers. Although their targets were the troops of the Light Division that were forming up there, it was mostly the town and its dockyards which were heavily hit. However this attack greatly affected Dutch morale, causing them to commence their withdrawal from the river into the polder further to the east. Nevertheless *II./InfRgt.16* continued to assess the threat of a Dutch attack across the Noord as still being high. To reinforce the bridgehead, two platoons from *7./InfRgt.16* were deployed on the northern ramps of the Dordrecht bridges. In the afternoon another air attack was commenced by the *Luftwaffe*. Again, the destruction was focused on the built-up area of Alblasserdam.[166] At about 1745hrs *II./InfRgt.16* observed

---

165 A good chance to establish a firm bridgehead on the western bank of the Noord had existed some hours earlier, if the most forward bicycle battalion from the Light Division had not been directed into Dordrecht and the swing-bridge had been closed at that time.

166 During the two air attacks on 11 May, 28 inhabitants of Alblasserdam had been killed, and 181 buildings had been destroyed or seriously damaged.

the movement of Dutch motor vehicles toward the south, causing them to fear an attack across the Noord at the island of Julia-Polder, which divided the river in two arms south of Alblasserdam. Therefore the two platoons recently arrived from *7./InfRgt.16* were deployed opposite this island. Over the course of the next few hours the apprehension on the German side turned out to be groundless, as the Dutch infantry on the western bank of the river close to Hendrik Ambacht returned to its eastern bank using a barge, which in the meantime was refloated. However, Dutch troops, including some artillery, continued to occupy the terrain on either side of Alblasserdam. They occasionally engaged the Germans opposite, but no further attacks were launched.

The decision to give up the thrust by the Light Division across the Noord was made by the commandant of Fortress Holland, after the divisional commander, Colonel van der Bijl, reported the failure of the attempts undertaken previously. As a result the important plan to Waalhaven airfield had remained unfulfilled. Serious faults in command and control by Lieutenant General van Andel and Colonel van der Bijl were the main reasons for the failure of the Light Division at the Noord. Had Lieutenant General van Andel requested information about the arrival times of the units of the Light Division in the area around Alblasserdam and their probable state of combat-readiness at that time, he would have been able to calculate that the division was unable to deploy along the start line for the attack west of the Noord on 11 May at 0500hrs. Coincidentally their arrival on time would not have even been possible had they have marched over the bridge in peacetime conditions. The effects of van Andel's neglect in informing Colonel de Bijl about the situation around Barendrecht and at the Dordrecht bridges was particularly detrimental, even if he had knowledge about these. The plan of van der Bijl to deploy his division with two task groups along the line Barendrecht-Bolnes would have required a preliminary attack, which due to a lack of information had not been planned for. The thought that van der Bijl may have built his plan upon the success of the attack of the 3rd Border infantry Battalion around Barendrecht on the night 10/11 May is irrelevant because he had not been informed about this action. The question how the presence of German troops in position at the bridges at Dordrecht would have affected the deployment of the left flank of van der Bijl's attack force is again hypothetical and therefore does not need to be pursued. Last but by no means least it has to be pointed out that Lieutenant General van Andel failed to provide the commands of the Light Division and of Group Kil with the same level of knowledge about his overall plan, thereby frustrating effective coordination between them. This measure should also have included the garrisons of Rotterdam and Dordrecht, which had remained independent, despite the fact that effective communication could have assisted them in making an effort to gain the initiative on Ijsselmonde and eliminating the German presence there.

In terms of the combat action, Colonel van der Bijl is to be blamed for poor tactical insight and lack of initiative. He had not felt under any pressure to transfer of his forces 70km from their staging area Tilburg/Eindhoven, across the Merwede and Maas and into the assigned line Dordrecht-Gorinchem. When he arrived with his battle HQ at 1740hrs in Molenaarsgraaf, about 12km east of Alblasserdam, he received the order for attack with his division against Waalhaven in less than 12 hours. Evidently, he had not grasped the operational importance of the bridge at Alblasserdam for his new mission. After he had called Lieutenant General van Andel for further details at 1840hrs, it had taken him until 2310hrs before he was able to obtain a picture regarding the conditions at the Noord; furthermore this was imprecise because of the dark. He had discovered that the swing-section of the bridge at Alblasserdam had not been closed; incomprehensibly he had not ordered the bridge to be made operational with priority. However the immediate use of the bridge by the first arriving bicycle infantry battalion would have quickly led to the establishment of a firm bridgehead on the western bank of the Noord and would probably have allowed more forces to follow without delay. Only under these conditions would it perhaps have been possible to meet the time-requirements for the concentration of his division in the eastern part of the island of Ijsselmonde. There is, however, ample reason to assume that prior to midnight on 10 May Colonel van der Bijl had disregarded the order for the time of his attack and instead had foreseen passage across the Noord only after dawn on 11 May. His order at 2240hrs to send the most forward unit of his infantry across the Merwede into Dordrecht, although there was no urgency for this action, confirms this. Besides neglect of the time-plan given by his superior without notifying him, Colonel van der Bijl had obviously not taken into account the threat of the *Luftwaffe* during a crossing-operation in plain daylight, all the more as the crossing-site along the Noord had not been protected by anti-aircraft weapons from the Dutch Anti-Aircraft Command and the Light Division had no weapons of this kind. Whether Colonel van der Bijl would have positioned all of his 16 field guns at the Noord prior to the start of the crossing in the remaining hours, so as to provide the best possible coverage of the operation, in the light of the actual development of the situation, remain unanswered. An even more serious offense against the general principles of command and control on the part of the headquarters of the Light Division, Group Kil and the garrison of Dordrecht, had been the lack of the exchange of complete information about ongoing and planned actions. Radio communication between the Light Division and Group Kil could have been established, if only by relay though the Dordrecht command. However, lack of tactical insight and of initiative, particularly on the part of Colonel van der Bijl, who should have shown interest in the situation of the areas forward of his troops hitherto unknown to them He also relied heavily on the command abilities of Lieutenant General van Andel, which had led to the neglect of coordination efforts. Early knowledge about the actions in progress under the command of Group Kil and the true situation at Barendrecht and the Dordrecht bridges may have induced Colonel van der Bijl to attempt a determined crossing of the Noord shortly after midnight another try. This would allow them to establish contact with the 3rd Border Infantry Battalion north of the Oude Maas and support the operation under way from the south against the bridges at Dordrecht by a thrust from across the Noord toward Zwijndrecht. However the time-window for actions of this kind closed after about 0600hrs on 11 May as the reinforced *II./InfRgt.16* arrived on the western bank of the Noord.

Obviously quite impressed by the first attack of the German dive bombers Colonel van der Bijl had reported the failure of his crossing-operation to the command of Fortress Holland. With this information Lieutenant General van Andel issued a new attack-plan for the Light Division which, even if contemplated very favorably, had to be regarded as adventurous. The plan involved leaving behind sufficiently strong covering-forces at the Noord; the division with the mosts forces was to cross the Merwede into Dordrecht. From there, it was to destroy the German forces south and south-west of the town, cross the Kil into Hoekse Waard and attack Waalhaven after crossing the Oude Maas. The 2nd Regiment of Hussars remained in Noord Brabant after being reassigned to the Light Division for this mission.[167] The new plan of Lieutenant General van Andel, at least initially, had obviously lacked any concept, regarding times for its execution as well as orders for cooperation with, and the support of other commands.[168]

On the island of Ijsselmonde south of Barendrecht the attempt by the Dutch failed to break through to Waalhaven from Hoekse Waard. The airfield was indispensible for the continued operations of *Fl.Div.7*, so it was important to protect it against threats from the south and west. Already on 10 May the commander of *InfRgt.16*, besides some troops from his regiment, were deployed alongside *II./FschJgRgt.2* with its three weak companies in the south of the island. While security forces from *I./InfRgt.16* was positioned along the northern bank of the Oude Maas between the lift-bridge south of Barendrecht, and the ferry-landing opposite Goidschalxoord, *II./FschJgRgt.2* was also posted in and around Barendrecht, from where it could also dominate by fire the northern ramp of the bridge. Still more to the west of Ijsselmonde, immediately upon its arrival in the morning, *1./InfRgt.72* had advanced toward the petroleum installation west of Pernis and toward Hoogvliet, and the bridge at Spijkenisse. However the company was stopped in front of these locations by strong Dutch forces.

Shortly prior to dawn on 11 May the Dutch 3rd Border Infantry Battalion, which because of detached sub-units was only 600 men strong, had reached its start positions for the crossing of the Oude Maas on either side of the southern ramp of the bridge south of Barendrecht. The attack-mission had planned to ferry two of its companies across the river at the ferry site at Goidschalxoord, about 4km west of the bridge. They then had to advance by the shortest route toward Waalhaven. Another company was to cross the river on a ferry about 3km east of the bridge to allow a flanking attack against the German elements near the northern ramp of the bridge. This attack was to enable the remaining company, together with the heavy machine-guns, mortars and anti-tank guns of the battalion, to move across the lift-bridge. After the two companies on the right flank had gained the height of the left flank, the actual attack was to be launched at 0400hrs. Group Kil was given overall command of the mission, although the 3rd Border Battalion had not formally been handed over to it by Group Spui. The security elements of Group Kil near the southern ramp of the bridge, two infantry platoons and some heavy machine-guns were ordered to support the assault across the bridge by fire. However they were not assigned to join the attack.

No information about the planned attack by the Light Division was passed to the 3rd Border Battalion. The message about the change of the time of attack to 0540hrs arrived at the HQ section of the 3rd Border Battalion shortly before the commencement of the crossing, was submitted without explanation. The change had no effect on the crossing plan, although it moved the attack into daylight.

Even though the ferry at Goidschalxoord was sunk on 10 May, this remained unknown to the 3rd Border Battalion and thus required the provision of alternate crossing vessals. However, all three companies either side of the bridge reached the northern bank of the Oude Maas unnoticed. On the left flank, immediately after the crossing, the forward

---

167 The Light Division had arrived north of the Merwede with its two bicycle infantry regiments, with three battalions each, and the two artillery detachments with eight guns each.

168 For reasons of objectiveness, it needs to be mentioned, that these measures, although unknown to the author, may have been passed on at a later time.

company moved off and reached a location 2km away from Waalhaven without contact with the enemy. The commander of the other company stopped his unit after the crossing and let them eat breakfast first. When the company finally followed behind its sister-unit, it was observed, reported and engaged by a German machine-gun-post from *I./InfRgt.16*. A shock troop of about 75 men from *2./InfRgt.16*, who were unobserved by the Dutch, quickly came to the support of the security post. In the sudden ambush by heavy machine-guns and mortars, the Dutch company lost some killed and wounded. Due to the noise of the gunfire in its rear, the forward company turned around and joined the fighting. However soon the Dutch ran out of ammunition and partly in full flight they retreated to the ferry crossing and were brought back across the Oude Maas with no further losses. According to plan the company on the right flank advanced to Heerjansdam. However, before it moved any further, the mayor of Heerjansdam reported the presence of strong German forces immediately in front of it. Without verifying the truth of this report the company commander moved his unit back across the Oude Maas. The reinforced company which was allocated for the advance across the bridge waited in vain for the appearance of its sister-unit at the northern ramp. Devoid of reports from the left and the right, at 1140hrs the company commander decided to storm across the bridge under the covering fire of the heavy weapons of the battalion, and of the machine-guns of the security detachment. Just prior to the start of the assault the chief of staff of Group Kil arrived south of the bridge and arranged for artillery support. This was executed at 1410hrs by a battery of 75mm guns against a German-occupied factory north of the bridge, subsequently the Dutch infantrymen rushed forward. The German defensive fire could not be silenced and the company, half way across the bridge, suffered four killed and 12 wounded, leading the commander to cease the assault. Covered by fire from the artillery battery the Dutch infantry managed to get back to the southern bank of the Oude Maas without further losses. With this action, the attack of the 3rd Border Infantry Battalion ended.

At 2145hrs reconnaissance-elements from *I./InfRgt.16* that were arriving at the northern bank of the river near Heerjansdam captured two small tankers that were anchored and with them their load of 3,600 tons of petrol.

At no time during the receipt of the mission and the preparation for its execution had the 3rd Border Infantry Battalion obtained an accurate and up-to-date picture of the enemy-situation. Again the command of Fortress Holland had failed to discover, collect, evaluate and disseminate all of the information which had actually been available from subordinate and independent commands. The transfer of the unit from Group Spui to Group Kil had not been triggered by the enemy situation. It had been directed by Lieutenant-General van Andel on account that the distance from the northern bank of the Oude Maas to the objective was considered shorter from the sector of Group Kil. A movement of the attack force across the bridge at Spijkenisse, which was in Dutch hands all the time, had probably never been considered.[169] There the attack force could have crossed the Oude Maas as if in peacetime, and afterward could have deployed for the attack without being threatened by

---

169   It may well be that this fact had remained unknown to the command of Fortress Holland. In the morning of 11 May the bridge at Spijkenisse, up to the area at Hoogvliet, had been protected north of the Oude Maas by two platoons from II/34th Inf.Rgt., a platoon from I/39th Inf.Rgt. and a heavy machine-gun platoon.

the enemy. The impulse for this option would have had to have come from Group Spui as Spijkenisse was located in this sector. Additionally the employment of II/34th Inf. Rgt., which already had elements north of the Oude Maas, would have constituted a more suitable solution than that of the deployment of 3rd Border Infantry Battalion, which had arrived exhausted and unfamiliar with the terrain in the north of Hoekse Waard. However it could have been used as a follow-on force behind II/34th Inf.Rgt.

On the airfield at Waalhaven the attacks of British bombers from midnight to dawn had resulted in the further destruction of administrative buildings and hangars. As the transport aircraft had taken off immmediatly after unloading their passengers and supplies, only a few Ju 52s that had been parked on the airfield were hit again. Losses in personnel, too, had been low. In the early morning, after the runway was cleared of debris, air transport traffic resumed, initially only in the form of single-plane landings.

Perhaps based on reports from two Fokker G-1 fighters used for reconnaissance over Rotterdam, but more likely as a result of their own observations, the two Dutch artillery batteries positioned in the north-eastern part of Rotterdam bombarded the airfield again from 1110hrs on. The bombardment was interrupted between 1340hrs and 1740hrs as the guns were moved to alternate positions in fear of German air attacks. The Ju 52s, which arrived before and had been parked at the edges of the airfield for unloading, managed to take off again. At 1430hrs, in order to avoid losses from artillery fire and bombing attacks on the airfield, a squadron of Ju 52s dropped containers with ammunition and rations by parachute near the command post of *InfRgt.16*. The supplies were immediately distributed among the troops. The high demand for anti-tank and mortar rounds, as a result of their use during the fighting for the bridgehead, could not be met. A Ju 52, which was damaged by ground fire during the resupply, had to conduct an emergency landing near Hordijk and afterward was parked there, well-camouflaged.

In case of a longer-lasting closure of the airfield due to artillery fire or bombing attacks, the commander of *InfRgt.16* was ordered to clear the obstacles placed along a part of the auto-route Rotterdam/Dordrecht slag flight restrictions by the Dutch so that it could be used as a provisional runway. Mainly Dutch prisoners, who had been captured the previous day, were used for this task. A number of the vehicles which were removed from the auto-route were used to motorize the troops. In spite of the flight restrictions for the airfield, half of *14./FschJgRgt.1* with six anti-tank guns had arrived unscathed during the morning and had immediately been dispatched for employment with *Gruppe Süd*.[170] At 1600hrs, *2./ InfRgt.72* was unloaded onto the airfield. In the evening, the battle HQ, the 3rd Company and elements of the 4th Company were also brought in, whereby the men of the two companies were partly landed on the auto-route. Other arrivals during the late afternoon and early evening were of elements of the battle HQ of *II./InfRgt.65* and some anti-tank and infantry guns from *InfRgt.47* and *InfRgt.65*. *I./InfRgt.72*, less its 1st Company, which was deployed against the petroleum installation and the bridge at Spijkenisse, were moved into provisional quarters in Barendrecht. There it took over some protective tasks together with the paratroopers from *II./FschJgRgt.2* and remained in readiness for missions to be assigned by the command of *Fl.Div.7*. With the exception of one Ju 52, which had to turn

---

170   The reliable after-action report of *7./FschJgRgt.1* mentions the arrival of a platoon of anti-tank guns, very likely from *14./FschJgRgt.1* in its position south of the Moerdijk bridges in the course of 11 May. It is not quite clear whether this half of *14./FschJgRgt.1* was landed on the airfield or on the auto-route. The second half of this company never showed up in the operational area of *Fl.Div.7* for unknown reasons.

back during the approach flight from Germany because of hits by anti-aircraft weapons, the newly-landed units from *I./InfRgt.72* on 11 May sustained no losses during their arrival.

With first daylight on 11 May the fighting for the bridges across the Nieuwe Maas renewed with increased intensity. The German paratroopers, infantrymen and engineers that were holding out in their shrunken bridgehead around the northern ramps of the bridges had not been attacked during the hours of darkness. The electric lighting on the bridges had not been turned off and so these had been continuously kept under fire, this meant that only a few soldiers had managed to get across as reinforcements. Shortly after dawn, Dutch artillery also joined the fighting by bombarding Noordereiland.[171] The fire on the bridges and their ramps was so intense that after a few attempts *Oberstleutnant* von Choltitz refrained from sending reinforcements and supplies into the bridgehead for fear of losses being too high. At this time the area was being defended by some 70 men,[172] but, as ammunition had become scarce, strict fire discipline was ordered. Strafing attacks by fighters against identified or assumed Dutch positions around the bridgehead at least temporarily provided for some relief for the exhausted defenders.

From midday onwards the Dutch Air Arm also made an appearance over the contested part of Rotterdam. At 1210hrs, in the absence of German fighter protection, two Fokker T-Vs flew an attack against the Willems Bridge. Of the 16 100kg bombs which were dropped only a few hit the northern ramp of the bridge. The effects were negligible but some of the bomb hits within the bridgehead had caused the collapse of already damaged buildings, some of which were still occupied by the Germans. At 1510hrs two Fokker T-Vs escorted by three D-XXIs attacked again. This time German fighter-protection was present, 12 Bf 110s fell upon the Dutch and managed to scatter their close formation. Again the D-XXIs proved to be dangerous opponents. In the ensuing aerial combat, two of the Dutch fighters were lost but not before they had shot down three of the Bf 110s. Before it crashed badly a T-V bomber also succeeded in damaging a pursuing Bf 110 so seriously that it had to conduct an emergency landing.

The bombing attacks had not led to the destruction or a blocking of the Willems Bridge, but had forced the Germans to abandon the houses that were hit by bombs. As the front and sides of the Dutch National Life Insurance building had remained standing, the Germans now made use of it as a strongpoint.

The Dutch endeavored to improve their positions around the bridgehead as they waited for the results of the artillery fire and the bombing attacks. The few attempted dashes of small groups against the insurance building in the course of the afternoon were easily checked by German covering fire from Noordereiland. The large Dutch passenger ship *Statendam* of the Holland-America-Line lay anchored at the Wilhelminekade and, at 1740hrs, it was set ablaze by the mortars and heavy machine-guns. It was consequently abandoned by the German machine-gun teams who had previously used it as a fire-base.

---

171   The artillery fire was delivered by the battery which on 10 May had been moved to the south-western part of Rotterdam-North in order to support the attack against the bridgehead.

172   In his after-action report, *Oberleutnant* Kerfin mentions a strength of two officers, seven non-commissioned officers and 34 other ranks able to fight for 11 May. He mentions also, however, that by 12 May a *Feldwebel* and 10 men from his platoon, a machine-gun-team from *11./InfRgt.16* and a number of stragglers had additionally been detected in the bridgehead.

Due to Dutch attempts to cross the Nieuwe Maas into Rotterdam-South, in the afternoon *Oberstleutnant* von Choltitz received *2./InfRgt.16* as a quick-reaction force. The release of this company from its assigned mission had become possible as renewed Dutch crossings of the Oude Maas from Hoekse Waard were deemed unlikely for the time being and *1./InfRgt.72* was considered sufficient for the protection of the air bridgehead on Ijsselmonde toward the west and with additional forces were available in Barendrecht.

In spite of the highly critical situation at the bridgehead north of the Nieuwe Maas, Student stepped back from his intent to give it up if needs be. *Oberst* Kreysing as well as *Oberstleutnant* von Choltitz now realized the importance of the bridges in Rotterdam for the conquest of the entire city. Student had moved his command post from Feyenoord into a café in Rijsoord, located halfway between the airfield and the bridges at Dordrecht, even though it could be quickly overrun if the attack of the Light Division across the Noord became a reality.

The intention of Colonel Scharroo to make the bridges across the Nieuwe Maas in Rotterdam unusable for the Germans by the use of air attack and weaken their strong positions on Noordereiland by fire had not been realized on 11 May. With the arrival of sizable parts of the allotted reinforcements, which included the staff of 11th Inf.Rgt., four infantry battalions (though incomplete), a mortar company and several anti-tank platoons, the situation for the garrison had notably improved. Colonel Scharroo deployed a small part of these forces with security missions along the northern bank of the Nieuwe Maas west of the the city. The mortars and anti-tank guns were positioned to fire at Noordereiland and the bridgehead. A platoon from IV/15th Inf.Rgt. was ferried across the Nieuwe Maas as reinforcement for the company from III/39th Inf.Rgt., protecting the petroleum installation west of Pernis. The majority of the additional troops were deployed along the unprotected northern and eastern edges of Rotterdam as a precaution against attempts of the Germans forces which had been identified around Delft and Ockenburg and those assumed to be east of Hoek van Holland, to penetrate into the city from the north and the west. However all of these measures were defensive in nature. Active support for the ground operations ordered by the command of Fortress Holland on the evening of 10 May for the retaking of Ijsselmonde were not considered by Colonel Scharroo. The reason for this neglect may have been that the exact arrival times of the reinforcements had not been known by the colonel, as in his position as an independent commander he had seen his priority as the protection of the city against potential threats from the north and east. In addition, no request had come from the commands of Fortress Holland or Group Kil, which had not bothered to inform the garrison commander about their attack plans for 11 May.[173] As reinforcements for Rotterdam were assigned directly by the commander-in-chief of the Dutch Field Army, it could not be wholly excluded that the command of Fortress Holland had never been informed about this measure.

On 11 May three quarters of the Dutch gold reserves, to the value of about 900 million guilders, were brought to England on two merchant-ships escorted by British destroyers.

---

173 This statement is supported by the results of the official examinations about the conduct of the Dutch armed forces, undertaken after the end of WWII.

Further attempts to also rescue parts of the Dutch gold stored in Rotterdam, failed. A guardship loaded at Vlaardingen during the night, carrying gold to the value of 22 million guilders, but was sunk shortly after its departure at Nieuwe Waterweg due to a magnetic mine. The commander of the British demolition teams, two of his men and 13 Dutchmen, lost their lives.[174]

In England, the 2nd Battalion Irish Guards, reinforced by a company of Welsh Guards, received the order to embark for Hoek van Holland. This operation was to cover the embarkation of the Dutch queen and other state authorities if the situation worsened.[175]

On the island of Dordrecht, firefights between small groups of men from *FschSan-Halbkompanie 7* and Dutch troops, advancing from the north and the east of the island,[176] were ongoing throughout the night 10/11 May in the polder south of Dubbeldam. The Dutch captured some of the isolated medical paratroopers after short actions and soon occupied again the former firing position of III/4th Art.Rgt. As *Oberst* Bräuer had already deployed all of his troops around Tweede Tol, including his staff and the regimental signals platoon for all-round protection, the last elements from *FschSan-Halbkompanie 7* who had not yet been called up were alerted at 0100hrs. With a group under Dr. Langemeyer they were deployed as reinforcement for the security post under *Oberleutnant* Platow east of Berkenhof. At 0210hrs the medical officers Dr. Lange and Dr. Gabler with 12 medical paratroopers and a wounded *Feldwebel* managed to fight through to this position.

After several thrusts of the Dutch against security elements in the north-east, east and south-east had been warded off and a counter-thrust had been successful, at about 0430hrs the Dutch cancelled their offensive actions and withdrew to the cover of their start positions prior to the appearance of the *Luftwaffe* over the contested terrain. This allowed for the removal of most men from the *FschSan-Halbkompanie* from the security positions. At about 1000hrs two more soldiers from this unit reached friendly lines from the drop zone of the 2nd Platoon. They reported that all other members of this platoon were most likely killed, wounded or captured. The strength of *FschSan-Halbkompanie* had now grown to four officers, 11 non-commissioned officers and 62 other ranks, of which a *Feldwebel* and three soldiers were wounded. Only one *Feldwebel* was known as killed at this time. Still missing, however, were two non-commissioned officers and 24 other ranks.

The intention of Dr. Lange to build up the medical aid station near the command post of *FschJgRgt.1* to become a main dressing-station had to be adandoned as most of the medical equipment required for it had not been removed from the drop zones. Nevertheless the medical abilities of the officers from *FschSan-Halbkompanie 7* were in great demand after bombardments by Dutch artillery on the barrack-camp near the regimental command post at 1700hrs, and again at 1830hrs, caused some casualties. After treatment, these men were brought under the protection of the Red Cross at a Dutch hospital in Dordrecht.

---

174 Another 20% of Dutch gold, which had been stored in a treasury building on the Boompjes in Rotterdam, had been captured by the Germans after the capitulation of Holland. Parts of the gold, which had sunk on the guard ship, were salvaged by the Germans and after the war by the Dutch.

175 The unit, which was designated 'Harpoon Force' was made up of 651 men. With the exception of four 3-inch mortars, it was equipped only with light weapons.

176 300 soldiers from III/4th Art.Rgt., who after the loss of their guns had withdrawn behind the Zuidendijk and parts of the 3rd Company from II/28th Inf.Rgt., positioned around Kop van't Land.

As renewed attacks by the Dutch from the area south of Dordrecht were assessed as highly probable during the hours of darkness, shortly prior to dusk *Oberst* Bräuer ordered parts of *FschSan-Halbkompanie 7* to be used as reinforcements to the security pickets in the north and east of the perimeter.

At about 0600hrs, five Ju 52s dropped 60 paratroopers into the polder, just south of the junction at Zeedijk-Schenkeldijk. They were part of a company of jump-trained soldiers from the parachute school, and the *FschJgErgäzungs-Btl*, commanded by *Oberleutnant* Moll, an instructor of the former. The company was formed prior to the airborne operation against Holland on the direct orders of Student and had been planned as the last reserve for parachuting in the case of utmost need. Without the consent of Student its employment on 11 May was ordered by the command of *Luftflotte 2*. Of the 12 Ju 52s from *2./KG z.b.V.1* which were used to transport the company, three had to turn back immediately after take-off because of adverse weather conditions. Three others had been shot down on the flight in by Dutch ground fire. One of these was able to conduct an emergency landing north of the Merwede, about 6km east of Dordrecht, whereby one of the paratroopers was killed. The other 14 passengers were captured by nearby Dutch forces from the Light Division after a short firefight, which cost the life of another paratrooper.

The men dropped with *Oberleutnant* Moll were engaged during the landing by two platoons of the 2nd Company I/28th Inf.Rgt. that were positioned nearby. This company was commanded by Ensign Marijs as all the officers had been either killed or wounded. In this action, some of the paratroopers were killed or wounded. The Dutch infantrymen then attacked and, after inflicting some more losses among the paratroopers, managed to capture 15 of them, including *Oberleutnant* Moll and two other officers. In the afternoon, Moll with the permission of the Dutch non-commissioned officer guarding him, returned to his men who were still fighting and convinced them that further resistance was hopeless. After he returned to the Dutch, who were running out of ammunition, he and Ensign Marijs agreed upon a ceasefire in order to avoid further needless bloodshed. Now, both sides left their cover to take care of their wounded. Toward the evening 33 paratroopers and 60 Dutch infantrymen, both sides fully armed, moved together to the farmstead at Tongplaat to the south. After the farm was marked with several Red Cross flags and the dead, (four Germans and one Dutch) were buried, all the men went to sleep in the barn, protected by a German and a Dutch sentry.

Around noon, three Ju 52s dropped paratroopers around the Zuidendijk south of Dubbeldam. These were aircraft with soldiers from *Kompanie Moll* aboard, which in the early morning had turned back to the jump-off airfield because of bad weather. The Germans, probably toatalling around 30 men, came down in terrain where Dutch troops were still conducting mop-up actions against the last isolated groups from *FschSan-Halbkompanie 7*. In a short time, the paratroopers lost four killed and a number of wounded. Unable to get organized, pick up their main arms or establish contact with the few still holding out men from the medical company in their vicinity, they were soon forced to give up the fight.

In the contested area around the bridges at Dordrecht, the early hours of 11 May passed by quietly, only now and then interrupted by firefights between the security elements of the paratroopers and the Dutch troops along the western edge of the town. However *I./ FschJgRgt.1* anticipated more action from the enemy against the bridges from Dordrecht with the onset of daylight. During a mop-up action early in the morning along the eastern bank of the Maas, a squad from Hoffmann's platoon succeeded in taking out three machine-gun-positions, and took 18 Dutch soldiers prisoner.

A short time later the expected threat to the bridges developed, but from an unexpected direction. At 0100hrs, *2./FschJgRgt.1* had relieved *4./FschJgRgt.1* in positions around the eastern bridge-ramps. A Dutch runner, captured at about 0215hrs by *Oberleutnant* Graf von Blücher, disclosed that his company was only 500m away from the southern edge of the German perimeter, followed by an entire battalion.[177] Shortly before dawn *4./FschJgRgt.1* was brought back into that perimeter. In an appropriate spot the company set up an ambush on either side of the auto-route, leading toward the traffic bridge. From here, in the first light of dawn, the paratroopers observed a Dutch infantry company, approaching in an almost peacetime formation. When it passed the Zeehaven at about 0510hrs, only 1.5km away from the traffic bridge, the ambush was sprung. Within seconds, 21 Dutch soldiers, among them three officers, were killed, and numerous others wounded. Many of the infantrymen who ran away in panic were captured by the pursuing paratroopers. The Dutch company behind the point unit had also received some fire but managed to rally in a small wood near the Zeehaven. Supported by mortars the pursuing paratroopers were forced back to their ambush positions. However, their security-elements remained well forward. They observed that the Dutch battalion was now rallying near the Zeehaven and for a short time was being fired at by other Dutch troops that were approaching from the north-east,[178] but retired to where they came from once their error became evident.

In order to obtain a better picture of the situation south-east of the bridges, at 1000hrs *I./FschJgRgt.1* deployed the reinforced platoon Hoffmann organized in three groups, against the built-up area. The action resulted in a great number of captured Dutch soldiers, but had to be broken off because of increasing resistance. At about 1100hrs *2./FschJgRgt.1*, which had remained in its position during the morning, also had contact with the enemy when a platoon of Dutch motorcyclists approached the bridges from Dordrecht. After a quick engagement directed by *Oberleutnant* Graf Blücher, a number of dead Dutch soldiers, ten motorcycles with sidecars and two heavy machine-guns remained on the road, while the surviving motor-cyclists hastily retired.[179]

---

177 II/28th Inf.Rgt. Its commander, Major Ravelli, had planned to let his troops rest in the chief house at Amstelwijk during the night. However, the chief of staff of Group Kil ordered him to immediately continue the advance toward the bridges. Complying, Major Ravelli ordered the assigned 2nd Company from III/34th Inf.Rgt. as point unit.

178 It was a company from the bicycle infantry battalion which had crossed the Merwede on the night 10/11 May in accordance with the new attack-orders for the Light Division. While the majority of this battalion, which had been placed subordinate to the garrison command of Dordrecht, had remained in the south-eastern part of the town, Lieutenant Colonel Mussert had deployed one company of it via Krispijn against the Zeehaven, which he believed to be in German hands. After this error was found out, the company had retired to Krispijn.

179 According to Dutch archives the attackers were the 4th Platoon of the machine-gun company from III/2nd Bicycle Infantry Regiment. The after-action report by *2./FschJgRgt.1* claimed 15 killed, whereas the more correct Dutch reports speaks of 6 killed.

After a short rest, at around midday *III./FschJgRgt.1* assembled for the continuation of the advance toward the south, in the south-eastern part of the defensive positions of *I./FschJgRgt.1*. *11./FschJgRgt.1* was weakened because of Kerfin's missing platoon and because of previous losses from Dutch artillery fire, and was left as reserve. *Hauptmann* Schulz was evidently well informed about the enemy-situation in front of his battalion, based on reports from troops in-place and by his own observations. What mattered now was to be able to act quickly and before the enemy of about the same strength as his battalion was active again.[180] He needed to keep losses to his force as limited as possible during the approach as he could not count on replacements. Therefore, in order to take the enemy by surprise and possibly cease fighting, he again proceeded to operate in a way that clearly violated the rules of war. He ordered prisoners who had been captured by *I./FschJgRgt.1*, be loaded onto a truck, or marched behind on foot, to be sent forward in the direction of the Dutch battalion which was again forming up for an attack near the Zeehaven. He and a number of his men followed behind as the prisoners were keen to keep their comrades at the Zeehaven from firing at them. The paratroopers behind the prisoners were intended to approach to close combat range. This malicious deception almost failed, when the outposts of Battalion Ravelli commenced fire on the truck at some distance. When its passengers, some of them now wounded, waved a white flag and calling out not to shoot, Major Ravelli, who was up front, passed out orders to his subordinate commanders and ceased fire. Supposing that the Dutch soldiers on the truck and behind it were reinforcements from Dordrecht, he, four other officers and several of his soldiers walked forward to meet them. Suddenly, *Hauptmann* Schulz and his men rushed forward from behind the prisoners, capturing the completely surprised group around the Dutch battalion commander. When Major Ravelli rejected the request by *Hauptmann* Schulz to order his battalion to surrender, he and more prisoners were headed off toward Krispijn, again in front of *Hauptmann* Schulz and some of his men. From this point Dutch troops commenced fire regardless of the prisoners up front. Again, *Hauptmann* Schulz attempted to force Major Ravelli to act as negotiator. As the Dutch officer stoutly refused, *Hauptmann* Schulz broke off the developing engagement and had his prisoners led back. He organized the majority of his 9th and 10th companies north of the Zeehaven and left behind a strong security-force in the south-western part of Krispijn. From here, at 1330hrs 11th and 12th companies had moved out toward Tweede Tol, only occasionally being engaged in short firefights with small groups of Dutch soldiers, mostly stragglers. At 1930hrs 11th Company arrived at the command post of *FschJgRgt.1* and was ordered to reinforce the perimeter. The remaining parts – the HQ section, a weak parachute platoon and a heavy machine-gun-squad – rested. 12th Company moved on to Willemsdorp, where it was to be assigned to *II./FschJgRgt.1*.

After the loss of most of its leaders the much-depleted Dutch Battalion Ravelli retired from the Zeehaven to the area around Amstelwijk. Pursuing troops from *III./FschJgRgt.1*, which bypassed Amstelwijk in the west, entered Wieldrecht, where they quickly overcame the few remaining soldiers from Battalion Ravelli who had retired into this village. However artillery and mortar fire from across the Kil forced the Germans to abandon it again. In late afternoon they reported that the remainder of Battalion Ravelli had now redeployed in Wieldrecht and commenced to set up positions there. In reaction *Hauptmann* Schulz

---

180   Between 1240 and 1440hrs Major Ravelli had contacted the commandant of the Dordrecht garrison in person. On this occasion Lieutenant Colonel Mussert had urged him to immediately resume his advance and to seize the bridges.

deployed his 10th Company for the attack and at 1940hrs the paratroopers assaulted Wieldrecht from the north and the south. One by one, the points of resistance were neutralized and the final Dutch officer was killed. Only a few of the defenders managed to escape the attack by swimming across the Kil. At 2130hrs the fighting came to an end and Battalion Ravelli ceased to exist. However 10th Company also suffered some considerable losses. Among the wounded was the senior platoon leader *Oberleutnant* Specht, who had taken over the company after the wounding of its commander. *Oberleutnant* Trebes now assumed command and he moved the company some distance back toward the north-east.

In the operational area of *Gruppe Süd* around Tweede Tol, the situation improved only slightly after the arrival of the weak *11./FschJgRgt.1*. Although the line of security posts in the north had been moved a good distance forward, there still was no secure line of communication along the Kil to *I./FschJgRgt.1* as the enemy was able to keep the route under fire from the western bank of the Kil and from the area south of Dordrecht. The lack of suitable weapons prevented efficient counter-measures against the enemy on Hoekse Waard. Ambushes by Dutch artillery from there and into the area around Tweede Tol throughout the day had hampered movement and caused losses time and again. The paratroopers fought back to the best of their abilities. They bombarded tug-boats and a barge on the western bank of the Kil with light mortar and at 1900hrs an observation-post on a watertower east of Gravendeel was forced to abandon its position, after it was fired at with anti-tank rifles. A reconnaissance patrol from parts of the battle HQ of *I./FschJgRgt.1*, which had remained in Tweede Tol, at about 1940hrs succeeded in pushing through to Wieldrecht. It returned with six prisoners and a captured machine-gun.

The enemy opposite the southern part of the air bridgehead of *II./FschJgRgt.1* did not continue offensive actions of the day before, but endeavored to strengthen positions in the nearby settlements. The parachute companies used the nighttime hours to improve their positions and to reconnoiter. At 0330hrs a platoon from *1/PiBtl.22*, parts of which had arrived in the operational area of *II./FschJgRgt.1*, was placed subordinate to its 7th Company on the right flank of the perimeter toward the south. It immediately commenced to reinforce the existing obstacles along the avenues of approach with anti-tank mines and booby-traps. A number of engineers from *1/PiBtl.22* also worked on the obstacles in front of 8th Company to the left of 7th Company.

The Dutch troops positioned in Lochtenburg kept the position of the 3rd Platoon from 7th Company in the south-west of Moerdijk under fire with heavy machine-guns from dawn. A reconnaissance patrol from 7th Company that was dispatched against Lochtenburg managed to get 200m in front of the village. There it was tied down by the fire of at least eight machine-guns. However it was forced to retire after a while, without losses, but with a machine-gun found on the way.

Around midday the commander of *12./FschJgRgt.1* arrived at the command post of *II./FschJgRgt.1* and reported that on order of *FschJgRgt.1*, his company was to take over the perimeter in the northern part of the battalion's air bridgehead. *Hauptmann* Prager ordered his 5th Company, to move into the area south of the bridges and to initially remain available as reserve. On the northern side of the traffic bridge, over the course of the morning the paratroopers finished the removal of the demolition charges, which had been interrupted on the day before when the Dutch artillery bombarded the bridge and *Leutnant* Tietjens had been wounded.[181] Early in the afternoon an anti-tank platoon from *14./FschJgRgt.1*, which arrived from Ijsselmonde, was placed subordinate to *7./FschJgRgt.1* and was deployed in its sector. The two Dutch infantry guns which had been captured the day before, were also positioned there.

From midday Dutch artillery increased its bombardment of the air bridgehead. Additionally the traffic bridge and its northern ramp were continuously kept under fire by heavy machine-guns from the south-eastern bank of Hollandsch Diep, particularly by fire from a large concrete casemate. The fire destroyed two trucks attempting to tow two captured guns across the bridge, on its northern ramp. This meant traffic travelling across the bridge was interrupted until the onset of darkness. German air attacks against the artillery batteries positioned on Hoekse Waard turned out to have little effect. Quite often the aircraft attacked dummy positions and only rarely detected the well-camouflaged guns as their crews stopped operating them in the presence of the aircraft and remained in cover.[182]

In the afternoon, two armored cars, motorcycle infantry and patrols on bicycles were observed in front of the sector of 7th Company. Several armored cars were also seen in front of 8th Company near Lage Zwaluwe. The origin of these troops initially remained unclear to the paratroopers, all the more since there was no indication of an imminent attack.

How critically the situation for *II./FschJgRgt.1* and for all of *Gruppe Süd*, could have developed on 11 May, was found out only after the end of the fighting for Fortress Holland.

During the execution of the Breda-variant of the French-British Dijle-plan, the French 7th Army (General Giraud) had moved forward by the 10 May. The covering and reconnaissance forces of its 1st Light Mechanized Division (1er DLM), which formed the foremost formation of 7th Army, consisted of two reconnaissance units – 2e GRCA and 5e GRDI[183] of Group Lestoquoi – and of 6th Cuirassier Regiment (6e RC). In the early hours of 11 May they arrived on the western bank of the Wilhelmina Canal between Tilburg and Oosterhout and about 4km east of Breda. Their mission was to cover the deployment of 1er DLM on its left flank and to reconnoiter with patrols toward the east. First units of the main force of this division, the reinforced Mechanized Dragoon Regiment (4e RDP) and the 74th Artillery Regiment arrived on the morning of 11 May from Oostmalle/ Belgium (about 25km east of Antwerp) and were deployed in a line from Tilburg to the area about 12km north-east of Turnhout. The 4th Cuirassier Regiment (4e RC) from 1er DLM, equipped with tanks (S-35 Somua and H 35 Hotchkiss) was still assembling around Oostmalle. The command post of 1er DLM was also located there. Following behind 1er DLM was the 25th Motorized Infantry Division (25e DIM), which was to occupy the area around Breda. An independently operating reconnaissance group under Colonel

---

181 The mine chambers, which had been built into three pillars of the bridge just above the surface of the water and which also had been loaded with demolition charges, however, had remained undetected.

182 The artillery on Hoekse Waard on this day was supplied with ammunition by a steamer, which had sailed along the Nieuwe Merwede and had passed underneath the Moerdijk bridges. Only the escorting motor torpedo boat was damaged by the fire of the paratroopers from the shore, so that it later had to be scuttled by the Dutch in Numansdorp.

183 A GRCA was the reconnaissance group of a French army corps, a GRDI that of an infantry division.

Beauchesne was tasked with covering the deployment of the forces following behind 1er DLM, and arrived with advance elements in the area around Breda. The main operational task of 7th Army, as determined by the French high command, was the coverage of the avenues of approach toward Antwerp. For the execution of this task, it was to connect with Dutch forces north of Tilburg and Belgian forces south of Turnhout. In order to protect Antwerp against a thrust by the Germans from the north-west of Holland, the occupation of the Dutch province of Zeeland by two French infantry divisions, in addition to the Dutch troops already deployed there, commenced.

During the course of the morning of 11 May, it became evident to the command of 7th Army that the supposed assignments of the new allies had not materialized. After the retreat of the Dutch III Army Corps and the Light Division across the Maas and Waal on the evening of 10 May, only the Peel Division remained in Noord Brabant. However after the penetration of the Peel-Raam Line at Mill by the Germans the division was forced back to the canal at Zuid-Willemsvaart. It had lost half of its infantry and all of its artillery during the fighting and withdrawal from the northern part of the Peel-Raam-position and so it was only able to occupy the western bank of the canal from south of Hertogenbosch to Helmond in a fragmentary way. South of Helmond, up to the junction of the Peel-Raam Line and the canal at Zuid-Willemsvaart, near the Dutch-Belgian border at Weert, the retreat had gone somewhat better. However the German *XI. Armee-Korps*, who were advancing on a wide front after the retreat of Belgian forces from the north-west of the province of Limburg, threatened the right flank of this disposition. As no positions had been prepared on the western bank of the canal at Zuid-Willemsvaart it was to be assumed that the Germans would quickly penetrate the weak forces of the Peel Division and would appear in front of the 1er DLM only a few hours later. This division would be threatened particularly on its left flank, as it was doubted that parts of the Peel Division in any fighting-strength would move back there. This threat could only be met by the timely insertion of 25e DIM for the defence along the western bank of the Wilhelmina Canal, between Tilburg and the Bergsche Maas. South of the line was occupied by 1er DLM and, because of the Belgian forces around Turnhout and the soon available armor-heavy 4e RC at Oostmalle, the situation looked better.

On the Dutch side, it was initially only the territorial commander of Noord Brabant, Colonel Schmidt, who realized that the deployment of 7th Army primarily served the operational objective of the French high command, to safeguard Antwerp. During conferences with the commanders of 1er DLM and 6e RC he was also able to perceive that no advance of complete French formations beyond the line Tilburg-Turnhout had been foreseen. As a consequence and in the light of the hopeless situation of his Peel Division, Colonel Schmidt saw no option other than to bring the rest of this division back behind the Wilhelmina Canal north-west of Tilburg and to task them with a mission within the operational scope of the French 7th Army. However he had no doubt that with the loss of the canal at Zuid-Willemsvaart, the fate of Noord Brabant was exclusively dependent on the further operations of 7th Army.

During his meeting with Colonel Schmidt the commander of 6e RC, Colonel Dario, was informed about the seizure of the Moerdijk bridges by German parachute forces for the first time. Schmidt, however, was unable to pass on precise information as the 6th Border Battalion on the morning of 11 May had been placed directly subordinate under the command of the Dutch Field Army and continuous communications to this battalion did not exist. The briefing by Colonel Schmidt resulted in Colonel Dario agreeing to dispatch reconnaissance in fighting-strength units against the Moerdijk bridges. This task he entrusted to Commandant (Major) Michon, who was the commander of the 2e Groupe d'Escadrons of his regiment. Commandant Michon formed a detachment with three platoons of AMD 178[184] from his 3rd squadron, two platoons with AMR 35 light tanks[185] assigned from 4e RDP, and his battle HQ, with which he intended to survey the area just east of Breda and to reconnoiter against the German air bridgehead at Moerdijk. At 1030hrs[186] Michon moved out from Tilburg. At the northern exit of Breda, Michon encountered the commander of the 6th Border Battalion. The latter briefed Michon about the situation and informed him that his battalion still had the mission to retake the Moerdijk bridges. Michon also learned that there was no communication with Dutch troops, who were assumed to be positioned more to the east and that German troops could already have reached Gertruidenberg (about 7km north of Oosterhout), where a bridge crossed the Bergsche Maas to Keizersveer. Commandant Michon immediately deployed a platoon each of AMR 35s and AMD 178s toward the Wilhelmina Canal at Oosterhout, and for the protection of the bridges across the small river Mark north of Breda. With the remainder of his force, he drove on to Terheijden (about 6km west of Oosterhout). From there, he dispatched a platoon of AMD 178s with the task of establishing contact with parts of the 6th Border Battalion, occupying Zevenbergen, Zevenbergschen Hoek, and Kalishoek and the last AMD platoon for reconnaissance to Wagenberg, Helkant, Hooge Zwaluwe and Lage Zwaluwe.[187] After a short while the patrol which was dispatched to Gertruidenberg reported the presence of Germans there.[188]

At 1230hrs, a detachment from the GRDI of 25e DIM arrived in Terheijden. It consisted of two AMD 178s and a platoon of motorcycle infantry led by a lieutenant. The detachment's mission was to escort the French General de Brigade Mittelhauser to the Dutch high command in Den Haag, where he was to take over the function of French liaison officer. It was only after he was acquainted with this action, that Commandant Michon decided to clear the Moerdijk Bridges in cooperation with the 6th Border Battalion. For this aim, he also assumed command over the escort and sent it to Zevenbergschen Hoek. However by this point it turned out disadvantageously for the intended attack, as his detachment, as well as the 6th Border Battalion, was spread out too thinly opposite the German air bridgehead and parts of the former had been dispatched for security missions to the east. Furthermore, coordination for the attack with the commander of the 6th

---

184 The Panhard AMD 178 was a lightly armored wheeled reconnaissance vehicle. It was armed with an effective 25mm gun and a coaxial machine-gun. It had radio equipment and a crew of four. Its range on roads was about 300km, its maximum speed 70km per hour.

185 The Renault AMR 35 was a lightly armored tank, for the support of motorized infantry. Its crew was made up of two men. It was in general armed with a 7.5mm machine-gun in a revolving turret. Some vehicles were alternatively equipped with a 13.2mm heavy machine-gun or a 25mm gun. Its range on roads was about 200km.

186 For reasons of simplicity, German times are used for the French actions as it was one hour ahead of French time.

187 These two platoons or parts of them had probably been observed and reported by soldiers from *II./FschJgRgt.1* during the afternoon of 11 May.

188 This report was wrong. An explanation may be that the Dutch security post at the bridge across the Bergsche Maas had been mistaken for German troops. It must be doubted that the patrol ever had gone forward sufficiently close to the bridge, as the Dutch had maintained their security there until 12 May. Therefore, the bridge could have used by the French until the night 11/12 May.

Border Battalion was still problematic. Considerable time was lost during the initial attack preparations. It was only once during that time that a short contact occurred between a patrol from Michon's detachment and a machine-gun-outpost of the paratroopers deployed at the hamlet at Blauwe Sluis.

While the French made their appearance in the western part of Noord Brabant, the Germans did not remain idle. Since the afternoon of 10 May the *Luftwaffe* had attacked the French 7th Army during its advance through Belgium,[189] making the commands of *Heeresgruppe B* and *Luftflotte 2* aware of the fact that its forward forces had crossed the Scheldt south of Antwerp. Reports from the aerial reconnaissance about the approach of French mechanized troops toward the line Oosterhout-Tilburg-Turnhout had not arrived prior to the late morning of 11 May.

Due to inadequate and temporarily interrupted radio communications, situation reports from *Fl.Div.7* to *Luftflotte 2* were missing or had arrived only garbled.[190] Therefore Kesselring ordered *Oberleutnant* Triebel from *Aufkl.Staffel 7*, who was placed under his command as liaison officer from *Fl.Div.7*, in a light aircraft, to the command post of the *Luftlande-Korps* in Rijsoord. He was ordered to bring with him the situation report from *Generalleutnant* Student. In his handwritten report, Student expressed his conviction that the operations in the area of *Fl.Div.7* could be accomplished in accordance with the mission.[191]

Whether *Oberleutnant* Triebel had reported at the command post of *Fl.Div.7* that an air attack against the enemy in front of *II./FschJgRgt.1* was underway, or whether Student was informed beforehand, cannot be known. In any case, *II./FschJgRgt.1* was made aware and was instructed to move back from its most forward positions to the main defensive line as a preventive measure against the effects of bombing. During the execution of this measure, however, two squads from *1/PiBtl.22*, working on obstacles in front of 8th Company, were not notified. Upon request of this company, a squad from 7th Company was sent forward and brought the engineers back. While this was under way, the announced air attack commenced at about 1730hrs. The He 111 and Ju 88 bombers from *III./KG 4* primarily bombed Zevenbergen and Zevenbergschen Hoek in front of the German air bridgehead. The paratroopers and engineers managed to reach the main defence-positions unscathed, despite some bombs landing close by. The two villages that had borne the brunt of the air attack were hard hit. In Zevenbergschen Hoek 35 inhabitants were killed and numerous others injured. About 150 buildings were destroyed or seriously damaged there and in adjacent settlements. The escort for General Mittelhauser, which had moved to Zevenbergschen Hoek, had five soldiers killed and an AMD 178 was damaged beyond repair by a near hit. Shocked by the air attack and obviously fearing more to come, Commandant Michon decided to immediately break off the unfolding preparations for attack of his detachment and to move back to 6e RC. Forced to take detours because of

---

189 The effects of these attacks on the personnel and material of the French was rather low. They had, however, not failed to reduce the morale of the French troops.

190 *General* (ret.) Trettner, who during the operations against Holland as a major was the operations staff officer in the command of the *Luftlande-Korps*, has on several occasions confirmed to the author the frequently interrupted or disturbed radio communications.

191 Student's report and appreciation of the situation during the night 11/12 May had been forwarded to Göring and Hitler in the latter's war-headquarters "Felsennest" in Münstereifel.

destroyed bridges and once more attacked from the air at Etten-Leur, it took until 0200hrs on 12 May before the detachment reached the south-western edge of Breda.

Immediately after the end of the bombing the paratroopers of *II./FschJgRgt.1* became active once again. With a captured Dutch 10.5cm gun which was assigned to 6th Company, they fired at observed enemy concentrations in Zevenbergschen Hoek. The fire caused an observation post in the steeple of the church in this village to be destroyed. One of the captured infantry guns, positioned with the 3rd Platoon of 7th Company, shelled motorized enemy troops in Lochtenburg. In the evening a patrol from 7th Company discovered that the Dutch had abandoned the village. In reaction it constructed a provisional barrier at the crossing over the drainage ditch at Roode Vaart, some distance north-west of Lochtenburg and remained as a security guard in that village throughout the night. With the onset of darkness patrols were also dispatched against the other settlements located in a semi-circle around the southern part of the air bridgehead. They detected that Lage Zwaluwe and all of the terrain south-west of it had also been abandoned by the enemy.[192]

The optimistic continuation of the operations of *Fl.Div.7* by *Generalleutnant* Student was built on his firm belief in the ongoing steadfastness of his troops, the skill of his subordinate commanders, the knowledge about further reinforcements and his judgment of the Dutch adversary after his unsuccessful endeavors to turn the tide during the day. However at this time he still lacked a clear picture of the Dutch forces between Alblasserdam and the area south of Dordrecht and obviously had underestimated how critically the situation for the air bridgehead at the Moerdijk bridges could develop if the French threw a great part of their arriving mechanized forces against it.

Of the isolated groups of *22.(LL)Inf.Div.*, only that under Dr. Wischhusen was able to report its movements on a regular basis by radio. For information about *Gruppe von Sponeck* and the defenders of Valkenburg, Student depended on reports from the command of *Luftflotte 2*, which, because of the unreliable radio communication, had arrived only sporadically.

During the night 11/12 May, he was informed that the German *XXVI.Armee-Korps* and the *9.Panzer-Division* were to relieve the paratroopers at the Moerdijk bridges. As their first task, they crossed the Zuid-Willemsvaart Canal south of Hertogenbosch and were about 45km away. In this area and to the south, much would depend on any encounter with the French.

The importance which Dordrecht had gained for the Dutch as a base for offensive actions against the Germans occupying the area east of the Kil and the bridges between the islands of Dordrecht and Ijsselmonde became plainly visible in the plans. Those developed during the course of 11 May instructed Colonel van der Bijl to clear the island of Germans using his division, supported by Group Kil and the troops still holding out in the south and south-west of Dordrecht In order to execute this order Colonel van der Bijl planned to move all of

---

192   After the departure of Are Michon and with the onset of darkness the units and sub-units of the Dutch 6th Border Infantry Battalion retired from their positions opposite the southern air bridgehead of *II./ FschJgRgt.1*, some of them on their own. Only parts of the battalion were later assembled by its commander south of the small river Mark, west of Breda. The morale of these soldiers, however, had been lost.

his division, except the covering force at the Noord, across the Merwede into Dordrecht and to the south of the town. After reaching the line Dordrecht-north–Kop van 't Land, three bicycle infantry battalions abreast, those in the middle and on the right being reinforced by the remainder from I/28th Inf.Rgt., were to advance through phase lines against the German positions between the bridges at Dordrecht and Tweede Tol. For this action an additional bicycle battalion was made available as a mobile reserve. The 2nd Motorcycle Battalion of the Hussars arrived around midday from Noord Brabant and, although in reduced strength, was deployed to push through to Wieldrecht ahead of the main attack and to establish contact with a reinforced company from the 3rd Border Battalion, to be ferried across the Kil on the night 11/12 May. Direct fire-support for the attack force was to be provided by the 2nd Artillery Detachment from the Light Division. After the elimination of the German resistance on Dordrecht, the attack was to be continued against Ijsselmonde and Waalhaven.

12 May – Whit Sunday

The activities of the isolated groups of *22.(LL)Inf.Div.* on this day again were mainly directed at survival.

After being rested at a farmhouse on its way toward Rotterdam, the force commanded by Dr. Wischhusen moved on again at 0300hrs, on the auto-route along the Delftsche Schie. Due to a lack of adequate transport, the wounded who were unable to walk were left behind at the farm under the care of a *Feldwebel* from the medical service with the intention of fetching them later. While the captured Dutch soldiers were taken along, the civilians who had been captured during the fighting on 10 and 11 May, were to be released by the medical *Feldwebel* at 0800hours.

After a short distance and still in the darkness, the point of the march column came across a Dutch security post and was engaged by machine-guns. Tracer fire from an aviation machine-gun mounted on a truck which approached the security post at full speed, was sufficient to make the Dutch retire. Just after dawn, at a bridge across a canal, the column again was fired at by machine-guns. One of the guns positioned in a farm complex was quickly neutralized, another one continued to dominate the bridge by fire. As there was no other way to advance other than across the bridge, the infantry gun of the group was brought forward. After a few rounds, the enemy, which consisted of an entire squadron of bicycle infantry, broke off the fight and retreated. Without further resistance, *Gruppe Wischhusen* now entered Overschie. The town where the Delftsche Schie split up into three canals was unoccupied by the enemy. However, in its southern part, at an open draw-bridge, a well dug in Dutch heavy machine-gun prevented any further advance. Consequently for the time being *Gruppe Wischhusen* settled down in all-round security positions with the main effort toward Rotterdam. At about 1000hrs the attempt to pick up the wounded, left north of Overschie, failed when the ambulance, dispatched for this task, was fired at on the way to the farm.[193]

Soon it was evident that the occupation of Overschie by the Germans had cut the shortest Dutch line of communication between Rotterdam and Delft. Throughout the course of the day seven ambulances approaching from Delft were captured together with their drivers. A truck from Delft, with the mission to pick up ammunition in Rotterdam,

---

193 The wounded and their caretaker had already been captured by Dutch troops, which had advanced from Delft.

suffered the same fate. In the afternoon it was recognized that the enemy had commenced to encircle *Gruppe Wischhusen* as fire from machine-guns was now also received from the north-east and the south-west. Some time later, and in spite of the defensive-fire, an armored car which was advancing from Rotterdam, managed to pass through Overschie toward Delft. The ambulance, for which the armored car served as escort, was allowed to follow unhindered. In the course of the night, thrusts by Dutch troops of reconnaissance in strength were launched from Rotterdam against the south-western edge of Overschie. They were easily warded off well in front of the German positions.

For the German group under *Oberst* Heyser, holding out in Valkenburg and in some farmsteads south and south-west of the village, it became evident at first light through movements of Dutch troops along the road from Katwijk aan Rijn that the enemy intended to attack again on this day.[194] In preparation for the attack from 0940hrs Valkenburg was heavily bombarded by artillery. The main targets were the church, townhall and the pastor's house. Hits on the roof of the church, which collapsed later, killed some of the Dutch prisoners that were confined in the building and one German soldier. As the church, in spite of its marking as a building protected by the Red Cross, remained a preferred target for the artillery, the 300 prisoners were moved to a workshop to the south of the village. In the assembly room of the town hall some injured soldiers from both sides were wounded again by the artillery fire. The civilian population also suffered tragic losses. Many inhabitants of the village assembled in the streets in order to move to Katwijk aan Rijn during a respite in the fighting, which the major and the Dutch artillery commander had arranged by telephone the day before. The ceasefire was carried out at the agreed-upon time with the inhabitants, waving white flags, being moved out to Katwijk.[195] The artillery did continue to fire for some minutes during this process and some civilians were injured.

When the artillery ceased fire at 1040hrs the Dutch infantry, supported by numerous flat trajectory weapons, advanced across the drainage ditch at Kleine Watering against the northern edge of Valkenburg. Progress, however, was slow, as buildings on the way were searched.

In the meantime the right bank of the Oude Rijn, between Haagse Schouw and Rijnsburg, was occupied by the Dutch.[196] An armored car which had appeared early in the day turned back after it had been hit by anti-tank rifle fire from the farmstead at Rijnvliet,

---

194 Early in the morning on 12 May I/9th Inf.Rgt. in Katwijk aan Rijn was ordered by the commander of 4th Inf.Rgt. to attack Valkenburg from the north and seize it. Two infantry companies and the machine-gun company from this battalion had been dispatched for this task. Fire-support was to be provided by III/2nd Art.Rgt. One platoon of 75mm guns of this unit was to move forward with the attacking infantry. Heavy machine-guns and anti-tank guns, positioned south-west of Rijnsburg, were to assist with flanking fire.

195 The then *Leutnant* Teusen, in a report about the actions of his platoon in the area around Valkenburg, noted that the Dutch artillery commander, during a complaining telephone-call by the major, had given as explanation for the ongoing artillery fire, that the approaching civilians had been identified as disguised paratroopers and moreover, that the artillery received the fire-order directly from Den Haag.

196 The territorial commander in Leiden had tasked the commander of 22nd Depot Battalion with the protection of the eastern bank of the Oude Rijn, as I Army Corps had not excluded crossing-attempts by the Germans from the West. Unity of command, however, had still not been established on 12 May for the area Haarlem-Leiden-Wassenaar.

which remained firmly in the hands of the paratroopers.[197] A patrol of two men from
6./FschJgRgt.2, ordered to reconnoiter toward Rijnsburg early in the morning, failed to
return.[198]

Dutch reconnaissance patrols made up of motor-cyclists from the hussars and of
infantry from a depot battalion, which probed later in the morning from Maaldrift toward
the north, were soon stopped by fire from the farms at Rijnvliet, Zonneveld and Torenvliet.
At about 1540hrs, the hussar motor-cyclists were taken out of the line and joined the 1st
Regiment of Hussars, who had moved from Wassenaar to Leiden.

Shortly after midday the Dutch infantry that were attacking from the north arrived
near Valkenburg. Advance elements even managed to penetrate into the north-western part
of the village. As they were not reinforced, they took up positions in sighting-distance of
the church. There streetfighting raged until 1640hrs. When Dutch artillery from across
the Oude Rijn commenced to bombard the village again, the isolated Dutch infantrymen
in Valkenburg abandoned the buildings, occupied by them and fell back upon the main
attack force. This, too, soon retreated to the north.[199] On the German side, the brunt of the
fighting in the afternoon was borne by 10./InfRgt.47, who lost five killed.

At about 1900hrs in the evening, Dutch infantry again advanced toward Valkenburg,
this time moving from the west.[200] The advance was slow because of the drainage ditches
crossing its path. However, before the actual attack commenced the Dutch retired again. For
some time the German defenders that were positioned at the western edge of Valkenburg,
particularly paratroopers from 6./FschJgRgt.2, delivered harassing fire.

For the units from II./InfRgt.47, firmly established in the dunes north and north-
west of Wassenaar since 10 May, the day went by without any serious challenge. This time
was therefore used to further improve positions along either side of the Wassenaarse Slag,
and to reinforce them with captured heavy weapons. A Dutch patrol advanced against
the forward strongpoint at 1500hrs, but promptly turned back when it was fired at from
a German outpost in the depression at de Pan, about 1000m north of Albertushoeve. A
Dutch infantry platoon, dispatched for reconnaissance against the Wassenaarse Slag at
1540hrs retreated again, when it came across German outposts which were positioned well
forward in the dunes around Groot Berkeheide. A small detachment, obviously sent out to
recover material left back in front of the Hotel Duinoord the day before, was ambushed by
the Germans and retreated without accomplishing anything.

The German force under Oberleutnant Martin which was isolated in the Staalduinse
wood south-east of Hoek van Holland was able to further improve its positions, as it was
again not attacked.

---

197 The vehicle was one of the three cars, which had been dispatched from Den Haag to Haagse Schouw on 11
     May. On 12 May at 0940hrs, all three had been ordered back to Den Haag for new missions.
198 The two soldiers were found killed near the left bank of the Oude Rijn after the end of the fighting in
     Holland.
199 The retreat of I/9th Inf.Rgt. was ordered for unknown reasons by 3rd Inf.Div. in spite of the favorable
     situation, reported by the commander of 4th Inf.Rgt. to the chief of staff of this division.
200 Two companies from II/9th Inf.Rgt. and a third covering the advance. The battalion had received its
     attack-order at 1425hrs as part of the plan to launch a pincer movement together with I/9th Inf.Rgt.
     However, the battalion did not leave its staging area before 1840hrs.

There were two reasons why the offensive operations of the Dutch against Valkenburg had not developed into being critical for its defenders and why the German force holding out in the dunes had not been threatened seriously on this day:

The commandant of Fortress Holland feared landings of German troops from the sea in north Holland, and in the area around Amsterdam. As such he had instructed the command of I Army Corps to maintain the fighting strength of its forces. This instruction was interpreted to the effect that actions against Valkenburg and the German force north of Wassenaar, were to be conducted only with single reinforced infantry companies and platoons for the time being, i.e. more or less as holding actions. An order to this effect was sent to the command of 3rd Infantry Division. This order quite obviously had not been passed on from there to 4th Inf.Rgt. as its commander had dispatched two battalions from 9th Inf.Rgt. for the attack against Valkenburg. As his report about the development of the situation at Valkenburg in the afternoon had not received any reply he withdrew I/9th Inf.Rgt., without instructions from 3rd Inf.Div., in front of the village. In the evening he viewed the belated attack of II/9th Inf.Rgt. as without a chance of success and so he also ordered it to retire.

The restrictions on the movements of the infantry against Valkenburg and the Wassenaarse Slag for 12 May had also been confusing. The dispersal of the men in difficult terrain, and the hardships they had to endure in the field, caused the command of 3rd Infantry Division to call for a regroup/rest. The task group of 1st Inf.Rgt. had not been affected by conditions of this kind, which, considering the loss of the greater part of I/1st Inf. Rgt., had certainly been weakened, but still had two uncommitted reinforced battalions.[201]

On 11 May General Winkelman had already ordered the sea transfer of as many of the German prisoners of war as possible to England, in order to remove them permanently from the establishment of the *Wehrmacht*. About 600 German soldiers, who had been confined in Scheveningen and Den Haag, arrived at Ijmuiden at 1840hrs on 12 May for shipment. Another 300 were being transferred from their present prison camps throughout the course of the evening.[202] When the Dutch ship *Westland*, planned for the transport, was sent to England and upon its return could not find the entrance into Ijmuiden because of the black-out, the 900 German prisoners of war were confined for the night in the basement of the town's fish hall. However the evacuation to England of the family of Princess Juliane from Ijmuiden on the British destroyer *Codrington* in the early evening was executed without any difficulties or incident.

The defenders of the bridgehead on the northern bank of the Nieuwe Maas were compressed into a small strip of terrain and were exposed to continuous fire from the surrounding positions of the Dutch. From midday onwards Dutch mortars also fired into the bridgehead. However there were no determined attacks by enemy infantry. The Dutch

---

201 III/1st Inf.Rgt., reinforced by sub-units from II/1st Inf.Rgt., the remainder of 4th Reserve Border Company, a platoon from 5th Company of the Depot of the Grenadiers and a heavy machine-gun platoon from II/4th Inf.Rgt., had taken over the protection of Wassenaar after the departure of the 1st Regiment of Hussars. In the afternoon, parts of III/16th Inf.Rgt from Den Haag had additionally been deployed as security forces along the south-western edge of Wassenaar. II/1st Inf.Rgt. had taken over the protection of Maaldrift and Landlust.

202 Dutch sources mention 117 pilots and other members of aircrews, but also prisoners from the *SS-AufklAbt* and members from the commandos, captured during the fighting at the Maas-Waal canal.

howitzers which were positioned in Kralingen continued to shell Noordereiland and Waalhaven. Counter-battery fire by the high-angle weapons at the disposal of *Fl.Div.7* and *InfRgt.16* was impossible because they lacked the required range.

The search for stragglers and missing in the bridgehead resulted in the establishment of contact with a squad of 11 men from Kerfin's platoon, who were positioned in the chambers beneath the traffic bridge, and with a machine-gun-team from *11./InfRgt.16* on the railway bridge. Both groups had remained in place and were supplied with ammunition and rations. Around midday an attempt to generate permanent contact with the soldiers defending from underneath the traffic bridge had to be given up, after one man was killed and four others wounded. In the afternoon, however, the defenders did manage to erect a machine-gun-position directed along the street that led to the Beurse station. From here some of the Dutch machine-guns, positioned in buildings along this street, were able to be silenced. At about 1800hrs, an attempt failed to establish contact across the traffic bridge with the troops on Noordereiland. Yet at 2000hrs two soldiers from the bridgehead did succeed in crossing the traffic bridge. For the first time, *Oberstleutnant* von Choltitz now received an extensive report about the situation north of the bridges. After nightfall the two runners returned to the bridgehead using the traffic bridge. They were accompanied by a *Feldwebel* from the medical service and a paratrooper from Kerfin's platoon, who had remained on Noordereiland. Using two stretchers the four soldiers took with them urgently required ammunition, medical material and some rations. After their arrival, the wounded were cared for in a more professional manner.

In spite of the loss of most of its modern combat aircraft and the dominance of the *Luftwaffe* in the airspace over Holland, the Dutch Air Arm continued to intervene in the fighting on the ground. Two Fokker C-Xs attacked the parking lot of Feyenoord stadium with eight 50kg bombs each as it was presumed to be a landing site for German aircraft. Two more Fokker C-Xs dropped 12 bombs on Waalhaven airfield, of which eleven impacted on the runway. In both cases the attacking aircraft managed to return to base without interference from German fighters. At about 2100hrs the British also appeared over Waalhaven with six Blenheim bombers and nine Swordfish torpedo bombers (these could also be used as conventional bombers, with a limited payload), of the Fleet Air Arm. However their bombs and machine-gun-fire caused little damage.

II./InfRgt.16 was still employed along the western bank of the Noord and it became evident during the course of the day that the enemy had given up his intent to force a crossing of the river. Although the eastern bank remained occupied by Dutch infantry fire had diminished considerably. The artillery however continued to regularly bombard the German position, but the mountain guns of *4/ArtRgt.22* were unable to provide counter-battery fire, as their range was insufficient. As the Dutch did not occupy the island of Sofia Polder *II./InfRgt.16* established a standing patrol on its northern tip. It reported shortly after 1330hrs that a Dutch column, consisting of 30-40 motor vehicles and bicycle infantry, was moving from the area east of Alblasserdam to the south. Thus the supposition of the command of *Fl.Div.7*, that the majority of the Light Division was to be employed via Dordrecht, was confirmed.

South of Barendrecht, a patrol from *I./InfRgt.72* detected that the lift-bridge across the Oude Maas was still protected from the southern bank of the river by infantry and some heavy machine-guns. However some enemy concentrations were no longer observed, so the command of *InfRgt.16* excluded renewed offensive actions for the time being.

During the course of the morning supplies were again dropped in the vicinity of the regimental headquarters at Hordijk, this time by He 111s. However, a number of the parachutes, fastened on the so-called 'supply bombs' did not land safely, ensuring a part of the dropped ammunition became unusable. The use of 'supply bombs' instead of the more reliable box-type containers was an indication that the *Luftwaffe* was running out of air-drop equipment.

About the same time as the supply drop took place, the two missing infantry gun platoons from *13./InfRgt.16* were unloaded on the airfield at Waalhaven.

The situation in the western part of Ijsselmonde was still considered unsatisfactory. Here Dutch infantry, which was assessed to be about a company in strength, and a number of anti-aircraft machine-guns[203] were firmly established in positions at the petroleum installation, about 2km west of Pernis. Their positions were protected on three sides by water. The elements from *1./InfRgt.72* opposite this Dutch position had attempted to gain some ground. The bridge across the Oude Maas at Spijkenisse and the eastern edge of the village of Hoogvliet were also still in the hands of the Dutch.[204] Those parts from *1./InfRgt.72* reinforced with at least one mortar from *4./InfRgt.72*, had been unable to make any progress there. When, about 1510hrs, an attempt failed to cross the Oude Maas in boats and a *Leutnant* and a *Feldwebel* from *1./InfRgt.72* had been killed during the attempt, all further offensive actions there were called off.

In light of reports received from the area around Dordrecht, Student saw his thoughts confirmed. His plans were to retain the bridges and neutralize the enemy operating in and from Dordrecht with all forces which could be made available. The information recived from *Luftflotte 2* – that the arrival of *9.Panzer-Division* could be counted upon during 13 May – provided encouragement. Until then, another 24 hours had to be sustained with the forces on hand. Their own actions, however, had to take into consideration not only the threat posed against the bridges at Dordrecht by the Dutch, but also the fact that French mechanized troops were only one or two marching hours away from the bridges at Moerdijk. Quickly, the plans to remedy the situation in Dordrecht and south of it, (developed the day before), were now put into effect by the staff of *Fl.Div.7*. As commander of the task force assembling near Waalhaven, Student placed the commanding officer of *ArtRgt.22*, *Oberstleutnant* de Boer.[205] The following forces were put under his command:

---

203 Originally, it was the 1st Company from III/39th Inf.Rgt. On 11 May a platoon from IV/ 15th Inf.Rgt. from the reinforcements for Rotterdam had additionally been assigned to this company. The 53rd and half of the 54th Anti-Aircraft Machine-Gun Platoons had also remained at the harbor area. Source: Report of Captain van Royen, who at that time was the commanding officer in this position.

204 The Dutch infantry at these locations was originally a platoon each from II/34th Inf.Rgt. and I/39th Inf.Rgt. and a platoon from 11th Machine-gun Company; on the morning of 12 May they had been reinforced by the 3rd Company from I/39th Inf.Rgt., two more heavy machine-guns, a mortar and some naval personnel.

205 There is no source explaining why Student had not placed the command of the operations against Dordrecht into the hands of *Oberst* Bräuer, in whose area of operation Dordrecht had been. It is, however, justified to assume, that he had not wanted to overburden the *Oberst*, and had wanted to keep him available as an adequate rank for coordination with the approaching *9.Panzer-Division*.

- *I./InfRgt.72*, commanded by *Major* Krüger, less its slightly reinforced 1st Company and a platoon from 2nd Company, the latter tasked with the protection of the airfield
- two incomplete companies from *II./FschJgRgt.2*
- units which had arrived from *4.* and *7./InfRgt.65*
- one platoon from *7./InfRgt.16*
- three anti-tank platoons from *Inf.Rgts.16* and *47*
- elements from *SanKp.7*
- three anti-tank guns from *FschPzAbwKp.7* (up to now in reserve)
- half of *FschGeschBttr.7* under *Oberleutnant* Loesch
- one battery from *II/ArtRgt.22*

Upon the arrival of the task force at the Dordrecht bridges, the forces from *I./* and *III./FschJgRgt.1* and from *1/PiBtl.22* in the area near Dordrecht were to join the operation.

A part of the heavy weapons which were planned for fire-support, namely the staff of *II/ArtRgt.22*, its 5th and parts of the 6th batteries as well as *14./InfRgt.47* (anti-tank), arrived just in time in 40 Ju 52s from *KGr z.b.V.9* and were unloaded between 0835 and 1100hrs. During this time, the two weak companies from *II./FschJgRgt.2* were relieved from their previous mission and were replaced by *I./InfRgt.16*, although this was not much stronger than a company.

While *Kampfgruppe de Boer* was assembling, Student made a surprise visit to the command post of *I./FschJgRgt.1*. Here he informed *Hauptmann* Walther about the mission and organization of *Kampfgruppe de Boer* and instructed him to support it with all available troops for an attack into the western part of Dordrecht, in the early morning of 13 May. Besides the 10th and elements of the 11th companies from *III./FschJgRgt.1*, which were already engaged in the fighting around Dordrecht, *Oberst* Bräuer also ordered its 9th Company, located in the south-western part of Krispijn, to join in the operation.

Throughout the course of the morning *Gruppe von Sponeck* managed to establish radio communication with the command of *Fl.Div.7*. Some proposals for a relief attack from the north of Rotterdam toward Overschie, which came up in the staff of *Fl.Div.7*, were turned down by Student immediately upon his return to his command post early in the afternoon. He now made it unmistakably clear that the resolution of the situation in the operational area of *Gruppe Süd* had to take ultimate priority.

There, the threat against the Dordrecht bridges (after the neutralization of the Dutch Battalion Ravelli) and against the bridges at Moerdijk after the retreat of the Dutch infantry and the French reconnaissance units, appeared reduced for the time being, in the light of the suspected attack of the enemy from around Dordrecht, the undiminished effects of the Dutch artillery fire from Hoekse Waard and the growing strength of the French forces in the area around Breda. Nevertheless the situation was anything but satisfactory. While the two operationally important pairs of bridges in the north and the south of the operational area of *Gruppe Süd* could be considered as tolerably well-protected by a combat-effective parachute infantry battalion each in prepared positions, the circa 3km long line of communication between them was safeguarded only by personnel from the staff and the HQ troops from *FschJgRgt.1*, and by the *FschSan-Halbkompanie 7*.

The arrival of the weakened *11./FschJgRgt.1* in the area around Tweede Tol had, to some extent, reduced pressure on the troops who had up to this point been employed for two days without rest, as parts of the company had immediately been moved into the outposts in the north and east. A platoon from *11./FschJgRgt.1*, reinforced by two heavy machine-guns in the early morning at 0330hrs, was dispatched against Wieldrecht. It cleared the village of a few Dutch stragglers and moved on toward the Zeehaven, leaving a small security element behind. At about the same time as the platoon from *11./FschJgRgt.1*, a shock troop of 20 men from *FschSan-Halbkompanie 7*, led by three medical officers from this unit, advanced along the railway toward the north. As they met no resistance it turned toward Amstelwijk after 2km, and came across the still operating medical aid station. Moving on in the direction of the Zeehaven, the shock troop met the platoon from *11./FschJgRgt.1*. Both forces now advanced together further to the north. Here they were fired on by Dutch machine-guns from the east. After a short while the commander of *III./FschJgRgt.1* appeared and ordered both forces to discontinue the advance. They arrived in Tweede Tol at about 1000hrs. A *Feldwebel* and four other ranks from the 2nd Platoon of the FschSan-Halbkompanie, having been isolated since their landing on 10 May, reached the German lines. They reported that they detected parts of *Kompanie Moll* in the farm at Tongplaat near the northern bank of the Merwede and guided a squad of men from the regimental staff under *Oberleutnant* Platow to that location. Upon its arrival at Tongplaat, *Oberleutnant* Platow assembled the soldiers of the *FschJg-Ergänzungs-Bataillon* under *Oberleutnant* Moll, as well as the Dutch soldiers under Ensign Marijs and led both parties back to the command post of *Oberst* Bräuer. There the *Oberst* disapproved vocally about the appearance of the Dutch soldiers with their weapons in their hands and ordered their immediate disarmament. However when *Oberleutnant* Moll explained the course of the fighting on 11 May and its end, *Oberst* Bräuer apologized for his manners. As a visible sign of his soldierly esteem for the Dutch commander he allowed Ensign Marijs retain his side-arm. His request to Marijs, to return to the local Dutch commander on the island of Dordrecht and, in view of the imminent arrival of the *9.Panzer-Division*, persuade him to discontinue fighting, was turned down by the former, who insisted on first observing the arrival of German tanks with his own eyes. *Oberleutnant* Moll and the men who returned with him were immediately deployed south of Tweede Tol.

In the course of the morning any remaining doubts in the command of *FschJgRgt.1* that the enemy was ready to attack against the lines of communication between the two pairs of bridges from the area south of Dordrecht vanished. This was after the greater part of the Light Division appeared to have crossed the Merwede. This assessment was reinforced when a group of 11 soldiers from *FschSan-Halbkompanie 7*, led by two medical officers and moving forward along the Zeedijk in an attempt to salvage medical equipment, received heavy fire from machine-guns and were forced to retire with one wounded.

Indeed, the plan of the commandant of Fortress Holland, to gain the eastern bank of the Kil using parts of the Light Division, then to cross this river at Wieldrecht and subsequently attack the German forces threatening Rotterdam from Hoekse Waard, had been set in motion since the early hours of 12 May. The attack in a south-westerly direction to the

Kil was to be conducted with three reinforced bicycle infantry battalions abreast and supported by one of the Light Division's artillery detachments. A fourth bicycle infantry battalion was also to be kept in reserve. The command of Group Kil was ordered to create a bridgehead at Wieldrecht simultaneously with the start of the attack of the Light Division, in order to support it during its final thrust to the Kil. Twelve 75mm field guns from 23rd Art.Rgt. were to direct their fire in front of the force. To allow the coordination of time and space during the attack, three phase-lines were determined – the first along the railway line Zwijndrecht-Sliedrecht, the second along the road Wieldrecht-Kop van't Land and the third from Tweede Tol to the dikes, protecting the island of Dordrecht in the south-west.[206]

At 1110hrs the bicycle battalion which was deployed on the left of the line reached the railway north-east of Dubbeldam and, bypassing the village, advanced toward the second phase-line without meeting resistance. The bicycle battalion in the centre, reinforced by the remainder of the 3rd Company from I/28th Inf.Rgt. advanced across the railway, but halted in Dorwijk, about 500m west of Dubbeldam, to allow other units to close up. The battalion on the right, on the way to the second phase-line, halted in the railway underpass just west of the station of Dordrecht, because the two artillery batteries from the Light Division had not yet deployed to their firing positions. At 1230hrs a company from the 3rd Border Infantry Battalion crossed the Kil from Gravendeel to Wieldrecht and drove off the few paratroopers from *11./FschJgRgt.1* who had been left there as sentries.

At 1310hrs the chief of staff of Group Kil and the commander of the attack force, who was present at the command post of the Dordrecht garrison, coordinated the action via telephone.[207] The conference resulted in a change to the operational plan: The initial objective of the attack was now the residential area of Krispijn. Accordingly, Krispijn was to be cleared of Germans by the battalion on the right that was attacking from the north. That in the centre was to attack via the cemetery of Dordrecht from the east. With Krispijn taken, the Light Division was then to pursue the original plan once again. From the bridgehead at Wieldrecht, a task force of three companies from Group Kil, after the taking of Krispijn by the Light Division, was to attack along the eastern bank of the Kil toward Tweede Tol, thereby forming the new right flank of the overall attack force.[208] However up to now the bridgehead at Wieldrecht was only occupied by the 80-man strong company from the 3rd Border Infantry Battalion, whereas two companies from 34th Inf.Rgt. planned to reinforce it were still kept available at Gravendeel.

As there was neither telephone nor radio communication from the commander of the attack force to the battalions nor such communications between these, the sending of orders and the movement of the centre battalion, as demanded by the changes to the plan, took considerable time. The battalion on the left was not instructed at all about the change.

At the same time a detachment from the 2nd Motorcycle Regiment of Hussars (2nd RHM) attempted to push through to Wieldrecht from Dordrecht in order to establish initial contact with the forces from Group Kil. The detachment consisted of a motorcycle company which was reinforced with a heavy machine-gun platoon and two anti-tank guns.

---

206 Once the attack force would have reached the third phase-line it would have been close to the northern part of the air bridgehead of *II./FschJgRgt.1*, but quite a distance away from the crossing-site at Wieldrecht. The question, of whether the commander of the Light Division had planned to also clear the northern ramps of the bridges at Moerdijk prior to moving on across the Kil, must remain unanswered.

207 Incomprehensibly, the paratroopers still had not cut the telephone cables across the bridges at Dordrecht.

208 Instructions for the coordination of fire and movement of the now very complicated operations obviously had not been arranged for, and therefore had borne the risk of failure from the very beginning.

As the column passed the roundabout north of Krispijn (Hugo de Groot-Plein) it was fired at by a forward sentry outpost from *9./FschJgRgt.1*, causing the detachment to split up. The heavy machine-gun platoon at the point of the column took the exit of the traffic roundabout leading toward Wieldrecht.[209] On its way, after a short firefight, it overran a machine-gun-team of the paratroopers, during which one of the Germans was killed and another captured. The Dutch also lost one man killed. When the platoon approaching Wieldrecht was mistaken for Germans by the soldiers of the 3rd Border Battalion it received heavy defensive fire, this caused seven dead and three wounded. It took some time before this error was realised. Unfamiliar with the locality the motorcycle company chose another exit from the traffic roundabout and near the Zeehaven came into contact with parts of *11./FschJgRgt.1*, who had been alerted and moved forward. In the ensuing firefight two of the motor-cyclists were killed and two more mortally wounded. Until the company was able to disengage and return to Dordrecht after nightfall, it also lost some of its soldiers as prisoners.[210] With four killed, *11./FschJgRgt.1* also suffered dearly. Moreover, *Hauptmann* Schulz, commanding *III./FschJgRgt.1*, was wounded twice and had to be taken back to Germany for medical treatment.

As reinforcement for *11./FschJgRgt.1*, the platoon under *Stabsfeldwebel* Hoffmann was sent on two trucks to the Zeehaven. When it arrived *11./FschJgRgt.1* had already beaten back the Dutch motorcycle company. *Hauptmann* Walther consequently deployed Hoffmann's platoon into the park of Amstelwijk, in order to keep up the line of communication between *I./FschJgRgt.1* and the command post of *Gruppe Süd* in Tweede Tol.

On preceding days of fighting for the Dordrecht bridges the 2nd and 4th companies of *FschJgRgt.1* had dug in on the eastern bank of the Oude Maas and from the morning were under fire continously from Dutch troops who were occupying the buildings of a factory near the bridges, at about 150m distance. As the Dutch fire could not be silenced by machine-guns and mortars, *Oberleutnant* Graf von Blücher, whose platoon had taken over the close protection of the traffic bridge, sent a small section forward to burn down the factory. This mission was successfully completed. Within half an hour, the factory buildings were ablaze and had to be abandoned by the Dutch. From this point on, the positions of the paratroopers at the bridges could only be engaged from more distant buildings.

Elements from *III./FschJgRgt.1* remained firmly established in the south-eastern part of Krispijn. Their main task was to prevent the enemy from an unhindered use of this area for the concentration of any offensive forces. During the fighting for Krispijn and in the area south of Dordrecht, *III./FschJgRgt.1* lost four killed from 11th Company, two from 9th Company and one from 10th Company. The positions of *I./FschJgRgt.1* were again shelled several times by Dutch artillery from Hoekse Waard. The fire hampered the movements of the paratroopers but caused only a few slightly wounded.

After the troops had assembled and received their orders, *Kampfgruppe de Boer* moved off shortly after midday toward the south. Its overall strength was about 550 men, but, as the number of requisitioned motor vehicles was insufficient, the movement was planned in two

---

209 *9./FschJgRgt.1* at that time was placed in defensive positions in the southern part of Krispijn.

210 For description of the actions of the motorcycle company and its losses, the very precise researches of A.M.A. Goossens are used, as the after-action report by *11./FschJgRgt.1* in this case is rather sketchy and exaggerates the Dutch losses.

parts. *Oberstleutnant* de Boer was to concentrate the majority of his force at the southern outskirts of Dordrecht, near the cemetery. The attack was directed to the north-west into the town in order to hit the Dutch forces opposing the bridges from the rear. Protection of the concentration area toward the south was to be provided for by forces from *FschJgRgt.1*.

At the time of departure of his force from near Waalhaven, *Oberstleutnant* de Boer was still unaware of the fact that the movements of the Dutch Light Division were already under way. Covered against observation from Dordrecht behind a dense screen caused by smoke grenades and supported by the fire of machine-guns and mortars from the positions of *I./FschJgRgt.1*, the first half of *Kampfgruppe de Boer* moved across the Dordrecht bridges without loss. Choosing a route through the part of Krispijn already occupied by paratroopers, it reached the area about 1km south of the cemetery by about 1430hrs. Here the troops dismounted from their vehicles, as the planned concentration area turned out to be occupied by Dutch forces. *Oberstleutnant* de Boer now formed two spearheads: on the left *2./InfRgt.72* (less one platoon) and on the right *3./InfRgt.72* (less one platoon). Each of the companies were reinforced by one heavy machine-gun and one 81mm mortar, and were separated by the railway between Breda-Dordrecht. The companies commenced advancing at 1530hrs with the initial mission to clear the concentration area at the cemetery of the enemy. From here, the *Kampfgruppe* was to attack into the town across the railway at Dordrecht-Sliedrecht at 1730hrs.

After the supporting two artillery batteries had reported their readiness for action, the bicycle battalion on the right of the attack-line of the Dutch Light Division moved out toward Krispijn from the area north of the station of Dordrecht. It had no communication with the battalion ordered to attack Krispijn from the east and did not wait for its appearance. Only the forward company came close to the northern edge of Krispijn. There it was pinned down by the fire of paratroopers from within the residential area. The follow-up companies were unable to get out of the railway underpass because of the fire directed against them. When the shells of the supporting artillery impacted among the attacking troops instead of in the enemy positions, the battalion retreated toward the station.

The bicycle battalion had moved out from Dordwijk belatedly in the direction toward Krispijn along the road between Dubbeldam and Dordrecht and had dispatched no patrols forward. At the junction of this road with the railway at Breda-Dordrecht, its forward company was surprised by *3./InfRgt.72*, which together with *2./InfRgt.72* on its left, had advanced fully combat-ready from the area south of the cemetery. The heavy machine-gun platoon formed the point of the Dutch company but was routed in an ambush. It lost one killed and three wounded and all of its motorcycles with sidecars, on which the heavy machine-guns were mounted. The infantry of the forward company withdrew in some disorder into the built-up area north of the railway crossing. From there, it took some effort to reorganize the men, considering that their commanding officer was mortally wounded. When the attempt of the Dutch failed to deploy one of the follow-up companies in an outflanking movement along the railway Dordrecht-Sliedrecht when it hit *2./InfRgt.72* advancing left of the railway Breda-Dordrecht, the movements of both sides came to a temporary standstill. Elements of the bicycle battalion, hit by *Kampfgruppe de Boer*, now reinforced positions near Dordrecht station.

It took until 1745hrs for *Kampfgruppe de Boer* to clear the planned concentration area near the cemetery of the Dutch soldiers positioned there, as such the attack across the railway into the town was shifted to 1800 hrs. Just in time the remaining troops of the *Kampfgruppe* arrived from Ijsselmonde. With one platoon from *3./InfRgt.72* and elements from *4./InfRgt.72*, a small reserve could now be formed. The forward deployment of artillery pieces and anti-tank guns, for the support of the infantry by direct fire, could not be accomplished, as these were unable to pass through the machine-gun-fire of the Dutch from the area around the station of Dordrecht. In the attempt, the crews of the anti-tank platoon provided by *FschPzAbwKp.7* lost two killed.

3./InfRgt.72, attacking on the right, succeeded in gaining about 150m ground north of the railway to the southern edge of the park at Merwesteijn against Dutch infantry, who stubbornly defended the streets and buildings. Then, the attack was halted due to the fire of anti-tank and machine-guns and could not be recommenced despite the introduction of the battalion reserve. Against dogged resistance, *2./InfRgt.72* on the left managed to take the railway at Dordrecht-Sliedrecht by 2000 hrs. As the contact between the two spearheads had become interrupted, *3./InfRgt.72* was redeployed from the southern edge of the park at Merwesteijn to the left until it was in touch again with *2./InfRgt.72*.

At nightfall the fighting in the southern part of Dordrecht slackened. During the night, both sides reorganized for the continuation of combat in the morning. Those elements from *II./FschJgRgt.2* which had followed from Ijsselmonde with the second part of *Kampfgruppe de Boer* were not committed to combat. East of Dordrecht, teams from *1/PiBtl.22* which had been assigned to the task force, had advanced to the small river Wantij by evening, which connected the Merwede and the Nieuwe Merwede north-east of Dordrecht. There they blocked some of the crossing sites in order to hamper movements by the Dutch.

On the Dutch side, the positions at the six bridges that connected the southern part of Dordrecht with the quarter of the town along the Merwede across a canal (Dutch term: *gracht*), were reinforced with a few heavy machine-guns, anti-tank guns and field guns and some additional depot troops. As the Germans discontinued their attack after nightfall, the Dutch infantry that had retired to the station and the built-up area north of it were able to reorganize, and to consolidate their positions. The depot troops opposite the Dordrecht bridges remained in their positions, as they were not attacked.

The reinforced bicycle battalion on the left, together with a battery of field guns for support, spent the afternoon waiting south-east of Duppeldam for the arrival of the center battalion, unaware of the changed plan. In the early evening, it was ordered by the commander of the Light Division to attack on its own against Tweede Tol along the Zeedijk.[211] It drove back an outpost of the paratroopers. Then its advance was met by elevated fire from Tweede Tol and thereupon discontinued.

Into the night the bridgehead at Wieldrecht remained occupied by a weak company from the 3rd Border Infantry Battalion and a few stragglers from the fighting of the day before. It was not reinforced with the two companies from 34th Inf.Rgt. that were waiting at Gravendeel, as the command of Group Kil had given up the plan for a thrust at Tweede Tol along the Kil as a result of the failed attack of the Light Division against

---

211 Because of the deficiencies in the initial phase of the attack of the Light Division, in the late afternoon Lieutenant General van Andel had ordered Colonel van der Bijl to assume command over the attack forces in person. The latter had moved to Dordrecht and as a first measure had done away with the phase-lines.

Krispijn. However no higher command was notified of this decision. A squad from the border infantry company, reconnoitering toward the east in the afternoon, was repelled by Hoffmann's platoon from the park at Amstelwijk. Nevertheless the staff of *I./FschJgRgt.1* saw the possibility of a renewed Dutch attack from the area around Wieldrecht against the Dordrecht bridges. This platoon was later reinforced with two anti-tank guns from an infantry regiment, which had been handed over to *I./FschJgRgt.1* for the defence of the Dordrecht bridges by *Oberstleutnant* de Boer, during the passage of his *Kampfgruppe*. However the Dutch remained content with a heavy artillery bombardment of Amstelwijk between 2200hrs and 2400hrs, which was delivered with the aim of preventing thrusts against the bridgehead at Wieldrecht.

On the evening of 12 May the command of *Gruppe Süd* still lacked a clear picture about the situation in and around Dordrecht. It was well informed by reports from subordinate units about the successful actions in Krispijn, along the Zeedijk and at Amstelwijk, but remained in the dark about the situation of *Kampfgruppe de Boer*, as well as about the strength of the enemy in Dordrecht, south-east of Dubbeldam and at Wieldrecht. Therefore, the highest degree of vigilance was required for the northern part of its operational area during the night and following morning. At nightfall, all of the uncommitted elements from *II./ FschJgRgt.1* and *FschSan-Halbkompanie 7* were deployed in the security line east and north-east of Tweede Tol. The seizure of Krispijn and of the area between the Zeehaven and Amstelwijk on 11 May turned out to be of considerable advantage for the retention of communication from Tweede Tol to the operational area of *I./FschJgRgt.1*. It was now not only possible to provide the forces at the Dordrecht bridges with supplies, which had plentifully been dropped at Tweede Tol, but also to establish a shuttle run for medical material and wounded between the main dressing station in Rotterdam-South and the units of *FschJgRgt.1*.

The air attacks requested by *Oberst* Bräuer during the afternoon against the Dutch artillery on Hoekse Waard had been somewhat ineffectual as the Do 17 bombers, despite their large numbers, achieved little.[212]

From midday on the main hope within the staff of *Oberst* Bräuer was directed toward the arrival of the first troops from *9.Panzer-Division* at the Moerdijk bridges, which was planned for this day.

In the air bridgehead of *II./FschJgRgt.1* no indication of an attack by the enemy from the south was perceived throughout the morning. The battalion commander was anticipating such an attack and during the night 11/12 May had moved his 5th Company from north of the bridges into the left flank of the main defensive line in the south and had retained only one of its platoons as reserve. However the Dutch troops who had been observed in the settlements in front of the positions of the battalion in the evening had vanished by morning. No trace was detected of the French who had been seen during the late afternoon of 11 May. Ongoing attacks by the *Luftwaffe* in the area around Breda and the noise of combat from the south-east, indicated that the enemy may still be present. Attempts by the Dutch to land some troops by boat on the southern bank of the Hollandsch Diep west

212 According to Dutch sources, only one of the permanently positioned 15cm guns was hit. 23rd Art.Rgt., with its 75mm guns, had not been found at all, as it had moved to an alternate firing position just prior to the air attacks and the bombers had attacked the dummy guns, set up in the former firing positions.

of Moerdijk had been prevented by an outpost from 7th Company which was deployed in the little port of Moerdijk. During the morning *II./FschJgRgt.1* used this time of relative calm, which was only occasionally interrupted by the fire of the Dutch heavy artillery from Hoekse Waard, and the machine-guns in the bunkers on the western bank of the Kil opposite the northern ramp of the traffic bridge, to improve its positions. During that time the obstacles along the avenues of approach from the south were removed in anticipation of the arrival of the forward elements of *9.Panzer-Division*. To prevent further landing attempts and engage the Dutch guard-boats and supply-barges, which still moved along the Hollandsch Diep, a captured anti-aircraft gun was positioned near Moerdijk and manned by paratroopers. However, after a few rounds were fired at a barge and a guard-boat the crew of the anti-aircraft gun was forced into cover by the precise fire of heavy machine-guns from across the Hollandsch Diep.

In the northern part of the air bridgehead *12./FschJgRgt.1* was not involved in any action. The remainder of *Kompanie Moll* was now posted along the eastern bank of the Kil just north of the operational area of *II./FschJgRgt.1*.

At 1632hrs, a patrol from *9.Panzer-Division* established first contact with combat outposts from *II./FschJgRgt.1* south of the traffic bridge; it was followed by an advance detachment. At 1700hrs its commander met *Hauptmann* Prager, who passed him on to *Oberst* Bräuer at Tweede Tol. From there he was brought by truck to the command post of *I./FschJgRgt.1*, where Student was present. Student told him that the report about the arrival of the first elements of *9.Panzer-Division* constituted the most precious gift for him that day, his 50th birthday. A short time later, the general was informed about a radio message from *9.Panzer-Division* to the command post of *Fl.Div.7*, in which it had reported its forward tanks at Oosterhout, about 18km south-east of the bridges at Moerdijk.

The *9.Panzer-Division* had advanced ahead of the other divisions of *XXVI.Armee-Korps* between Hertogenbosch and Eindhoven and formed from its main forces two *Kampfgruppen* capable of combined-arms combat.[213] *Kampfgruppe Apell* in the north consisted of the HQ of *Inf.Brig.9*, *I./PzRgt.33*, *II./Schützen-Rgt.11*, *FlakAbt.94*, *I./Art.Rgt.102*, *PzJgAbt.50* and some logistics troops. After crossing the canal at Zuid-Willemsvaart south of Hertogenbosch against reminants of the Dutch Peel Division it had advanced until nightfall without further resistance to the area around Oosterhout. The mission of this task force was to establish contact with *Fl.Div.7* across the bridges at Moerdijk. The southern *Kampfgruppe*, led by the commander of *Schützen-Rgt.11*, *Oberst* Theodor von Sponeck,[214] had driven through Tilburg in the afternoon. The area remained unoccupied by the enemy, and by 2030hrs the group had moved on toward Breda. An advance company from *I./Schützen-Rgt.11* bypassed a road barrier at the entrance to this town and about 2300hrs crossed the small river Mark over an unoticed bridge at Ginneken, a suburb of Breda. Immediately thereafter, it was attacked by French armored cars and motorcycle-infantry. The attack was repelled but the company, despite the support of the

---

213 The operations of *9.Panzer-Division* and of its adversaries in the western part of Noord Brabant, resulting in the relief of *Fl.Div.7*, are deliberately given some room in this part of the book, as there is little literature available which depicts the events of both sides in the context of the German thrust against the south of Fortress Holland. It is also meant to provide some insight into the organization of the opposing forces, their missions and the operational and tactical principles governing their conduct.

214 Theodor von Sponeck had been a cousin of the commander of *22.(LL)Inf.Div.*

self-propelled heavy infantry guns of *sIG.Kp.701*, was unable to gain further ground against the continued resistance of the French reconnaissance forces.

Formed from *Aufkl.Rgt.9* of the *9.Panzer-Division*, a reconnaissance detachment was deployed in front of each *Kampfgruppe*. *Aufkl.Abt.Lüttwitz* advanced in front of *Kampfgruppe Apell* and was placed subordinate to it. It consisted of the staff of I./*Aufkl. Rgt.9*, 3./*Aufkl.Rgt.9* (motorcycle infantry), the infantry gun platoon, two heavy mortar squads and an anti-tank gun, all from 4./*Aufkl.Rgt.9*, four armored reconnaissance patrols from 5./*Aufkl.Rgt.9*, a battery from I./*Art.Rgt.102*, a platoon from 3./*PiBtl.86* and a platoon from *FlakAbt.94* (three SdKfz 6/2 halftracks with 3.7cm anti-aircraft guns). The detachment moved west through the area between the Wilhelmina Canal north of Tilburg and the southern banks of the rivers Bergsche Maas and Amer, which had not been occupied by the French. Retiring units of the Dutch Peel Division had either been surprised and captured, or quickly driven off. On 12 May at 0525hrs, Colonel Schmidt, the commanding officer of the Peel Division and at the same time territorial commander of Noord Brabant, unexpectedly encountered the point of *Abt.Lüttwitz* at Dongen while on his way to Tilburg. With him, thre officers and about 30 men of his staff were captured. At about 0900hrs Dutch elements that were protecting the bridge across the Wilhelmina Canal at Dongen were driven off after a short firefight. In order to safeguard the left flank of *Kampfgruppe Apell*, the bridge was subsequently destroyed.

At 1400hrs the reconnaissance detachment moved across the Wilhelmina Canal at Oosterhout and following its advance-party arrived at the Moerdijk bridges shortly prior to 1700hrs. Only a few of its vehicles crossed the traffic bridge, liaised with the paratroopers north of it and then rested. The majority of the detachment was deployed to protect the arrival of *Kampfgruppe Apell*, in front of the southern air bridgehead of II./*FschJgRgt.1*. Some of its elements advanced toward the south-west just past Zevenbergen, without encountering French forces.[215] They captured more soldiers of the routed Peel Division who had attempted to seek refuge in the west.

The anti-aircraft platoon and the artillery battery from *Abt.Lüttwitz* were deployed in support of II./*FschJgRgt.1* immediately after their arrival. While the battery engaged the Dutch machine-gun casemates on the western bank of the Kil opposite the traffic bridge, the 3.7cm guns of the anti-aircraft platoon succeeded in sinking one of three Dutch boats, which came near the Hollandsch Diep at about 1730 hrs and forced the other two to turn back.

The Dutch forces which were not attacked on 12 May were employed for the protection of the bridge across the Bergsche Maas at Keizersveer. Here, a squadron of hussars occupied field positions on the southern bank of the river, while half a company of infantry, anchoring itself on two large concrete-casemates and armed with anti-tank and heavy machine guns, was established around the northern ramp of the bridge. In the early morning stragglers from the Peel Division had made their escape toward the north across this bridge. With the appearance of *Kampfgruppe Apell* around Oosterhout, this route into Fortress Holland had been closed for the soldiers of the Peel Division, as well as for the French 1er DLM, who were not aware of it for almost two days.

---

215 The French reconnaissance forces around Breda in the morning of 12 May had hesitantly carried out the order of General Giraud, to form the right flank for the protection of Antwerp, along the line of Breda-Moerdijk. In the early afternoon, this action stopped, after Giraud had sent a new order to now establish the defensive line west of Breda.

In Den Haag, late in the evening, the Dutch high command listening to a broadcast on Radio Bremen learned about the arrival of the first German forces at the Moerdijk bridges. A deliberate attack against Rotterdam and the loss of the city must be expected after the arrival of sufficiently strong German ground forces in the south of Fortress Holland and as the collapse of the Grebbe Line was now imminent, on the night 12/13 May General Winkelman took the decision to concentrate on the area of Den Haag-Leiden-Amsterdam and to commence immediately with preparations for its defence. In order to gain time he intended to have Rotterdam defended for as long as possible.

In Dordrecht neither Lieutenant Colonel Mussert nor the staff of Colonel van der Bijl were informed about the fact that the Dutch high command or Lieutenant General van Andel had almost completely excluded the intervention of the French across the Hollandsch Diep on the evening of 12 May. This was in spite of the report by Ensign Marijs, who after being given the opportunity to observe the first German vehicles at Tweede Tol, had been released to Dordrecht by *Oberst* Bräuer with the intention of convincing the commanders there of the hopelessness of further resistance. In the evening these still counted on the arrival of French tanks during the coming day. At midnight, Colonel van der Bijl assumed command over the garrison troops in Dordrecht.[216]

13 May

In spite of the enforced abandonment of the Grebbe Line on the evening of 12 May the Dutch high command was confident that the so-called 'New Waterline' which blocked the entrance into Fortress Holland from the east and the avenue of approach into Noord Holland across the fortified enclosure dam could be retained for some time. However, the complete loss of the islands of Dordrecht and Ijsselmonde and presumably also of Hoekse Waard should be contemplated within the next 24 hours, if the German *9.Panzer-Division* and the forces following behind it could not be prevented from crossing the Moerdijk bridges or the attack of the Light Division failed to achieve its objectives.

After the neutralization of the territorial command under Colonel Schmidt, and the non-appearance of the French liaison staff, General Winkelman and his staff lacked knowledge about the operations of the French 7th Army in Noord Brabant. Based on what little information they had received on 12 May, they were quite sure that serious offensive actions by the French against the bridges at Moerdijk must now be excluded. They therefore saw the attempt to destroy these crossing-sites by artillery fire and air attacks as the only way method remaining to them. If the arrival of strong German ground forces on Ijsselmonde within a day or two could not be prevented by the destruction of the Moerdijk Bridges and the retaking of the Dordrecht bridges, the destruction of the bridges across the Nieuwe Maas by demolition became imperative in order to keep up the defence of Rotterdam for as long as possible. However, before this measure could be realized, the German bridgehead around the northern ramps of these bridges needed to be eliminated. The order for this was issued to Colonel Scharroo during the night 12/13 May.

At 0330hrs General Winkelman informed Queen Wilhelmina and the cabinet about the situation in the south-west of Holland, recommending that the sovereign should depart

---

216 Because of the activities of his own chief of staff, Lieutenant Colonel Mussert had been relieved of his post by the commander of Group Kil, who had accused him of lacking leadership and loyalty. After Mussert had protested against this measure, he was re-appointed as garrison commander by Lieutenant General van Andel shortly after midnight, but was placed subordinate to the commander of the Light Division.

for England without delay. He explained that this act would serve as an unmistakable signal to the world that Holland was willing to continue the war against Germany on the side of its allies. After some initial hesitation Queen Wilhelmina accepted General Winkelman's petition. Escorted by a few armored cars and some police troops she proceeded to Hoek van Holland. There at 1100hrs she embarked on the British destroyer *Hereward* and later in the day arrived safely in England. In the evening, most of the members of the cabinet followed her on the British destroyer *Windsor* As was directed by the Queen, the responsibility for the continuation of the struggle in Holland now rested in the hands of General Winkelman.

After the failed attempt on 12 May the 900 German prisoners of war, who had been assembled in the port area of Ijmuiden, were shipped to England on board the steamer *Phrontis* in the early morning. Escorted by the British, and despite an unsuccessful German air attack, the ship reached Dover the same day. Another shipment of prisoners, as well as the further transfer of Dutch naval and merchant vessels to England, was also planned.[217]

In order to influence the Dutch high command's plans regarding Rotterdam Lieutenant-Colonel Wilson, furnished with far-reaching command-authority, was sent from Den Haag to Rotterdam during the course of 13 May. As his first action he initiated attacks against *Gruppe von Sponeck* in Overschie. Colonel Scharroo, however, retained his function as the commander of the Rotterdam garrison.

At 0530hrs the German bridgehead around the northern ramps of the bridges across the Nieuwe Maas in Rotterdam was attacked by Dutch marines. However the defenders inside the insurance buildings and nearby positions succeeded in repelling the onslaught. It was only now that the artillery fire, planned to support of the attack, commenced. It fell short and so was discontinued after a short time.[218] In the meantime, an assault troop from the Dutch marines to the strength of about a platoon moved forward in the cover of the pier and at about 1000hrs had managed to gain the northern ramp of the traffic bridge. During their advance, the marines were initially fired at from behind by the defenders of the insurance building, causing them to lose two killed. When the assault troop reached the middle of the bridge, the Germans were fully alerted. Their defensive fire erupted from all sides, forcing the marines to retire. However, only a few of them were able to get back to their start positions. Others found cover in the lower structure of the bridge and held out there.[219] Two armored cars that approached from the Beurse station firing their 37mm guns, stopped their advance after one of them was damaged by mortar fire.

After this final attempt to eliminate the German bridgehead, the Dutch garrison command restricted its actions to the defence of the northern bank of the Nieuwe Maas. For this purpose it deployed, under the command of the staff of 25th Inf.Rgt., seven companies of infantry, supported by a number of heavy machine-guns, anti-tank guns and mortars.

217 Arrangements for the evacuation of the Dutch navy and merchant fleet and for the destruction of port facilities in the case of emergency had been made by the commander-in-chief of the Dutch Navy, Admiral Furstner prior to the German attack without the knowledge of the Dutch government.

218 The six 81mm mortars, which had also been planned for the support of the attack, had not all been brought to bear, because their commanding officer had seen no possibility to direct their fire at the insurance building.

219 During the night of 13/14 May a small number of them had jumped into the Nieuwe Maas and had escaped by swimming. Others had got away during the German air attack on Rotterdam during the afternoon of 14 May.

The German positions on Noordereiland were to be engaged primarily by intensive artillery fire.

On the German side, at around 1600hrs *Oberstleutnant* von Choltitz accepted the offer by two citizens from the occupied part of Rotterdam to negotiate the cessation of fighting in Rotterdam with the Dutch garrison commander. After a few hours both returned without achieving their goal. They reported that during talks Colonel Scharroo announced the complete destruction of Noordereiland by artillery fire but had also asked for the dispatch of German officers as negotiators. However, von Choltitz had regarded this as impracticable for the time being, as the bridges were hit by impenetrable Dutch fire. It was so efficient that the garrison of the bridgehead was manned by a mere two officers and no more than 60 other ranks. Furthermore they could not be supplied and provided with a few reinforcements until the night 13/14 May. For the first time a telephone cable was laid to the northern bank of the Nieuwe Maas on the same night. As the command of *InfRgt.16* was aware of the plan to commence the attack for the conquest of Rotterdam without delay after the arrival of ground forces, in reaction *3./InfRgt.16* and some uncommitted elements from *1/PiBtl.22* were brought forward to Rotterdam-South.

From the point of view of the command of *Fl.Div.7* and *InfRgt.16* the situation in the western part of Ijsselmonde remained unsatisfactory. An attack by elements of *1./InfRgt.16* against the Dutch positions at the petroleum port west of Pernis had failed, causing both sides some losses. The destruction of ships which were loaded with crude oil and of some of the large oil tanks in the port area during the afternoon, had, however, allowed the conclusion that the enemy intended to retire from there across the Nieuwe Maas.[220] The retreat was executed during the first hours of darkness unhindered by the Germans, who had proven too weak in numbers to overcome the strong Dutch positions. A thrust by other parts of *1./InfRgt.72* from Hoogvliet against the bridge at Spijkenisse supported by a heavy mortar was also unsuccessful against the numerical superior Dutch holding force.

Generalleutnant Student also worried about the situation at the lift-bridge south of Barendrecht. Here only the weak *II./FschJgRgt.2* reminaed after the departure of *Kampfgruppe de Boer*. They were left for the protection of the northern bank of the Oude Maas, where a renewed thrust by the Dutch from Hoekse Waard against Waalhaven could not be completely excluded.[221]

At the Noord crossing operations by strong Dutch forces were no longer expected after the departure of the majority of the Dutch Light Division across the Merwede. Nevertheless, *II./InfRgt.16* remained tied down there with the majority of its troops.

A supporting air attack against Dutch artillery positions east of Alblasserdam, flown in the morning by the Ju 87s from *12./LG 1*, triggered aerial combat which lasted from

---

220 On 13 May at 1540hrs, as a preparatory measure for the retreat, about 80 British troops, accompanied by Dutch engineers, crossed the Nieuwe Maas into the petroleum port and blew up a number of tankers and oil tanks. After they had retired, the reinforced 1st Company from III/39th Inf.Rgt. followed them to the northern bank of the Nieuwe Maas. A considerable amount of the oil supplies, however, had not been destroyed and later were utilized by the Germans.

221 As a matter of fact, such an action was planned with the Dutch Light Division.

0610 to 0840hrs. Here a German squadron was attacked by 12 British fighters and was supported by two fighter squadrons from *JG.26*. When the sky over Alblasserdam was clear again, four of the German dive bombers and two Bf 109s had been shot down and the British had lost five fighters in total.

Gruppe von Sponeck, in the northern part of Overschie, west of the auto-route toward Delft, and *Gruppe Wischhusen*, in the south of the town, still had no direct contact with one another. This was despite a distance of just 4km between them. *Gruppe von Sponeck* was surrounded to the north by enemy forces, but had its outposts still positioned well forward. An attack from the north, launched at about 0300hrs by three detachments of Dutch infantry to the strength of a company each, supported by heavy machine-guns and anti-tank guns, was carried forward to a distance of about 2.5km in front of the German main line, before being discontinued.[222] One of the armored cars supporting the infantry was damaged by defensive fire, at which point both vehicles retired.

Since daybreak *Gruppe Wischhusen* had been receiving intensive and well-aimed fire from the machine-guns of the Dutch infantry that were advancing from Rotterdam. For the most part, the enemy used heavy ammunition, which pierced the thin walls of the buildings, consequently their defenders sought cover in the basements and in their dug-outs. Nevertheless, one of them was killed and several others were wounded. Shortly after midday Dr. Wischhusen was informed about the presence of another German force in the northern part of Overschie. He reported this information in person, without delay, to *Generalleutnant* Graf von Sponeck. Once the procedures for the coordination of the two groups were laid down, Graf von Sponeck appointed an officer from the combat arms as the new commander of *Gruppe Wischhusen*. However in the meantime a determined attack by Dutch infantry, supported by two armored cars, developed against the southern part of Overschie. At 1640hrs, the attackers advanced over the bridge across the Schie Canal. The German sentries, commanded by *Oberleutnant* Eckleben, were partly cut off and suffered some losses in killed and wounded. Additionally, a number of soldiers were captured. As the Dutch armored cars had not kept up with the infantry the attack was eventually repelled by the deployment of Genz's platoon of Parachute infantry.[223] Although the Dutch infantry had retired behind the Schie Canal after its attack had been halted, the new German commander decided to take the positions back about 500m into the town's interior under cover of darkness, in order to reduce the effects of the Dutch machine-gun fire. However, before this action could be taken, at 1840hrs the enemy again launched attacks against Overschie, this time simultaneously from the north and the south. In the north, a detachment of infantry, supported by anti-tank guns and heavy machine-guns, succeeded in entering the forward buildings of Overschie. In this attack the defenders lost several men killed and wounded and a number of prisoners. By nightfall the Dutch, who had lost two killed, retired again and took the prisoners with them. The attack of a company of infantry against the southern part of Overschie was unsuccessful mainly because the

---

222 At 0540hrs the companies had been ordered to retire to Delft. This order initially was met with disbelief and was executed only at 1240hrs, after it was confirmed that the attack force had occupied the planned anti-tank positions around Den Haag.

223 The attackers had consisted of two platoons from III/21st Inf.Rgt., which had been sent to Rotterdam as part of the reinforcements. The crews of the armored cars had refused to accompany the infantry into the built-up terrain. One of the vehicles, hastily withdrawing under fire, had run over some of the infantrymen behind it. One soldier was killed and two others, among them the company commander of the force, were seriously injured.

three heavy machine-guns in support were forced into cover by German machine-guns and at nightfall halted fire all together.[224] The defenders were now able to execute the planned shift of their positions towards the centre of the town.

As a result of the ongoing encirclement of his forces *Generalleutnant* Graf von Sponeck suspected the enemy would launch an attack on the coming day. He did have some doubts about his troop's morale because his soldiers had shown unmistakable signs of a reduced will to carry on, with the exception of the parachute infantry, who fought on relentlessly. In his radio report to the command of *Luftflotte 2* in the evening he expressed his concerns accordingly.

On 13 May the German troops that were holding out in Valkenburg and in the dunes north and north-west of Wassenaar were still surrounded by enemy forces. On this day Valkenburg was not attacked by infantry, but was shelled several times by artillery. Within the village were the prisoners, who since the previous day had been lodged in a garage in the southern part of the village. The civilian population was also still lodged there and had suffered most from these bombardments. As food for the captured Dutch soldiers became scarce several of them, with the approval of their captors, had been allowed to collect provisions in the village. The reduced supervision was used by a few determined men to make their escape and return to their own lines. *Oberst* Heyser sent two of the prisoners to the commander of the Dutch 4th Inf.Rgt., Colonel Buurman, with the offer to exchange the wounded Dutch soldiers in Valkenburg for captured German soldiers. Colonel Buurman not only rejected this offer, but also retained the two negotiators and questioned them again about their former units. The German strongpoint in the farmstead at Zonneveld, about 900m south of Valkenburg, was hit very heavily by the Dutch artillery. As the Dutch infantry advancing against Valkenburg was hampered considerably by the fire from Zonneveld in the course of the past two days, Colonel Buurman had ordered intensive bombardment of the area from 0640hrs on, to be undertaken by two batteries from III/2nd Art.Rgt. This caused the buildings of the farm to be heavily damaged and set ablaze, its defenders abandoned them and retired to the strongpoint at Rijnvliet, about 500m to the east. For the inhabitants of Valkenburg who had sought refuge in Zonneveld the bombardment was particularly tragic, as many of them were injured and eleven died of their wounds.

No determined attacks were launched against the German force established in the dunes north-west of Wassenaar. However combat patrols from the areas around Katwijk and Wassenaar were sent forward against German outposts in front of their main positions throughout the day. Most of them failed to achieve their goals.

The order to advance with a reinforced infantry platoon from III/1st Inf.Rgt. along the Wassenaarse Slag to the beach which was issued by the commander of 3rd Inf.Div. was rejected by the commanding officer of III/1st Inf.Rgt. as ill-considered.

In preparation for an assault mission between 0600 and 0740hrs the Albertushoeve Hotel was shelled by artillery. The effect of this attack was negligible, only one round impacted on the building and its garrison remained unharmed.[225] The assaulting force, a

---

224 According to Dutch sources, it was the lack of tracer ammunition which had prevented an efficient support after nightfall.

225 A platoon from III/6th Art.Rgt. had fired 57 rounds from the area around Poelgeest and afterward had wrongly reported the destruction of Albertushoeve.

reinforced platoon from the 1st Company of 4th Inf.Rgt., was dispatched from the area around Katwijk with the mission to seize Albertushoeve but was halted by the fire of a German outpost, positioned in the depression at De Pan, about 1km north of the hotel. At 1000hrs, after the arrival of considerable reinforcements, the Dutch resumed the attack and managed to drive the Germans from the depression. As they had retired some distance after the engagement, the Germans re-occupied De Pan. A Dutch counterthrust finally forced them to give up their positions. Except for one Dutch soldier who was killed during the counterthrust, only a few men were wounded on both sides during the hour-long engagement. Albertushoeve was not attacked again as the Dutch troops, who had grown to a strength of almost three companies and were supported by heavy infantry-weapons, had been ordered to retire toward Katwijk and Valkenburg airfield prior to nightfall.[226]

Combat patrols against the German positions in the dunes were also dispatched from the areas around Wassenaar and Den Haag. An infantry platoon, moving from Oostdorp (about 1 km north of Wassenaar) in the direction of the Wassenaarse Slag turned toward the south-east after receiving fire from a German outpost shortly after leaving the village. More successful was a patrol which operated in a motor-boat along the drainage ditch at Zijlwetering. It captured a German officer and seven other ranks in a mill without meeting any resistance. A patrol from Den Haag was undertaken by soldiers of the 5th squadron of the 3rd Hussar Regiment in the afternoon. However they were ambushed by Germans, causing two non-commissioned officers and seven hussars to be captured.

In the morning, the commander of the German troops around the Wassenaarse Slag had dispatched an *Unteroffizier* of the medical service to the Dutch lines north of Wassenaar. He delivered a proposal to convey the seriously wounded Dutch and German soldiers from the German-held area to Dutch medical installations. Upon approval by the commander of 1st Inf.Rgt., the regimental medical officer of 1st Inf.Rgt. had driven to the German positions with two ambulances, taken over eleven Dutch and four German seriously wounded men and had brought them to the hospital in Leiden. The Dutch and the German medical officers had separated after the agreement and planned to repeat this procedure the next day.

The absence of deliberate attacks by the Dutch against the village at Valkenburg and into the dunes north-west of Wassenaar, had, on the one hand, been brought about by the decision of the commander of I Army Corps to preserve his own forces for deployment against the still suspected introduction of German reinforcements by sea or from the air. On the other hand, the initiation of the anti-tank line for the protection of Den Haag, Leiden and Amsterdam, directed by the Dutch high command in the early morning, had already led to changes in the availability of the forces opposing the German troops left over from *22.(LL)Inf.Div.* Colonel Buurman was forced to release II/9th Inf.Rgt., III/2nd Art. Rgt. and II/6th Art.Rgt. (less two batteries), from his command immediately upon this

---

226 According to Dutch sources, the commander of III/4th Inf.Rgt., upon the failure of the assault troop, on his own initiative had reinforced it with a company from II/4th Inf.Rgt., two of his own platoons and part of his machine-gun company. At about 1300hrs, he assumed command over the two remaining platoons of the 1st Company from I/4th Inf.Rgt. at the airfield, and had also dispatched them for the attack against Albertushoeve. In the late afternoon, however, the commander of 4th Inf.Rgt. had ordered the attack force back to its start positions by order of the directive from 3rd Inf.Div. of the day before, to omit any large-scale attacks for the time being.

decision. Moreover, he had to keep I/9th Inf.Rgt., II/4th Inf.Rgt. and the heavy weapons at the regimental level, ready for deployment in the envisaged anti-tank line. 1st Inf.Rgt., deployed in the area of Wassenaar-Maaldrift had not been affected by the reorganization but nevertheless had not been used for offensive actions as a result of the order from 3rd Inf.Div.

In spite of the arrival of *Aufkl.Abt.Lüttwitz* at the Moerdijk Bridges during the evening of 12 May and its deployment with the majority of its forces in a protective screen south of the air bridgehead toward the south and south-west, the positions of *II./FschJgRgt.1* on either side of the bridges had remained fully occupied during the night 12/13 May. This was because surprise actions by the enemy had not completely been excluded. From 0440hrs on Dutch heavy artillery from Hoekse Waard bombarded the bridges, with the aim of destroying them. The effects, however, were dismal, as only a few of the shells, which were fired at a low tragectory, hit the upper structures of the bridges.

Prior to sunrise, *Kampfgruppe Apell* from *9.Panzer-Division* arrived on the southern bank of the Hollandsch Diep with its forward units. Despite the ongoing artillery fire *I./PzRgt.33* set out to cross the traffic bridge, *Oberst* Apell, accompanied by a radio vehicle, moved ahead of his tanks in order to establish contact with *Generalleutnant* Student. At around 0600hrs Student was on the way from his command post to Dordrecht and met with *Oberst* Apell south of the bridges. After the *Oberst* reported the composition of his *Kampfgruppe*, Student directed him to employ the forward tank company to support the troops fighting in Dordrecht. The other units of *I./PzRgt.33* were to drive across the traffic bridge at Dordrecht farther to the north. *I./ArtRgt.102* was ordered to fight the Dutch artillery on Hoekse Waard from positions on the southern bank of the Hollandsch Diep. The battalion from *Schützen-Rgt.11* was to remain south of the Moerdijk Bridges at his disposal. However one of its companies was to be placed subordinate to *Aufkl.Abt.Lüttwitz*.

Kampfgruppe Apell was yet to begin the crossing of the Hollandsch Diep, when at 0519hrs an air attack was flown against the traffic bridge, as a last attempt by the Dutch Air Arm to destroy it. A Fokker T-V bomber, escorted by two G-1 type fighters, approached the bridge, and in two passes dropped two mine bombs of 300kg each. The first bomb missed the target and the second grazed a pillar of the bridge, but turned out to be a dud. During the flight back the bomber and one of the fighters were shot down over Ridderkerk by Bf 109 fighters that had arrived in the airspace over Fortress Holland. The columns of *Kampfgruppe Apell* now began to cross the traffic bridge immediately after the end of the air attack and were only occasionally hampered by the fire of Dutch artillery from Hoekse Waard.

After a relatively calm night which was utilized for reorganization and resupply, *Kampfgruppe de Boer* was preparing to resume the attack into Dordrecht. The start time for the attack was then shifted and an air attack by dive bombers was announced to take place between 0600hrs and 0630hrs. This attack did not take place. At about 0630hrs, Student arrived at the command post of *I./InfRgt.72*. He expressed his acknowledgment of the deeds of the troops of the day before to the assembled tactical leaders and informed them about the arrival of the first tanks of *9.Panzer-Division* on the island of Dordrecht. He also decorated *Oberstleutnant* de Boer and *Major* Krüger with the clasp for the Iron Cross Second Class and the commanders of the 2nd, 3rd and 4th companies of *I./InfRgt.72* with the Iron Cross First Class. Prior to the main attack a platoon from *3./InfRgt.72* seized the station of Dordrecht after a fire-preparation of five minutes by the six mountain guns assigned to the *Kampfgruppe*. The defenders of the station had retired during this into the built-up area to the north. From here, infantry from a bicycle battalion engaged the Germans in and around the station, causing the inhabitants of Dordrecht, who had sought refuge in the station on the day before, to come under fire from both sides.

The planned attack of *Kampfgruppe de Boer* was further delayed as Dutch troops north of the station commenced to move forward against the railway. Moreover concentrations of Dutch infantry in the area south-east of Dordrecht, accompanied by anti-tank-guns and field guns, indicated a planned attack toward the west from there.[227] When the report arrived that German tanks had already bypassed Dordrecht on their way toward the north, *Kampfgruppe de Boer* resumed the attack at 1300hrs, crossing the railway turning toward the north. At point of the attack was *3./InfRgt.72* followed by elements of *4./InfRgt.72* and *2./InfRgt.72*. The battle HQ of *Oberstleutnant* de Boer and *Major* Krüger was immediately behind the point company and had moved into a building where they were fired at by a Dutch anti-tank gun which had been set up in a barricade to the north. The fire killed three soldiers of the staff and wounded *Major* Krüger and the commander of his 3rd Company. Eventually two platoons from 3rd Company, which had moved forward along side-streets, managed to overrun the barricade and disable the anti-tank gun. Nevertheless, the assault of the *Kampfgruppe* was discontinued and at about 1500hrs its infantry was moved back to the area around the station. As Dutch infantry from north of the station launched a counter-thrust,[228] a bombardment of the station area by Dutch artillery was suspected and the situation in the east of the town was still unclear. Accordingly, *I./InfRgt.72* was moved some distance further to the south-east in order to set up a secure perimeter. The station and its immediate vicinity was protected by a few sentries who succeeded in holding up the Dutch infantry from the north, who then retreated.

With the arrival of first elements of *9.Panzer-Division*,[229] the situation on the island of Dordrecht began to change decisively in favor of the Germans. The reinforced forward

---

227 Unknown to the German side the attack plan for the Light Divison, because of the development of the situation in the late afternoon of 12 May, had again been changed. The attack force now had just to gain the roads leading from the Moerdijk bridges past the area west of Krispijn, in order to block them against the German forces arriving from the south.

228 For the defence of the six bridges across the canal in the northern part of Dordrecht, I/1st Bicycle Infantry Regiment, reinforced by a company of navy personnel and the railway engineer platoon, had been assigned the three bridges in the east, and II/1st Bicycle Infantry Regiment the three in the west. It was the latter which had conducted the counter-attack.

229 9.Pz.Div. at that time had been the weakest armored formation in the *Wehrmacht*, as it was yet to receive its full complement of tanks. According to its table of organization, dated 1 May 1940, it had in its *I.Abteilung* five Pz II and one Pz III in its HQ Company, and in its three other companies a total of 14 Pz II, 34 Pz III and 11 Pz IV tanks. The *II.Abteilung*, which should have been identical to the *I.Abteilung*, consisted of 27 Pz I, 15 Pz II, 4 Pz III and 5 Pz IV tanks. The headquarters and the signals platoon of *Pz.Rgt.33* had 3 Pz I (should have been 5 Pz II)) and 1 Pz III tanks.

company from *I./PzRgt.33*,[230] which had been ordered to support *Kampfgruppe de Boer* after it had received its instructions, advanced in single file along the Zeedijk toward the east. About 4km east of Tweede Tol it came across a reinforced Dutch bicycle battalion,[231] moving toward the west. Many members of the Dutch unit had mistaken the German tanks for French ones and were completely surprised, and after taking considerable losses withdrew in disorder. The fire from the tanks also hit the command post of the 2nd Bicycle Infantry Regiment, which was located a short distance further to the east and added to the general confusion. During an air attack against the field guns which were positioned behind the infantry, the advance of the tanks was interrupted but then resumed. This led to a great number of Dutch soldiers being captured. As most of the company's tanks at the junction of the Schenkeldijk and the Zeedijk had turned toward the north in order to support *Kampfgruppe de Boer*, the remaining tanks ended the pursuit and taking the captured Dutch soldiers with them, settled down in a secure position at Haaswijk, about 1km east of Dubbeldam. The twenty tanks that were advancing along the Schenkeldijk toward the north came across another reinforced Dutch bicycle battalion in a concentration area just south-west of Dubbeldam.[232] After a short firefight, during which two of the tanks were damaged by 75mm field guns, the Dutch infantry were driven back and retreated toward the north-east.[233] However most of the assigned field guns and anti-tank-guns were left behind. A small element of the retreating infantry and a few of the heavy weapons made their way into the Merwede quarter of Dordrecht ready to continue the battle.

In Dordrecht, while *I./InfRgt.72* was still in the process of seting up a defensive line south of the railway, 20 tanks from *3./PzRgt.33* which had overcome the Dutch south-west of Dubbeldam, began to arrive at the square in front of the station from 1540hrs. Their fire quickly drove away the Dutch infantry who had advanced into the streets just north of the station. Immediately thereafter they organized into three or four attack teams, and without waiting for escorting infantry (as is the custom in urban combat), they set out along several streets in the direction of the bridges across the canal north of Dordrecht. At four of the five bridges the teams were quickly repelled. It was only at the Vriese Bridge on the eastern flank of the Dutch canal positions where a team became involved in severe fighting. Beside some infantry the position at the bridge was guarded by a 75mm field gun and a 47mm anti-tank gun. The tanks approached the bridge along side-streets and then appeared directly in front of it. The two leading vehicles, a Pz III and a Pz II, were immobilized by the fire of a Dutch field gun, the driver of the latter was killed. Both tank crews dismounted and scrambled to the rear. By this time the other tanks of the team had destroyed the field gun and forced the crew of the anti-tank gun into cover. Now, two tanks (Pz IVs) crossed the bridge, turned toward the north-west and managed to advance another 100m to a street in the Bagijnhof area and a square. Here at the location of two Dutch command posts, they came across defended barricades and trenches. An anti-tank gun scored a hit on the turret of the leading tank, which killed its commander. The tank which followed behind was

---

230 The reinforcements had been a platoon of 4 Pz IV tanks from 4th Company and the Pz II tanks from 2nd Company.

231 One of the two battalions from 2nd Bicycle Infantry Regiment, which in the morning of 13 May was ordered to attack Tweede Tol.

232 It had constituted the second half of the attack force from 2nd Bicycle Infantry Regiment, directed against Tweede Tol.

233 Like its sister unit, which was hit hard at the Zeedijk, this battalion had eventually retired to the northern bank of the Merwede across the railway bridge west of Sliedrecht.

also damaged by anti-tank fire. Nevertheless, both tanks were still able to withdraw. The two immobilized tanks in front of the Vriese Bridge now were also salvaged. Well into the afternoon all the tank attack teams returned to the area near the station, some of the tanks now being low in ammunition and fuel.[234]

In the meantime *Kampfgruppe de Boer* formed up for the continuation of the attack in a direction toward the canal. The thrust was to be conducted in close cooperation between the infantry and tanks. Shortly after 1700hrs the task force set out; the point was formed by an infantry squad, followed by two tanks, *I./InfRgt.72*, 3rd Company, battle HQ and 2nd Company and paratroopers from *II./FschJgRgt.2*. They met with some occasional fire on their way but the troops advanced to the canal, taking the southern bank and, protected by sentries, now took time to rest. Behind the attack force, other troops cleared the streets and buildings of any remaining Dutch troops. Any further thrusts across the bridges were avoided during the oncoming darkness, as it was thought that the northern bank of the canal was still being defended by the Dutch. However the morale of the defenders of the Merwede quarter of Dordrecht was shattered after witnessing the approach of German tanks at the canal bridges and as a result of the developing situation in the south east of the island of Dordrecht. Consequently by late afternoon the commander of the Light Division had decided to give up the town. By 2040hrs the majority of his troops deployed in Dordrecht, covered by a rearguard at the canal under Lieutenant Colonel Mussert, and crossed the Merwede to its northern banks. Throughout the course of the night 13/14 May the rearguard at the canal-bridges evacuated their positions and crossed the Merwede at the ferry site between Dordrecht and Papendrecht unmolested by Germans. Some of the Dutch troops deployed for the attack against the station, and in particular the 1st Company from II/1st Bicycle Infantry Regiment 1, the railway engineer platoon and a number of naval personnel, were cut off north of the Spui bridge on the western flank of the canal positions and were captured by the advancing Germans. Already late in the afternoon elements of *I./* and *III./FschJgRgt.1* had cleared the quarter of Dordrecht north of Krispijn, thereby decreasing the pressure on the defenders of the bridges across the Oude Maas.

By the afternoon the end had also come for the Dutch bridgehead at Wieldrecht. A German tank, reconnoitering toward this village, was fired at by machine-guns and by artillery from across the Kil. To remove this obstacle nine tanks were summoned for the attack. Their fire dispersed the 4th Company of the 3rd Border Infantry Battalion, of which some soldiers were killed and about 40 captured. Others had managed to hide out and to swim across the Kil later. The reinforced 3rd Platoon from *3./FschJgRgt.1*, under Hoffmann and located in the park at Amstelwijk, had not been involved in the fighting at Wieldrecht, but had later taken over the Dutch prisoners from there and had arranged for their transport to a collection site.

German columns, which mostly consisted of units from *9.Panzer-Division*, were able to incessantly cross the bridges at Moerdijk throughout the day and the first tanks arrived on Ijsselmonde in the afternoon. A short time later the commander of *9.Panzer-Division*, Generalmajor Ritter von Hubicki, reported to the command post of *Fl.Div.7* in Rijsoord. *Generalleutnant* Rudolf Schmidt, the commanding general of *XXXIX.Armee-Korps*,

---

234   The main armament for the Pz II was a 2cm gun, for the Pz III a 3.7cm gun and for the Pz IV a short 7.5cm gun, firing high explosive shells.

arrived at Ijsselmonde in the evening; in this function he was responsible for the conduct of further operations against Fortress Holland from the south. His mission was assigned by the commander-in-chief of *18.Armee* and was to seize Rotterdam, relieve the encircled *Gruppe von Sponeck* at Overschie and initially push his forces forward to the Oude Rijn between Leiden and Utrecht. Placed subordinate to him in *XXXIX.Armee-Korps*[235] were the *9.Panzer-Division*, the *SS Leibstandarte Adolf Hitler*[236] following immediately behind the *9.Pz.Div.* the *254.Inf.Div.* (still in reserve), and a number of combat-support units from *18.Armee* and *XXVI.Armee-Korps*. According to a directive from the *OKW* dated 8 November 1938, *Generalleutnant* Schmidt, in his function as overall commander of the ground forces in the operational area of the *Luftlande-Korps*, was also responsible for the relief and extraction of the parachute and air-landing forces. Therefore he assumed command over *Fl.Div.7* immediately after his arrival at Ijsselmonde. He lacked organic corps-level troops in his *ad hoc* corps, particularly signals units and so he had to depend almost solely upon the staff of *Fl.Div.7* for signal communications to superior and supporting higher commands. These communications, however, remained unreliable.

Under the leadership of *Generalleutnant* Schmidt, his subordinate commanders, Student and Ritter von Hubicki, as well as *Oberst* Kreysing, immediately set out to develop the order for the attack against Rotterdam, to be conducted on 14 May. Based on the knowledge and the preparatory measures of these commanders, the following was laid down as the attack-order:

The attack by ground forces was to commence after fire preparation by the artillery and the *Luftwaffe*, with two *Kampfgruppen* in front. When these had gained sufficient ground in the northern part of Rotterdam, a third *Kampfgruppe* was to be passed through them toward Delft. The majority of *9.Panzer-Division* was to advance toward Utrecht.

It was organized as follows:

- *Kampfgruppe Apell*: II./*Schützen-Rgt.11*, one company from I./*PzRgt.33*, 2./ *PiBtl.22*, *PzAbwAbt.50*, *schw.ArtAbt.629*, HQ *ArtRgt.577*, II/*ArtRgt.577*, *Batt.698*, flame-throwers and shock troops from army-level *PiBtl.52 (mot.)*. The *Kampfgruppe* was to cross the Nieuwe Maas over both bridges.
- *Kampfgruppe Kreysing*: Two companies from *InfRgt.16*, 7./*InfRgt.65*, 1/*PiBtl.22*, I./*ArtRgt.102*.[237] The *Kampfgruppe* was to cross the Nieuwe Maas with boats and small ships at the village of Ijsselmonde.
- *Gruppe C*: Reinforced *LAH* and one company from II./*PzRgt.33*. The *Kampfgruppe* was to follow Apell across the Maas bridges.

---

235 The command of *XXXIX.Armee-Korps* was generated in January 1940, but had not yet received organic corps-level troops and formations.

236 In the military forces initially formed by personnel of the SS, the formations above company and battalion had been designated *Standarte*. The first of them was the *SS Leibstandarte Adolf Hitler*. It had originally been used as the personal guard of Adolf Hitler. For the campaign against Holland the three existing *Standarten* had been organized into the *SS-Verfügungsdivision*. At that time the *LAH* had consisted mainly of infantry, and some units with supporting weapons.

237 In the course of the attack-preparations, this group was reinforced by 13./*InfRgt.16* (six infantry guns), 14./*InfRgt.16* (four anti-tank guns), 5./*ArtRgt.22*, half a machine-gun platoon from 12./*InfRgt.16* and five machine-guns from *InfRgt.65*.

Fl.Div.7, after the seizure of Rotterdam, was to provide for the security of the city. For this mission, it was to be reinforced by the HQ of *PzRgt.33*, a heavy artillery detachment and *II./PzRgt.33* (less one company). The leadership for the negotiations for the surrender of Rotterdam was to be in the hands of *Generalleutnant* Student.

The *254.Inf.Div.*, still in reserve, was to gain the area south of Rotterdam on the evening of 14 May with two regimental-size combat groups, and Dordrecht with a third one. From there the division was to follow behind *9.Pz.Div.* on 15 May.

The time for the start of the attack was set for 14 May at 1530hrs.

To protect the bridges along the line of communication Moerdijk-Rotterdam against air attacks the following anti-aircraft forces were to be deployed: *I./FlakAbt.49* at the Moerdijk bridges, the two light batteries from *FlakAbt.242* at the Dordrecht bridges, and the three heavy batteries from *FlakAbt.242* at the bridges across the Nieuwe Maas in Rotterdam.[238]

Not all of *9.Panzer-Division* was immediately available for commitment to Fortress Holland. Its southern *Kampfgruppe* remained committed in the area around Breda and east of the town. After *PzPiBtl.86* constructed a bridge across the Wilhelmina Canal north of Breda, shortly after midday on 13 May *II./SchtzRgt.10* established itself in a bridgehead on the western bank of the Mark Canal, west of Oosterhout. An armored patrol in the early hours of 13 May was sent forward in support of the infantry company and tied down west of the bridge at Ginneken where it was shot up. Of the four tanks that had been dispatched to Breda, two Pz IIs and one Pz IV, were engaged by numerous French armored cars (AMD 178) just west of the town, in the area of Princenhage. After the two Pz IIs had become ineffective, the Pz IV continued the fight, and was able to destroy three of the AMD's before it was immobilized by a hit to its engine. Despite the negative outcome of the fight for the Germans, the French reconnaissance forces subsequently retired some distance toward the west. This facilitated the advance of the majority of *I/Schützen-Rgt.11* in support of its forward company at Ginneken. Air reconnaissance had reported the advance of French troops from the south-west and west and *I/Schützen-Rgt.11* was tasked with an offensive mission immediately west of Breda. There at 1130hrs it routed and captured French troops who attacked on foot from the interior of Breda.[239] Subsequently elements from *II./PzRgt.33* occupied the town which had been evacuated by its inhabitants and cleared it of French stragglers. *2/PzAbwAbt.543* and the engineer platoon of *I/Schützen-Rgt.11* were deployed south of Ginneken to protect the left flank of *Gruppe von Sponeck*. Even further to the south detachment Bentele of *AufklRgt.9*, cooperating with *Gruppe von Sponeck*, kept in contact with French forces in the area of Zundert on the Dutch-Belgian border. As it became evident in the afternoon that the French had commenced retrograde movements in front of the entire sector of *XXVI.Armee-Korps*, the exhausted *I/Schützen-Rgt.11* was allowed to rest in its security positions.

---

238 *FlakAbt.242*, a mixed motorized unit, was provided by the *Luftwaffe*. It was equipped in its two light batteries with 3.7cm guns and in its three heavy batteries with 8.8cm guns, four per battery. The unit had arrived in its area of operations during the evening of 14 May.

239 During the advance of the southern task force of *9.Pz.Div.*, toward the west, Breda had not been occupied. The leader of a French reconnaissance unit, which by error had been left behind, had decided to destroy his vehicles and to attempt a sortie on foot.

Aufkl.Abt.Lüttwitz, which was still reinforced by a company from *PzPiBtl.86*, now reverted to the command of *AufklRgt.9* for reconnaissance and protection in the direction towards Antwerp. The detachment was initially delayed by French reconnaissance forces at the River Dintel, about 12km south-west of Moerdijk. After a short time it succeeded in taking possession of the insufficiently destroyed Dintel Bridge at Standaarbuiten and in removing the mines to its approaches. While the majority of the detachment remained in Standaarbuiten for the night 13/14 May, its motorcycle infantry, reconnoitering across the bridge toward the south, was engaged in street fighting with French sentries in Oudenbosch, just 2km south of the bridge.

The forward elements of the *LAH*, which was on the move from the attack-sector of *X.Armee-Korps* to *XXXIX.Armee-Korps*, unexpectedly came across a reinforced squadron of Dutch hussars as it passed through Gertruidenberg.[240] After an effective ambush the hussars retired to prepared field positions near the southern ramp of the bridge at Keizersveer, which was manned by elements from the security force of the bridge and by stragglers from the Peel Division. There they joined the defenders. An attack by a battalion-size task force from the *LAH* which was launched at about 1540hrs was repelled with losses. The defenders had the support of anti-tank guns and heavy machine-guns from two large concrete-casemates located at the northern ramp of the bridge. The attack of the *LAH* was resumed at 2000hrs and by about 2130hrs the Dutch had moved back to the northern bank of the Bergsche Maas. Here they found cover behind two steel gates blocking the bridge for vehicular traffic. At 2205hrs the bridge was blown up and completely destroyed, causing the SS troops to discontinue the attack and resumed their march toward the bridges at Dordrecht. The engagement around Gertruidenberg was the last deliberate combat of Dutch troops on the terrain of Noord Brabant. They had lost two men killed.[241]

A number of stragglers from the Dutch Peel Division had made their way into Zeeland. There the territorial commander attempted to integrate them into the defence of Walcheren, Zuid Beveland and Zeeuws Vlanderen with little success.[242] Some elements from the Peel Division also joined the French reconnaissance forces that had retired into the most western corner of Noord Brabant on either side of Bergen op Zoom. There, they were deployed for the protection of the approaches toward Antwerp together with parts of the French 1er DLM.

On the German side, the *SS Standarte Deutschland* of the *SS-Verfügungsdivision*, reinforced with artillery and engineers at the divisional level and with *MG-Btl.15* from the *Heer* was tasked with the seizure of the province of Zeeland. The *SS-Standarte Germania* was to protect its left flank.

---

240 The squadron had advanced from the bridge across the Bergsche Maas south of Keizersveer with the aim to establish contact with French forces.

241 The losses of the *LAH*, which must have been considerably higher, had officially not been reported, probably for reasons of the unit's connection with the name of Adolf Hitler. In any case, the number of 13 killed from the *LAH*, registered in Holland, of which 7 had died in the final fighting in Rotterdam on 14 May, should be considered untrustworthy.

242 On the Dutch side the 38th and 40th Infantry Divisions, the 14th Border Infantry Battalion and an incomplete artillery regiment had been deployed for the defence of the province of Zeeland. Six coastal batteries protected the mouths of the Scheldt. On 11 May the French had landed their 68th Inf.Div. on Walcheren and Zuid Beveland, whereas Zeeuws Vlanderen had been occupied by parts of the French 60th Inf.Div.

The urgency of the quick fall of Rotterdam was now expressed by an addendum to the order by *General der Artillerie* von Küchler. It stated that during negotiations regarding the surrender of the city, if necersary, its destruction was to be announced and in the case of a refused surrender, was to be executed. Considerable pressure on this matter was also exerted by Göring, who wanted to have his friend Graf von Sponeck extricated and therefore urged the start of the attack as early as possible. For this reason he requested for the provision of air attack forces against Rotterdam on 13 May.

The commanders who were involved in the preparations for the attack had no doubt that it would succeed only with heavy artillery and air support. The Dutch had strong garrisons in Rotterdam and unfavorable conditions were generated by the densely built-up city, with its numerous port facilities and canals traversing it in its southern part. The utilization of this artillery and air support was considered completely legitimate in accordance with the rules of war, as Rotterdam had the statute of a defended city. Based on this legal argument, an intensive fire-preparation by the artillery and the *Luftwaffe* had begun and from the standpoint of the responsibility of the commanders for the soldiers entrusted to them, this action appeared to be imperative, if only to keep losses in personnel and material within acceptable limits. However, the decision by *General der Flieger* Kesselring to have the preparatory air attack executed by *KG 54*, which was equipped with He 111 bombers, did not fully involve *Generalleutnante* Schmidt and Student.[243] Schmidt and Student were aware of the risk which would come from area-bombing to the population who, despite the decision of the Dutch military to defend Rotterdam, had not been evacuated. Furthermore there was considerable risk to the irreplaceable cultural heritage in the city's interior. Therefore the commanders, in agreement with the liaison officer from *KG 54*, determined that only the Maas station, close to the Nieuwe Maas in the south-east of the city and a narrow strip immediately north of the bridges, were to be targets for the attacking aircraft. The most important decision taken by *Generalleutnante* Schmidt and Student to avoid unnecessary threat to the inhabitants of Rotterdam and for the architectural heritage of the city, was to carry out the artillery bombardment only in the case that the request for surrender was refused. In this instance the bombardment was set for 14 May 1440hrs and the air attack was to end with the last bomb dropped at 1528hrs. The defenders were to be informed about the consequences should they refuse to surrender and so Article 25 of The Hague Convention for Land Warfare would also be met.

Early in the evening the command of *Fl.Div.7* decided to utilize the arrival of elements from *I./PzRgt.33* on Ijsselmonde for the seizure of the bridge south of Barendrecht and for the elimination of enemy positions at its southern ramp. Thus, a threat to the forces concentrating for the attack against Rotterdam and for the firing positions of the supporting

---

243 It has not been possible to definitively identify the reason for the use of level bombers instead of dive bombers, which would have been much better suited to attack point-targets. The range of the Ju 87 would have sufficed, as their attack against Alblasserdam proved. A plausible reason for the use of He 111s may have been, that almost all of the dive-bomber formations of the *Luftwaffe*, including those from *VIII.Flieger-Korps* of *Luftflotte 2*, had been summoned for the support of the crossing of the Maas by *Panzergruppe von Kleist* on 13 May, and its further support on 14 May. The thought that Göring had a vital interest in scoring a decisive success for his *Luftwaffe* by destroying parts of Rotterdam by level-bombing and thereby to speed up the surrender of the Dutch should not be excluded. During the Nuremberg war crimes trials in 1945, he evaded answering this question.

artillery would be disposed of. An indication of the existence of this threat was given when the weak company of *II./FschJgRgt.2* was safeguarding the area south of Barendrecht. Here, during the course of the day they had to repel a thrust of Dutch troops across the bridge that may have been the reconnaissance for a later offensive action.

The attack across the bridge was to be conducted as a raid by a few tanks. At 1850hrs *I./PzRgt.33* was ordered to roll up the Dutch positions south of the bridge with a tank platoon. *Leutnant* Grix from the staff of *I./PzRgt.33*, who was tasked with the mission, decided to employ the staff platoon consisting of his tank (Pz III) and four Pz II tanks. The commander of the sentries at the bridge reported that no anti-tank guns or field guns were observed at the southern bank of the Oude Maas near the bridge.[244] Based on this information Grix commenced his raid at 2000hrs. While two of the tanks provided fire-support the other three, led by the Pz III crossed the bridge at high speed. Shortly before reaching the end the Pz III was hit by an anti-tank round which wounded the driver and the loader. More hits by the Dutch anti-tank guns then rendered the tank unusable and its crew evacuated. In the meantime the two subsequent tanks were also put out of action, killing one member of the crew and badly wounding one of the tank commanders. The remainder of the crews now retreated under machine-gun fire, which slightly wounded some of the soldiers. Around 2200hrs one of the disabled tanks exploded. Continuously fired at by mortars and machine-guns all of the surviving crew members, of whom a further seven were wounded, finally made their way back across the bridge into cover at 2300hrs. Inadequate reconnaissance, a lack of support from high-angle weapons and a reckless over-estimation of their own combat power had resulted in the failure of the raid. Nevertheless its intended aim was not only met, but even surpassed. Immediately after the German tank thrust was repelled the commanding officer of the 3rd Border Infantry Battalion, who was responsible for the protection of the bridge, decided to halt his mission. During the night 13/14 May all troops of Group Kil retired across the Spui river to the islands of Putten and Voorne; making the way to Hoekse Waard free for the Germans to pass. When the positions at the petroleum installation near Pernis were also given up in the evening it was only the bridgehead at Spijkenisse which firmly remained in Dutch hands on Ijsselmonde. The Germans had sufficiently strong forces for the surveillance of this part of the island. The security of the concentration area south of Rotterdam was made safe. As there were no indications of another attack by the Dutch across the Noord toward the west and in spite of the return of the Dutch Light Division to the northern bank of the Merwede, the German commanders in front of Rotterdam now directed all of their efforts toward the task manifested by the order of *18.Armee*.

Throughout the struggle there was no sign of the mixed battalion of British Guards that had landed at Hoek van Holland to allow the evacuation of the Queen of the Netherlands and her cabinet. After an attack by German bombers against Hoek van Holland along the Nieuwe Waterweg on 13 May the British hastily abandoned their positions after the loss of 11 killed and about 20 wounded. From there they embarked for England on three British destroyers. Much equipment was left behind.

---

244   However this information was sketchy, as in fact three infantry platoons, eight heavy machine-guns and two anti-tank guns from the 3rd Border Infantry Battalion had been positioned close to the southern ramp of the bridge.

On the morning of 13 May the Dutch high command had still hoped to delay the German attack from the south into the core of Fortress Holland. They hoped this could be achieved by the destruction of the bridges across the Hollandsch Diep and the Nieuwe Maas and also allow them time for the defence of the New Waterline by a counter-attack at the Grebbe Line.[245] However by the evening it had become apparent that all of these intended actions had failed in their aims. In Rotterdam and at the Grebbe Line it had been the inability of those in charge to employ the readily available forces without 'ifs or buts', and to ensure their cooperation.

For the defence of Rotterdam, the chances were still considered good in the light of the considerable strength of the troops assembled there and of the highly suitable terrain. In order to gain time for the establishment of the anti-tank line around Den Haag, the prolongation of the defence of Rotterdam by further strengthening its garrison was most important. This however made it necessary to open the lines of communication into the city from the north by eliminating the German force at Overschie as quickly as possible.

The intervention of French or even British forces in the struggle for Fortress Holland was a forlorn hope, particularly as it became apparent that the development of the situation east of Brussels would quickly lead to the abandonment of the last French positions on Dutch soil covering the avenues of approach toward Antwerp.

14 May

At 1040hrs the attack-order of *XXXIX.Armee-Korps* was handed out to the subordinate commanders and the troops moved into their start positions. Three officers, among them the intelligence officer (Ic) from the corps staff, crossed the traffic bridge in Rotterdam under a flag of truce shortly before 1140hrs.[246] Their mission was to pass a letter from *Generalleutnant* Schmidt to the Dutch garrison commander which requested the surrender of the city. The German officers arrived at the command post of Colonel Scharroo and handed the document to him, conforming to the requirements of the Geneva Convention, a copy of which they had brought with them for the mayor of Rotterdam and the municipal council. The requirement for the decision by the garrison commander was set for 1300hrs. The request for the surrender contained an unmistakable indication about the consequences of its refusal. *Generalleutnant* Schmidt had purposefully chosen the lapse of the ultimatum for 1300hrs even though the attack was not planned before 1445hrs. This gave some freedom of action toward both sides should an initial refusal of surrender occur. Unknown to him was the timetable set by the command of *Luftflotte 2*, in which the attack by *XXXIX.Armee-Korps* was set for 1530hrs, as determined by *Generalleutnant* Schmidt the day before.

Colonel Scharroo and Lieutenant Colonel Wilson took offense at supposed mistakes in the document, for instance a missing signature and the exact demands of the requesting German commander.[247] Nevertheless, they immediately informed General Winkelman about the ultimatum and asked for his decision. As this did not arrive immediately the

---

245 For this counter-attack four infantry battalions and some artillery had been made available.

246 Although the events which led to the unfortunate air bombardment of Rotterdam are only partly related to the general subject of this book, they are laid out here in some detail, in order to make the reader acquainted with this subject, as it has been discussed for many years. The data assembled here and their evaluation by the author are thought to draw a picture, which comes as close as possible to the truth.

247 According to regulations in the rules of war these entries were not required. After the war, this was confirmed during a judicial examination of the events which had led to the air bombardment of Rotterdam.

German officers were asked to leave again, under the condition that a Dutch negotiator would be sent as soon as the decision of the commander-in-chief had arrived, but in any case prior to the expiration of the ultimatum. The German delegation returned to the command post of *Generalleutnante* Schmidt and Student in Rijsoord at 1240hrs. As the officers were under the impression that the Dutch garrison commander was willing to accept the requested surrender, *Generalleutnant* Schmidt immediately had a teletype-message sent to the command of *Luftflotte 2*, in which he requested the postponement of the air attack in reference to the ongoing negotiations. The receipt of this message was confirmed by the command of *Luftflotte 2* at 1242hrs.[248]

Despite the appeal by the mayor of Rotterdam to carefully weigh the potential destruction of the city against the little time which he gained by any further defence, General Winkelman decided to reject the ultimatum. He instructed Colonel Scharroo at 1325hrs. Colonel Scharroo now ordered his adjutant, Captain Backer, to formally deliver the rejection of the ultimatum. Backer arrived at Noordereiland at 1400hrs. Informed about his presence, *Generalleutnante* Schmidt, Student and Ritter von Hubicki arrived twenty minutes later. Having read the response Schmidt immediately dictated a new letter. Now he not only requested the surrender of the city without delay, but also determined the conditions for its execution. At 1455hrs he signed the document with his name and rank and handed it over to Captain Backer.

Immediately after the receipt of the document Captain Backer was led back across the traffic bridge and suddenly the bombers of *KG 54* approached Rotterdam from two directions, completely unexpectedly. Horrified, *Generalleutnant* Schmidt now realized that his earlier request for the postponement of the air attack had not been followed. Desperately, he and some other officers tried to prevent the air-bombardment by firing red signal flares, which had been agreed upon with the *Luftflotte* command in such a case. However the signals were not seen by the bomber group as they approached from the west. The group was formed of 57 He 111s led by the formation's commander, *Oberst* Lackner. The group dropped its 250kg and 50kg bombs over the previously determined targets. In the smaller bomber group formed of 36 He 111s and approaching from the south, only its commander, *Oberstleutnant* Hoehne, saw the red signal flares, but only after his first group of aircraft had dropped its bombs. Nevertheless by radio he passed the code for turning away to the aircraft behind him.

According to the statement of *Oberst* Lackner after the war, shortly prior to the take-off of *KG 54* from the airfields at Quakenbrück, Hoya and Delmenhorst at 1330hrs, he had received the message from the directing staff of the formation that *Generalleutnant* Student had pointed out that red signal flares must be looked for if negotiations with the garrison of Rotterdam were still ongoing. Inexplicably Student, in this radio message, had not mentioned the method for postponement of the air attack which *Generalleutnant* Schmidt had sent to the command of *Luftflotte 2* about 40 minutes earlier. As it cannot be assumed that Student's message was conveyed even incompletely to the commander of *KG 54*, the commanding general of the *Luftlande-Korps* must be blamed for this neglect. This attitude is possibly as a result of the 'fog of war' effect, but nevertheless it weighs heavily on the reputation of *Generalleutnant* Student, who was aware of the request of *Generalleutnant* Schmidt and should have asked for its outcome. There is no doubt about

---

248 Unfortunately, it has not been possible to find out at what time Kesselring had approved the request and at what time and in what way his decision was passed on to *Flieger-Korps Putzier*.

Color photographs and maps

Netherlands 1940 A view across the Kil waterway from the polder south of Tweede Tol. The opposite bank is on the island Hoekse Waard, which was held until almost the end of the fighting in May 1940 by the Dutch. The water tower at De Wacht was used by the Dutch as an observation post. (Photo by courtesy of A.M.A. Goossens)

Netherlands 1940 Terrain at the southern edge of the island of Dordrecht, looking toward the Nieuwe Merwede. Parts of a reinforced *Fallschirmtruppe Kompanie* under *Oberleutant* Moll had jumped into the polder seen on the left side of the photo early in the morning of 11 May 1940 and became engaged with a weak company of the Dutch I/28th Infantry Regiment. (Photo by courtesy of A.M.A. Goossens)

Crete 1941 The old coastal road close to the western access to the old bridge across the Tavronitis river. Elements of the *SturmRgt* landed here and in the riverbed in nine gliders in the morning of 20 May, suffered heavy losses but succeeded in overcoming the New Zealand infantry. Hill 107, on which the majority of the reinforced New Zealand 22nd Infantry Battalion was entrenched, looms in the background to the right. The new bridge and road did not exist in 1941. (Courtesy of the Archiv des Bundes Deutscher Fallschirmjäger)

Crete 1941 View along the eastern bank of the Tavronitis, looking toward its mouth, located on the left side of the photo, and to the western part of the airfield Maleme (right of the photo). This terrain, occupied by infantry from the New Zealand 22nd Infantry Battalion and numerous anti-aircraft guns, was mainly seized by the *3.Kompanie* of the *SturmRgt.* on 20 May. (Courtesy of the Archiv des Bundes Deutscher Fallschirmjäger)

Crete 1941 View from the northern slope of Hill 107 looking toward the lower Tavronitis valley and the airfield at Maleme. C Company of the New Zealand 22nd Infantry Battalion was entrenched around the airfield, supported by numerous anti-aircraft guns. By the time German landings commenced on 21 May, Hill 107 had been abandoned by its defenders. In the background to the left is the Rodope Peninsula. The buildings in the center did not exist in 1941. (Courtesy of the Archiv des Bundes Deutscher Fallschirmjäger)

Crete 1941 View from the eastern slope of Hill 107 looking east. To the left are the villages of Pirgos and Dhaskaliana. The latter, and the terrain nearer to the center, are where the New Zealand 23rd Infantry Battalion was located, with the 21st Infantry Battalion further to the right. When the reinforced *III./SturmRgt.* landed on 20 May it encountered both of these units. Further to the rear are the heights around Modhion, from where the New Zealand artillery fired on the airfield at Maleme. (Courtesy of the Archiv des Bundes Deutscher Fallschirmjäger)

Crete 1941 View from the eastern slope of Hill 107 along the coastal strip toward the east. The built-up area in front is Pirgos. There, the remnants of the 5. and *6.Kompanien* of *FschJgRgt.2* and of parts of *FschSanAbt.7* held out until relief, after they had been dropped as reinforcements to *Gruppe West* on 21 May. The unsuccessful counterattack of the New Zealand 5th Brigade was launched along the coastal strip on 22 May, the advance of *Gruppe Ramcke* commencing along it on 23 May. (Courtesy of the Archiv des Bundes Deutscher Fallschirmjäger)

Crete 1941 View of Cemetery Hill, located just south of Galatas, from the south. On 20 May it was defended by soldiers of the Greek 6th Regiment. The *Fallschirmtruppe* of *9.Kompanie* of *III./FschJgRgt.3* came down immediately in front of the hill. They launched their assault with the weapons they had carried on the jump, and despite suffering heavy losses, succeeded in seizing the hill and capturing more than a hundred of their opponents. In the afternoon, however, they were forced to give up their gains and to withdraw to the forward slope of the hill. (Photo courtesy of the author)

Crete 1941 View from Cemetery Hill just south of Galatas into the valley, which stretches to the south-west, to Alikianou. The regimental staff and the 1st and 2nd battalions of *FschJgRgt.3* were dropped around the prison, which can be seen in the center. Further to the rear runs a spur, where *FschPiBtl.7* landed as flank protection. The slopes to the left rear were occupied by the Greek 6th Regiment. (Courtesy of the Archiv des Bundes Deutscher Fallschirmjäger)

Crete 1941 View from the high ground just south-east of Galatas looking north-east, to where the Greek 6th Regiment occupied positions on 20 May. In the center, on the left side, is Karatsos. The slope further to the left formed part of the defensive positions of the New Zealand 19th Infantry Battalion. Behind this slope and further in the background are the suburbs of Chania, with the Akrotiri Peninsula rising behind them. In the background on the right is Perivolia. The terrain rises steeply in direction toward the White Mountains. After the area around Galatas had been cleared from its defenders, *FschJgRgt.3* advanced in the low ground toward Chania, with *GebJgRgt.100* on its left and *GebJgRgt.141* on its right. (Courtesy of the Archiv des Bundes Deutscher Fallschirmjäger)

Crete 1941 Typical terrain on the Akrotiri peninsula. A number of *Fallschirmtruppe* from *Sturmgruppe Altmann* were seriously injured when their gliders crashed into the rocks. Widely dispersed after the landing, the force was overcome by the Northumberland Hussars of CREFORCE, who were positioned on Akrotiri. (Courtesy of the Archiv des Bundes Deutscher Fallschirmjäger)

Crete 1941 View from the south-western tip of the Akrotiri Peninsula across the western end of Souda Bay. The bright green in the center is the Commonwealth soldiers' cemetery. On the opposite bank of the Bay are the port installations of Souda. On 27 May the 19th Australian and 5th New Zealand brigades made a defensive stand in the terrain to the right of them, stretching towards the chain of hills, anchored on '42nd Street'. The lead battalion of *GebJgRgt.141* suffered heavy losses during a counterattack there. *GebJgRgt.85* initiated its outflanking move towards the east along the crest of the hills. (Courtesy of the Archiv des Bundes Deutscher Fallschirmjäger)

Crete 1941 The German cemetery on Hill 107. In the background can be seen Maleme airfield. (Courtesy of the Archiv des Bundes Deutscher Fallschirmjäger)

Crete 1941 The Commonwealth cemetery at Chania, with a view of Souda Bay. (Courtesy of the Archiv des Bundes Deutscher Fallschirmjäger)

Skagerrak
Schweden
Kattegat
Alborg
1.Zg.4./FschJgRgt 1
III./I.R. 159
Tyborøn
Viborg
Jütland
Århus
Helsingborg
Helsingør
Öre-Sund
Røskilde
Kopenhagen
Malmö
Fredericia
Esbjerg
Middelfahrt
Kolding
Haderslev
Odense
Großer Belt
Seeland
Køge
Nyborg
Korsør
Fünen
Kleiner Belt
Abenrå
Vordingborg
Masnedø
4./FschJgRgt.1(-)
Tønder
Nykøbing
Laaland
Falster
Flensburg
Schleswig
Gjedser
Husum
Fehmarn
Kiel
Rendsburg
Warnemünde
N
Neumünster
Lübeck
KEY:
Airlanding of German troops
Disembarkation of German troops
Parachute assaults
Kilometer
0
50
100

1. Actions of *4./FschJgRgt 1* in the area of *Weserübung Süd*

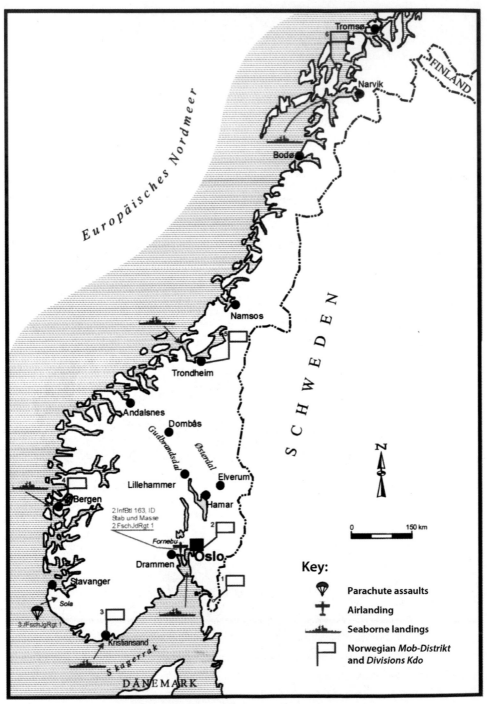

2. Norway at the beginning of *Weserübung Nord*

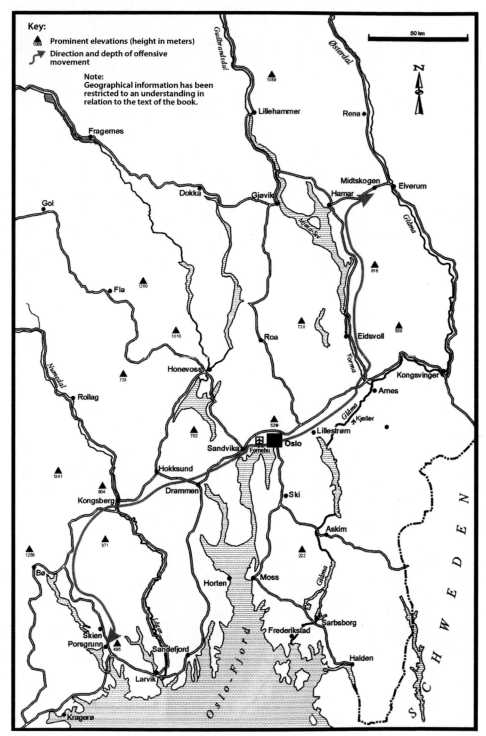

3. The area around Oslo and the offensive actions of *Abteilung Walther*

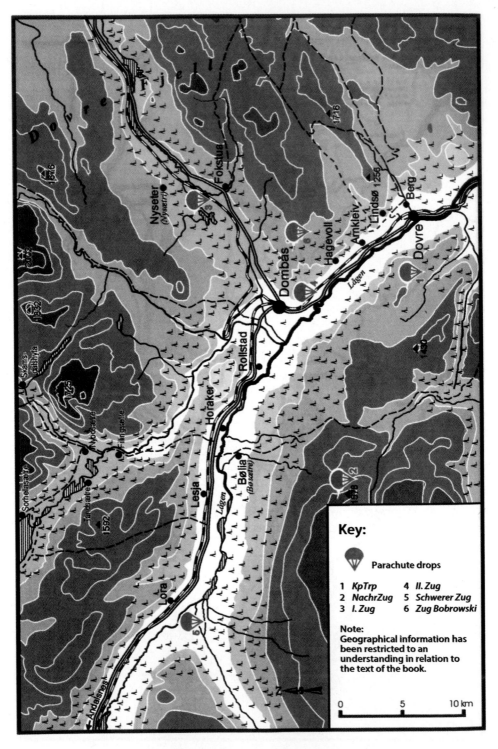

4. The actions of reinforced *1./FschJgRgt* 1 in the Dombås area

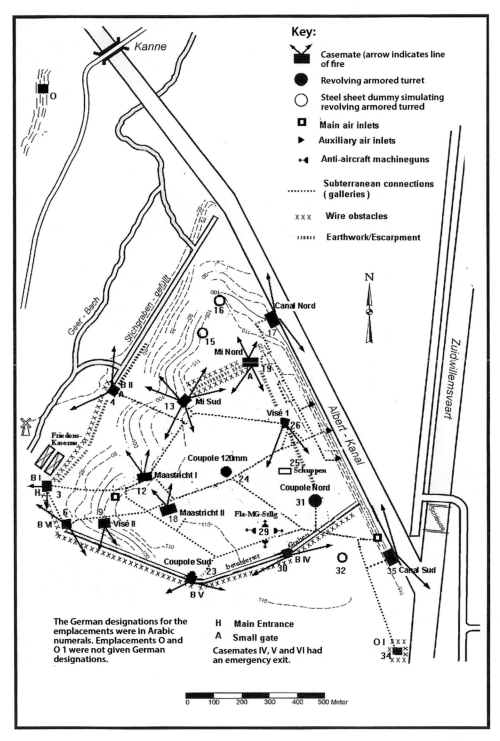

Key:

Casemate (arrow indicates line of fire

Revolving armored turret

Steel sheet dummy simulating revolving armored turred

Main air inlets

Auxiliary air inlets

Anti-aircraft machineguns

Subterranean connections (galleries)

x x x Wire obstacles

Earthwork/Escarpment

N

Kanne

O

Geer - Bach

Stichgraben - gefüllt

O 16

15

Canal Nord

17

Mi Nord

19
A

B II
A

4   13   Mi Sud

Visé 1

26

Friedens-Kaserne

Coupole 120mm

24

Schuppen

25

Coupole Nord

Maastricht I

31

B I
H   3

12

6   9   18   Maastricht II   Fla-MG-Stllg

B VI   Visé II   29

Graben

Coupole Sud   betonierter   30   B IV   32   35   Canal Sud

23

B V

Albert - Kanal

Zuidwillemsvaart

Schleuse

The German designations for the emplacements were in Arabic numerals. Emplacements O and O 1 were not given German designations.

H   Main Entrance
A   Small gate

Casemates IV, V and VI had an emergency exit.

O 1   34

0   100   200   300   400   500 Meter

5. The Albert Canal 10 May 1940

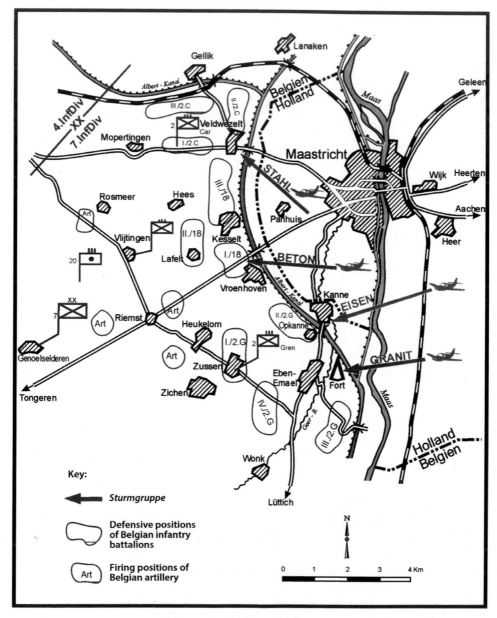

6. Fort Eben-Emael

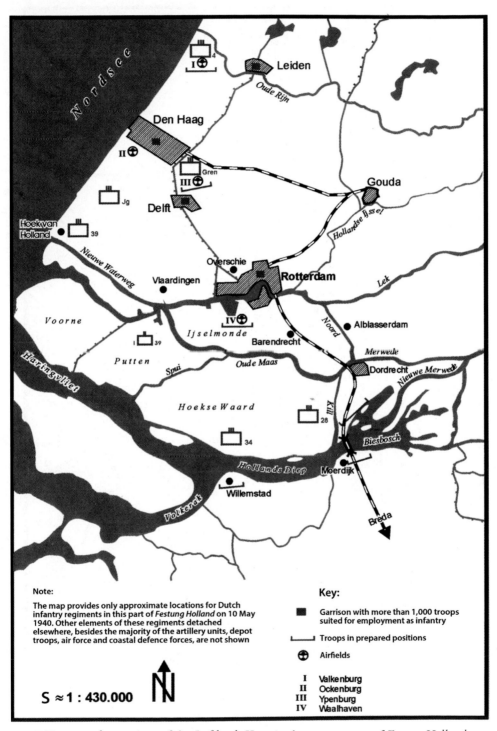

Note:

The map provides only approximate locations for Dutch infantry regiments in this part of *Festung Holland* on 10 May 1940. Other elements of these regiments detached elsewhere, besides the majority of the artillery units, depot troops, air force and coastal defence forces, are not shown

S ≈ 1 : 430.000

Key:

■ Garrison with more than 1,000 troops suited for employment as infantry

⌐___⌐ Troops in prepared positions

⊕ Airfields

I   Valkenburg
II Ockenburg
III Ypenburg
IV Waalhaven

7. The area of operations of the *Luftlande Korps* in the western part of *Festung Holland*

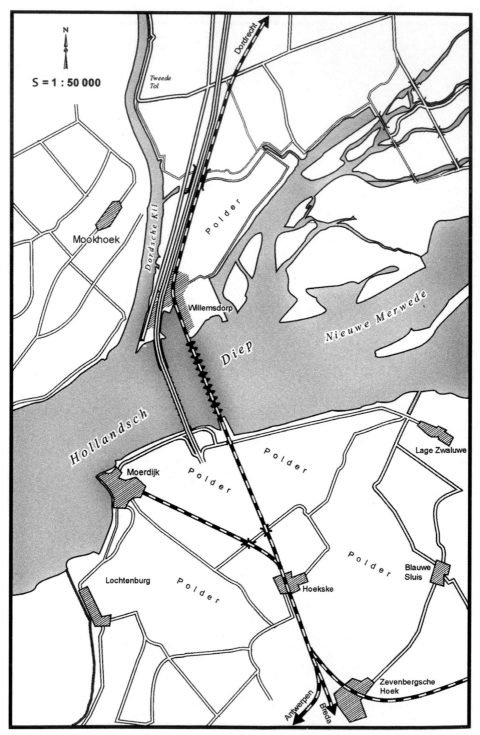

8. The bridges at Moerdijk

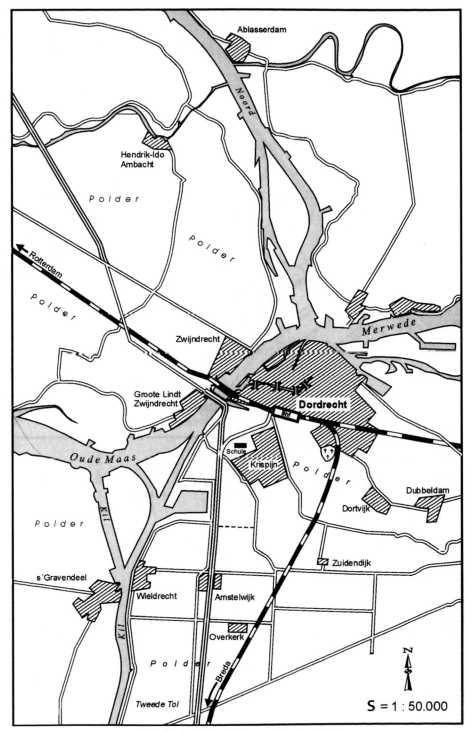

9. Dordrecht and the Oude Maas bridges

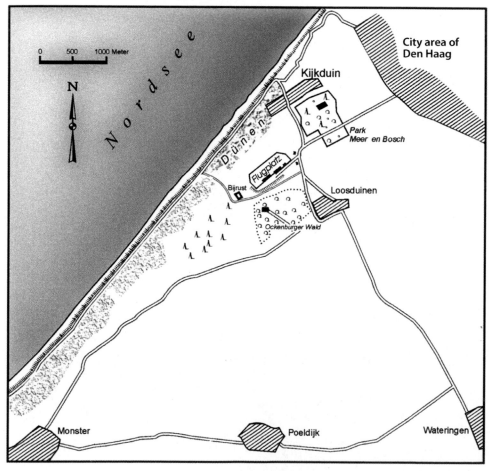

10. Ockenburg airfield

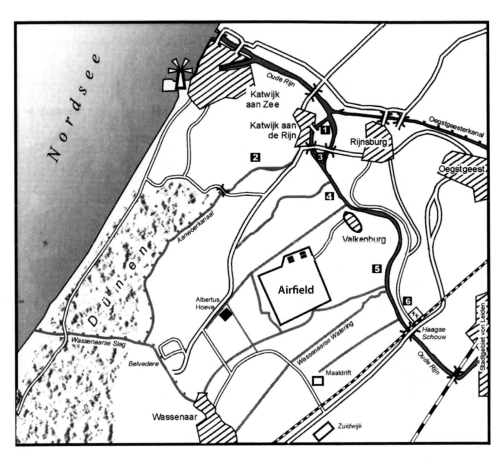

Nordsee

Oude Rijn

Katwijk
aan Zee

Katwijk aan
de Rijn

Rijnsburg

Oegstgeesterkanaal

Oegstgeest

1

2

3

4

Valkenburg

Aanvoerkanaal

5

Duünen

6

Albertus
Hoeve

Airfield

Wassenaarse Watering

Haagse
Schouw

Stadgebiet von Leiden

Wassenaarse Slag

Belvedere

Maaldrift

Oude Rijn

Wassenaar

Zuidwijk

N

0   1   2 Km

Key:

1 Seminary

2 Pumping station

3 Stone quarry

4 Brick yard

5 Rijnvliet farmstead

6 Stone quarry

Drainage ditch

Tram line

Lighthouse

11. Valkenburg airfield

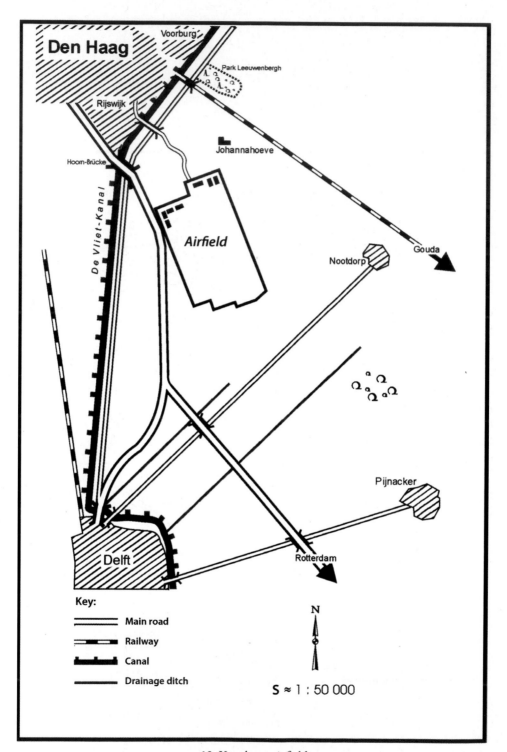

12. Ypenburg airfield

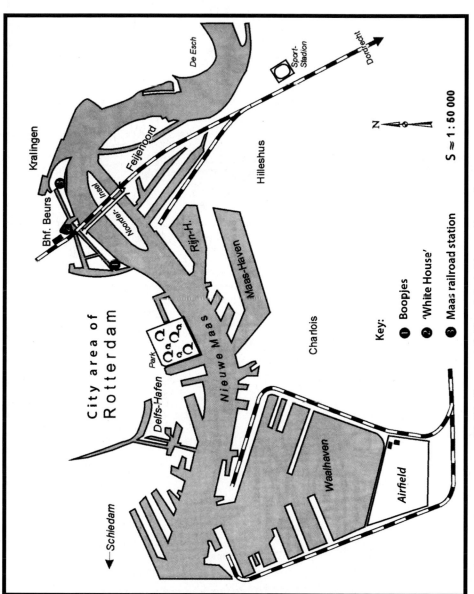

13. Waalhaven airfield and the bridges at Rotterdam

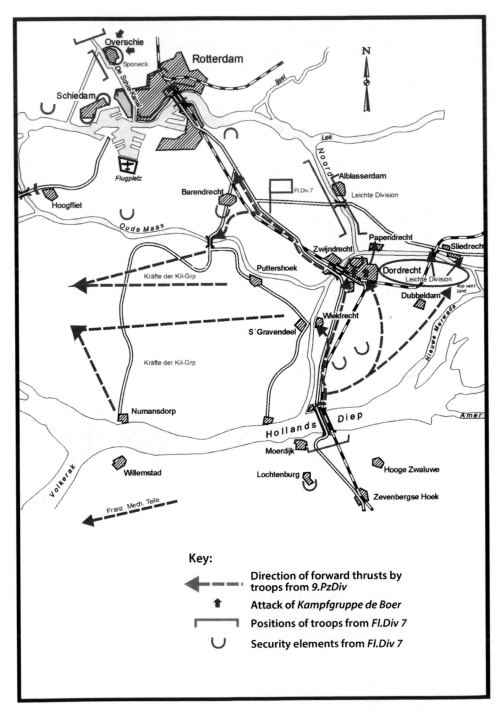

14. The situation in the operational area of *Fliegerdivision 7*, mid-day on 13 May 1940

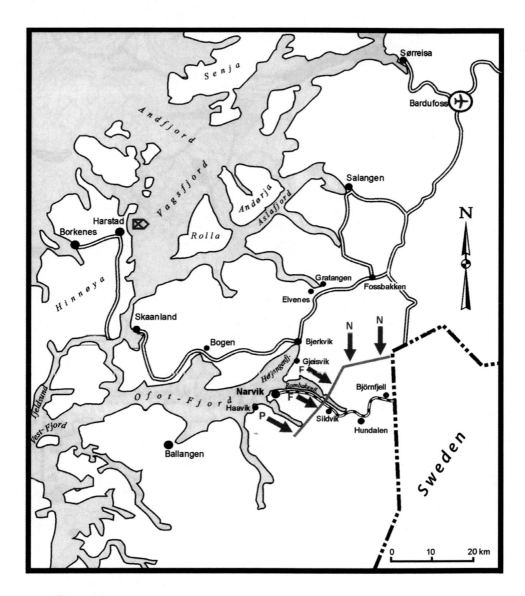

15.Narvik and its environs, situation on 1 June 1940

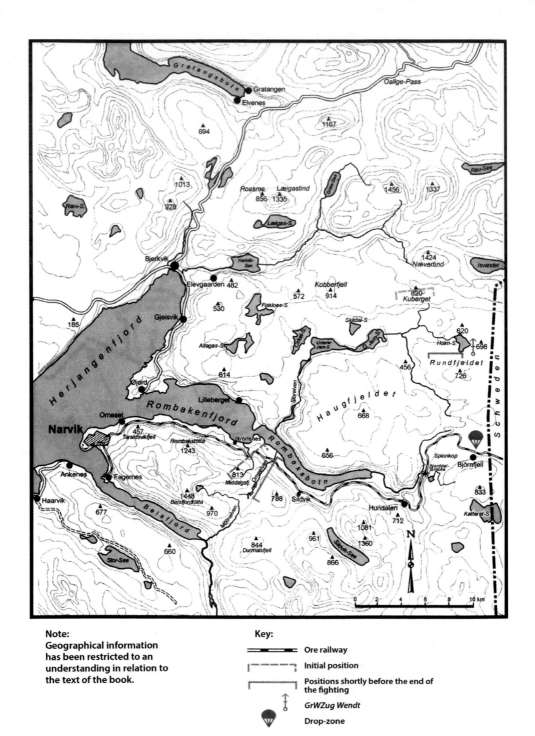

16. Narvik area of operations – actions of the *Fallschirmtruppe*

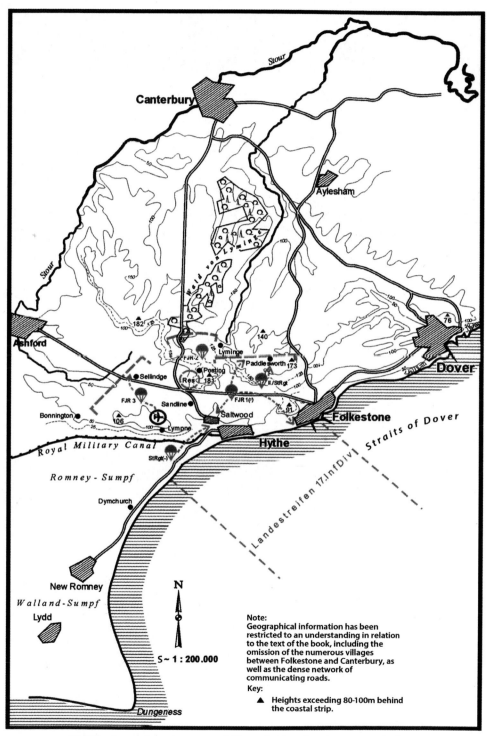

17. The planned employment of *Fliegerdivision 7* in Operation *Seelöwe*

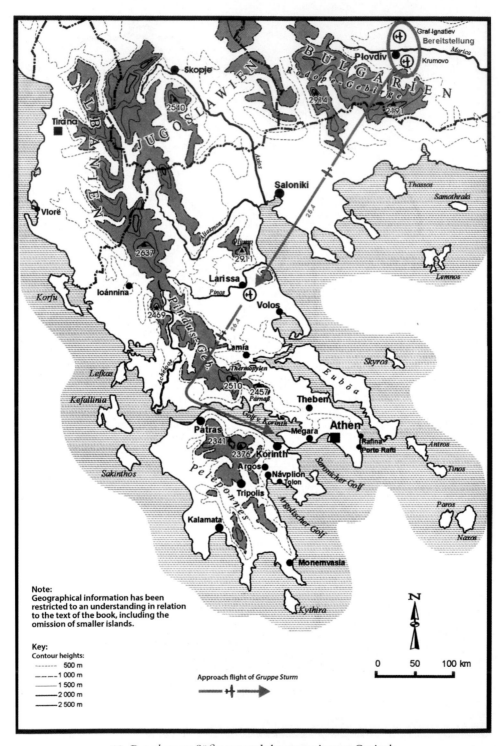

Note:
Geographical information has been
restricted to an understanding in relation
to the text of the book, including the
omission of smaller islands.

Key:
Contour heights:
.... 500 m
--------1 000 m
————1 500 m
————2 000 m
————2 500 m

0   50   100 km

N

Approach flight of *Gruppe Sturm*

18. *Detachement Süßmann* and the operations at Corinth

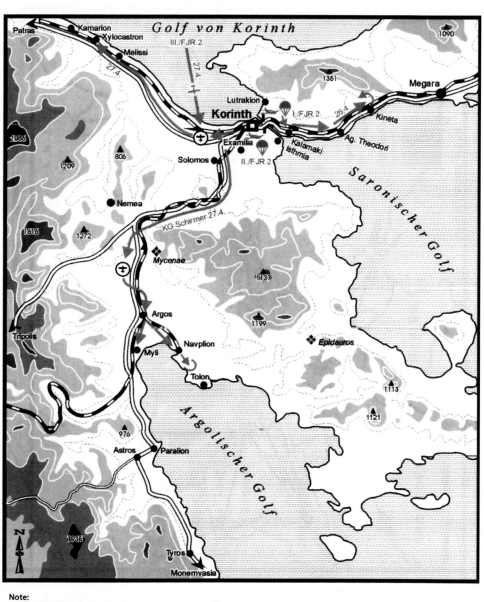

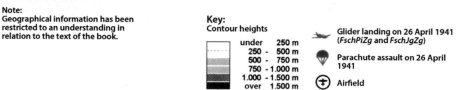

Note:
Geographical information has been restricted to an understanding in relation to the text of the book.

Key:
Contour heights

under	250 m
250 -	500 m
500 -	750 m
750 -	1.000 m
1.000 -	1.500 m
over	1.500 m

✈ Glider landing on 26 April 1941 (*FschPiZg* and *FschJgZg*)

⛂ Parachute assault on 26 April 1941

⊕ Airfield

19. The operations area of *Gruppe Sturm* in the Isthmus of Corinth and beyond

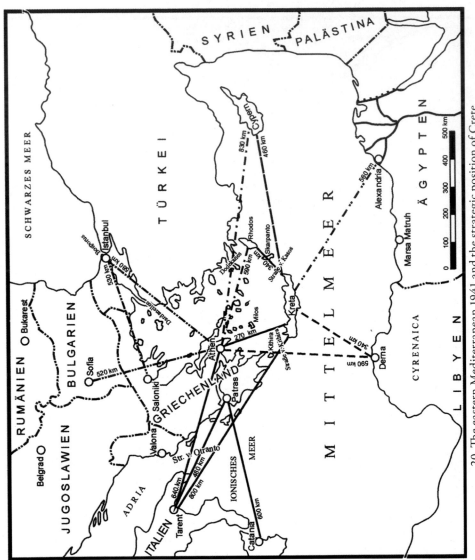

20. The eastern Mediterranean 1941 and the strategic position of Crete

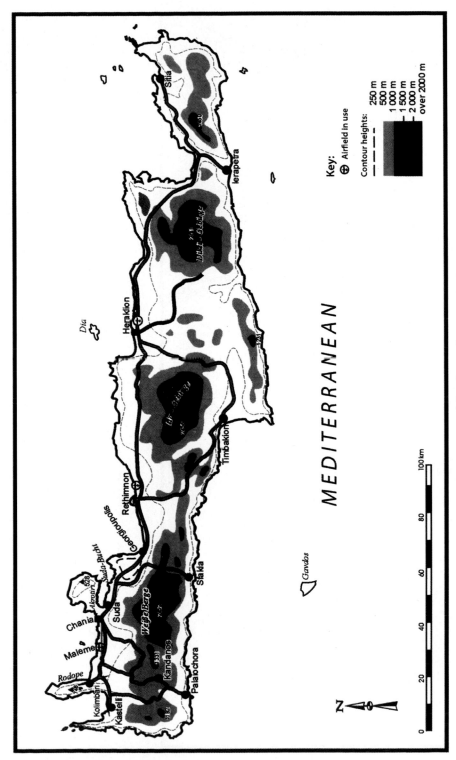

21. Crete 1941, with key lines of communication

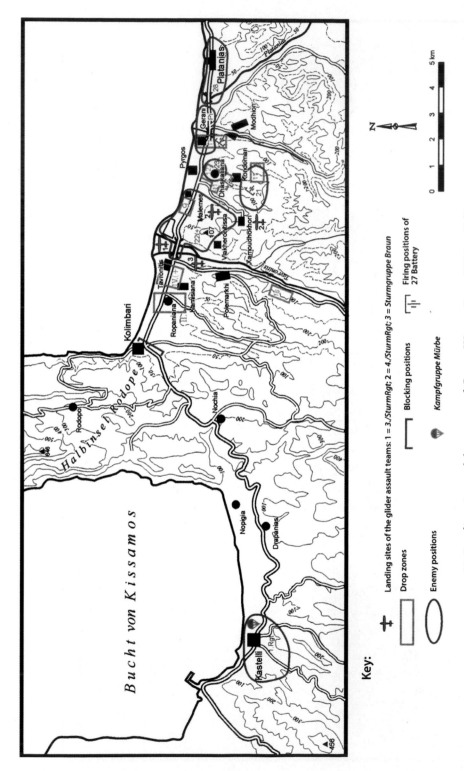

Key:

Landing sites of the glider assault teams: 1 = 3./SturmRgt; 2 = 4./SturmRgt; 3 = Sturmgruppe Braun

| | Firing positions of 27 Battery |

| | Blocking positions |

| | Drop zones |

| Kampfgruppe Mürbe |

| | Enemy positions |

22. Landing sites and drop zones of *Gruppe West* on Crete, 20 May 1941

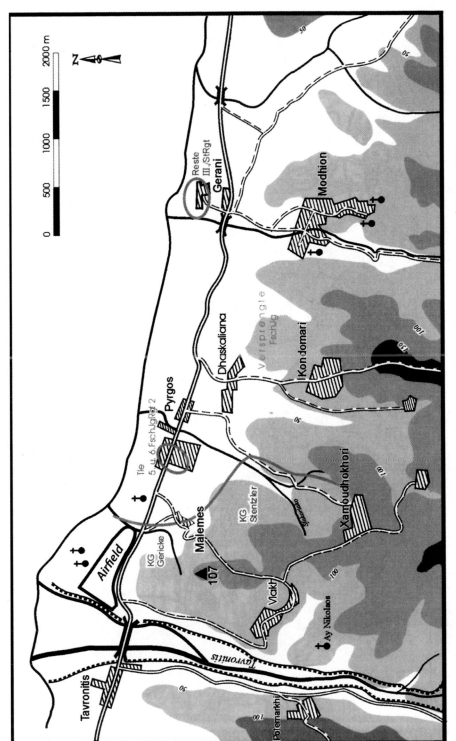

23. Area of operations and forward positions of *Gruppe West*, Crete, evening of 21 May 1941

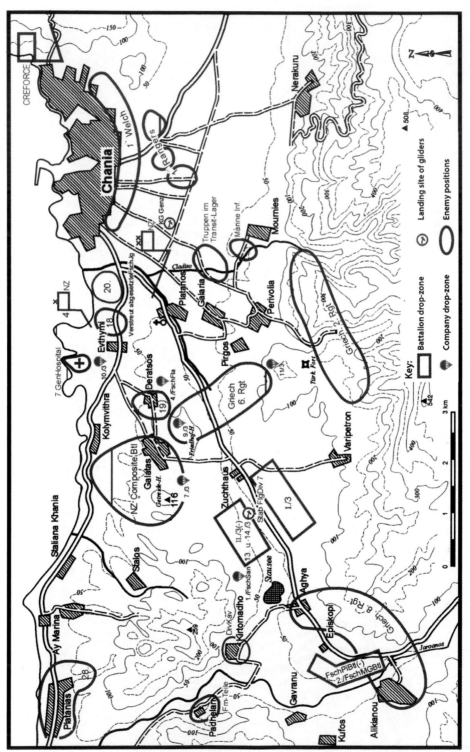

24. The parachute assault of *Gruppe Mitte*, Crete, 20 May 1941

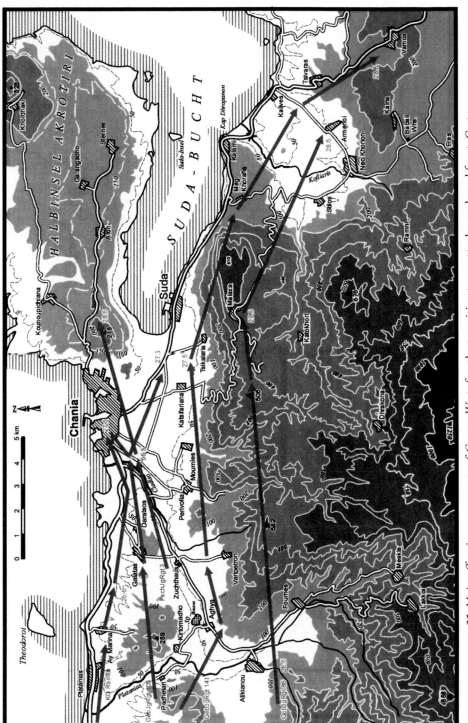

25. Main offensive movements of *Gruppe West* after the transition to an attack on a broad front, Crete

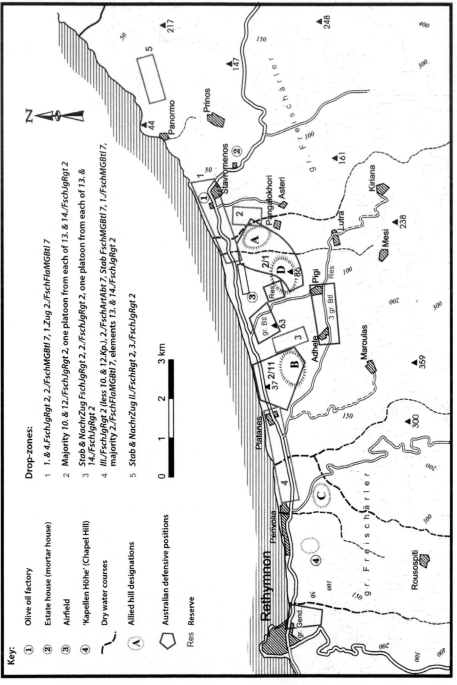

Key:

① Olive oil factory

② Estate house (mortar house)

③ Airfield

④ 'Kapellen Höhe' (Chapel Hill)

⌇ Dry water courses

Ⓐ Allied hill designations

⬠ Australian defensive positions

Res Reserve

Drop-zones:

1 1. & 4.FschJgRgt 2, 2./FschMGBtl 7, 1.Zug 2./FschFlaMGBtl 7

2 Majority 10. & 12./FschJgRgt 2, one platoon from each of 13. & 14./FschJgRgt 2

3 Stab & NachZug FschJgRgt 2, 2./FschJgRgt 2, one platoon from each of 13. & 14./FschJgRgt 2

4 III./FschJgRgt 2 (less 10. & 12.Kp.), 2./FschArtAbt 7, Stab FschMGBtl 7, 1./FschMGBtl 7, majority 2./FschFlaMGBtl 7, elements 13. & 14./FschJgRgt 2

5 Stab & NachZug II./FschJgRgt 2, 3./FschJgRgt 2

26. The area of operations around Rethymnon, Crete – situation during the parachute assault, 20 May 1941

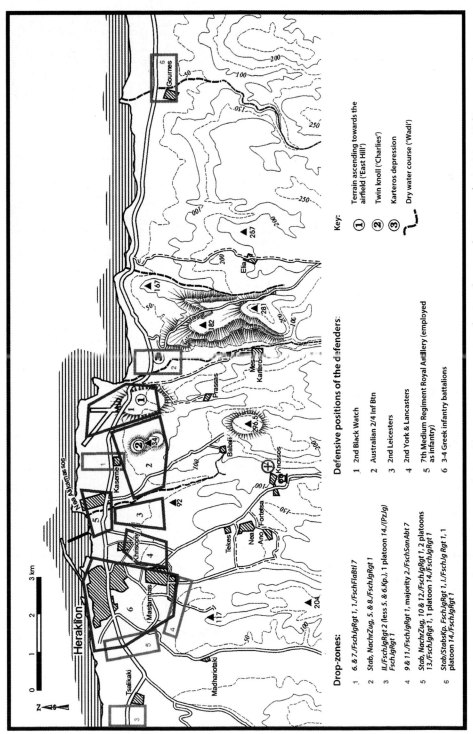

Drop-zones:

1 6. & 7./FschJgRgt 1, 1./FschFlaBtl 7
2 Stab, NachzZug, 5. & 8./FschJgRgt 1
3 II./FschJgRgt 2 (less 5. & 6.Kp.), 1 platoon 14./(PzJg) FschJgRgt 1
4 9 & 11./FschJgRgt 1, majority 2./FschSanAbt 7
5 Stab, NachzZug, 10 & 12./FschJgRgt 1, 2 platoons 13./FschJgRgt 1, 1 platoon 14./FschJgRgt 1
6 Stab/StabsKp. FschJgRgt 1, I./FschJg Rgt 1, 1 platoon 14./FschJgRgt 1

Defensive positions of the defenders:

1 2nd Black Watch
2 Australian 2/4 Inf Btn
3 2nd Leicesters
4 2nd York & Lancasters
5 7th Medium Regiment Royal Artillery (employed as infantry)
6 3-4 Greek infantry battalions

Key:

① Terrain ascending towards the airfield ('East Hill')
② Twin knoll ('Charlies')
③ Karteros depression
〜 Dry water course ('Wadi')

27. Area of operations around Heraklion, Crete – situation during the parachute assault, 20 May 1941

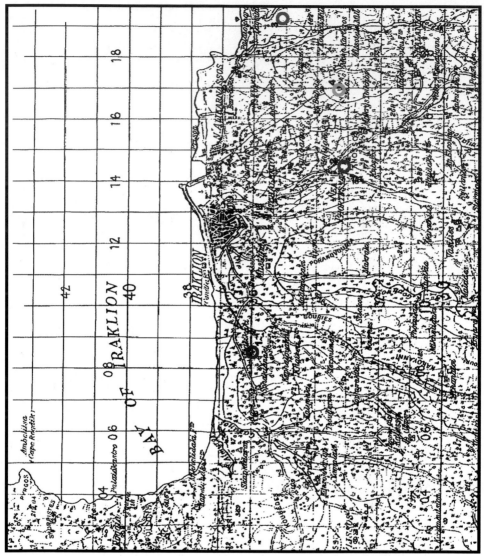

This excerpt from an enemy map (scale 1:100,000) shows the intensive land-use and cut-up terrain around Heraklion.

Key:

1 Main dressing station of 2./FschSanAbt 7
2 British field hospital
3 Karteros depression
4 Hill 296.5

28. Heraklion and its environs (map extract)

the fact that Schmidt's request was taken into account at the command of *Luftflotte 2* and that the decision taken had been passed on as a directive to the command of *Flieger-Korps Putzier*. It is clearly confirmed by the attempts to recall *KG 54* by radio and a last effort undertaken by the operations officer from the staff of *Luftflotte 2*, who had tried to catch up with the formation in a fast Me 108 in order to attempt to convey the decision by short-range wireless, but it came too late. The chances are that a knowledgeable member of the staff of *Luftflotte 2* could have called the directing staff of *KG 54* by telephone in order to pass the decision for the postponement of the air attack in good time. That this did not happen is simply a matter for hindsight.

There is no doubt that complete reliance was placed on the efficiency of remote communications methods from the commands of *Luftflotte 2* and *Flieger-Korps Putzier*, as well as from the directing staff of *KG 54* to the bombers in the air. The establishment of a code word to be passed by radio in the case that *KG 54* was to drop its bombs over an alternate target clearly indicated this attitude. However practical experience had not yet been available in this field. Therefore it had not been taken into consideration that the long aerials of the He 111 were retracted, once the aircraft had formed up for the attack. This no longer allowed communication with them by radio over long distance. As ground-to-air radio communication had also been impossible because of a lack of compatibility with the radio sets between the ground and flying forces, this method of exercising control over the bombers had also been non-existent.

The firing of red signal flares from the ground was to be used as a last resort to prevent the air attack and was agreed upon by the commands of *Luftflotte 2* and *XXXIX.Armee-Korps*. The procedure to date had not been practiced and therefore had not been proved reliable. Standing operational procedures for identification purposes, however, did exist to mark friendly positions and vehicles by swastika flags or colored panels and forward lines to be indicated by white Very lights. Additional procedures such as stationing low-flying aircraft over the target area with their radio tuned to the same frequency as that of the approaching bomber formation, would have allowed the detection of signal flares from the ground and guide the actions of the attack-aircraft respectively, yet this had not been taken into consideration, although the means had been available.

In Rotterdam disaster ran its course. Although only high explosive bombs were dropped by *KG 54* in accordance with its tactical mission, many buildings in the densely built-up target areas quickly caught fire, caused by short-circuits of interrupted electrical cables and by hits to gas pipes and stores with combustible materials. Furthermore a strong wind from the west set more and more buildings ablaze. Despite the numerous bodies of water in the southern part of Rotterdam, the first attempts of the municipal fire brigade to quench the flames were impeded by the lack of efficient firefighting devices. The boats and ships furnished with pumps and hoses mostly lacked the crews to operate them. When the wind in the evening shifted east, the fires then spread to the up to now undamaged old city.

The effects of the air attack on the defenders of Rotterdam were immediately evident. By 1615hrs the destruction of Rotterdam had been reported to General Winkelman by Lieutenant Colonel Wilson, who had returned to Den Haag. During his report a message arrived at the Dutch high command from the garrison commander of Utrecht, who reported an ultimatum for the surrender of the city in the case of its refusal its bombardment was announced. General Winkelman had already approved the surrender of Rotterdam after the receipt of Wilson's report but now considered the options for the defence of Holland with his staff and most important subordinate commanders. However he quickly concluded that a continued defence was hopeless and would only increase suffering of the civilian population. Therefore at 1700hrs his men were directed to lay down their arms and end the fighting.

By 1640hrs Colonel Scharroo had already ordered the ceasefire of his troops and immediately drove to Noordereiland. There, at 1700hrs, he met with *Generalleutnante* Schmidt and Student to offer the capitulation of Rotterdam. He was upset about the fact that the time he had been allowed for his decision was not granted by the Germans. *Generalleutnant* Schmidt expressed his apprehension but stated that he could only offer his deep regrets for the events. At 1800hrs Colonel Scharroo signed the capitulation document. By 2030hrs the first complete German units were moved into the southern quarters of the city north of the Nieuwe Maas which were stricken by destruction and fires. The message concerning the capitulation of Rotterdam was sent by radio from the command post of the *Luftlande-Korps* to the command of *Luftflotte 2*. For reasons unknown it was received not before 2030hrs and was not available in decoded form until 2115hrs.

Earlier in the day Göring had decided to delay the relief of *Gruppe von Sponeck* which had been planned for this day, as he was preparing another massive bombing attack, this time striking the northern part of Rotterdam. The air attack was to be executed at 2030hrs but the renewed bombing of the city was eventually prevented by a radio message from *Generalleutnant* Schmidt at 1855hrs, who reported that the north of Rotterdam was already occupied by his troops.[249] How the bombardment of the north of Rotterdam could have delayed the occupation of the city and the relief of *Gruppe von Sponeck*, need not to be examined here in the light of the actual events.

In the meantime *Generalleutnant* Student had been seriously wounded. *Generalleutnant* Schmidt had tasked Student with the negotiation of the details for the capitulation of Rotterdam. As such Student drove to the command post of Colonel Scharroo which was located in a building in the north-west of the city on the second floor. During the negotiations fighting broke out on the street in front of the building, in which advance elements of the *LAH* had come across a Dutch infantry battalion, which were assembled ready to surrender. In a state of confusion and nervousness both sides commenced fire at each other. When *Generalleutnant* Student stepped to the window of the room in °rdᵉr to get a picture of the situation he was hit in the head by a stray German bullet. Only the skill of a Dutch surgeon, quickly summoned, saved his life. The general later was conveyed to Germany for an operation by a specialist, and in total his recovery took nine months.

On the night 13/14 May the Dutch high command ordered withdrawal of most of the troops from the Grebbe Line to the so-called New Waterline and the ongoing firm retention of the approach into Noord Holland at the closure dike. They appreciated the situation and as such believed this could provide a good chance to successfully continue the struggle for the core area of the country. However, as a prerequisite, Rotterdam had

---

249 The bomber formation tasked with the mission to bomb the north of Rotterdam had taken off at 1900hrs and therefore had not been informed about the contents of Schmidt's radio message. It had, however, been possible without difficulties, to reach the formation shortly after its take-off by radio and to turn it back.

to be held until the anti-tank positions around Den Haag had been established. In order to meet this aim the elimination of the German forces still holding out at Overschie and at Valkenburg/Wassenaar had to be undertaken. Overschie was to be captured by three infantry battalions, reinforced with field guns, anti-tank-guns and heavy machine-guns and under the direction of the commander of the Jager Regiment. An additional battalion from the area around Delft was to act as reserve. Two armored cars with 37mm guns were attached to the attack force.

The start of the attack was scheduled for 0900hrs but was delayed until 1040hrs by obstacles that were erected by the defenders of Overschie and by air attacks, as well as inadequate coordination between the attacking forces. These did not reach the built-up area of Overschie until 1340hrs. The leading battalion which advanced along the old road was successful in driving the Germans back from a mill and a factory toward the interior of the town. The results of the devastating air attack against Rotterdam shocked the attack forces so much that their advance was halted for a while. Nevertheless, until late in the afternoon they were at the northern edges of Overschie. When news about the capitulation of Holland arrived at 1940hrs the attack was discontinued and all task forces retired toward the north. Already by 2200hrs the forward elements of the *LAH* had established contact with *Gruppe von Sponeck*. At this time, the *LAH* was the only German force from *XXXIX. Armee-Korps* that had managed to pass through Rotterdam.

On the morning of 14 May the command of the Dutch 1 Army Corps had ordered renewed attacks by the units around Katwijk and Wassenaar against the German forces holding out in the dunes and in Valkenburg. These attacks were to be directed by the commander of 4th Inf.Rgt. Except for the a few patrols, which were all repelled by the Germans, no determined offensive actions were undertaken during the course of the day. In the afternoon 3rd Inf. Div. ordered an attack against Albertushoeve and Rijksdorp which was to commence at 1940hrs.

The German commander in Valkenburg finally succeeded in reaching an agreement for the evacuation of all females and children and males under 16 and over 60 years of age for the morning of 14 May. For this purpose a ceasefire until 1000hrs was arranged. However as the evacuees, carrying two white flags, approached Katwijk they were stopped by shots in the air from Dutch sentries in front of the village. The Dutch sentries thought that German soldiers, disguised as civilians, were attempting to break into the Dutch positions. It took long-lasting deliberations with the commander of 3rd Inf.Div. before the evacuees were permitted to enter Katwijk.

At about 1740hrs, elements from 4th Inf.Rgt., supported by mortars and anti-tank guns, commenced the advance against Albertushoeve – this was earlier than ordered by 3rd Inf.Div. They succeeded in driving back the German outposts. The directive arrived at the command post of 4th Inf.Rgt., where it was to destroy any documents relating to the defensive positions on the coast and the eastern front of Fortress Holland, as it had now become evident that the end of the struggle for Holland was near. The attack forces in front of Albertushoeve were halted and at 1940hrs the command of 3rd Inf.Div. were instructed about the ceasefire. However the commander of 4th Inf.Rgt. remained unaware of this until 2010hrs, when the message about the capitulation of Holland was passed to him by the territorial command in Leiden. Immediately Colonel Buurman ordered his troops back from the contested areas. The Dutch troops employed in the area of Katwijk-Leiden-Wassenaar in the five days of the war had lost 185 men – all had been in vain.

On the morning of 14 May Dordrecht was handed over to *Oberst* Bräuer as the last Dutch rearguards under Lieutenant Colonel Mussert retired at dawn to the northern bank of the Merwede. The negotiations for surrender were commenced on the night 13/14 May by the mayor of Zwijndrecht with the assistance of two other citizens. Soon the mayor of Dordrecht, who had moved to Papendrecht, joined them. Neither the command of the Light Division nor that of the garrison of Dordrecht participated in anyway at all; therefore the Dutch military representation at the negotiations consisted of a lieutenant colonel, who, by accident, was still present in the town. During its complete occupation, in which parts of *I./* and *III./FschJgRgt.1* had been employed and later been quartered in the town, the remaining groups of Dutch stragglers were captured.

A regimental *Kampfgruppe* from *254.Inf.Div.* had arrived in Dordrecht and in the eastern part of the island in the course of the afternoon was engaged in a few firefights with elements of the Light Division across the Merwede. The attempts made by this *Kampfgruppe* to cross the river failed due to the Dutch defensive fire. The railway bridge west of Sliedrecht was blown-up after the last units of the Light Division had crossed it.

The life of Lieutenant Colonel Mussert was to end on this day in a tragic way. He had established his command post in Sliedrecht upon accomplishment of his mission in Dordrecht. Many officers from the Light Division, and some of those from the garrison troops of Dordrecht, incorrectly suspected him to have supported the Germans in the recent fighting. The captain in charge of the Sliedrecht sector decided to arrest Mussert for a court-martial. Mussert strongly protested against being arrested and as a result the lieutenant who accompanied the captain wounded him with four pistol shots so seriously that he died in hospital shortly after midnight.[250]

On 14 May the Dutch still held the area immediately north of the bridge at Spijkenisse. This area was only occupied by the Germans after the capitulation of Holland. The old fortress of Willemstad, about 12km west of Moerdijk, was attacked at about 1400hrs on 14 May by a patrol from *AufklRgt.9* consisting of eight armored cars. The defence of the fortress rested in the hands of a Dutch infantry company that were reinforced with a few heavy machine-guns. After a first assault against one of the old forts from the east had failed its garrison surrendered and the attack was renewed. After fire was directed against the main fort and German reinforcements arrived the commandant of the fortress surrendered Willemstad at 1620hrs. However the fighting continued for a while as parts of the garrison had not received the surrender instructions. During this time, a number of Dutch soldiers made their escape across the Hollandsch Diep. It was only in the early evening, that the commander of the reinforced patrol reported Willemstad and its surroundings as taken.

---

250 In an examination of the events undertaken by the Germans, the lieutenant had pleaded self-defence and therefore was sentenced as guilty. After the war, he was rehabilitated by the Dutch authorities. Even at that time, treasonable behavior by Mussert was not apparent.

Forces of the southern *Kampfgruppe* from *9.Panzer-Division* were deployed with security-missions west and south of Breda, since the early morning of 14 May they had no contact with French troops, as those in front of them had moved away in the direction of Antwerp. Therefore only elements of *AufklRgt.9* were left in security positions at Zundert and along the Dintel-river near Standaarbuiten. After *II./PzRgt.33* had marched into the area south of Rotterdam in the morning, other parts of *Gruppe von Sponeck* – *I/Schützen-Rgt.11*, the staff of *Schützen-Rgt.11*, one company from *PzAbwAbt.543* and *s.InfGeschKp.701* – followed at 1730hrs and in the evening arrived in and around Barendrecht.

Despite superior numbers the last of the French forces, after a brief engagement with the approaching reinforced *SS Standarte Deutschland* at Bergen op Zoom and Woendrecht, gave up the most western part of Noord Brabant. In the evening forward elements of the *Standarte* gained the Bath line which covered the avenues of approach toward Zuid Beveland and Walcheren and was manned by the Dutch 14th Border Infantry Battalion. The artillery *Abteilung* assigned to the *Standarte* immediately commenced the bombardment of this position.[251]

In spite of the declared capitulation of Holland 339 German prisoners of war, among them a number of soldiers from *Fl.Div.7*, were shipped to England from Ijmuiden on the Dutch steamer *Texelstroom* in the evening of 14 May.[252]

Everywhere in the area of the *Luftlande-Korps*, as on the other fronts on Dutch territory affected by the capitulation, weapons ceased to sound by the evening, whilst the command of the German *18.Armee* issued orders for the complete occupation of Holland and the *OKL* commenced the transfer on Dutch soil of the first flying formations and anti-aircraft troops. The priorities for the command of the *Luftlande-Korps* were the establishment of contact with the isolated groups of *22.(LL)Inf.Div.*, medical care for the wounded and the relief of the exhausted parachute and air-landing forces in the formerly contested areas. A few days after the signing by General Winkelman and *General der Artillerie* von Küchler of the capitulation document in Rijsoord on 15 May, the transfer of the parachute and air-landing troops, initially to assembly areas in eastern Holland and then to their home garrisons was started. As additional employments of these forces in the west had not been planned for, their reconstitution and enlargement was to be undertaken with greater emphasis.

The struggle for the south-western part of Fortress Holland had ended with quite different results for the two major formations employed from the air. It had quickly become apparent that the mission for *22.(LL)Inf.Div.* was impracticable, but *Fl.Div.7* had succeeded in

---

251 The Bath line was taken by the SS troops almost without a fight on 15 May. However the struggle for the province of Zeeland lasted until 27 May.

252 This act rightfully was regarded by the German side as an offense against the Geneva Convention. The examination of this event after the occupation of Holland, however, had not led to serious consequences for the Dutch officer who had commanded this action, as he was able to credibly prove that he had not been informed about the capitulation at this time.

conquering and retaining the three pairs of bridges that were imperative for the thrust of mechanized ground forces from the south into Fortress Holland. There were various reasons for the different outcome of both operations. To analyze them completely and with all their particularities would by far go beyond the purpose of this volume. Therefore only those factors that had a direct impact on the employment of the parachute force during their deployment to Holland will be discussed below.

The preparation for parachute assault by air attack forces

It was the aim of the parachute assaults to surprise the enemy at the objectives to be seized and catch them at a low state of combat-readiness. As a result the plans of attack against Fortress Holland had not foreseen any longer lasting preparatory air attack operations in advance of the actual commitment of the paratroopers. The parachuting was to be conducted toward the end of the first air attacks against the enemy protecting the objectives. Therefore only a narrow time window was available for the bombardment from the air. Moreover, the proportion of air attack forces assigned to *Flieger-Korps z.b.V.* for the neutralization of the seven objectives to be seized had been rather scarce, all the more as a considerable part of them initially had to be employed to fight the Dutch Air Arm. As the task had only been partly accomplished on the first day of the fighting, and the Royal Air Force had also made its appearance on this day, it was impossible to release the majority of the fighters of *Flieger-Korps z.b.V.* for the strafing of enemy ground forces.

The narrow time-window for the preceding air attack operations and the limited numbers assigned had been a hindrance. However the types of assigned aircraft had not allowed for a sufficient weakening of Dutch anti-aircraft forces prior to the arrival of the first air transport formations over the objectives. There are also some indications that the efficiency of the Dutch heavy anti-aircraft guns had been underrated. This proved to be a disadvantage, particularly in the operational area of *22.(LL)Inf.Div.* Although the number of transport aircraft shot down with paratroopers aboard was remarkably low, partly owing to the fact that the Dutch heavy batteries had been stricken by technical problems and many of the anti-aircraft machine-guns were unreliable. Numerous Ju 52s evading anti-aircraft fire had deviated from their course prior to dropping their passengers. The dispatchers, riding in the aircraft with the command elements of the main and sub-units, often lost their orientation over the mostly similar looking terrain and had released their passengers at random.[253] Those of the dispatchers who did attempt to find the predetermined drop zones had not realized that the aircraft were flying 50m per second, causing further disorientation.

It is quite certain that the employment of dive bombers, with their ability to hit point-targets, would have served the purpose of destroying anti-aircraft guns much better than level bombers. However dive bombers had been assigned to *Flieger-Korps Putzier* only in small numbers and for limited periods of time.[254]

The high commands of the *Luftwaffe* and the *Heer* had to accept that the chances of surprising an enemy at an operational level in future combat operations with the use of

---

253   The insufficient training and experience of the dispatchers was self-induced by the parachute force, as these soldiers had very often been detailed to the air transport formation only shortly prior to combat employment. In late 1940/early 1941 *XI.Flieger-Korps* had therefore established a training installation for dispatchers at Freiburg/Breisgau.

254   Serial production of the Ju 87 B had commenced in 1938. In 1939, only 143 had been produced. It had been the production of 603 Ju 87 during the year 1940 that finally allowed for their massive use.

parachute forces had diminished after Holland. Consequently the aspect of fire-preparation from the air now had to be looked at with increased importance.

The outcome of the parachute assaults

At the time the *Wehrmacht* launched its offensive in the West *Fl.Div.7* was still in the process of forming up. For its employment in Holland only four jump-trained parachute infantry battalions, one of them less a company, and one additional company, had been available for parachuting. The formation of *Sturmabteilung Koch* required fully trained personnel to the strength of about three companies. The 50 Ju 52s for the delivery of the assault detachment to its objectives had reduced the air transport avalability for the air-landing troops until the afternoon of the first day of the fighting. As all of the 42 DSF 230 gliders that had been acquired by then had been needed to land *Sturmabteilung Koch* at the bridges across the Albert Canal and Fort Eben-Emael, the command of *Fl.Div.7* was unable to make use of this well-suited transport means to facilitate surprise point-landings of combat teams. The shortage had also deprived the command of the possibility to employ parts of three companies from *II./FschJgRgt.2* in the initial parachute assaults who were not yet jump-trained. The outcome of the fighting for Ypenburg airfield might have been completely different if it had been possible to land glider forces immediately in the rear of the Dutch defenders at its northern edge at the same time as the parachute drop of *I./FschJgRgt.2*. The glider forces could have been used to neutralize those Dutch positions during the initial phase of the fighting which later turned out to be particularly strong, like those at the bridge south of Barendrecht.

All of the parachute units that were tasked with the assault from the air had a common mission. This was to seize the assigned objective undamaged and retain it until the arrival of ground troops. For the first part of the mission they had been organized, armed and intensively trained. There was little practical experience, with the exception of *3./FschJgRgt.1* which had seized the airfield at Stavanger-Sola in Norway by parachute assault and to some extent *4./FschJgRgt.1* after its bloodless parachuting in Denmark. Consequently the leaders of the parachute units were forced to rely on experiences gained during field exercises and on lessons learned during theoretical tactical training. However the advantage of combat experience which was gained by a number of soldiers of *I./FschJgRgt.1* and *I./FschJgRgt.2* during their employment as infantry in Poland and Norway must also be noted. Trusting in the effects of surprise, the morale of all ranks and the superb infantry armament, the command of the *Luftlande-Korps* was convinced that the paratroopers would be able to seize the assigned objectives quickly. In order to forestall counter-measures by the Dutch, the start of the air-landing on all four airfields to be seized was determined 30 minutes after parachuting.

The forces of *FschJgRgt.1* planned for the seizure of the pairs of bridges at Moerdijk and Dordrecht were to accomplish these tasks initially on their own. At short notice they could only be reinforced by the staff and two companies from *I./FschJgRgt.1* which had been determined as the regimental reserve, as all other units assigned to the regiment first had to be landed on Waalhaven on 10 and 11 May.

The evaluation of the parachute assaults in Holland after the end of the operation had shown that some of the determining factors for success or failure had only come up during their execution.

Even in the final phase of planning only scarce knowledge was available about the Dutch forces around the Ypenburg and in Delft and their defensive posture. Relying on the effects of surprise and the fighting value of the paratroopers, the command of the *Luftlande-Korps* nevertheless had believed *I./FschJgRgt.2* was capable of clearing Ypenburg in the calculated time so that the first wave of the air-landing troops could be brought in as planned. The commander of *I./FschJgRgt.2* planned to assault the airfield from three sides and neutralize all of the Dutch forces deployed along its edges within 30 minutes. However this was condemned to fail from the very beginning. The two companies dropped west and south of the airfield had unexpectedly landed in strongly occupied security zones which had been established forward of the actual airfield. There for the greater part they part remained tied up in bitter fighting throughout most of the time determined for the seizure of the airfield, which led to high losses. As the main effort of the Dutch forces along the northern edge of the airfield had not been identified as such, the company which was dropped north of it had not received the mission to attack it. Instead they were ordered to take possession of the bridges across the de Vliet Canal for the thrust of *22.(LL)Inf.Div.* against Den Haag. Dropped widely dispersed and soon coming across numerically superior Dutch forces arriving from Den Haag, the company was forced to defend its position and had been routed in parts. As the plan of attack of the battalion commander simply had not worked at any time in the face of the disposition and aggressiveness of the Dutch forces, his mission was doomed to fail.

The parachute assault of *III./FschJgRgt.1* against the airfield at Waalhaven had played out completely differently, although it was planned in a similar pattern to that against Ypenburg. Its quick success with relatively low losses in personnel had primarily been achieved. The defenders had not factored in the use of airborne or landing troops and neglected a defence plan that included measures to prevent their use. Moreover contingency plans for the support of the airfield were not factored into any regional or national defence plan. One particular weakness of the defence of the airfield was that the commander of III/ JgRgt had neglected to occupy potential drop zones for paratroopers near the airfield and to direct his two companies left aside from its direct defence to conduct *ad hoc* counter-attacks against landing paratroopers without specific orders. The artillery detachment that was quartered in the north-west of Rotterdam and equipped with modern long-range guns was not tasked with supporting the troops defending the airfield from the very beginning of an attack. Therefore *III./FschJgRgt.1* had not only found undefended drop zones but had also been able to assault without delay the Dutch positions directed towards the runways. In summary, the success of the parachute assault against the airfield at Waalhaven, besides the surprise achieved and the determined actions of the paratroopers, was mainly attributed to a failure of defence that was not well reasoned and comprehensively prepared. Had the information available about the employment of German parachute and air-landing forces in Operation *Weserübung* been properly evaluated and passed on, it should have led to the decision to provide more troops for the defence of airfield at Waalhaven. This was particularly so as it had constituted the only installation of this kind in the south of Fortress Holland. These troops would have been readily available from the forces that were kept back in fear of the unlikely threat of amphibious landings by the Germans in Westland and on the island of Putten. Some of their 47mm anti-tank guns that were positioned and well dug-in at the airfield could have caused a similar effect on landing German transport aircraft as the 37mm guns of the armored cars at Ypenburg. The subordination of I Army

Corps and of depot troops under Lieutenant General van Andel had, on the morning of 10 May, brought no immediate improvement for the defence of Waalhaven. It was only after the loss of the airfield and the perceived serious threat to the entire south of the Dutch core defensive area that measures for its retaking were finally considered. The whole of the military potential available to van Andel after the change of command structure still had not been enough. In addition, the unreasonable decision of the Dutch high command to maintain the independence of the garrison of Rotterdam was detrimental to counter-measures. After the second day of fighting in Holland it had kept combat troops to the strength of about a regiment unavailable for Lieutenant General van Andel's use.

The commander of *III./FschJgRgt.1* correctly regarded the quick neutralization of the Dutch ground air-defence in the vicinity of the airfield as a key prerequisite for the landing of transport aircraft. Against air attacks and the effects of long-range artillery, he had to depend on the *Luftwaffe*. Fortunately for him both threats developed only hours after the start of the air-landings, so the actions of his troops had not been disturbed by them. Moreover, as the artillery bombardment was interrupted numerous times, its effects on flight operations had remained within acceptable limits. Acceptable as this situation was for the air-landing of troops on Waalhaven in the early stage of the airborne operation it may have prevented the commands involved from recognizing the full risk of the domination of airfields by the artillery of the enemy in future operations of this kind.

In the parachute assault against the bridges at Moerdijk, the factor of surprise had worked well. Here, the Dutch deployed considerable forces for their protection. Additionally these could depend on a number of heavily-armed large concrete casemates that dominated the bridges. As the command of Group Kil was responsible for the protection of the bridges it regarded the employment of parachute forces immediately after the start of the German attack as unlikely. This was because the lines in the east of Noord Brabant and the agreed-upon occupation of the area Breda/Tilburg by French troops meant an attack by German ground forces from the south had not been anticipated for the forseeable future, and as such the garrison of the bridgehead south of the Hollandsch Diep had not been put into the highest state of alert during the night 9/10 May. This appreciation of the situation, in conjunction with the planned retirement of the Light Division across the traffic bridge at Moerdijk, had also led to the decision to not prepare the explosive charges in both bridges for ignition in order to prevent any unintentional destruction. The only troops under full alert, based on the country-wide order of the night 9/10 May, had been the ground anti-aircraft units at and in the vicinity of the bridges. The heavy 25th Art.Rgt. from Hoekse Waard and I/17th Art.Rgt. from the Beerpolder area on the island of Dordrecht had been planned as support for the troops in the bridgehead. However as the artillery command had been thinking in the terms of support to the situation of Group Kil it had not prepared for rapid support in front of the bridgehead and had not yet established an observation post there.

The well-coordinated elements of *II./FschJgRgt.1* that were tasked with the seizure of the bridges, had been dropped after the end of the preparatory air attack, so that neither the crews of the anti-aircraft machine-gun platoons or the security posts of the infantry, which had taken cover during the air attack, nor the majority of the bridgehead garrison in their quarters, had found the time to meet the assault of the forward shock troops of the paratroopers from their positions. The parts of the garrison which was deployed in a security screen in a semi-circle, some distance forward of the southern ramps of the bridges, was too far away from the initial scene of the fighting and quickly had seen themselves attacked from the rear. The overriding mission of *II./FschJgRgt.1* was to seize both bridges undamaged. Without the bridges the entire operational plan of *Heeresgruppe B* for the attack against Fortress Holland from the south would have been seriously threatened.

Whereas the parachute assault was a complete success and caused relatively low losses, a critical situation had developed south of the bridges in the late afternoon and early evening of 10 May. There the advancing Dutch 6th Border Infantry Battalion had managed to drive back the paratroopers into the original Dutch positions around the southern ramps of the bridges and had forced them to give up all of the previously occupied settlements except Moerdijk. As a result of the late and inaccurately delivered supportive artillery fire from Hoekse Waard the commander of the 6th Border Infantry Battalion had shifted the continuation of his attack to 11 May. The most promising chance to defeat paratroopers, by attacking them at the earliest possible time after landing with all forces in the vicinity of the drop zone and to continuously press home the attack, had not been recognized and consequently was missed. How principles like this had not found their way into the military doctrine of the Dutch ground forces, how sketchy the situation in the south of Fortress Holland was for the commands responsible for its protection and how the insensitive the reaction was from the Dutch higher command after informed about the scope of the German airborne attack became particularly evident in the case of the 3rd Border Infantry Battalion. This unit was initially under the command of III Army Corps and like the 6th Border Infantry Battalion was deployed quite unnecessarily for surveillance toward the Dutch-Belgian border, between Bergen op Zoom and Rosendaal. On the morning of 10 May at 0840hrs and quite some time after the parachute assault against the strategically important bridges at Moerdijk had become known to the Dutch Spui and Kil commands, the battalion had received the order to move, at 1040hrs, into the area around the old fortress at Willemstad. On its way it was to close the obstacles along the small rivers Dintel and Mark. At 1240hrs the forward company and the staff arrived at Willemstad, soon followed by the majority of the unit. By 1440hrs at the latest Group Spui had known about the presence of the 3rd Border-infantry Battalion around Willemstad. At this time it was instructed about the use of the unit for an attack from Hoekse Waard against Waalhaven. At about the same time, or not much later, the command must also have become aware about the advance of the 6th Border Infantry Battalion against the German air bridgehead at the Moerdijk bridges as its support by artillery from Hoekse Waard was being arranged for. However at no time had it taken the opportunity to retake the bridges at Moerdijk which offered itself due to the presence of two quite strong infantry battalions in front of them. Therefore they had taken no action to initiate their concerted attack. Instead it slavishly clung to an order from the command of Fortress Holland, which had disregarded the inter-relations between time and space. For *II./FschJgRgt.1* inadequate information and coordination among the Dutch commands involved in the operations immediately south of the Hollandsch Diep and even more the lack of vigor and initiative of the commanders and staffs on the tactical level, had proved a distinctive stroke of luck, which had saved it from a serious crisis.

The seizure of the bridges at Dordrecht by the paratroopers of the 3rd Platoon of *3./FschJgRgt.1* had been possible by the coincidence of several conditions. The protection of the bridges was made the responsibility of the garrison command of Dordrecht. However this had detailed only small guard elements for this task, at the time of the parachute assault it had only had a few men and moreover had been inadequately equipped with arms and ammunition. Group Kil did not feel competent for the security of the bridges, although it was responsible for all of the island of Dordrecht, except the town itself, and should have been aware of the fact that no Dutch combat troops had been present on the western bank of the Oude Maas around Zwijndrecht. The bravery and resoluteness of the men of the 3rd Platoon from *3./FschJgRgt.1* and those few who had managed to reach the bridges from the drop zone of the majority of this company stands as a good example of their morale. Nevertheless their chances for success would have been limited had they came across combat-ready infantry positioned at the bridges.

Luck was on the paratroopers' side, and the anti-aircraft machine-guns of the two platoons positioned at the bridges could be brought to bear neither against the approaching Ju 52 with with Hoffmann's platoon aboard, nor against the area where it dropped its cargo. Therefore the paratroopers had been able to assemble without losses, quickly pick all but one of their weapon containers and assault the bridges according to plan. The soldiers of the Dutch anti-aircraft machine-gun platoons had been forced to fight as infantry, for which they had neither been trained nor armed.

The retention of the bridges until the arrival of the two parachute companies from Tweede Tol became possible only because the command of the garrison of Dordrecht or that of Group Kil had prepared contingency plans for their retaking. Over the several hours that Hoffmann travelled to the bridges the garrison command of Dordrecht had failed to form a counter-attack force from its 1,600 depot troops. It had concentrated entirely on fighting the paratroopers who had been dropped at the southern edge of the town and endeavored to establish unity of command. This attitude, on the one hand, worked in favor of the paratroopers at the bridges but on the other had accelerated the defeat of the majority of *3./FschJgRgt.1*. The drop zone for this unit was selected in complete ignorance of the strength and dispositions of the Dutch garrison of Dordrecht. Additionally the commander of *3./FschJgRgt.1* had wrongly assessed the enemy and his ability to react immediately after the landing and had decided to first gain freedom of movement along the railway leading to the bridges by an attack, instead of avoiding this probably well protected route. The attempt to realize this decision was thwarted by the unexpectedly stubborn resistance of a platoon of railway engineers and had allowed the Dutch to bring up depot troops of considerable strength to the scene of the fighting. The rest of the engagement at de Polder and its end are well known and require no repetition here. The failure of the Dutch garrison commander to recognize the importance of the bridges at Dordrecht for the coherence of the line along the Oude Maas and to summon his forces for an *ad hoc* counter-attack had been a clear indication that he was overburdened in his function as a tactical commander.

The parachute assaults with one company each against the airfields at Ockenburg and Valkenburg contributed little to their seizure. Mistakes during the approach flight had caused two-thirds of *3./FschJgRgt.2*, who were tasked with the seizure of the airfield at Ockenburg, to be dropped about 10km away from the objective and therefore they were unable to accomplish their mission. The remaining platoon, also landed some distance away, fought for the airfield together with the first airlanded troops. The parts of *6./FschJgRgt.2* that had to seize the airfield at Valkenburg were also dropped inaccurately so that they reached the airfield only at the start of the air-landing. However the temporary blocking of the road from Amsterdam to Den Haag just west of the Oude Rijn had proven to be very efficient. One platoon of *6./FschJgRgt.2* managed to prevent the Dutch from quickly moving additional forces into the threatened areas around Valkenburg and Wassenaar.

In the aftermath it can be said that although the employment of the two parachute companies for the seizure of the airfields of Ockenburg and Valkenburg had, for the greater part, gone astray, it had added to the confusion of the Dutch commands and had tied down forces. Nevertheless it could have led to serious setbacks for the air-landings if the airfields had been better defended.

The abilities of parachute forces to prevail and to persevere

The armament and equipment of the parachute units had been tailored for parachute assault and the temporary retention of seized objectives until the arrival of relief forces from the air or ground. As the techniques to facilitate the drop of heavy weapons were still under development, the paratroopers, beside arms carried along by the individual soldier during the jump, had to rely on the weapons which were dropped with them in containers. These in general included submachine-guns, rifles, machine-guns, light and medium mortars and anti-tank rifles. All weapons which required transport within a Ju 52 had to be provided to them after they had been airlanded. As gliders had not been available for *Fl.Div.7* the option to land at least anti-tank guns in gliders in conjunction with parachuting was also ruled out. With the weapons initially on hand, the paratroopers not only had to prevail in the parachute assault but also had to persevere at their objectives until the arrival of relief forces. Fortunately they had been spared counter-attacks supported by armored vehicles, as these could not be mustered by the Dutch, and the French opposite the Moerdijk air bridgehead had missed the opportunity to turn the situation to their advantage. Nevertheless counter-attacks by armored forces had to be anticipated in future parachute operations against an up-to-date equipped enemy and solutions therefore had to be found to strengthen the anti-tank capability of the parachute units.

With the exception of the parachute assault against Ypenburg the Dutch forces at the objectives had been surprised in a low state of combat-readiness. In order to prevent them from interfering against the assault during its weakest phase – the landing, the gathering of the main armament and the assembly – a high degree of coordination of time and space with the supporting combat aircraft was required. This coordination had worked extremely well in the parachute assault against the Moerdijk bridges, where detailed and accurate intelligence had been gathered beforehand. The air attacks against the forces at the airfields had been handicapped by the requirement to leave the runways undamaged for the subsequent air-landings. For the latter this had no negative effects, as the dispositions of the Dutch forces had been faulty.

According to the principal task of the parachute infantry, three requirements had consistently been met:

First, the requirement of a high number of automatic weapons, as each squad was equipped with two machine-guns with a high rate of fire. These could be handled in combat by one soldier if necessary. In combination with the heavy machine-guns and medium mortars of the heavy weapons company, fire-superiority could quickly be achieved and maintained during forward movement against the Dutch infantry, who in most cases were less well-equipped.

Second, was the high physical fitness of all soldiers. They had volunteered for service in the parachute force and had been accepted only after demanding medical and athletic examinations. Thereafter they received a hard training in infantry combat. Maximum effort was also used to ensure the individual had aggressive spirit.

Third, was the education of the soldier as a fighter, capable of thinking in the terms of the mission and of acting on his own in these terms, should orders fail to arrive. Quite often small combat teams or individual soldiers acting independently, had considerably added to the success of a mission.

Student had not yet considered the employment of the parachute force as a pivotal element in the operational level of warfare or had seen its ability for combined-arms combat. For protection against strong counter-attack the paratroopers remained dependent on heavy weapons or at least on the continuing support of the *Luftwaffe*. Techniques to drop heavy weapons ready for use with parachutes had not yet been developed at the start of the campaign in the West. DSF 230 gliders would have allowed for the delivery of heavy weapons organic in *Fl.Div.7*, although only after some alterations – the anti-tank guns had to be somewhat modified, and the mountain guns had to be dismantled into two. For the air-landing of these weapons loaded into Ju 52s runways of 100m in length were required. However these were rare in the operational area of the *Luftlande-Korps* and first had to be seized. The alternate use of sections of Dutch auto-routes had, as the realities had shown, been risky and had only been possible after sections had been cleared from the obstacles placed on them. The lack of ability of high-angle weapons to properly counteract the more numerous Dutch artillery was a disadvantage throughout the operations of the *Luftlande-Korps*. The limitations in the load capacity of the Ju 52 had not permitted the supply of anything larger and heavier than the 75mm mountain guns. However these sufficed neither in number, nor in range, for counter-battery fire against the medium and heavy Dutch artillery. Despite numerous attempts the combat aircraft of the *Luftwaffe* also never achieved a lasting effect against the Dutch artillery batteries. Attention had to be directed towards overcoming this weakness for future airborne operations, as it would, as events in Holland had shown, reduce the freedom of action of the parachute and air-landing forces employed. A promising solution had been seen in the construction and acquisition of more spacious gliders. This process had already started, but had not yet gone beyond a developmental and trial phase of a few prototypes. Another technical approach started with the development of recoilless guns – because of their reduced weight they could be dropped by parachute from the Ju 52. Both innovations were seen as remedies to the lack of heavy weapons in the parachute units' inventories.

Methods to direct combat aircraft to targets on the battlefield by ground radio had technically been resolved but had not proceeded far enough for use by the parachute units. Therefore, the existing procedure was used. This involved the request for air support being sent by radio from the command of *Fl.Div.7* to the command of *Luftflotte 2*. From there, the request was transferred as missions to *Flieger-Korps Putzier* or other aviation formations. Due to the length of the time required for this procedure the requests had to be sent out well in advance. Close air support in a suddenly and unexpectedly changing situation could only be provided for, if combat aircraft without a predetermined mission had been in the air over the contested area, and had been able to recognize the agreed-upon signs on the ground, requesting support from the air.

The high commands of the *Luftwaffe* considered the established procedures for requesting and directing combat aircraft for ground support as satisfactory, such that even after the end of the fighting in Holland no efforts were undertaken to introduce ground-to-air radio communications for the parachute and air-landing forces.

Final comments

The statement by Student after the war that the success or failure of airborne operations is a very narrow line could also be applied to the employment of the *Luftlande-Korps* in Holland. The failure of *22.(LL)Inf.Div.* to seize Den Haag stood against the successful opening and retention of the entrance into Fortress Holland from the south by *Fl.Div.7*. Here, for the first time, a complete parachute infantry regiment had attacked from the air. Even though its units had parachuted in at different key points along an axis of more than 20km, they had still accomplished their aim at the operational level.

In spite of the knowledge about the existence of a parachute force in the *Wehrmacht*, and although provided with indications about its employment techniques by the command of the Dutch armed forces, the deployed troops had been surprised by the parachute assaults. Nevertheless, the commandant of Fortress Holland together with those of Rotterdam, Dordrecht and Leiden, would have been able to direct troops of far superior strength almost everywhere against the parachuted and airlanded German forces. On the morning of 10 May, about 20,000 troops from the field forces and depots and 60-80 artillery pieces had been available near the objectives attacked. After alterations in command relations on the evening of 10 May, these numbers had grown to about 55,000 men and about 150 artillery pieces although not all of these had been sufficiently close for immediate employment in the contested areas.

The command of the *Luftlande-Korps* had determined eight objectives to be seized by attacks of parachute and air-landing troops. Almost 7,000 men from *22.(LL)Inf.Div.* and the assigned *InfRgt.72* had been airlanded between the morning of 10 May and the late afternoon of 12 May. However most of the troops had succeeded in holding out until the capitulation of Holland. About 3,700 soldiers from *Fl.Div.7*[255] had arrived on Dutch soil, almost 90% on the first day of the fighting.

Except at Ypenburg, the Dutch side had not exploited the excellent force proportion which existed in the operational area of the *Luftlande-Korps* in the window of time between the start of the fighting and the arrival of German mechanized troops for attacks in overwhelming strength. They had used their units piecemeal and often failed in unity of command during their counter-attacks. German air superiority, which had existed from the very beginning of the fighting, cannot be regarded as a major reason for this attitude. It certainly hampered some of the movements of the Dutch ground forces and a few times

---

255   This number derives from the following calculation:
- Four parachute infantry battalions at their war establishment, with around 610 men each (3 companies with 144 men each, a heavy weapons company with about 120 men, the staff and the signals platoon with about 60 men). (For the purpose of this calculation, *6./FschJgRgt.2* has been added to *I./FschJgRgt.1*, which had arrived less one company);
- *II./FschJgRgt.2* with not more than 300 men (air-landed);
- two half-companies of the parachute medical service with a total of 250 men;
- *LuftNachrKp.7* with about 100 men;
- staff and motorcycle platoon of *Fl.Div.7* with about 60 men;
- staff and signals platoon of *FschJgRgt.1* with about 60 men;
- two half parachute anti-tank companies and *FschGeschKp.7* with about 200 men total;
- *Kompanie Moll* with about 120 men.

restricted their combat actions, but had not, as the losses by air attack indicate, reduced their strength. The essential reason for not utilizing the high numerical superiority of the Dutch ground forces for determined early attacks against the air bridgeheads of *Fl.Div.7* was the hesitation of the Dutch high command and the command of Fortress Holland to deal with the threat on hand with all forces available nearby and to disregard for the time being suspected German deployments of additional troops from the air, or from the sea against the Fortress. The initial confusion about the situation which was created by the sudden and unexpected appearance of Germans, together with unclear and contradicting reports from subordinate commands, had contributed to this hesitation. However an early threat against the southern approaches to Fortress Holland had been ruled out. General Winkelman and Lieutenant General van Andel had completely relied on the timely arrival in the area of Tilburg/Breda of the French 7th Army with its impressive fighting strength and high mobility. Moreover the Fortress had also been considered well protected in the east by the planned retreat of III Army Corps and the Light Division, across the Waal and the Nieuwe Merwede. That German *Heeresgruppe B* and the *OKL* counted on a successful thrust of mechanized ground forces through the lines in Noord Brabant, to the bridges at Moerdijk and from there into the heart of Fortress Holland and as a preceding action planned to occupy the axis of Moerdijk-Rotterdam by an airborne operation, had not been conceived as a viable operational approach by the Dutch High and Fortress command.

The protection of Ypenburg was set up on a realistic appraisal of the probable course of a German airborne operation against it and was able to revert to readily available counter-attack forces. Yet both of these prerequisites for success were lacking at the airfield at Waalhaven. The commandant of Fortress Holland had not seen a threat by parachute and air-landing forces in the opening phase of the war; he had placed little attention toward preparations against it himself but had left it to the tactical leaders to act on their own initiative in this regard. This succeeded at Ypenburg, but failed at Waalhaven. With regard to the airfields at Ockenburg and Valkenburg the direct defences had been too weak. However, it was the initiative of tactical leaders in their surroundings which had led to their recapture. In both cases, well-positioned Dutch artillery had prevented the Germans from clearing the airfields of stranded transport aircraft for renewed use.

The decision by the Fortress command to keep back large parts of I Army Corps between Haarlem and Den Haag, in case of amphibious landings from the North Sea or additional airborne operations north of the Oude Rijn, had turned out to be of considerable advantage for *Fl.Div.7*. These forces had remained unavailable for commitment in the south-west of Fortress Holland almost to the end of the fighting.

The intention to retake Waalhaven with a division-size attack across the Noord, supported by offensive actions from Hoekse Waard, resulted from an assessment that it constituted the end of the only naval axis through which the Germans, for the time being, could feed their operations along the Rotterdam-Moerdijk route. It could have become the single most dangerous threat to the accomplishment of the mission of *Fl.Div.7*. However as it had turned out both the plan for the execution of this mission and the quality of the leaders tasked had prevented its realization. The decision for the attack was made on the afternoon of 10 May. The commander of the Light Division, which was to carry out the main attack, had not received a warning order by this time and so had not sped up the movement of his forces, finding them spread out over a distance of more than 25km (up to five marching hours on foot) at the time of receipt of the attack order. This meant that the timing for the attack could not be met. Moreover, an incorrect assessment of the situation at the bridges at Dordrecht by the Fortress command, and a lack of information about this situation by the commander of the Light Division, had induced the latter to send his first battalion across the Merwede. Lack of initiative and daring by this commander also prevented the establishment of a firm bridgehead on the western bank of the Noord during the night 10/11 May and thereby prevented the platform needed for his follow-on forces to attack the airfield at Waalhaven during the course of 11 May.

During its employment in Holland, the German parachute force lost 270 men killed or mortally wounded, totaling about 7.2% of its personnel. About 350-370 soldiers from *Fl.Div.7*, including a few wounded[256] had been shipped to England as prisoners of war, this was between 9 and 10% of its strength. If the ratio of killed to wounded soldiers, requiring treatment is set as 1:2 for *Fl.Div.7*, according to the after-action reports of the units, another about 500 men or 14% of the strength of the employed forces, had been put out of action. Thereby the overall losses in personnel of *Fl.Div.7* at the end of the fighting in Holland can be estimated to be about 30%.

With 309 men killed and probably more than 500 shipped to England and 500 wounded, the losses of *22.(LL)Inf.Div.* were slightly higher than those of *Fl.Div.7*.

The air transport formations had lost 70 of their aircrews killed, most of them during the fighting for the airfields. A number of aircrew, such as fighter pilots and the crews of other aircraft, had fallen into Dutch hands. Altogether about 120 men had also been shipped to England. The permanent losses among the aircrews of transport aircraft were particularly serious, as quite a number of the officers and high-ranking NCOs had been drawn from *Luftwaffe* training installations.

The losses in transport aircraft had been appallingly high. Of the 430 Ju 52s furnished for the airborne operation in Holland, more then 200 were totally beyond repair. Additionally, a considerable number of Ju 52s had been damaged so seriously that they had to undergo lengthy repairs or even had to be cannibalized for spare parts. The renewed employment of the parachute and air-landing forces made it necessary to quickly replace the losses of the air transport arm. The resistance of the Dutch armed forces, except those who still had held out for a short while in Zeeland, those unaffected in the overseas possessions of the Netherlands and those who had escaped to the Allies, had terminated to some degree after the air bombardment of Rotterdam and the announced destruction of Utrecht, after General Winkelman had assessed the overall military situation on the contested Dutch territory as hopeless. The air attack against the defended parts of Rotterdam requested by *Generalleutnante* Schmidt and Student was executed because of a 'fog of battle' at the time. These circumstances were fatal, when the surrender of the city without further fighting was imminent. Its tragic results for the inhabitants and its architecture – about 800 men, women and children were killed, around 80,000 left homeless and more than

---

256 The number mainly derives from the evaluation of the after-action reports of *I./FschJgRgt.2* and of *3./FschJgRgt.1*, as well as from rather detailed researches of the Dutch military historian, Lieutenant-Colonel (ret.) E.H. Brongers, published in *ARMEX Defensiemagazin* May 1984 and *Mars et Historia* May/June 1990. Of the about 370 soldiers from *I./FschJgRgt.2* captured around Ypenburg, 270 had been shipped to England. About 80 men from *3./FschJgRgt.1*, after its defeat at Dordrecht, probably 10 from *Kompanie Moll*, after the emergency landing of their Ju 52 at Werkendam, and maybe a few from *FschSan-Halbkompanie 7*, had shared their fate.

60,000 buildings destroyed – will remain unforgotten. However there can be no doubt that the air bombardment would have taken place anyway if the garrison commander had refused to surrender the city even after the expiration of the expanded ultimatum. From a purely military perspective the termination of fighting in Rotterdam immediately after the air attack and the capitulation of Holland probably saved more lives than those that had been lost in the city by German bombs. Immediately after the end of the employment of the parachute and air-landing forces in the campaign in the West the work on the "lessons learned" by General Student and his staff, pertaining to their future role within the *Wehrmacht* continued, fostered by Göring. Thereby ideas and experiences gained in Holland and Belgium were evaluated. Soon, plans for new missions were to be considered as part of this work.

The deep channel of the Albert Canal on the eastern side of Fort Eben-Emael. The plateau on the upper left part of the photo is the surface of the fort. In the foreground, on the right, is the lock of the Zuidwillems Canal, which leads to Maastricht.

The bridge across the Albert Canal at Kanne was blown up in the face of the landing of *Sturmgruppe Eisen*. The group's report, indicating that the bridge could be used by vehicles following minor repairs, proved to be over-optimistic. The embrasures of Emplacement O, at the foot of the plateau of Fort Eben-Emael, are clearly visible in the background.

Fort Eben-Emael after its capture. This is casemate Maastricht 1 (German designation Werk 12). Behind each embrasure was a 7.5 cm gun. One of the guns was neutralized by *Sturmtruppe Arendt*.

Fort Eben-Emael after its capture. One of the two caponiers which covered the Albert Canal below the fort. They were each armed with one quick-firing gun, three machine-guns and two searchlights. They resisted *Sturmgruppe Granit*, and were later put out of action by troops mopping up.

Fort Eben-Emael after its capture. The revolving armoured turret armed with twin 12 cm guns, Coupole 120 (*Werk 24*), was twice attacked with 50 kg shaped charges. However, they could not penetrate the 28 cm thick armour. The guns, which did not come into action during the assault, were finally put out of action by pushing 1kg demolition charges down their barrels.

Feldwebel Wenzel (with bandaged head) and the men of his Sturmtrupp shortly after the capture of Fort Eben-Emael. Their faces show the strain of the preceding combat.

Some of the men who captured Fort Eben-Emael, photographed shortly after the action. (Bundesarchiv, Bild 146-1971-011-27, photo: Büttner)

Following the completion of his mission, *Hauptmann* Koch reports back to the commanding general of *VIII.Flieger-Korps*, *General der Luftwaffe* Freiherr von Richthofen, at Köln-Ostheim airfield. (Courtesy of Werner Müller)

The western exit of the bridge at Veldwezelt shortly after the end of the fighting, with German motorcyclists moving across it. A bunker, thought to dominate the bridge with its anti-tank gun and heavy machine-guns, can be seen to the left. It was neutralized and seized by men from *Sturmtruppe Ellersiek* during the first assault by *Sturmgruppe Stahl*. The mobile steel fences either side of the roadway blocked the bridge against vehicles.

One of the very effective 75mm anti-aircraft guns used by the Dutch, seen here during a training exercise – over 80 were in service in 1940.

An M 38 Landsverk light armored car, of which the Dutch had procured 24 for their Light Division from Sweden. It had good firepower, with a 37mm gun and three machine-guns. However, its thin armor made it vulnerable.

The bridges across the Hollandsch Diep near Moerdijk, a photo from a few years before 1939. To the left is the road bridge. The highway to Rotterdam was still incomplete in 1940.

The bridges over the Oude Maas at Dordrecht, a photo taken from
the north, over Zwijndrecht. Dordrecht is at the upper right.

The bridges over the Nieuwe Maas, in Rotterdam, seen from the northern part of the
city shortly before the outbreak of war. In the background is the densely-populated
island of Noordereiland. From the right, the Boompjes leads towards the road bridge.

Part of the old port in the north of Rotterdam, east of the railway bridge over the Nieuwe Maas, a photo from the the 1920s. The prominent building in the center is the 'White House'. In the background is the eastern tip of Noordereiland. The buildings along the bank of the Nieuwe Maas just left of the railway were a part of the initial German bridgehead.

The command post of *FschJgRgt.1* at Tweede Tol. The regimental commander, *Oberst* Bräuer, is standing. To the left of him, seated, the *Ordonnanz-Offizier*, *Leutnant* Graf von der Schulenberg. In the background is the railway over the Zeedijk. (Courtesy of A.M.A. Goossens)

A Dutch barracks near Tweede Tol which served as a collection point for German parachutes and supply containers. (Courtesy of A.M.A Goosens)

At Dordrecht, near the eastern exit from the road bridge over the Oude Maas. Officers from *I./FschJgRgt.1*, from left *Stabsarzt* Dr. Müller, *Oberleutnant* Grötschke (*2.Kp.*), *Hauptmann* Gericke (*4.Kp.*). (Courtesy of A.M.A. Goossens)

Troops moving towards the fighting on the island of Dordrecht. They
probably belong to *II./FschJgRgt.2*, which was not jump-trained at the time,
as although they wear jump overalls they are still equipped with regular
Wehrmacht steel helmets and boots. (Courtesy of A.M.A. Goossens)

One of the bunkers in the park of Amstelwijk following its capture
by a *Sturmtruppe* under *Leutnant* Graf von Blücher. The bodies of
two Dutch soldiers killed during the assault can be seen.

The lift bridge across the Oude Maas south of Barendrecht. The area around its southern end remained firmly in Dutch hands until the evening of 13 May. (Courtesy of A.M.A. Goosens)

Some of the Ju 52s destroyed during the attempt to land troops on the airfield at Ypenburg.

The northern outskirts of Valkenburg shortly after the end of the fighting. Destruction caused by Dutch artillery fire can clearly be seen. Rear left is the church steeple – about 100 Dutch prisoners were initially housed in the church until it, too, became the target of Dutch shellfire.

Aerial resupply. The He 111 bomber was capable of dropping 8-10 so-called 'supply bombs' by parachute, each with a load of 250 kg. From a distance, such supply drops were sometimes mistaken by Dutch troops for drops of *Fallschirmjäger*.

Salvaging supply containers could be risky if under enemy fire.

The operations center in the command post of *Fl.Div.7*, in a guest house in Rijsoord, during a conference. *Generalleutnant* Student sits by himself, on the left. The officer standing in front of the map table is the head of the operations section, *Major i.G.* Trettner. (Courtesy of A.M.A. Goosens)

A team from the motorcycle platoon of *Fl.Div.7* attached to its HQ for messenger, escort and guard duties. (Courtesy of A.M.A. Goosens)

Following the end of fighting around the bridges at Moerdijk *Fallschirmtruppe* from *II./FschJgRgt.1* examine a French AMD armored car destroyed in Zevenbergschen Hoek during an air attack late in the afternoon of 11 May 1940. A soldier from the relief force is also with them. (Courtesy of A.M.A. Goossens)

Forward reconnaissance elements from *9.Panzer-Division* reach Tweede Tol at 18.00 hours on 12 May 1940, where they are greeted by the staff of *FschJgRgt.1*. From left, *Hauptmann* Rau (*Adjutant*), *Oberst* Bräuer, *Leutnant* Graf von der Schulenberg.

First contact between men of a *Fallschirmjäger* medical company and a *Pz III* tank from *PzRgt.33* on the island of Dordrecht.

Troops from the *SS Leibstandarte* moving through the devastated and
burning quarters of Rotterdam north of the Nieuwe Maas to relieve
Gruppe von Sponeck at Overschie. (Courtesy of A.M.A. Goossens)

Part IV

The *Fallschirmtruppe* during the time between operations in Holland and the Balkans Campaign

1

Fallschirmtruppe reinforce the defense at Narvik

After attempts by the Allies failed to establish positions in central Norway, blocking the land and sea lines of communication to the German forces that had landed in Trondheim,[1] they directed their attention toward the north of Norway. With the cooperation of the Norwegian armed forces the region was to be retained at all costs. The essential points to hold were the town of Narvik and the ore railway leading from the town to Sweden. Although the landed German task force was still cut off from its land lines of communication and the transport of iron ore from the port to Germany was stopped by interdiction at sea, it had to be assumed that the *Wehrmacht* would quickly seek to link up with the defenders in central Norway and bring to bear superior air assets against the blockading fleet. The early elimination of the German beachhead at Narvik could reduce the urgency behind the German thrust toward this port and buy time for an unmolested build-up of Allied positions in northern Norway. Moreover only the elimination of the German beachhead would generate the opportunity to systematically destroy the ore-loading installations in the port of Narvik and the ore railway up to the Swedish border. The previous plans of the Allies for the occupation from Narvik of the Swedish ore deposits and the ore port of Lulea on the coast of the Baltic Sea,[2] were put aside due to the actual development of the situation.

The landing of German troops at Narvik had primarily been undertaken as an intervention against recognized or assumed threats by the Allies. The terrain and climatic condition of the region beyond the Arctic Circle led to the use of mountain troops for this task. Their number was determined by the transport capacity of the ten destroyers that were assigned for this mission – *GebJgRgt.139* from the *3.Gebirgs-Division*, with its three battalions and units at the regimental level; one platoon from *GebPiBtl.83*, a naval artillery detachment, an advance command of *I./FlakRgt.32* and the battle HQ of *3.Gebirgs-Div.* under its commander, *Generalmajor* Dietl – altogether about 2,000 soldiers. Supplies for the anticipated commitment to this isolated position and some heavy weapons should have reached Narvik on cargo ships and tankers in advance of the task force as these had been sent prior to the start of *Weserübung Nord*. The reaction of British naval forces that were already operating in the Norwegian Sea had partly thwarted German plans. While the mountain troops had been able to occupy Narvik and its hinterland, including the ore railway, with little loss, the supply ships, except one tanker, had been sunk or captured by British naval forces on the way to their destination. Determined actions by British naval units on 10 and 13 April also resulted in the loss of all the German destroyers in the fjords around

---

1   The plan to regain Trondheim – Operation Hammer– was dropped as impracticable already on 20 April 1940.
2   It was Plan Avonmouth. Compare Derry, p.145.

Narvik. However about 2,600 sailors had managed to reach shore and been integrated into *Kräftegruppe Dietl*, mostly as autonomous units under the command of naval officers.[3]

There was no difficulty in arming the naval personnel adequately from stocks of captured Norwegian depots. However they lacked the training and experience for ground combat. Moreover the loss of the supplies had strongly impacted on the sustainability of the entire task force. Remedy of this situation could only be expected by air for the foreseeable future, but only to a limited extent due to the lack of landing sites for transport aircraft required to drop or land reinforcements and re-supply. As transport aircraft could fly round trips from Trondheim only with additional fuel tanks, their loads were reduced respectively. Sea planes would allow supplies and personnel to be landed in the fjords around Narvik, but they had an even further reduced load capacity because of their specific construction. Moreover the extremely unstable weather conditions in northern Norway prior to the start of the Arctic summer had not allowed for regular flight-plans. The presence of British combat aircraft also proved to be quite troublesome. Operating from aircraft carriers the British could appear in the airspace over Narvik very suddenly. As amphibious operations by the Allies threatened Narvik directly they had not been undertaken immediately after the success against the German destroyers. *Generalleutnant* Dietl, who was promoted to this rank after the successful landing of his task force, was able to initially concentrate his efforts toward the north. Here the troops of the Norwegian 6th Division, which had been mobilized or brought along from the Finnish border, appeared in considerable strength. The German commander therefore decided to deploy only one of his mountain infantry battalions – *II./GebJgRgt.139* – together with some naval troops, and a few salvaged or captured heavy weapons for the defense of Narvik. He ordered the commander of *GebJgRgt.139*, *Oberst* Windisch, to defend the desolate and rugged terrain in the north with a task group, composed of *I.* and *III./GebJgRgt.139* and some supporting naval units. The use of *I./GebJgRgt.139* in *Gruppe Windisch* became possible after the remainder of the garrison of Narvik had withdrawn toward the south-east, and been neutralized by this battalion.

The operational area around Narvik displayed many peculiarities that were previously unknown to the command of the task force and its troops. The town, located at the eastern end of the Ofot Fjord which stretched about 60km inland from the Vest Fjord, had developed from an unimportant settlement of fishermen into a community of several thousand inhabitants, after the significance for the export of iron ore deposits from around Kiruna in Sweden was recognized at the turn of the century. For this reason, a port was sought which was free of ice throughout the year.

About 10km west of Narvik the Ofot Fjord, like the stretched-out fingers of a hand, split up into four smaller fjords; the Herjangsfjord toward the north-east, the Rombakenfjord toward the east, the Beisfjord toward the south-east and the Skjomenfjord toward the south. Located on a rocky peninsula between the Beisfjord and the Rombakenfjord, Narvik proper was made up of two distinctively different parts. The quarter of Frydenluns on the peninsula at Framnes, with its rocky edge dropping steeply down about 100m into the Ofot Fjord, was covered with typical Norwegian houses built of wood. Beyond the peninsula stood the administration and business buildings, mostly built of stone and concrete. On

---

3   The seizure of Narvik is covered by a number of sources, such as Rohwer-Hümmelchen, Derry and Ziemke. The course of the fighting at Narvik, based on war diary entries of participating commands and units is quite correctly depicted by Buchner.

the beach of the large natural basin in the south of the peninsula an ore-crushing work and a loading pier had been constructed. The latter, with a length of about 400m, offered space for the mooring of ships of any size. Immediately east of the town the bare elevation of the Taraldvikfjell (477m) rose steeply. Behind it, across the entire width of the peninsula, loomed an almost impassable mountain range with the Fagernessfjell (1,270m), the Rombakstötta (1,243m), the Beisfjordtötta (1448m) and the Middagsfjell (818m) as the highest elevations. At the southern edge of this mountain range only a narrow road led inland along the steep northern bank of the Beisfjord. However the slopes descending to the southern bank of the Rombakenfjord provided room for the ore railway. From the port area of Narvik, it covered a distance of almost 40km, initially on the rocky southern slopes of the Rombakenfjord and at its narrow end the Rombaksbotn. From there it swung north and, after circumventing the high ground near the Björnfjell, turned to the east to the Swedish border which, as the bird flies, was only 30km from Narvik. Constructed in the year 1902 the single-track electrified railway[4] continuously climbed about 600m from the port, through a number of tunnels and across several bridges to the Swedish border. Along the second half of the line, a number of small settlements had grown up at the train stations of Sildvik, Hundalen and Björnfjell. Just east of Hundalen an almost 50m high bridge traversed the Norddalen.

The only tolerable road connection from the north led from Tromsö, 250km away via Bardufoss and along the eastern bank of the Hejangsfjord to the entrance of the Rombakenfjord. From here a car ferry operated to Narvik. The only additional road connection into the greater area of Narvik led from Trondheim, about 600km to the south, via the port of Bodö which was 200km away, to the Beisfjord. This road, however, was intersected by several fjords, which could be crossed only by ferries.

Where the steeply descending rocks had offered some space at the banks of the fjords, such as at the entrances to the Beisfjord and the Rombakenfjord opposite of Narvik, small settlements with a few buildings, their inhabitants mostly earning their living from the sea, had grown. A denser chain of settlements had developed along the northern and eastern banks of the Herjangsfjord, which stretched out north of Narvik to the north-east. The interior of the region up to the Swedish border, except the small settlements along the railway, was uninhabited. The terrain in the hinterland of Narvik was characterized by elevated plateaus with bare rocky summits (Norwegian designation: fjell) formed by the movement of glaciers during the Ice Age. Mostly around 600m high, these were grouped closely together and separated by depressions which contained small lakes and brooks. At the start of operations, the elevations were still covered with some deep snow. Protection against fire could only be found by hiding behind solitary rocks, piling up rubble or building snow-walls. The small birch woods in some of the depressions, with the thin stems of their trees, offered only very limited possibilities to obtain timber for the construction of field positions.

The situation of the troops deployed on the open ground was further impeded by the bad weather conditions. In May the nighttime temperature dropped below freezing. Snowfall, sopping-wet sleet, icy fog and frequent strong winds prevented the clothing of the soldiers in the field ever drying. Movements through the rugged, snow-covered terrain lasted endlessly and sapped away the strength of the men who rarely were fed adequately.

---

4   After the electricity plant near Troeldal was destroyed by naval gunfire, the Germans made use of some steam locomotives to maintain the rail traffic.

It was therefore only by utilizing all the resources available in the operational area and through the utmost care of the leaders, that the combat-effectiveness of the troops could be maintained to the greatest possible extent. Nevertheless, in the face of the critically developing situation in early May the mission of *Kräftegruppe Dietl* appeared to be greatly endangered if reinforcements of personnel, the provision at least of combat-essential supplies, and early relief were not brought to bear. The fact that on 23 April neutral Sweden had permitted the transfer by train of a few cars containing clothing and medical material, accompanied by thirty signals soldiers in civilian attire, was a fortunate event. During the return trip of the train a number of highly specialized personnel of the *Kriegsmarine* were brought back to Germany. The change in light conditions was to the advantage of the resupply flights as May marked the beginning of the Arctic summer and transport aircraft could now approach the area around Narvik in the hours of night and drop soldiers and material. These conditions, however, also added to the difficulties of combat operations as the enemy now also used the night for movements and attacks, meaning that the troops in the field positions almost never found time for a fitful rest.

The intention of the Allies to take the area around Narvik into their own hands in cooperation with Norwegian forces in northern Norway, became obvious with the landing during 14-18 April of the British 24th (Guards) Brigade, and numerous support troops into the small port of Harstad on the island of Hinnoya, about 40km north-west of Narvik. The proposal by Admiral of the Fleet, the Earl of Cork and Orrery, who since 20 April was responsible for operations against Narvik, to use these troops for a *coup de main* against the town, had not been followed by Major General Mackesy who commanded the ground forces. The hopes of Admiral Lord Cork to achieve the surrender of Narvik after a bombardment by his fleet, which included the battleship *Warspite*, and subsequently landing a battalion there, had also come to nothing, as the effects of the bombardment had been assessed as too ineffectual. A part of the Norwegian 6th Division, which had attacked from the north simultaneously with the bombardment, had succeeded in occupying the area around Gratangen, at the end of a fjord of the same name and about 30km north of Narvik. A German counterattack on 24 April, however, led to the shattering of one of the two Norwegian battalions committed and to the retaking of Gratangen.[5]

After the arrival of the 27e Demi-Brigade of the French mountain troops (Chasseurs Alpins) with three battalions and two companies of light tanks,[6] commanded by General de Brigade Béthouart, on 27/28 April further troops followed – the 13e Demi-Brigade of the French Foreign Legion with two battalions on 5 May and the Polish Mountain Brigade[7] with four battalions on 9 May. After a hesitant start to their relationship, Admiral Lord Cork and Major General Mackesy agreed upon a new plan. They planned to attack

---

5   These descriptions, as do most of those about later events on the Allied side, strongly lean upon the report of Admiral of the Fleet, The Earl of Cork and Orrery, to the British Admiralty, in which the reports of Lieutenant General Auchinleck and Major General Mackesy were enclosed.

6   These were the 342e and 343e Companie Autonome de Chars with 15 Hotchkiss H 39 and 15 Renault FT 17 tanks. Not all of these vehicles, however, were employed.

7   This formation, with its Polish designation Brygada Strzelcow Podhalankich, commanded by the Polish Colonel Bohusz-Szyszko, was only by name a mountain brigade. Most of its officers and non-commissioned officers had escaped to France after the defeat of Poland. Its lower ranks were mainly made up of Polish miners, who before the war worked in France.

the area held by the Germans from two sides in cooperation with the Norwegians. On 28 April two battalions of French mountain troops, reinforced with artillery and three tanks, were brought ashore near Sjövegan, about 20km north of Gratangen. On 1 May one of these battalions, advancing toward the south in the valley of Labergdal came across German outposts, but failed to establish contact with the 7th Brigade of the Norwegian 6th Division,[8] which had moved forward further to the east. For the attack against the German beachhead from the south the 1st Battalion South Wales Borderers from the 24th (Guards) Brigade reinforced with artillery, was brought across the Ofot Fjord to Hasvik, on the peninsula between the Skjomenfjord and the Beisfjord. Here it was joined by the 3rd Battalion of the French 27e Demi-Brigade. However the occupation force contented itself chiefly with securing the area around Hasvik. This allowed the Germans to succeed in regaining the village of Ankenes and the elevation just south of it, with *6./GebJgRgt.139* which had been ferried across the Beisfjord. It was only after the arrival of the Polish brigade on 14 May that the Allied offensive commenced from the south, initially with three Polish battalions that were brought to Haarvik.

On the northern flank of the front, the offensive was unleashed on 12 May. With fire support from British warships the 13e Demi-Brigade of the French Foreign Legion, with five tanks and twelve guns assigned, landed during the night 12/13 May on the northern and north-eastern banks of the Herjangfjord. Against the inexperienced men of *Marine-Bataillon Kothe* they quickly occupied the area around Bjerkvik and Elevgaarden on 13 May and with forward elements advanced along the coastal road to Øjord, at the entrance to the Rombakenfjord opposite Narvik. Along the northern sector of this front, the Norwegian troops that were well accustomed to Arctic conditions and appropriately equipped, attacked on 12 May and pushed back the opposing *Kampfgruppe* under the commander of *I./GebJgRgt.139*, *Major* von Schleebrügge. Additionally task *Gruppe Windisch* was threatened in its rear by the landings in the Herjangsfjord and on its left flank by the battalions of the French 27e Demi-Brigade. Accordingly it was ordered to fall back onto positions along the line Mebyfjell (south of Elevgaarden)-Lake Fiskloes-Lillebalak (572m)-Kobberfjell (914m)-Kuberget (820m). During the withdrawal to this line the troops lost most of their supplies and heavy weapons. This withdrawal enabled the 27e Demi-Brigade to further advance toward the south from the area around Gratangen and link up with the 13e Demi-Brigade around Bjerkvik.

The start of the offensive by the Allies was accompanied by considerable changes in their command structure and task organization. On 13 May, Lieutenant General Auchinleck assumed command over all British ground and air forces in Norway, under the new designation North-Western Expeditionary Force. At this point Major General Mackesy was relieved of his command and replaced by General de Brigade Béthouart who was given command over all Allied ground forces deployed in the area around Narvik.

After the Allies had surrendered central Norway and further resistance by Norwegian troops was unlikely, a few independent British companies were brought in with the task of blocking the road from Trondheim to the north, between Mo I Rana and Bodø. Soon, they were reinforced with elements of the 24th (Guards) Brigade from Harstad. After Lieutenant General Auchinleck had taken over command he made the decision to employ the entire 24th (Guards) Brigade and some support troops for the occupation of the port of

---

8   The command of 6th Div, had formed the 6th and 7th field brigades. Each consisted of two infantry
     battalions and an artillery battery.

Bodø and the blocking of the coastal road. The transfer of these forces was initiated without delay, so that by the start of the offensive at Narvik on 12/13 May no British combat troops remained.[9] In Maalsevdal the king and the government of Norway had found quarters and close by in Tromsø the build-up of a base for the Allies also commenced.

After the decision was made to retain the area around Narvik despite the efforts of the Allies to retake it, *Gruppe XXI* received the mission, in conjunction with the newly-created *Luftflotte 5* (*Generaloberst* Milch) to make use of all means in order to enable *Gruppe Narvik* to hold out.[10] Until its relief on the ground the mission had to be accomplished exclusively by air, as reinforcing and resupplying it by sea had proved impossible due to the large presence of Allied naval forces in the sea regions opposite central and northern Norway. By reason of the force ratio after the landings of the Allies and of the dismal climatic conditions it was out of the question to seize the nearest airfield at Bardufoss, about 80km north of Narvik.[11] Consequently, the air-landing of troops and material became impossible. Reinforcements and supplies to sustain *Gruppe Narvik* had to be delivered by means of air drops or by sea plane.

The execution of these tasks immediately caused major problems for the commands of *Gruppe XXI* and *Luftflotte 5*. Many of the flying formations, including all except two of the air transport groups, had already been removed for the attack in the West. Moreover, most of the transport aircraft that remained in Norway, as a result of their limited range, could only reach the area around Narvik from the base at Trondheim. Even from there, it was only possible for the Ju 52 and only if additional fuel tanks were applied. This requirement reduced their load capacity so only ten paratroopers could be taken aboard. Better suited, because of their larger range, were the scarce, but obsolete, Ju 90. They were primarily used for cargo flights. Flying boats with an adequate loading capacity, such as the Do 24 and Do 26, could be employed but only in very small numbers, as these aircraft with their extended range were required for their major role of reconnaissance over the sea. Fortunately, a pronounced threat to the own flight movements by Allied air forces had not yet developed in the air space over Narvik, as the deep snow prevented them from using the airfield at Bardufoss. Furthermore the Blackburn Skua planes, operating from the aircraft carrier *Ark Royal* in the Lofoten Sea, only had limited capabilities as fighters. A considerable threat, particularly for the sea planes landing in the fjords, however, was seen in the strong anti-aircraft capability of British warships. Nevertheless sea planes had succeeded in landing the *3./GebJgRgt.138* and an anti-tank gun from *GebPzAbwAbt.48* by 7-10 May for the loss of but one of their numbers.

Almost no chance was seen for the possibility to quickly drop parachute troops in adequate strength in order to counter the critical situation of *Kräftegruppe Dietl*, as all of the fully trained units of this kind, as of 10 May, were engaged in the West. The only uncommitted paratroopers that remained were those who had been liberated from Norwegian captivity on 5 May after their unfortunate mission at Dombås. These were quartered in Oslo and were not particularly physically fit. Nevertheless these were now

---

9   The transfer of 24th Brigade lasted until 20 May, when the Polish troop transporter *Chorbry* and the British cruiser *Effingham* had been lost. During 29-31 May the troops deployed around Bodø had to be evacuated, as German relief forces for Narvik had approached and the *Luftwaffe* had attacked vigorously.

10   *Gruppe Narvik*, which on 14 May was placed directly subordinate to the *Wehrmacht* high command (*OKW*), was returned to the command of *Gruppe XXI*.

11   This was foreseen in the initial operation plan for *Kräftegruppe Dietl*.

planned for immediate parachuting as reinforcement for *Gruppe Narvik*.[12] On 10 May the replacements for the paratroopers who had been killed or seriously wounded at Dombås, as well as the provision of jump equipment for the entire company was arranged for. On 11 May 35 men from the *FschJgErgäzungs-Btl* in Wittstock and their jump equipment arrived in Oslo. The company was now armed from the stocks of *Gruppe XXI* and organized into a HQ section, five heavy machine-gun teams, three parachute infantry platoons, and a signals platoon. On 12 May at 1300hrs the HQ section, the heavy machine-gun teams and two squads of paratroopers (from *1./FschJgRgt.1*), under its new leader *Leutnant* Becker, were flown to Trondheim. Bad weather had prevented take off until 14 May at 0800hrs. At 1145hrs the paratroopers, three officers and 63 other ranks, were dropped 400m north of the station at Björnfjell in the vicinity of the command post of *Gruppe Narvik*. The drop zone was so small that only three men from each aircraft could jump in one approach.

In the meantime the situation of *Kräftegruppe Dietl* took a turn for the worse. Along its northern front Norwegian troops had maintained their pressure. Particularly in the Kuberget sector, where *1./GebJgRgt.139* was deployed as the principal unit of *Gruppe von Schleebrügge*, an attack by superior Norwegian forces was expected every hour. On the peninsula between the Herjangsfjord and the Rombakenfjord the enemy had taken firm hold of the area around Øjord and had also pushed forward to the south, with advance elements from the area west of Hartvik (east of Elevgaarden) in the direction of Mebyfjell. Here *3./GebJgRgt.138* had to be inserted quickly after it had been landed by sea planes. The warships which were entering the Rombakenfjord almost every day kept Narvik and its outer positions along the southern shore of the fjord under constant naval gunfire. This was causing further damage in the town and losses among the defenders. At the southern flank of the front, at Ankenes, *6./GebJgRgt.139* came under pressure from Polish troops who were attacking there, after a counter-attack by *7./GebJgRgt.139* had failed with considerable losses.

Gruppe von Schleebrügge, defending the sector at the Kuberget, reported that a large-scale attack by the Norwegians was imminent. As such the paratroopers, under *Leutnant* Becker, who had just assembled after parachuting, were ordered to march to this sector around noon. With completely inadequate equipment for mountain warfare – even greatcoats and rucksacks were missing – the force immediately set out and arrived at about 2330hrs in the camp at the base of the Kuberget range, which rose in front of them to heights between

---

12   It is rather incomprehensible that reinforced *1./FschJgRgt.1*, after its liberation, was not immediately transferred to Germany, in order to join the ranks of their fellow paratroopers in the operation against Holland. This measure would have been the most logical one as the number of jump-trained paratroopers for employment against Fortress Holland had been shockingly low, so that *Generalleutnant* Student was obliged to form a last reserve even from jump-trained personnel of the parachute school and the *Fallschirmjäger-Ergänzungs-Bataillon*. In this context a view by *Major* (ret.) Mößinger, who served as a *Leutnant* in *1./FschJgRgt.1* at Dombås and Narvik is of interest. He suspected that the company had not been transferred back to its battalion to avoid unrest among the fellow paratroopers because of the events which led to their unlucky employment at Dombås. The fact that in his memoirs by Götzel Student dedicates but two pages to the involvement of paratroopers in the battle for Narvik, could well mirror his uneasiness in this matter.

790 and 860m. Requested to hasten their pace, the soldiers left behind what little baggage they carried along, including the blankets they had been issued in Björnfjell, and climbed up to the positions of the mountain troops. They arrived at 0100hrs and were informed that the attack had been beaten off. Exhausted and without warmth-preserving equipment – the baggage left back at the landing site had disappeared – the paratroopers took over the positions assigned to them, mostly in cracks between boulders, behind stone walls and in snow-holes. At dawn they realized that the Norwegians were opposing them from commanding positions higher up.

At 1100hrs on 16 May the Norwegians attacked again. During the fighting which lasted for twelve hours, they succeeded in seizing Height 794, about 1.5km west of the Kuberget, that was occupied by two heavy machine-gun teams and a squad from *1./ FschJgRgt.1*. Further advances by the enemy, who was highly mobile with ski equipment and heavily supported by artillery and mortars, were blocked.

On this day, the signals platoon assigned to Becker parachuted in with 22 men at Björnfjell. It was planned to bring the platoon in on 15 May. During the approach flight along the coast, the Ju 52 with the platoon aboard encountered the anti-aircraft fire of Allied warships in front of Narvik and was forced to turn back. Despite the fire from Swedish anti-aircraft guns, the approach flight along the Norwegian-Swedish border had gone well. According to its training and equipment the platoon being employed by *Generalleutnant* Dietl was to establish and maintain radio and wire communication from his command post. The platoon leader, *Oberleutnant* Gerhold, was made commander of the drop zone.[13]

On 18 May, the remainder of reinforced *1./FschJgRgt.1*, *Leutnant* Mößinger and 74 men with 12 light machine-guns, was dropped at Björnfjell and immediately marched to the Kuberget. There, the paratroopers and mountain troops on 17 May had retaken Height 794 in a counterattack. The location was subsequently occupied by a company of sailors. However as the Norwegians had resumed their attack against the Kuberget on 18 May and had been beaten off only by great effort, the situation there remained very critical.

After the arrival of the paratroopers under *Leutnant* Mößinger, on 19 May *1./ FschJgRgt.1* took over the sector at the Kuberget. The worn-down *1./GebJgRgt.139* was withdrawn from the lines – it had lost in action 13 killed, 25 wounded, 27 missing besides 7 seriously ill. The width of the sector required the deployment of all three parachute infantry platoons abreast. The equipment left behind by the departing mountain troops, like blankets and tarpaulins, made the stay on the rocky, snow-covered ground somewhat more acceptable. However, to bring forward across the rugged terrain, even the minimum amount of ammunition, rations, water and timber, took great effort. Observed high-angle fire almost continuously hit the positions of the paratroopers, and enemy snipers were always lurking for targets. Losses therefore were unavoidable: 3 paratroopers were killed and several others, among them *Leutnant* Mößinger, wounded. Nevertheless, the morale of the soldiers of *1./FschJgRgt.1* remained unbroken despite the bitter experience at Dombås. When, the enemy landed troops on the northern bank of the Rombakenfjord at Troedal during the early morning of 21 May, and advanced with them toward the east, where the Lillebalak could only be held after a desperate counter-thrust and when the Kobberfjell was seriously threatened. *Generalleutnant* Dietl decided to take back the entire northern

---

13   In this function, Gerhold had done well. He had, for example, succeeded in reducing the high loss-rate of dropped containers with mortar ammunition to about 5 %, after he had found out that these were overloaded at the resupply base.

front. The new defensive line was to run along the Stornelven Valley, climbing from the Rombakenfjord toward the north-east, along the southern edges of the two Jern lakes, along the Holmelven Valley, including Point 620, north of Lake Holm, and from there to the Swedish border.

As part of the withdrawing task *Gruppe Windisch*, *1./FschJgRgt.1*, unobserved by the enemy, abandoned the Kuberget and fell back to its new sector located along the Holmelven brook, almost at the end of the right flank of the new line. It made use of the northern elevations of the Rundfjeldet massif (726m), which offered good fields of fire for the machine-guns. On the right of the paratroopers, up to the Swedish border, *3./GebJgRgt.138* (up to now the reserve of *Gruppe Narvik*), had been inserted. It was reinforced by a platoon of sailors.

On 23 May *1./FschJgRgt.1* moved back into the new line, establishing outposts in front of the main line of defense. As the enemy did not follow up initially, the company used the time from 24 to 27 May unhindered, for the construction of field positions and shelters. For the first time, German combat aircraft made their appearance over the sector and attacked the Kuberget several times, dropping bombs.

In the southern part of the operational area the situation of *Gruppe Narvik* quickly deteriorated. Enemy artillery, setting up positions at the tip of the peninsula between Herjangsfjord and Rombakenfjord as well as daily naval gunfire at Narvik and against the positions along the southern bank of the Rombakenfjord, indicated that an attack against the town from the sea was imminent. At Ankenes, where *II./GebJgRgt.139* had to replace its worn-down 6th Company by the 8th Company, the pressure of Polish units and French mountain troops was increasing.

Although the holding of the German beachhead became increasingly threatened, its defenders were made aware of various actions by higher command that they had not been written off and the landing of reinforcements was regarded as a priority. The intention of the German high command to resolutely continue the struggle for the area around Narvik became particularly evident when on 23 May at 2245hrs an officer and 65 other ranks from *2./GebJgRgt.137* were dropped by parachute at Björnfjell. On the next day, at 2200hrs, 55 soldiers from *1./GebJgRgt.137* followed by the same method. On 25 May at 1000hrs and 1900hrs, one more officer and 53 men from both mountain infantry companies also parachuted in.[14]

Of even more importance for the survival of *Kräftegruppe Dietl* was the decision by high command to send additional *Fallschirmtruppe* to Narvik. On 21 May, only two days after the return of *I./FschJgRgt.1* from Holland, the operations staff (Ia) of the commander-in-chief of the *Luftwaffe* had ordered the battalion to be combat ready by 24 May, for commitment by *Luftflotte 5* at Narvik.[15] Hastily *I./FschJgRgt.1*, with its new 1st Company under *Oberleutnant* Fischer, was filled up with soldiers from the *Fallschirmjäger-*

---

14   108 volunteers from *1./GebJgRgt.137* under *Oberleutnant* Schweiger and 113 from *2./137* had received a short jump-training lasting eight days at the parachute school in Wittstock. As the mountain soldiers, despite their marginal training, had only two injured during the landing, the training time for the men of the parachute force was soon also reduced.

15   Student states that Göring had ordered the employment of the entire *FschJgRgt.1* and a parachute battery. This statement, which differs from the publications of a few other authors, must be considered as correct, as shortly prior to the end of the fighting in Narvik the transfer of *II./FschJgRgt.1* had been initiated.

Ergänzungs-Bataillon and other units, before receiving the missing complement of its equipment. From 24 May on the battalion, which totaled 25 officers and 735 other ranks[16] and commanded by *Hauptmann* Walther, was transferred in three groups to Trondheim. *Gruppe A* was transferred by rail to Ålborg and from there by air transport; *Gruppe B* by rail to Frederikshavn from there by sea transport to Narvik and air transport; *Gruppe C* by air transport via Oslo. Inclement weather hindered the movements by air so all parts of the force were not assembled in Trondheim until 30 May. On the way to Trondheim, a Ju 52 was shot down by Norwegian anti-aircraft weapon near Rena, in the southern part of the Østerdalen,[17] causing the deaths of the aircrew, and from *I./FschJgRgt.1 Oberleutnant* Eckleben, the battalion's administrative officer and nine other ranks.

On 26 May, first elements of *I./FschJgRgt.1* – three officers, including *Hauptmann* Walther, and 63 other ranks – were dropped at Björnfjell by nine Ju 52s. During the approach flight, the aircraft with the commanding officer of *2./FschJgRgt.1, Oberleutnant* Tycska and nine other paratroopers aboard, was attacked and destroyed by British Gladiator fighters[18] near Sulitjelma, about 75km east of Bodø. All ten men managed to leave the crashing aircraft by an emergency jump, but this left two of them injured on landing. After a few days marching seven of these paratroopers were able to establish contact with German troops advancing toward Bodø. *Oberleutnant* Tycska and the two injured men were released by the Norwegians after a short captivity.

Bad weather and the lack of transport aircraft prevented any further delivery of paratroopers into the contested area around Narvik until 28 May. On this day, 46 men were dropped. Again, the aircraft were attacked during the approach flight by British Gladiators, this time over the Saltdalen Valley, south-east of Bodø. One of the planes, with ten paratroopers aboard, was set ablaze. Five of the men were able to leave the crashing Ju 52 by an emergency jump. The others, together with the aircrew, lost their lives in the crash. Another Ju 52 of this formation was also badly damaged by the fire of the Gladiators. Returning to Trondheim it clipped a mountain on the way but was able to conduct an emergency landing. Its passengers, *Leutnant* Schmelz and the HQ section of *3./FschJgRgt.1* as well as the aircrew, remained unscathed and, after two days, managed to reach troops of the *2.Gebirgs-Div.* on their way to Narvik.

On the next day at 0445hrs, Ju 52s dropped two officers and 63 other ranks near Björnfjell and a further 61 men, all from *I./FschJgRgt.1* at about 2230hrs.[19] Although the command of *Luftflotte 5* had recognized that the enemy now was operating in the airspace

---

16   This strength, taken from the battalion's after-action report, is considerably higher than that for Holland. Reasons are probably that the heavy weapons platoons of the rifle companies were brought up to regular parachute platoons and that at least parts of the battalion train (29 motor vehicles are mentioned in the after-action report) had been taken along.

17   Obviously, some Norwegian troops were still present and active in this region despite the fact that German forces had moved along the Østerdalen on their way to Trondheim during April.

18   The intercepting Gladiators were from 263 Squadron, which had been brought along from England on the aircraft carriers *Furious* and *Glorious* together with 46 Squadron (Hurricanes). 263 Squadron was operating with 14 Gladiators from the airfield at Bardufoss since 23 May. The after-action report of this squadron, as well as that of *Leutnant* Keuchel from *4./FschJgRgt.1* and the war diary of *Generalleutnant* Dietl confirm the date of the loss of this Ju 52, whereas the action-report of *I./FschJgRgt.1* erroneously states 25 May.

19   The available sources provide no information about the units of these paratroopers. The after-action reports, however, allow for the assumption that it was reinforced platoons from the 3rd and 4th companies.

above Narvik with Gladiators and even with the efficient Hurricane fighters,[20] no escorts from Me 110s had yet been made available for protection of the air transport.

Neither the defenders of Narvik, nor any of the German high commands at that time, had any idea that the time for the entire landing force of the Allies was running out. The high-flying plans of Lieutenant General Auchinleck, to retain northern Norway by means of the requested reinforcements, came to nothing. On 24 May a directive from the British chiefs of staff arrived by teletype, ordering all Allied troops and naval units to withdraw from the Norwegian operational area. This was in order to make them available for the continuance of the developing struggle in the West and ward off the envisaged threat to the Britain itself.[21] Prior to that the ore railway and the port installations of Narvik were to be completely destroyed, for which the seizure of the town was seen as desirable. For the time being the withdrawal order was kept top secret, particularly from the Norwegians. General de Brigade Béthouart, who had not been informed about the decision of the British chiefs of staff until 26 May, initially regarded the order as against the honor of the French soldier to forsake the Norwegians, but then accepted the facts. It was he who urged most strongly for the execution of the already initiated operations for the seizure of Narvik, because the planned evacuation could best be screened by doing so, and the morale of the Allies would be bolstered. Moreover, the clearing of the area around Narvik would have to be preceded by that around Bodø, as on 25 May the forward elements of the German *2.Gebirgs-Div.* had already advanced to Rokland, located only 15km south of the Saltfjord in front of Bodø.

Following the bombardment of Narvik and the German positions identified along the banks of the fjords around the town for several hours, at 0400hrs on 28 May a battalion each of the French Foreign Legion and Norwegians was brought ashore across the Rombakenfjord near Orneset, east of Narvik. Attacking German combat aircraft, which for the first time included dive bombers, succeed in sinking a landing boat and damaging the anti-aircraft cruiser *Cairo*, which served as the naval command ship. This caused the arrival of reinforcements for the landing force, including three tanks, to be delayed until 1100 hrs. When British fighters from Bardufoss managed to drive away the German bombers and naval gunfire helped overcome a crisis among the landed troops, after a successful German counter-thrust from the Taraldsvikfjell, the seizure of Narvik was continued. The advance of Polish troops to the Beisfjord south-east of Ankenes, bypassing the defenders there and forcing them to withdraw, contributed to the overall success of the operation. At 2200hrs General de Brigade Béthouart reported the occupation of Narvik. Its garrison, which had mainly consisted of naval troops, withdrew in an easterly direction and tried to establish contact with other German units in the area. Its heavy weapons, however, were lost. In the evening a force consisting of scratch elements of various German units, in the southern part of the battlefield held a line running from the Hestefjell (778m), 3km south-west of the end of the Beisfjord to the Skavtua (663m) and on the opposite side of the Beisfjord from Fagernes across the mountains to Tunnel 4 at Forneset, a good 6km east of Narvik. With

---

20   The aircraft carriers also brought along 46 Squadron of the R.A.F. It was stationed on the airfield at Bardufoss from 26 May on with 14 Hurricanes.

21   Compare the Earl of Cork and Orrery report and Derry, p.213.

the advance of the Allies into the fjords around Narvik the delivery of reinforcements by sea planes finally came to an end for the Germans.[22]

The critical situation in the southern part of his operational area forced *Generalleutnant* Dietl to employ the paratroopers of *I./FschJgRgt.1* as they arrived without waiting for their formation as complete units. On 27 May, *Leutnant* Keuchel, with a platoon from *4./FschJgRgt.1*, was ordered to the southern tip of the Beisfjord with a mission to set up a rallying position along the Lakselven brook for the troops withdrawing from the area around Ankenes and to reinforce the naval company which was deployed there. The commander of *II./GebJgRgt.139*, *Major* Haussels, directed the arriving paratroopers to occupy a rallying position along the Mölnelven brook at Kvanta, about 2 km further to the north-east.

The paratroopers who were dropped on the morning of 29 May were to be deployed without delay. As the front in the south become unstable, *Leutnant* Rottke from *3./FschJgRgt.1*, was ordered by *Generalleutnant* Dietl to repel the reported thrust of Polish troops across the Aksala (961m) with two platoons of this company and a platoon each of mountain and naval troops under his command. Rottke's force, moving off at 1200hrs, was brought in a freight train from Björnfjell to the station at Hundalen, about 3 km east of the end of the Beisfjord. As the railway from there onward could be hit by observed fire from Allied warships, the ascent to the Aksala was accomplished on foot. After the force reached the height, and the report about approaching Polish troops turned out to be wrong, it was directed by means of runners to return and to set up positions about 2km further to the north, on the slopes west of the small settlement of Sildvik.

On this day the battle HQ of *3.Gebirgs-Div.* realized the loss of Narvik and the extent of the gains made by the Allies. Consequently *Hauptmann* Walther received the mission to relieve *Marine-Kompanie von Freytag-Loringhoven*, withdrawing along the ore railway, with a hastily scraped together unit of troops and to stop the enemy there. Walther's detachment consisted of the heavy machine-gun platoon from *3./FschJgRgt.1*, some hastily formed naval companies and half of the original signals platoon of *I./FschJgRgt.1* under *Stabsfeldwebel* Scheurig. They moved via rail to Hundalen and then on foot to Tunnel 4 at Forneset. There it met with *Marine-Kompanie von Freytag-Loringhoven*. As an incursion of Polish troops across the mountains in the southern part of the Narvik Peninsula was reported, *Hauptmann* Walther dispatched his heavy machine-gun platoon to the 1,400m+ high mountain range south of Forneset. After climbing for several hours the platoon discovered that the report was wrong and was ordered back into the valley of the Orneelven brook, about 6km east of Tunnel 4, where the defense was to be continued later. In the evening, the platoon under *Leutnant* Keuchel also reported to *Hauptmann* Walther, after it was relieved by the rallying parts of *II./GebJgRgt.139* along the Mölnelven brook. It was deployed on the Middagsfjell (813m), about 3km south of the entrance to the Rombaksbotn. *Abteilung Walther* was able to retain the area around Tunnel 4 until late in the afternoon and relieve the remnants of the defenders of Narvik and the Taraldsvikfjell, who withdrew along the ore railway, although a British destroyer in the Rombakenfjord delivered heavy fire against the positions and Tunnel 4 from a distance of 1-1.5km from

---

22   Until 26 May, *2./GebJgRgt.138*, first elements from *6./GebJgRgt.138* and a few mountain and anti-tank guns had been brought in by this way. It had then been the threat from the air that had drastically demonstrated the end of the sea plane actions, when on 28 May two of the large Do 26, landing in the Rombaksfjord, were destroyed by Hurricanes and some of their passengers were taken prisoner.

1720hrs on. Throughout the course of the night the enemy pushed back *II./GebJgRgt.139*, which was fighting in the mountains left of *Abteilung Walther*, with the remnants of three of its companies and some naval troops. This caused the deep left flank of the detachment to be threatened and its position became untenable. At 2300hrs the order arrived to move back to positions along the Orneelven brook. Here, the already established heavy machine-gun platoon of *3./FschJgRgt.1*, with its well-directed fire, enabled the mountain and naval troops under *Major* Haussels to disengage from the enemy and to fall back. At about this time, *Leutnant* Rottke and his two parachute platoons released from their previous task, reported to *Hauptmann* Walther at his command post. One of these platoons now relieved Keuchel on the Middagsfjell and the other was placed subordinate to *Oberleutnant* Götte.[23] This officer was now in charge of all sub-units of *I./FschJgRgt.1* in *Abteilung Walther*. *Hauptmann* Walther did not intend to fall back directly to the Orneelven position, but to fight for time in front of it. For this purpose, he selected the line Middagsfjell–Strömnen Peninsula.

While the main effort of the Allies clearly rested in the southern part of the contested area, they become active again also on the northern front, against the withdrawing task *Gruppe Windisch*. It was particularly its left flank, where *III./GebJgRgt.139* and the two weak companies of *I./GebJgRgt.137* were employed, that came under increasing pressure from the artillery supporting French mountain troops and Norwegian infantry. In front of the sector of *Gruppe von Schleebrügge* with *1./FschJgRgt.1* and mountain troops to its right, for the enemy was content the time being with reconnaissance and bombardment by high-angle weapons. Nevertheless, another paratrooper was killed here.

On 30 May bad weather and the strained air transport situation prevented any further delivery of forces by air. The day saw *Abteilung Walther* given up Straumsnes at the ore railway about 2km west of the Strömnen Peninsula. To the left of the detachment *II./GebJgRgt.139*, positioned on the eastern slope of the Beisfjordtötta along the Mölnelven Valley and on the Durmalsfjell (884m) east of the valley, was attacked by superior Polish forces. The Polish forces succeeded in flanking the movement to the south and, under the cover of dense fog, seizing the Durmalsfjell to advance toward the Aksala mountain, located 4km further east. Counterthrusts by *II./GebJgRgt.139* failed to drive the enemy back. This caused all German troops fighting along the ore railway and in the mountains south of it to become endangered of being cut off.

In this situation all combat actions along the ore railway at 1900hrs were handed over to *Hauptmann* Walther. He immediately reacted by withdrawing the troops which were still engaged along the ore railway west of the Strömnen Peninsula. On the northern front the left flank of task *Gruppe Windisch* was pushed back further east in bitter fighting. As a consequence all of the mountain troops sustained heavy losses. *Gruppe Narvik* did not receive air support during the morning of 31 May as the aircraft of the Allies were employed for attacks on German ground forces, particularly along the railway between Sildvik and

---

23   In the after-action report for Narvik of *I./FschJgRgt.1*, Götte is mentioned as leader of the 2nd Company. This company, however, had been commanded by *Leutnant* Tycska. It remains unresolved, whether Götte, who before was Walther's adjutant, had taken over the command of the 3rd Company after Tycska had failed to arrive, or whether he had actually commanded the 4th Company for Narvik because of the absence of *Hauptmann* Gericke.

Björnfjell. For the first time Norwegian combat aircraft, under the escort of British fighters, attacked German positions at the Rundfjeldet where the command post of *I./GebJgRgt.139* was located.

Despite the fog and sleet which prevailed over the northern part of the operational area on 31 May the uncommitted elements of the staff of *I./FschJgRgt.1*, the battalion's medical detachment under *Unterarzt* Dr. Scheffler and the heavy mortar platoon of the 4th Company were dropped at Björnfjell unmolested by enemy aircraft. While the staff elements and the medical detachment moved off to *Hauptmann* Walther's detachment, the heavy mortar platoon was ordered to set out for Height 698, where, on the extreme right flank of task *Gruppe Windisch* at the Swedish border, a platoon from *I./GebJgRgt.139* was established. Lacking a guide familiar with the terrain, moving for hours in deep snow and dense fog and heavily laden with its four 8cm mortars and their ammunition, the mortar platoon eventually became lost. Only after firing signal flares was it located by a ski patrol of mountain troops and conveyed to its position. On the way the platoon leader was wounded by enemy machine-gun-fire, meaning a *Feldwebel* was forced to assume command. The latter directed the positioning of the mortars, partly on the forward slope of Height 698, behind some boulders and only about 200m away from the enemy.

Abteilung Walther was not attacked during 31 May and was able to set up a line along the Middagsfjell –Strömnen Peninsula. The detachment now consisted of:

- paratroopers gathered in *Kompanie Götte* – 2 officers and 94 other ranks
- the *Marine-Kompanien Meissner, Fuchs, von Freytag-Loringhoven* and *von Diest*, altogether 15 officers and 342 other ranks
- Keuchel's parachute platoon– 2 officers and 51 other ranks
- Kersten's parachute platoon– 1 officer and 45 other ranks
- the battalion-staff and personnel of the signals platoon, altogether 45 men.[24]

The soldiers of the detachment had, for the greater part, fought for days without hot food and under adverse weather conditions and consequently they were exhausted. Some help was given when in the railway station of Sildvik a provisional kitchen was established. From there it was possible to deliver hot food by light trolleys along the railway and then by hand-carried containers to the troops. During the afternoon, friendly combat aircraft attacked the enemy in front of the detachment; the first bombs were dropped on their own positions because of a prematurely fired signal. Fortunately, the losses were light. As *II./GebJgRgt.139*, positioned left of the detachment in its rear, remained under heavy enemy pressure and gave up some ground, the detachment's left flank also had to be withdrawn some distance.

Admiral Lord Cork and Lieutenant General Auchinleck could note with satisfaction that the evacuation of Bodø was close to completion and accomplished without great losses, despite the fact that *Luftflotte 5* had vigorously attacked there. In order to further delay the

---

24   A heavy mortar platoon under *Leutnant* Bittner, which is mentioned in the battalion's report, could not be traced.

advance of the *2.Gebirgs-Div.* toward Narvik small units with blocking missions were left behind along the route.

Upon Churchill's directive the political and military commands of the Norwegians were still kept in the dark about the decision of the Allies to completely withdraw from Norway. Therefore the Norwegian troops in the north of the contested area, confident about the ongoing support of their Allies, prepared for the seizure of the Rundfjeldet and the Haugfjell adjoining to the west. These were the last massifs in front of the area around Björnfjell still retained by task *Gruppe Windisch*. However the loss of Björnfjell would force the Germans to either surrender or cross the Swedish border to internment.

On 1 June the left flank of the exhausted troops of task *Gruppe Windisch* were pushed back to the western and northern edge of the Haugfjell. After they seized Height 620 the Norwegians were repelled several times with heavy losses in their attacks east of Lake Holm. As a result of the advance of the enemy behind its left flank *Abteilung Walther* was again threatened with envelopment and the anticipated frontal attack would not allow for an orderly withdrawal. This led *Hauptmann* Walther, in the early hours of 1 June, to obtain approval from *Generalleutnant* Dietl to fall back on the Orneelven position. The withdrawal commenced at 0330hrs with the evacuation of equipment and gear followed by the naval companies and covered by the paratroopers. Between 1000 and 1200hrs new positions were occupied for their entire width. The main line of defense was behind the Orneelven brook. From where it flowed into the Rombaksbotn the troops were deployed as follows: north of the ore railway, a platoon of naval troops as sentries in a house in Orneelven; Naval *Marine-Kompanie Meissner* between the Rombaksbotn and the railway; *Marine-Kompanie Fuchs*, with Kersten's platoon subordinate, south of the railway on the ascending slope up to the ridge; *Marine-Kompanie von Freytag-Loringhoven* in positions projecting to the south-west; Keuchel's platoon on the left flank. Parts of *Kompanie Götte* were deployed as sentries on either side of the railway. Its other parts were organized into shock troops and kept ready behind *Marine-Kompanie Meissner*. The heavy machine-gun platoon of *3./FschJgRgt.1*, under *Feldwebel* Rothärmel, was split up into its two squads along the front line. *Marine-Kompanie von Diest* was initially divided up between other units and sub-units. The detachment's command post and the telephone exchange, with wire connections to all sectors, being located in Tunnel 10. The sector in front of the main line between the Rombaksbotn and the railway was strengthened by mine obstacles and booby traps. Tunnel 8 was prepared for demolition. On this day *Abteilung Walther* did not engage with the enemy, the enemy only probed in the sector of Keuchel's platoon, but this was unsuccessful.

After the evacuation of Bodø the Norwegian government now considered an armistice of its own independent from the actual military situation. However the Allies decided to inform King Haakon and his cabinet on 1 June about their decision to give up Norway. This task was accomplished by the British ambassador. General Ruge, the Norwegian commander-in-chief was to be informed on 2 June. At this time admiral Lord Cork and Lieutenant General Auchinleck evidently had received the news that the evacuation of the greater part of the British Expeditionary Corps in France and numerous French troops from the beaches around Dunkirk had almost been completed, although all of their heavy equipment had to be left behind. Early in the morning of 2 June several Norwegian infantry companies attacked against Height 698, close to the border with Sweden and east of Lake Holm. However they were beaten off by the mountain troops and sailors positioned there, although this was only after fighting at close quarters. About the same time a destroyer bombarded the position which had been cleared by *Abteilung Walther* the day before. Later in the course of the morning, however, artillery and heavy mortars opened up against the detachment's new sector. Any further attacks by infantry failed to materialize, so *Hauptmann* Walther sent out reconnaissance patrols from both flanks of his sector. These reported that the terrain along the railway up to the previous positions was still unoccupied by the enemy, but that French troops sat on Height 638 to the south.[25]

After *2.Gebirgs-Div.* had occupied Bodø on 1 June the increasingly critical situation for *Kräftegruppe Dietl* caused *Luftflotte 5* to now concentrate its attacks against the Allied warships in the fjords to the west and north-west of Narvik. For the first time *Abteilung Walther* enjoyed massive air support as 10 dive bombers,[26] eight level bombers and four Me 110s attacked enemy troops along the ore railway. The fighters from the aircraft carriers *Ark Royal* and *Glorious*, which arrived west of the fjords[27] as well as those from Bardufoss, prevented serious damage among the naval units and claimed high losses among the attacking German aircraft.

As the air transport situation on the German side improved, on 2 June two weak parchute platoons, under Spany and Süttner, were again flown to Björnfjell. As with previous efforts, the approaching transport aircraft were attacked by British fighters. One of the Ju 52s had to turn off and cross the border to Sweden where it was shot down by anti-aircraft guns. Five paratroopers and two of the aircrew managed to parachute from the crashing plane although some of them suffered serious injuries. The remaining six paratroopers and one member of the aircrew were either killed by the fire of the fighters and anti-aircraft guns or perished in the crash. The other Ju 52s managed to drop their officers and 44 other ranks at 1445hrs without further incident.[28] The critical situation in the sector of *Gruppe von Schleebrügge* at the Swedish border meant that those paratroopers were immediately sent to this location, where they arrived by 1825hrs. Opposite the sector of *Hauptmann* Walther's detachment, on 3 June the enemy's ground forces also remained quiet. Walther therefore dispatched patrols in order to gather intelligence. One of them, advancing along the ore railway with a mission to bring in prisoners and to occupy an elevation just west of the main defense line, was fired at by French heavy machine-guns from Height 638 and failed to accomplish its goals. Another, led by a *Feldwebel*, managed to force its way into a position of French troops under the protection of the heavy machine-guns of Rothärmel's platoon

---

25   The after-action report of *I./FschJgRgt.1* mentions French mountain troops. The evaluation of sources of the Allies, however, show that at least along the railway, French foreign legionaries from Narvik were also present.

26   These had been Ju 87 Rs from *I./StG 1*, which compared with the Ju 87 B, had a considerably extended range.

27   The aircraft complement of *Ark Royal* was replenished with 24 Skua and 21 Swordfish, whereas *Glorious* had brought along only 6 Sea Gladiators and 6 Swordfish, as it was to take aboard the fighters from the airfield at Bardufoss upon its evacuation.

28   The after-action report of 263 Squadron mentions 6 approaching Ju 52s, probably from *KGr z.b.V.107*. This corresponds with the number of paratroopers dropped from the remaining five aircraft, which is also confirmed in *Generalleutnant* Dietl's diary.

and inflicted considerable losses among its defenders. The slackening pressure by the enemy now allowed *Hauptmann* Walther to send up to one-third of his troops back to a rest area in Sildvik daily, where opportunities were created to dry the ever-wet clothing and treat the bad colds that became widespread among the men.

In front of the centre and right flank of task *Gruppe Windisch* the enemy remained active. Several times the Norwegian troops attacked across the Holmelven Brook east of the upper Jern Lake and against Height 698. However they were repelled each time. The heavy mortar platoon of the paratroopers considerably contributed to the retention of Height 698. The heavy fighting on the extreme right flank of task *Gruppe Windisch* continued throughout 4 June. There, the Norwegians, through the interplay of artillery fire and infantry attacks, sought to enforce a breakthrough to the Rundfjeldet well into the night. Again, the fire of the heavy mortars of the paratroopers proved highly effective.

Contrary to that it remained quiet on 4 June in the sectors which had previously been attacked by French and Polish troops. However the warships remained particularly active as were the artillery and the air forces of the Allies. As the Germans later discovered, their mission was to cover the evacuation of the beachheads. Already on the night of 3 June the first 4,700 soldiers were embarked on destroyers, which then brought them to transports entering in pairs the Vågsfjord north of Harstad. The embarkation of a further 4,900 men was planned for the night 4/5 June.[29]

On 5 June Norwegian troops again attacked the extreme right flank of task *Gruppe Windisch*. The defenders were able to close incursions by counterattacks of local reserves but anticipated a large-scale attack in the days to come. In the south, destroyers entering the Rombaksbotn and artillery continued to bombard *Abteilung Walther*.[30] After two air attacks the rail carriage which was serving as *Hauptmann* Walther's command post was moved into Tunnel 8, however, its brakes failed, and the carriage rolled downward toward positions occupied by the enemy. The soldiers working in the command post managed to disembark in time but all the unit's documents and maps remained inside. A patrol from *Kompanie Götte*, which reached the carriage after it had stopped on the Strömnen Peninsula, found out that it was emptied of its contents. *Generalleutnant* Dietl, angered by this, subsequently issued a directive to all subordinate commanders with instructions in detail, advising how to deal with maps and operation orders.

On the night 5/6 June another 5,100 Allied soldiers were embarked. The Norwegians had now taken over the sector of the French mountain troops north of the Rombakenfjord. On 6 and 7 June bombardment by artillery and naval guns against the German troops in the southern part of the combat area continued with undiminished intensity. On 7 June Allied aircraft again attacked positions and installations of the defenders in the south and the new command post of *Abteilung Walther* in the railway station at Sildvik was hit. The Germans still assumed that the Allies were reorganizing their forces and a landing at the southern end of the Rombaksbotn could not be excluded; two anti-tank guns, two light anti-aircraft guns, a heavy machine-gun and several anti-tank rifles were positioned in the

---

29   With hindsight it becomes evident that the Germans had not detected the start of the evacuation of Narvik. This was prepared in such way that 15 large transports had been assembled in a waiting area about 180 sea miles away from the Norwegian coast, where they had been protected by warships. The first convoy with evacuated soldiers had sailed for Scapa Flow still on 4 June and had arrived there safely.

30   Mines, which had been dropped by German aircraft into the Strömnen defile and the Tjelsund leading from the Vest Fjord toward Harstad, had been neutralized by the Allies in no time.

sector of *Hauptmann* Walther north-east of Sildvik, close to the fjord in order to engage destroyers, approaching with landing troops. In addition to this measure *Generalleutnant* Dietl ordered a firm connection between *Abteilung Walther* and *II./GebJgRgt.139*, which was to be positioned in the area around Hundalen in the coming days, covered by strong rearguards. These actions indicated that the battle HQ of *3.Gebirgs-Div.* was still ignorant of the true intentions of the Allies.

Opposite *Abteilung Walther* French troops were still observed on 7 June. In the sector of *Gruppe von Schleebrügge* the offensive actions by the Norwegians carried on without interruption, the defenders were now close to exhaustion because of continuous fighting and adverse weather conditions.

On 7 June, when a platoon from *2./FschJgRgt.1* under *Leutnant* Graf von Blücher was dropped at Björnfjell, *Oberst* Meindl,[31] the commander of *GebArtRgt.112*, jumped together with the paratroopers. He did this jump without any preliminary training. Immediately after landing he assumed command of the southern part of the operational area. Von Blücher's platoon was no longer involved in combat actions.

During the nights 5/6 and 6/7 June the Allies were able to evacuate more than 10,000 of their ground forces unhindered. On 7 June the first fighters from Bardufoss were flown out to the aircraft carrier *Glorious*. King Haakon VII, the Crown Prince and the government of Norway also left their country for Britain on the same day, leaving from Tromsø on the British cruiser *Devonshire*, and avoiding capitulation or remaining in a position to continue the war against Germany. The commander-in-chief of the Norwegian armed forces, General Best, was authorized to execute their demobilization and resume negotiations about the capitulation of the country with the Germans after the withdrawal of the Allies.

On the night 7/8 June the remaining 4,600 soldiers of the Allied landing force were brought aboard transports. The rearguard was embarked on destroyers in the early morning of 8 June, while aircraft from *Ark Royal* covered the embarkation and the departure of the last convoy. *Glorious* took aboard the seven Hurricane fighters which still operated from Bardufoss and steamed for England, escorted by two destroyers.[32]

It was only due to the reports of *Abteilung Walther* and *Gebirgs-Btl Haussels* reporting the complete withdrawal of the enemy in front of them that in the early hours of 8 June the battle HQ of *3.Gebirgs-Div.* came to the conclusion that the Allies had given up the struggle

---

31   Eugen Meindl, born 1892 and served as an artillery officer in the First World War. He stayed in the German armed forces after the war. He commanded *GebArtRgt.112* during the campaign in Poland and was promoted to *Oberst*. He then transferred over to the parachute force during his stay in Narvik. In September 1940 he assumed command of the newly created *Luftlande-Sturmregiment* and led it during the airborne assault of Crete, where he was seriously wounded. He won the *Ritterkreuz* on 14 June 1941 and was commander of *Division Meindl* and later commanding general of *XIII.Flieger-Korps* in Russia. Then promoted to *Generalleutnant* in January 1943 he returned to the parachute force after 1943 as commanding general of *II.FschKorps*. He was promoted to *General der Fallschirmtruppe* in April 1944. He saw intensive and continuous combat with *II. FschKorps* in France, initially in Normandy. He was awarded the *Eichenlaub* to the *Ritterkreuz* in August 1944 and *Schwerte* to the *Ritterkreuz* in May 1945. He was in captivity until 1947 and died in 1951.

32   On this day, however, *Glorious* was found west of the Lofoten by the German battle-cruisers *Scharnhorst* and *Gneisenau*, which had arrived from the south. After a short engagement, the aircraft carrier and the two escorting destroyers had been sunk. More than 1,400 British seamen and 28 of the 32 pilots from the aircraft aboard perished.

for Narvik. Thereupon *Abteilung Walther* was tasked immediately with the reoccupation of the line Strömnen Peninsula– Middagsfjell and ordered to dispatch patrols along the ore railway toward Narvik. A similar order was sent to Haussels. However, when task *Gruppe Windisch* attempted to gain insight into the situation of the opposing Norwegian forces, by sending out patrols probing on the left flank, they were repelled. In front of the sector of *Gruppe von Schleebrügge* on the right flank, a soldier was killed during reconnaissance action and two others were taken prisoner. All doubts about the end of the fighting for Narvik and indeed for all of Norway vanished when, on 9 June at 0115hrs, *Generalleutnant* Dietl was informed by *Gruppe XXI* that the King of Norway and his government had left the country for good and when *Abteilung Walther* reported the unopposed entry of Narvik already the day before. Later in the morning a Norwegian negotiator arrived in the positions of *Gruppe von Schleebrügge*. From then on no shot was fired again by the Norwegians.

On 10 June the so-called 'Norwegian Northern Army' surrendered. The paratroopers of *I./FschJgRgt.1* took no part in negotiations with the Norwegians. The battalion assembled in Narvik where it stayed subordinate to *Oberst* Meindl, who was made military commandant of the town. Until 16 June it was detailed for clearing up tasks, as the enemy had left behind large amounts of weapons, ammunition and other equipment. On 11 June von Blücher's platoon also arrived in the town, followed by the 21 soldiers of the battalion under *Hauptmann* Wich, who had been dropped on 9 June. On the occasion of officially informing his men about the capitulation of Norway on 12 June *Hauptmann* Walther also awarded 26 Iron Crosses 2nd Class to members of his unit. On the morning of 17 May the old *1./FschJgRgt.1* and other elements of the battalion, which had been employed at the northern front, also arrived in Narvik.

Of the 760 soldiers of *I./FschJgRgt.1* brought to Trondheim 375 had been dropped at Björnfjell. The remainder, because of weather conditions and lack of transport aircraft, had not been committed, including the new *1./FschJgRgt.1*. Together with the 164 officers and other ranks of the reinforced old 1st Company of the battalion, 539 paratroopers had reinforced *Kräftegruppe Dietl*. Including those killed in crashes of transport aircraft during the approach flight, two officers, two non-commissioned officers and 24 other ranks of *I./FschJgRgt.1* had been killed and two officers, 16 non-commissioned officers and 23 other ranks had been wounded. The Allies had taken with them as prisoner three non-commissioned officers and two other ranks. Four other soldiers remained missing.

On the afternoon of 17 June, with the arrival of German naval units with reinforcements and supplies arrived in Narvik, all parts of *I./FschJgRgt.1* were embarked on the cruiser *Nürnberg* and arrived without incident in Trondheim on 18 June at 1100hrs. After unification with the parts of the battalion which had remained there it was transferred by rail to Oslo, from there on the steamer *Isar* to Ålborg and from there again by rail to Stendal, where it arrived on 23 June at about 2300hrs.

At Narvik paratroopers had been employed as reinforcements for troops in combat for the first time. As previously in parachute missions, during the initial phase of *Weserübung* the command of *Fl.Div.7* had no influence on the planning and execution of the employment of these troops. Decisions about their transport, as well as about their use, had been made by commands which were not always aware of the necessary experience needed and which sometimes placed their own requirements and interests as paramount. This was particularly evident during the delivery of paratroopers to their destination, when the Ju 52s transporting them had to fly without fighter escort despite the clearly perceived air threat. 22 soldiers of *I./FschJgRgt.1*, 70% of its killed and missing, had become the victims of direct and indirect effects of the enemy's fighters as a result of this incomprehensible mistake.[33]

Despite the dismal conditions on the battlefield for the construction of shelters, the losses of the paratroopers in ground combat had been relatively low. The main reason for this fact was that they did not have to conduct a parachute assault. However it was understood that the parachute units lacked the equipment for combat under Arctic conditions. Organizational deficits had also been detected in the capability to fight over a longer period of time. As in Holland, the lack of organic heavy weapons for defense was clearly perceptible. As ground-to-air radio communications had again been non-existent the only hope for the troops on the ground was that friendly aircraft, beginning to operate in the airspace over Narvik, would direct their attention not only against the warships of the Allies, but also against their artillery and mortars. However this hope was often in vain so that the paratroopers, supported only on rare occasions by the few guns of the mountain troops, were almost continuously at the mercy of the enemy's high-angle weapons. The remarkable effects of the only heavy mortar platoon of *I./FschJgRgt.1*, even though its benefits had chiefly been enjoyed by the mountain troops, had demonstrated that an increase of more organic heavy weapons was the right one.

The delivery of the paratroopers in 'packets' which was enforced by adverse weather and lack of transport aircraft, besides the critical situation of *Kräftegruppe Dietl*, did not permit the employment of *Bataillon Walther* as a whole. Employed in company and platoon-sized units, the paratroopers again, and this time under adverse terrain and weather conditions, had proven the morale and perseverance of their units and moreover had gained invaluable combat experience.

How strongly the German high command counted on the capability of the parachute force to play a main role in the retention of the area around Narvik until the arrival of relief troops on the ground became apparent with the employment-plan of II./*FschJgRgt.1*. This battalion, upon its return from Holland, had been quickly reinforced and made ready for parachuting into the area around Narvik as reinforcements. After a road march to Frederikshavn and sea transport to Oslo, it was transferred to the airfield at Trondheim-Størdalen, where it arrived on 8 June. However the withdrawal of the Allies from Norway had made parachuting unnecessary. A short time later, it was transferred back to its home garrison in Stendal.

During the struggle for Narvik the German high command again had undeniably experienced the flexibility of the Allies, provided by a strong, versatile and competently commanded navy. Whether, and in what way the views gained thereby influenced its plans and decisions for the future employment of parachute troops, will be illustrated later.

---

33   It needs to be pointed out, however, that *Luftflotte 5* initially had only limited resources for the air war and from the very beginning of its mission in Scandinavia, had also been forced to protect the south of that region against the rather frequent and vigorous incursions of British bombers.

2

The parachute force is enlarged from a still-incomplete Division to a *Flieger-Korps*

On 11 May 1940, after the attack in the West had gained some impetus, Hitler, evidently impressed by the spectacular achievements of *Sturmabteilung Koch* at the Albert Canal and the successful seizure of the bridges at Moerdijk, Dordrecht and of the airfield at Waalhaven by parachute infantry battalions, had ordered the immediate enlargement of the parachute force. The staff of *Fl.Div.7* was made aware of this decision after the return of the majority of its troops to their home garrisons, by a directive of the *OKW* on 22 May. This directive contained no information about the final strength of the parachute force, but marked out that it had to be ready for parachute undertakings in its new size, at the latest by the end of August. The *Heer* and the *Luftwaffe* was instructed to recruit volunteers for the parachute force from all their units.

In the staff of *Fl.Div.7* the *OKW* directive was correctly interpreted as going far beyond the existing expansion plans. Building upon the experiences with *Sturmabteilung Koch* the formation of an *Luftlande-Sturmregiment* which was capable of both parachuting and landing with gliders was planned from the outset. With the former assault detachment and its leader, soon promoted to major, combat experienced personnel for the formation of a glider assault battalion in the new regiment were readily available.

The parachute infantry company was now organized like those of *I./FschJgRgt.1* during its employment in Narvik; it had three identical platoons, each consisting of the command team with the platoon leader, his assistant and two soldiers, three squads, each with a squad-leader and eleven soldiers and a support team with five soldiers, equipped with one light mortar and an anti-tank rifle, altogether 45 men instead of the former 36. Each squad still had two light machine-guns. In each squad the commander, his assistant and a runner were also equipped with submachine-guns, thus the firepower of the company increased considerably. Moreover, a number of telescopic sights were issued for the riflemen.[1] As the personnel of the company's HQ section, to which a medical officer was added, remained restricted to one plane-load, the combat strength of the parachute infantry company was only slightly larger than that of its previous organization. It also required a change to the previous loading plans and the addition of a thirteenth man in some of the Ju 52s, if the company was to be transported for parachuting by one squadron of twelve aircraft. All heavy infantry weapons were now concentrated in the heavy weapons company of each parachute infantry battalion – eight heavy machine-guns in two platoons and a mortar

---

1   The information by Dach about 14 men in the parachute squad is erroneous. This has been confirmed by several veterans of the parachute operations against Corinth and Crete. The error by Dach may have occurred, as on the days after the start of the airborne assault against Crete, a number of Ju 52s, because of aircraft losses and damage, were loaded with 14-15 paratroopers as reinforcements.

platoon with six 8cm mortars.[2] As the strength in personnel in the heavy weapons company was slightly lower than that of the rifle companies, the combat strength of a parachute infantry battalion, including its staff and signals platoon, was between 560 and 580 men.

After the successes of the parachute force in the opening phase of the campaign in the West, which was cleverly exploited by propaganda, there had been no lack of volunteers, many of them now even with combat experience. Therefore the formation of new parachute units proceeded with great speed. Up to early autumn 1940 the three parachute infantry regiments were established as follows:

FschJgRgt.1, commanded by *Oberst* Bräuer, with
- HQ
- *I.Bataillon* / *Major* Walther
- *II. Bataillon* / *Hauptmann* Burckhardt[3]
- *III. Bataillon* / *Major* Schulz
- 13th (Nebelwerfer) and 14th (anti-tank) companies

Home garrison for the regiment was Stendal.

FschJgRgt.2, commanded by *Oberst* Sturm, with
- HQ
- *I. Bataillon* (completely rebuilt after its disaster in Holland) / *Hauptmann* Kroh [4]
- *II. Bataillon* / *Hauptmann* Pietzonka
- *III. Bataillon* / *Hauptmann* Wiedemann
- 13th (recoilless guns) and 14th (anti-tank) companies.

Home garrison for the regiment was Berlin-Reinickendorf, except *II. Bataillon*, stationed in Döberitz.

FschJgRgt.3, commanded by *Oberst* Heidrich [5]
- HQ

---

2   The precise caliber of the mortar was 8.14cm. It was the model which was introduced into the infantry regiments of the *Heer*. Its maximum range was 2.4km. A model developed particularly for the parachute force, with a shorter barrel, reduced weight (26kg) and a range of but 1.1km had not yet been issued.

3   The battalion was re-built, as the old I*I./FschJgRgt.1* as a whole was transferred as cadre to *FschJgRgt.3*, in order to have a complete combat-experienced unit there.

4   Hans Kroh. Joined the *Regiment 'General Göring'* as *Oberleutnant* of the police in April 1936. From October 1937 he was director of training at the parachute school in Stendal. In January 1939 assigned to the staff of *Fl.Div.7* until after the end of the campaign in Holland. Commander of *I./FschJgRgt.2* from summer 1940. He commanded the battalion during the airborne assaults at Corinth and Crete receiving the *Ritterkreuz* on 21 August 1941. Later he was employed in Russia before gaining promotion to *Oberstleutnant* in November 1943. From December 1943 on he was commander of *FschJgRgt.2*. *Eichenlaub* were added to his *Ritterkreuz* on 6 April 1944. From May 1944 given with the command of *2.FschJgDiv*. He was promoted to *Generalmajor* on 13 September 1944. *Schwerte* were then added to the *Eichenlaub* on 12 November 1944. He was captured in Brest at the end of April 1945. He joined the German *Bundeswehr* as *Oberst* in June 1956 and was promoted to *Brigadegeneral* and assigned the command of the German *1.FschDiv*. in September 1957. He was then promoted to *Generalmajor* in July 1959 before retiring in October 1962. He is now deceased.

5   *Oberst* Heidrich was extricated from the command of *InfRgt.514* during the campaign in the West, in order to build up and command *FschJgRgt.3*.

- *I.Bataillon / Hauptmann* Freiherr von der Heydte,[6] garrison in Wolfenbüttel
- *II.Bataillon / Major* Derpa, garrison in Braunschweig
- *III.Bataillon / Major* Heilmann, garrison in Magdeburg
- 13th (Nebelwerfer) and 14th (anti-tank) companies, garrison in Braunschweig.

With *II./FschJgRgt.3 Oberst* Heidrich also received *II./FschJgRgt.1* under his command. They were the former *Fallschirm-Infanterie-Bataillon* of the *Heer*, which, in the early days of the parachute force he had built up and trained as its commander. *Major* Heilmann[7] was provided a subordinate, whose experience as a platoon leader, company commander and battalion commander in the infantry was invaluable.

As the weapons issued to the gun companies of the infantry regiments turned out to be unsuited for parachuting, those in the parachute infantry regiments received the 10.5cm Nebelwerfer, the Do-Gerät 38 and the only recently developed recoilless light gun LG 40 L. 15.5.[8]

---

6   August Freiherr von der Heydte, born 1907. He undertook General Sstaff training and joined the *Fallschirmtruppe* in August 1940. After his parachute training he was made commander of *I./FschJgRgt.3*. He led the battalion during the airborne assault on Crete and received the *Ritterkreuz* on 9 July 1941. Employment in Russia from September to December 1941 and in North Africa from February to April 1942. Thereafter he undertook a role as operations staff officer of *2.FschJgDiv.* in Italy. After convalescence he was made commander of *FschJgRgt.6* in the West from February 1944 on and promoted to *Oberstleutnant* in August 1944. *Eichenlaub* were added to the *Ritterkreuz* on 23 October 1944. He served as commander of the parachute-drop during the German offensive in the Ardennes. He was taken into U.S. captivity in December 1944 and discharged from the accusation of commitment of war crimes. Nevertheless he was released as late as July 1947. After the war he gained a professorship in jurisprudence, before dying in 1994.

7   Ludwig Heilmann, born 1903. Left the *Reichswehr* as non-commissioned officer after several years in the infantry. He joined the *Heer* again as *Leutnant* in July 1934 and was platoon leader, company commander and staff officer in the infantry July 1934 to June 1940. He took parachute training in June 1940, prior to his assignment as commander of *III./InfRgt.423*. He transferred to the *Luftwaffe* in August 1940 and was assigned the command of *III./FschJgRgt.3*. Then he was promoted to *Major* in November 1940. He led his battalion during the airborne assault on Crete. Thereafter he received the *Ritterkreuz* on 14 June 1941. He commanded his battalion as *Major* and *Oberstleutnant* from August 1941 to November 1942 in the East. Thereafter he was tasked with the command of *FschJgRgt.3* until June 1943. From then on he was commander of *FschJgRgt.3* in Italy. He led his regiment on Sicily and in the Cassino battles. *Eichenlaub* were added to his *Ritterkreuz* on 2 March 1944 and *Schwerte* on 15 May 1944. Tasked with the command of the *5.FschJgDiv.* in November 1944. He served as *Generalmajor* from December 1944 in the West (Ardennes). He was in British captivity from March 1945 to August 1947 and died in 1959.

8   The main equipment in the three gun companies was not homogenous. After-action reports of the units and input of veterans reveal the following: *13./FschJgRgt.2* was equipped with the LG 40 (probably 6 of them), for the parachute assault against the Corinth Canal. For the airborne assault against Crete *13./FschJgRgt.3* was equipped with the Nebelwerfer (probably 9), and the Do-Gerät 38 (3 launchers). *13./FschJgRgt.1* also had the Nebelwerfer (probably 6). The Nebelwerfer was constructed like a mortar. Its caliber was 10.5cm. Stripped into three parts of 34-36kg each, it was dropped by parachute in containers. Its maximum range was 3,025m. The Do-Gerät consisted of a 53kg heavy frame of metal-grating with a built-in launching-chute for the projectile, which had a caliber of 15cm and a weight of 40kg. The maximum range of the projectile was 5,500m. Because the charge of the projectile consisted of gunpowder, its trajectory could be well observed by the enemy. The unreliability of the projectile did not allow it to engage precise targets. The LG 40 L.15.5 was of 75mm and a weight of 145kg. Its maximum range was 6,800m. For parachuting, it was transported on the undercarriage of the Ju 52, with a bundle of parachutes attached to it. Its layout as a recoilless weapon made it easy for the enemy to identify its firing position after each shot by the enormous amount of dust thrown up. Moreover, it required a safety

The *Luftlande-Sturmregiment* was organized into four battalions, three of them parachute infantry battalions. The fourth, planned as combat support, had a company with 12 Nebelwerfers, one with 12 anti-tank guns, one with 6 light anti-aircraft guns and an engineer company. There were no additional units at the regimental level, with the exception of a headquarters company. The regiment was commanded by *Oberst* Meindl, who, in August 1940, had transferred from the mountain troops. The regiment was stationed as follows:

- Staff and HQ company in Hildesheim
- *I.Bataillon* / *Major* Koch, in Hildesheim
- *II.Bataillon* / *Major* Stentzler, in Quedlinburg
- *III.Bataillon* / *Major* Scherber, in Halberstadt
- *IV.Bataillon* / *Hauptmann* Gericke, in Helmstedt.

From 1 July 1940 onwards *Fallschirm-Maschinengewehr-Battaillon 7/ FschMGBtl.7* was built up in Gardelegen. Most of its officers and non-commissioned officers were volunteers from the *Heer* who were transferred to the *Luftwaffe* after having passed parachute training. The other ranks chiefly arrived from various units of the *Luftwaffe*. The battalion was commanded by *Major* Erich Schulz. It consisted of a staff, a security platoon, a rather large, fully motorized signals platoon and three rifle companies. Each of the latter were composed of two heavy machine-gun platoons with four heavy machine-guns in each, and a mortar platoon with four 8cm mortars. The combat strength of a rifle company being 125 men, the battalion did not attain combat readiness before spring 1941.

Fallschirm-Flugabwehr-Maschinengewehr-Bataillon 7 / FschFlaMGBtl.7 was built up from scratch from June 1940, initially under *Major* Derpa in Halberstadt. In late 1940 it was moved to an airfield near Quedlinburg and taken over by *Hauptmann* Baier. The battalion was organized into the staff, the signals platoon and four rifle companies. The main armament of each of the latter consisted of six anti-aircraft guns (2cm on a tripod mounting).[9]

The formation of the *Fallschirm-Pionier-Bataillon* in June 1940 in Dessau-Kochstedt commenced with some difficulties. One of them was that all of the soldiers from the engineer arm available in *Fl.Div.7* were used as cadres for the *Sturmregiment*. Problems were also caused in that the engineer branch of the *Heer*, because of its own enlargement plans and the ongoing demanding preparations for Operation *Seelöwe*, was *very* hesitant to release volunteers to the parachute force from among its ranks. Nevertheless, until late 1940, *FschPiBtl.7* was built-up with the staff and four companies under the command of

---

distance of 80m behind its barrel. For these and some other reasons, the gun did not meet the expectations of the parachute force. Only 50 weapons of this model were actually built.

9   The weapon was the 2cm mountain anti-aircraft gun, which from 1940 on was issued specifically to the mountain and parachute troops. Its weight in the firing position was 286kg. For transport and delivery by parachute, it could be stripped into eight parts. It could, however, also be dropped as a whole by means of a parachute bundle. Without the heavy plate protecting its crew from the fire of infantry weapons the weight of the weapon was considerably lower. Its maximum range against targets on the ground was 4,800m. In its air-defence role, it could engage targets up to 3,700m high. As ammunition, high-explosive and armor-piercing shells were available. Rate of fire was 220 rounds per minute.

the recently-promoted *Major* Liebach. Lack of training and equipment, however, prevented combat-readiness being achieved during the requested time.[10]

With *FschPzAbwKp.7*, now designated as *Fallschirm-Panzerjäger-Kompanie 7 / FschPzJgKp.7*, as cadre, *Fallschirm-Panzerjäger-Abteilung 7 / FschPzJgAbt.7* was formed in June 1940 in Salzwedel, initially under *Hauptmann* Krüger. The detachment was made up of staff, signals platoon and three companies. Each of the latter was organized into three platoons with four 3.7cm anti-tank guns (3.7cm Pak) each. Two heavy Zundapp 750cc sidecar motorcycles were assigned to each Pak and its ammunition trailer. At the end of August the detachment was moved to the training area of Munsterlager for enhanced training. This included parachuting of the complete detachment together. During this time *Hauptmann* Schmitz took over command from *Hauptmann* Krüger. Like all units of *Fl.Div.7* the detachment sent off a detail for the reconnaissance of staging areas in northern France, for the possible employment of the parachute force in the invasion of England – Operation *Seelöwe*.

Shortly after the return of *FschGeschBttr.7* from Holland to its new garrison in Halberstadt the build-up of *Fallschirm-Artillerie-Abteilung 7/FschArtAbt.7* commenced. The detachment consisted of the staff and three batteries. Each of the latter was now equipped with four 75mm 36 L/19.3 mountain guns, which were more effective than the previously used Skoda gun. The command of the detachment was placed into the hands of *Major* Bode. The recently developed *Kettenkrad* was planned as a towing vehicle for the guns, instead of the heavy sidecar motorcycles. As parachuting of the guns was still out of the question, these had to be landed as a whole by Ju 52 or stripped in two parts into two gliders (DSF 230). However the construction of lightweight guns more suited for parachuting was under way. Already by March 1941 the 2nd Battery of the battalion was equipped with four 10.5cm 40/2 lightweight guns.[11] Split into four parts and packed into containers, the gun was dropped by parachute from the Ju 52. For the time being, the heavy sidecar motorcycle, dropped from the undercarriage of the Ju by means of a quintuple parachute, remained the tow for the gun and its ammunition trailer.

At about the same time the medical company was enlarged to become *Fallschirm-Sanitäts-Abteilung 7/FschSanAbt.7*, initially in Stendal and soon in the newly constructed barracks in Brandenburg/Havel. It consisted of staff, three parachute medical companies and an airborne medical company with a main dressing station. The detachment was initially commanded by *Oberstabsarzt* Dr. Neumann. When he was transferred to the *Luftlande-Sturmregiment* as its chief medical officer, *Oberstabsarzt* Dr. Berg assumed command of it. Medical soldiers, as in previous campaigns, were initially planned to act as combat troops, and intensive infantry training was conducted on the training area at Sennelager.

As gliders were now available in increasing numbers the enlargement of the present glider detachment could also be realized. On 27 July, *Luftlande-Geschwader 1/LL.Geschw.1* was built up at Hildesheim, initially with the staff and two glider groups. On 28 August a third group was set up in Braunschweig-Waggum. *Oberstleutnant* Wilke, who had proven his soldierly abilities as leader of an air transport group in Holland, was tasked with the

---

10   Compare Austermann, pp.30 and 38.

11   At the instigation of *Fl.Div.7*, the gun was developed in the Army Armament Office under *Oberst* Dr Dornberger. Its weight in the firing position was 388kg, its maximum range 7,950m and its rate of fire 6-7 shells per minute. It was moved for short distances by means of a wheeled carriage. A demonstration of the weapon had taken place in January 1941 on the firing-range at Jüterbog.

command of the wing. A glider with a large load capacity was not yet available , the Go 242 Goliath was at this time being developed in the Gotha works.

In general the provision of personnel for the enlargement of the parachute force met with very few difficulties except, to some extent, the formation of the engineers. A veritable challenge however was the timely parachute training of between 3,000 and 4,000 soldiers who had additionally volunteered as paratroopers. In this regard the establishment of another *Fallschirmjäger-Ergänzungs-Bataillon* in Helmstedt under *Major* von Carnap turned out to be of advantage.[12] In order to generate sufficient training slots, Parachute School I (*Oberleutnant* Zierach) was reopened in Stendal and Parachute School III under *Hauptmann* Vogel newly set up in Braunschweig-Breutzen beside Parachute School II (*Major* Primus) in Wittstock.

In addition to the enlargement of the parachute force and the introduction of new weapons, some attention was also dedicated to the methods of parachuting. The RZ 1 parachute was increasingly replaced by the RZ 16. This gave the paratrooper a lesser opening shock during the unfolding of the canopy and tended to cause less oscillation. However the problem of quickly disposing of the harness after landing remained unresolved. Another improvement was the introduction of camouflage canopies; experience had shown that the white canopies strewn on the ground had been used by enemy artillery and aircraft as target markers.

For the drop containers, a standardized size came into use. Its spring system, made to absorb the shock on landing, was also improved. Furthermore, the number of containers was markedly increased as the daily consumption rate for supplies for the now complete *Fl.Div.7* was calculated at 60 tons of ammunition and 15 tons of highly concentrated food. Therefore 750 containers were required per day if all supplies were to be brought by air.

The trailers for the transport of supplies on the ground, with a load capacity of 500kg, were now constructed such that they could be folded up and loaded into the transport aircraft for parachuting. Progress had also been achieved for the parachuting of some of the heavy weapons, particularly for the 3.7cm Pak and the 2cm anti-aircraft gun. Attached between the wheels of the undercarriage of the Ju 52, they could now be dropped by quintuple parachutes. However, because of the longer opening procedure of these parachute bundles the transport aircraft for parachuting had to fly at 250-300m altitude. Weapon crews and other personnel jumping from the same aircraft were therefore exposed in the air to the enemy's defensive fire for longer periods of time and were more scattered on the ground after landing.

By increasing the number of radio sets the feasibility of establishing and maintaining communication after landing between units and superior commands was also improved. *Fallschirm-Nachrichten-Kompanie 7 / FschNachrKp.7*'s equipment consisted of 80-watt short-wave radios, which under good conditions had a range of more than 200km, they also carried 15-watt and backpack short-wave radio sets (*Tornister-Funkgeräte*). All radio sets of the parachute force could be dropped by parachute. For this specific chests were required, whereas the backpack radio sets were dropped in normal containers in which they could also be moved around after landing. The delivery of the 80-watt radios was also planned for using gliders.

---

12   *Fallschirm-Ergänzungs-Bataillon 1/FschErgBtl.1* under *Major* von Kummer was located in Stendal.

Radio teams of *FschNachrKp.7* were generally used to reinforce the signals platoons of the parachute infantry regiments and the *Luftlande-Sturmregiment* as these, besides backpack radios, contained just one 80-watt radio. The signals platoons of the battalions/detachments were exclusively equipped with backpack radios. Their range was limited to just a few km. Radio communication between the regiments was not planned. The accumulators and anode batteries of the larger radios which were required to operate them lasted for about 2-3 days. There was equipment available in the signals platoons of the regiments to recharge these batteries. However the teams with backpack radios had to be supplied with new batteries. Reliable radio communication over large distances was guaranteed only by the 200-watt sets. They had to be provided by corps-level signals detachments. For their delivery into the operational area of parachute troops, two gliders were required per set.[13]

Already in summer 1940, *General der Flieger* Student (promoted to this rank on 29 May) had taken an active role in the progress of his troops from hospital. By late 1940 he was back to duty. On 1 January 1941, as planned the month before by the *OKL*, the corps for the parachute force was activated and Student was nominated as its commanding general. His staff was located in Berlin-Reinickenforf, as in the case of the parachute division, this formation also received a "cover" designation of *XI.Flieger-Korps* and parts of the staff of *Fl.Div.7* were transferred into the corps staff. On 15 December the proven *Major i.G.* Trettner was assigned as operations staff officer (Ia). At the same time *Generalmajor* Schlemm[14] joined the corps staff as chief of staff.

Directly subordinate to the corps command were the *Luftlande-Sturmregiment*, *FschMGBtl.7*, *FschSanAbt.7* and, from *Fl.Div.7*, the transportation company and the air reconnaissance squadron. *Luft-Nachrichten-Regiment 41 / LnRgt.41* was also added to the troops at corps-level as its 1st Company was parachute-trained, *XI.Flieger-Korps* thus received an organic signal formation at the operational level. The parachute replacement battalions and the parachute schools were also placed subordinate to the corps command. On 1 January 1941 *Oberst* Ramcke,[15] who initially was tasked with the development of heavy weapons for the parachute force, was appointed commander of its training institutions.

---

13   Regarding the radio equipment of the parachute force, see Thote.

14   Alfred Schlemm, born 1894. Chief of Staff of *XI.Flieger-Korps* from December 1940 to February 1942. Thereafter, until summer 1943 he undertook command assignments in the East. He was promoted to *Generalleutnant* in June 1942. From summer 1943 he was on assignments in Italy. In January 1943 he was promoted to *General der Flieger*. After convalescence from January 1944 to October 1944 he became the commanding general of *I.Fallschirm-Korps* in Italy (Anzio). He received the *Ritterkreuz* on 11 June 1944. From November 1944 to March 1945 he served as the commander-in-chief of *1.Fallschirm-Armee* in the West as *General der Fallschirmtruppe*. He was in British captivity from March to May 1945 and died in 1986.

15   Bernhard Hermann Ramcke, born 1889. Joined the parachute force after successful parachute training in August 1940 and became commander of the training institutions of the force from January 1941 to February 1943. During this time he was also the commander of the *Sturm-Regiment* on Crete after the wounding of *Generalmajor* Meindl. He was promoted to *Generalmajor* in July 1941 and received the *Ritterkreuz* on 21 August 1941. From April 1942 to February 1943 commander of *FschJgBrig.1* in North Africa. He was given *Eichenlaub* to the *Ritterkreuz* on 31 August 1942 and promoted to *Generalleutnant* in December 1942. In February 1943 tasked with the build-up of *2.FschJgDiv.* and with its reconstitution after its return from the East. From June 1944 to August 1944 he was the commander of the division,

On 21 January 1941 *Generalleutnant* Süßmann was assigned the command of *Fl.Div.7*. Again he was an officer who was advanced to the top of this division but who lacked experience as a tactical leader in ground combat operations and whose career had taken place exclusively within the *Luftwaffe*, with little attention to command principles and techniques of ground forces.[16] *Major i.G.* Graf von Üxküll was appointed principal staff officer of *Fl.Div.7*.

Due to the negative experiences with the *ad hoc* special purpose air transport combat groups, the post of an Aviation Commander (*Flieger-Führer*) was created in the staff of *XI.Flieger-Korps*. It was led by *Generalmajor* Conrad. The request to place all Ju 52 formations for training and employment in war under the command of the *Flieger-Führer* was not followed by the *Generalquartiermeister* of the *Luftwaffe*, who decided to keep the employment of these formations in his own hands. However he directed that the additional special purpose air transport combat groups were to be formed again from aviation schools, and were to be assembled as such that sufficient time could be warranted for the instruction of their planned employment by *XI.Flieger-Korps*.

In January 1941, as part of the preparations for Operation *Marita*, but also for the employment of German forces in North Africa, in addition to *KG z.b.V.1*[17] and the staff of *KG z.b.V.2*, the *KGr z.b.V.40*, *50* and *60* were assembled. In February *KGr z.b.V.101*, *104* and *105* were also established.

---

then until September 1944 he was the commandant of fortress Brest. During this time he was promoted to *General der Fallschirmtruppe* and awarded the *Schwerte und Brillanten* to the *Ritterkreuz*. On 20 September 1944 he was taken into U.S. and then British captivity before being handed over to the French in December 1946. In March 1951 he was sentenced to five years in prison for alleged war crimes during the defense of Brest. He was prematurely released in June 1951 and died in 1968.

16 The abstention from naming an experienced commander from the *Heer*, who, after the campaigns of 1939 and 1940 would have been available without doubt, probably must be put down to Göring's endeavors for prestige. Student's role in the nomination of Süßmann remains unclear.

17 During the period December 1940 to February 1941, its *III.Gruppe* was flying reinforcements and supplies for the Italian forces in Albania from the airfield at Foggia.

3

The role of the parachute force in the military-strategic planning of the German High Command between Autumn 1940 and Spring 1941

Once it had become apparent that Great Britain, now governed by Churchill, was not willing to end the war against Germany and at most would accept the *status quo ante bellum* as a basis for peace with the Axis powers, the supreme German command found itself in a situation without a military strategic concept for the continuation of armed conflict. It was surprised by the quick and complete success of the campaign in the West. Hitler, in particular, had counted on peace negotiations with the British after the capitulation of France. The determination of the British to resist became visible when on 3 July 1940 the British Royal Navy attacked French naval units in the port of Mers-el-Kebir, in order to neutralize their possible use by the Axis powers.

Prior to the outbreak of war only the General Staff of the *Luftwaffe* had studied a possible military conflict with Britain. A directive by the General Staff of the *Luftwaffe* on 4 July 1939 to *Luftflotte 2*, which was designated to conduct the air war against Britain, in a realistic appreciation of the risks and chances of success, had foreseen only air attacks against energy and supply installations of the British military economy. After the conclusion of the campaign in Poland, when Hitler expressed his determination to wage war against the Allies offensively, the *Kriegsmarine* commenced its deliberations about its tasks after a successful attack in the West. In connection with this Raeder, on his personal initiative, on 15 November 1939 had established a small special staff under the chief of the Directorate for Naval War (*Seekriegsleitung*), *Vizeadmiral* Schniewind. This staff was to deal with a potential invasion of Britain. Five days later the special staff forwarded the results of its work in the form of *Studie Rot*. The study, with respect to the success of an invasion, was rather sceptical in its basic tenor not the least because at the time of its origin, the jump-off ports had to be selected exclusively on German territory. For the main the study dealt chiefly with maritime and navigational aspects.[1] Consequently within the high command of the *Wehrmacht* (*OKW*) the study had been shelved.

On 13 December 1939, in the high command of the *Heer* (*OKH*), *Generaloberst* von Brauchitsch commissioned the development of a study with the codename *Nordwest* to deal with an invasion of Britain. It primarily looked at options to seize London. Its assumptions were based on the English Channel and North Sea ports being controlled or in German hands but the core of the British expeditionary corps being still engaged in France. The landing was to take place in the south-east of England, between the mouth of the Thames and The Wash. *Fl.Div.7*, reinforced with *InfRgt.16* from the *22.(LL)Inf.Div.*,

---

1   Compare Kieser.

was to seize the ports of Great Yarmouth and Lowestoft on the Norfolk coast by airborne assault, so that an infantry division and a bicycle brigade could be brought ashore there.[2] The landing of an infantry division was also planned for Holleslay Bay near Ipswich. Up to eight armored and additional infantry divisions were then to follow in a second and third wave. The *Luftwaffe* and *Kriegsmarine* would be given intensive covering and supporting missions. *Generaloberst* von Brauchitsch and *General der Artillerie* Halder approved of the *Heer* study and had it passed on to the Directorate for Naval War and the commander-in-chief of the *Luftwaffe* for examination and comments.

However on 30 December the *OKL* declared itself unable to conform to the plans of the *Heer*. The main reason related to the achievement of absolute air superiority over England as a prerequisite for the undertaking. Moreover, it pointed out that the strongest air defense of the enemy probably lay within the chosen area of operations.

The Directorate for Naval Warfare rejected the study with reference to the strength of the British Home Fleet. Its outspokenly strong comments revealed its view about the ignorance of the *Heer* planners in matters of amphibious operations. From that time on the subject was ignored by all of the high commands.

On 21 May 1940, *Admiral* Raeder, in a conversation with Hitler, brought up again the invasion of England. He emphasized the importance of absolute air supremacy for the operation. Very much to the liking of Raeder, Hitler directed that no preparations for an invasion were to be initiated for the time being. Nevertheless, he had not stopped planning within the Directorate for Naval War. In a new approach by means of *Studie England,* which the special staff forwarded to Hitler on 27 May, some of the deliberations of the *Heer* were included. Without a specific directive the work for the assembly of a landing fleet also commenced. In the face of the clearly recognized navigational difficulties the doubts of the Directorate for Naval Warfare about the successful outcome of an amphibious operation on the English coast thereby had grown even greater.

When no offers of resolution by Great Britain were received after the capitulation of France, *Generalmajor* Jodl accepted that the war would go on. In a memorandum dated 30 June – the day on which the British Channel Islands were occupied by the *Wehrmacht* – he put forward his deliberations about further military conflict with Great Britain. In order to make the opponent ready to accept peace, he foresaw the smashing of the military economy in Great Britain from the air as the principal approach. Furthermore he requested the interdiction of this country's imports from abroad. He regarded an invasion as possible only after the achievement of air supremacy.[3]

The high commands of the *Heer* and the *Kriegsmarine* had independently continued with their invasion plans, although the *Kriegsmarine* had seen only the time-periods of 20-26 August and 19-26 September as suitable for amphibious operations. It was at this point that the *OKL* also entered the stage yet again. *General* Jeschonnek made known that 25,000 airborne troops, of which 6-7,000 were to be paratroopers, would be available for

---

2   It is quite conceivable that the author of study *Nordwest, Major i.G.* Stieff, had sought the advice of Student about the use of parachute and air-landing forces, although Student's memoirs lack any mention of it. No reasonable basis, however, exists for the statement of Kühn (p.58), that Student had planned the use of *Fallschirmtruppe* against the debarkation ports of the Allies returning from Dunkirk.

3   Compare Irving, p.193 and Klee, p.61.

an invasion. On 11 June the *OKL* advised the *Heer* about the availability of about 400 Ju 52s and 110 gliders. On 16 June, these numbers were raised to 450 Ju 52s and 150 gliders.[4]

In the meantime the need for action became apparent, as Hitler instructed the heads of the *Wehrmacht* to initiate preparations for an invasion of England within a short timeframe, which may become necessary under certain circumstances. On 13 July he approved a plan for the invasion, which *General der Artillerie* Halder and *Vizeadmiral* Schniewind had drawn up together. On 16 July he signed *OKW* Directive No. 16 for the preparation of an amphibious operation against England.[5] The operation received the codename *Seelöwe*. The purpose of the operation was the neutralization of Britain as a basis for the continuation of the war against Germany. The landing was to be carried out in the form of a surprise crossing of the Channel on a wide front between Ramsgate and the area west of the Isle of Wight. The British air forces were to be subdued to such an extent that they would be unable to oppose the crossing with a combat power worth mentioning. The intervention of British naval forces against the landing was to be prevented mainly by laying extensive minefields on either side of them. All preparations for the invasion had to be completed by mid-August. In the part of the Directive which dealt with the role of the *Luftwaffe* Hitler laid down, "For the use of parachute and air landing troops, I request proposals, examined in cooperation with the *Heer*, whether it may be expedient to keep the parachute and air-landing troops available as a quickly employable reserve in the case of an emergency."

The command of the *Kriegsmarine* now had to solve the problem of generating with great effort (and with considerable detriment to inland shipping) a landing fleet practically from scratch, that would suffice the demands of all three *Wehrmacht* services. At least the same priority had to be dedicated to the task to neutralize the British air force, its ground organization and supporting industry. In a conference with the commanders-in-chief of the *Heer* and the *Kriegsmarine* on 31 July Hitler rightfully emphasized this task as an indispensable prerequisite for the success of the invasion. On 1 August he signed Directive No. 17, which dealt with the conduct of the air and naval war against England. On 4 August, based on this directive the *OKL* initiated the intensified air war against England. Due to the weather conditions the day of the first major air attack – *Adlertag* (Eagle Day) – was not to be before 13 August.

During a conference with Hitler on 31 July the controversial views of the Directorate for Naval Warfare and the high command of the *Heer* about the concept of landing operations became evident. The former had seen itself unable to carry out the landing of the two armies of *Heeresgruppe A*[6] between Worthing and Folkestone. Hitler therefore decided, in an *OKW* directive dated 16 August, that the main effort in the initial phase of the landing was to be undertaken by the *16.Armee* between Hastings and Folkestone. In the sector of the *9.Armee* between Brighton and Bexhill, only the first echelon from three divisions, i.e. six regimental combat groups, were to be landed initially.[7]

---

4   In his 16 July 1940 diary entry, Halder confirms the content of the report by Jeschonnek. The number of paratroopers provided by Jeschonnek was considerably exaggerated by this time.

5   Der Führer und Oberbefehlshaber der *Wehrmacht*, *OKW*/WFA/L Nr. 33160 g.Kdos, Chefsache, FHQ.

6   On the side of the *Heer*, *Heeresgruppe A* was tasked with the conduct of *Seelöwe*.

7   The controversy about the landing plan until Hitler's decision is documented in the war diary of the *OKW* in the records for 5, 9, 12 and 13 August 1940 (see Schramm).

On 29 July the Directorate for Naval Warfare already reported that it could not meet the date of 15 August for the completion of the landing preparations. The *OKW*, in its directive, had foreseen the time-period 19-26 September for the execution of the amphibious operation. As such the final date was to be ordered 8-10 days in advance.

Influence on the change in the initial landing phase of *Heeresgruppe A* had also been exercised by the attitude of the *Luftwaffe* command, concerning the use of its parachute troops. Already in early August, the differing perceptions of the *OKH* and the *OKL* clearly became visible, when the latter wished to employ the *Fallschirmtruppe* as mobile reserves, only after the establishment of the beachhead, according to the view Hitler provided in his Directive No. 16. This had been rejected by the *Heer* command as they had seen parachute assaults for the seizure of initial beachheads as mandatory and had allocated 7,000 men for this task. It had even offered to transfer soldiers fit for parachute training from its own ranks, should the *Luftwaffe* lack appropriate numbers. Throughout the course of the further coordination process between the services the *OKL* somewhat departed from its initial position. It did not agree to the request of *Heeresgruppe A* to employ two parachute-regiments for the seizure of Brighton and the heights north of Beachy Head, rather it intended to retain at least a part of its parachute force as a quick reaction reserve.[8] The ideas of the *OKL* were then integrated into the planning directive.

Göring, whose flying formations had become heavily involved in the air battle over Britain, had issued directives to *Luftflotten 2* and *3* on 27 August, pertaining to the employment of air resources for the support of Operation *Seelöwe*. On 5 September a supplemental order for the cooperation of the *Flieger-Korps* with the armies during the initial landings followed.

Regardless of the *OKW* directive of 16 August, in which a landing at Brighton in the initial phase of *Seelöwe* was given only a supportive function, the *Heer* for a while continued to plan for the use of parachute troops there, too. On 12 September their employment in the initial phase of the landing operation had finally been planned in the sector of *16.Armee*. During a conference with *Heer* representatives, *Generalfeldmarschall* Kesselring of *Luftflotte 2* agreed on the use of two parachute-regiments and two battalions of glider troops for this army. However on 18 September a new directive was issued by the command of *Luftflotte 2*, in which an operation of *Fl.Div.7*, north-west of Folkestone, was ordered exclusively by parachute drop.[9]

The staff of *Fl.Div.7*, commanded by *Generalmajor* Putzier (during the convalescence of Student), was included in the planning for the end of August early September. Advanced parties of the division had been sent to staging areas around Saint Quentin, in northern France. About this time the build-up of a depot for supplies which were to be delivered by air after the landing of troops was also commenced near Laon. The material to be flown in with the paratroopers in the initial assault was assembled on Dutch airfields. The air transport formations *KG z.b.V.1* and *2* and the special purpose combat groups, which had been on call at the flying schools of the Chief of Training of the *Luftwaffe*, were also transferred to France at the end of August.

---

8   This perception of the *OKL* had shown little appreciation of the realities, as the parachute force at this time was handicapped in its mobility on the battlefield after its landing, and due to its lack of combat power stood little chance of successfully fighting a conventionally armed opponent in open terrain.

9   The use of gliders was abandoned, as it was recognised that the enemy increasingly was blocking their potential landing sites.

By mid-September the *Luftwaffe* had still not been able to wear down the British fighter arm. One of the reasons for this failure was that its bombers, upon Hitler's directive, had been attacking British cities from 6 September on.[10] Consequently, combat power was diverted from the main mission. This had already helped the hard-hit Royal Air Force to regenerate and to efficiently fight back; the German side had not used 11 September as the date for the start of the preliminary actions for *Seelöwe*. The landing was now to take place on 24 September. Despite the determination Hitler continued to display to the public his doubts about the success of an invasion of England, which worried him from the very beginning of the planning process, now increasingly gained the upper hand, even though he had disguised them with other matters.[11] He apparently even disclosed to *Reichsmarschall* Göring, in a face to face conversation at the end of August, that he was considering the preparation for a landing in England primarily as a means to exert pressure on the British, in order to change their mind about continuing the war.[12]

On 14 September, in a conference with the commanders-in-chief of the *Wehrmacht* services Hitler disclosed his intent to postpone his decision about *Seelöwe* to 17 September. However the preparations for the operation were to be continued in order to deceive the enemy and to further make him direct his defense efforts to southern England. An order by the Command Staff of the *Wehrmacht*[13] issued on the same day emphasized this measure as particularly important. As Hitler had taken no decision by 17 September the *OKW*, upon request by the Directorate for Naval Warfare, on 19 September had been ordered to discontinue the deployment of the invasion forces.

Up to that time the commands tasked with the conduct of *Seelöwe* on the operational level had continued with preparations for the envisaged date of the landing. Regarding the use of paratroops the *Heer* command had not followed a proposal by the *OKL*, to drop *Fl.Div.7* in the area New Romney–Kingsnorth–Bonnington–Dymchurch, in order to support from there the advance of the *35.Infanterie-Division* from its landing beach toward Ashford.[14] Thereupon *Fl.Div.7*, subordinate to *Luftflotte 2* until its arrival on British soil, would receive the following missions on 18 September:

- Opening of the passages across the Royal Military Canal in Hythe and west of it for the *17.Infanterie-Division*;
- Safeguarding of the amphibious landings by blocking the roads leading from Canterbury toward Folkestone;
- Employment of parts of the Division in support of the actions to seize Dover during the progress of the operations.[15]

---

10   In his Directive No. 17, Hitler had reserved the decision about bombardments of this kind explicitly for himself. When, by a navigational error, German bombs had been dropped on London for the first time on 24 August, Churchill immediately ordered a retaliatory raid on Berlin for the next day. This was executed with 80 bombers. As British air attacks on German cities thereafter had continued, on 4 September Hitler announced retaliatory attacks on British cities. See Cartier, pp.251-252.

11   Irving, p.211, mentions respective remarks to Raeder on 13 August and to the just promoted field-marshals on 14 August.

12   Götzel, pp.168-180, recounts at some length Student's memories about his conversation with Göring in this matter on 2 September. Kurowski, p.127, mentions that Student, in an interview with him after the war, had remembered Göring's words on this occasion as: "Der Führer will gar nicht nach England."

13   The *Wehrmachtsführungsamt/WFA* had received the new designation on 8 August 1940.

14   See Schenk, pp.315-316.

15   See Klee, pp.162-163 and Schenk, p.315.

In the staff of *Fl.Div.7*, these missions had been transposed as follows:[16]

The first wave of paratroopers was to be dropped simultaneously with the sea landing of the advance elements of *17.Infanterie-Division*. It was to consist of *Kampfgruppe Meindl* (two reinforced parachute infantry battalions) and *Kampfgruppe Stentzler*.[17] The former was to open the passages across the Royal Military Canal in Hythe and west of the town. This was to prevent flanking actions of the enemy against the sea landing by pushing forward combat effective elements to the line Hythe–Saltwood (1km north of Hythe). *Kampfgruppe Stentzler* was initially to seize and hold the high ground south-west of Paddlesworth (4km north of Folkestone).

The second wave was to be dropped about an hour later. It was to be composed of *Kampfgruppe Bräuer*, *FschJgRgt.2* and *FschJgRgt.3*. *Kampfgruppe Bräuer* was to consist of a parachute infantry battalion, the parachute engineer-battalion and the anti-tank companies of all three parachute regiments and, after landing north of Sandling Park (3km north of Hythe), together with the subordinate *Kampfgruppe Stentzler* it was then to seize Sandgate (just west of Folkestone) from the rear and retain the heights west of Paddlesworth. Another parachute infantry battalion of *Kampfgruppe Bräuer* was to be dropped south of Postling (5km north of Hythe) as divisional reserve.

FschJgRgt.2 was to seize the heights north of Postling and defend them against attacks from the North. *FschJgRgt.3* was to safeguard the landing operation of *17.Infanterie-Division* toward the west and seize the airfield at Lympne (5km north-west of Hythe) with one of its battalions.

Depending on the development of the situation additional units of *Fl.Div.7*, equipped with heavy weapons, were to be brought in by air about five hours after the first landings utilizing the airfield at Lympne.[18] At the earliest possible time *17.Infanterie-Division* and the tanks of *PzAbt.B*, with their amphibious capability and supported by *Kampfgruppe Meindl*, were to cross the Royal Military Canal and neutralize the enemy north of it.

By the end of July Hitler had made known his conviction that above all the Soviet Union, as the greatest perceived threat, had to be neutralized by military means. In early September, he disclosed his intention to hit the British in the Mediterranean region during the winter of 1940/41.[19] After deciding in early October to maintain preparations for an invasion of England until spring 1941 only as a means of political and military pressure and, if by that time still necessary, to again contemplate an invasion, the high commands of the *Wehrmacht* quickly turned toward new tasks. While the *Luftwaffe* continued its struggle in the air against the British Royal and Merchant navies and began to improve the operation of cross Atlantic convoys, the *Kriegsmarine* began to prioritisef U-boat construction over invasion preparations. As part of this measure the advanced parties of *Fl.Div.7* were

---

16   The operation plan of *Fl.Div.7* does not exist anymore. It has, however, been possible, to extract its vital contents from an order of *17.Inf.Div.*, which had regulated cooperation with *Fl.Div.7*.

17   Both combat groups together made up the majority of the *Luftlande-Sturmregiment*.

18   Deviating from the original intention of the *OKL*, which was to retain a part of the parachute force as a quick reaction reserve, all of the available regiments and detachments of *Fl.Div.7* had received firm missions for the first day of the invasion. The employment of the division, as explained above, is also confirmed in the report of the chief of the *Wehrmachtsführungsstab*, *Generalmajor* von Greiffenberg, recorded in the *OKW* diary for 23 September 1940.

19   On 6 September, he had revealed to Raeder, who had proposed to attack the British positions in the Mediterranean, that, in the case of a cancellation of *Seelöwe*, he intended to clear the situation there in the winter 1940/41.

transferred back to their home garrisons and the air transport groups, formed from the training organizations of the *Luftwaffe*, were also relocated. Only the depot for air resupply material near Laon remained untouched.

From early August onwards the *OKW* resumed deliberations for the conquest of Gibraltar and support of the Italian offensive into Egypt. Yet, although Hitler was quite keen for an operation against Gibraltar, he made clear his thoughts that the Mediterranean region was the domain of Mussolini.

After his decision to postpone the invasion of England until at least spring 1941, Hitler pursued the task of winning Spain over to the side of the Axis powers, as the conquest of Gibraltar, now designated as Operation *Felix*, would have to be launched from this country. On parallel lines the high commands of the *Heer* and the *Luftwaffe* energetically pushed ahead with the military preparations for *Felix*. In Directive No. 18, dated 12 November 1940, dealing with the further conduct of the war against Great Britain, the instructions for *Felix* had taken up considerable space. In Directive 18 (a) dated 27 November, the plans for *Felix* were laid out in more detail. However when General Franco unmistakably stated his view that he did not want to have Spain drawn into the war under the prevailing conditions, the preparations of the *Wehrmacht* for *Felix* were suspended by Directive No. 19 (b). Up to this time the command of the parachute force had not participated in any of the planning for *Felix*.

When, around the turn of the year 1940/41, the situation of the Italians in Albania and North Africa had deteriorated dramatically, the conquest of Gibraltar was again considered by the Germans, in spite of Franco's attitude. For the first time *General der Flieger* Student had also been called in. In order to pay regard to General Franco's sensibility about the deployment of numerous German troops on Spanish soil, Göring obviously addressed the use of *Fallschirmtruppe* against the 'rock' to Hitler. At any rate Student, who had been taken along by Göring for consultations at Hitler's Berghof, received the mission to examine the chances of success of an airborne assault against Gibraltar by the latter. During the return trip to Berlin, Göring had expanded on the idea and tasked Student to also examine the prospects of airborne missions against the Suez Canal, Crete, Cyprus and Malta.[20] Based on a thorough appreciation of the situation in the staff of *XI.Flieger-Korps*, Student reported to Göring that Gibraltar could not be seized from the air, but that all other options would stand a chance of success.

In early 1941 the necessity for planning an airborne operation on the French Mediterranean coast also arose. The attempts by Hitler to achieve the cooperation of Vichy France with the Axis powers in the war against Great Britain had taken a disappointing course in the winter of 1940, despite the fact that General Pétain's regime was heavily involved against the de Gaulle movement for the French possessions in central and north-western Africa and Syria, as the latter was militarily supported by Great Britain.[21] On the German side, the outcome of this struggle was considered dubious and therefore the threat was perceived that French

---

20   This expansion of Hitler's mission by Göring reveals how strongly the latter's thinking toward an extension of the war against Great Britain had already been developed.
21   Compare Schreiber, pp.529-530.

North Africa could go over to the enemy. In this instance Hitler planned the occupation of the remainder of France, thereby safeguarding the French Mediterranean coast against any landings of the enemy from a possibly hostile French North Africa. The planning for this operation was designated *Attila* and initiated with Directive No. 19 dated 10 December 1940. A substantial goal of *Attila* was to prevent with all effort the defection to the enemy of the French Navy, of which parts of considerable strength were assembled in Toulon.

In mid-December Hitler ordered an examination of employment options for parachute and air-landing forces in Operation *Attila*. Against the plans of the *OKL*, which saw almost no chance of success in an operation of this type, Student was ordered in January 1941 to examine the prospects for an airborne assault of *XI.Flieger-Korps* against the naval port of Toulon. The evaluation of aerial photos and the findings of a secretly undertaken reconnaissance by Student's orderly officer, *Hauptmann* Schacht, had led to the result that the mission could be accomplished, albeit with considerable difficulties. In order to seize warships anchoring in the port of Toulon gliders were to land immediately beside them on the piers or even on their decks. Paratroopers were to be dropped over the airfield at Toulon and troops that were air-landing there, were to take possession of the city proper and its port. Naval artillerymen, brought along in gliders, were to occupy the French coastal guns in the port in order to use them, should the British Mediterranean Fleet appear.

On 25 January Hitler approved Student's plans. However further planning within the parachute force did not take place as the development of the situation feared for French North Africa had not occurred. Furthermore the need for military action arose in the south-east of Europe.

In the Balkans Hitler wanted peace and endeavored to safeguard the Rumanian petroleum, which was indispensable for the *Wehrmacht*. By an intensive interplay between territorial concessions for the Soviet Union concerning Rumania, a protective attitude toward this country and Bulgaria, and by a moderating influence on his Italian ally, he had managed to generate a situation that played into his hands between July and early October 1940. With the establishment of a military mission to Rumania and the arrival of the first formations of the *Heer* and the *Luftwaffe*, declared as 'instructors', in the third week of October the protection of the oilfields could be now regarded, to some extent, as guaranteed for the near future.

During the time of Hitler's endeavors to win over Spain and Vichy France for his plans, only the support of the Italians in their thrust into Egypt with an armored formation and some air assets had been contemplated. Soon, however, the German high command found itself in a tight spot regarding the situation in the Mediterranean region.

On 28 October, not totally unsuspected by the *OKW*, the Italian armed forces attacked Greece from Albania. Hitler quickly overcame his disappointment about the lack of timely information by Mussolini and believed the promise of his ally, that he would soon bring the attack against Greece to a successful end.

Within the senior command of the *Wehrmacht*, an action of this kind by the Italians was contemplated just a few days prior to the actual event. Consequently, the advantages of an occupation of Greece as well as the consequences of a failure of such an attack had been addressed. Probably based on a statement by Hitler that the possession of Crete would quickly bring the conduct of the war in the eastern Mediterranean to a successful conclusion for the Axis powers,[22] the island had been included in the appreciation of the situation by the Command Staff of the *Wehrmacht*. The representative of the *Luftwaffe* in the operations section of this staff, however, assessed the threat from there against the Rumanian oilfields as inconsequential.

On 28 October, before the attack of the Italians against Greece had become known, Jodl had once more taken up the subject of Crete and had elaborated as follows:

A military action by the Italians against northern Greece and the port of Piraeus would certainly lead to the occupation of Crete by the British. Thereby, the link between Italy and Libya would be threatened permanently. An Italian surprise action against Crete in general would be possible and could be masked relatively easily. It would, however, require the full employment of the Italian battle fleet. As such an operation could not really be counted upon, and an Italian amphibious operation against Crete would hold out the prospects of success only if the British naval squadrons in the eastern Mediterranean had been weakened. Therefore the following course of the operation is considered feasible:

1. Continuation of the Italian offensive into Egypt for the seizure of Mersa Matrue at the earliest possible time.

2. Attack against the British Alexandria squadron with all available means after the fall of Mersa Matrue.

3. Start of the operations against Greece and simultaneous occupation of Crete after the British squadron has been weakened sufficiently.

The intention to make the contents of this note the subject of a conversation between Jodl and the Italian military *attaché* in Berlin never occurred as a result of the start of the Italian campaign against Greece.

A few days after the Italians launched their offensive, Jodl's apprehension in relation to Crete proved true. British ground forces from Egypt were landed on Crete. Moreover, the utilization of Souda Bay by the British Mediterranean Fleet had been recognized. On the German side this led to an extension of Directive 18, which was still under development. The *OKH* was now instructed to undertake preparations to occupy, together with the Bulgarians and in concert with the Italian operations, Greek Macedonia and Greek Thrace, thus generating the preconditions for the employment of German air forces against the British airbases from which the Rumanian oilfields could be threatened.

As a result of its style Directive 18 was to be regarded as a contingency plan. With the arrival of British air forces on the Greek mainland,[23] but even more by the undisguised efforts of Churchill to bring about a Balkan front against the Axis powers, including Greece,

---

22   Halder noted Hitler's statement in his daily diary for 24 October 1940. It is important as such, as it may have influenced Hitler's decision in favor for Crete and against Malta a few weeks later.

23   As part of Operation *Barbarity*, the first squadron of Blenheim bombers arrived on 4 November 1940. Up to the end of November, two squadrons of Gladiator fighters, three squadrons of Blenheim bombers and some anti-aircraft units had been stationed on the Greek mainland.

Yugoslavia and Turkey, solid plans for a military intervention were quickly developed by the German side.

At the end of November 1940 the military situation of Italy in its war against Greece had deteriorated dramatically, and the British naval squadrons ruled the Mediterranean almost unopposed.[24] Combined with the fact that the Italian armed forces in North Africa faced a disastrous defeat during the British counter-offensive launched on 9 December, the German high command came under pressure. The initial German remedial actions to assist the Italians in North Africa consisted of the dispatch of German air forces to southern Italy and western Libya, effective from 15 December on (soon, the entire *X.Flieger-Korps* would also be brought along from Scandinavia) and the acceleration of the preparations for the transfer of mechanized ground forces with offensive capabilities to Tripolitania. Most of all, however, the contingency planning undertaken for Greece in Directive No 18 came to life with Directive No. 20 of 13 December. As such Operation *Marita* intended to bring at least the Aegean coast of Greece and the area around Saloniki into German hands.

For the parachute force Directive No. 20 only contained the indication that it could become necessary as part of the air war to occupy British bases on Greek islands by airborne missions. The deliberations by the Command Staff of the *Wehrmacht* about an airborne operation against the island of Lemnos, from where the sea lines of communication between the Black Sea and the eastern coast of Greece could be threatened, was dropped, as the *Fallschirmtruppe* had been planned for a mission in Operation *Attila*.

The command of *XI.Flieger-Korps* took no part in the planning process for the campaign against the Soviet Union, which increasingly determined the deliberations and actions of the German supreme military authorities. The execution of this campaign at the start of the dry season in 1941 had become most probable, notably after Directive No. 21 *Barbarossa* was signed by Hitler on 18 December 1940. It had only been in one of Hitler's numerous instructions for *Barbarossa* that he implied the lack of need for the *Luftlande-Korps* in the initial phase of the operation in the East, but to keep it available as a reserve for possible missions at a later stage or in the case of an emergency.[25] This guidance probably brought about proposals for the use of parachute and air-landing forces in piece-meal actions, which were forwarded to the Home Defense section of the Command Staff of the *Wehrmacht* in mid-March 1941, although they were not further pursued at the time.[26]

Hitler's decision to first resolve the situation in Greece, which he saw as increasingly threatening for his entire Balkan strategy, would soon bring with it the employment of the parachute force in this area of war.

With the transfer of the German *12.Armee* (*Generalfeldmarschall* List) to Rumania, ordered between 3 January and 28 February 1941, and the build-up of supply stores for *VIII.Flieger-Korps* (*General der Flieger* Freiherr von Richthofen) in Bulgaria, the die had definitively

---

24   This had contributed to the successful raid of British carrier aircraft against the Italian battle-fleet in Taranto on 11/12 November, in which three Italian battleships had been put out of action for a considerable time, as well as some ineffective encounters of Italian naval units with the British Alexandria and Gibraltar squadrons.

25   Compare the *OKW* war diary for 4 February 1941 in Schramm.

26   This supposition has been supported by *General* (ret.) Trettner in a statement to the author in late 2004, after which the staffs of *XI.Flieger-Korps* and *Fl.Div.7* had not been involved in any deliberations of the *Heer* about the employment of parachute and air-landing troops in *Barbarossa*.

been cast for the execution of *Marita*, as it could not be expected that Greece would yield to the demands of the Axis powers, which were equal to a request for complete surrender.

On 25 February 1941 Hitler decided to commence with the bridging of the Danube along the Rumanian-Bulgarian border on 28 February and to enter Bulgaria on 2 March. The situation in Libya could now be regarded as subordinate as it showed signs of improvement after successful air operations by *X.Flieger-Korps* and the arrival of the first German ground forces. As part of the preparations for *Marita*, the planning for the seizure of the island of Lemnos from the air was reconsidered. The *OKL* and the Directorate for Naval Warfare had stated that they did not attach any importance to the possession of the island. The commander-in-chief of the *Heer*, however, insisted on its seizure, as he saw it as a possible threat against the left flank of *12.Armee's* advance into Greece.[27] On 16 March the *OKW* issued a directive stating that Lemnos was to be occupied via an airborne attack only if it was weakly occupied by British forces.

At this time the arrival of British, New Zealand and Australian ground forces on the Greek mainland[28] was recognized by the Germans. But, as air reconnaissance over the Greek islands was marginal, the military status of Lemnos remained unknown.

On 22 March the *OKL* reported that a reinforced parachute regiment was to be used for the mission against Lemnos, now designated *Hannibal*, in such way that its employment from Plovdiv/Bulgaria could commence on day 8 after a warning of seven days. However, *Hannibal* could be launched only three days after the start of the attack of *12.Armee* across the Greek-Bulgarian border at the earliest, as only after this time could the flying formations which were required for guarding the air transport of the paratroopers and air operations in their support, be drawn away from this army. Consequently Jodl instructed *AOK 12* and *VIII.Flieger-Korps* to determine the time for *Hannibal* in cooperation during the course of the attack.

Prior to these events, on 19 March the command of *XI.Flieger-Korps* was ordered to transfer that parachute force which the *OKL* had agreed upon for the seizure of Lemnos to Bulgaria. As the corps command and *Fl.Div.7* had commenced planning for this operation some time earlier, during the initial deliberations for it in the Command Staff of the *Wehrmacht* the organization of the force planned for *Hannibal* was already established. Designated as *Detachement Süßmann*, it comprised the staff of *Fl.Div.7*, *FschJgRgt.2*, *3./FschArtAbt.7*, *3./FschFlaMGBtl.7*, two platoons from *FschPiBtl.7*, *1./FschSanAbt.7*, elements of the air reconnaissance squadron and *I./Luftlande-Geschwader 1*. For air transport from the area around Plovdiv to Lemnos the command of *KG z.b.V.2* (*Oberst* Heyking) was placed subordinate to *Fl.Div.7*. It received *I.* and *II./KG z.b.V.1*, *KGr z.b.V.60* and *102* as well as an additional squadron of Ju 52s as tow aircraft for the gliders.[29] *Generalleutnant* Süßmann, commanding *Fl.Div.7*, was in charge of the entire force.

---

27   Compare the war diary of the *OKW* for 3 and 4 March 1941. Student's memories in Götzel, p.190, that the Directorate for Naval Warfare had also requested the seizure of Lemnos in the renewed planning, are incorrect.

28   The British Operation *Lustre* (the dispatch of an expeditionary corps to Greece) was realized with the arrival of the first convoy in Piraeus on 7 March 1941. The core of the expeditionary corps consisted of the New Zealand Division, the Australian 6th Division, each with three brigades, and the hastily organized 1st British Armoured Brigade. The British General Wilson was given the command of this corps. The R. A. F. in Greece was subordinate to Air Vice-Marshal d'Albiac.

29   The allotment of these transport aircraft is that for the parachute operation against the Corinth Canal on 26 April. It is assumed here, that it was also valid for the planned operation against Lemnos, as there

On 19 March, ahead of the final approval of this organization by the *OKW*, the advance party of the detachment led by the chief of staff of *XI.Flieger-Korps*, *Generalmajor* Schlemm, flew from Berlin-Staaken to Vienna. There, in the evening, Schlemm was given an outline instruction about the mission of the detachment by the commander-in-chief of *Luftflotte 4*, *Generaloberst* Löhr, who was tasked with the conduct of the air war in the eastern Mediterranean region. He ordered the subordination of *Detachement Süßmann* to *VIII.Flieger-Korps*. Upon arrival of the advance party at the command post of *VIII. Flieger-Korps* in Sulu Dervent/Bulgaria on 20 March, Schlemm received detailed orders. The permanent airfields at Plovdiv and Graf Ignatiev, as well as the provisional airfields at Malo Konare and Golemo Konare were assigned as staging areas and jump-off points for the detachment for the mission against Lemnos. Plovdiv and Graf Ignatiev were also used by aircraft of *VIII.Flieger-Korps*.

First air transport formations and parachute units arrived in Bulgaria on 22 March. The forces were moved by rail, including the gliders, and needed considerably more time as the deployment of *12.Armee* was still ongoing and the wintry conditions also hampered rail traffic.[30]

Shortly before 5 April, the originally planned date for the start of *Marita*, *Detachement Süßmann* was assembled in its staging area. Upon the overthrow in Belgrade of its government, on 27 March Hitler had decided to also attack Yugoslavia. The detachment remained untouched by the hastily undertaken re-organization of the attack forces and the redistribution of their missions. The date for the now simultaneous attack against Yugoslavia and Greece was fixed for 6 April.

After parts of the *12.Armee*, supported by *VIII.Flieger-Korps*, overcame the dogged resistance by some of the fortifications along the Bulgarian-Greek border and advanced into north-eastern Greece, the air reconnaissance squadron of *XI.Flieger-Korps* collected intelligence over Lemnos. It soon became apparent that the island had no military garrison worth mentioning. Therefore, only a short time later, *Hannibal* was abandoned.[31] Instead *12.Armee*, regardless of the undiminished mastery of the eastern Mediterranean by the British fleet after the heavy strike against the Italian navy west of Crete on 28/29 March,[32] contemplated an amphibious landing of ground forces on Lemnos.[33]

Due to the rapid advance of *12.Armee* on the Greek mainland, parts of the air transport formations assigned to *Detachement Süßmann* were to be used for aerial resupply and redeployment missions for *VIII.Flieger-Korps*, which was now moving its bases into Greece. No use was yet made of the parachute forces around Plovdiv with the exception

---

were no changes in the composition of *Detachement Süßmann* between its arrival in Bulgaria and its employment against the Corinth Canal.

30   Götzel, at that time assigned to the quartermaster section of the staff of *Fl.Div.7* and therefore involved in the movements, reports in the journal *DDF* 4/1956, pp.2-4, that one company of *FschJgRgt.2* had been on the rail for 15 days.

31   The option for an airborne assault against Lemnos, however, was still maintained in Hitler's Directive No. 27, dated 13 April 1941.

32   The engagement, known as the naval battle of Cape Matapan, had cost the Italians three heavy cruisers and two destroyers sunk, and the battleship *Vittorio Veneto* damaged, whereas the British had lost just one carrier aircraft.

33   By this method, Lemnos was occupied without resistance on 25 April 1941.

of *FschJgRgt.2*, which was redeployed from the two provisional airfields to the newly constructed airfield at Krumovo.

On 21 April, the day on which *Generalfeldmarschall* List in Larissa accepted the capitulation of all Greek troops north of the Gulf of Corinth, the Yugoslav armed forces also capitulated. Four days earlier an event took place which was to have enormous effects on the parachute force. Student, ruminating on the continuous set-backs in the build-up of the parachute force after the campaign in Poland, on the absence of missions after the cancellation of operations *Seelöwe*, *Attila* and *Hannibal* and of the non-involvement his troops in *Barbarossa*, became increasingly concerned about their morale and their reputation in the public eye, the latter also being important for the recruiting of volunteers. Student therefore began to look for possibilities for a new spectacular parachute and air-landing mission. Probably inspired by conversations with Göring, who had his doubts about Hitler's intention to attack the Soviet Union, and who was for extending the war against Great Britain into the Near East, where one of the Empire's vital veins rested on the petroleum wells, Student had busied himself with employment options for *XI. Flieger-Korps* in this region. According to Göring's thoughts, Crete and Cyprus were to be occupied as springboards on the way to the Near East. However this appeared to only be possible by parachute and air-landing troops, as long as the dominance of the eastern Mediterranean by the British fleet remained unbroken. However against Göring's ideas stood Hitler's decision to engage Great Britain in Egypt and the Near East only after the suppression of the Soviet Union, i.e. during the winter 1941/42.[34] It had to be assumed that the presence of the *Luftwaffe* in the Mediterranean would be reduced to the bare minimum for its employment in *Barbarossa* and so a decisive weakening of the British Alexandria squadron, regarded as mandatory by Jodl prior to the seizure of Crete, would also become doubtful. Mandatory for an attack against Crete was Hitler's decision on 18 March to occupy the entire Greek mainland. Then the *Luftwaffe* would be brought into a position to attack Crete from bases in the south of the Peloponnese, using aircraft with restricted ranges and to reach out far into the waters off the island.

On 20 April, under his own initiative, Student traveled to the forward command post of the commander-in-chief of the *Luftwaffe* which had been set up for the Balkan campaign at the Semmering, about 80km south of Vienna. Here he intended to make use of Göring's ideas about a strategic thrust into the Near East[35] in order to bring his parachute force and himself back into the game. Crete, therefore, almost exclusively, came up as a first objective. Göring ensured that Student was granted time to report the status of combat readiness of *XI. Flieger-Korps* to Hitler personally, who at that time kept track of the Balkan campaign from his special train parked in front of a tunnel at Semmering. The report was also to be used to discuss deployment options of the corps in the Mediterranean region. However prior to this event, a conversation regarding the general strategic environment

---

34   This decision had finally been drawn up in Hitler's Directive No. 30, dated 23 May 1941, i.e. three days after the start of the airborne assault against Crete.

35   Whether Göring had ever proposed this idea to Hitler, like Raeder, is doubtful. Raeder had drawn up a memorandum about the significance of the Mediterranean region for the further conduct of the war and on 14 November 1940 had presented it to Hitler. During the presentation, he had also proposed to postpone the military conflict with the Soviet Union until after the victory over Great Britain, if by that time still necessary. See Gundelach, Band 1, p.39.

for the Mediterranean took place in Hitler's saloon carriage. The discussion was attended by Göring, *General der Flieger* Jeschonnek, *Generalfeldmarschall* Keitel and Jodl. Student was accompanied by the operations staff officer of *XI.Flieger-Korps*, *Major i.G.* Trettner. While Göring and Jeschonnek were keen on taking Crete, as Göring was still guided by his idea to carry the war into the Near East, Keitel and Jodl saw the priority as the conquest of Malta. This British island fortress was located only 58 sea miles away from the southern tip of Sicily and had been attacked minimally from the air by the Italians; nevertheless it soon emerged as a thorn in the side of the Italian sea-lanes to North Africa. The operations of the German *X.Flieger-Korps* against the island and the sea convoys delivering reinforcements and replacements had brought British actions against the sea transports from Italy to Libya, steered from Malta, almost to a standstill but had not led to a permanent removal of the threat. [36] Jodl, the strategic head in the *OKW*, arrived at the conclusion that the reduction of German air power in the Mediterranean at the start of *Barbarossa* would quickly lead to a serious threat to the sea-lanes to North Africa in his assessment of the importance of Malta for the conduct of the war. This would then impact on the reinforcement and resupply transports for German forces now fighting there and have troublesome effects on Hitler's intended offensive actions against the British Empire in the Near East, after the campaign against the Soviet Union. Therefore, Jodl's position was in preference for a conquest of Malta.

Student offered mainly tactical reasons for the taking of Crete in preference to Malta. He argued that the long northern coast of Crete was better suited to establish a foothold than the smaller island of Malta where the enemy could better concentrate his forces and move his reserves faster.

While the discussion was still ongoing Hitler appeared. He listened to the pros and cons for Crete and Malta and then asked Student whether Crete actually could be taken from the air. Upon the latter's confirmation, he immediately decided for Crete, remarking that there was still enough time for the conquest of Malta.[37] However he insisted that the landing of forces from the sea had to be planned for in addition to the attack of Crete from the air. He also pointed out in the light of *Barbarossa* that the operation had to take place as soon as possible. When Student referred to the head-start required for the movement and the staging of forces, Hitler held out the prospect for the date of attack as "around 15 May" but did not fully commit to its execution. At the end of the conference he disclosed the reasons for his decision regarding Crete, pointing out the importance of the Rumanian oil fields for the advance of the *Wehrmacht* in Russia, as these could be attacked by the British from Crete. Furthermore he stated his conviction that the supply route through the Dardanelles would be safe from the British fleet after the conquest of Crete. In his argument he left no doubt that the conquest of Crete solely served his present primary aim, the destruction of the Soviet Union. Consequently in his concluding remark, that the conquest of Crete would constitute a "nice-to-have" conclusion to the campaign in Greece,[38] he unmistakably revealed the fact that there was neither apprehension nor support by

---

36   Five days prior to the conference at the Semmering, four British destroyers, operating from Malta, had engaged an Italian convoy of five transports, escorted by three destroyers, and had sunk all of the transports and one destroyer.

37   The above delineation of the course of the conference on 21 April 1941 leans upon Student's memories in Götzel, pp.198-200, on his elaboration *Angriff ohne Kenntnis der Lage* and on a comment by Trettner regarding essay about Crete by Dr. Roth, published as supplement to *DDF* 4/2001.

38   See Vogel, p.488.

him for Göring's and Raeder's deliberations as to the further conduct of the war in the eastern Mediterranean. As there had also been no proposals for an operational level use of *XI.Flieger-Korps* in *Barbarossa* by the high commands of the *Luftwaffe* and the *Heer* up to now, this subject did not come up during the conference on 21 April. Therefore Hitler only had to decide between the two options for *XI.Flieger-Korps* in the Mediterranean region.

At any rate Student achieved his main goal by Hitler's decision, namely a new combat mission for the whole of the parachute force and thus the objective most desired by him. As a plain commander of troops, he had been admitted to the military-strategic aspects of the subjects discussed on 21 April and was asked whether a successful execution of an airborne assault against Crete could be accomplished. He answered this question positively without restrictions.[39]

---

39   For that reason, the criticism of Student on 21 April 1941 by some military historians seems unjustified.

4

Reinforced *Fallschirmjäger-Regiment 2* seizes the Isthmus of Corinth

eneral der Flieger Student hurried back to Berlin from the Semmering and with the staff of *XI.Flieger-Korps* commenced planning for the conquest of Crete, despite the fact that they still lacked a definitive directive. Meanwhile, the force under *Generalleutnant* Süßmann in Bulgaria became involved in *Marita*. Probably as a result of Hitler's fear that the Corinth Canal could be blocked by the enemy, on 22 April the *OKL*, the *OKH* and *Armeeoberkommando 12/AOK 12*, were ordered by the *OKW* to examine the possibilities for an operation by parachute troops against the Isthmus of Corinth. As the *OKH* and *AOK 12* had beforehand reported about the importance of the canal and the only bridge which crossed it for the operations of ground forces and having spoken positively for a parachute assault against it, the decision was made to complete its execution without delay.

The *OKW* directed the commander-in-chief of the *Luftwaffe* to commence with preparations. The aim of the mission was the seizure of the bridge across the Corinth Canal so as to enable the troops of *12.Armee* to quickly enter the Peloponnese. Beyond this aim they wanted to block the Isthmus against forces of the British expeditionary corps that were withdrawing from the north toward the Peloponnese, though this was not laid down explicitly, mainly because that blocking would occur anyway by the seizure and retention of the only bridge across the Corinth Canal.

As directed by Göring, the commander-in chief of *Luftflotte 4*, *Generaloberst* Löhr, issued the order for the execution of the mission on 22 April. As it was available at short notice *Detachement Süßmann* was tasked with the mission. The overall control of the operation was assigned to *General der Flieger* Freiherr von Richthofen, commanding the *VIII.Flieger-Korps*. The general was greatly opposed to it as he considered the engagement of his flying formations against the anticipated evacuation operations of the British expeditionary corps as a priority and saw detrimental consequences for the supply of his corps in the temporary loss of the air transport formations, but had to accept the decision taken by the highest command level. However he determined that the airborne assault by *Detachement Süßmann* was to be conducted only after the *Heer* seized Thebes, which was only 60km away from the Corinth Canal.[1] Prior to the commencement of the planning process for the airborne mission, the situation in the Greek war zone[2] developed as follows:

After hard fighting and with considerable losses the defense of northern Greece undertaken by Australian and New Zealand forces was overcome by parts of the reinforced

---

1   See Richter, p.193, and Götzel, p.192.
2   For the subsequent short presentation of this situation, the respective parts of Buchner and Playfair have been evaluated.

5.Panzer-Division and the *6.Gebirgs-Division*. However the skillful defenders had managed to escape the danger of an impending envelopment of their left flank by mountain and motorcycle-infantry with the majority of their forces. The German command remained ignorant of the decision of the British commander-in-chief Middle East, General Wavell, made known to the King of Greece on 21 April, to evacuate the British expeditionary corps from the Greek mainland. The Germans had perceived withdrawal movements but remained in the dark about the further intentions of the enemy, in particular, whether, protected by the Gulf of Patras, the Gulf of Corinth and the Saronian Gulf, he would continue the defense on the Peloponnese. Therefore the air operations of *VIII.Flieger-Korps* were initially directed against this region. During the afternoon of 23 April *VIII.Flieger-Korps* succeeded in destroying most of the still operational British Hurricane fighters on the airfield at Mykene (the remaining six aircraft were transferred to Crete the next day), allowing it to achieve unrestricted air superiority over southern Greece. It now could direct its efforts against the evacuation of the British expeditionary corps, which in fact had commenced in the night 24/25 April. However this task turned out to be complicated as the embarkation of the troops of the enemy took place simultaneously at several locations, sometimes away from ports and always during the hours of darkness. Moreover, the troops assembled for embarkation disciplined themselves so skillfully during daytime that they were seldom detected from the air.[3]

At noon on 25 April the advance detachment of the *5.Panzer-Division* entered Thebes. South of Thebes, at Tatoi, a New Zealand brigade group once more blocked the advance of *5.Panzer-Division* but was forced to retreat during the course of 26 April. Covered by the rearguard actions of the New Zealanders, an Australian brigade group of almost 6,000 men was embarked at Megara, about 30km away from Tatoi, during the night 25/26 April. By the morning of 26 April nearly all of the troops which were designated for embarkation from ports on the Peloponnese, among them three brigade groups, were brought across the Corinth Canal. On the night 25/26 April General Wilson, the commander-in-chief of the expeditionary corps, moved his headquarters to Myli, about 45km south of Corinth, despite the loss of large amounts of heavy equipment and supplies, expressing his satisfaction about the present course of the evacuation operation. The German *12.Armee*, after resistance around Thebes was broken, directed the efforts of its most forward troops towards Athens, about 25km away.

Immediately upon the receipt of the mission to seize the bridge across the Corinth Canal by a parachute assault, *Detachement Süßmann* commenced with preparations for this operation.[4] The staff of *FschPiBtl.7* and two of its companies were summoned to Plovdiv from Dessau-Kochstedt as reinforcements. For their transfer, two provisional squadrons were formed from the Ju 52s placed at the disposal of the parachute-schools. As the distance

---

3   In the night 24/25 April about 12,000 troops, including the 5th NZ Brigade Group, had been embarked from Porto Rafti in Attica and Navplion on the Peloponnese in the evacuation operation, designated as 'Demon', under the competent direction by Vice-Admiral Pridham-Wippell.

4   For the course of the mission from the German side, the following sources have been used: Gefechtsbericht Korinth der Gruppe Sturm, in Götzel, 'Wie es zur Luftlandung bei Korinth kam', in *DDF* 4/1956, pp.2-4; report by *Oberleutnant* von Roon, commanding *3./FschJgRgt.2* at Corinth in *DDF* 9/10 1984, pp.6-8; remarks and two aerial photos provided to the author in March 2008 by *Brigadegeneral* (ret.) Hans Teusen, who commanded a platoon of *6./FschJgRgt.2* in the operation.

from Plovdiv to the Isthmus of Corinth was beyond the range of the Ju 52, Larissa, located in the Thessalian Plain, was chosen as the jump-off base for the parachute assault. A transfer of the paratroopers by land to the base had to be excluded because of poor road conditions, the lack of motor transport and the probable short reaction time between the receipt of the order and its execution. The transfer by air, however, also posed considerable problems. In the meantime two air transport groups had been diverted to the support of the German forces in North Africa, quite a number of transport aircraft still remained detached to *VIII. Flieger-Korps* and the combat readiness of the Ju 52 formations had decreased due to overuse. Thus, only about 140 transport aircraft were available for the mission against the Corinth Canal. This meant that the parachuting of the complete *Detachement Süßmann* in one single flight was not possible. In addition to that restriction, stores of aviation fuel on the airfield at Larrissa, also used by units of *VIII.Flieger-Korps*, were insufficient for multiple flights of the air transport formations to Corinth and allowed for the employment of only one air transport group for a resupply mission after the landing of the *Fallschirmtruppe*. Even for the return flight of the Ju 52s from Larissa to their bases in Bulgaria, fuel had to be brought with the aircraft.

During the morning of 25 April the order for the parachute assault on the morning of 26 April arrived at the command of *Detachement Süßmann*. *General der Flieger* Freiherr von Richthofen repeatedly expressed his opposition to the mission and justified it with the strained air transport situation and his view about the priority of the employment of his forces against the British evacuation fleet. Göring, however, took the side of *Generalfeldmarschall* List, who requested the execution of the airborne mission.[5]

Generalleutnant Süßmann delegated direct command of the parachute assault to the commander of *FschJgRgt.2*, *Oberst* Sturm. As the preparations of the detachment had been completed for the greater part by the arrival of the execution order, the transfer of the elements planned for the actual parachute assault commenced without delay early in the morning of 25 April. Nevertheless this action took up valuable time until late in the evening, so that the last air transport squadrons touched down on the packed airfield at Larissa in the darkness. There was almost no time for the rest or supply of troops, as final arrangements for the start of operations still had to be complete. During this time, the following units arrived at the airfield: staff and signals platoon of *FschJgRgt.2*, *I./FschJgRgt.2* (*Hauptmann* Kroh), *II./FschJgRgt.2* (*Hauptmann* Pietzonka), one-third of *13./FschJgRgt.2* (guns), half of *14./FschJgRgt.2* (anti-tank), *3./FschFlaMGBtl.7* (less one platoon), the parachute engineer platoons Häffner and Brohm and half of *1./FschSanAbt.7*. *3./FschArtAbt.7* was to follow in gliders with three guns. The remaining parts of *Detachement Süßmann* were initially to stay behind at Plovdiv-Krumovo.

Throughout the course of the evening of 25 April *Generalleutnant* Süßmann also moved with his forward command element to the command post of *VIII.Flieger-Korps*, which since 24 April had been in the seaport of Volos, about 45km south-east of Larissa. Against his instructions, Süßmann retained the two squadrons formed from the Ju 52 of the parachute schools, as they were urgently required to deliver aviation fuel from the Plovdiv area to Larissa.[6] The tactical leaders of *Gruppe Sturm* were instructed about the

---

5   See Richter, pp.444-448 and Vogel, p.474.
6   The fuel was pumped through a newly constructed pipeline from the Rumanian oilfields to the northern bank of the Danube and shipped from there by tankers to the Danube port of Russee. There it was loaded into fuel wagons, and brought by rail into the area around Plovdiv. There it was filled into 200-liter barrels

terrain in the operational area as precisely as possible by means of maps and aerial photos. The intelligence produced the following picture.

The hub of the operational area was formed by the Corinth Canal, which was cut into the rocks of the Isthmus at its most narrow part, 6.4km in width. Built between 1881 and 1893 it connected the Saronian Gulf in the south-east with the Gulf of Corinth in the north-west. It was cut into the rock of the Isthmus up to 60m deep with almost vertical walls. It was 24m wide at its top and 21m at sea-level, 8m deep. About 3km from its northern entrance the canal was crossed by its only bridge, which was of solid steel construction, being traversed by the road and railway line leading from Athens along the coast of the Saronian Gulf. North of these lines of communication and east of the canal the terrain descended from the 1,300m high Gerania Mountains, to the coast of the Saronian Gulf. Another road led from the settlement of Loutraki, located at the Gulf of Corinth, about 4km north of the bridge, toward the site of the bridge. The town of Corinth had 20,000 inhabitants and was built on the flat beach of the Gulf, a good 3km west of the bridge. Here, the road divided. One arm bypassed an airfield about 4km west of the town and led along the northern coast of the Peloponnese to Patras, on the Gulf with the same name. The other arm turned to the south, through mountainous terrain to Argos a town about 35km south of Corinth, then to Myli, on the coast of the Argolian Gulf and from there across the Peloponnese to the sea-port of Kalamata on the Messenian Gulf. Another airfield was located some distance south of Mykene. At Argos, a division of the road ran to the sea ports at Navplion and Tolon on the northern shore of the Argolian Gulf. Only a short distance west of the road division at Corinth, a mountain ridge with central massifs of more than 2,300m high rose steeply south of the coastal road and stretched toward the west.

On 25 April bombers and fighters of *VIII.Flieger-Korps* attacked the anti-aircraft positions of the enemy which had been detected in the vicinity of the Corinth Canal. Immediately after the decision to evacuate the Greek mainland the command of the British expeditionary corps concentrated its remaining anti-aircraft forces of 16 Bofors guns for the protection of any retrograde movements, but also against possible German airborne attacks, on the Isthmus of Corinth, along the road to Argos and on the nearby airfield.[7] Initially only the remainder of the 4th Hussars Regiment from the British 1st Armoured Brigade was tasked with the surveillance of the northern coast of the Peloponnese, including the Corinth Canal, a length of 110km. It consisted of 12 light Mark VI tanks, six Bren Gun Carriers and one armored car.[8] On 24 April the New Zealand 6th Field Coy of engineers was summoned from Thebes and prepared the bridge across the Corinth Canal for demolition. Moreover it assembled some boats for the construction of ferries at the southern entrance of the canal, in case that bridge was destroyed prematurely by the enemy.

On this day the command of all troops deployed at the canal was given to Brigadier Lee. His sector of responsibility included terrain on either side of the canal and the areas around

---

and flown by Ju 52 to the airfield at Larissa. In Larissa, the transport aircraft returning from the Corinth area had to be refilled from these barrels by means of hand-pumps.

7   The description of the forces on the British side involved in the fighting on the Isthmus of Corinth is primarily based on the Official History of New Zealand in the Second World War.

8   The Mark VI was armed with two machine-guns in a turret. The Bren Gun Carrier was constructed mainly for the transport of heavy infantry weapons. It was only lightly armored and open-topped.

Corinth and Argos. He was instructed to be prepared for German air-landings on the two airfields which were located in his sector. During the evening of 25 April Brigadier Lee retained some of the troops on their way to the Peloponnese, these being three companies and two platoons from the Australian 2/6 Infantry Battalion, B Coy/19th (NZ) Infantry Battalion, 6th (NZ) Field Coy and one engineer platoon from the British 7th Armoured Division Field Squadron. At about 0230hrs on 26 April C Squadron from the Cavalry Regiment of the New Zealand Division, still equipped with a few wheeled armored cars and reinforced with the remainders of the Bren Gun Carrier platoons from the 22nd and 28th (NZ) Infantry Battalions, also arrived.

Brigadier Lee formed the so-called Isthmus Force for the direct defense of the bridge across the Corinth Canal. It was composed of B Coy/19th Infantry Battalion, 6th Field Coy, one platoon of 122nd Light Anti-Aircraft Artillery Regiment, a British engineer platoon and C Squadron/NZ Divisional Cavalry. The force was placed subordinate to the commander of B Coy/19th Infantry Battalion. This officer positioned one of his infantry platoons in the Gerania mountains, about 7km north-west of the bridge and deployed the remaining two platoons of his company in the hilly terrain about 500m north of the bridge. A company from 2/6 Infantry Battalion was also positioned in the area immediately east of the bridge. However the commanders of the two forces deployed east of the canal were not informed about each other's presence. C Squadron/NZ Divisional Cavalry was in the process of setting up positions about 2km west of the western bridge ramp. In the immediate vicinity of this ramp four heavy anti-aircraft guns were being positioned. Some of the 37mm and 40mm guns were dispersed in positions around the bridge. Others were set up further to the west and south-west. 6th Field Coy prepared positions about 500m south of Corinth. Two of its squads, planned as demolition teams, were kept standing by about 1km north of the bridge, near the western bank of the canal. In the buildings between Corinth and the northern entrance of the canal the 4th Hussars established their command post. A company of 2/6 Infantry Battalion moved into a position on the slope about 3km south of Corinth, just north of a small village. The remainder of 2/6 Inf, the staff, one company and two platoons, together with a few heavy and some Bofors anti-aircraft guns, were deployed for the protection of the nearby airfield.

For direct defense along the Corinth Canal and the immediately adjoining terrain, Brigadier Lee had 900 soldiers from the expeditionary corps at his disposal.[9] A considerable number of Greek soldiers, who had not felt bound to the capitulation arrangements of their high command, were also present some distance east of the canal, in the settlements south of it and in the area around Patras. Joint combat operations with the expeditionary corps, however, had not been planned.

On 26 April *Gruppe Sturm* took off for the parachute mission against the Isthmus of Corinth from the airfield at Larissa between 0430 and 0600hrs.

The approach flight of the air transport took place in the following formations: *KGr z.b.V.102* with *Untergruppe Pietzonka*, *KGr z.b.V.60* with *Untergruppe Kroh*, *I./KG z.b.V.1* with *3./FschFlaMGBtl.7* and half of *14./FschJgRgt.2*, *I./LL-Geschwader 1* with

---

9   This number has been taken from Allied sources. As the reports of *Gruppe Sturm* show, the overall number of soldiers from the expeditionary corps, who, for one reason or another had been present on 26 April in the sector assigned to Brigadier Lee, must have been considerably higher.

the regimental staff. This was conducted at a height of more than 2,000m across the Pindus Mountains. The most forward section consisted of six Ju 52s, towing the gliders with the parachute engineer platoon of *Leutnant* Häffner aboard (reinforced 2nd Platoon of *3./FschPiBtl.7* – 54 men) which was to land 12 minutes ahead of the first wave of the paratroopers at both ramps of the bridge across the Corinth Canal to take possession of it. South of the Pindus mountain range the air transport formations, except the six towing aircraft, descended to 30m above the surface of the Gulf of Corinth and flew protected from observation by the morning haze over the water toward the east. The gliders unhooked the cables of the towing aircraft at about 20km distance from the objective at 1,200m height and commenced the dive. The Ju 52s with the main force aboard ascended to parachuting height in the vicinity of the drop zones and reduced their speed.

During the time of the approach flight of *Gruppe Sturm*, combat aircraft of *VIII.Flieger-Korps* attacked identified positions of the enemy on either side of the Corinth Canal. Only fighter-bombers with machine-guns and dive bombers, due to their capability of hitting targets precisely, were used, to prevent an unwanted destruction of the bridge by bombs going astray. Some of the anti-aircraft guns around the canal were thus put out of action and the crews of the remaining weapons, as well as the infantry in their field positions, were forced to take cover.

The six gliders with Häffner's platoon aboard came down on either side of the bridge at about 0610hrs, coming in as air attacks ceased, and hidden against observation until the very last moment by the haze and the smoke from the impacting bombs. Five of them touched down about 100-200m from the bridge. The sixth glider, attempting a landing on the western ramp of the bridge, crashed into its foundation block. Both the pilot and the medical sergeant behind him were hurled onto the road. The remaining eight soldiers were stunned and injured by the impact, and initially unable to join the fighting although they managed to leave the glider. The crews of the other gliders fought through to the bridge site, taking only a few losses from scattered fire by the totally surprised defenders. Here, a number of them neutralized the few guards at the bridge and commenced to remove the explosive charges from the steel framework and cut the ignition cables, while others prevented the crews of nearby anti-aircraft guns from occupying their weapon pits, which they had left during the air attacks.

Shortly before 0640hrs the first wave of paratroopers of *Gruppe Sturm* arrived west of the canal. These were two companies each of the two parachute infantry battalions – 2nd and 4th companies of *I./FschJgRgt.2* and Brohm's engineer platoon (east of the canal), and 5th and 6th companies of *II./FschJgRgt.2*.[10]

West of the canal *5./FschJgRgt.2*, under *Oberleutnant* Thiel, reinforced with a heavy machine-gun platoon from the 8th Company, was dropped first. With just the weapons to hand the paratroopers seized the railway station near the bridge, three positions nearby and a number of motor vehicles that had been abandoned by their drivers and passengers during the air attacks on the road to Corinth. This also allowed for the capture of a considerable

---

10   The times for the landing of the units of *Gruppe Sturm*, found in its after-action report, must be regarded as approximate. Only the time for the explosion of the bridge, which was exactly 0700hrs, is definitively confirmed by two aerial photos, all others have been slightly adjusted by the author. However there is no doubt that the first wave of the paratroopers was dropped about 10-15 minutes later than originally planned, probably because the leading air transport formation had lost some time ascending to parachuting height and by reducing their speed for the drop. The adjusted times also correspond better with those found in the respective Australian and New Zealand histories of the Second World War.

number of enemy soldiers. Afterwards the company set up positions along a perimeter around the western ramp of the bridge, at about 1km distance. Under *Hauptmann* Schirmer *6./FschJgRgt.2* was dropped two minutes after *5./FschJgRgt.2*. Its 1st Platoon under *Leutnant* Teusen put four light anti-aircraft guns out of action and set up for the close protection of the engineers working on the bridge immediately west of it. The other two platoons of the company advanced against the column of motor vehicles on the road toward Corinth, which had not been attacked by *5./FschJgRgt.2*.

The staff and the signals platoon of *II./FschJgRgt.2* jumped as part of the first wave of the battalion. *Hauptmann* Pietzonka suffered a double fracture of an ankle on landing and was carried to his command post, which was being established a short distance from the canal. Here, he tasked *Hauptmann* Schirmer with tactical command of the battalion. During the mopping-up actions in the drop zone of the force around the command post, the battalion's orderly officer, *Oberleutnant* Dohmes, was killed. *Leutnant* Schallnas from *3./FschFlaMGBtl.7* with his HQ section, jumped with the battalion-staff and shortly thereafter met the same fate.

East of the Corinth Canal, in the area of operations of *I./FschJgRgt.2*, Brohm's parachute engineer platoon jumped first. Its mission was to seize the road and railway bridge about 4km east of Kalamaki and to prevent its destruction. However it was dropped incorrectly and came down in the defile about 10km north-east of Kalamaki, immediately on the shore of the Saronian Gulf. One of its squads landed in the water, causing one soldier to be drowned and two weapon containers to become lost. Three other men were also injured on the landing ground. Nevertheless, without further losses, the platoon overcame a number of Greek soldiers who fired at them during the landing and captured 20 of them. Subsequently, Brohm cleared the village of Aghia Theodori on the coastal road about 10km north of the canal from Greek stragglers. There it was joined by the 3rd Platoon of *2./FschJgRgt.2* under *Leutnant* Kühne. Together the platoons now advanced along the coastal road toward a barracks in the village of Kineta, about 6km further to the east. When this was found abandoned they moved on in the direction toward Megara. However by now they were continuously involved in firefights with Greek stragglers. Just west of Megara they successfully removed the explosive charges from a railway bridge. It was at this time that both platoons were ordered to fall back into the defile west of the village of Aghia Theodori and to act as combat outposts for *Untergruppe Kroh*. On the way to the new location the parachute engineer platoon unexpectedly became involved in a firefight with troops of the British expeditionary corps that were advancing from the east. Before it was able to disengage the platoon lost two killed and four wounded.

The 2nd and 4th companies of *I./FschJgRgt.2*, except two plane loads, were correctly dropped east of the canal with the battalion-staff. The paratroopers first cleared the drop zone and then advanced toward the canal. Enemy infantry, to the strength of about a company, which were positioned east of the bridge, were quickly overrun and most of the soldiers of B Coy, 19th (NZ) Infantry Battalion were captured. The subsequent attack against a hill to the north met with stronger resistance.

While the fighting on both sides of the canal was ongoing and the parachuting of *Gruppe Sturm* continued, the engineers of Häffner's platoon completed the removal of explosive charges from the bridge structure. These were piled on the bridge, to be carried away afterward. At this moment, at exactly 0700hrs, the bridge blew up in a tremendous explosion and plunged down into the canal. Several engineers who were still working on the bridge, and a military war correspondent, *Sonderführer* von der Heyden, who had accompanied the engineer platoon, were instantly killed.[11] Some of the men from Teusen's platoon, located in protective positions close to the western ramp of the bridge, were injured by steel splinters.

Despite the loss of the bridge the paratroopers continued with their missions. West of the canal, parts of the 5th and 6th companies that were advancing further to the west, come across the remainder of C Squadron/NZ Divisional Cavalry and the assigned two Bren Gun Carrier platoons east of Corinth. As these were still in the process of recovering from the preceding air attacks they were surprised by the sudden onslaught of the paratroopers. Between eight and ten of the armored vehicles were destroyed or captured in the first minutes and most of their crews were taken prisoner. However about 40 of the New Zealanders, with two armored cars and five Bren Gun Carriers managed to escape toward the south along a sunken road, unobserved by the attackers. When this road ended at a deep ravine the vehicles were pushed over, at least denying them to the enemy. Their crews were later found by Greeks and conveyed across the mountains to Navplion. The company from 2/6 Infantry Battalion, which was positioned north of Examilia, was not drawn into the fighting and was able to retreat on its own toward the south.

After landing *7./FschJgRgt.2* dispatched two platoons against Corinth. On the way to the north-western entrance of the Corinth Canal the third platoon encountered some resistance from field positions and buildings along its western bank. Nevertheless the platoon succeeded in overrunning the command post of the 4th Hussars and capturing most of its personnel. In the meantime *8./FschJgRgt.2*, two platoons from *3./FschFlaMGBtl.7* and two anti-tank-guns, that were the remaining parts of *Untergruppe Pietzonka*, also landed safely west of the Corinth Canal and secured their drop zones. The two anti-tank guns set up firing positions south of the road leading from the blown bridge toward Corinth. *Hauptmann* Pietzonka now assigned two-thirds of the 7th and 8th companies, one anti-tank gun and one light anti-aircraft gun to *Hauptmann* Schirmer with the mission to build a protective screen against the town. However the mission was quickly overcome by events, as the 6th and 7th companies from *II./FschJgRgt.2* entered the outskirts of Corinth. *Leutnant* Rühle from 6th Company penetrated the town in one of the Bren Gun Carriers, of which 6th and 8th companies had captured one each in working condition, despite the fact that it was occupied by a considerable number of troops. He managed to get hold of the town's mayor and the Greek military commandant of Corinth, to escort them safely to *Hauptmann* Schirmer. After a short exchange of views with the latter the two Greek authorities declared themselves willing to hand the town over to the German officer in charge. They were then brought to the regimental command post, which had been set up at a road junction about 1.5km west of the destroyed bridge after the Regimental Staff had landed at 0730hrs. At 1100hrs *Oberst* Sturm met the two Greek officials and requested the unconditional surrender of Corinth by 1300hrs or else it would be attacked by dive bombers. The bluff worked and the Greek mayor surrendered the town unconditionally. Its occupation by German troops was completed at 1300 hrs.

In the meantime parts of the 7th and 8th companies of *II./FschJgRgt.2*, assigned to *Hauptmann* Schirmer, attacked into the town on their own. Two platoons and the HQ section from 6th (NZ) Field Coy stubbornly resisted the advance from a lemon grove at

---

11   Of the various reports about the reasons for the explosion, the most credible is that a lucky hit by a British anti-aircraft gun had ignited the pile of explosives.

the edge of Corinth. When their situation became hopeless they managed to break out in small groups. Most of them eventually reached the port of Kalamata, where they too were evacuated on 27 April. Another platoon of 6th (NZ) Field Coy, with the exception of about 20 men, was captured in an air raid shelter. The few Greek troops in Corinth, consisting exclusively of staff, administrative and logistical personnel, offered no organized resistance. *Hauptmann* Schirmer's 6th Company bypassed Corinth in a southerly direction. On the way it occupied a barracks where it captured three anti-aircraft guns, two light and one heavy. At 1400hrs a reinforced *II./FschJgRgt.2* formed a defense line toward the south from the eastern entrance of the Corinth Canal, to the position of *6./FschJgRgt.2* south-west of Corinth. About this time, *Oberst* Sturm also moved to Corinth, from where he began to establish personal contact with subordinate units. Incomprehensibly, no attempt was undertaken to occupy the airfield at Corinth.

Together with the first paratroopers of *II./FschJgRgt.2*, a shock troop from *1./FschSanAbt.7*, led by *Oberarzt* Dr. Mallison, had also entered Corinth. Not yet marked as medical personnel, the shock troop confiscated a Greek military hospital and immediately prepared the operating rooms for the surgical treatment of wounded. The main dressing station of *1./FschSanAbt.7* was moved to the hospital, leaving behind only a collection point for wounded in the original location. At about 1530hrs a Ju 52 dropped medical supplies at the hospital. Shortly afterwards a medical Ju 52[12] landed at the hospital, loaded the first seriously wounded and took off again. Some transport aircraft delivering supplies also touched down at the hospital and after unloading, took wounded aboard. So by 1700hrs 37 of them were on their way to a German military hospital in Salonika. Among them was *Hauptmann* Pietzonka, who handed over command of his battalion to *Hauptmann* Schirmer.

In the operational area of *Untergruppe Kroh*, *3./FschJgRgt.2*, under *Oberleutnant* von Roon, had finally arrived shortly after the canal bridge had been blown, even though it should have been dropped before the staff of *I./FschJgRgt.2*. Two of its platoons came down as planned and attacked the village of Kalamaki from the north. The village was occupied after a short fight because the Allied and the Greek troops there immediately made for the high ground north of the railway and coastal road. A ferry, which was found in Kalamaki, was immediately utilized, but it started to sink with the first truck aboard. As a result work commenced to construct a provisional bridge with boats found in the small port of Kalamaki. With the support of engineers from platoon Häffner, the bridge was ready in the early afternoon and constituted the only permanent crossing site for troops and light vehicles for the time being. As the telephone exchange in Kalamaki still worked communication across the canal was soon possible again via commercial lines. A platoon from *14./FschJgRgt.2* (anti-tank), dropped in support of *I./FschJgRgt.2*, arrived at Kalamaki without difficulties and set up positions on the eastern edge of the village toward the east. The platoon from *13./FschJgRgt.2*, which had also been assigned to *I./FschJgRgt.2*, however,

---

12   Two of these aircraft, which had specifically been prepared for the air transport of seriously wounded, had been assigned to *Gruppe Sturm*.

was dropped wrongly into the Gerania Mountains. The salvage of the individual loads of its two recoilless guns turned out to be extremely difficult and time consuming.

The third platoon of *3./FschJgRgt.2* was dropped incorrectly south-east of Corinth, west of the canal. It advanced toward its eastern entrance near Isthmia and captured an anti-aircraft battery, which had already been abandoned by its crew. At about 1345hrs the gliders with guns of *3./FschArtAbt.7*, which had been brought along from Plovdiv/Bulgaria via Larissa arrived near the regimental command post of *Gruppe Sturm*.[13] A situation report from *VIII.Flieger-Korps*, about a possible enemy attack against the Isthmus of Corinth from the north-east, caused these guns to be assigned to *Untergruppe Kroh*. At 1900hrs their commander reported to the command post of *I./FschJgRgt.2* and in the course of the night managed to bring along his two guns.

As the two platoons positioned in combat outposts of *Untergruppe Kroh*, in the defile west of Aghia Theodori, were attacked several times before midnight and *VIII.Flieger-Korps* had warned of a strong thrust by the enemy from the east within the next few hours, they were finally withdrawn into the main defensive line of *I./FschJgRgt.2* just east of the Corinth Canal.[14]

Except for the sporadic exchange of shots during reconnaissance or mopping up actions, the fighting in the operational area of *Untergruppe Pietzonka* came to a temporary end in the evening of 26 April. Since the start of the glider and parachute assault, the sub-group, now commanded by *Hauptmann* Schirmer, had taken 554 soldiers of the British expeditionary corps as prisoners; among them were 19 officers and more than 450 Greek soldiers. Among the heavy equipment captured undamaged were 14 heavy and 10 light anti-aircraft guns, two Bren Gun Carriers, about 50 trucks and numerous smaller motor vehicles. However considerable units of the British expeditionary corps and some brigade groups were known to have reached the area around Argos and Navplion. As the position which was occupied by *Hauptmann* Schirmer's force in the evening was thought to be vulnerable to a counter-attack from the south it was relocated as of 1000hrs. A counter-attack had indeed been initiated in the morning. This was based on an erroneous report by the command of the 4th Hussars, that just a hundred or so German paratroopers had been dropped near the Corinth Canal. Two companies from the 26th Battalion of the 6th (NZ) Brigade and a number of its Bren Gun Carriers had been dispatched as reinforcements from the area around Argos to the Isthmus, in order to support the still intended movement of the 4th (NZ) Brigade Group to the Peloponnese. Informed by stragglers on the way toward Corinth about the true dimensions of the German parachute assault and attacked from the air, the commander of the reinforcement column decided to stop the further advance of his force and initially occupy a blocking position at Solomos, about 7km south of Corinth.

---

13 For transport by gliders, the guns had to be taken apart into two loads. One of the gliders with parts of a gun had to conduct an emergency landing, still on Bulgarian soil. Therefore only two of the intended three guns had arrived in time. The third gun was delivered after the end of the fighting on the Isthmus of Corinth.

14 4th (NZ) Brigade Group, which in the morning of 26 April had delayed the advance of 5.*Panzer-Division* south of Thebes, indeed, had planned to move across the Corinth Canal to its embarkation port on the Peloponnese. It was its advance forces which had clashed with parts of Kroh's group in the course of 26 April. When the German parachute mission against the Isthmus of Corinth was recognized to its full extent, General Wilson had turned the Brigade Group around toward Porto Rafti on the coast of Attica, where 4,600 of its soldiers had been embarked in the night 27/28 April. Its forward troops, however, had been drawn into the fighting on the Isthmus, and were captured there. See Davin, Volume 2, p.422.

There, the force covered the rearward lines of a company of the Australian 2/6 Infantry Battalion, from the area north of Examilia and provided motor transport for this company further to the south. A German reconnaissance patrol, which had pursued the retreating Australian company from Examilia, was ambushed in the ravine in front of Solomos and was almost totally wiped out.

In the ports of Navplion and Tolon, about 40km south of Corinth, covered by the remainder of Lee's task force and by the 26th (NZ) Infantry Battalion from the greater area around Argos, about 4,500 soldiers of the British expeditionary corps, among them the headquarter troops of General Wilson, were embarked during the night 26/27 April. As no further opportunity for an evacuation from these ports had been seen, the evacuation fleet had attempted to take aboard as many soldiers as possible. Therefore at daylight on 27 April they were still within the range of German dive bombers. These promptly attacked and managed to sink the transport *Slamat,* the Polish destroyer *Wryneck,* and the British destroyer *Diamond,* causing the loss of more than 500 soldiers and sailors.[15] Furthermore about 2,200 soldiers of the expeditionary corps, mostly administrative and logistic personnel, were left behind for good on the coast of the Argolian Gulf. On 26 April General Wilson had passed command over all remaining forces of the expeditionary corps on the Greek mainland to the commander of the New Zealand Division, Major General Freyberg, and left for Alexandria in a flying boat. In addition to the evacuations in the Argolian Gulf, about 8,700 soldiers of the expeditionary corps, including the two almost complete Australian 16th and 17th Brigade Groups, were evacuated during that night from the port of Kalamata for Egypt.

Owing to the uninterrupted replenishment of aviation fuel on the airfield at Larissa, in the course of the late afternoon of 26 April the air transport formations which had returned from their tasks at the Isthmus of Corinth were able to move I*II./FschJgRgt.2,* a great part of the staff of *Detachement Süßmann,* and additional medical troops from the area around Plovdiv to Larissa. There, they were earmarked for delivery by air into the operational area of *Gruppe Sturm* on 27 April.

At dawn on 27 April, when attacks by the enemy from the north-east failed to materialize, *1./FschJgRgt.2* pushed forward reconnaissance in front of its entire sector. Two platoons from its 2nd Company, advancing toward Kineta, came across motorcycle-infantry of the *5.Panzer-Division* at Aghia Theodori. These light troops moved onto the Corinth Canal and crossed it using the provisional bridge at its eastern entrance. As a consequence the combat operations of *Untergruppe Kroh* definitively came to an end. From its overall personnel strength of 30 officers and 973 other ranks, it had lost five killed, five wounded and 13 missing. On the side the enemy, about 1,120 soldiers had been captured, with about 380 of them belonging to British, New Zealand and Australian units. In view of the now approaching advance forces from *5.Panzer-Division,* at 1730hrs *Hauptmann* Kroh received the order from *Oberst* Sturm to move his sub-group to Corinth.

As *Untergruppe Pietzonka* was not counter-attacked, its positions, abandoned at nightfall on 26 April, were reoccupied shortly after first daylight on 27 April. At the

---

15   See Richter, p.171.

western entrance of the Corinth Canal, four of the captured heavy anti-aircraft guns were positioned against possible attacks by British naval forces. On the orders of *Oberst* Sturm, all Greek soldiers captured so far during the parachute mission were now released and sent home.

At about 1100hrs, a liaison officer from *5.Panzer-Division* arrived by light reconnaissance aircraft at the regimental command post. However it was not seen as necessary to accept his offer for an acceleration of the arrival of advance forces, and for the relief of the *Fallschirmtruppe*.

About this time, *1./FschJgRgt.2*, which was deployed to protect the regimental command post, was ordered to move to Corinth. Swinging far to the south the company suddenly came across elements of the enemy, which still held out in the park-like ruins of ancient Corinth. It took a costly flanking movement, which cost nine killed and four wounded, before the company managed to drive the enemy off. Its 3rd Platoon now advanced toward the airfield at Corinth, about 3km further to the north, at the beach of the Gulf of Corinth. On the way to this objective the platoon captured about 80 soldiers of the expeditionary corps, among them 14 officers. When it reached the undefended airfield at about 1345hrs, it found some Ju 52s in which *Generalleutnant* Süßmann and parts of his staff had arrived.[16]

By 1430hrs *Generalleutnant* Süßmann and *Oberst* Haseloff, the commander of *5.Schützen-Brigade* from *5.Panzer-Division*, who had driven ahead of his troops, shook hands at the command post of *Gruppe Sturm*. Around 1500hrs, probably based on an agreement between *Generalleutnant* Süßmann and the operational staff officer of *5.Panzer-Division*, *Oberst* Sturm ordered *Hauptmann* Schirmer to immediately seize the airfield at Mykene, utilizing captured motor vehicles. Before *Hauptmann* Schirmer's task force was ready to move the staff of *II./Schützen-Regiment 13*, the 1st and 8th companies of this regiment and three 15cm guns from *8./ArtRgt.116*, led by the commander of *II./Schützen-Regiment 13*, *Oberstleutnant* Kieler, managed to cross the Corinth Canal over the provisional bridge of the paratroopers. However the bridge had broken down under the weight of the third gun and as such the connection between both banks of the canal had to be maintained with boats until the arrival of engineers from the *5.Panzer-Division* with bridging equipment.

For the advance toward Argos, task force Schirmer was now placed subordinate to *Oberstleutnant* Kieler. It was to advance to Argos ahead of Kieler's troops. There, it was to wait for the arrival of the 15cm guns prior to the further advance toward Navplion.[17]

At 1640hrs Schirmer moved off toward Argos. On the way Schirmer was informed by a report dropped from reconnaissance aircraft that the area around Argos was unoccupied by the British expeditionary corps. Therefore he decided to immediately pass through the defile north of Argos and occupy the nearby airfield. On the abandoned airfield the task force discovered a number of damaged British fighter aircraft, some anti-aircraft guns and

---

16   A statement by Buchner (p.193), indicating the airfield at Corinth was seized by the paratroopers on 26 April after heavy fighting, is contradicted by the after-action report of *Gruppe Sturm*. The latter makes also clear that the commander-in-chief of *Luftflotte 4*, *Generaloberst* Löhr, arrived together with *Generalleutnant* Süßmann on 27 April for a short visit on the Isthmus of Corinth, but had left earlier than Süßmann.

17   See Plato, pp.128-129.

about 8,000 liters of aviation fuel.[18] Leaving behind a parachute platoon, an anti-tank gun and a light anti-aircraft gun for the protection of the airfield, *Hauptmann* Schirmer hurried on. At 1915hrs his task force arrived in front of Argos. Although the 15cm battery had not yet made its appearance *Hauptmann* Schirmer sought out the mayor of Argos and the Greek garrison commandant, who immediately surrendered the town to him. The task force then moved on for about 8km toward Navplion. There, under the protection of sentries, it rested for some hours. During the night a platoon from *1./FschJgRgt.2* delivered an 80-watt radio set. By means of this communication, *Gruppe Sturm* ordered *Hauptmann* Schirmer to advance to Navplion and Mily early in the morning of 28 April and return from there to the area around Corinth after the arrival of follow-on forces from the *5.Panzer-Division*.

During the afternoon of 27 April, *III./FschJgRgt.2* landed on the airfield at Corinth and was initially kept in readiness there. With the departing transport aircraft a number of the less seriously wounded paratroopers were taken back to German medical installations in the north-east of Greece. A patrol from *1./FschJgRgt.2*, moving along the coastal road, unexpectedly met elements of the *2./AufklAbt* from the *SS Leibstandarte Adolf Hitler* at Xylokastron, about 30km west of Corinth. The *Leibstandarte*, which began crossing the Gulf of Patras on 26 April and in the meantime had gained control over Patras and its port, had not been informed about the actual situation at the Isthmus of Corinth. Four of its companies therefore were sent from Patras by train for the relief of *Gruppe Sturm* late in the afternoon of 27 April. As there was no need at all for their presence, they returned to Patras on the morning of 28 April for the subsequent advance along the western part of the Peloponnese.

At dawn on 28 April, *5./FschJgRgt.2* occupied Mily, which had been cleared of the enemy. The 7th and 8th companies of Schirmer's task force, supported by sub-units of the motorcycle-infantry from *5.Panzer-Division*, took possession of the town and the port of Navplion. There was no sign of the British expeditionary corps with the exception of the wreck of the troop transport *Ulster Prince*, which after some bomb hits listed alongside the pier of the port. However in the town the paratroopers captured the general who was in command of all Greek troops on the Peloponnese, except for those in Patras. The Greek general declared himself willing to surrender all troops under his command. This intention, however, caused some difficulties, as the telephone system on the Peloponnese had partly broken down and radio contact between Schirmer and *Gruppe Sturm* was not reliable.

Schirmer's 6th Company in the meantime bypassed Navplion and around midday approached Tolon. There it was confronted by numerically superior British troops, who had not yet given up hope of being evacuated from this port. In the ensuing fighting *6./FschJgRgt.2* lost three killed and 14 wounded and were forced to fall back some distance toward Navplion. Upon Schirmer's situation report, *Oberst* Sturm immediately dispatched a reinforced company from *III./FschJgRgt.2*, still available elements of *3./FschFlaMGBtl.7* and a platoon each of the regimental-level gun and anti-tank companies, in support of Schirmer.

---

18   After the termination of the evacuation at Navplion and Tolon in the early hours of 27 April, the elements from the Isthmus Force and 26th (NZ) Infantry Battalion, covering the approaches from the north, had moved off for their own embarkation at Monemvasia, in the south-east corner of the Peloponnese.

In the meantime *Oberleutnant* Knobloch, Schirmer's adjutant, had won over a captured British officer as a negotiator with the stranded British forces at Tolon. He had obviously been able to convince him about the (non-existent) presence of numerous German troops close to Tolon, of the imminent arrival of armored forces and of a pre-planned dive-bomber attack. How effective his ruse was became visible a few hours later. At about 1900hrs 72 officers and 1,200 other ranks formed up at Tolon to march into captivity. In addition numerous enemy wounded were transported by ambulances to the field dressing station, which the medical officer of Schirmer's task force had set up in Navplion. The amount of booty was also considerable, although most of the about 500 motor vehicles of the enemy were made permanently unusable.[19]

The task force of 5.*Panzer-Division* under *Oberstleutnant* Kieler moved off from the Isthmus of Corinth late in the evening of 27 April and in the early hours of 28 April commenced to cross the Peloponnese in a direction toward the port of Kalamata. In the course of this day it was joined by two 8-wheeled signals reconnaissance armored cars. These had used the light war bridge, which in the meantime had been constructed across the southern part of the Corinth Canal by the engineer battalion of 5.*Panzer-Division*.

After the capitulation of the British troops at Tolon *Hauptmann* Schirmer was driven to Corinth. For the first time since the employment of his task force *Oberst* Sturm and *Generalleutnant* Süßmann now received a complete and precise report about the situation on the coast of the Argolian Gulf, as most of the radio traffic from there was garbled. As this region was now considered safely in the hands of troops from the 5.*Panzer-Division* Schirmer's force was ordered back to the Isthmus. The reinforcements for Schirmer, which had reached the area around Argos, were called back earlier.

With the return of *Untergruppe Pietzonka* from the south, the mission of *Gruppe Sturm* on the Peloponnese had definitively come to an end. Of its overall strength of 28 officers and 830 other ranks, the sub-group had lost four officers and 43 other ranks in killed, wounded and missing. As it had taken the brunt of the fighting, it alone had captured more than 1,900 soldiers of the British expeditionary corps on the Peloponnese, among them 91 officers.

After the end of the campaign by the *Wehrmacht* on the Greek mainland, *Detachement Süßmann* was moved into quarters around Corinth and Megara. The fighting on the Peloponnese had cost the detachment 65 killed, 89 seriously and 123 less seriously wounded and 17 missing. With eight killed and 18 wounded, the losses of Häffner's parachute engineer platoon was particularly high. During its involvement in the actual fighting, 1./*FschSanAbt.7* had also lost four killed, 20 wounded and two missing. Among the killed was the commander of *FschSanAbt.7*, *Oberstabsarzt* Dr. Berg.

---

19   The most effective method to make motor vehicles unusable was to drain off the motor-oil and to then let their motors run until the cylinders had stuck.

With the seizure of the Isthmus of Corinth the parachute force again proved its value as a military instrument with high shock effect. The command of the *12.Armee* had evidently firmly counted on the success of the requested parachute assault, although it had been well aware of the enemy's ability to cleverly and expertly block the advance routes of its ground forces and thereby generate the time required for the destruction of the bridge across the Corinth Canal. In this context it is interesting to note that the command of *12.Armee* evidently did not realize that most of the British expeditionary corps had already crossed the Corinth Canal on the way to the embarkation sites on the morning of 26 April. Seen from this point of view the decision to seize the Isthmus of Corinth by a parachute assault had mainly served the purpose of generating the conditions for an unhindered crossing of the canal upon the arrival of mechanized ground forces, independent of the availability of the only existing permanent crossing site. As a result of the masterly executed evacuation operation *Demon* by Vice-Admiral Pridham-Wippell, the plan to capture a large portion of the British expeditionary corps on the Peloponnese had failed.

On the side of *Detachement Süßmann* and *VIII.Flieger-Korps*, the planning for and the preparation of the parachute operation on the Isthmus of Corinth had been extremely well thought-out. One of the most important aspects was the use of a glider force immediately prior to the parachuting of the majority of the assault force, utilizing the surprise effect of a fully combat-ready platoon against the bridge. In order to achieve the desired success the cooperation between the supporting combat aircraft and the glider force had to be accomplished in such a way that the former by their suppressive fire, prevented the anti-aircraft weapons in the vicinity of the bridge from firing against the landing gliders, whereas as their first combat-action their passengers had to neutralize the anti-aircraft positions before the crews of the guns were able to man them and to open fire against the approaching transport aircraft. How efficient this method of attack had been, was confirmed by the fact that not one of the Ju 52s was lost in the airspace over the Isthmus.

The gallantry and skill of the paratroopers of *Gruppe Sturm* went without saying. Nevertheless their quick success was also built on the fact that the defenders on the Isthmus of Corinth consisted of a scratch force from British, New Zealand and Australian units which had never fought together before and had lacked any cohesion. Brigadier Lee, who was assigned as their commander, had been the artillery officer of I Australian Corps and as such was neither known by the detached troops, nor was he overly familiar with ground combat at the tactical level. It was therefore no wonder that the troops left behind on the Isthmus, with the feeling of all soldiers for a cause lost, had primarily seen their escape and survival as their main focus at the start of the parachute assault. This explained why the about 900-1,000 defenders with a great many heavy weapons and a number of lightly armored vehicles at hand, had only in a few cases fought to the best of their abilities and, in some cases, had prematurely left the battlefield.

The decision to make use of the absolute air supremacy of the *Luftwaffe* such that the attack force was flown in and dropped in one formation, had proved correct. It had not been seen as necessary to seize the airfield at Corinth by parachute assault, as it had not been defended at all and landings had been planned for the remainder of *Detachement Süßmann* only after the occupation of Corinth and of all of the operational area on either side of the canal.

Some experience was also gained for future parachute missions. For the first time heavy weapons had been dropped by parachute together with troops. The planning and execution of the resupply with aviation fuel by the staff of *Detachement Süßmann,* for which the two squadrons of Ju 52s put together from the aircraft of the parachute schools were used, was also noteworthy; these had been retained in the zone of operations against the orders of Berlin. As in previous operations, the ability of the troops to come up with makeshift solutions had helped to solve a serious problem.

The opportunity to employ *Detachement Süßmann* in an earlier phase of the campaign in Greece had obviously never been contemplated. After the British had given up the defense of the Aliakmon line and of the Olympus mountain range and had conducted a fighting withdrawal toward the south, the seizure and blocking of the Domokos Pass at the southern end of the Thessalian Plain, 65km south of Larissa, by *Detachement Süßmann,* could have prevented the escape of strong elements of the ANZAC Corps, until the 5. and *2.Panzer-Divisions* of the *12.Armee* approached from the north. Without doubt this operation could have led to the end of the planned resistance by the British expeditionary corps and to its piecemeal defeat, at a time when its evacuation had not yet been considered by the Middle East Command.[20]

The second reason has to be seen in the attitude of Student himself. He remained in his headquarters in Berlin during the transfer of *Detachement Süßmann* to Bulgaria for the execution of Operation *Hannibal,* as well as after the start of *Marita,* and obviously had paid little attention to the fighting in Yugoslavia and Greece. As neither the *OKW* nor the high command of the *Heer* had thought about an operational-level role for *XI.Flieger-Korps* in Operation *Barbarossa* and as Student had also not developed his own ideas for this use, as one should have expected, he had concentrated his efforts on the build-up of his parachute corps and its employment according to Göring's views about the extension of the war against the British Empire in the eastern Mediterranean and the Near East. The sudden use of *Detachement Süßmann* against the Isthmus of Corinth certainly must have been against his own intentions. His assertion after the war that he was informed about this operation only after its execution is, however, difficult to understand. There can be no doubt that *Generalleutnant* Süßmann had informed him immediately after the receipt of the execution order from *Luftflotte 4.* In addition the measures related to the reinforcement of the detachment, with further parts of *FschPiBtl.7* and the assignment of aircraft from the parachute schools for their transport to Bulgaria had not gone unnoticed by his staff in Berlin. More to the point, in light of the command arrangements for *Detachement Süßmann* and the involvement of Göring and *Generaloberst* Löhr, Student evidently accepted having no more influence on its use at Corinth.

How much the *OKL* was willing to comply with Hitler's intuitions became clearly visible when Göring ordered the employment of *Detachement Süßmann* at the Isthmus of Corinth despite the fact that only a few days prior to this operation Hitler had decided to take Crete using parachute forces and calculations about the required strength of these forces had not yet been made.

---

20   *General* (ret.) Trettner, in his response to a question by the author on 9 September 2005, pointed out that *12.Armee* had probably not requested the support by parachute forces, as the quickly changing situation on the ground had not provided for the required preparation time for a parachute operation of this kind and dimension. This argument, however, disregards the fact that Süßmann's detachment during the time in question, i.e. between 18 and 20 April, had been completely assembled and kept combat-ready for employment at short notice. Moreover, the range of the Ju 52s would have permitted it to fly from around Plovdiv to an area north of Lamia without refueling.

The employment of parachute troops on the Peloponnese had, as in the previous operations in Belgium and Holland, ended with their quick relief by ground forces. Some of the lessons which were important for the planned operation against Crete were not remembered, because the paratroopers had not been forced to fight a conventionally-armed or determined enemy. Despite the tremendous armament efforts of Germany, the issue of equipping the parachute force with organic means for the air transport of its forces and for fire support from the air remained unresolved. Both elements had to be drawn away from other users for every operation, which not only had a negative impact on the accomplishment of their other tasks, but was also time consuming and costly in effort. Therefore airborne operations on a large scale would always require approval at the highest command level.

Part IV Photographs

An aerial view of Narvik from the north. Beyond the harbour, flowing into it, lay the Beisfjord. To the right, in the background, lay Åndalsnes, with the Åndalsnes-Fjell rising from there towards the left.

The Narvik area of operations. When the thaw began, the depressions in the ground filled with water. The elevation in the background is the Koppasfjellet near Bjerkvik, seen from the west.

The Narvik area of operations. A paratrooper coming down on the
drop-zone near Björnfjell station. The drop-zone was so small only
three men could jump from each Ju 52 during each approach.

The Narvik area of operations. Björnfjell with its railway station, along the ore-railway from
Sweden to the port of Narvik. In the foreground are bomb craters from British air raids.

Landing near Björnfjell. The number of jump injuries was relatively small.

The Narvik area – a German aircraft, probably a He 111, drops supply containers near Björnfjell.

The Narvik area of operations. The ore railway bridge over the
Norddalen, target of repeated British air raids.

The Narvik area of operations. Lake Holm looking to the north, seen
from the positions of *1./FschJgRgt.1* from 24 May 1940.

The Narvik area of operations. *Fallschirmjäger*, navy soldiers and *Gebirgsjäger* before going into action. In the centre, with scarf, is *Hauptmann* Walther, commander of *1./FschJgRgt.1*.

The Narvik area of operations. A view from the positions of *1./FschJgRgt.1* at the Kuberget, north toward the Naevertind (1,424 m).

Following the operations in Holland, the dropping by parachute of heavy weapons and equipment was introduced. Here an anti-tank gun is dropped using five parachutes.

A towing section, consisting of a Ju 52 and a DFS 230 glider. If released from a high altitude a distance from the target, gliders could often land with an element of surprise.

A view of a DFS 230 glider from the side. The wheels were only attached at the beginning of the flight, and were soon released. The wooden landing ski under the nose was wound with barbed wire to reduce the distance of skidding on landing. Later on, the gliders were equipped with braking parachutes. Serial production of the glider had commenced during preparations for the invasion of the United Kingdom, so more than sixty of them were available for the assault on Crete.

Weapon containers being loaded into the stowage shafts of a Ju 52. They bore different colored markings for the units, with numbers for the sub-units. The aluminium cylinders at the bottom of the containers are shock-absorbers.

The loading of a mountain gun into a Ju 52, here one
belonging to *FschArtAbt.7*, was cumbersome.

The LG 7.5 40L/15.5 recoilless gun. *13./FschJgRgt.3* was armed with these during the
assault on Crete. The gun had previously been used by *Gruppe Sturm* on the Isthmus
of Corinth. A further development of this weapon, the 10.5 cm LG 40/2, was issued
to *2./FschArtAbt.7* for the assault on Crete, and proved its worth at Perivolia.

In order to parachute-drop heavy weapons and motorcycles, they had to
be attached to the underside of the Ju 52 – here a 3.7 cm Pak.

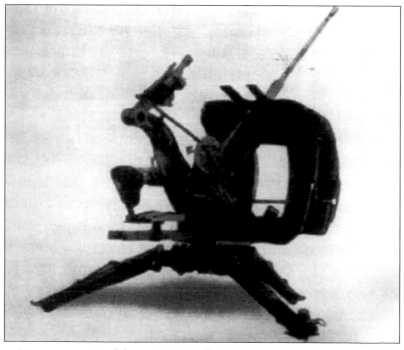

A 2 cm mountain Flak 38 gun, specially constructed for mountain troops
and parachute troops, and used on Crete by *FschFlaMGBtl.7*.

The area of operations around Corinth. A view of the Isthmus of Corinth from
the south a short time after the German occupation. A bridge built by German
engineers can be seen crossing the canal. To the right of the canal is the landing
area of *I./FschJgRgt.2*. In the foreground is the village of Kalamaki.

The area of operations around Corinth. South of the narrow coastal strip, along the northern
edge of the Peloponnese, extends an area of deeply-cut mountainous terrain. In a stroke
of luck for the Germans, it was left undefended by the British expeditionary force.

Fallschirmtruppe preparing for the assault on Corinth. (Bundesarchiv, Bild 146-1977-122-16)

A *Fallschirmtruppe* command post during the operations around
Corinth. (Bundesarchiv, Bild 146-1977-122-15)

As can be seen, the 6 gliders from *Leutnant* Häffner's engineer platoon came down either side of the bridge.

Legend:

1 Railway and road bridge
2 Landing sites of gliders
3 Parachutes
4 Parked vehicles
5 Hastily-dug field positions

6 Well-prepared field positions
7 Machine-gun nest
8 Anti-aircraft guns
9 Bomb craters

This aerial photo, taken by a reconnaissance airplane of on 26 April 1941 at 0659 hours, shows the Corinth Canal and the terrain either side of it shortly after the landing of Gruppe Sturm. The bridge across the canal is still intact.

The key is identical to that of
the preceding photograph.
Scale 1:8,000.

This aerial photo, taken at 0701 hours on 26 April 1041, documents the destruction
of the bridge across the Corinth Canal. The bridge had blown up a minute earlier,
and its smoke can be clearly seen, drifting in a north-westerly direction.

A pause in the fighting for a group of *Fallschirmtruppe*, Corinth.
(Bundesarchiv, Bild 146-1977-163-04A)

26 April 1941 – negotiations are conducted regarding the surrender of
Corinth. From left to right – the Greek military commander at Corinth, *Oberst*
Sturm, *Leutnant* Frank (killed on Crete). (Courtesy of Rudolf Müller)

Corinth, 26 April 1941 - the mayor of Corinth at the command post of *Gruppe Sturm*, negotiating the surrender of the town. In the foreground, resting on packs, is the injured commander of *II./FschJgRgt.2*, *Hauptmann* Pietzonka. In the background, to the right, wounded are loaded into confiscated trucks to be transported to the hospital in Corinth. (Courtesy of Rudolf Müller)

Corinth, 26 April 1941 – although fighting continues, a *Feldwebel* from *1./FschJgRgt.1* finds the time to have a photo taken of himself and some of his comrades. (Courtesy of Rudolf Müller, a former member of *7./FschJgRgt.2*)

Corinth, 27 April 1941, around 1430 hours. *Oberst* Sturm arranges for co-operation with the relief forces from *5.Panzer-Division* with the commander of its *5.Schützen-Brigade*, *Oberst* Haseloff, who arrived ahead of his troops. To the left, with his back to the camera, is *Generalleutnant* Süßmann, commander of *7.Flieger-Division*. (Courtesy of Rudolf Müller)

Part V

The *Fallschirmtruppe* in the battle for Crete

1

The German plan of attack and the provision of the troops for Operation *Merkur*

On 25 April Hitler signed his Directive for the Conduct of the War No. 28, which detailed Operation *Merkur*.[1] It stipulated that the occupation of the island of Crete was to be prepared, thereafter to function as a base for the air war against Britain in the eastern Mediterranean. The overall command for the operation was placed into the hands of the commander-in-chief of the *Luftwaffe* (*Ob.d.L.*). For its execution he was to draw primarily on the troops of the *Luftlande-Korps* and the forces of the *Luftwaffe* already deployed in the Mediterranean region. The *22.(LL)Inf.Div.*, which was subordinate to the *Ob.d.L.*, was also to be employed as a part of the *Luftlande-Korps*. The *Heer* was tasked with earmarking suitable reinforcements from its forces in Greece, including a mixed armor detachment, for transfer to Crete by sea. The *Kriegsmarine* was to secure the sea lines of communications prior to the start of the occupation of Crete and, as far as necessary, to make arrangements with the Italian Navy. The instruction that the transport movements to Greece should not delay the deployment of *Barbarossa* and with the intention that the *Luftlande-Korps* was to be made available, as a whole or in part, for new assignments soon after the occupation of Crete, emphasized the priority of the invasion of the Soviet Union. Moreover, Hitler still reserved the order for the execution of *Merkur* to himself.

Göring tasked the commander-in-chief of *Luftflotte 4*, *Generaloberst* Löhr, with overall command of operations for the conquest of Crete and *VIII.* and *XI.Flieger-Korps* were placed directly subordinate to him. *VIII.Flieger-Korps*, which had already deployed part of its forces on Greek territory in early May, commenced moving its flying formations to airfields around Athens and in the Peloponnese after the end of the fighting. Replacements were brought along for aircraft and aircrews lost during the fighting. A considerable number of aircraft, however, were to be flown back to Germany for basic overhaul. Those that remained were also kept busy, as they were employed for air cover during the occupation of some of the larger Greek islands by the *Heer*, such as Skyros and Chios, in the northern Aegean Sea.[2]

General der Flieger Freiherr von Richthofen intended to attack Crete intensely from the air for at least four days prior to the airborne operation. This would demoralize the defending ground forces by repeated air attacks against their positions.

Admiral (*Süd-Ost*) Schuster was tasked with the direction of operations at sea. He was confronted with the problem that he neither had enough German warships, nor suitable

---

1   For the complete text of Directive No. 28 see Hubatsch, pp.115-116.
2   The northern Cyclades had been occupied by Italian troops at about the same time.

means for the transfer of heavy equipment to Crete. He initially planned to bring the first sea transports into Souda Bay three days after the start of the airborne attack. For the protection of the sea transport movements and mine clearing operations, he succeeded in obtaining from the high command of the Italian Navy (*Supermarina*), the 10th and 16th Torpedo Boat Flotillas with a few boats, about ten minesweepers, a section of fast patrol boats from the 13th Flotilla (*MAS*) and four motorboats that were armed with heavy machine-guns. After he had not been granted rail transport for the requested Siebel ferries, he ordered the requisition of a large number of *caïkes*, typical Greek wooden motorised sailing boats used for coastal shipping and fishing, and some of the smaller steamers still available, for the transport of troops and equipment.

With the receipt of Directive No. 28 and in view of the possible date for the attack, the deployment of the troops and their equipment to Greece became the overriding and most urgent task for the command of *XI.Flieger-Korps* in Berlin. The troops had already been put on the highest state of readiness by warning orders well in advance. Of considerable advantage now was that about ¼ of *XI.Flieger-Korps* was already assembled in southern Greece. This situation not only reduced the amount of the required transport movements to a high degree, but also allowed for the preliminary preparation of staging areas for the arriving troops by those already present. Nevertheless the small quartermaster section of the corps command under *Oberstleutnant* Seibt faced a tremendous burden.

The rail movement of about one hundred train-loads commenced on 27 April. By 2 May they were complete, and by 8 May in Arad/Hungary and Craiova/Rumania. From there the movement to the staging areas in southern Greece continued for a distance of about 1,500km by means of motor vehicles on unfinished roads, mostly through mountainous terrain and across often only temporarily-repaired bridges. The responsibility for the provision of supplies along the route and the war bridges across the Danube at Turnu Magurele-Sofia-Larissa-Athens rested with the *12.Armee*. Eight days had been scheduled for the road movement. At least the gliders of the *Luftlande-Geschwader*, stripped into their parts, could be brought by rail to Skopje in southern Yugoslavia. There they were fitted together by the accompanying technical platoon and towed by Ju 52s to the airfield at Tanagra, east of Thebes.

The transport of supplies and the containers for their storage for parachuting was also time- consuming. Fortunately in early 1941 the quartermaster section on the staff of *XI.Flieger-Korps* calculated the amount of resupplies needed for parachute missions, so that adequate rates were available for the duration of the fighting on Crete, estimated to be ten days. The gathering of supplies and containers required in large numbers, had to be conducted from several storage areas; from the supply depot at Laon, which had been set up for Operation *Seelöwe*, from the air park in Gardelegen, a *Luftwaffe* establishment in Lower Saxony and finally from material stores in Berlin. From these locations, the supplies were brought by rail to the Rumanian Black Sea port of Constanza and subsequently by ship through the Dardanelles to the Greek port of Piraeus. The further distribution was done by motor vehicles. The 1,500 tons of supplies for *Detachement Süßmann* was transported by ship from the port of Burgos to Piraeus after the end of the fighting on the Greek mainland.

Immediately after the receipt of Hitler's Directive No. 28 Student had sent most members of his headquarters to Greece while he remained in Berlin with a small working staff in order to develop the plan of attack for *XI.Flieger-Korps*.[3] First of all the conditions he had to examine the conditions prevailing in the objective's area.

Crete, 8,400km², is the fifth largest island in the Mediterranean. It is 120km away from the south-eastern tip of the Peloponnese and 320km from the coast of the Cyrenaica. From west to east it is almost 260km long. Its width from north to south varies between 12km and 40km. Only about 3% of its entire surface is made up of flat terrain, which is almost exclusively found along its northern coast and in the extreme east. The larger settlements, with the capital Chania (36,000 inhabitants in 1941) and Heraklion (43,000 inhabitants in 1941) are the main ports for regional sea traffic. Souda Bay, protected by the mountainous peninsula of Akrotiri and stretching from Chania toward the north-east, is named after the town and port at its southern coast and is suited for large ships. Halfway between Chania and Heraklion is Rethymnon (10,000 inhabitants in 1941), another small port. Its appearance, like those of the other two sea ports on the northern coast, is marked by the architectural remains of numerous former conquerors of Crete, particularly the Romans, the Venetians and the Turks. Along the entire northern coast, from Kastelli at the Bight of Kissamo in the west to Sitia in the north-east, a road connects the settlements. In 1941 its surface was broken stones resting on rock and as such it was all-weather. However for long distances it was single-lane carriageway, particularly where the mountains came close to the northern coast, and the road wound in narrow serpent-like bends between steep cliffs and deep ravines. The coastal strip up to the first slopes rising toward the south is covered to this day by extensive olive groves and, where the soil permits, vineyards. There are no large wooded areas although rows of trees, scrub and sometimes hedges are found in depressions and along the courses of rivulets, which during the summer months are mostly dried out. Along a road which leads through a wide valley from Chania for about 12km toward the south-west to the small town of Alikianou were located a prison and a large reservoir, Lake Agia.

Immediately west of the village of Maleme about 15km east of Chania a military airfield had been constructed on the coast. It was about 1km long and a little less than 500m wide. Its runway was made of gravel and there were no service buildings on the airfield. About 5km east of Heraklion, also immediately at the coast, an airfield for civilian passenger traffic was under construction. One of its two 1.4km long and 50m wide runways was ready for use, although it lacked tarmac. A provisional airfield also existed about 5km east of Rethymnon. Its unfortified runway had a length of about 1km. At Kastelli-Pediada, in the north-west of Crete, the construction of another airfield had also commenced.[4]

South of the coastal strip in the north of Crete, steep, almost bare, rocky terrain rises continuously along almost the whole length of the island toward four mountain massifs; in the west the Lefka Ori, with its highest peak of 2,452m; in the middle, the Ida Mountains with the 2,456m high Mount Idi; further east the Dikti Mountains, up to 2,152m in height; and finally the Ornon Mountains near the eastern end of Crete, 1,100m high. The peaks of more than 2,000m height are covered with snow for almost the entire year. The

3   At first glance this decision by Student seems to be somewhat strange, as he had made no use of the possibility to obtain an early personal view about the conditions of his troops in their staging areas and to establish contact with other commands involved in Operation *Merkur*. It can, however, be explained by the fact that he was well aware of the head-strong personalities of *Generaloberst* Löhr and *General der Flieger* Freiherr von Richthofen and therefore had attempted to present them with a thoroughly developed operational plan of his own upon his arrival in Greece.

4   There are no indications that the German air reconnaissance had identified the construction site.

numerous valleys leading from the mountain massifs toward the north are cut deep into the rock. However, only a few of them contain some water during the summer months. In the south the mountain massifs drop down steeply toward the sea and only rarely offer space for small settlements and fishing ports.

Only four roads tolerably suited for the use of motor vehicles crossed the mountainous terrain from coast to coast in 1941:

- From the area around Maleme to the small port Palaeochora on the south-western coast.
- From Souda Bay across the Askifou plateau, to a precipice close to the small fishing port of Sfakia on the southern coast.
- From Heraklion to the small port of Timbakion on the southern coast.
- From Heraklion toward the east along the northern coast to Sitia with a diversion to Lerapetra on the southern coast.

Away from these through-roads and some footpaths the entire mountainous terrain south of the northern coastal strip was only scarcely inhabited. The 430,000 inhabitants of Crete, if not from mainland Greece, were formed by the harsh life of farmers, fishermen and shepherds. In their centuries-long struggle for survival against the numerous conquerors of the island, the native Cretans maintained an archaic social order and developed a particularly strong desire for freedom.

The German operational maps, which had been produced hastily from aerial photos and Greek geographical groundwork, were only of restricted value, despite their large scale, as they were badly studied and lacked a sufficiently clear impression of the elevation as well as of the ground coverage.

During the development of his operational plan Student largely groped in the dark regarding the numerical strength of the enemy on Crete and the composition of his forces. The German high command was aware of the landing of British and Commonwealth ground forces on Crete immediately after the start of the Italian attack against Greece and had also observed the unloading of large parts of the British expeditionary corps in Souda Bay after its evacuation from the Greek mainland. However, as the waters around Crete and the island itself could not be surveyed from the air during night-time, almost no intelligence became available as to the whereabouts of these troops or the movements of British ships to and from Crete during the hours of darkness. Nevertheless in early May the strength of Crete's garrison of ground forces from the British Empire was estimated at one division of about 15,000 men.[5]

Basing his assessment of the enemy on Crete on this intelligence, General Student was quite certain that the British garrison command had concentrated its forces for the defence of the island along its northern coast and was prepared for the initiation of a German attack by parachute and air-landing forces. Therefore he began with the opinion that the enemy had deployed at least an infantry battalion for each of the aerodromes at Maleme and Heraklion and a somewhat weaker force for the airstrip at Rethymnon. He also assumed that there were strong reserves in the mountains, just south of the coastal road. In the light

---

5   See Schramm, war diary entry of the *OKW* for 7 May 1941.

of the importance of Souda Bay he expected the main effort of the defence in the western part of Crete and presumed a strong group of forces in the area around Alikianou, about 12km south-west of Chania.

Student viewed the early seizure of at least one of the airfields as essential for the success of *Merkur* and, as Holland had taught him, he could not afford to stake all in one venture by conducting a parachute assault against a single airfield. Consequently, he decided to attack all three of them in the initial phase of the operation. He rejected the option of dropping the *Fallschirmtruppe* on plateaus in the interior of Crete and to subsequently attack the defenders from the rear, as he was aware of the fact that the endurance of his forces for the fighting he anticipated was not warranted, if only because of the anticipated early withdrawal of the majority of the flying formations of the *Luftwaffe* in preparation for *Barbarossa*. His operational plan foresaw a direct attack on the two airfields which were suited for the landing of a large number of transport aircraft, using a reinforced parachute regiment each, and the airfield at Rethymnon by parts of a regiment. The main forces of the enemy along the road Chania-Alikianou were also to be attacked by a reinforced parachute regiment. Units of paratroopers landing at the north-western tip of Crete close to Chania and on the peninsula at Akrotiri were to prevent the enemy from moving forces unhindered to the focal points of the initial fighting. Thus, General Student planned the landing of paratroopers at seven different locations along the northern coast of the island. The main effort of the operations was later to be established by the air-landing of troops from the *Heer* on the two large airfields, which were to have been occupied by this time.[6]

On 7 May Student reported to *Generaloberst* Löhr in Saloniki and traveled to Athens in order to assume personal command over *XI.Flieger-Korps*, which was assembled in southern Greece. Quickly, he discovered that the situation there was unsatisfactory.

The forces to be brought along from Germany had still not arrived, as a considerable part of them had to be halted temporarily in the area of Kozani to let an Panzer division pass on its way to the north. Thus, the date of the attack, announced by Hitler as "around 15 May" could not be met.

The delivery of supplies by sea from the Black Sea coast in Rumania was delayed by the threat of enemy submarines and minefield. As decided by the *OKW* on 5 May, the *22.(LL)Inf.Div.*, which according to Directive No. 28 had been planned to be part of *XI.Flieger-Korps*, would not be available for Operation *Merkur*, but remained deployed for the protection of the Rumanian oilfields around Ploesti. Alternatively, the *5.Gebirgs-Division* was now earmarked for *Merkur*.[7] For the greater part, this division was equipped with heavy weapons suited for air transport, but had no experience in this form of mission.

There were only a few acceptable airfields for the large numbers of transport aircraft which now began to arrive in Greece together with those that had undergone an overhaul

---

6   See CMH Publication 104-13, Washington D. C. 1989, which was put together for the Historical Division of U.S. EUCOM by former high-ranking German officers, among them Student, Meindl and von der Heydte. This describes the method planned by Student, describing so-called 'oildrop tactics'. Like oildrops, several air bridgeheads, without an initial main effort, were to grow together in the course of an airborne operation.

7   Some sources give as reason for the decision of the *OKW* the lack of motor transport for *22.(LL)Inf.Div.* Mühleisen, p.31, assumes that *Generaloberst* Löhr had brought about the assignment of *5.Gebirgs-Div.* because of the experience of its soldiers in mountain warfare.

in Germany. In order to meet the most pressing space requirements for their stationing the dried-out Kopais Lake, north-west of Thebes, was to be used as a provisional airfield. The ground organization of the *Luftwaffe* in Greece was considered as totally inadequate for the coming operation. Immediately after the end of the fighting on the Greek mainland, *Luftflotte 4* had removed two of its three deployed airfield service commands (*Flughafen-Einsatzkommandos*) from this area. Most of its airfield commands and the majority of its signals troops and ground transport columns were also moved, in preparation for Operation *Barbarossa* – only those elements of its organization which were considered absolutely essential for the support of *VIII.Flieger-Korps* remained in Greece. Due to its limited command and logistic elements *XI.Flieger-Korps* was in no position to make good these reductions. The assignment of two higher column commanders as advisers from the command of *Luftflotte 4* was of little help.

The provision of aviation fuel for the air transport fleet remained unresolved, in that adequate amounts of aviation fuel could not be guaranteed for any extended operational period beyond that planned for.

While the arriving troops and their staffs drew up plans for the airborne attack and for the air transport training of the units of *5.Gebirgs-Division*, *Oberst* Ramcke and some experts had been brought in from Germany to enable the senior command to begin the process of coordinating these plans. It immediately became apparent that von Richthofen disagreed with the operational plan laid out by Student. He thought himself unable to rely on the air resources that had been made available to him, as he was required to provide adequate air support simultaneously at all drop zones, as planned by Student. Therefore he proposed a distinct main effort for the initial landing of the parachute forces, permitting him to concentrate his bomber and fighter formations for the best possible use. However Student did not budge, as he considered the weight of direct air support of less importance than its correct timing; that is, during the final phase of the approach flight of the transport aircraft and the gliders, and during the parachute drops, with the aim of suppressing the anti-aircraft weapons of the enemy. For this task he believed that fighter-bombers and fighters with their machine-guns were particularly suited, as these aircraft would also be able to protect the approaching air transport formations against attacking enemy fighters. Dive and level bombers were assessed by him as more suited to attacks against newly-detected targets after the landing of paratroopers. From this time on he also regarded combat against the British Mediterranean Fleet as the principal mission of the bomber formation, in order to prevent it from interfering in the fighting along the northern coast of Crete.

Student's perception about the inter-relations of air attack and parachute forces clearly reflected his experiences from the parachute assaults at Stavanger, Holland and also Corinth.[8] Seen from this point of view, his operational plan for the initial attack of his parachute forces was conclusive. However it was built around only a weak occupation of Crete by the enemy[9] and did not bear in mind the initial restricted numbers of fighter-

---

8   *VIII.Flieger-Korps* had worked together with parachute forces only during the airborne attack against the Isthmus of Corinth.

9   The intelligence section of *12.Armee* had assessed the garrison of Crete as one division with two infantry regiments (six battalions), an artillery regiment, and some remnants of British and Greek forces which had escaped from the Greek mainland. See Gefechtsbericht Kreta of *XI.Flieger-Korps*.

bombers and fighters in the complement of *VIII.Flieger-Korps*. As the two commanding generals could not come to terms, they asked for the decision of the commander-in chief for *Merkur*. *Generaloberst* Löhr, on the basis of the traditional principles for command and control, was also hoping for a clear main effort in the initial phase of the operation, however, he recognized the logic behind Student's approach, emphasizing the early seizure of one of the airfields, which he too considered as conditional for the conquest of Crete. After reconciliation with Göring, he therefore decided to conduct the parachute assault initially against the west of the island, and subsequently against the airfields further to the east. By this method of attack he saw himself in a position to fully support the paratroopers in both major operational areas.

At about the same time it was also decided to direct the first sea transport of troops and equipment required in the initial phase of *Merkur* not into Souda Bay but to open beaches on the north-western coast of Crete.

The planning in the staffs of the commands at the operational level was now adjusted to meet the course of action and the force missions resulting from the decision of *Generaloberst* Löhr, and the units now planned to carry out their preparations. On the airfields in southern Greece provided for the *Fliegerführer* of *XI.Flieger-Korps*, *Generalmajor* Gerhard, the air transport formations returning from overhaul in various locations in Germany, Austria and Czechoslovakia, commenced to land.

They were assigned to *KG z.b.V.1* (*Oberst* Morzik), *KG z.b.V.2* (*Oberst* von Heyking) and *KG z.b.V.3* (*Generalmajor* Buchholz), and stationed as follows:

- in Dadion (today: Amfiklia), north of the Parnass mountains: one group and the staff of *KG z.b.V.1*
- in Megara: two groups
- in Corinth: one group
- in Topolia: three groups and the staff of *KG z.b.V.2*
- in Tanagra: two groups, half of *I./Luftlande-Geschwader 1* and the staff of *KG z.b.V.3*
- in Eleusis: the other half of *I./Luftlande-Geschwader 1*.[10]

The overall number of combat-ready Ju 52s, subordinate to the air commander of *XI.Flieger-Korps*, was around 500. The transport aircraft were to be parked close together

---

10   The numbers of air transport groups and their designations differ in the available sources. The Gefechtsbericht Kreta of *XI.Flieger-Korps*, which has been used above, is considered the most reliable although it does not state the origin of the 72 Ju 52s which were used as towing aircraft for the gliders in the first wave. In this wave around 500 Ju 52s (503 according to the Gefechtsbericht, 493 according to Bekker, p.263, took off for Crete on the morning of 20 May. For the air transport of paratroopers, the Gefechtsbericht states the following allocation:
- *KG z.b.V.1* with *I.* and *II./KG z.b.V.1* (two groups)
- *KG z.b.V.2* with *KGr z.b.V.101, 102* and *105* (three groups);
- *KG z.b.V.3* with *KGr z.b.V.40, 60, 106* and *II./KG z.b.V.172* (four groups).
These nine groups, if one counts a number of their aircraft as disabled on 20 May, together with the 72 tow aircraft, made up the c 500 Ju 52s which were to fly in the morning of 20 May 1941. *KGr z.b.V.104*, which Morzik, p.6, mentions as present on 20 May, could stand for any other group of the report above mentioned erroneously in the Gefechtsbericht, or could have been part of the fleet of the tow aircraft.

on their airfields. The airfield at Mykene which had originally been planned for them was also assigned to *VIII.Flieger-Korps* on 15 May at short notice. Additional airfields for the air transport fleet, such as at Almyros and Atalanti, turned out to be unusable. Adding to these difficulties was the fact that the dispatchers that had been provided for the parachute force were without any practical experience for the task lying ahead of them.

As *Luftflotte 4* had withdrawn most of its ground organization for the management of flight operations other than those for *VIII.Flieger-Korps*, *XI.Flieger-Korps* was forced to hastily put together airfield commands from its own troops. The fact that long distance communications from the assigned airfields to operational-level commands in Athens, and a lack of their own signal personnel and equipment, thus having to depend on Greek telephone cables, turned out to be of particular disadvantage as these were of poor quality and sometimes subject to sabotage.

In the meantime the assignment of the troops from *12.Armee* planned for *Merkur* was accomplished. Beside *5.Gebirgs-Division* under *Generalmajor* Ringel, *XI.Flieger-Korps* received:

- *Kradschützen-Bataillon 55* and *II./PzRgt.31* from *5.Panzer-Division*
- *Leichte FlakAbt.73* and *Flak-Btl.609*
- Some other detachments for combat and combat support, in particular elements from *PiBtl.659*, altogether 160 men, and their equipment for general engineering tasks on Crete.

Elements of *6.Gebirgs-Division* (*Generalmajor* Schörner), *II./FlakLehrRgt* and *I./FlakRgt 23* with staff, two heavy batteries and one light battery were kept available for potential employment in *Merkur*.

VIII.Flieger-Korps also had its flying formations ready for employment. *Lehrgeschwader 1 / LG 1*, equipped with the He 111, was deployed on the fully operational airfield at Tatoi, the commercial airfield of Athens and the airfield at Eleusis. The former was one of the most important bases of the former Greek air forces. The latter was also used by the air reconnaissance squadron of *XI.Flieger-Korps* and half of an air transport group with two squadrons of gliders. The transport squadron of *XI.Flieger-Korps* was stationed in Phaleron. *Kampfgeschwader 2 / KG 2*, equipped with the long-range Do 17, was moved to Menidi on the eastern coast of Greece. The aviation groups equipped with Me 109 fighters, Me 110 fighter-bombers and Ju 87 dive bombers were distributed on the airfields at Mykene, Molai and Githio in the eastern Peloponnese, due to the shorter range of these aircraft. As had been agreed with the Italian Air Force command for the Aegean (*Aeronautica d'Egeo*), *III./StG 2*, with 40 Ju 87s, was stationed on the island of Scarpanto (today known as Karpathos), about 90km north-east of the eastern tip of Crete and *II./KG 4*, with 40 He 111s, in Gadura on Rhodes. Due to their sufficiently long range the Ju 88 bombers remained on station on their base in Bulgaria, subordinate to *Luftflotte 4*.[11]

For its initial employment against Crete *VIII.Flieger-Korps* thus had at its disposal: 18 (6) long-range reconnaissance aircraft in five squadrons, 180 (110) bombers in six groups,

---

11   Bekker, p.280, reports that on 22 May two groups of Ju 88s (*I.* and *II./LG 1*) were stationed in Eleusis, probably after they had been moved forward from Bulgaria.

132 (101) dive bombers in four groups, 110 (84) fighter-bombers in three groups and 112 (97) single-engined fighters in three groups. *Luftflotte 4* additionally had 17 long-range reconnaissance aircrafts, 29 (22) bombers and five (2) air-sea rescue aircraft. *XI.Flieger-Korps* participated with 12 (4) reconnaissance-aircraft. Thus the overall number of aircraft for combat and reconnaissance missions in *Merkur* on 17 May was 615 (441).[12]

On 14 May *VIII.Flieger-Korps* commenced its preparatory air attacks. However these could not be flown with the intensity intended as the requested aviation fuel had not yet arrived. Consequently the corps command initially had to cope with the supplies left over from *Marita* and captured stocks.[13] The fighters and bombers of the R.A.F. on Crete were quickly destroyed or forced to evacuate to Egypt.[14] Good results were also achieved against enemy merchant ships in Souda Bay. However the mission to spot and attack the ground forces on Crete was rather ineffective. Efforts to silence the anti-aircraft weapons of the British cruiser *York*, which had run aground in Souda Bay, were unsuccessful until the end of the preparatory air attacks.[15] An attempt by the commander of the reconnaissance squadron of *XI.Flieger-Korps*, *Oberleutnant* Holthoefer, to land an Me 110 on the air strip at Rethymnon to gain a clearer picture about the enemy there ended with his death.

On 12 May, the operational order of *XI.Flieger-Korps* was given.[16] The mission stated that the first priority was the occupation of the Island of Crete as a base for the conduct of the air war in the eastern Mediterranean and its retention against possible counter-attacks until the relief by forces of the *Heer*.

Its third priority reflected the intended course of action. *XI.Flieger-Korps* was to initially seize the airfields and the most important towns of the island by surprise attacks from the air with strong parachute advance detachments and assault troops. In order to achieve optimal support from *VIII.Flieger-Korps*, and in particular fighter protection, the first attack would be conducted in two waves. The first wave was to be against Chania and the airfield at Maleme, the second wave against Heraklion and Rethymnon. The initial forces were to be reinforced with more parachute and air-landing troops as well as sea transports (these were to be the third and further waves) until the entire Corps had been landed on the island.

The arrival of the waves over the drop zones was fixed as follows: first wave at Y hour; second wave at Y plus eight hours.

---

12   See Gundelach, p.204. Playfair, referring to German sources, gives the overall number on 17 May of 716 (514). The numbers in brackets reflect the combat-ready aircraft.

13   The latter were quite considerable, as at Drapetzonia alone, near Piraeus, 1,500 tons of aviation fuel left behind by the British expeditionary corps was secured. See Playfair, p.130.

14   Data from the office of the chief of *Luftwaffe* training, which is available at the BA-MA, indicate that during 14-18 May alone *JG 77* shot down 7 Hurricane and 2 Gladiator fighters. British sources state that 4 Hurricane and 3 Gladiators were combat-ready on Crete on 19 May.

15   The heavy cruiser *York* was seriously damaged on 26 March by a daring attack of manned torpedoes of the Italian Navy, and was run aground. On her deck, which had remained above water, the medium artillery (10.2cm) and the 40mm and 2cm anti-aircraft guns had remained operational.

16   This order – GenKdo *XI.Flieger-Korps*, Abt I a, Br. N. Nr. 4341 g. Kdos., dated 12 May 1941 – is enclosed as Annex III in the Gefechtsbericht Kreta of *XI.Flieger-Korps*.

The detailed course of action for the first day of the fighting was developed by Student and his staff jointly with the commanders of the regiments and independent units. It stated:

First wave – *Gruppe West*
Luftlande-Sturmregiment under *Generalmajor* Meindl, reinforced with *1./FschArtAbt.7*, *FschFlaMGBtl.7* and *3./FschSanAbt.7*, to seize the airfield Maleme after landing with gliders and parachutes.

First wave – *Gruppe Mitte*
FschJgRgt.3 under *Oberst* Heidrich, reinforced with *FschPiBtl.7* (less its 3rd Company but with *3./FschFlaMGBtl.7* and 1st Platoon from *1./FschPzJgAbt.7* attached) and *1./FschSanAbt.7*. After parachuting into the basin along the road Chania-Alikianou this force was to engage with strong enemy forces there and advance toward Chania as far as possible. *FschPiBtl.7*, dropped in the area around Alikianou, was ordered to protect the rear of *FschJgRgt.3*. Immediately after *FschJgRgt.3* had cleared the drop zone the commander of *Fl.Div.7* and his battle HQ would land there by glider. Subsequently he was to assume the command of *Gruppe West*.

The following were tasked with independent missions in the vicinity of Chania:

1./Luftlande-Sturmregiment under *Oberleutnant* Genz, was to neutralize a heavy anti-aircraft battery positioned south of Chania after the landing by glider.

2./Luftlande-Sturmregiment under *Hauptmann* Altmann. After landing with gliders, this was to put out of action the anti-aircraft positions on the Akrotiri Peninsula and tie down the enemy forces there.

Second wave – *Gruppe Ost*
FschJgRgt.1 under *Oberst* Bräuer, reinforced with *II./FschJgRgt.2* (less its 5th and 6th companies), *1./FschFlaMGBtl.7* and *2./FschSanAbt.7*, after parachuting was to seize the airfield and the town of Heraklion.

Second wave – *Gruppe Sturm*
FschJgRgt.2 (less 2nd battalion) under *Oberst* Sturm, reinforced with the *2./FschArtAbt.7*, *FschMGBtl.7* (less 3rd Company) and *2./FschFlaMGBtl.7* after parachuting in, was to seize the air strip and the town of Rethymnon.

As, according to the plan of Student, the majority of the *5.Gebirgs-Division* was to be airlanded on the airfield at Heraklion, *Gruppe Ost* was placed subordinate to *Generalmajor* Ringel.

Because of the restricted staging capacities of the airfields in southern Greece, the parachute regiments were to be deployed in packets. This turned out to be particularly cumbersome for the communication of orders and the revision of the status of their preparations. Although the reason for the splitting of the initial attack forces into two waves was explained as necessary for the support of *VIII.Flieger-Korps*, Student, in view of the available air transport capacity, could not have missed the fact that only because of the decision of *Generaloberst* Löhr had it become possible to attack the four initial major objectives from the outset, with about twice the strength of troops than that foreseen by him in his original operational plan.[17] With the employment of *Sturmgruppen Genz* and *Altmann* outside of the initial operation area of *Gruppe Mitte* and the parachuting of a combat element at Kastelli in the north-west of Crete, he nevertheless did include his favored 'oil drop tactics' into the operation plan.

During the coordination of the course of action with the command of *5.Gebirgs-Division*, which in the meantime moved from Chalkis to Athens, Student maintained the idea that the majority of the mountain troops could be airlanded at Heraklion and from there could advance toward the west, whereas *Gruppe West* and *Mitte* would attack toward the east.

Admiral Süd-Ost was able to requisition and assemble a fleet of more than 60 small motorised sailing boats, with considerable effort, for the sea transport of reinforcements and some heavy equipment. He thereupon received the order from the command of *Luftflotte 4* to form two light echelons. Differening to the initial plan of *Admiral* Schuster, the first echelon was to land on the first day of the attack on the open beach west of Maleme, the second wave to land one day later east of Heraklion. After coordination with the command of *XI.Flieger-Korps*, *Admiral* Schuster formed the *1.leichte Seetransportstaffel* with 25 motorised sailing boats (*caïques*) under *Fregattenkapitän* Devantier. It was to convey about 2,500 soldiers, including the parachute units *3./FschPiBtl.7*, *2./FschPzJgAbt.7*, *3./FschArtAbt.7*, *8./FschJgRgt.3* and the train of *FschMGBtl.7*. From *5.Gebirgs-Division* II./*GebJgRgt.100* and the 13th and 14th Company of this regiment plus other *Heer* units subordinate to *XI.Flieger-Korps*, including *PiBtl.659*, were added to the squadron. As protection against air attacks two batteries of *FlakLehrRgt.* were distributed among the boats. Each boat, in addition to its Greek crew, was manned by three German naval ratings. Five small Italian minesweepers were to sail in front of the squadron.

The *2.leichte Seetransportstaffel*, comprising 38 motorised sailing boats, was to convey almost 4,000 men to Crete including *III./GebJgRgt.85*, *3./FschPzJgAbt.7*, signal troops of the *Luftwaffe*, anti-aircraft units and the trains of the combat and combat support units employed on Crete. It was led by *Fregattenkapitän* von Lipinski.

Each of the *leichte Seetransportstaffeln* was assigned one of the large Italian torpedo boats as its leading vessel. Due to the age of the boats of the squadron, their pace would only be 4-7 sea miles per hour, therefore the transfer to Crete could not be accomplished in one day. In order to meet the scheduled landing of the *1.leichte Seetransportstaffel* on the north-western coast of Crete, it was to be assembled one day prior to the start of the attack at the island of Milos,[18] located almost half-way between Attica and the northern coast of Crete. Anti-aircraft weapons positioned there provided some protection against air attack. The distance from Milos into the Bight of Kissamo required another 18-20 hours of sailing, of this the last 6-8 hours would be in darkness. Without air cover during that time, and close to the north-western coast of Crete, the squadron would be seriously threatened by British

---

17 This aspect and its importance for the actual course of the operations in the first two days of the attack is not even mentioned in Student's memoirs, although landing with only about half of the strength of the *Fallschirmtruppe* at each of the four primary objectives according to Student's original plan probably would have led to the failure of *Merkur*.

18 Milos was occupied by German troops on 5 May 1941.

naval forces which may be on patrol there. On 16 May the last batch of gliders, which had to be brought along by tow aircraft from Skopje, arrived on the airfield at Tanagra.

On 16 May, *Generaloberst* Löhr conducted a final conference with the commanding generals, *Admiral Süd-Ost* and the key staff personnel in the hotel Grande Bretagne in Athens, during which he was briefed about the status of preparations. After this he ordered the start of the attack on Crete for 20 May, two days later than originally planned. His decision was primarily determined by the fact that extra aviation fuel for the air transport movements was now on the way. On 17 May a tanker from the Rumanian Black Sea coast arrived in Piraeus. After the Corinth Canal was cleared of the debris from the blown bridge by naval divers (brought along by aircraft from Kiel, Germany), a ship laden with 8,000 barrels, each filled with 200L of aviation fuel, and a small tanker was able to reach Piraeus on the same day. As specialized tankers were not available the fuel had to be delivered to the jump-off airfields by the assembled trucks of the units of *XI.Flieger-Korps*.[19] There, the aircraft were filled up by means of hand pumps. It was late in the evening of 19 May before all the Ju 52s were filled up, mainly with the help of paratroopers, who had to sacrifice their rest for refueling. The storage of fuel on the airfields for another two sorties, as originally planned by the air commander of *XI.Flieger-Korps*, was not yet possible at that time, as there were not enough barrels available and the empty ones first had to be brought back to the ships for refilling. The command of *XI.Flieger-Korps* therefore had to rely on the delivery of fuel for the second sortie of the Ju 52s on 20 May, prior to their return from the first sortie.

Admiral Süd-Ost requested shifting the landing of the *1.leichte Seetransportstaffel* to 21 May because of observed movements of British naval forces in the waters around Crete, and the command of *XI.Flieger-Korps* agreed. However no change took place for the assembly of both squadrons at Milos on 19 May.[20] After one of the Italian torpedo boats which had been planned as leader vessels had not shown up in time, *Lupo* was now ordered to lead the *1.leichte Seetransportstaffel*, whereas *Saggitario* was to lead the *2.leichte Seetransportstaffel*.

Probably none of the higher commands involved in the preparations for *Merkur* had considered it would be possible to surprise the enemy with the airborne attack, as stated in the operational order. It seemed likely that the enemy was aware of the deployment of the parachute force to southern Greece and the assembly of hundreds of transport aircraft there. This was all the more probable as many Greeks on the mainland were still using their eyes and ears to help the British, and the U.S. embassy in Athens had unimpeded radio communication with Crete.[21] An indication of the awareness of the enemy regarding the imminent operation against Crete was the attack by British bombers against the jump-off

---

19   This measure was steered by the higher column commanders detached from *Luftflotte 4*. The assembly of the transport vehicles was particularly cumbersome, because about 1,800 trucks of *VIII.Flieger-Korps* had been withdrawn from Greece for *Barbarossa* on 14 May.

20   The *2.Schiffsstaffel* had to be brought along from Chalkis for this purpose. Another squadron made up of seven steamers and planned to transport supplies and heavy vehicles, had also been assembled.

21   The warning of the British joint chiefs of staff about a possible German attack against Cyprus and Syria, passed in mid-April to Middle East Command, had been overcome by events, as the British, who had been able to decode the highly secret radio communications of the *Luftwaffe* by means of ULTRA, had a complete and continuous picture of German intentions and the status of preparations directed toward Crete since the end of April 1941.

airfields, a few nights prior to the start of *Merkur*. As they had little effect[22] not too much thought was given on the German side.

Hitler was fully engaged in the preparations for *Barbarossa* and only in passing kept track of the promising developments in the Near East;[23] consequently he dedicated almost no attention to the planning for *Merkur*.

After a final conference with Student on 19 May, the commanders of the parachute units instructed the troops about their initial objectives and the intended course of action. Late in the evening the loading of the aircraft of the first wave with the equipment to be dropped was accomplished and the troops assembled on the airfields ready for embarkation, General Student reported the conclusion of all preparations to the command of *Luftflotte 4*. However some deficiencies remained unresolved: the paratroopers would have to fight in the anticipated high temperatures on Crete in the same thick woolen uniforms which they had worn in the snow in Norway. Tropical clothing which was stored in Rumania and Bulgaria for them had not yet been delivered. Moreover, the overly fat and salty food which was provided as combat rations by no means complied with the conditions of a deployment in the sub-tropical climate of Crete. Although late, the supply of drinking water was fortunately dealt with when the quartermaster of *XI.Flieger-Korps* arranged for the production of 25,000 bottles of mineral water per day, with a factory in Athens.[24]

A last uncertainty about the start of the attack developed on 19 May, when the chief meteorologist of *Luftflotte 4* predicted the approach of a front of bad weather from the west. However Student remained unmoved by this, all the more, as Brand, the meteorologist on the staff of *XI.Flieger-Korps*, clung to his previous prediction about good conditions for the airborne attack, based on his year long observation of the weather in the Mediterranean region.

---

22   In the time frame 13-20 May, Wellington bombers from 37, 38, 70 and 148 Squadrons had flown 42 attacks against German airfields in southern Greece from Egypt during the hours of darkness. 27 Squadron had also bombed some of the islands occupied by the *Wehrmacht*.

23   In Iraq the pro-Axis potentate Rashid Ali al-Gaylani had risen against the British, and had asked for German military support. While the British had reacted immediately in strength against the rebel movement, the German support for Rashid Ali had remained half-hearted and was limited to the deployment of a few *Luftwaffe* aircraft and to the purchase of some weapons for the rebels from Vichy-controlled Syria. The uprising therefore had quickly been smashed and had also led to the loss of Vichy Syria by the end of July 1941.

24   Because of the lack of containers, it must be doubted that large amounts of this water was dropped over Crete.

2

Enemy dispositions for
the defence of Crete

The importance of Crete as a naval base and an objective was recognized by the British political and military authorities prior to Italy's entry into the war. Therefore, forces for the occupation of the island had been kept ready in case of Greece being drawn into the conflict.[1] The dispatch of British troops to Crete had consequently taken place on Italy's attack against Greece.[2] Between 19 November and early December 1940 two infantry battalions (2nd York and Lancs and 2nd Black Watch), two Commandos, the staff of an anti-aircraft regiment with a heavy and a light battery,[3] an engineer company, a field hospital and another medical unit had arrived and had been placed under the command of 14th Brigade. In March the Commandos were withdrawn and instead an infantry battalion of the 1st Welch Regiment was sent.

In the light of the development of the war on the Greek-Italian front and the restrictions of the freedom of action of the Italian naval forces by the British Mediterranean squadrons, the concern that the Italians could commence an operation for the conquest of Crete never arose. The Greek supreme military command had firmly counted on the protection of Crete by the British Mediterranean fleet, when it had transferred its 5th Infantry Division from the island to the Greek mainland shortly after the start of the Italian attack.

During the transfer of elements of the R.A.F. and of the British expeditionary corps to Greece through operations *Barbarity* and *Lustre*, Souda Bay and the airfields at Maleme and Heraklion were used as intermediate bases and refueling points for naval vessels, merchant ships and aircraft. For the purpose of flight control and aircraft reporting, the 252 Air Ministry Experimental Station (AMES) was set up in the mountains south of the airfield at Maleme.

During the employment of the British expeditionary corps in Greece the Middle East Command had paid little attention to Crete and had economized its forces and resources to the utmost for operations in several areas. However with the evacuation of the troops from the Greek mainland the island moved into the focus of the British political and military authorities. Crete had not only been used for the debarkation of troops evacuated from

---

1   These dispositions had become visible in the response to questions about the campaigns in Greece and on Crete by the then premier-minister of New Zealand, Fraser, provided by the United Kingdom chiefs of staff. See *Official History of New Zealand in the Second World War 1939-45*, Volume II, p.502.

2   For the examination of the dispositions of the British for the defence of Crete, the following sources have primarily been consulted: Playfair; *Official History of New Zealand in the Second World War 1939-45* Volume II; *Australia in the War of 1939-1945*, Series One/ Army. Only additional sources therefore will be indicated in footnotes.

3   The heavy anti-aircraft batteries of the British and the Empire forces generally had been equipped with 3.7 inch (9.8cm) guns, the light batteries with the highly efficient 40mm Bofors gun.

Greece, but had quickly developed as a factor in the plans for the further conduct of the war in the eastern Mediterranean. Up to this point the directive by Churchill from 18 April had given priority to the victory in Libya above all other military operations of the Middle East Command. In principle this had not altered, even after the forced withdrawal from Greece. Subsequent to the loss of the Greek mainland and its outlying islands, the strategic planning for the period just prior to the outbreak of the war between Italy and Greece and the denial of the possession of Crete to the enemy so as to safeguard their own positions in the eastern Mediterranean had become paramount. In line with Churchill's thoughts, forces returning from Greece and those already stationed on Crete were to be used for the defence of the island. Middle East Command, though, pointed out that substantial reinforcement of the remnants of the R.A.F., which had escaped from the Greek mainland to Crete, could not be provided at that time. However to the best of its abilities it had immediately initiated the replacement of lost equipment and the provision of supplies for the troops of the expeditionary corps who were to remain on Crete.

A significant military support for the defence of the island could not be expected from the Greek side. Most of the Greek soldiers brought there towards the end of the fighting on the mainland were raw recruits. For the greater part, they carried only their personal equipment and heavy infantry weapons and ammunition remained scarce. By the assignment of personnel for mentoring from the Commonwealth units on Crete, efforts were made to improve the combat efficiency of the Greek troops. On 23 April their subordination to the British island commandant was requested from George II, the King of Greece. He arrived with his cabinet on Crete and readily agreed.

With a fine sense for the history and the traditions of the Cretan people, the British succeeded in winning over the greater part of the population to their cause and rousing their readiness to resist against invaders in age-old ways.[4] Of considerable benefit for these activities was that the Greek king and his government had not sought security in Egypt but had come to Crete. Thereby they gained the allegiance of the majority of the Cretan population.

On 25 April the first evacuation transport from Greece arrived in Souda Bay and was unloaded there. Until 29 April about 25,000 British and Empire troops of the expeditionary corps were brought ashore on Crete, about as many were conveyed directly to Egypt, among them the majority of the Australian 6th Division. For days after the official end of Operation *Demon* small groups of stragglers had also reached the island by a number of adventurous methods. All of the heavy equipment of the expeditionary corps, however, was left back on the Greek mainland. While most of the evacuated combat troops had brought along their small arms and machine-guns, the large numbers of service support troops arrived without any weapons. Resources for logistical support on Crete were scarce to non-existent and nobody had been prepared to deal with the situation that developed regarding the new role of the island.

---

4   The activities of the British archeologist and secret service officer Pendleburg had been particularly successful in this field in the area around Heraklion. See Mühleisen, p.21.

On 26 April Major General Weston arrived on Crete as commander of forces from the British Mobile Naval Base Defence Organization (M.N.B.D.O.) which had been sent to Crete. He was also assigned the post of island commandant.

On 27 April, Wilson, the hitherto the commander-in-chief of the British expeditionary corps, reported back to General Wavell at Headquarters Middle East Command. His appreciation of the possibility of defending Crete successfully was not overly optimistic. He believed a combined air and sea landing was the most likely tactic to be used by the Germans against Crete. He pointed to the lack of sufficiently large air forces for the protection of the island as a particular weakness, as it would allow the almost unhindered approach of German airborne troops. Moreover, the fleet would be threatened by massive air attacks to the extent that the losses of ships would make it almost impossible to prevent landings from the sea. Seen under these conditions, he regarded three brigade groups, an additional highly mobile infantry battalion, the M.N.B.D.O. and strong anti-aircraft forces, deployed along the northern coast of Crete, as necessary for the defence of the island. Even then, he had given the chances of success as low.

On the same day the Joint Intelligence Committee of the British war cabinet issued an appreciation of the enemy situation, according to which a German attack against Crete was regarded as certain and imminent. Churchill had passed this information to Wavell on 28 April and called upon him to tenaciously defend Crete. In this context he had spoken of the anticipated German airborne attack as a good opportunity to "kill German paratroopers".[5]

Also on this day the number of Greek combatants on Crete, commanded by General Skoulas, had been declared by Minister-President Tsouderos. About 7,500 soldiers in ten regiments, 1,000 trained reservists and about 2,500 gendarmes, who were considered an elite, were based on the island.[6]

On 29 April the commander of the New Zealand Division, Major General Freyberg, who had directed the evacuation operations on the Greek mainland, arrived on Crete together with soldiers of his 6th Brigade Group. His responsibility as the highest military representative of his country in the Mediterranean theater of war meant he endeavored to quickly re-unite his division, which had been landed on Crete with the majority of its combat and combat-support troops and re-establish its full fighting strength. This he had seen as possible only in Egypt. While he had inspected his troops already assembled around Souda Bay his 6th Brigade Group, which had not been unloaded, had been transported to Egypt without his knowledge.

On 30 April Wavell flew to Crete in order to confer with the senior commanders present and with the Greek government about the defence of the island on the basis of Churchill's directive. As proposed beforehand by Churchill, he offered Major General Freyberg command over all troops stationed on Crete, including the Greeks. In the meantime they were designated as CREFORCE. Freyberg was surprised by this offer as he had intended to re-constitute his division in Egypt. Therefore he hesitated with his response and took counsel with Prime Minister Frazer. The latter, informed by Freyberg about the

---

5   It is certain that knowledge about the German airborne attack against Crete at this early time could only have come from ULTRA, probably by the decoding of radio messages from the commander-in-chief of the *Luftwaffe* and/or from *Luftflotte 4* to *XI.Flieger-Korps* upon publication of Directive No. 28.

6   In his detailed study 'Greek Ground Forces in Crete and their Small Arms Nov 1940-May 1941' Mehtidis states that 11,500 soldiers and more than 1,000 gendarmes were organized in units. He also states, that about 3-4,000 armed civilians had to be added to this number.

present condition of the New Zealand Division and about the preparations on Crete, asked Churchill to make his choice either for adequate equipment and supplies for the troops on Crete, or for the abandonment of the island. Churchill attempted to convince Frazer about the importance of occupying Crete, for the war in North Africa and guaranteed the provision of the equipment required for the defence of the island. At the same time, via the British Chiefs of Staff, he requested the formal appreciation of General Wavell about the chances of success for the defence of Crete. Wavell saw the problem of logistical resupply as the main constraint for a successful defence of the island. Churchill, in his decision to retain Crete, was encouraged by the commander-in-chief of the Mediterranean fleet, Admiral Cunningham, who on 1 May declared that it was imperative to deny the enemy the use of the island for as long as possible. He argued that in German hands Crete would:

- increase difficulties for the supply of Malta, which was the key in the struggle against the sea lines of communication of the Axis to North Africa;
- offer the enemy the opportunity to reinforce his offensive air-operations in North Africa
- permit the enemy to operate against Cyprus with light naval forces.

The convincing efforts and the firm will of Churchill resulted in the approval of Frazer to appoint Major General Freyberg as commanding officer of the troops on Crete and to keep the majority of the New Zealand Division on the island. Thereupon Freyberg assumed command as desired by Churchill. Immediately after his appointment as overall commander, Freyberg set out to prepare Crete against a German attack, codenamed *Scorcher*. With CREFORCE Order No. 3, dated 3 May, he announced assumption of command and formed four sectors for the defence of the northern coast of Crete:

- Sector Maleme and Galatas: under Brigadier Puttick, who was also tasked with the command of the New Zealand Division.
- Sector Souda Bay: under Major General Weston as commander of the M.N.B.D.O.
- Sector Rethymnon: under Brigadier Vasey, commanding the Australian 19th Brigade.
- Sector Heraklion: under Brigadier Chappel, commanding the British 14th Brigade.

A small reserve was to remain under the direct command of Major General Freyberg.[7]

The troops commenced their preparations on the basis of the CREFORCE Operational Instruction No. 10, issued on 3 May, and the successive orders of the sector commanders. The initially critical material situation in the meantime improved considerably:

- The M.N.B.D.O., with its 2,200 Royal Marines (amongst them the novelist Evelyn Waugh) beside other equipment received two heavy anti-aircraft batteries, 14 coastal guns (15.8 and 10.5cm) which could also fire against ground targets, some Military Police and port service personnel.

---

7   The units assigned to each sector have been left out here, as they were subject to several changes prior to the German attack.

- From the stocks of the Middle East Command, 49 field guns had been sent to Crete. With the exception of a few British 3.7-inch guns these were of French and Italian origin, and partly arrived without sighting devices. Moreover, only about 300-400 rounds per gun were made available. As the weapons were sent without crews they had been taken over by artillery units that returned from Greece.
- 6 infantry tanks[8] from the 7th Royal Tank Regiment (7th R.T.R), and 16 light tanks from the 3rd Hussars, as well as a number of additional heavy and light anti-aircraft batteries were also landed.

With the delivery of large amounts of small arms and light automatic weapons it became possible to equip the command and logistic troops, who, for the greater part came back from Greece without weapons. They could now be integrated alongside the infantry. A very useful reinforcement were the 20-30 anti-aircraft machine-guns of the ground personnel of the R.A.F. They were mainly positioned around the airfields, but were also used to protect 252 AMES and the newly established 220 AMES, east of the airfield at Heraklion. In order to increase the mobility of the troops and for the transport of supplies, trucks had been brought to the island[9] although their number was considered inadequate for the coming tasks. For the transport of the larger coastal guns some heavy towing vehicles had also been landed. However the delivery of Bren Gun Carriers had been rather unsuccessful as only ten were salvaged from a ship with 35 of these vehicles aboard, after it was sunk in Souda Bay in a German air attack. Fortunately, the three infantry battalions of 14th Brigade had brought along their full complement of 13 of these lightly armored tracked vehicles during their early deployment to Crete. Some of them were handed over to other units.

The supply situation had also developed in an acceptable way. Between 29 April and 19 May about 15,000 tons of army supplies had been unloaded in Souda Bay. German air attacks, particularly from 14 May on, had made the unloading of ships increasingly difficult. Of the 15 ships entering Souda Bay, eight had been sunk or seriously damaged. Due to the ongoing air threat, only ships with a speed of about 30 knots, mainly destroyers and other small warships, had been able to enter and leave Souda Bay. In order to stay out of the range of German dive bombers during daylight, they arrived after nightfall at around 2300hrs and departed the next morning no later than 0300hrs. However this meant that the daily output of unloading had dropped to about 100 tons per day. Nevertheless it was possible, beside the improvement of the stocks of the units, to build up a large number of stores in the defence sectors. The stocks of ration packs, fuel and lubricants was 80,000 rations and 5,000 gallons for Maleme and Galatas, 40,000 rations and 5,000 gallons for Rethymnon and 60,000 rations and 10,000 gallons for Heraklion. Stocks of tropical clothing were considered adequate.

The composition of CREFORCE, including the forces already mentioned, had also developed apace. In the period between 5 and 14 May 3,200 Britons, Palestinians and Cypriots, 2,500 Australians and 1,300 New Zealanders had been removed from the island to Egypt in three sea transports. With the exception of a contingent of about 450 men from the Australian 2/1 Machine-gun Battalion, these were troops with no tasks in the

---

8   These were the heavily-armored model Matilda II, armed with a 40mm gun and a machine-gun. The standard ammunition for the German 3.7cm anti-tank gun had proved ineffective against the armor of this tank.

9   By this measure the 231st Motor Transport Company was filled up to its full complement of 94 trucks.

impending fight. On the other hand, on 16 May, the British 2nd Battalion Leicestershire Regiment was brought to Heraklion and on 19 May the 1st Battalion Argyll and Sutherland Highlanders, together with two Matilda II tanks.[10] The Argyll and Sutherlands were initially deployed for the protection of the plateau of Messara, which was considered suitable for airborne landings.

With the arrival of a British Royal Navy hospital, equipped with tents, the number of beds for wounded was brought up to 660. However the plan to remove about 14,000 Italian prisoners of war from the fighting in northern Greece and Albania, who were confined in several camps from the island, remained unsucessful.

The promises and first noticeable efforts of the superior commands to improve the defence of Crete induced Major General Freyberg to let Churchill know on 5 May that he faced a German airborne attack with a degree of confidence. The scarce air forces for the protection of the air-space over the island remained a cause for uneasiness. Of the fighters and bombers that had returned from the Greek mainland only 36 were combat-ready on 9 May. Of these 24 were stationed on the airfield at Maleme and the rest on the airfield at Heraklion. A short time later the Blenheims had been flown off to Egypt. The Hurricanes and Gladiators had taken up the fight against the attacking formations of the German *VIII. Flieger-Korps.* On 13 May only 6 Hurricanes and some Gladiators were left available for the commander of the R.A.F. on Crete, Group-Captain Beamish. On 17 May another 10 Hurricanes were brought over from Egypt. On 19 May, Beamish ordered the transfer of the last three of each Hurricanes and Gladiators to Egypt, after a Hurricane was shot down in aerial combat that day, and the two remaining Fulmars of 805 Squadron of the Fleet Air Arm had been destroyed on the airfield at Maleme. From then on, Freyberg had to set all his hopes on the support of air-assets from Middle East Command.

Admiral Cunningham, with his peculiar energy, had arranged the dispositions of his naval forces. He had directed his plans mainly for the defence against German sea landings and additionally for possible support of the ground battle by the guns of his warships. He had seen the coastal sectors at and near Heraklion and Rethymnon, but also the Bight of Kissamo, as potential objectives for German landing actions. Therefore he directed that a task force be formed for each of these sectors, composed of cruisers and destroyers. These naval forces cruising in the coming days in the waters north of their assigned sectors during the hours of darkness were to destroy approaching German sea transports. A covering and support force, consisting of two battleships and a number of destroyers, was to be kept ready in the waters west of Crete during these operations. Prior to daybreak all task forces were to withdraw into the waters south of Crete, out of the range of the majority of the German combat aircraft. The parts of the Alexandria Squadron which were not directly

10   These two tanks had been all Middle East Command had released for Crete from a convoy with 240 brand-new tanks, among them 80 Matilda II, which had arrived in Egypt around 10 May. Churchill had proposed to Wavell that one of the ships of the convoy divert to Souda Bay and unload 12 Matilda II there. Wavell, who because of his view about the situation in North Africa had been of the opinion that every single one of the arriving tanks was needed there, had reported to Churchill that he had arranged for the delivery of tanks to Crete. He had, however, referred to the already delivered tanks and thus had consciously ignored Churchill's desire.

employed in the interdiction-operations – the two remaining battleships, the only still available aircraft carrier in the eastern Mediterranean, two cruisers and several destroyers – were to stand by as reserve. A few motor torpedo boats, stationed in Souda Bay, were to take over reconnaissance missions for the fleet.

The numerous changes in the composition of the troops for the defence sectors caused by the arrival of forces at different times, the ongoing study of the terrain and resulting new missions was completed by 16 May, the date which the German attack could be expected. The plan for the defense of Crete was now codenamed *Colorado*.

On this day Major General Freyberg reported to General Wavell by teletype that he was convinced that Crete could be retained. Based on his appreciation of the situation, that the assault from the air would be combined with sea landings, which was also shared by Middle East Command, he then instructed the sector commanders to prepare from the very beginning against both methods of attack. He attached parts of the available anti-aircraft weapons and coastal artillery to the sectors, but left them subordinate to the original commands. Not subordinate to the sector commanders were the ground personnel of the R.A.F. as well as both AMES, altogether about 560 men.[11]

Maleme / Galatas Sector

Brigadier Puttick, in command of the New Zealand Division, tasked the 5th Brigade with the defence of the airfield at Maleme and with the protection of the coast between the mouth of the Tavronitis River in the west and the area on either side of the mouth of the Platanias River in the east. As the bird flies the sector was a little more than 8km long.

Brigadier Hargest, the commander of 5th Brigade, deployed the forces subordinate to him as follows:

- The 22nd Battalion, 644 men, in an area comprising the airfield and village of Maleme and the high ground around Hill 107, which dominated both.
- The 23rd Battalion, 571 men, in an area on the high ground around the settlement of Dhaskaliania, south of the coastal strip, about 1.5km east of Hill 107. The 18 guards and convicts of a field punishment camp on the western edge of the village of Modhion were to join the battalion in the case of an attack.
- The 21st Battalion, 376 men, in an area on the high ground immediately south of the 23rd Battalion.
- The combined engineer units, 7th Field Coy and 19th Army Field Corps Coy, 364 men, employed as infantry in an area of resting on several groups of houses along the coastal road north of Modhion.
- The 28th (Maori) Battalion, 619 men, in an area, including the mouth of the Platanias, the village of Platanias, and the high ground stretching from there to the south-east. In this location Brigadier Hargest established his command post.

Of the anti-aircraft forces that were assigned to 5th Brigade, 10 40mm Bofors from the 156th LAA Battery and the Australian 7th LAA Battery were positioned along the

---

11   The subsequent data for units and their strength primarily have been extracted from Davin, who has undertaken the effort to list these completely and in detail for all of CREFORCE.

length of the airfield at Maleme. Between these weapons, several anti-aircraft machine-guns, manned by R.A.F. crews were also placed. Near Hill 107, two 9.8cm anti-aircraft guns from C Battery of the M.N.B.D.O. were set up. Two 10.5cm coastal guns of the same origin were set up on a summit north-west of Hill 107, with the line of fire directed toward the airfield and the coast. Of the two platoons from the 27th (New Zealand) Machine-gun Battalion with eight heavy machine-guns, one was deployed so that it could dominate the valley of the Tavronitis, including the steel girder bridge which the coastal road crossed the river by. The second platoon was positioned in squads east of Maleme, from where it could fire onto the airfield. Another platoon from 27th Machine-Gun Battalion was placed subordinate to the 23rd Battalion.

The two infantry tanks assigned to 5th Brigade were released to the 22nd Battalion. There, together with three Bren Gun Carriers from the 1st Welch and a platoon of infantry they formed the battalion reserve. Of the remainder of the 5th (New Zealand) Field Artillery Regiment, which was partly re-equipped with guns, C Troop of 27th Battery, with four French 75mm field guns, was positioned with unhindered lines of fire along the coastal road toward the west, on a hill north-west of Modhion. It was to provide direct fire-support for the 5th Brigade. The guns were set up in the open as they had to be laid directly because of a lack of sighting equipment. Likewise for direct fire-support for 5th Brigade A Troop from 27th Battery, with two British 3.7 inch howitzers, was positioned in the area of the 21st Battalion and B Troop of this battery, with three captured Italian 75mm guns, in that of the 23rd Battalion.

Hargest's request to be reinforced with an infantry battalion for the protection of the coastal strip west of the Tavronitis was not granted by the command of the New Zealand Division. In order to at least survey the possible route of advance into the area south of Hill 107 by enemy forces landing west of the river, Hargest ordered one platoon from the 21st Battalion forward to a summit about 500m south-west of Hill 107.

In his order for the intended course of action, Hargest determined that in the case of an attack against the airfield at Maleme the 23rd and 21st Battalions must be ready for intervention after the shortest possible time. For such a case the 28th Battalion and the engineer detachment were initially to continue the protection of the coast.

In summary, for the direct defence of the airfield at Maleme and the high ground around Hill 107, more than 1,200 soldiers with 16 heavy weapons (40mm and larger, as well as about 60 light, heavy and anti-aircraft machine-guns) stood ready.

The field positions, mainly dug-outs and lengths of trenches, were completed and well camouflaged against observation from the air. The camouflage profited from the dense coverage of undergrowth on the high ground and olive groves and vineyards in the coastal strip and along the slopes. The most threatened approaches to the positions were blocked by barbed wire, which arrived in large amounts just in time. For the protection of 252 AMES, which was located about 2km south-east of Hill 107, the commander of 22nd Battalion had detached his engineer platoon. Near Hill 107 the observation post of A and B Troops from 27th Battery was set up. From there telephone communication existed to the gun positions.

The 10th (NZ) Brigade was formed as late as 14 May, and since 17 May had been commanded by Colonel Kippenberger. They were given the mission to defend the area north and south of the large village of Galatas against landings from the air and sea. From the 100m high hills that surrounded Galatas, the coastal strip in the north as well as the road, leading in a wide valley from Chania in a south-westerly direction, past a prison and the reservoir at Agia toward Alikianou, could be dominated by fire.

After several changes in its composition the 10th Brigade now consisted of the Greek 6th Regiment, the Greek 8th Regiment, the remainder of the New Zealand Divisional Cavalry, employed as infantry, and a mixed unit made up from logistical troops and artillerymen, designated as the 1st New Zealand Composite Battalion. Colonel Kippenberger deployed his troops as follows:

The Composite Battalion, the soldiers of which were inexperienced in infantry combat, established itself with the majority of its forces in a position toward the west and south, on the hills south-west and south of Galatas. Supply soldiers and artillerymen, organized into two strong companies were dug in on Red Hill and Ruin Hill, west of Galatas. Another force of artillerymen was placed on Wheat Hill about 500m west of Galatas. The more than 300 men from the Petroleum Company of the New Zealand Division were positioned on and in front of Pink Hill, immediately south-west of Galatas. The Divisional Maintenance Company of 274 men covered the coastal strip north of Galatas. As Pink Hill offered excellent observation into the basin beyond the prison, Colonel Kippenberger set up his forward command post there.

The Greek 6th Regiment, made up of 30 officers and 1,350 other ranks, was established in positions which stretched toward the south-east from the southern edge of Galatas for about 2.5km via Cemetery Hill across the basin to high ground where an ancient Turkish fort stood. However the regiment possessed only a small amount of automatic weapons.

The Greek 8th Regiment, consisting of 40 officers and 800 other ranks, occupied an area on the high ground between the eastern edge of Alikianou and the Agia reservoir. From there they dominated the part of the road Chania-Alikianou which passed through the basin. If required, this regiment was also to reinforce the guards of the Italian prisoners of war, who were confined in tent camps at Fourmes and Sines, south of Alikianou.

The detachment of the Divisional Cavalry, about 300 men, designated as 'Russell Force' was deployed in the small settlement at Kirtomadho, about 1km north-west of the reservoir. Due to its limited combat effectiveness, it was to withdraw in the direction toward Galatas in the case of an attack.

The 10th Brigade received direct fire-support from 28th Battery, which had three Italian 75mm guns set up in a firing position south-east of the village of Daratsos. The 1st Light Troop, Royal Artillery, which was planned for general fire-support for the New Zealand Division, was positioned with its four British 3.7 inch howitzers 1km south of Daratsos and was also able to direct its fire into the sector of the 10th Brigade.

For air-defence only one platoon from the Australian 7th LAA Battery with two 40mm Bofors guns was available. The shortage in automatic weapons, particularly in the Greek units, was to some extent compensated by the subordination of one heavy machine-gun platoon from the 27th New Zealand Machine-Gun Battalion and two troops from the 156th LAA with two machine-guns. Some officers and non-commissioned officers from the New Zealand engineers were posted as advisers to the two Greek regiments.

The 4th New Zealand Brigade, under its commander Brigadier Inglis who had returned from Egypt on 17 May, detached its 20th Battalion as reserve to the command of the New Zealand Division. This battalion of 637 men occupied an area on either side of the coastal road immediately west of Chania. The 18th and 19th Battalions of 4th Brigade, together with the brigade staff and the signals platoon, formed the reserve of CREFORCE. Both infantry battalions were also deployed in defence areas:

- 18th Battalion, less B Company, about 550 men, on either side of the coastal road around the village of Evthymi, about 2km west of Chania. There, Brigadier Inglis set up his command post.
- 19th Battalion, 565 men, in and around Daratsos. For the protection of the artillery south of the village, a platoon of the battalion was to be detached during the night 19/20 May.

Assigned to 4th Brigade in its role as reserve were C Squadron of the 3rd Hussars, with ten light tanks, a heavy machine-gun platoon and a platoon of light anti-aircraft guns. The brigade reconnoitered possible counter-attacks toward Maleme, Alikianou and Heraklion; its 19th Battalion additionally looked toward the Akrotiri Peninsula. The fully equipped and motorized 1st Welch, presently under the command of Major General Weston, was planned to reinforce 4th Brigade for counterattacks.

B Company of 18th Battalion was detached for the protection of the King of Greece and his cabinet, whilst the members of the Greek government and the British Military Mission, which were also brought to Crete, found quarters in buildings about 1km south-west of Chania. The king and his family, escorted by a platoon from B/18th Battalion and accompanied by the British military *attaché* Colonel Blunt, moved to quarters in the village of Perivolia, about 3.5km south-west of Chania.

The 1st Greek Regiment, about 1,000 men and directly subordinate to the command of the New Zealand Division, was sent to the north-western part of Crete, into the area around Kastelli. Organized into two battalions its mission was to protect this area against landings from the air and sea and safeguard a fuel depot, which had been set up for the airfield under construction, however only about 600 rifles were available for its soldiers. The New Zealand Division dispatched a few officers and NCOs to train and advise these troops. About 50 well-trained and fully armed gendarmes formed the reserve of the regiment. It was also joined by about 200 members of the local homeguard, led by a certain Kondopirakis, a veteran from the fighting against the Turks in the 1920s. They were equipped with a variety of weapons.

A military college, 17 officers with about 300 cadets, which was set up after its evacuation from the Greek mainland in Kolombari, in the southern part of the Rodope Peninsula, was not yet included in the defensive measures. As a precaution its members, who were fully armed, had been organized into two companies.

The 7th General Hospital was clearly recognizable from the air as a medical installation by the Red Cross and was quartered in the barracks of a former Greek military hospital and in additional tents on a piece of terrain protruding into the sea north of Evthymi. However its location was poorly selected, it was on a beach suited for landings and moreover was immediately adjacent to the positions of the 18th Battalion.

The command post of the New Zealand Division was established in the eastern part of its sector. From there wire and radio communications existed to the brigades and to the HQ of CREFORCE. Brigadier Puttick was convinced that he had met the twofold defence mission by his chosen dispositions, which he coordinated beforehand with Major General Freyberg, to the best of his abilities. However he did not think his divisions was in the position to occupy the area west of Tavronitis from the very beginning. In his mind not enough time had been left prior to the anticipated German attack and so he also canceled his plan from 13 May to transfer the 1st Greek Regiment into this area.

Souda Bay Sector

For the defence of this sector, which included the capital Chania and the area south of it as well as Souda Bay and the Akrotiri Peninsula, the sector commander Major General Weston, had a strong but disorganised force at his disposal with his 15,500 men. His most important task was the protection of the port installations and berths in Souda Bay from air attack and the landing of parachute troops.

Twenty-six heavy anti-aircraft guns had been designated for air defense (7.9, 9.8cm and 16 40mm guns). Most of them were positioned on the Akrotiri Peninsula and around the western end of Souda Bay. Additionally a battery with two 40mm and 20mm guns each could be employed, which remained combat ready on the grounded heavy cruiser *York*. For defence against naval forces or sea landing troops entering Souda Bay, two coastal guns (15.8 and 10.5cm) were positioned south of the entrance to the Bay and another two 15.8cm coastal guns on a height at its western end. A platoon from the 27th New Zealand Machine-Gun Battalion, with four machine-guns positions, was also present, and an anti-torpedo net was drawn across the entrance to the Bay.

The infantry units deployed were as follows:

The 1st Welch, about 850 men, in an area covering the approaches toward Chania from the south. The 9th Battalion KRRC (King's Royal Rifle Corps), who had been considerably weakened during the fighting in Greece, about 400 men, divided into companies for the protection of the approaches toward the Akrotiri Peninsula. A battalion formed from the 2/2 and 2/3 Battalions of the Australian 16th Brigade (16th Australian Infantry Brigade Composite Battalion), 450 men, in a position at Kalivia, on the coast south of the entrance to Souda Bay. The 17th Australian Infantry Brigade Composite Battalion, formed from the 2/4 and 2/5 Battalions, of about 350 men positioned at Cape Dhrapanon, protruding from the south into the entrance of Souda Bay. The Greek 2nd Regiment, a little more than 900 men, directed toward the north in positions in the mountainous terrain about 4km south of Chania, with its left flank adjacent to the Greek 8th Regiment.

Of the remainder of the combat support forces brought to Crete from the Greek mainland, some units had taken over the protection of the ascents to the Akrotiri Peninsula as infantry. The Australian 2/2 Field Regiment, due to a lack of guns, was employed as infantry positioned along the precipice, about 1.5km west of Cape Dhrapanon. The majority of the assigned engineers, together with more than 1,000 Palestinian and Cypriot pioneer troops and port service and security personnel of the M.N.B.D.O. were deployed in an around the port of Souda. Also under the control of the Souda sector command was a transit camp at Platanos, about 1km south-west of Chania. About 700 soldiers, originally planned for transfer to Egypt, were assembled there. Scantily equipped with small arms, they were now designated as the 'Royal Perivolians'. There were almost no troops in Chania proper as its closely-packed medieval buildings and narrow streets could have easily become a trap during bombing attacks. For the protection of the command post of Major General Weston and some command installations established in the town's citadel, an element from the 106th Light Anti-Aircraft Regiment RA (Royal Artillery) had been detached. A number of Italian prisoners of war were also confined in the town prison. A short distance north of the positions of the Greek 2nd Regiment, in the village Mournies, the tent hospital of the Royal Navy was set up. For the immediate medical care of the troops in all of the western part of Crete, two company-size medical units – 168 and 189 Field Ambulance – were available. Souda Bay was marked by the effects from the almost daily attacks of the *Luftwaffe*: in the Bay, with their superstructures partly above the surface of the water and still burning, rested eight large merchant ships and a tanker. A number of other ships, among them the British corvette *Salvia*, were unable to leave the Bay because of the damage suffered. Overlooking Chania and the terrain south of it, the headquarters of Major General Freyberg was set up in an area with quarries and caves, about 1.5km north-east of the town. By means of the radio and telegraph station, located near the transit camp, good communications existed to Middle East Command and to all sectors on Crete. Including the signal elements the special staff sections and the liaison staffs from the R.A.F. and the Royal Navy, the headquarter organization comprised about 400 men.

Rethymnon / Georgioupolis Sector

The sector stretched from Georgioupolis, at the south-western edge of the Bight of Almyros, along the coast via Rethymnon and was commanded by Brigadier Vasey, the commander of the Australian 19th Brigade. He was tasked with the mission to prevent the enemy from seizing Rethymnon and its airstrip as well as from landing in the Bight of Almyros on either side of Rethymnon.[12] Of the forces assigned to him he had the Australian 2/7 Infantry-Battalion (680 men), the Australian 2/8 Infantry Battalion (380 men), a battery with six Italian 75mm guns from the Australian 2/3 Field Regiment, the 100-strong Australian Engineer Field Company (less one platoon) and a platoon from the 106 RA deployed in the area around Georgioupolis. For coastal protection two 10.5cm guns of the M.N.B.D.O. were also positioned there. Brigadier Vasey established his command post in Georgioupolis proper.

However the majority of his forces were planned for the defence of the airstrip east of Rethymnon. Its runway passed along the shore and to the south was surrounded by three 60-100m high elevations, with vineyards on their northern and olive groves on their southern slopes, in the east Hill A, in the south Hill D and in the west Hill B. There was little danger of the landing of parachute troops in the rocky, mountainous terrain on either side of Rethymnon, which restricted the coastal strip to a width of about 800-1,000m and was intersected by ravines every 1-1.5km. Therefore the sector commander of Rethymnon, Lieutenant Colonel Campbell, was able to concentrate the majority of his forces at the airstrip and on the shore.

The Australian 2/1 Infantry Battalion, of about 620 men, were completely equipped with small arms and machine-guns, but with only two 8cm mortars and two Bren Gun Carriers, and was to defend Hill A with one company, a heavy machine-gun platoon from the 2/1 Machine-Gun Battalion and two attached Italian 75mm guns from the 6th Battery of the Australian 2/3 Field Regiment. The majority of the battalion, three infantry companies occupied Hill D and its slopes. From there the airstrip could be dominated by fire along its entire length.

The Australian 2/11 Infantry Battalion, which was 640 men strong, was deployed with three of its companies on Hill B and either side of it. Another company was kept ready

---

12   For the subsequent presentation of the preparations in the sectors Rethymnon and Heraklion, the official history *Australia in the War of 1939-1945*, Series One, has been used.

some distance toward the south-east as a quick reaction force. Attached to the battalion were two 100mm guns and a platoon from the 2/1 Machine-Gun Battalion.

The Greek 4th and 5th Regiments, altogether about 2,300 men, were organized in four battalions. One battalion was positioned in the saddle between Hill D and Hill B. The other three battalions were placed as reserve into the area around the two small villages of Adhele and Pigi, located in a basin about 1.5km south of the airstrip. These settlements were connected with the coastal road by a track, leading along a valley to Platanes and by a path toward the north through a gorge of a stream. The coastal road from Rethymnon passed the airstrip close to the shore to the small village of Stavromenos and its olive oil factory, located about 800m further to the east. At Platanes a road branched off via Pigi and Adhele and passed east of the Ida Mountains to the small port of Timbakion on the southern coast.

The two Matilda II infantry tanks from the 7th R.T.R., assigned to the sector command, were hidden under olive trees on the path which led toward the north along the gorge.

On order of the sector commander no Australian troops were based in Rethymnon. The garrison of Rethymnon consisted only of the personnel of the local training school of the Greek gendarmerie, about 900 men, well trained, armed and with high morale. The protection of the settlement of Perivolia, stretching along the coastal road about 1.5km east of Rethymnon, as well as of Hill C, located just south of the settlement, was also handed over to the gendarmes. In the area around Rethymnon numerous armed civilians were also positioned, who in some areas were led by Greek officers.

As no anti-aircraft weapons had been issued to Lieutenant Colonel Campbell, he attached great importance to perfect camouflage against observation from the air. The success of this became evident on 16 May, when aerial photos, salvaged from a German reconnaissance aircraft that crashed near the airstrip, had shown but one position.

Lacking equipment, the assigned engineers had been unable to place mine fields. The large amounts of barbed wire received did, however, enable the troops to liberally protect their positions with wire entanglements. The runway of the airstrip was provisionally blocked with fuel-barrels filled with sand and rocks.

Campbell established his command post on a northern spur of Hill A. Altogether he had about 4,500 combat and combat-support troops at his disposal.

Heraklion Sector

The sector, stretching from the area around Heraklion for about 7km toward the east, was placed under the responsibility of the commander of the British 14th Brigade, Brigadier Chappel. Heraklion was the most populated town on Crete and surrounded on the landward-side by a 6-10m high solid stone-wall with a few gates. Only on the north-western edge of the town had the wall been broken up to generate space for the coastal road, leading to its interior. In front of the wall, new, partly extended living-quarters were built. Heraklion still has a harbour, which is protected against the sea by a neck of land. A long jetty protrudes into the harbor which allows even large ships to berth. Immediately south-east of the harbour is the settlement of Alikarnassos and about 15km farther to the south-east was a large barracks. The airfield, with two intercrossing runways, was located directly on the shore, about 5km east of Heraklion. Toward the south the elevated ground of the airfield was bounded by two heights; in the west the rock-strewn twin summits of the 'Charlies' and in the east the East Hill. Between the airfield and these heights, the coastal road from Heraklion passes across a dry river valley and then, along the shore, via the village of Gournes, about 8km east of the airfield, toward the most eastern part of Crete.

The terrain south of Heraklion and its airfield initially ascends only slightly in the direction toward the saddle between the Ida and Dikti Mountains and is agriculturally intensively used to grow olives, grapes and corn to this day. From Heraklion, the main line of communication toward the south leads across the eastern spur of the Ida Mountains to Timbakion. Another road to the east passes the ruins of ancient Knossos about 6km away from Heraklion into the mountain range, but ends shortly before the southern coast of Crete.

Brigadier Chappel deployed the forces assigned to him as follows:

The British 2nd Black Watch of about 860 men, fully equipped, directly on the airfield and on East Hill.

The Australian 2/4 Infantry Battalion of about 550 men, which had brought back from Greece only one light machine-gun per platoon and three 8cm mortars without bases, and therefore was reinforced with four heavy machine-guns and six Bren Gun Carriers from 14th Brigade, on and around the 'Charlies'.

The 2nd Leicesters, with about 630 men, as reserve, but dug-in immediately west of the 2/4 Infantry Battalion. They had been landed in Heraklion by two cruisers as late as the night of 15/16 May and therefore had brought along no vehicles.

The 2nd York and Lancs, 740 men, were fully equipped, in an area south-east of Heraklion. The battalion also provided contact with the garrison of Heraklion, which consisted of a Greek garrison battalion with about 800 men and the Greek 3rd and 7th Regiments, altogether about 1,800 soldiers.

Of the assigned tanks Brigadier Chappel placed a Matilda II each at the eastern and western edge of the airfield under camouflage. The six light tanks were positioned or covered at the south-eastern corner of the airfield.

The twelve assigned 40mm anti-aircraft guns (eight from the Australian 7th LAA Battery and four from the British 156th LAA Battery) and four heavy AAA (Anti-Aircraft Artillery) guns from the M.N.B.D.O. and some twin anti-aircraft machine-guns were positioned around the northern edge of the airfield.

The nine 100mm and four 75mm guns from the British 234th Medium Battery received firing positions south-west of the airfield.

The sector at Heraklion was particularly well provided with medical forces. The British 7th Medical Rgt with about 450 men and a medical company from the 189 Field Ambulance set up their installations mainly in Nea Alikarnassos. Here, Chappel established his command post.

Not counting command and control troops, logistical troops, pioneer, medical forces and R.A.F. Ground personnel Brigadier Chappel had about 6,600 highly trained and well-equipped soldiers at his disposal, plus eight tanks, 14 AAA guns and 15 artillery pieces for the defence of his sector.

After the publication of CREFORCE Operational Order No. 3 and Operational Instruction No. 10 Major General Freyberg granted the sector commanders far reaching freedom of action for the preparations of the defence of the island and had mainly stayed in his headquarters. There, he had let himself be briefed about the progress of the preparations but spent almost no time in gaining an impression of his own. After 16 May he initiated no more changes in the dispositions and the mission of the troops, as he anticipated the start of the German attack on any day thereafter. Whether he had known about the shifting of this attack from 18 to 20 May because of the fuel situation is not clear. At any rate, the troops, resting in the highest state of alert, had not been informed about it.

With a high degree of probability, the take-off of the German air transport formations from the airfields in southern Greece in the early morning of 20 May had been reported to him via communications between the U.S. Embassy in Athens and his headquarters. Shortly before 0800hrs,[13] while observing the approach of the Ju 52 formations toward the northern coast of Crete from the heights above Chania in front of his headquarters, Major General Freyberg turned around to his escort and said "They are on time!"

---

13   The British time on Crete was one hour behind the German time. German time is used in the subsequent study of the fighting.

3

The assault from the air

Att 0415hrs on 20 May the fighters, bombers and transport aircraft of the *VIII.* and *XI.Flieger-Korps* commenced take off toward Crete in a carefully-planned order. The majority of the formations of *VIII.Flieger-Korps* were to attack once more in the accustomed pattern against previously identified targets. Immediately prior to the arrival of the gliders and transport aircraft over the operational areas of *Gruppen West* and *Mitte*, dive bombers and fighter-bombers, protected by fighters, were to attack the positions of the enemy strongly for 20 minutes and thereafter to silence his AAA weapons during the final approach of the gliders and the parachuting of the assault troops.

I./SturmRgt. commanded by *Major* Koch, organized into dive glider assault groups, including one made up from the command platoon of the *SturmRgt.* under *Major* Braun,[1] took off with their tug-squadrons from the airfields at Eleusis and Tanagra. *1./SturmRgt.* (less its 3rd Platoon), under *Oberleutnant* Genz and *2./SturmRgt.* (reinforced by the 3rd Platoon from *1./SturmRgt.*), under *Hauptmann* Altmann, were to neutralize the identified heavy AAA batteries south of Chania and on the Akrotiri Peninsula, if possible prior to the arrival of the first air transport formations. The other three assault groups were facing similarly difficult tasks. Shortly before the parachuting of the majority of the *SturmRgt.*, 108 soldiers of *3./SturmRgt.* under *Oberleutnant* von Plessen, were to take out the AAA and machine-gun positions at the western and northern ends of the airfield at Maleme. *Sturmgruppe Braun* was to destroy the enemy positions at the Tavronitis Bridge. *4./SturmRgt.* under *Hauptmann* Sarrazin, joined by Koch and parts of his battle HQ totaling 108 men, had a tent camp situated immediately south of Hill 107 as an objective which was identified as quarters for troops. Additional gliders of *I./LL Geschwader 1* were provided for the radio teams of *LnAbt.41* and the signals platoon of the *SturmRgt.*, for half of *1./FschArtAbt.7* (*Hauptmann* Schram) and for *Generalleutnant* Süßmann and his battle HQ.[2]

As the Ju 52 flew slower than the other transport aircraft when towing gliders, they had to take off some time ahead of these. In order to drop the parachute forces of *Gruppen West* and *Mitte* as entire battalions, an orderly sequence had to be calculated for the assembly in the air of the respective formations. The time required for this assembly and the actual duration of the flight of the towing aircraft, however, could only be roughly calculated. Therefore it remained uncertain whether the glider assault groups assigned to *Gruppe West* would be able to arrive over the operational area with the intended 15-30 minutes headstart against the parachuting of *III./SturmRgt.*, which was to attack Maleme from the east.

---

1 *Major* Braun had occupied the post of the staff major in the staff of the *SturmRgt.* This post was generated to have an officer of some rank available for special tasks. Accordingly, the staffs of the battalions of the *SturmRgt.* had a staff captain or an *Oberleutnant*.

2 The evaluation of all relevant and reliable sources confirms the already mentioned number of 72 gliders for *Merkur*: 9 for *Sturmgruppe Braun*, 9 for *Sturmgruppe Genz*, 15 for *Sturmgruppe Altmann*, 12 for *3./SturmRgt.*, 12 for *4./SturmRgt.*, 5 for the radio sets assigned to the *SturmRgt.*, 5 for the commander of *Fl.Div.7* and his battle HQ, 4 for ½ *1./FschArtAbt.7* and 1 for the radio set with *I./SturmRgt.*

At 0415hrs *1./SturmRgt.* took off with all nine gliders from the airfield at Tanagra. Its primary mission was to take out the 234th Heavy Anti-Aircraft Battery positioned with its four 9.8cm guns, about 1km north-east of the village of Mournies. The approach flight developed badly, two of the gliders with soldiers from the 2nd Platoon aboard suffered snapped towing cables while the aircrafts were still far out over the sea. The fate of its passengers remained hidden to the other tugs, which continued their flight.[3] These were fired at by heavy AAA guns before they had even reached the coast. The gliders therefore were prematurely unhooked, disturbing their flight order. After the tow aircraft turned off at about 0715hrs the gliders commenced their dive still under fire from AAA. The commander of the 2nd Platoon, *Leutnant* Mahrenbach, was killed and his deputy seriously wounded as a result of this fire. The premature unlatching meant that the 1st Platoon, which with the three gliders was to directly attack the AAA position, could not land there and instead came down some distance to the north, toward Chania. The glider with the dead Mahrenbach aboard touched down at a road junction near the southern outskirts of Chania. It crash-landed and all of its passengers, except one paratrooper, were seriously injured. While the injured moved toward the noise of the fighting from the AAA position, the unwounded paratroopers cleverly covered their rear against about a company of enemy troops, who approached on trucks from Chania to join the fighting and finally forced them to abandon their mission.

One glider of the command platoon of *1./SturmRgt.* with *Oberleutnant* Genz and the assigned medical officer, *Oberarzt* Dr. Stehfen aboard, came down in the midst of the AAA position and the others two landed nearby. Led by Genz the men of the command platoon, soon joined by the approaching 1st Platoon, overcame the soldiers of the heavy AAA battery in bitter close combat. When the fighting was over only seven of the 180 enemy forces remained unscathed. The two parachute platoons also lost a considerable number of killed and wounded. Among the latter was *Leutnant* Toschka, the commander of the 1st Platoon. Fortunately the radio set which was assigned to *Sturmgruppe Genz*, remained undamaged.

The surviving men of the assault group were continuously involved in firefights against enemy troops nearby but now established themselves in all-round defence in the position with its four heavy guns, in order to wait for the planned relief by elements of *Gruppe Mitte*. Shortly after 1000hrs Genz was informed by *FschJgRgt.3*, that *I./FschJgRgt.3*, tasked with the relief of his assault group had become tied-down in front of Perivolia and received the order to fight through to this location. Immediately thereafter the radio of the assault group was hit by small arms fire and became unusable.[4]

The enemy in front of the assault group in the meantime had received reinforcements and approaching tanks had been reported. This caused Genz to set out in a south-westerly direction with 25 combat-effective paratroopers. The wounded were left behind under the initial care of Dr. Stehfen and several other soldiers. About 500m away from the AAA

---

3   The after-action report of *XI.Flieger-Korps* mentions but one glider lost over the sea. More reliable is the war diary of *FschJgRgt.3*, printed in excerpts in *DDF* May/June 1991, pp.17-23. There, the number of missing is stated as 3 non-commissioned officers and 13 other ranks from *1./SturmRgt.* This corresponds with the number of passengers in two gliders (less the glider pilots).

4   The after-action report of *FschJgRgt.3* mentions that the relief action was ordered shortly after 0945hrs. Until that time, Genz had requested reinforcements via radio. The time 0930hrs, found for the order to fight through in Kurowski, is erroneous.

position the group around Genz was forced to temporary revert to the defence; Dr. Stehfen and nine more men caught up with it.

Circumventing the enemy in front of it toward the south, and with a reconnaissance party scouting ahead, the assault group continued its movement after nightfall and progressed about 5km. While passing through the village of Perivolia, which was occupied by the enemy. Genz managed to deceive the security guards with the help of his good knowledge of the English language.[5] By Genz's ruse the group was able to extract itself from the enemy another two times after short firefights.

The employment of 2./SturmRgt. against the AAA units on the Akrotiri Peninsula failed from the start. Due to a navigational error, the towing aircraft flew in the direction of Cape Dhrapanon and noticed the error only when they were almost level with Rethymnon and as they turned back the flight order of the formation was completely lost. Upon approaching from a new direction after the unhooking, and amidst AAA fire, most of the glider pilots lost their orientation. About an hour behind the original plan and widely dispersed, the gliders went down. On the rocky mountainous terrain of the Akrotiri Peninsula a number of them crashed and their passengers suffered high losses. The heavy AAA battery which the assault group was initially tasked with taking out, proved to be a dummy position. Furthermore as most of the gliders came down within the area of the Northumberland Hussars the paratroopers who remained combat-effective were unable to unite into larger groups. Therefore on 20 May the greater part of Kompanie Altmann was overwhelmed. Most of its soldiers, among them the company commander and two more officers, were captured. Only a few small groups managed to escape into the desolate, waterless surroundings.[6] The command of XI.Flieger-Korps remained ignorant about the fate of the reinforced 2./SturmRgt. until the end of the fighting on Crete.

In the operational area of Gruppe West, the assault groups from the 3rd and 4th companies of the SturmRgt., brought along in gliders from the airfield at Eleusis, landed almost simultaneously at about 0715hrs, as the attacks by dive bombers and fighter-bombers diminished.[7]

3./SturmRgt., organized into a command platoon and three rifle platoons each with three gliders,[8] had been given the mission to take out the AAA and field positions along the western and north-western ends of the airfield at Maleme. As the glider with the platoon leader of the 3rd Platoon aboard had to conduct an emergency landing on the island of Antikytira after its towing cable snapped,[9] the platoon arrived with only two-thirds of its

---

5   Perivolia was occupied by staff from the Greek 2nd Regiment. Poor knowledge of the English language by the Greek soldiers and the darkness had saved the situation.

6   As a result of a lack of water and ammunition these too soon had to surrender to enemy search parties. The after-action report of XI.Flieger-Korps states the losses of Sturmgruppe Altmann as 108 men, 48 of them killed and 36 wounded. Among the killed were Oberleutnant Ebner. All of the captured paratroopers, except the three officers, who had been brought to Egypt – Hauptmann Altmann, Oberleutnants Mohr and Rümmler – had been liberated during the seizure of Chania.

7   The subsequent description of the employment of the Luftlande-Sturmregiment mainly relies on the war diary of this formation (KTB Kreta des LL-Sturmregiments), available at the Bundesarchiv Militärarchiv under the signature BW 57/47.

8   The remaining personnel of the company had been assigned to the regimental signals company, which was used as infantry.

9   The passengers of this glider had again joined the battalion on 24 May.

combat strength. Under violent incoming fire two gliders of the command platoon made a forced landing on the beach north-west of the airfield. Their passengers, except for a few bruises, remained uninjured and combat effective. However when one squad attacked an AAA position nearby it was completely decimated in the open terrain. Shortly thereafter the company commander, *Oberleutnant* von Plessen, was also killed as he led an assault against another AAA position. While under fire the medical officer that was attached to the command platoon, *Oberarzt* Dr. Weizel, set up a collection point for wounded in some cover. Together with two other men he carried three seriously wounded to this point and provided medical care for them.

The 1st and 2nd Platoons came down immediately west and close to the mouth of the Tavronitis River. Under close range fire the platoon leader of the 1st Platoon, *Leutnant* Musyal, was seriously wounded. The platoon leader of the 2nd Platoon, *Oberfeldwebel* Arpke, was temporarily put out of action after his glider crashed. In both platoons *Feldwebel*s took over command and led their soldiers in the attack against the AAA and field positions along the western side of the airfield. Here *Oberjäger* Schuster proved his abilities as he took out two AAA positions by himself. Despite suffering considerable losses the two platoons succeeded in clearing most of the airfield's western edge within a short time. However heavy fire from the eastern edge of the airfield and from the northern slope of Hill 107 soon forced them to take cover in the bed of the Tavronitis and withdraw from action. At this time the 3rd Platoon landed with its two gliders near the village of Tavronitis and after a short fight captured 30 of the enemy there, managing to establish contact with the other platoons. At about 0930hrs *Oberarzt* Dr. Weizel assumed command over *3./SturmRgt.* At about 1000hrs the company held a line on the eastern bank of the Tavronitis from the eastern ramp of the bridge to the coast. There, its soldiers were largely protected against the flat trajectory fire from the eastern edge of the airfield, but remained involved in firefights against the survivors of a platoon from C Company of 22nd Battalion, who continüd to defend the airfield.[10]

4./SturmRgt. under *Hauptmann* Sarrazin and the battle HQ of *Major* Koch had lost four of their twelve gliders over the sea during the approach flight, when their towing cables snapped.[11] Hampered during their downward dive by defensive fire and the German dive bombers still in the air, the gliders came down widely dispersed. While two of them touched down directly in the abandoned tent camp, several others landed on the western slope of Hill 107, between the positions of parts of D Company/22nd Battalion and the platoon from 21st Battalion, which was dug-in farther to the south-east. Some more landed south-east of Hill 107. The assault group was further weakened when three gliders were blown up on landing, *Hauptmann* Sarrazin being killed. Split up in small groups, the paratroopers, despite heavy losses, offered fierce a resistance. Finally a group of survivors, among them the seriously wounded Koch, managed to fight through toward the west to

---

10   Davin, p.102, gives the initial strength of C Company as 117 rifles, 7 light, one heavy and 6 Browning machine-guns. Well dug-in, the company had lost only 6 men during the air attacks, all from the platoon along the south-eastern perimeter of the airfield.

11   Two of these gliders had managed to conduct an emergency landing on a small island close to the coast of Crete. The passengers, only slightly injured managed, re-established contact with friendly forces after a few days. The other two gliders had landed in the sea. All except three of their passengers had been saved by sea rescue.

other parts of the *SturmRgt.*, which, in the meantime, had been dropped there. The dead, among them *Oberleutnants* Gerbershagen and Hoffmann from Koch's battle HQ, as well as the seriously wounded, remained behind. Small groups of paratroopers that were unable to extract themselves from the enemy were able to find some cover in the intersected terrain south-east of Hill 107, from where they kept on fighting.

Only a few minutes after the landing of *Sturmgruppen von Plessen* and *Sarrazin*, *IV./ SturmRgt.* under *Hauptmann* Gericke, the regimental signals company under *Oberleutnant* Osius (employed as infantry), parts of the HQ company and *3./FschSanAbt.7* (less one platoon) under *Stabsarzt* Dr. Siebert, were dropped as the first wave of *Gruppe West*. Attached to *13./SturmRgt.* was *3./FschFlaMGBtl.7* under *Oberleutnant* Theuerling, with three of its 2cm antiaircraft guns. The majority of these troops came down in the flat terrain covered with olive groves and vines, between the villages of Kamisiana and Tavronitis. The commander of the *SturmRgt.*, *Generalmajor* Meindl, jumped together with *Hauptmann* Gericke. They had just left their Ju 52 when it received a direct hit from an AAA gun and crashed with some of its passengers still aboard. Although injured on landing *Hauptmann* Gericke managed to retain command over his battalion. Much of the heavy equipment dropped by parachute became unusable on landing in olive trees. The losses among the sidecar motorcycles, which were required as towing vehicles, were particularly high.

Together with the parachuting elements of the first wave of *Gruppe West* were four gliders with radio teams aboard[12] and another four which carried two mountain guns from *1./FschArtAbt.7*. They commenced the dive toward their landing sites but the landing of the half-battery took an unfortunate course. One of the gliders, with a gun aboard, crashed, killing all of the members of the crew and destroying the gun. Even more serious was the loss of the long-range radio sets: the two gliders which carried the 200-watt transmitter also crashed, killing all members of the radio team and totally destroying the set. In the crash of the third glider the 80-watt radio set was rendered useless and the adjutant of Meindl and two more soldiers were seriously injured. Fortunately the other 80-watt set, which landed in the fourth glider, was only damaged. Using parts of the unusable set the regimental signal officer managed to make it fit for use after several hours of work. It was with this set that communication could be established from 1100hrs with the wireless centre of *XI.Flieger-Korps* at Loutra, near Athens. The first reports transmitted by the *SturmRgt.* were assessed as quite optimistic by the staff of *XI.Flieger-Korps*.

The *Fallschirmtruppe* who came down immediately west of the Tavronitis met with almost no resistance in their drop zone as the field positions there were unoccupied. Therefore they were able to assemble unhindered and to pick up their equipment with ease. As they could not be engaged by the weapons of the defenders on the western slope of Hill 107, they were only being fired at by anti-aircraft guns and heavy machine-guns positioned some distance away from Hill 107.[13]

---

12   A fifth glider, with the 80-watt radio set for *I./SturmRgt.* aboard, had to conduct an emergency landing in the sea about 15km north of the Cretan coast. Its passengers had later been picked up by air-rescue aircraft.

13   The request by the commander of 22nd Battalion to change the line of fire of the two coastal guns on the north-western slope, so that they could direct their fire against *Fallschirmtruppe* landing west of the Tavronitis, had been turned down by the gun commander with reference to his mission, the defence against sea landings.

3./FschSanAbt.7 attacked the buildings of Tavronitis west of the bridge, and in close combat cleared them of the ground personnel of the R.A.F. who occupied them. Subsequently the company set up a dressing station in the vicinity.

16./SturmRgt. (engineers) under *Oberleutnant* Hoefelt was dropped, as planned, west of the Tavronitis Valley, about 2km south of the airfield, with the mission to protect the right flank of the *SturmRgt.* along the road to Kandanos. During its advance southwards, it was time and again involved in firefights with armed Cretan civilians.

During the parachuting of the first wave of *Gruppe West*, the assault group under *Major* Braun, parts of the regimental staff and the combat platoon came down belatedly under heavy machine-gun fire in nine gliders near the western ramp of the Tavronitis Bridge. Still seated in his glider *Major* Braun was killed together with several other passengers. The Regiment's orderly officer, *Oberleutnant* Schächter, was also seriously wounded. Nevertheless the assault group took out the defenders near the western bridge ramp and cut the ignition cables on the bridge, which had been prepared for demolition.

At about 0800hrs Meindl and his battle HQ arrived at the Tavronitis Bridge. However, after recieving a short situation report, he moved forward from the river bed to get a personal picture of the situation, but was seriously wounded by machine-gun fire. Resting on a litter he remained in command of *Gruppe West*, but gave control of the actual fighting to *Major* Stentzler, commanding *II./SturmRgt.* This battalion, except its 6th Company, was planned as the reserve of the *SturmRgt.* At about 0800hrs and 45 minutes behind schedule the battalion was dropped without resistance in the area around Ropaniana, a small settlement, located immediately south-east of the Rodope Peninsula.

The 6th Company, led by *Oberleutnant* Pissin, was given the mission to protect *Gruppe West* from the area around Kolimbari from the west and the Rodope Peninsula. The unit consisted of the HQ section with an assigned radio set, the 1st and 3rd Platoons and an anti-tank gun from *14./SturmRgt.* An independent mission was assigned to a detachment under *Leutnant* Mürbe, consisting of the 2nd Platoon, the heavy machine-gun squad and the light mortar team from 6th Company, two anti-tank guns from *14./SturmRgt.*, an engineer squad from *16./SturmRgt.*, a radio team and a medical officer, altogether totaling 72 men.[14] Its mission was to find out about the situation in the area around Kastelli and if possible secure the Bight of Kissamo for later sea landings.

After it assembled the 6th Company advanced toward Kolimbari. On the high ground south of this village, where the coastal road leads through a pass, it came across two platoons of Greek soldiers and a number of armed civilians in dug-in positions. In a hard fight, during which the company lost one killed and five wounded, the enemy was forced to withdraw to the Rodope Peninsula. 18 Greek soldiers and several armed civilians were captured. The latter were shot on the spot.[15]

---

14   As the correct composition of *Kampfgruppe Mürbe* is not completely available in the German literature about *Merkur*, it has been put together here from several sources. The Gefechtsbericht Kreta of *XI.Flieger-Korps* gives its strength as 72 men. Davin, pp.173-174, mentions 76 men from New Zealand sources, 74 men from a German source.

15   This event, which obviously was substantiated solely by the fact that civilians had participated in the fighting, is mentioned only in the company's after-action report. It had clearly constituted an offence against the rules of war, which were enclosed in the paybook of every German soldier. In the third order it was stated that an enemy who has surrendered may not be killed, even a partisan or a spy. The latter would find their punishment in court. An examination in more depth of this event, which, according to the company's after-action report was repeated on 23 May and may also have triggered some of the cruelties

Kampfgruppe Mürbe was dropped from six Ju 52s at 0725 hrs, too close to Kastelli and was attacked during landing by troops of the Greek 1st Regiment, members of the Home Guard and civilians armed with a variety of weapons. *Leutnant* Mürbe was killed at 0745hrs and the commander of the 2nd Platoon at 0800hrs. At 1015hrs the radio team sent a final report which said that communications would end as the team had to fight, too. Later at 1100hrs the detachment's last pockets of resistance were overwhelmed. It lost 48 killed and of the survivors, 22 men, mostly wounded, were captured. Two soldiers initially managed to escape and hide in the surrounding countryside. The prisoners were beaten and threatened with death by the civilians. They were then protected by the New Zealand officers and non-commissioned officers with the Greek 1st Regiment and brought into the safety of the prison of Kastelli and into the terrain some distance away from the village. By means of the detachment's radio set, which was captured intact, attempts were undertaken to mislead *Gruppe West*.[16]

The employment of *III./SturmRgt.* under *Major* Scherber, reinforced with two anti-tank guns from *14./SturmRgt.* and two anti-aircraft guns from *3./FschFlaMGBtl.7*, was a disaster from the outset. Delays generated by bad conditions during take-off from Mykene had caused a number of issues. Futhermore the air transport formation with the reinforced *III./SturmRgt.* aboard arrived in the airspace east of Maleme as late as 0900hrs, nearly an hour and a half later than its sister-battalions west of the Tavronitis. *Major* Scherber received the mission to attack Maleme from the east with his force. In order not to drift out into the sea during the parachuting, because the slopes which ascended from the area south-west of Maleme and from Pirgos had been thought unoccupied by the enemy and as a result of crass navigational mistakes by the dispatchers, the 11th and 12th companies were dropped on the slopes and dispersed over a distance of about 2km. The 10th Company parachuted about 1.5km further to the west, at and north of Modhion. The 9th Company came down with one component immediately west of Pirgos and with the other about 1.5km south of Hill 107. Almost everywhere the parachute soldiers landed amongst enemy positions that were fully combat ready. A number of men came down directly in front of the rifle barrels of dug-in New Zealanders.

The losses were atrocious. The 11th and 12th companies were almost completely destroyed in the areas of the New Zealand 23rd and 21st battalions. The 10th Company also suffered badly as during landing they were assaulted by the New Zealand engineers, deployed in and north of Modhion, and by the convicts of the field punishment camp who had been armed. A group of paratroopers, who established themselves in a building near the beach, were attacked by two platoons from the New Zealand 28th Battalion after guns from 27th Battery directed their fire against them. According to enemy reports several Germans were killed and two officers and eight men captured. The parts of the 9th Company, and the one or two anti-tank guns, which had been dropped immediately east of Maleme, suffered considerable losses in the fight against the headquarter company of the

---

committed by civilians against German killed and wounded in the western part of Crete, is beyond the subject of this book.

16 There is no doubt that *Kampfgruppe Mürbe* fought fiercely until the end, as demonstrated by the losses of 57 killed and 62 wounded from the Greek 1st Regiment alone, including one of the advisers. See Davin, p.174.

New Zealand 22nd Battalion that was deployed as infantry in the village. Soldiers from the AAA guns, who escaped from the airfield, directed the fire of the captured anti-tank guns against their former owners. Finally, a number of paratroopers dropped east of Maleme, among them the wounded company commander, succeeded in fighting through to the Tavronitis River. On the way, they overran a platoon from the New Zealand headquarters company in its positions at the southern edge of Maleme.

Only small groups of *III./SturmRgt.* managed to disengage from the enemy. Most of them settled down in the intersected terrain south of the coastal road and from here contributed to the disquieting of the New Zealand troops, who preferred to remain fixed in their positions. Most of the officers of *III./SturmRgt.* were killed, among them its commander. *Oberleutnant* Trebes, the officer in the battalion staff, managed to assemble a number of the scattered paratroopers and in the course of the morning to fight through to the west. On the way the group took out an AAA gun in a position east of the airfield. Later in the morning Trebes was again involved in combat. He led paratroopers from *13./SturmRgt.* and from the 1st Platoon of *3./SturmRgt.* in the attack against the R.A.F. camp south of the Tavronitis Bridge. Soldiers from the *13./SturmRgt.* thereafter positioned some of their 10cm Nebelwerfer in this location.

By reports of soldiers arriving from the drop zone of *III./SturmRgt.*, the command of the Regiment was informed for the first time about the failure of the mission of this battalion at around 1000hrs. The true dimensions of the disaster however remained hidden until later.[17]

Soon it became apparant that the strength and combat value of the enemy along the coastal strip east of Maleme had been greatly underrated.

Around midday on 20 May, orders by the regimental commander, who was resting in the dressing station in Tavronitis, began to take effect. As *III./SturmRgt.* had not appeared in the embattled area according to plan the only option promising success was the attack on the airfield and the dominating Hill 107 from the west. *I./SturmRgt.*, except its reinforced 6th Company, continued to press forward against Kolimbari, now abandoned its role as reserve and was brought forward from the area around Ropaniana. *Major* Stentzler, with his 5th and 7th companies swinging out to the south, was to attack Hill 107, thereby releasing

---

17   In the context of these events some clarification is considered necessary about the numbers of *Fallschirmtruppe* dropped or landed on the morning of 20 May. With the 430 Ju 52s available for parachuting about 5,160 men theoretically could have been dropped, if all aircraft had been filled with 12 men each. However the available sources state that, including the passengers of the gliders, only 4,320 men were actually transported to Crete – about 1,400 less than theoretically possible. Thus only 30% of the capacity of the Ju 52s was required for the transport of equipment. Looking specifically at *Gruppe West*, it is known from reliable sources that 1,860 men were dropped or landed with gliders in the morning of 20 May. Subtracting the 324 men of the assault groups, the c.40 men in the gliders with the radio teams and the half battery, the 180 men of the regimental signals and headquarter companies and the estimated c.160 men of the assigned combat support units, altogether about 700 men, about 1,160 men remained for *II., III.* and *IV.* battalions of the *SturmRgt.* Counting the units of *IV./SturmRgt.*, only about 300 men, it becomes evident that the two parachute battalions of the *SturmRgt.* could not have jumped with more than about 430 men each, unless it is assumed that their transport aircraft had been loaded with more than 12 men. As regards the fatal losses of *III./SturmRgt.*, the list contained in Winterstein states 356 for the entire duration of the fighting on Crete. Therefore the number of c. 400 men killed in the actions of 20 May is largely correct only when those of the reinforcing units are added.

the elements of the assault-group which still held out there. The 8th Company, together with those from *IV./SturmRgt.*, was to engage the defenders on the western and northern slopes of Hill 107. Parts of *Bataillon Gericke* and remnants of *I./SturmRgt.* were to advance against the western slope of Hill 107 and along the southern perimeter of the airfield as far as possible. At the regimental command post, which was established in field positions of the enemy in an olive grove immediately south of the village of Tavronitis, the signals officer of the staff, *Oberleutnant* Goettsche, maintained radio communication with the wireless centre of *XI.Flieger-Korps* by means of the only operational 80-watt radio. Radio communication also existed to the staffs of *II.* and *IV./SturmRgt.*

From 1000hrs on enemy artillery which was directed from Hill 107 fired into the area west of the Tavronitis and into the eastern part of the airfield. Undiminished heavy fire was also directed against the paratroopers along the western edge of the airfield. Here parts of *15./SturmRgt.* had also intervened in the course of the morning and together with *Oberjäger* Schuster and his men succeeded in taking out an anti-aircraft gun, which had dominated the airfield. During this action the company commander of *13./SturmRgt.*, *Oberleutnant* Dobke, was killed. Any further advance toward the east was however denied by the enemy.

Upon the first encouraging report from the *SturmRgt.* the staff of *XI.Flieger-Korps* had cause for hope that Maleme would soon be open for air-landings, as such at about 1230hrs the air commander sent *Major* Snowadski, with a small staff and a wireless station in two Ju 52s to the airfield. Snowadski was to become the airfield commandant. It was only during the landing run that the pilots of both aircraft realized the airfield was still dominated by the enemy. They accelerated again and although both aircraft were damaged, managed to return to the Greek mainland. There, *Major* Snowadski provided Student with a clearer though less favourable picture of the situation in the area around Maleme shortly after 1500hrs. About the same time a wireless message from the *SturmRgt.* confirmed the content of this report.

At 1500hrs the attack of the *SturmRgt.* against Hill 107 was launched. In the early evening hours, the outflanking thrust of the 5th and 7th companies, under *Oberleutnants* Herterich and Barmetler, came across enemy positions south of Hill 107. Some time earlier, the regimental medical officer Dr. Neumann and a scratch force from the regimental combat platoon and *I.* and *III./SturmRgt.*, was able to gain a foothold on the north-western slope of the height by utilizing the effects of renewed air attacks and leading a frontal attack against Hill 107, albeit suffering heavy losses. The thrust had been against R.A.F. ground crew, who eventually fled from their camp.

At about 1700hrs, as they assessed their gains, the paratroopers were attacked by two Matilda II tanks to their complete surprise, accompanied by about a platoon of infantry that were advancing along the northern slope of Hill 107 toward the Tavronitis Bridge.[18] Quickly the soldiers that were facing the counter-thrust composed themselves and took up the fight with all the weapons at hand. While the attack of the enemy infantry that were

---

18   Reports from the *SturmRgt.* to the command of *XI.Flieger-Korps* confirm the surprise of the troops, at least in the area around Maleme. The intelligence report of *XI.Flieger-Korps*, dated 16 May (Feind-Nachrichtenblatt Kreta Nr. 4 des GenKdo XI FlgKorps), however, had indicated the presence of about 30 light tanks on Crete.

advancing south of the coastal road was broken up under heavy losses by defensive fire, one of the tanks stopped on the coastal road. The other pushed forward in the dry bed of the Tavronitis River up to and under the bridge. Here it came to a halt after several hits from an anti-tank gun; the crew dismounted and was captured.

The efforts of the *SturmRgt.* to gain a solid hold on Hill 107 continued until nightfall. At that time its 5th and 7th companies worked their way to the southern foot of Hill 107. There they interrupted the advance when the situation ahead of them was assessed as unclear. All elements of the *SturmRgt.* now prepared for the anticipated counter-attack, for which it was certainly suspected that the enemy had sufficiently strong forces at his disposal just east of Hill 107. Nevertheless, *Gruppe West* intended to resume the attack for the seizure of Maleme and Hill 107 in the early morning of 21 May. However ammunition was urgently required, particularly for the anti-tank guns, as well as medical supplies. These were requested by radio and were promised for delivery.

However, unbeknownst to all German commands that were involved in *Merkur*, the situation in the operational area of the *SturmRgt.* was to change decisively in its favour during the course of the night 20/21 May.

The reinforced New Zealand 22nd Battalion, tasked with the defence of Maleme and Hill 107, had been able to retain its positions during the fighting on the morning of 20 May, except those along the western perimeter of the airfield and those to the south of Tavronitis Bridge, although most of the AAA weapons there had been taken out. At this time the commanding officer of 22nd Battalion, Lieutenant Colonel Andrews, assessed the situation as sufficiently stable and denied the demand of his C Company for the employment of the battalion reserve. Contacting the HQ of the 5th Brigade, he only requested the re-establishment of physical contact by the 23rd Battalion to those parts of his battalion which could no longer be reached from Hill 107. This request was turned down by the brigade commander, with the explanation that the 23rd Battalion was also involved in fighting against paratroopers. Only a short time later, the fighting in the area of 23rd Battalion had developed favourably for the New Zealanders, who had lost only seven killed and about 30 wounded. Nevertheless the battalion commander, Lieutenant Colonel Leckie, omitted to establish contact with the 22nd Battalion on his own initiative. The New Zealand 21st Battalion also remained in its positions after it had beaten off the paratroopers, particularly after a platoon, sent out at 1130hrs toward the 252 AMES, reported the area to be free of enemy froces. About an hour prior to this event Brigadier Hargest had reported to the New Zealand Division that the main effort of the German airborne assault probably would be directed against the 22nd Battalion.

Throughout the course of the afternoon the situation for the 22nd Battalion deteriorated due to the relentless attacks and undiminished vigor of the German paratroopers. At 1700hrs Andrews requested the prepared counter-attack by the 23rd Battalion. However, yet again he was turned down. Upon his report at about 1830hrs, that the counter-thrust of his reserve had failed and that he would be forced to fall back with his troops unless supported by the 23rd Battalion, Hargest replied "If you must, you must!" About half an hour later, however, Hargest informed Andrews that he had detached a company each from the 23rd and 28th Battalions as reinforcements, which were expected to arrive around midnight. At about 1715hrs, Hargest reported this intention to Brigadier Puttick, probably in order to gain his agreement.

After it came under fire from mortars shortly after 1600 hrs the command post of the 22nd Battalion had been moved to the south-east, into the area of B Company.[19] As communication to his two forward deployed companies could not be established from this location Andrews assumed that these, for the greater part, had been annihilated. Consequently, the enemy would be able to bypass Hill 107 to the north. As paratroopers in some strength – parts of the 5th and 7th companies of the *SturmRgt.* – had commenced to probe toward the gap between his A Company around Hill 107 and B Company, Andrews also feared that the former could be cut-off. Consequently he decided to withdraw A Company on the ridge south of B Company and ordered the execution of this action. Between 2100 and 2130hrs he reported it to the brigade commander.[20] When, shortly prior to 2200hrs, the company commander of A Company/23rd Battalion arrived at the command post of 22nd Battalion, he received the mission to occupy Hill 107, which had been abandoned by A Company/22nd Battalion. This was even though his unit was still on the move – incomprehensibly its route was chosen via the 252 AMES and the village of Xamoudochori. Beginning to establish itself in field positions around Hill 107, A Company/23rd Battalion had time and again been engaged in firefights with paratroopers close-by. The officer from the 22nd Battalion who was provided as guide was killed in these engagements. Physical contact with A Company/23rd Battalion had at least been established by the remnants of the platoon from the 21st Battalion, which before had been deployed on the left flank of 22nd Battalion.

During this time, Andrews made the decision to fall back with his A and B companies to the positions of the 21st and 23rd Battalions, with A Company/23rd Battalion covering this move before being ordered to withdraw afterward. Shortly after midnight he initiated the retreat of his two companies and, on 21 May at 0200hrs, also the withdrawal of A Company/23rd Battalion. Just prior to dawn the retiring companies near Xamoudochori met A Company/28th Battalion, which at 1900hrs on the previous day had been detached as reinforcements, but had lost their way and had been continuously forced to fight scattered paratroopers on the way. Sometime before the company had reached Hill 107 and found its environs vacated. Everywhere it had detected enemy movements. After they had picked up about 60 soldiers from the initial defenders, who had missed the withdrawal of their units, they moved off toward the south-east.

Parts of C and D companies of the 22nd Battalion, which Andrews had assumed to be annihilated, had remained in their original positions. Until the early morning of 21 May C Company retained positions along the coastal road and the south-eastern edge of the airfield. When a reconnaissance patrol had observed only enemy troops toward the northern slope of Hill 107, at about 0420hrs the company commander ordered the retirement of his force toward the south-east, past Hill 107. On the way several soldiers from A and B companies, who had been asleep in their emplacements, were picked up. At about 0600hrs, in a small wood some distance west of the defence area of 21st Battalion, the company sought cover

---

19 About an hour later, Lieutenant Colonel Andrews had also sent away about 160 walking wounded, among them Germans, accompanied by the battalion's medical officer and medical personnel toward the east. Until daybreak on 21 May this group had not yet reached the positions of the 21st Battalion and had rested. During the entire day it was safeguarded against air attacks by recognition panels laid out by German wounded.

20 Davin, p.112, states that the response by Brigadier Hargest has not been documented. He remarks, however, that Hargest may not have grasped the importance of this report.

from German air attacks. Here, it discovered the resting HQ company and the remainder of D Company.

After receiving a report about the evacuation of the positions in his rear, the company commander of the latter divided the men around him into three groups and ordered their withdrawal. While the groups retiring past Hill 107 and along the coast, which were mainly ground crew of the R.A.F. and crews of the AAA and coastal guns, managed to avoid contact with the enemy, the platoon withdrawing toward the south in the Tavronitis Valley had been surrounded and, except for a few men, was forced to surrender.

After several fights against paratroopers the HQ Company, moving toward the west, went off in a southerly direction at around 0300hrs as a reconnaissance patrol had found the positions of B Company/22nd Battalion vacated.

During the evening of 21 May the litter-cases among the wounded soldiers in the former dressing station of the 22nd Battalion, who had been left under the care of some medical staff, were taken into German custody by the advancing paratroopers. The Germans among them were returned to the care of their own forces.

The examination of the events on the side of the enemy in the north-western part of Crete on 20 May makes clear that the abandonment of Hill 107, key for the defence of Maleme, must be attributed to a variety of reasons. There is no doubt that disrupted or disturbed telecommunications adversely contributed to the vague and incomplete picture of the situation at the senior command levels of the New Zealand 5th Brigade. More serious consequences developed from the offhand assigned missions for a number of units to defend against landings from the air as well as from the sea. It had been the overemphasis of the threat from the sea that prevented the occupation of the area immediately west of the lower valley of the Tavronitis River by combat troops, although it had clearly constituted a base for an attack of parachute forces against Maleme. The threat seen from the sea had also resulted in complicated relief plans in the case of a counter-attack into the positions of the New Zealand 22nd Battalion. The 23rd Battalion was planned to first relieve it in the area of the 28th (Maori) Battalion, but not before another unit had taken over the positions of the latter. The ongoing fighting against scattered paratroopers south-east of Maleme and the fear of additional landings of paratroops along the coastal road between Maleme and Platanias prevented these relief operations late in the afternoon of 20 May.[21] Thus the disastrous employment of *III./SturmRgt.* had helped *Gruppe West* in the struggle for its air bridgehead, as remaining paratroopers of the latter continued to fight in their drop zone and contributed in tying down the enemy opposing them.

The lack of energy and initiative displayed by the command of the New Zealand 5th Brigade, and the commanders of the two battalions deployed immediately east of Hill 107, had hindered the defence.[22] The continuous attacks of the *Luftwaffe*, dominating the skies over Crete during the hours of daylight, doubtlessly had endangered the movements of the

---

21   The level of concern about additional landings of paratroops in the command of the New Zealand Division is evident by the fact that Brigadier Puttick had given way to a request by the commanders of the 10th and 4th Brigades, around noon, to release the 4th Brigade for a counter-attack toward Alikianou, not before the evening and only under restrictions. See Davin, p.166.

22   In their studies of Freyberg as commander today's New Zealand historians, particularly Laurie Barber and John Tonkin-Covell, regard Brigadier Hargest as primarily responsible and reproach him for incorrect appreciations of the situation and for his lethargic attitude.

defenders. This should have been anticipated beforehand. Therefore, the relatively short distances from the defence areas of the 23rd and 21st Battalions should have been overcome after nightfall. The course of actions relating to the support of the 22nd Battalion had shown that movements of this kind had not been sufficiently reconnoitered.

In studying these findings it appears quite justifiable to draw the following basic conclusion from the course of the fighting for Hill 107 on 20 and early 21 May. The most promising chance to prevent the German parachute forces from establishing an air bridgehead west of Maleme, which would have resulted in an all-out immediate counter-attack using all available forces nearby, remained unused. This was not because of the failure of the troops or their insufficient combat-strength, but because of the attitude of their commanders, who had clung to their initial plans and lacked the will to take risks.

Oberst Heidrich, who commanded *Gruppe Mitte* was, like most of his soldiers, assaulting an enemy from the air for the first time. This commenced on 20 May from 0715hrs. The drop zone which was chosen for the Group stretched along the road Chania-Alikianou between the village of Daratsos, located east of the heights around Galatas and the small settlement of Episkopi, about 6.5km farther to the south-west, about 1.8km north-east of Alikianou. The road led through a valley, which at the prison in the middle of the drop zone, was almost 3km wide, narrowing to about 1.6km at the water reservoir of the Agia Lake and then passed into another basin north-east of Alikianou. From the heights around Galatas and the high terrain on either side of the valley, which ascends to about 100m and in the south to more than 300m, almost all of the drop zone could be observed completely. Olive groves, which ascended from the base of the high ground on either side of the valley to its crest, prevented observation from the air. The medium-high vegetation in the valley, which was mostly vines, corn and bushes, prevented aerial observers seeing that the terrain was rocky and rugged.

Gruppe Mitte was tasked with the mission to tie down the reserves of the enemy, which were assumed to be located along Prison Valley, to subdue them as much as possible and seize the high ground around Galatas. Subsequently it was to muster forces for a thrust toward Chania. The main purpose of the seizure of the dominating terrain around Galatas was to pave the way for *Gruppe West*, advancing along the coastal road.

The first unit dropped on the approach from the north after taking off from Tanagra was *III./FschJgRgt.3*, commanded by *Major* Heilmann. The battalion was reinforced with *4./FschFlaMGBtl.7*.[23] Although the terrain offered some distinctive features for navigation, the companies of the battalion which were to be dropped immediately south and east of Galatas came down widely dispersed.

The 9th Company and the battalion staff with *Major* Heilmann landed on high ground about 800m north-east of the prison, just south of Galatas and Daratsos, between the positions of the dug-in enemy there, and immediately suffered high losses. Nevertheless, the paratroopers, who were mostly armed only with the submachine-guns, pistols and hand

---

23   The number of 47 Ju 52s, assigned for the transport of this reinforced battalion, allows us to conclude that it was not brought along with its full complement of paratroopers and probably did not number more than 480 men. Whether *4./FschFlaMGBtl.7* was dropped with all six of its 2cm anti-aircraft guns is no unclear. According to its wartime establishment, the unit was also equipped with a number of heavy machine-guns and some anti-tank rifles.

grenades carried along for the jump, were able to seize the hill and the cemetery immediately north of the road Chania-Alikianou. In close combat the soldiers of the defending Greek 6th Regiment were overcome and the machine-guns positioned on the hills were taken out. About one hundred Greeks were captured. Those Greek soldiers who were not killed or captured fled in disorder partly into Galatas, partly into the defensive positions of the New Zealand 19th Battalion in the area around Daratsos. *Major* Heilmann and some of his soldiers advanced to the outer buildings of Galatas. However, there the paratroopers were forced to cease the assault because of the heavy defensive fire and of increasing losses. The conquered hills around noon were still in the hands of the Germans. Some paratroopers, who occupied some houses on the southern edge of Galatas, managed to hold out until nightfall.

The 10th Company under *Oberleutnant* Pagels was dropped correctly, but all by itself, on the flat coastal strip about 1km north-east of Galatas, close to the installations of the 7th General Hospital[24] and the New Zealand 6th Field Ambulance. Parts of the company, which came down in the area of the New Zealand 18th Battalion, were fired at during landing and were quickly overwhelmed. The paratroopers who were dropped further to the west, among them *Oberleutnant* Pagels, quickly advanced to the tented camp of the 7th General Hospital. There they took the medical personnel and the patients into captivity. In the course of the morning the company commander discovered the enemy in considerable strength, including armored vehicles, was approaching from the east. Thereupon he decided to fall back toward Galatas where he intended to link up with his own forces. The majority of the medical personnel and the patients that were able to walk were taken along under guard. On the way about 100 medical soldiers and about 40 patients of the New Zealand 6th Field Ambulance were also captured. During this action the commander of this unit was mortally wounded resisting. After a rest, during which the area was marked by Red Cross panels against air attacks and the prisoners were fed from captured stocks of food, the column set out in a direction toward Daratsos at about noon, as probing armored vehicles had indicated that enemy combat troops were approaching.

Almost all of the 11th Company was dropped in the wrong place and on high ground about 2.5km east of the prison. Fired at from the positions of the Greek 2nd Regiment in the south and attacked by Cretan armed civilians near Perivolia,[25] the paratroopers, led by *Oberleutnant* Lange, fought their way through to the drop zone of *I./FschJgRgt.3* south of the prison, its actions on the way contibuting to the disintegration of the southern flank of the Greek 6th Regiment. The incorrect landing of these caused the King of Greece and the members of his government, who were quartered in Perivolia near the drop zone, to hastily set out into the mountains in the south-east in the direction of the southern coast of Crete, under the escort of a platoon from the New Zealand 18th Battalion.[26]

The HQ section of *11./FschJgRgt.3* was dropped correctly on the road immediately south-east of Galatas. Unimpressed by the absence of the majority of his unit its commander,

---

24   Its installations on 18 May had been attacked by a single German aircraft, as a result of which 5 soldiers, among them 3 medical officers, had been killed. There were no more direct air attacks afterward.

25   These civilians are also mentioned in Davin, p.145.

26   Some time prior to the German attack General Wavell had instructed Freyberg to have the King and his government remain in Crete for psychological reasons, even if the island was attacked – see *Australia in the War of 1939-1945*, Series One, Army, p.214). The King and his entourage, after a strenuous foot march of several days, were to cross the White Mountains and to be brought to Egypt from the small port of Roumeli on 24 May by the British destroyer *Decoy*.

Oberleutnant Kersten, with his few men, advanced toward Galatas. All of them were later killed in an ambush by New Zealand troops.

The 12th (heavy weapons) company, led by *Oberleutnant* Volquardsen, was also incorrectly dropped. Parts of it landed east of the prison. Other parts came down right over the Agia Lake, causing a number of solidiers, among them a platoon leader *Leutnant* Schimkat, to be drowned. Some of the heavy weapons were also lost in the lake. The company assembled south of the prison and later gave support to the fight of *I./FschJgRgt.3*.

4./FschFlaMGBtl.7 under *Oberleutnant* Matthies parachuted immediately south of Daratsos into the area of the New Zealand 19th Battalion and the fire-position of the four field howitzers of the 1st Light Troop. From the beginning of the landing the company suffered high losses. Four of its officers were killed and the commander of the *FschFlaMGBtl*, *Hauptmann* Baier, who jumped with the company, was seriously wounded. The company was unable to hold out in the southern part of the area of the 19th Battalion but succeeded in taking out the crews of the field howitzers and in warding off counter-thrusts from the area around Daratsos, by employing three or four of its anti-aircraft guns. During the ongoing fighting one of the captured field howitzers was turned around and used to fire at the three field guns of F Troop/28th Battery which were positioned in the area of the 19th Battalion.

I./FschJgRgt.3, commanded by *Hauptmann* Freiherr von der Heydte, was dropped as planned into the area around the prison almost simultaneously with *III./FschJgRgt.3*. Only one platoon was dropped erroneously near the wireless station at Platanos in the immediate vicinity of the CREFORCE transit camp and about 1.8km south-west of Chania. From here, it was attacked and quickly cut up.[27] *I./FschJgRgt.3* were given the mission to clear the terrain south of the road Chania-Alikianou of the enemy, to build a security-screen toward Perivolia and to establish protective positions toward the south near Lake Agia.

AAA fire from the heights around Galatas caused the first losses among the paratroopers during the approach-flight of the air transport formation. Immediately after landing the paratroopers of 2nd and 4th companies stormed the prison where a supply depot was suspected to be located, there they captured about 20 Greek soldiers and a heavy machine-gun. To find and salvage the weapon containers in the unwieldy, overgrown terrain turned out to be extremely difficult. *Hauptmann* Freiherr von der Heydte deployed his 2nd and 3rd companies under *Oberleutnants* Knoche and Straehler-Pohl to clear the drop zone from the enemy. As ordered by *Oberst* Heidrich beforehand, these two companies were subsequently to advance via Mournies in direction of Souda. A reconnaissance patrol with sufficient fighting strength was immediately sent ahead. The 1st Company, which after the death of is commander, *Oberleutnant* Hädrich, was being led by *Oberleutnant* Hepke, was made ready to seize the high ground around Galatas, where the forward elements of *III./FschJgRgt.3* had become bogged down. When the two patrols that had been sent ahead reported the staging area for the attack as being occupied by the enemy, *Oberleutnant* Hepke decided to proceed with an entire company assault. With some losses this goal was achieved. About 200 Greek soldiers were captured during this action and the booty consisted of an infantry gun, two anti-aircraft machine-guns, a wireless vehicle and a truck. A platoon of

27   At this time the transit camp was occupied by about 700 troops from various non-combat units who were in the process of receiving arms.

the battalion which was employed to the right of the 1st Company with the mission to establish contact with *Sturmgruppe Genz* at the wireless station north-west of Mournies[28] overran three field positions that were occupied by British and Greek soldiers, capturing 55 of them. With only 10 men left for the mission during its further advance the platoon met strong resistance in front of Perivolia and was forced to fall back on the 1st Company.

II./FschJgRgt.3, commanded by *Major* Derpa, brought along from Dadion, parachuted with the staff, its 5th and 6th companies under *Oberleutnants* Staab and Liers and the attached 13th company led by *Oberleutnant* Voss, shortly after 0815hrs as planned along the road between the prison and Lake Agia.[29] The battalion's mission was to form the reserve at the disposal of the regiment commander and then to assemble in an olive grove east of the prison. As late as 1100hrs the 13th company had only managed to make ready three of its Nebelwerfer and two Do-launchers for firing. From then on these weapons were employed in fire-missions against the heights south-west of Galatas. Under the direction of its company commander, *Oberleutnant* Neuhof from the 7th Company was dropped tight over Pink Hill, just south-west of Galatas. It instantly assaulted the hill which was protected by wire entanglements and defended by parts of the New Zealand Composite Battalion. The paratroopers were able to inflict heavy losses on the enemy, but then were halted in front of the barbed wire. The company commander was killed. A counter-attack from Galatas then forced the men to withdraw some distance downhill.[30]

Oberst Heidrich, his battle HQ and the regimental signals platoon also jumped with *II./FschJgRgt.3*. They came down north of the prison, which in the meantime was seized by parts of *I./FschJgRgt.3*. The command post of *Gruppe Mitte* was now set up in a building just north of the prison.

The 14th (anti-tank) company under *Oberleutnant* Günther was dropped ahead of *II./FschJgRgt.3*. Dispersed over several areas, it came down east of Lake Agia and lost eight killed and a number of wounded by fire from the slopes to the north-east of the lake. It took until noon before the soldiers could break free from the engagement with the enemy and make ready for firing two anti-tank guns of the 3rd Platoon, and one each of the 1st and 2nd Platoons. One anti-tank gun had fallen into the lake and another into the positions of the Greek 8th Regiment. The other six guns were destroyed on landing or remained lost.

The regimental engineer platoon was somewhat better off as all of its weapon containers had been located. However, of the six sidecar motorcycles, loaded with engineer-material, only one could be salvaged.

At about the same time as *II./FschJgRgt.3*, *1./FschSanAbt.7*, led by *Stabsarzt* Dr. Mallison, was dropped near the prison. As the medical soldiers did not have to fight, the main dressing station was receiving wounded shortly after their landing.

---

28   This station was assigned to *Sturmgruppe Genz* as an additional objective. However, the *Gruppe* had not made it to this location.

29   Due to lack of transport aircraft, the 8th Company had not joined the battalion but had been planned to arrive on Crete by sea. It had, however, been dropped at a later time with the majority of its men and equipment.

30   Davin, p.160, reports that the counter-thrust was led by Captain Forrester from the British Military Mission with about 200 soldiers of the scattered Greek 6th Regiment, who had been joined by numerous armed civilians. The presence of these civilians is also confirmed in German original sources.

The parachuting of *FschPiBtl.7* commenced at 0800hrs. The battalion, commanded by *Major* Liebach, was reinforced with *3./FschMGBtl.7* led by *Hauptmann* Schmidt W. and the 1st Platoon from the *1./FschPzJgAbt.7* under *Leutnant* Sempert. It had left behind its 3rd Company, which was to follow with the heavy equipment by sea transport. The battalion's mission was to occupy the area east and north of Alikianou and protect the rear of *FschJgRgt.3*. A combat detachment, consisting of *3./FschMGBtl.7*, the temporarily-assigned *2./FschPiBtl.7* and the anti-tank platoon, was to seize the bridge across the Jaroanos River, just east of Alikianou and to establish a bridgehead for the later thrust into this town. Due to delays during the take off-of the aircraft from Topolia, with *FschPiBtl.7* aboard, only *3./FschMGBtl.7* and the anti-tank platoon, brought along in nine Ju 52s from Tanagra, were dropped at 0800hrs. Their parachuting commenced several seconds late so that they came down about 700m south-west of the planned drop zone. Yet the navigational error turned out to be fortunate as the original landing site was occupied by parts of the Greek 8th Regiment. The losses sustained by the fire from the Greek positions on the high ground north-east of Alikianou were tolerable and thus the landed forces were able to assemble rather quickly and to attack the enemy north of them in the rear. Most of the heavy machine-guns were positioned with their lines of fire directed toward the south and the south-west. The mortars found cover in a depression. Already a short time later, communication with *FschJgRgt.3* was established by radio and patrols.[31]

2./FschPiBtl.7 under *Oberleutnant* Tietjen was dropped at around 0900hrs from 10 Ju 52s immediately north of the forces already landed. Its men were also fired at from the high ground, ascending east of the road. The loads were dropped too soon and therefore were mostly lost. In the unwieldy terrain and under the fire of the enemy, only a portion of the weapon containers could be salvaged and the weapons which fell into the hands of the enemy were immediately employed against their former owners. The initial mission of *2./FschPiBtl.7* was to seize the bridge across the Jaroanos. Together with this unit a patrol each from the 1st and 4th companies of the engineers were dropped. They were to reconnoiter the tented camps near Skines and Fourmes, about 5km south-west of Alikianou. There more enemy troops were suspected.[32] During the clearing of the drop zone, a number of soldiers from the Greek 8th Regiment as well as armed Cretan civilians, who had occupied some of the houses there, were overcome. A platoon from *2./FschPiBtl.7*, which advanced against the Jaroanos Bridge, was soon held up by defensive fire. Its commander, *Leutnant* Schoenperlen, was killed. The two patrols were also unable to get across the river. Additional troops from the 2nd Company, advancing shortly after 1030hrs, succeeded in taking out three camouflaged field positions in front of the bridge, causing eight Greek soldiers to be killed and 14 captured. However the thrust across the bridge again failed as did another attempt undertaken after six heavy machine-guns from *3./FschMGBtl.7* had been sent as reinforcements. An attack by dive bombers, which *Oberleutnant* Tietjen requested at 1245hrs, failed to materialize after a non-commissioned officer of the anti-tank platoon erroneously reported the taking of the bridge to *FschJgRgt.3*. The troops of *FschPiBtl.7*, deployed north and north-east of Alikianou, thus contented themselves with safeguarding the occupied terrain.

---

31   See also Klitzing, pp.36-37.

32   This assessment was erroneous. In the already mentioned intelligence report No. 4, the tent camps had clearly been identified as prison camps. The report of an agent had even given the numbers of the Italian prisoners of war confined there, as well as of their guards.

Only a short time after the staff of *FschJgRgt.3* had set up its command post in the prison four gliders with parts of the staff of *Fl.Div.7* and radio teams aboard landed about 1km to the west. However the division commander, *Generalleutnant* Süßmann, was not with them. After the members of the division staff were conveyed to the prison, *Oberst* Heidrich was informed about the fate of the general. After the HQ section had taken off from Eleusis in five gliders, both wings of the glider with *Generalleutnant* Süßmann aboard had been torn off, probably caused by the wake of a bomber passing too close. The towing cable had snapped and the body of the glider had plunged down onto the rocks of the small island of Aegina, where it was destroyed. As was found out later, all passengers – the general, his two adjutants, an orderly officer, the divisional medical officer and the glider-pilot – had perished. *Oberst* Heidrich now assumed command of *Fl.Div.7*, but also retained command over his regiment.[33] The battle HQ of the Division, directed by the operations-officer, *Major* Graf von Üxküll, settled down in the administration building of the prison. Its most important function for the time being was to establish and maintain radio communication with the command of *XI.Flieger-Korps*. By means of the 80-watt transmitter this was achieved at about 1300hrs.

From the very beginning of the operations of his force *Oberst* Heidrich recognized the importance of the heights around Galatas. At about 0945hrs he obtained a sufficiently clear picture of the situation in the operational area of *Gruppe Mitte*, to bring his will to bear upon the cooperation of his units. As a priority, he recognized the need to get the attack of *III./FschJgRgt.3* in front of the heights south and south-west of Galatas going again. Therefore he immediately had *5./FschJgRgt.3* moved to this location and *I./FschJgRgt.3* was ordered to initially cease its flanking movement toward the north-east and to advance against the heights east of Galatas.

Thereupon *Hauptmann* von der Heydte formed a combat detachment of a platoon from the 2nd Company, two platoons from the 3rd Company and a heavy machine-gun squad from the 4th Company and employed it for attack just right of the road Chania-Alikianou. The detachment, led by *Oberleutnant* Knoche, despite heavy artillery and mortar fire succeeded in seizing two hills, baptized 'kleiner Burgberg' and 'grosser Burgberg'. Here they captured 60 enemy soldiers and four heavy machine-guns. Subsequently it set up positions on both hills. The detachment was supported by elements of *11./FschJgRgt.3* who had advanced from their drop zone toward the north. They were now integrated into the defence. In the late afternoon the detachment was able to turn away an attack by a company of New Zealand infantry supported by Bren Gun Carriers, which developed south of the road. During this attack one of the Carriers was destroyed by the fire of an anti-tank rifle.[34] As the attack of his 1st Company was held up, von der Heydte now shifted his main effort to this unit and reinforced it with the still uncommitted elements of the 4th Company – a heavy machine-gun platoon and the mortar platoon. He let one platoon from Knoche's detachment swing toward the 1st Company in order to prolong its right flank. A platoon from the 2nd Company, which was set free after parts of *II./FschJgRgt.3* had interfered

---

33   This decision occurred as there was no communication to the *SturmRgt.*, which moreover was directly subordinate to *XI.Flieger-Korps*.

34   The attacking force was C Company of the NZ 18th Battalion. It had lost one officer and two more men in the destroyed Bren Gun Carrier.

in front of Galatas, was deployed left of the 1st Company with the mission to clear the terrain of enemy stragglers. This action became possible because parts of *12./FschJgRgt.3*, which in the meantime had come forward, had also been inserted into the attack front. The paratroopers from *I./FschJgRgt.3* that were positioned on the uncovered slopes in front of Galatas suffered considerably under the undiminished heavy defensive fire from above. It was there where *Oberleutnant* Hädrich was killed and the signal officer of the battalion, *Oberleutnant* Mäckh, was seriously wounded.

At about 1400hrs, *III./FschJgRgt.3* reported that its attack against the heights east of Galatas, despite the reinforcement with *5./FschJgRgt.3*, had stalled and a counter-attack from Galatas was in progress. The latter was halted, but only with considerable losses. A further advance of the battalion, however, was no longer possible with its decimated and exhausted troops.

As combat activities were now reduced, at 1435hrs *Oberst* Heidrich summoned his three battalion commanders to his command post. After these briefed him about the situation of their units, he ordered a halt to offensive actions for the time being and reorganized his troops. The thrust against the heights at Galatas was to be resumed in the late afternoon after renewed fire preparation. At 1440hrs he reported his intentions by wireless to the command of *XI.Flieger-Korps*.[35] The fate of *10./FschJgRgt.3* remained unknown and became apparent only later in the fighting for Crete. This unit, numbering less than 50 men after losses in the area of the New Zealand 18th Battalion and because a number of its soldiers had been dropped widely dispersed, had moved toward Daratsos with about 300 prisoners after resting. North of this village they were fired at from the area of the New Zealand 19th Battalion, whereby three prisoners from the New Zealand 6th Field Ambulance were killed. In the fighting a number of paratroopers were killed and many others were captured. At about 1700hrs the engagement ended. The liberated medical soldiers and patients, together with the captured paratroopers, spent the night 20/21 May in the area of the 19th Battalion.

In order to provide an adequate impetus for the attack, at 1530hrs *Oberst* Heidrich released the uncommitted *6./FschJgRgt.3* under *Oberleutnant* Stangenberg. The command of the three companies of *II./FschJgRgt.3* was taken over by *Major* Derpa.

Supported by *FschJgRgt.3*, fighting in front of Galatas, after bitter combat the 6th Company succeeded in conquering Hill 116, or Ruin Hill. In this action *Oberleutnant* Stangenberg was wounded.

In the area of *FschPiBtl.7* no progress was achieved during the afternoon against the Jaroanos Bridge. One of the patrols tasked with reconnoitering toward Skines and Fourmes advanced in the direction of Alikianou via the hamlet of Kufos. At about 1830hrs, 300m beyond Kufos, it was fired at by riflemen positioned in trees, causing the death of one soldier. Reporting the situation to *FschPiBtl.7* the patrol retired to Kufos. There, the two soldiers who had been left back as a security screen were attacked by armed civilians; among them were a number of women. After the two parachute engineers shot some of the attackers, those remaining were quickly driven off.

---

35   However, the time for the renewed attack, the morning of 21 May, was transmitted.

At around 1600hrs supplies were dropped for the first time, together with a small number of soldiers from the *FschPiBtl.* who had had to have been left behind in Greece. The supplies and men came down widely dispersed between Alikianou and Kirtomahdo and mostly fell into the hands of the enemy. Only those of the parachute engineers and the containers which come down immediately in front of the positions of *2./FschPiBtl.7* could be recovered, with the exception of one soldier, who was killed in the heavy enemy fire.

By the evening the 1st and 4th companies of *FschPiBtl.7* gained some ground toward the north-east and cleared it of Greek soldiers who were holding out there. At the pump station near Kirtomadho, the New Zealand advisers to the Greek 8th Regiment that took shelter there were encircled. Kirtomadho proper was thus abandoned by the enemy.

As *Major* Liebach was of the opinion that the mission of his battalion, to protect the rear of *FschJgRgt.3*, could be achieved also from the area north-east of Alikianou, he concentrated the still available parts of his 2nd Company, *3./FschMGBtl.7* and the anti-tank platoon in a hedgehog position around his command post, at the cross-roads just west of Episkopi. The salvaged supplies were to be brought to this location, too.

At about 2000hrs *Major* Derpa ordered his 6th Company, now led by *Leutnant* Cramer, to abandon Hill 116 despite the fact that the hill, seized after bitter fighting, constituted the key for the conquest of the area around Galatas. He reported this measure to the Regiment, but before the counter order arrived, the 6th Company had already given up the hill and retired to the unoccupied Wheat Hill. While it was in the process of setting up a renewed defence, it was hit at about 2130hrs by a counter-attack by two companies of New Zealand infantry, and three light tanks and was thrown back almost to the foot of the hill. There it was able to hold fast, as the enemy ceased the attack.[36]

After the retreat from Hill 116 and Wheat Hill *Oberst* Heidrich became aware of the exposed position of the remnants of *III./FschJgRgt.3*. Assuming that this battalion would come up against a large-scale counterattack, which he anticipated for the coming morning, he decided to give up all of the slopes south-west of Galatas that were still held by some of his forces. The depleted *II./FschJgRgt.3* and the remainder of *III./FschJgRgt.3*, commanded by *Major* Derpa, were now to set up a blocking position north of the prison. As the left flank of the still fully combat-effective *I./FschJgRgt.3* would thus be exposed to flanking movements of the enemy, this battalion was also to retire abreast of the position of the other units. The order for these actions was issued at 2300hrs.

The first battalion to move was *I./FschJgRgt.3*, east of the road Chania-Alikianou. In its new position, its elements were deployed from left to right as follows: 2nd Company, parts of 12th Company, 1st Company, 11th Company and 3rd Company. Behind these, in support, were the 4th Company and parts of the 13th company. *II./FschJgRgt.3* moved next. Its 7th Company set up positions about 500m east of the prison, its 6th Company

---

36   The counter-attack was ordered by the New Zealand Division with the mission to clear the area around the prison with a battalion from the 4th Brigade and tanks. Precautionary thinking on behalf of the commanders of the 4th Brigade and the 19th Battalion, however, had resulted in the reduction of the attack force to A and D companies from the 19th Battalion and to three light tanks from the 3rd Hussars. Upon the request by the commander of the 10th Brigade, who had seen the left flank of his brigade endangered by the use of companies from the 19th Battalion, the attack was cancelled. The order, however, had not reached the attack force in time. After the initial success, it fell into disorder and stopped in the conquered terrain. In the morning of 21 May it was withdrawn.

joining to the north. The 5th Company and the remnants of *III./FschJgRgt.3* formed the reserve, behind the 6th Company. The staffs and the signals personnel of *FschJgRgt.3* and *Fl.Div.7* prepared positions around their command posts. *Major* Heilmann was temporarily assigned to the regimental staff.

In anticipation of a counter-attack *FschPiBtl.7* was drawn closer to the centre of the operational area of the group. At about 2100hours *Major* Liebach was ordered by the battle HQ of *Fl.Div.7*, to immediately take over the protection of the area around the prison, along the line pump station Kirtomadho-Agia-Varipetron (2km south of the prison), toward the north-west, west, south and south-east. The 1st and 4th companies of the battalion were quickly able to form the right flank of the new protective line, as they were close by. In order to occupy the left flank, the 2nd Company, anti-tank platoon, staff, walking wounded, prisoners and *3./FschMGBtl.7*, in that sequence, moved off from their present locations at about 2145hrs. In the light of the urgency for the new mission and because of a lack of transportation, the seriously wounded were to be left behind under the care of medical personnel. Large quantities of material, including ammunition, were also left behind. During the march in rugged terrain the anti-tank guns soon had to be abandoned, after their breech blocks were removed. A short while later, most of the containers were also left behind. Continuously fired at from Greek positions along the slopes east of their route the troops, utterly exhausted, reached the new deployment area just prior to daybreak. One platoon from *3./FschMGBtl.7* arrived at the command post of *FschJgRgt.3* at about 2300hrs, but had been held back there because of the perceived critical situation. At 0400 hrs, *Major* Liebach reported the accomplishment of the mission to the command post of *Fl.Div.7*.

During the course of 20 May *Oberst* Heidrich increasingly realised that the planned operation of *Gruppe Mitte* could not be brought about. The supposition that strong enemy forces could be deployed along the road Chania-Alikianou, which had triggered the employment of the Group, indeed, had proven correct. However, unlike the assumptions of *XI.Flieger-Korps*, it had not been British Imperial reserves that were to tie down and to weaken the men, but mainly Greek troops firmly positioned for a defence against airborne landings.

The intended thrust against Alikianou also developed unfortunately. Here parts of the Greek 8th Regiment had fought unexpectedly bravely from strong field positions, so that even at the end of the first day the threat against the rear of *Gruppe Mitte* had not been overcome.

No support at all from the air had been provided for on 20 May. Air attack forces doubtlessly could have been mustered for this task, as the attacks by dive bombers against Chania between 1400hrs and 1500hrs had shown. The non-appearance of the *Luftwaffe*'s combat aircraft over the operational area of *Gruppe Mitte* can only be explained by the current thinking in the commands of the VIII and the *XI.Flieger-Korps*, that the paratroopers could seize the heights at Galatas by themselves. When this had failed in the afternoon the complicated request procedures for close air support in conjunction with the shift of the air support priorities to *Gruppe Ost* prevented any timely reaction with air attack forces over Galatas.

There was also unease about the increasing shortage of ammunition. Some replenishment had occurred in the afternoon. However as most of it was dropped incorrectly, it remained unavailable for the troops.[37]

A request by *Oberst* Heidrich at 1515hrs in his function as temporary commander of *Fl.Div.7*, to immediately reinforce *Gruppe Mitte* with *FschJgRgt.2* for the thrust against Chania, was refused by the staff of *XI.Flieger-Korps*, as the commitment of the second wave was on the way and a change of plans at that time was considered impossible. Certainly Student was also against this measure.

Whether the intention of *Oberst* Heidrich to resume an all-out attack on 21 May could be realized, became dependent on the actions of the enemy. For the time being, however, *Gruppe Mitte* had lost the initiative. Its losses were not yet fully known but were regarded as considerable.[38]

As in the area around Maleme, CREFORCE had reckoned with airborne landings in the basin between Chania and Alikianou and had undertaken preparations to parry them.[39] The instruction by Major General Freyberg to safeguard the north of Crete against attacks from the air and sea had led to the situation whereby the connecting link between the sectors of Maleme and Chania were formed by troops who had to be considered to be second rate. Whether the heights around Galatas had been identified to their full extent as an important blocking position toward the west and the south is doubtful, as just a few days prior to the German attack, the first-class 1st Battalion Welch Regiment were removed from the area south of Galatas into the CREFORCE reserve and replaced by the insufficiently equipped, though somewhat reinforced Greek 6th Regiment. The occupation of the heights by troops not trained as infantry, while two infantry battalions of the 4th Brigade were retained at the coast as reserves for a number of contingencies, also suggests a clear recognition of the value of the Galatas Heights was lacking. These two battalions could as well have served in a reserve role from the area around Galatas, thereby placing the command of the 4th Brigade with responsibility for its defence, while the second-rate New Zealand troops would have sufficed for the coastal defence.

In the sector of Chania, during the evening of 20 May Major General Weston ordered the Australian 2/8 Infantry Battalion from Georgioupolis forward and had it deployed between the positions of the 'Royal Perivolians' in the transit-camp and the Greek 2nd Regiment, in order to strengthen the area against a possible thrust of the enemy against Souda. The staff of the Australian 19th Brigade and its 2/ Infantry Battalion received warning orders for a transfer into the western part of his sector. A definitive joint decision by Puttick, Weston and Freyberg, to settle the situation in the north-western part of Crete by an immediate counter-attack with all available forces, however, did not occur.

During the morning of 20 May, while the staff of *XI.Flieger-Korps* still waited for the first reliable news about the course of the operations of *Gruppen West* and *Mitte*, those

---

37   The origin of these resupply sorties remains unclear. They may have been drawn from the assigned Ju 52s, but may also have been provided by *Luftflotte 4*.

38   The casualty list of *FschJgRgt.3* at the BA-MA, lists 313 killed in action for 20 May 1941. By the end of the fighting on Crete, the Regiment had lost another 60 men killed.

39   The subsequent description of the events on the side of the defenders for the area around Galatas is mainly based on Davin, pp.162-169.

commands which were to set in motion the employment of the second wave of the airborne forces were already under great strain. From the perspective of the air commander of *XI.Flieger-Korps*, the air transport of the first wave had gone well so far, as of the 503 Ju 52s employed only seven had been lost over Crete. From this time onward, however, difficulties had arisen, which had not been anticipated, and for which consequently no counter-measures had been prepared.

A large number of the transport aircraft that were returning from Crete between 0900 and 1000hrs became unusable for the second wave as a result of the damage received over Crete or during landing on the ill-suited airfields. As a consequence, considerable and time consuming changes in the air transport plans had to be initiated. Even then it became evident that the operational aircraft would not suffice to load all of the forces planned for the parachute assaults at Heraklion and Rethymnon, although the about 70 Ju 52s, which had towed the gliders with troops and equipment of the first wave, became available for the parachuting of the second wave. The air transport fleet still lacked between 40 and 50 Ju 52s, mainly at the airfields of Topolia and Megara. Here the highest-ranking commanders of the parachute units had to make the decision on the spot as to which units should be left behind. In Topolia, this had been the 4th and 12th companies from *FschJgRgt.1*, both equipped with heavy infantry weapons. At Megara, it had probably been *Hauptmann* Schirmer who determined that the 5th and 6th companies of his *II./FschJgRgt.2* had to stay behind. General Student and his staff obviously had not been able or willing to exert their influence on these decisions. This resulted, in particular, in the weakening of the force planned for Heraklion, which according to the operation order should have been sufficiently strong to ensure the seizure of the airfield, for the intended landing of the majority of the *5.Gebirgs-Division*.[40]

The refueling of the Ju 52s by hand was more tedious than planned, as the aviation fuel that was brought along in barrels had arrived only after the landing of the aircraft.

Therefore, shortly before noon, it became evident that the start of the take-off of the second wave, fixed for 1300hrs, could not be adhered to on most of the airfields. More loss of time was likely, as dust rising from the runways of the airfields during take-off would make it necessary to plan intervals of five minutes between waves.

During this time the lack of sufficient and secure telecommunications from the jump-off airfields of the air transport formations to the staffs of the air commander and the *XI.Flieger-Korps* became perceptible in a particularly dreadful way. The airfield commands had been unable to report the developing delays or the insufficient transport capacities in good enough time to the command of *XI.Flieger-Korps*. The coordination of the chronological tables for the air-movements between the VIII and the *XI.Flieger-Korps* had been left undone, in most cases, for this reason.[41] Therefore, *III.Flieger-Korps* sent off the air attack forces that were planned to cover the last phase of the approach-flight and the parachuting of the second wave at the originally fixed times. As the fuel of the combat

---

40   The Gefechtsbericht Kreta of *XI.Flieger-Korps* notes that the initial strength of the reinforced *FschJgRgt.1* for Heraklion, because of lack of air transport capacity, had to be reduced by about 600 men. According to calculations by the author, it had been only about 480 men.

41   *General* (ret.). Trettner, at that time operations officer of *XI.Flieger-Korps* has characterized the consequences of the deficiencies in the telecommunications system on 20 May, mainly caused by *Luftflotte 4*, as "catastrophic". See his report 'Unternehmen *Merkur*. Die Luftlandeschlacht um Kreta', published in *DDF* March/April 1991, pp.6-8.

aircraft suited for this task allowed only a limited time over the objectives, most of them were forced to turn back prior to the belated arrival of the air transport formations.

Not all of the problems experienced during the take-off of the second wave, however, were in relation to insufficient telecommunications for the coordination with the *VIII. Flieger-Korps*.

With some degree of certainty it can be assumed that during the course of the morning of 20 May the command of the *XI.Flieger-Korps* was informed about the delays of two air transport formations of the first wave because of adverse airfield conditions, as well as about the difficulties encountered in bringing aviation fuel to the airfields. As the conditions on the airfields could not be improved, and in fact were worsening due to the increasing dry heat, delays were caused in the take-off of the transport aircraft of the second wave. A shift of the start-time of the air attack forces should have been arranged with *VIII.Flieger-Korps* late in the morning. General Student and the heads of his staff, most of whom had also been pilots, certainly must have been aware of the restricted flying times of the fighter-bombers and the dive bombers.

It appears therefore, that too much confidence by the command of *XI.Flieger-Korps* was placed in the abilities of the air commander and commodores of the air transport formations, to nevertheless bring in the second wave in an orderly fashion despite the developing difficulties.

For its commitment at Heraklion, *FschJgRgt.1*, commanded by *Oberst* Bräuer, was reinforced with *II./FschJgRgt.2* (*Hauptmann* Schirmer), *1./FschFlaMGBtl.7* (*Oberleutnant* Timm) and the greater part of *2./FschSanAbt.7* (*Truppenarzt* Dr. Langemeyer).

Oberst Bräuer organized his force into four combat groups:

- *II./FschJgRgt.1* (*Hauptmann* Burckhardt), reinforced with *1./FschFlaMGBtl.7*, a platoon from *13./FschJgRgt.1* (3 Nebelwerfer 10.5cm) and a platoon from *14./ FschJgRgt.1*;
- *III./FschJgRgt.1* (*Major* Schulz), reinforced with two platoons from *13./ FschJgRgt.1* and a platoon from *14./FschJgRgt.1* (3 3.7cm anti-tank guns);
- *I./FschJgRgt.1* (*Major* Walther), reinforced with a platoon from *14./FschJgRgt.1*;
- *II./FschJgRgt.2*, reinforced with a platoon from *14./FschJgRgt.1*.

The combat groups, with the staff of the regiment and the regimental signals platoon together with *I./FschJgRgt.1*, were to be dropped in this sequence at short intervals beginning at 1515hrs. *2./FschSanAbt.7* was to parachute together with *III./FschJgRgt.1* south-west of Heraklion where it was later to set up the main dressing station for *Gruppe Ost*.

Delays during the preparation phase at Topolia and adverse conditions at this airfield prevented an uninterrupted take-off of the air transport formations as a whole. This meant that take-off lasted, largely unknown to the command of *XI.Flieger-Korps*, more than three hours, resulting in the disorder of the planned sequence and air movement toward Crete.

II./FschJgRgt.2 – staff, signals platoon, 7th and 8th companies – was dropped as the first combat group from 25 Ju 52s at 1630hrs about 4km south-west of the township of Heraklion. Its mission was to protect the attack of *Kampfgruppe Schulz* against Heraklion toward the west. Its drop zone was unoccupied by the enemy, so that, except for a few injuries during the landing, no losses occurred. Only the 1st Platoon of the 7th Company led by *Oberleutnant* Zimmermann, which was dropped 2km too far to the east and came down immediately in front of field positions occupied by Greek and Australian soldiers, lost some killed and wounded, among them the platoon leader. However, with the support of other sections of the company the remainder of the platoon managed to overcome the resistance. At about 1700hrs, *Bataillon Schirmer* effectively blocked the approaches from the west toward Heraklion. However it was involved in firefights with Cretan irregulars throughout the day.[42]

III./FschJgRgt.1 was dropped at 1730hrs about 1km south of Heraklion with the 9th Company under *Oberleutnant* Singer, the 11th Company led by *Oberleutnant* Becker and *2./FschSanAbt.7*. At this time, the fighter-bombers which were detached to suppress AAA units and the troops on the ground during the approach flight of the transport aircraft and the landing of the paratroopers had returned home after using up their ammunition. As the enemy had set up a deep system of field positions and dug-outs in a semi-circle forward of the entrances to the town, the paratroopers received heavy fire whilst in the air. While the 9th Company and the parachute medical company came down far enough away from the enemy-positions to escape the full force of the fire from there, a platoon of the 11th Company which descended right over them and landed in their midst was almost completely destroyed.

Immediately after the hasty assembly, and with only the weapons taken along for the drop, the three companies attacked the Greek positions in front of them across the almost open terrain and succeeded in taking out or driving off their defenders. Among the high losses of the paratroopers was that of the commanding officer of the 9th Company. Behind the taken position towered the enormous 10-12m high town wall of Heraklion from which British and Greek soldiers had excellent fields of fire, causing further losses among the paratroopers.

A short time later transport aircraft with the 10th Company under *Oberleutnant* Egger, the 12th Company under *Oberleutnant* Vosshage, *Major* Schulz with his staff and the assigned platoons from the 13th and 14th companies aboard arrived over the contested area, where they received massive fire from AAA guns. A Ju 52, which was hit before its passengers could be dropped, crashed into the town wall. As the infantry fire from there was too heavy, the landed troops assembled some distance to the west. From here they were employed by *Major* Schulz to clear the living quarters west of the old township of Heraklion. This task was achieved shortly before midnight after lengthy fighting and with the cooperation of previously landed companies of the battalion and parts of the medical company. The quarter was to serve as the jump-off point for the assault against the interior of Heraklion, to commence in the coming hours of darkness. *Major* Schulz decided to conduct the attack along the beach and through the western gate in the town wall, as he considered climbing the defended wall as impossible. The anti-tank platoon, assigned to *II./FschJgRgt.2* was also integrated into the attack force. The company commander of *14./FschJgRgt.1*, *Hauptmann* Grasmehl, who had jumped with *Kampfgruppe Schulz*, now had two anti-tank platoons at his disposal.

During the ongoing fighting in front of the town wall Dr. Langemeyer with part of his company set up a dressing station some distance more to the west. A short time later the

42   War diary of *II./FschJgRgt.2* stored at the BA-MA, signature RL 33/46.

first seriously wounded brought back, under fire, by medical staff were operated on here. Surgical treatment was also provided by *Oberarzt* Dr. Kirsch, who himself was seriously wounded by a shot to the chest.

While the situation in the west and south-west of Heraklion gave rise to the hope that the original plan of attack could be executed despite being considerably behind time, a drama enfolded for *Gruppe Ost* on and around the airfield of the town. It was to be seized by the reinforced *II./FschJgRgt.1*. It was planned to drop an assault group each at the western and eastern end of the airfield. *1./FschFlaMGBtl.7* was assigned to the western assault group. As the sequence of the approach flights became disordered when *FschJgRgt.1* left Topolia, the transport aircraft with *1./FschFlaMGBtl.7* aboard had already commenced to drop its passengers when those with the parachute battalion approached the drop zones at about 1750hrs.[43] The defenders were fully alerted since the start of the airborne attacks in the west of Crete and were instructed about the methods of these attacks. The German air attack forces which were planned to cover the final approach flight of the air transport formations toward the airfield and the parachuting here had flown back after using up their ammunition. The skillfully camouflaged and-Oder weapons of the airfield defence suffered almost no losses by the air attacks and many had even not been detected. Upon the approach of the transport aircraft, the crews of the anti-aircraft guns and the automatic weapons removed the camouflage on their positions and commenced firing. Several Ju 52s were hit, set ablaze and crashed before they were able to drop their passengers.[44] A number of paratroopers were also shot during the descent, however many more were hit by the precision fire of riflemen immediately after landing and during the cumbersome removal of parachute harnesses.[45]

The western assault group of reinforced *FschJgRgt.1*, led by *Hauptmann* Dunz, consisting of the 6th and 7th companies of the battalion and of *1./FschFlaMGBtl.7*, was almost entirely cut down within 20 minutes of landing by the crossfire of the 7th Medical Rgt, employed as infantry around Nea Alikarnassos, the artillerymen of the 234th Medium Battery, firing from their gun positions with small arms, and the two companies from the Australian 2/4 Infantry Battalion positioned in the northern part of the area of this unit. Against the few combat effective men of the assault group, the tanks which were undetected in the staging area now advanced firing and together with the counter-attacking Bren Gun Carrier platoon from the 2nd Leicesters, completed the disaster for the Germans. However a few of the paratroopers managed to retire into the solidly-built barracks about 800m

---

43   The time of the arrival of *II./FschJgRgt.1*, besides those sources of the former enemy, has been taken from the report of Bernd Bosshammer, 'Neun Tage zwischen Leben und Tod', written after the war. Bosshammer had been dropped as a *Feldwebel* in *5./FschJgRgt.1* over Heraklion and had been seriously wounded after the landing.

44   *Australia in the War of 1939-1945*, Series One, Army, p.281 states that 15 Ju 52s were shot down at Heraklion on 20 May 1941.

45   There are quite controversial judgments about the numbers of paratroopers who were hit while descending. Some reports, particularly those of the former enemy, speak of high numbers. Dr. Heinrich Neumann, in his response to a report about the medical service during *Merkur*, points out that only a very small number of dead paratroopers with their harness still on had been found in the operational area of *Gruppe West*. Käthler mentions that trials with paratrooper dummies had shown that 30,000 rounds from machine-guns and rifles had been required to achieve one hit on a descending paratrooper.

south-east of Nea Alikarnassos. An even smaller number escaped by swimming along the coast toward the east. There they reached other groups from *FschJgRgt.1* and reported the outcome of the fighting.

The eastern assault group, consisting of the 5th and 8th companies from *II./FschJgRgt.1* and the assigned platoons from the 13th and 14th companies from the regimental units of *FschJgRgt.1*, led by *Hauptmann* Burckhardt, came down immediately east of the positions of the 2nd Black Watch. The drop zone of the group was planned to be the wide valley of the small stream at Karteros. Fired at from the heights which separated the valley from the airfield, the assault group suffered considerable losses during landing, but was lucky as the valley protected them from observation by the enemy. The paratroopers who came down within the positions of the 2nd Black Watch were quickly dealt with by small teams of the Scots. With hastily scraped together soldiers of his assault group, who did not find the time to pick up their main arms from the weapon containers, *Hauptmann* Burckhardt assaulted the heights in front of him. The commanding officer of the 5th Company, *Oberleutnant* Herrman, who had temporarily became blind after being hit in the head during the descent, joined the assault, leaning on his *Oberfeldwebel* until he collapsed. The uncoordinated and weak forces conducting the assault under *Hauptmann* Burckhardt broke under the fire of the defenders of the heights. Among others, the company commander of the 8th Company, *Oberleutnant* Platow, was killed. After the failed thrust *Hauptmann* Burckhardt managed to assemble about 60-70 men of his assault group at the foot of a rocky elevation on the eastern side of the Karteros Valley. Small groups of paratroopers, among them many wounded, were able to hide in the intersected, rocky terrain in front of the positions of the 2nd Black Watch, hoping to find their way toward the east after nightfall. The Scottish soldiers wisely abstained from searching the terrain for stragglers in the oncoming darkness. Only one of the tanks, at about 2130hrs, drove firing along the road leading through the Karteros depression toward the coast, causing some losses among the paratroopers, who found cover in the ditch alongside the road. After a short time, however, the tank returned to the airfield.

The full extent of the catastrophe for the reinforced *II./FschJgRgt.1* remained hidden to the command of *FschJgRgt.1* during the night 20/21 May. Only near the end of the fighting in the area around Heraklion was it found out that the assault group had lost more than 300 killed, among them 12 officers and about 100 wounded, including eight officers. This was almost 90% of its combat strength.

I./FschJgRgt.1, commanded by *Major* Walther, was initially to form the reserve of *Gruppe Ost* but was not dropped according to the operational plan. Its 3rd Company had parachuted according to the original timetable, at 1515hrs, but came down near Gournes which lay more than 10km east of Heraklion – luckily the drop zone turned out to be unoccupied by the enemy. The majority of the battalion parachuted as late as 1840hrs. The 2nd Company, which was to seize a wireless station about 2km west of Gournes, was dropped about 5km too far to the east.[46] It arrived a few hours later at the assembly area of the battalion. From there the wireless station was occupied without resistance.[47]

Oberst Bräuer, who with his staff and signal elements, had been dropped around 1840hrs near Gournes, intended to gain a personal picture about the situation at the airfield at Heraklion which he assumed to be taken. Together with a platoon from *2./FschJgRgt.1*, led by *Ritterkreuz* holder *Oberleutnant* Graf von Blücher, he moved off and arrived shortly prior to midnight on the eastern slope of the height ascending toward the airfield. Unexpectedly, the group received fire from there causing the *Oberst* and the members of his staff who accompanied him to retire some distance to the east. During this time he was informed by stragglers of *II./FschJgRgt.1* that the parachute assault against the airfield had completely failed. As he neglected to bring a radio set he had no communication with his units. In order to make good his mistake he established his command post behind a rocky knoll just east of the Karteros depression, about 1.5km east of the enemy-occupied height. From here he then had wireless communications with *XI.Flieger-Korps* in Athens and to all three of his still combat-effective battalions.[48] *Oberleutnant* Graf von Blücher and his platoon remained in contact with the enemy and, as he had received no orders, he decided to attack toward the airfield and succeeded in breaking into the forward positions of the 2nd Black Watch. There, the platoon was surrounded by the enemy, but established itself in all-round defence in the rocky terrain.

As at Maleme, the attempt to seize the airfield, which was important for the continuation of the airborne operation, had failed from the onset. For both airfields the assault was planned in the same pattern by the landing of parachute troops at both ends of the runway and the use of converging attack. In both cases, however, the combat-power and the morale of the defenders had been completely underestimated, resulting in fatal consequences. For Maleme, it remained questionable whether the *SturmRgt.* would be able to gain a firm foothold in the first hours after landing, if the area immediately west of the Tavronitis River was occupied by combat-ready and experienced enemy troops.

The decision to commit the second wave according to the original operation order despite the delays and disorder at the jump-off airfields of the air transport formations and the disrupted interaction between the close air support and the parachute forces had, in the end, rested with the command of *Luftflotte 4*. When first indications about the actual strength and combat power of the enemy in western Crete arrived at the *Luftflotte* command, and the hitherto prevailing feeling of an

---

46   The impression that the drop zone for *I./FschJgRgt.1* had been selected at Gournes, created in the after-action report of the *XI.Flieger-Korps* and in Student's memoirs, veils the truth. It is dubious that *Oberst* Bräuer had selected a drop zone which would have placed his reserve more than two hours' march away from the scene of the actual fighting, unless one imputes a grave fault in his command management. That the battalion was dropped at the wrong location is confirmed by Mößinger, at that time the orderly officer of *I./FschJgRgt.1*, who states, that it was planned to parachute into the Karteros valley, close to the airfield.

47   The wireless station was part of the 220 AMES of the R.A.F. and was protected by a platoon from the 2nd Black Watch. Upon the receipt of reports about the start of the German airborne attack in the morning of 20 May, the installation was abandoned.

48   The long-range communication had probably been established by transmitters of *1./Luftnachrichten-Kompanie 7*, of which radio teams had been dropped with *Gruppe Ost*.

easy victory in the west[49] began to fade, it evidently still did not see a requirement to change the plans for Heraklion and Rethymnon as air reconnaissance reported weak defences around the airfields there. Options, like shifting the use of the second wave to Maleme in order to overcome the critical situation there, or to shift the parachute attacks against the airfields at Heraklion and Rethymnon to 21 May after at least some of the problems related to the organization and the take-off of the second wave, as well as its interaction with the close air support had been straightened out, had obviously not been considered. The command of *XI.Flieger-Korps* had not intervened, at least partly because of insufficient telecommunications that had prevented it from receiving a full picture of the problems for the start of the second wave. Of much more weight was the strong will of General Student to cling to the original plan, pertaining to the airfield at Heraklion, where he still had in mind the landing of the majority of the *5.Gebirgs-Division*.[50] The favourable reports of the air reconnaissance for the airfields at Heraklion and Rethymnon certainly encouraged him in his view, even though they were confirmed to be incorrect by 20 May. As for the problems related to the lack of interaction between the close air support and the parachute forces, as well as to the disarray in the arrival of the latter over the objectives, he and his staff relied on the determination of the paratroopers in battle and on the ability of their tactical commanders to overcome them. However these virtues met with particular difficulties at Heraklion. While the thrust of the forces of *Gruppe West* aimed at one objective, though from different directions, *Kräftegruppe Bräuer* from the very beginning had to seize the airfield, as well as the town and port of Heraklion.[51] This approach risked the failure of both tasks, even if all the troops initially planned for *Oberst* Bräuer had been made available.

In reality both tasks were unaccomplished on 20 May. It is true that complete ignorance of the strength and fighting abilities of the enemy in the Heraklion sector was the major reason for these failures. The peculiarities of this sector had been little considered by the commands of *XI.Flieger-Korps* and *Fl.Div.7*. When noting its operational importance, a coherent and sufficiently strong defence should have been anticipated, despite the favorable intelligence evident by their assessment of Heraklion proper. It should have become clear from the outset of planning that the enemy would undertake the utmost possible efforts to retain the largest settlement on Crete with the best port in the north-eastern part of the island. Even though no experience had been gathered by the parachute force about combat in extended built-up areas, a look at the tactical manuals of the *Heer* would have revealed the potential difficulties for the conquest of Heraklion.[52] This may explain why the assignment of an engineer company or even of the *FschPiBtl.7* as a whole with the specific training and

---

49   In a letter to the author in 2005, *General* (ret.) Trettner pointed out that *Luftflotte 4* initially had a "euphoric" view about an easy victory on Crete, whereas *XI.Flieger-Korps* was quite conscious about the difficulties of the airborne operation.

50   According to calculations undertaken after the war by *Brigadegeneral* (ret.) Gericke, the initial strength of *Gruppen West* and *Mitte* was 4,320 men in total. That for Heraklion and Rethymnon, prior to the reduction mentioned beforehand, was 4,340 men.

51   The rationale behind the two-fold mission for *Kräftegruppe Bräuer* remains unmentioned in the Gefechtsbericht Kreta of *XI.Flieger-Korps*, as well as in Student's memoirs. Some formulations in the former, however, give rise to the assumption that Student, following his theory of 'oildrop tactics', had been the driving factor behind it.

52   The principal manual of the *Heer*, H. Dv. 300/1 – Truppenführung, covered combat in built-up areas in its numbers 552-558 and had left no doubt about the difficulties which could be encountered.

equipment of these soldiers for combat in built-up and fortified areas was never taken into consideration.

Although *Oberst* Bräuer probably had little influence on the strength and composition of his task force during the initial phase of the development of the operational plan for the airborne attack, it is quite certain that he ordered how it was to fight. He was evidently confident of the correctness of the intelligence reports for his sector, and assigned the tasks for his units accordingly. Nevertheless, doubts in his abilities as a tactical commander on the ground – he had never received a thorough training in the command and control principles of ground forces, and had never led a company, let alone a battalion of parachute infantrymen in combat – appear to be justified by the following findings.

The lack of gliders for his mission[53] and the preparation of the defenders, which should have been anticipated after the events in western Crete, had deprived *Oberst* Bräuer of any chance to achieve at least some tactical surprise. Nevertheless he had one of his battalions dropped in the immediate vicinity of the airfield and over the supposedly strongest air-defence and had weakened it by dividing it into two parts.

Quite incomprehensible was his decision to assign the *1./FschFlaMGBtl.7* to the directly assaulting *II./FschJgRgt.1* instead of using this unit, with its effective 2cm guns, in a supporting role at some distance to the airfield.

The battalion planned for the taking of Heraklion was assigned a drop zone too close to the built-up area of the town. Therefore it suffered considerable losses and first had to retire some distance for assembly in preparation for the assault. Despite the obviously weak strength of this unit for the task of clearing the old part of Heraklion with its large area of solidly built, dense living and administrative quarters, he ordered an entire battalion (though only with two companies and the staff present) to protect its rear toward the west.

Although the battalion foreseen as reserve was dropped wrongly at more than 10km distance from the airfield, *Oberst* Bräuer did not move to the west immediately after landing, so that he would have been able to quickly support the assault force if this had achieved some success. By neglecting to take along a radio set during his personal reconnaissance he had lost valuable time to gain control of his battalions.

For his mission to seize the airstrip at Rethymnon and the town proper, *Oberst* Sturm[54] organized his task force as follows:

---

53   Seen in the aftermath, the importance placed on the airfield at Heraklion for the entire airborne operation would have justified assigning *Sturmgruppen Genz* and *Altmann* to *Kräftegruppe Bräuer* for the preliminary attack against the anti-aircraft weapons there, instead of their only limited value around Chania as part of the 'oildrop tactics' favored by Student.

54   Alfred Sturm, born in 1888. Served as a fighter pilot in WWI after 1915. After the war, among other assignments, he was a company commander in the infantry. He transferred to the *Luftwaffe* in 1933 and to the *Fallschirmtruppe* in June 1940. From July 1940 he was commander of *FschJgRgt.2*, leading it in the parachute operations at Corinth and on Crete. He received the *Ritterkreuz* on 9 July 1941. Gained a promotion to *Generalmajor* in August 1941 and from winter 1941 was employed in the Russia. After convalescence in October 1942 he was made commander of the ground combat school of the *Luftwaffe*. He gained a promotion to *Generalleutnant* in August 1943. He undertook some additional assignments in a regional command of the *Luftwaffe*, in the *OKW* and as commander of a division-sized *Kampfgruppe*. Retired from active duty in January 1945 and was in captivity from April 1945 to June 1947.

- *I./FschJgRgt.2* (less its 2nd Company), reinforced with *2./FschMGBtl.7* and a platoon each from the 13th and 14th companies of *FschJgRgt.2*, commanded by *Major* Kroh, was to parachute on both ends of the runway of the airstrip and to seize it for possible air-landings:
- *III./FschJgRgt.2*, reinforced with *1./FschMGBtl.7, 2./FschArtAbt.7*, the majority of *2./FschFlaMGBtl.7* and elements from the 13th and 14th regimental companies, commanded by *Hauptmann* Wiedemann, was to come down east of Rethymnon and to seize the town;
- The staffs of *FschJgRgt.2* and *FschMGBtl.7, 2./FschJgRgt.2* and a platoon each from the 13th and 14th companies were to be dropped between the two reinforced battalions and to form the reserve.

Kräftegruppe Sturm, taking off from the airfields at Megara, Tanagra and Corinth, was also delayed during the start of its air transport formations for up to one hour, so that the planned suppression of the enemy defenses by close air support aircraft during the approach and landing of the parachute forces did not occur. Moreover, the attacks, which were flown by about twenty combat aircraft and fighters at about 1500hrs, had little effect against the well-protected and concealed defenders.[55] Only the Greek 4th Regiment, which was positioned between the Australian infantry battalions, moved away to the south under the intensity of the air attacks but was quickly brought back.

At 1545hrs, 15 minutes after the end of the air attacks, the first air transport formations with soldiers of *Kräftegruppe Sturm* aboard, approached the assigned sector from the east along the coast. However the problems during take-off resulted in the disarray of the planned arrival sequence, causing confusion over the objective area. The Ju 52s with the 10th and 12th companies of *FschJgRgt.2* joined the formation of *Kräftegruppe Kroh*. The 3rd Platoon of the 12th Company was reduced to one plane load, which was dropped over the olive oil factory at Stavromenos, as one of its aircraft had remained back damaged on the airfield, a second had to conduct an emergency landing on the island of Milos and a third was shot down over Rethymnon.[56]

Over the course of the next 35 minutes, *Kräftegruppe Sturm* was dropped on a strip of ground along the coast of about 12km in length and about 1km wide between Perivolia, about 2 km east of Rethymnon and the hamlet of Stavromenos. No longer suppressed from the air the defenders directed their fire against the approaching transport aircraft with all available weapons, causing many planes to deviate considerably from the final route to their drop zones. *III./FschJgRgt.2* and its assigned reinforcements, but without its 10th and 12th companies, was dropped correctly with the majority of its troops immediately south-east of Perivolia with sub-units, however, at the village of Platanes, about 1km to the east. During

---

55   The crew of an Me 110, which was shot down south of Perivolia, was able to join the paratroopers.
56   The presence of the 10th and 12th companies with *Sturmgruppe Kroh* is mentioned for the first time in the report of this group on 26 May as "remnants of the 10th and 12th companies". Alfred Grunau, who was a member of *12./FschJgRgt.2* on Crete, mentions the commitment of this company in a report, stored under signature BW 57/167, in the BA-MA. Willi Weier, who had also been a member of *12./FschJgRgt.2* on Crete, has confirmed in a letter to the author that the paratroopers from the 10th and 12th companies, as far as they had arrived on the battleground around Rethymnon, were dropped together with *Sturmgruppe Kroh*.

the final approach the transport aircraft received heavy defensive fire.[57] One Ju 52 with soldiers from *1./FschMGBtl.7* aboard was shot down and another was set ablaze forcing it to conduct an emergency landing near Platanes. Two more aircraft were damaged so badly that they had to land after they dropped their passengers.[58] The defensive fire now switched to the descending and landing men of *Kampfgruppe Wiedemann*. It came from Greek gendarmes, located in Perivolia and from the defensive positions of the Australian 2/11 Infantry Battalion, which was established on and around Hill B.[59] The soldiers of *1./ FschMGBtl.7* were unable to find all of their containers which held their heavy machine-guns and mortars on the drop zone, which was covered by high vines and was being swept by fire. All three platoon leaders of this unit (*Oberleutnant* Helfenbein and *Leutnants* Mohr and Reichel) as well as its *Oberfeldwebel* were killed shortly after landing. The company commander, *Oberleutnant* Laun, was seriously wounded and as such the remainder of the company was now led by non-commissioned officers.[60] *2./FschFlaMGBtl.7*, led by *Oberleutnant* Kerrut, also suffered its first losses during the landing, and only part of its heavy weapons could be salvaged. *2./FschArtAbt.7* parachuted shortly after 1600hrs from 20 Ju 52s. Three of its four recoilless guns and two of the four sidecar motorcycles, which were dropped with parachute bundles, could be made ready for use. As the battery was not being fired at during landing it initially suffered seven injured. A part of the containers with ammunition for the guns, however, remained undiscovered in the broken terrain. At about 1630hrs the battery assembled at the eastern edge of Perivolia. It was at that time that losses occurred from infantry fire from Hill C, located about 1km south of Perivolia.

As this was happening *Hauptmann* Wiedemann and a number of his paratroopers forced their way into Perivolia and cleared the village from Greek gendarmes, supported by the guns of the parachute artillery battery, firing over open sights. A subsequent thrust toward Rethymnon, however, was broken up by heavy defensive fire from the eastern outskirts of the town. A group of paratroopers who occupied a height with a small chapel and cemetery on top of it, located about 500m south-west of Perivolia, was more successful. It was baptized the '*Kapellenhöhe*' (Chapel Hill) by the Germans. The parachute artillerymen were ordered to seize the defended height south of Perivolia. The heavy weapons that were supporting the attack managed to destroy one of the bunkers on the height. The assaulting machine-gun teams and riflemen of the battery, however, were halted by defensive fire.[61] In the light of the unclear situation *Hauptmann* Wiedemann considered a renewed attack into the darkness as holding forth little promise; therefore he decided to take up a defensive posture until at least daybreak. He deployed a part of his 9th Company (*Oberleutnant* Begemann), reinforced with a heavy machine-gun-squad, along the western end of Perivolia, between the beach and the coastal road. The 11th Company (*Oberleutnant* Pabst) was posted between the coastal road and the '*Kapellenhöhe*'. The majority of the 9th Company was positioned on this height. The assigned elements of the 14th Company established itself along the southern perimeter of Perivolia. Parts

---

57   This fire had mainly been delivered by anti-aircraft and light machine-guns, as CREFORCE had not assigned anti-aircraft guns to the Rethymnon sector.

58   Their crews later joined *Kampfgruppe Wiedemann*.

59   In addition to three companies of 2/11 Infantry Battalion and five mortars, two 100mm guns and a platoon from the Australian 2/1 MG Battalion were positioned on and around Hill B.

60   See also the reports by members of the company in Klitzing, pp.18-27.

61   For the description of the fighting of *2./FschArtAbt.7* in the area around Perivolia, the report by Mündel, 'Der Igel von Rethymnon', published in *DDF* April/May 1971, pp.10-11, has also been used.

of *1./FschMGBtl.7* and *2./FschArtAbt.7* took over the defence toward the east. The heavy machine-guns of *1./FschMGBtl.7* were unfortunately only of limited value, as none of their mountings had been salvaged.

Shortly after 1800hrs, parts of the Australian 2/11 Infantry Battalion, with the support of artillery, conducted a counter-attack from the south-west. The artillerymen that were stopped some distance in front of Hill C were driven back to the eastern edge of Perivolia. Here, in action with other parts of *Kampfgruppe Wiedemann*, they succeeded in preventing the attackers from entering the village. While mopping up the terrain in front of the German positions they captured a number of paratroopers, who had remained there in isolated positions. Shortly prior to daybreak on 21 May they retired to their positions.

Kräftegruppe Kroh parachuted at 1545hrs, almost one hour late and partly over incorrect locations. *2./FschMGBtl.7* under *Oberleutnant d.R.* Dr. Büttnert came down as planned on the coastal road just east of Stavromenos. Unfortunately one plane-load of its men was dropped over the sea and all of them drowned. As first unit of *I./FschJgRgt.2* the 4th Company, commanded by *Hauptmann* Morawetz, landed within the effective range of the Australian 2/1 Infantry Battalion (with the two heavy machine-gun platoons from the 2/1 Machine-Gun Battalion). The company suffered heavy losses during the descent and immediately after landing. Among the numerous killed were the company commander and all of his officers. Only a few minutes later the 1st Company under *Oberleutnant* Schindler came down alongside the 4th Company. It also had a considerable number of losses before the paratroopers were able to get to their weapon containers. The elements of both companies which landed inside the positions of the enemy, on the strongly defended Hill A, protected by wire-entanglements, were almost completely wiped out. The Germans had named Hill A the *'Weinberghöhe*. Only a few small groups of paratroopers were able to take up the fight.[62] The parts of the 1st and 4th companies that came down north-east of the *'Weinbergshöhe'* immediately began to advance toward the airstrip. However they were unable to gain much ground and at 1630hrs were stopped 600m in front of Hill A. At 1715hrs *Major* Kroh and his 3rd Company led by *Oberleutnant* von Roon, arrived in the area about 400m east of this hill. This group, which also included the battalion staff and the signals platoon, had been dropped wrongly on a beach about 4km east of the olive oil factory. *Major* Kroh immediately deployed the 3rd Company, *2./FschMGBtl.7* and remnants of the 1st and 4th companies for the attack against the *'Weinberghöhe'*. Supported by the fire of an 8cm mortar, at about 1800hrs the 3rd Company managed to gain the northern slope and established a defensive perimeter. A short time later *2./FschMGBtl.7* and the remainders of the 1st and 4th companies joined the attack and succeeded in overrunning the Australian artillerymen, who had retired to a north-western spur of Hill A. At 1930hrs the whole height was in German hands. From there a number of paratroopers fought their way forward to the airstrip during the onset of darkness. There they captured the dismounted crews of two Matilda II tanks.[63] However they were then forced to ground and had to

---

62 It had, however, not been in vain. *Australia in the War of 1939-1945,* Series One, Army, p.258 reports that two heavy machine-guns on Hill A had been taken out and the crews of two guns there was forced to withdraw. Thus the isolated groups of paratroopers had probably contributed quite efficiently to the later conquest of the hill.

63 *Australia in the War of 1939-1945*, pp.259 and 261, reports that at 1615 hrs these tanks had already been sent off from their staging area north of the hamlet of Pigi for the attack against the paratroopers east of

establish themselves for defence. At about this time, *Major* Kroh, through reports from subordinate units, discovered that his group had lost about 400 men in killed, wounded and missing.

The forces planned as reserve led by the commander of *FschMGBtl.7 Major* Schulz, which had been joined by *Oberst* Sturm, his battle HQ and the regimental signals platoon, were dropped shortly before 1600hrs on the beach west of the airstrip, with *2./FschJgRgt.2* under *Oberleutnant* Jahnke, to the north of and on Hill B, within the heavily wired positions of the Australian 2/11 Infantry Battalion and the Greek 4th Regiment. During the final approach flight a Ju 52 with soldiers from the 13/FschJfRgt 2 aboard was shot down and crashed. The regimental signals platoon parachuted about 8km to the east. The only 80-watt transmitter which was provided for *Kräftegruppe Sturm* was destroyed on landing and as such there was no possibility of establishing communication with the wireless stations around Athens.[64] The paratroopers coming down in the defensive areas of the enemy took heavy losses during the descent, as many of them drifted in front of the field positions of the enemy. Most of the remainder were killed, wounded or captured immediately after they hit the ground. Only a few found cover between the vines, among these being *Oberst* Sturm, who landed with about ten soldiers of his battle HQ. The parts of the reserve which came down near the beach also took some losses, but were better protected from observation by the high vines around them. Therefore, *Major* Schulz succeeded in assembling a few men of his staff and retreated along the coast toward Rethymnon. At about 2230hrs he arrived at the location planned as the command post of *Kräftegruppe Sturm*, but only found the adjutant of *Oberst* Sturm, *Oberleutnant* von Reitzenstein and the incorrectly dropped HQ section of *I./FschJgRgt.2*. Moving on along the coastal road to the east he established contact with elements of *Kampfgruppe Wiedemann* during the night 20/21 May. As the regiment commander was believed to be missing, he now assumed command of *Kräftegruppe Sturm* as its highest ranking officer.

As at Heraklion *Kräftegruppe Sturm* failed to parachute and assemble under the cover of air attack forces. Compared to Heraklion, however, no immediate assault against the airstrip and Rethymnon had been planned for, in view of the strength and composition of the troops. Instead the attack against both objectives was to commence after the assembly of the forces nearby. It was impossible to bring this plan to fruition for several reasons, as most of the enemy dispositions remained undetected by air reconnaissance. The drop zones for *Kampfgruppen* Kroh and Wiedemann had been chosen in areas which, for the greater part, were dominated by enemy fire, thereby preventing the intended orderly assembly of both of them. This also applied to the reserve force under *Major* Schulz. Here, however, parachuting at incorrect locations was the main reason for its loss. The faulty parachuting of the staff of *I./FschJgRgt.2* and its 3rd Company revealed shortcomings in the training of

---

Hill A. However, one of them had got stuck just north of the airstrip, whereas the other had plunged into the dry bed of a stream. As the tanks had not been destroyed by the advancing paratroopers, they were salvaged by the Australians on 21 May and were brought to action again with new crews.

64   See also Thote. The regimental signals platoon had reached *Sturmgruppe Kroh* on 21 May.

dispatchers although this turned out to be of decisive advantage, as these soldiers had been able to join the fight in good order after a short time.

The struggle for the initial objectives

During the evening of 20 May the command of *XI.Flieger-Korps* realized that the situation for its troops fighting on Crete had become critical. It was now understood that the strength and preparations of the enemy on the island had been considerably underestimated. The losses reported up to then had been appalling. *Gruppen West* and *Ost* had not been able to seize the airfields that were assigned to them as primary objectives. *Gruppe Mitte* managed to clear most of its drop zones, but remained surrounded by the enemy and had not gained ground toward Chania. The situation at Rethymnon remained obscure as no wireless communication with the task force existed. Furthermore the capture of the airfield at Heraklion by *Kräftegruppe Bräuer* had to be regarded as a complete failure and the attack against the town proper was yet to commence. *Gruppe West* had achieved at least a partial success by advancing to the western edge of the airfield at Maleme and gaining a foothold on the slopes of Hill 107. By means of sea transport the movement of troops to the north-western coast of Crete had been initiated, thus a substantial reinforcement of *Gruppe West*, including heavy weapons, could be expected, although the enemy in the area of Kastelli/Kissamo was posing a threat to the landing. The struggle of *Gruppe West* was impeded by the loss of its energetic leader and by an increasing shortage of ammunition.

Despite the overall situation neither Student nor Löhr considered discontinuing the battle for Crete, which would result in the sacrifice of more than 7,000 *Fallschirmtruppe* on the island. Nevertheless a way now had to be found to generate the prerequisites for the air-landing of the troops assigned to *XI.Flieger-Korps* from the *12.Armee*. In view of the terrain conditions on Crete this could only be achieved by the seizure of at least one of the two principal airfields. However, for the time being, the command of *XI.Flieger-Korps* and of *Fl.Div.7*, still on the Greek mainland, was looking for *ad hoc* solutions to improve the critical situation of its troops fighting on Crete. As it was realised that a large number of troops in the second wave had been left behind because of a lack of air transport capacity, a plan was being organized to drop these men no later than 21 May, as this was seen as the fastest method to bring reinforcements to Crete. Energetic officers, with *Oberst* Ramcke leading the way – he ceased his supporting role in the preparation of the *5.Gebirgs-Division* for its air transport – commenced to collect and organize the paratroopers who had been left behind.

21 May

During the early hours of 21 May it became evident from wireless reports from *Gruppe West* that the *SturmRgt.* was in the process of occupying all of Hill 107 which had previously been given up by the enemy. As the airfield at Maleme was no longer under fire from there, after a short conference with his closest staff, Student decided to form the main effort for the further landings in the western part of Crete.[1] Without delay he initiated the necessary measures.

As the signals officer of the *SturmRgt.* had reported that the airfield at Maleme was still under fire by enemy artillery and his forces were still defending at its eastern edge, *Hauptmann* Kleye, an experienced pilot on the corps staff, was ordered to land with a Ju 52 on the airfield and to assess the chances for the air-landing of troops from the *5.Gebirgs-Division* at this location. He was furthermore to take along urgently required ammunition.

Oberst Ramcke, with the paratroopers gathered by him and the still available units of *FschPzJgAbt.7*, was to parachute west of the Tavronitis River as reinforcement for *Gruppe West* and was subsequently to assume command over this group.

Admiral Süd-Ost was directed to let the two *leichte Seetransportstaffeln*, assembled at the island Milos, immediately set sail to the north-western coast of Crete.

While these actions were initiated, the command of the *Luftflotte* was informed about Student's decision and was requested to adjust air support for 21 May accordingly.

At 0600hrs *Hauptmann* Kleye landed his Ju 52, not as originally planned on the beach west of the mouth of the Tavronitis, but on the airfield proper. His aircraft was immediately taken under fire from the north-eastern corner of the airfield. Approaching paratroopers quickly unloaded the ammunition which it had brought along. After he received a report from *Hauptmann* Gericke, that Hill 107 was in German hands and that advance elements of the *SturmRgt.* had reached the eastern perimeter of the airfield, *Hauptmann* Kleye succeeded in taking off again and despite the damage to his aircraft he landed safely near Athens. His report to the command of *XI.Flieger-Korps* about the situation of *Gruppe West* immediately triggered the need for additional measures.

Gruppe West was directed to order all aircraft needed for the landing of troops and supplies on to the airfield on 21 May. From the point of view of *XI.Flieger-Korps* this task was also imperative for the operations of *Kräftegruppen Bräuer* and *Sturm*, as these would have to be resupplied from the air for quite some time, requiring all of the available containers and parachutes for heavy loads.

As the further course of the operation now depended on the timely and firm conquest of the airfield at Maleme, and the capability to retain it against the anticipated counter-attack, General Student decided to drop the still-available 5th and 6th companies from *FschJgRgt.2* under *Oberleutnants* Thiel and Nagele, as well as parts of the 2nd and 3rd companies from *FschSanAbt.7* under *Oberarzt* Dr. Hartmann, at 1500hrs on the coastal strip west of Platanias. The preceding air attacks took place from 1400 to 1500hrs, against the jump-off areas of the enemy's counter-attack forces assumed around Maleme and Pirgos.

---

1   There are considerable differences between Student's memoirs and the after-action report of *Luftflotte 4* regarding the decision-making in Athens during the night 20/21 May. For logical reasons, supported by the actual events, the former's version has been adopted by the author. The statement in the above-mentioned document, that the decision to build the main effort in the area of Maleme had been made in the command of *Luftflotte 4* by the evening of 20 May, and the commander of the *5.Gebirgs-Division* appointed as new commander of *Gruppe West*, must be strongly doubted. It would have meant a serious disregard for the existing command hierarchy.

In co-ordination with parts of the *SturmRgt.* advancing toward the east, the threat to the airfield was to be eliminated once and for all.[2]

At daybreak on 21 May and after preceding air attacks, paratroopers from several units of the *SturmRgt.*, led by Dr. Neumann, advancing along the north-western slope, and the 5th and 7th companies under *Major* Stentzler, attacking from the south-west, completed the conquest of Hill 107. Time and again the attackers came across enemy soldiers who had been left behind during the retreat. Most of them had escaped toward the east. Others, who continued to fight on, were quickly overcome. Around noon both forces established themselves in a protective line along the eastern slope of Hill 107. One of the combat patrols, probing toward the east, gained the area in the vicinity of the command post of the New Zealand 23rd Battalion, before being repelled by a counter-attack. During the morning hours *IV./SturmRgt.* was engaged in firefights with elements of the enemy still holding out at the north-eastern and eastern perimeters of the airfield. The battalion prepared for the attack against the village of Maleme, which was to commence after an air attack announced for 1400hrs.

Shortly prior to 0800hrs the HQ company of *FschPzJgAbt.7*, its 1st Company (less the platoon with *FschPiBtl.7*), its 3rd Company and a company formed from left-behind paratroopers,[3] led by the commanding officer of *FschPzJgAbt.7*, *Hauptmann* Schmitz, was dropped from 42 Ju 52s. The force came down together along the coast between Kolimbari and Tavronitis. Of the 20 anti-tank guns and their towing vehicles, dropped by means of parachute bundles, only a few were usable[4] and three of the descending soldiers drifted out to sea and drowned. By 1100hrs the force had assembled around Tavronitis and placed sentries toward the south and west. At 1300hrs, *Hauptmann* Gericke directed *Hauptmann* Schmitz to detach four of his anti-tank guns to support the attack against the village of Maleme. When these guns, drawn by sidecar motorcycles, crossed the Tavronitis bridge at full speed at about 1500hrs, the first soldiers of the gun-crews were killed by sniper fire.

At about 1000hrs the signals platoon of *FschMGBtl.7*, which had been left behind on the Greek mainland with a few more soldiers from this battalion, was dropped from three Ju 52s south-west of Ropaniania. After reporting to *Hauptmann* Gericke the platoon was assigned to the reserve of *Gruppe West*.[5] The other soldiers, under *Leutnants* Kurz and Feyerabend, were apportioned to *FschPzJgAbt.7*.

Shortly after 1100hrs three Ju 52s from *6./KG z.b.V.1* touched down on the rock-strewn strip of sand west of the mouth of the Tavronitis, after their pilots observed that the airfield was under fire from artillery. The aircraft brought along urgently required ammunition. Under the direction of *Hauptmann* Kleye, who had flown along with a small team of supply soldiers, they were hastily unloaded. As the aircraft were not targeted by the

---

2   In his memoirs (Götzel, p.268), Student stated that he had anticipated the concentration of the enemy's counter-attack forces in the area Maleme-Pirgos, so that the drop zone would be unoccupied. He had, however, neglected to have his assumption verified by aerial reconnaissance.

3   The Gefechtsbericht Kreta of *XI.Flieger-Korps* speaks of a company of paratroopers, formed from members of *FschJgRgt.2*, led by *Leutnant* Klein.

4   The description of the employment of *FschPzJgAbt.7* is primarily based on the account of five of its members who had fought on Crete. It was published in *DDF* March/April 1986, pp.3-7. The account provides also for the correction of the time of parachuting, which in the war diary of the *SturmRgt.* is wrongly given as 1500hrs.

5   Its platoon leader, who on 20 May had erroneously boarded a Ju 52 with soldiers from *FschJgRgt.1*, had jumped with these at Heraklion.

enemy, two of them that remained ready for take-off – the third had lost its undercarriage during the landing – were loaded with wounded. Among those was *Generalmajor* Meindl, who by now was in a critical state. In a masterpiece of piloting, the two aircraft managed to take off again and at 1425hrs landed safely on the airfield at Megara.[6]

In the early morning of 21 May *6./SturmRgt.* under *Oberleutnant* Pissin, occupying the pass through which the coastal road led south of Kolimbari, was tasked with the advance toward Kastelli in order to establish contact with *Kampfgruppe Mürbe*. Around noon, a patrol from the company, consisting of two squads on a captured vehicle, moved off in the direction of Nochia, located about 4km south-west of the pass. At the exit of the pass the patrol came under fire from a larger unit of Greek soldiers. After the loss of one killed and four seriously wounded, it retired. The resistance of the enemy could be broken only after the deployment of stronger forces, including the assigned anti-tank gun, shortly before nightfall. Unfortunately, a supporting air attack by fighter-bombers and dive bombers also hit the company. Another three of its soldiers were wounded and the anti-tank gun with its towing truck were destroyed.

At 1500hrs 27 Ju 52s carrying troops for the attack against the airfield at Maleme arrived from the east, approaching their drop zones. As the enemy, contrary to Student's assumption, remained in his defensive areas, the two parachute companies and the parachute medical platoons were dropped within and near the positions of the engineer units of the New Zealand Division on either side of Gerania, and at the western edge of the defensive area of the 28th (Maori) Battalion. The men of *5./FschJgRgt.2*, coming down between Gerania and the Platanias Valley, were cut up during the drop, causing all of its officers and NCOs to become casualties. The fight against these paratroopers was joined by C Troop of the 27th Battery, in firing positions south of Gerania. The paratroopers from the 5th Company, who landed in the western part of the defensive area of the 28th (Maori) Battalion at about 1750hrs, were also neutralized, except for a small group which continued to holdd out. The medical soldiers who were dropped in the area around Gerania also suffered considerable losses, including many killed. *Oberarzt* Dr. Hartmann, most of the remainder were captured. Nevertheless, *Assistentarzt* Dr. Schuster managed to gather about 25 men. *6./FschJgRgt.2*, which came down west of the positions of the New Zealand engineers, was also decimated during the landing. While retiring along the coastal road toward the airfield, the company came under fire from the defensive area of the New Zealand 23rd Battalion. At nightfall, about 80 paratroopers of this unit, led by *Oberleutnant* Nagele, established themselves in the eastern part of Pirgos.[7]

On the basis of the situation reports submitted by *Gruppe West* in the course of the morning of 21 May, Student decided to plan the landing of the first *Gebirgsjäger* on the airfield at

---

6   The event is reported by one of the pilots who participated in it in – Schaug, p.81. Differing to the war diary of the *SturmRgt.*, *Leutnant* von Könitz is not named as the pilot who had flown back *Generalmajor* Meindl. Whether *Leutnant* von Könitz had flown on his own to Crete cannot be verified.

7   See also Davin, pp.189-190.

Maleme on this day, despite the fact that it was still under fire from enemy artillery and despite the risk that it could be lost again in an expected counter-attack. Student had this decision carried through against the opposition of *Generaloberst* Löhr around noon. As both Student and Löhr had issued orders to the commander of the *5.Gebirgs-Division*, *Generalmajor* Ringel, without proper synchronization, the latter was confronted with differing missions.[8]

At about 1600hrs a group from *KG z.b.V.3* approached the airfield at Maleme from Tanagra in the west, carrying the reinforced *II./GebJgRgt.100* and elements from the staff of this regiment, together with its commander *Oberst* Utz. As the enemy artillery had reopened its fire on the airfield the Ju 52s touched down amidst the impacts of the shells; mortars and flat trajectory weapons from the area east and south-east of the airfield joined the artillery fire. A number of transport aircraft received direct hits during the landing run. Others were wrecked in the shell-craters or crashed into already destroyed planes. The mountain infantry and the regimental staff fortunately had only slight losses during the unloading. *Oberst* Utz, however, was to refrain from using the battalion as a whole. As arranged with *Hauptmann* Gericke, he reinforced the attack of the *SturmRgt.* against Maleme with the 7th Company and sent the 8th Company off to toward the south-west in support of *16./SturmRgt.* in order to safeguard the road leading to Kandanos. The remaining two companies were kept ready to counter enemy forces, which were reported approaching from that direction.[9] Almost all of the transport aircraft which remained intact on the airfield were loaded with wounded by the men of *3./FschSanAbt.7*[10] before taking off again.

Together with the mountain troops the airfield command at Maleme, under *Major* Snowadski, was brought along as ordered by the air-commander of *XI.Flieger-Korps*. It immediately took over the task of administering landings and maintaining the airfield ready for use. The 20 Ju 52s that remained on the airfield, destroyed or seriously damaged, were towed to its edges by means of a captured tractor.

Simultaneously with the parachute attack at Gerania and Pirgos, *Hauptmann* Gericke ordered the start of the thrust against Maleme from the west, thus utilizing the preceding air attack. At 1700hrs the attack force was still involved in fighting for the village. It had succeeded in occupying its western part, but still met stubborn resistance from buildings in

---

8   The war diary of the HQ section of the *5.Gebirgs-Division*, RH 28-5/1 in the BA-MA, states that at 1245 hrs *Generalmajor* Ringel had been tasked by the command of *XI.Flieger-Korps* to immediately assume the command of all ground forces on Crete and to clear the island of the enemy from west to east. At 1430hrs it states that *Generalmajor* Ringel, in a personal conversation with *Generaloberst* Löhr, had just received the mission to bring the airfield at Maleme firmly into his own hands, and to safeguard it for the landing of follow-on forces.

9   The report later turned out to be wrong. It may have been generated as the result of a successful misleading of *Gruppe West* by means of the radio set which had been captured by the Greeks at Kastelli, but possibly also by an erroneous aerial reconnaissance report. Aircraft that were dispatched to the south-west of Crete late in the afternoon of 21 May had not detected any enemy there. See also Gefechtsbericht Kreta of the *XI.Flieger-Korps*.

10   After the loss of its commander this unit was led by *Oberarzt* Dr. Dietzel.

the east of the settlement.[11] For the final conquest of the village and mopping up a company from *FschPzJgAbt.7* was additionally deployed.

At 1800hrs *Oberst* Ramcke and 550 paratroopers gathered by him in the area around Athens, including the almost complete 4th and 12th companies from *FschJgRgt.1*, was dropped on the coastal plain north of Tavronitis. Unfortunately one flight of Ju 52s dropped its passengers over the sea, and of the 35 paratroopers dropped, only 10 could be rescued. After a short situation report by the signals officer of *SturmRgt.* at 1815hrs *Oberst* Ramcke assumed command of *Gruppe West*. Student directed that the attack against Chania was to commence on 22 May. Ramcke decided to continue the thrust along the coastal road energetically during the night and dispatched *Kompanie Kiebitz*, which had been dropped with him, as reinforcement to *Kampfgruppe Gericke*. *Kompanie Klein* had landed together with *FschPzJgAbt.7* and was sent to *II./SturmRgt.* on the eastern slope of Hill 107. At the onset of nightfall and from his command post the *Oberst* issued the order for an attack toward the east in the early morning of 22 May to the assembled commanders of the units of *Gruppe West*. He intended to advance with the parachute forces along the coastal road, whereas *Oberst* Utz was to hit the enemy west of Platanias in the flank and the rear.

Around this time the village of Maleme was taken in its entirety. Sentries were pushed out further to the east as an enemy counter-attack was anticipated during the night, but, with the failure of the landing of parachute forces in the area of Gerania and Pirgos, *Oberst* Ramcke refrained from the thrust of the *SturmRgt.* to the east during the hours of darkness. The sentries in front of Maleme were drawn back to the eastern edge of the village. The final hours of 21 May remained quiet, except for occasional firefights which could be heard from the area around Pirgos-Modhion-Kondomari. In Athens, Student continued to believe that the existing worries of the Airfleet command about an attack of the enemy against the air bridgehead from the south-west were unjustified.

As proposed by the commander of the 5th (New Zealand) Brigade, the New Zealand Division decided to launch the counter-attack to recapture the airfield at Maleme and Hill 107 during the night of 22 May.[12] As Brigadier Hargest and Brigadier Puttick were keen for the uninterrupted protection of the northern coastal strip against sea landings and insisted on the occupation of the defensive areas of the 20th and 28th Battalions, which were planned as offensive forces by other troops, the planning for the counter-attack was done at the highest command level. During a conference at the CREFORCE command post during the afternoon, which was attended by the commanders of the 4th (New Zealand) Brigade and the 19th (Australian) Brigade, it was decided that these forces were to conduct the relief of the counter-attack forces. Major General Freyberg shared Puttick's anxiety about the coastal positions and was in line with Puttick about the strength of the counter-attack.[13] Puttick, neither at the time of his decision nor in the hours afterward, was able to obtain a clear picture of the situation in the area around Maleme. Although the loss of Hill

---

11   Davin, p.188, states that the loss of Maleme was reported at 1800hrs and that by that time probably only stragglers from the NZ 22nd Infantry Battalion and armed civilians had still put up some fight in the eastern part of the village.

12   The utterly complex command arrangements made during the planning for the counter-attack are described at great length in Davin, pp.192-206. They have been laid down here only in their essential parts.

13   Davin, p.201, states, that Major General Freyberg probably had clear indications about the start of German sea transports at this time.

107 had been reported to him at about 0400hrs, he had not endeavored to gain a personal view of the situation in the sector of his 5th Brigade.

The orders for the coordination of troop movement for those involved in preparation for the counter-attack were issued at the command of CREFORCE at 2010hrs.

The Australian 2/7 Infantry Battalion and the Australian 2/1 Machine-Gun Company from the area around Georgioupolis, now subordinated to the 4th (New Zealand) Brigade, were to relieve the New Zealand 20th Battalion south-west of Chania. The Australian 2/3 Field Regiment and an anti-tank platoon, also brought along from Georgioupolis, were to be placed under the command of the New Zealand Division. The artillery was to be positioned such that it could fire on the airfield at Maleme. The command post of the 19th (Australian) Brigade, the 2/8 Field Coy (engineers), and an Australian medical company were ordered to move to the area around Stilos. The 1st Argyll and Sutherland Highlanders, which up to now had protected the Messara plain near Timbakion against airborne landings, was summoned as reinforcement for the garrison of Heraklion.

Upon returning to his command post, Brigadier Puttick instructed the 5th Brigade by telephone about the plan for the counter-attack shortly after 1900hrs, and subsequently dispatched a liaison officer to verbally pass on the details. With the commanders of the attack force also present at the command post of the 5th Brigade, the intended course of action was now as follows:

- Staging for the attack, with the 20th Battalion to the right of the coastal road and the 28th Battalion to its left is to take place about 300m west of the Platanias stream. It is to be completed after the relief and movement of the 20th Battalion by 22 May 0100hrs.
- Advance on either side of the coastal road, with the assigned platoon of the 3rd Hussars ahead on the road.
- Start of the attack after completion of the advance at 0400hrs, with Pirgos as the first objective.
- From Pirgos, after a rest of 30 minutes, attack with the 20th Battalion against the airfield, from the cemetery of Maleme on both sides of the road and with the 28th Battalion against Hill 107, so that its left flank touches Hill 107.
- Retirement of the 20th Battalion to the northern slope of Hill 107, thereby relieving the 28th Battalion, which is to return to its original area.
- Forward movement of the 21st Battalion to the line Xamoudochori-Hill 107.

An objective further to the west, planned at eliminating the German air bridgehead, was not mentioned. The 23rd Battalion, the defensive area of which was to be traversed by parts of the attack, was informed about the attack plan by liaison officer around midnight. Although it was to participate in the final phase of the attack, the 21st Battalion was not informed until 0400hrs on 22 May.

The hopes of *XI.Flieger-Korps* and *Gruppe West* to improve the situation in the north-western part of Crete by sea landings in the Bight of Kissamo on 22 May, came to nothing in the hours between 21 and 22 May.[14] *1.leichte Seetransportstaffel*, carrying *3./FschPiBtl.7*, *2./FschPzJgAbt.7* and all of their equipment on the way to Crete had been ordered back to the island of Milos early in the morning of 21 May, after it received a warning about British warships cruising in the waters north of Crete.[15] At around noon it was confirmed that the sea area north of Crete was free of British naval units, and the squadron, on the orders of *Admiral Süd-Ost*, set sail again for Crete. A few hours later *2.leichte Seetransportstaffel*, which in the meantime had also arrived at Milos, also followed. The six-hour interruption of the voyage of *1.leichte Seetransportstaffel* was to have devastating consequences. The squadron's low cruising speed meant it sailed into the darkness and lost the protection of air cover. Informed by air reconnaissance about the approach of a boat convoy from Milos, British naval units set course for the waters north of Crete. Shortly prior to 2300hrs, Force D, consisting of the cruisers *Dido, Orion* and *Ajax* and four destroyers, came across *1.leichte Seetransportstaffel* about 20km north of the Bight of Kissamo. During 2½ hours of fire from the British ships, two small steamers and 10 motorised sailing boats were sunk. The escorting Italian torpedo boat *Lupo* under Commander Mimbelli, attempted to protect the German convoy against the overwhelming force of the enemy and was heavily damaged by 18 hits. Nevertheless by her valiant fight she enabled the motorised sailing boats to escape toward the north. The losses in personnel of the German convoy were grave. Of the embarked soldiers from the parachute force many perished, so did most of those from the artillery battery, a large number of the 1st and 2nd Platoons from the anti-tank company, and almost all of the 2nd Platoon from the engineer company, among them *Leutnant* Häffner, who only a few weeks before proved his excellence at Corinth. However a considerable number of the shipwrecked were picked up by the sea rescue services and by Italian patrol boats during the course of 22 May. Some men travelling in rubber boats or swimming even managed to reach the coast of north-western Crete or the outlying small islands after several days.[16] It was a blessing in disguise for the 1st and 2nd Platoons from *3./FschPiBtl.7* and the 3rd Platoon from *2./FschPzJgAbt.7*, as their transports had not caught up with the convoy and were not targeted by the British warships.[17]

The command of *Gruppe Mitte* anticipated attacks by the enemy along the road Chania-Alikianou and from the area around Alikianou at first light on 21 May. However, the attacks did not materialize, as the enemy was too occupied with solidifying his positions around the German air bridgehead, which had suffered considerably during the fighting the day before. For that purpose the New Zealand Divisional Cavalry, about 300 men, which had retired from the area around Kirtomahdo in the evening of 20 May, was inserted into the gap that had developed between Pink Hill and Cemetery Hill. Behind it the remainder

---

14   For the description of the events around the *leichte Seetransportstaffeln*, the following sources have been used: Schenk, pp.21-23, Playfair, pp.136- 137 and *Australia in the War of 1939-1945*, Series One/ Army, p.231.

15   The warning had probably been provided by combat aircraft from *Luftflotte 4*, stationed on the Dodecanese, which at daybreak had attacked British naval units on the way to the covering force west of Crete. South of the Straits of Kaso the cruiser *Ajax* had been damaged by German aircraft and the destroyer *Juno* had been sunk by Italian aircraft intervening from Rhodes.

16   After the end of the rescue actions, 297 soldiers of the *leichte Seetransportstaffeln* had been reported as killed, the majority of them from *III./GebJgRgt.100*. See also Gundelach.

17   These sub-units later had been brought to Crete by aircraft or had been used as cadres for new units.

of the Greek 6th Regiment was kept ready in the event of counter-attacks. A company from the 19th Battalion was moved forward onto the eastern slope of Cemetery Hill. At noon it attacked from this location alongside elements of the New Zealand Divisional Cavalry and supported by the fire from the mortars of the 19th Battalion, the guns of F Troop from the 28th Battery and three light tanks against the top of Cemetery Hill. It succeeded in pushing back parts of *III./FschJgRgt.3*, which during the night, had again occupied the height.[18] As it was hit shortly after its occupation by precisely directed fire from German mortars, causing the counter-attack forces considerable losses, the area was abandoned again and for the time being remained no man's land. The troops positioned along the coast north and north-east of Galatas and on the high ground along the eastern rim of Prison Valley spent 21 May clearing their positions of isolated paratroopers and improving their emplacements. The plan to attack in the direction of the prison was not pursued again in the light of the preparations for the retaking of Hill 107, which was planned from noon.

In view of the strength of the positions of the enemy blocking the approaches toward Chania and of the threat to the air bridgehead from the south, *Oberst* Heidrich saw no chance of resuming the attack on 21 May. As he had been informed about the improving situation in the area of Maleme he now wished to utilize the progress made to achieve his assigned mission. He continued with the reorganization of his forces, to plan, and, to a limited extent, carry out his next moves. In the morning one of the shock troops that were employed for this purpose managed to overcome the New Zealand advisers of the Greek 8th Regiment who were entrenched at the pump station. In the morning the remainder of *Sturmgruppe Genz*, three officers and 21 other ranks, managed to reach the positions of *I./FschJgRgt.3*. During this action *Oberarzt* Dr. Stehfen and a *Feldwebel*, who had been sent ahead by *Oberleutnant* Genz for reconnaissance, were killed. Supplies and particularly ammunition were dropped within the protected zones on this day. Furthermore the anti-tank positions were also improved, as the platoon from *FschPzJgAbt.7* succeeded in salvaging and making ready for use again the guns which had been left behind during the retreat in the night. An air attack against the heights of Galatas at about 1000hrs, and attentive sentries, ensured that the exhausted troops found some rest and the possibility to improve their positions. The medical officers and soldiers under *Truppenarzt* Dr. Mallison were able to treat the numerous injured and wounded within the protection of the prison. Among them was *Gefreiter* Max Schmeling[19] who was injured during the landing on 20 May.

---

18   The after-action report of *FschJgRgt.3* does not mention this event. As, according to Davin, p.200, five mortars and 10 light machine-guns of the Germans had been destroyed during this attack, it may have been *12./FschJgRgt.3*, which had been hit.

19   The German boxing idol trained as a paratrooper at the start of the war. This deed was greatly emphasized by Nazi propaganda. The veteran paratrooper Willi Weier, who spent much time with Schmeling after the war, as a professional hunter accompanying him on hunting trips, passed the following information to the author in October 2005, which Schmeling personally provided to him: Schmeling, well-known throughout the Western world and therefore important for the National Socialist regime, was removed from active military service soon after his employment on Crete and assigned functions in the care of captured Allied officers.

In the operational area of *Gruppe Sturm*, a platoon from *3./FschJgRgt.2* and parts of *2./FschMGBtl.7* reached the middle of the airstrip at daybreak on 21 May. At 0400hrs, when *Kampfgruppe Kroh* commenced its attack aimed at taking the airstrip, the enemy to the strength of about a company, launched a thrust from the area around Hill D in the direction of the *Weinbergshöhe* (Hill A). It was repelled but the action by the enemy led to the cancellation of their own attack. The enemy then reinforced the original attack force considerably. Utilizing the effects of the bombing attack of a single German aircraft on the forward line of the paratroopers, which caused losses and led to some confusion, at 0800hrs the enemy resumed the attack from around Hill D with four assault groups, each about a company strong. The main force of the attackers enveloped the *Weinbergshöhe* from the south while other units outflanked it from the west. The attack was a complete success and at about 0900hrs, this key terrain was again in the hands of the enemy. As a result the two guns, which originally were positioned here, were won back and a considerable number of paratroopers captured. The markedly depleted *Kampfgruppe Kroh* had to fall back onto the olive oil factory near Stavromenos, about 1,800m north-east of the *Weinbergshöhe*. Here its soldiers set up positions behind the brick walls of the factory building. Stavromenos, immediately south-east of the factory, where the coastal road turned toward the south, was also included in these positions. There some of the heavy weapons that were still available— three 2cm-anti-aircraft guns and two anti-tank guns – were positioned. On the enemy side the *Weinbergshöhe* was occupied by artillerymen from 2/3 Field Regiment. In the meantime these had been able to equip themselves with captured German weapons. An attack by a Greek battalion against the olive oil factory which was planned for this day could not be carried out, as the Greeks first had to clear the approaches of groups of paratroopers still holding out there. This action took until nightfall to complete.

Around noon a shock troop, commanded by the commander of the signals platoon of *I./FschJgRgt.2*, *Oberleutnant* Rosenberg, succeeded in liberating more than 50 of their comrades-in-arms near the beach, who were captured during the counter-attack of the enemy against the *Weinbergshöhe*. There were almost no weapons for these men but they did become available as reserves.

Groups of paratroopers that had been dropped widely dispersed further to the south on the previous day were mainly from the 2nd Company, as well as almost certainly from the 10th Company, and they continued to fight against Greek soldiers in that area. One of these groups seized a dressing station that had been established in the village of Adhele. However during its further advance toward the north it was repelled in front of the positions of the Australian 2/11 Infantry Battalion, and consequently had to retire into the mountains. Another group, moving through the village of Pigi toward the airfield, fell into an ambush by Greek soldiers, and for the most part was captured. The small hamlets of Babali and Prasses, which were occupied by other small groups of paratroopers, were given up during the course of the day against superior enemy forces.

During the evening *Oberst* Sturm and the few men of his staff were taken prisoner by soldiers from the Australian 2/11 Infantry Battalion after they ran out of ammunition and the situation became hopeless for them.

The combat group defending Perivolia and on the 'Kapellenhöhe', now led by *Major* Erich Schulz, was continuously under fire by Australian artillery and snipers from the area around Hill C. From 0730hrs until about 1430hrs, Do 17 bombers attacked enemy emplacements at the eastern edge of Rethymnon and near Hill C in concentrated runs.

Despite the dispersed air recognition panels some of the bombs impacted between friendly positions and caused losses. Most of the supplies dropped in the afternoon by six Ju 52s could be salvaged. However no ammunition for the 10.5cm guns was delivered, as 7.5cm shells had erroneously been packed into the transport aircraft.

Shortly after 1600hrs a Greek battalion attacked Perivolia from Hill C. It was stopped by defensive fire about 400m in front of the village and then retired. An attack by Greek gendarmes, launched simultaneously from the eastern part of Rethymnon, also failed to get through. Shortly prior to midnight, parts of *9./FschJgRgt.2*, deployed on the *'Kapellenhöhe'*, were also attacked but were able to retain their positions.

Due to the lack of wireless-communication with *Gruppe Sturm* the command of *XI.Flieger-Korps* remained without a clear picture of the situation west of Rethymnon.

In the sector of *Kräftegruppe Bräuer III./FschJgRgt.1*, reinforced with parts of the regimental 13th and 14th companies,[20] launched its assault against Heraklion on 21 May, shortly before 0230hrs. *Major* Karl-Lothar Schulz organized his forces into two shock-groups: The 11th Company (*Oberleutnant* Becker) was to advance along the beach to the inner port, while the 10th Company (*Oberleutnant* Egger) to its right, was to enter the town through its western gate. Elements from the 9th and 12th companies and from *2./FschSanAbt.7* were assigned to each of the shock troops. With his battle HQ and a heavy machine-gun platoon, *Major* Schulz formed another combat team, which he led in person.

The attack was opened up by the 11th Company along the beach. After short preparatory fire by the mortars of the assigned platoon from *13./FschJgRgt.1* in front of the western gate, in order to explode any mines placed there, *Major* Schulz and his team, together with the shock-group of the 10th Company, assaulted the western gate. Fire from two anti-tank guns and heavy machine-guns forced the defenders to take cover. In hard fighting, during which the paratroopers relied mainly on their hand grenades, the barricades that protected the gate on its inner side were stormed. For hours the shock-groups fought their way along the streets of the town leading to the port and citadel. At the request of *Major* Schulz, shortly after 0800hrs *Hauptmann* Schirmer sent a reinforced platoon from his 7th Company, under *Oberleutnant* Schrader and a composite platoon made up from the men of his staff and signals platoon, led by *Leutnant* Krückeberg, into the attack. After a short while both platoons closed up with the shock-groups. At 1040hrs Becker's group gained the inner port, followed by Egger's. About this time the resistance of the Greek garrison of the town was, for the most part, was broken. Only the citadel at the north-eastern corner of the port was still vigorously defended. At around noon and in a square close to the port the commanders of the shock-groups were summoned by *Major* Schulz, who had fought his way to this location with his combat team. Here the officers provided their commander with situation reports and waited on further orders. At this time it was discovered that the assault force was desperately low on ammunition and hardly able to continue the fight, particularly in the case of a counter-attack by Commonwealth troops from outside of the town. In this situation a small group of Greeks was escorted to *Major* Schulz. The group

---

20   In his report 'Meine Kriegserlebnisse 1940-1945' Ernst H. Simon, who had jumped west of Heraklion as a member of the 1st Platoon of *13./FschJgRgt.1* and after the war had achieved the position of the technical director of Lufthansa, reports that the commander of this company, *Oberleutnant* Wehner, was killed during the descent.

consisted of the mayor of the town, its military commandant, two other officials and a lady of German origin as interpreter. The Greek officer and the mayor declared the capitulation of Heraklion. *Major* Schulz immediately accepted and had a record about the results of the negotiations prepared.

In the meantime the Australian brigade command reacted to the situation in Heraklion and dispatched parts of two infantry battalions in order to retake of the town, in complete disregard of the capitulation arrangements of the Greeks.[21] As parts of the German assault force near the port were almost encircled by the counter-attacking enemy and running out of ammunition, at around 1600hrs *Major* Schulz decided to give up the dearly won old parts of Heraklion and establish positions in the west outside of the town wall. By wireless communication with the command of *XI.Flieger-Korps*, which had been established a few hours earlier,[22] resupply with ammunition and an air attack was urgently requested, at the time when *Major* Schulz had decided to abandon Heraklion.

Later in the afternoon the requested ammunition was delivered by Ju 52 on the delay for marked drop zone, some distance west of the town. It was immediately distributed among the paratroopers, who now, despite their exhaustion, were confident that they could hold their positions. At about the same time they also requested that dive bombers were used to attacke the town, particularly the area around the citadel. The bombing attack evidently discouraged the enemy from closing with the paratroopers.

In order to generate unity of command in the area west of Heraklion, in the evening *Oberst* Bräuer placed *II./FschJgRgt.2* under the command of *Major* Schulz.

A lack of experience in combat in defended built-up areas within the parachute force quite explains why the enormous amount of ammunition and explosives that were required for this type of operations had not been provided beforehand. When this deficiency became apparent during the fighting in Heraklion it was too late to overcome it, as the time until the delivery of ammunition would be at least two hours following a request by radio. The critical shortage of ammunition, alongside the exhaustion of his men caused *Major* Schulz to give up Heraklion.

While the reinforced *III./FschJgRgt.1* was struggling for Heraklion, *Bataillon Schirmer* was continuously involved in firefights with Cretan irregulars and scattered Greek soldiers, who time and again attempted to advance toward the town through the vineyards, losing two killed and two wounded.

To the south-west *Truppenarzt* Dr. Langemeyer and parts of his *2./FschSanAbt.7* set up the main dressing station of *Gruppe Ost* in the small mountain village of Tsalikaki, about 4km from Heraklion, in the course of the morning. It was protected by a platoon from *9./FschJgRgt.1*. As the supply drops in the afternoon also included medical material, the wounded could now be treated properly. *Oberarzt* Dr. Kirsch, despite his chest wound,

---

21　According to *Australia in the War of 1939-1945*, Series One/ Army, p.284, a platoon each from the 2nd Leicesters and the 2nd York and Lancasters had been tasked with the counter-attack. The source also states that a number of Greek troops and armed civilians, obviously unaware of the capitulation, had also continued to fight. If one follows the German reports of the renewed fighting for Heraklion, it becomes quite evident that more than just two British infantry platoons conducted the counter-attack.

22　The signals officer of *III./FschJgRgt.1*, *Oberleutnant* Kappel, was able to recover one of the two containers with a radio set late in the morning and to establish communication with the command post of *Oberst* Bräuer and, by teletype, with Athens. It may, however, also be that the latter was achieved by means of an 80-watt-transmitter from *1./LnAbt.41*, from which four radio teams had been assigned to *2./FschSanAbt.7*.

conducted the most urgent surgery. The wounded from the aid station and the collection points near Heraklion were eventually brought to Tsalikaki.

Around the airfield at Heraklion the fighting gained in intensity again at daybreak. It was only during the course of the afternoon that *I./FschJgRgt.1* arrived from the area around Gournes behind the elevation at the eastern rim of the Karteros depression, where on its northern spur, the observation post of the regimental staff was positioned. The battalion was so delayed because it had waited in vain for the return of a platoon from the 1st Company under *Leutnant* Lindenberg, which during the evening of 20 May had pursued enemy soldiers that were retiring from the wireless station near Gournes.[23]

Oberst Bräuer ordered *Major* Walther to attack the airfield with his battalion right away. Covered only by the fire of a few heavy machine-guns, the three rifle companies deployed from their approach march and traversed the circa 800m-wide Karteros Valley. On the slope ascending to the elevation east of the airfield, they were hit by the fire of almost invisible field positions of the defenders and from mortars. Incurring heavy losses, the assault was brought to a stand-still. Thereupon the companies retired to the bottom of the valley, where they found at least some cover.

At daybreak the platoon of *Oberleutnant* Graf von Blücher, which had penetrated a short distance into the positions of the 2nd Black Watch in the night, could be observed from all sides, and in the course of the morning was annihilated. Only very few of the men, most of them wounded, managed to escape toward the east into the vineyards and the stone huts that were scattered there. *Oberleutnant* Graf von Blücher was among the killed.[24] The few men from *II./FschJgRgt.1* who had held out isolated in the Greek barracks south-west of the airfield were also overwhelmed by noon.

Late in the afternoon the paratroopers east of the airfield were resupplied from the air by several Ju 52s that dropped ammunition, medical material and replacements for the lost heavy weapons.

In the evening of the second day of the fighting around Heraklion *Oberst* Bräuer ordered the end of all offensive actions against the airfield for the time being. Thereupon *I./FschJgRgt.1*, which had been joined by the remnants of *II./FschJgRgt.1* and its commander, was withdrawn behind the elevation east of the Karteros depression. Here it prepared for the defence.

During the evening of 21 May, and contrary to *Luftflotte 4*, the command of *XI.Flieger-Korps* assessed the crisis of the battle for Crete as over.[25] Despite the still anticipated strong counter-attack the area around Maleme was regarded as under firm control after the arrival of three battalion-sized formations and numerous heavy weapons. There was also a good chance to further reinforce *Gruppe West* with forces of three to four battalion-sized combat groups, by landings from the air and the sea in the course of the coming day. Following

---

23   In a letter to the author, Kurt Barank, who was a member of *I./FschJgRgt.1* on Crete, stated that during the night 20/21 May, when resting, the platoon was surrounded by Greek soldiers. These had attacked at dawn, when all but two of the 36 men of the platoon had been killed.

24   The death of *Oberleutnant* Graf von Blücher is all the more tragic in that both of his brothers were also killed as paratroopers during the fighting around Heraklion. The parents were informed about the death of their sons only four weeks later, upon the return of *FschJgRgt.1* from Crete.

25   See also the appreciation of the situation of *XI.Flieger-Korps*, memorized by Student in Götzel, pp.275-280.

the arrival of *Oberst* Ramcke the command of the *SturmRgt.* was again in firm hands and the presence of the HQ of *5.Gebirgs-Division* from 22 May on was expected to positively affect the cohesion of operations in the west of Crete, Student was confident that the attack toward the east could be pushed forward on the coming day. Even if *Gruppe Mitte* was unable to revert to the attack, its air bridgehead constituted a veritable thorn in the side of the enemy and tied down a number of his forces, which thereby remained unavailable to settle the situation at Maleme. Student regarded the role of *Gruppe Ost* at Heraklion in a similar way. However the situation at Rethymnon remained unclear to him; only pilot-reports were available about the ongoing fighting and the airstrip was still in the possession of the enemy. In order to realize his intention of the conquest of Crete from the west, he had to rely for all other contested areas upon the valor and endurance of his *Fallschirmtruppe*. However their adequate re-supply from the air and their support by combat aircraft was mandatory for this task. His request to fly to Crete on 22 May was forwarded in the course of the day, as he wished to gain a personal picture of the situation there, but he was was turned down by *Generaloberst* Löhr, probably on the orders of Göring. Student thereupon instructed his Chief of Staff, *Generalmajor* Schlemm, to fly to Crete on the morning of 22 May for an appreciation of the situation and to report back to him in the evening.

22 May

At dawn ten motorised sailing boats of the unfortunate *1.leichte Seetransportstaffel* made fast progress to the port of the island Milos and came under the protection of the AAA batteries positioned there. The *2.leichte Seetransportstaffel* steamed on toward the north-eastern coast of Crete on a more easterly course. The officer in charge, *Fregattenkapitän* von Lipinski, was quite certain about reaching the landing beach during daylight under the protection from the *Luftwaffe*. Indeed, the first two groups from *StG 2 'Immelmann'* had taken off from the airfield at Molai in order to attack the British naval units, which the day before had been detected in the waters north-west of Crete.[26] This was Force C, four cruisers and four destroyers, which during the night had searched the waters north of Heraklion for German convoys in vain, and now was en-route to rendezvous with the main force. At about 0700hrs it came across the *2.leichte Seetransportstaffel* 25 sea miles south of Milos. The German convoy was escorted by the Italian torpedo boat *Saggitario*. While under attack from two British cruisers, it attempted to provide the possibility of escape for the convoy by laying a smoke screen. Just as Force C was ready to commence its work of destruction and had already sunk one of the motorised sailing boats, the Ju 88s from *I./LG 1* appeared over the action. The German bombers immediately attacked the British warships through a barrage of anti-aircraft guns. Alternating with the Do 17's from *KG 2* the Ju 88s attacked for more than three hours, causing serious damage to the cruisers *Naiad* and *Carlisle*. Force C now ceased to pursue the German convoy and steamed toward the Straits of Kythira, where it was to meet the main force, which, after the integration of Forces A, B and D and of reinforcements from Alexandria, now consisted of two battle ships, five cruisers and 19 destroyers. By that time the main force was being attacked by every combat aircraft the *VIII.Flieger-Korps* was able to muster. Even Me 109s in the role of fighter bombers were employed. Between 1230hrs and 1600hrs the cruiser *Gloucester* and

---

26   The discussion of the actions of the British Mediterranean Fleet and the German *VIII.Flieger-Korps* on 22 May and the days thereafter is primarily based on the evaluation of Playfair, pp. 136-140, and Bekker, pp.278-281.

the destroyer *Greyhound* were sunk and the battleship *Warspite* was heavily damaged. Now the British naval force, including Force C, steered toward Alexandria in order to escape from the range of most of the German bombers. On the way the battle ship *Valiant* was also damaged by a bomb hit. The cruiser *Fiji*, which reached the waters west of Crete belatedly after a rescue operation, was seriously hit by the bomb from a single Me 109 fighter-bomber at 1745hrs, and at 1915hrs was sunk by the bomb of another Me 109. In the meantime the German *2.leichte Seetransportstaffel*, after the loss of but one of its boats, safely reached Milos again.

The cost paid by the British Mediterranean Fleet for its employment on 22 May was high. However it had ensured that for a number of days the German command did not dare to reinforce or supply its troops on Crete from the sea. As long as was considered impossible to keep the British Mediterranean Fleet away from the waters north of Crete, the battle for the island had to be fought exclusively with troops brought along and supplied by air.

The German *leichte Seetransportstaffeln* were now ordered back to Piraeus. The units suited for transfer to Crete by air, mainly from the parachute and mountain troops but also motorcycle infantry and the transport squadron of the *XI.Flieger-Korps*, were speedily assigned to the air-commander.

During the night 21/22 May, in the operational area of *Gruppe West*, the *SturmRgt.* was able to reorganize its forces along the line eastern edge of the airfield–east of Maleme–eastern slope of Hill 107–east of Xamoudochori. On its left flank was *Kampfgruppe Gericke* with the 13th and 14th companies of the *SturmRgt.*, the remnants of *III./SturmRgt.*, parts of *3./FschFlaMGBtl.7*, *4./FschJgRgt.1* (*Oberleutnant* Kiebitz), and *7./GebJgRgt.100*, altogether about 650 men. On its right flank was *Kampfgruppe Stentzker*, with *II./SturmRgt.* (less its 6th Company) and Klein's parachute company, altogether totalling 550 men. The remainder of *I./SturmRgt.*, as far as they were part of *Gruppe West*, were gathered under the command of *Oberstabsarzt* Dr. Neumann. The sub-units of *FschPzJgAbt.7* which were not assigned to *Kampfgruppe Gericke*, about 140 men, were being kept available as *Kampfgruppe Schmitz*. *1./FschArtAbt.7* under *Hauptmann* Schram now disposed of two guns for general fire-support.

Oberst Utz, in agreement with *Oberst* Ramcke, took over the western and southern part of the operational area. *16./SturmRgt.* in sentry posts about 5km south of Tavronitis along the road toward Kandanos and *6./SturmRgt.*, advancing toward Kastelli, were placed under his command. *8./GebJgRgt.100* was kept ready for the reinforcement of positions toward Kandanos.[27]

At dawn on 22 May *Kampfgruppen Gericke* and *Stentzler* moved forward toward the east and with their forward elements reached the high ground south of Pirgos and the western edge of this village. Here they were halted by fire from elevated positions. Almost along the entire line of *Gruppe West* the advance of enemy forces now occurred.[28] Upon a report from *Kampfgruppe Stentzler* about enemy tanks in front of Maleme, two anti-tank guns from *FschPzJgAbt.7* were brought forward to the eastern edge of that village. However the

---

27   For the task-organization of *Gruppe West* during the night 21/22 May see also KTB Kreta des *LL-Sturmregiments*.

28   As German sources hardly mention the counter-attack of the 5th (NZ) Brigade, its description mainly depends upon Davin, pp.218-222.

report turned out to be incorrect. Instead, a single tank advancing along the coastal road toward Pirgos was put out of action by one of the two anti-tank guns there. 'A' company of the New Zealand 20th Battalion managed to push back parts of Kiebitz's company, which was deployed along the coastal strip east of the airfield. They reached the north-eastern corner of the airfield, from where they fired with anti-tank rifles at the landing transport aircraft. The counter-attacking *7./GebJgRgt.100* forced the enemy to retire after a short time. The two companies from the 20th Battalion, which followed behind the lead unit, were intercepted in the north-eastern part of Pirgos by about 80 paratroopers from the 5th and 6th companies of *FschJgRgt.2*, under *Oberleutnant* Nagele, and the remainders of the medical platoons under *Unterarzt* Dr. Schuster. The combat caused considerable losses on both sides before the enemy companies, hit by a counter-attack into their right flank, were forced to retreat toward the south-east across the coastal road behind the 28th (Maori) Battalion. This unit fought forward to a line, stretching from the eastern outskirts of Pirgos, to the forward bounds of the defensive area of the 23rd Battalion. The advance of the 28th Battalion to that line had troublesome effects on the Germans as the Maoris, from the right flank, were able to direct their fire to the eastern edge of Maleme. This was primarily felt by the crews of the two anti-tank guns positioned there – by about 1100hrs all but one had become casualties from machine-gun and sniper fire.

At 0600hrs the New Zealand 21st Battalion attacked with three companies against the right flank of *Kampfgruppe Stentzler*. It succeeded in re-occupying the abandoned station of 252 AMES at around 0730hrs, and at about 0900hrs dislodged the sentries of the paratroopers from Xamoudochori. Two of its companies advanced toward Vlakheronitis, however, they were forced to ground by defensive fire about 600m in front of the village.

At about 1130hrs the command of *Gruppe West* assessed that the attack by the enemy has lost its impetus for the time being.[29] The initial successes had partly come about by the fact that the exhausted paratroopers had been surprised while asleep.[30] As the enemy was now posted with relatively fresh troops close by, *Oberst* Ramcke considered that an immediate counter-attack would lead to unexceptable losses. He therefore decided to wait for the arrival of further reinforcements by air in order to outflank the enemy in front of *Gruppe West* by envelopment from the south, as planned. He was confident he could retain his present positions with the forces available. *3./SturmRgt.*, by gathering its dispersed parts, was brought up to somewhat more than 50 men, and still led by Dr. Weitzel, being placed under the command of *Kampfgruppe Stentzler* in the evening. It was to join this force on Hill 107 the following morning.

Between 1000hrs and 1200hrs the reinforced *I./GebJgRgt.85* under *Major* Dr. Treck was landed at Maleme airfield under the fire of enemy artillery. Again transport aircraft

---

29   Davin, p.213ff, offers as an explanation for this situation – that the relief of the NZ 20th Battalion in its positions by the Australian 2/7 Infantry Battalion had taken so long, that the former had arrived around Pirgos only piecemeal.

30   Davin, p.213, mentions a report describing the German *Fallschirmtruppe* as "helpless" during the hours of the night. This assessment, although somewhat exaggerated, could hold true in view of the shortcomings in the training of the *Wehrmacht* for combat at night, in urban areas and in extended woods prior to and during the the first years of the war.

were destroyed by direct hits or crashed during landing, but there was little loss among the mountain infantry. The battalion was placed subordinate to *Oberst* Utz, who, in line with the intended course of action, immediately dispatched it for the enveloping thrust in a south-easterly direction against the dominating Hill 259 (Mount Monodhendri). As the bird flies the distance to the objective was only 10km, but the route led through rugged terrain with almost no information available about the enemy there. From Hill 259 the distance to the command post of *Gruppe Mitte* was a mere 3km. The battalion, however, had no mission to establish contact there as after the occupation of Hill 259, it was to turn toward the coast to pave the way for *SturmRgt.*, advancing along the coastal road.

At about 1630hrs the pressure by *Gruppe West* was also increased against the enemy who had advanced beyond Xamoudochori.[31] The enemy initially retreated to this village but around 1500hrs withdrew to its original positions in the east.

Shortly after 1200hrs the reinforced *I./GebJgRgt.100* under *Major* Schrank was also airlanded. The enemy artillery still fired on the airfield, but not continuously, as infantry guns of the mountain troops from Hill 107 and dive-bomber attacks forced the enemy gunners to take cover. The newly-arrived mountain infantry battalion assembled, and was then dispatched at 1500hrs behind *I./GebJgRgt.85* for the southern envelopment of the enemy between *Gruppen West* and *Mitte*.

Following close behind the air transport formation which landed *I./GebJgRgt.100*, 17 Ju 52s landed with *4./FschSanAbt.7* aboard. This unit operated the field hospital of the parachute force. Five of these aircraft which had to land on the beach, because of the congestion at the airfield, were seriously damaged but with little harm to their passengers. The hospital equipment was transported to Tavronitis under artillery fire. There the main dressing station of *3./FschSanKp.7* was taken over by the new arrivals and expanded. By 1800hrs the first seriously wounded had received surgery by specialists flown in. Even prior to the arrival of *4./FschSanAbt.7*, *Oberarzt* Dr. Schuster had reported at the main dressing station for duty, after he and some of his medical soldiers managed to fight through from Pirgos.

Shortly after midday, *Generalmajor* Schlemm with a small staff and a radio team also landed on the airfield. After a short situation briefing by Ramcke, he directed the further flow of forces and supplies in action with the Corps HQ in Athens.

Late in the afternoon the New Zealand 28th (Maori) Battalion retired from Pirgos and the area immediately south of the village to the high ground around Kondomari, in order to escape the increasing German fire, however one of its companies moved back to its original positions around Platanias. On the way it came across a number of paratroopers south of the Platanias Bridge and captured some of them.[32] *Kampfgruppe Gericke*, following close behind the retiring Maoris, occupied Pirtgos where they established contact with the paratroopers under *Oberleutnant* Nagele, who held out there and had considerably disturbed the counter-attack of the New Zealand 20th Battalion.

---

31 Although nowhere mentioned in the German after-action reports, it had probably been the as yet-uncommitted 5th and 6th companies from *II./GebJgRgt.100*, which had additionally been employed in that area.

32 It is quite certain that these paratroopers, most of them wounded, were stragglers from *III./SturmRgt.*

As the 20th Battalion moved back into the northern part of the positions of the 23rd Battalion near Dhaskaliana, the 28th Battalion occupied the ground in front of it, and the remainder of the 22nd Battalion moved into the gap between the 21st and 23rd Battalions, five depleted New Zealand infantry battalions[33] were positioned in an area of about 8km in length and 1km in depth just about 3km away from Hill 107.

In the afternoon, Major General Freyberg believed the situation of the New Zealand Division to be acceptable, and at 1700hrs ordered it to continue the counter-attack. In addition to the troops from the 5th (New Zealand) Brigade, he had planned to use the 4th (New Zealand) Brigade with the 18th Battalion and the Australian 2/7 Infantry Battalion as well as the 1st Welch, which was also assigned to this brigade. The command of the New Zealand Division, however, arrived at a different picture of the situation. Without obtaining a personal impression on the battlefield or interrogating his commanders, Brigadier Hargest reported that his troops were exhausted and after the 4th Brigade had referred to the threat of a breakthrough by the Germans in a direction toward the coastal road, Brigadier Puttick came to believe that the counter-attack could not be resumed. He passed his view on early in the evening to Freyberg, and urged him to agree to a withdrawal of the 5th Brigade. Freyberg initially remained indecisive and therefore shortly prior to 2100hrs sent his chief of staff to the command post of the New Zealand Division. There a final decision was made to move back the 5th Brigade, leapfrogging during the night 22/23 May on the line of the forces fighting at Galatas.

In his situation report to General Wavell in the afternoon, Freyberg requested to land the British 2nd Queen's Royal Rgt not as planned by Middle East Command at Timbakion, but at Souda Bay. General Wavell did not comply with this request. He did, however, announce the employment of fighters over Crete for 23 May and their subsequent stationing on the island. Differing from Freyberg's request, he proposed to reinforce the defence around Chania with troops from Rethymnon and replace these forces from Heraklion, once the 1st Argyll and Sutherland Highlanders arrived.[34] Wavell obviously accepted Freyberg's decision to withdraw his forces from the area east of Maleme, which the latter reported to him during the night, justifying this measure with the improvement of the force-ratio between CREFORCE and the German forces in the area around Galatas.[35]

In the operational area of *Gruppe West*, GebPiBtl.95 (*Major* Schätte) was airlanded in the afternoon. Together with it, a battery with six mountain guns from *GebArtRgt.95* and the second half of *1./FschArtAbt.7* arrived. At this time the airfield of Maleme was hardly ever under artillery fire.[36] The primary hindrance for its use now constituted the c 100 destroyed

---

33　The 21st Battalion, which had arrived from the Greek mainland already reduced in strength, reported losses in killed, wounded and missing for the period 20-22 May of 3 officers and 114 other ranks.

34　This proposal can be considered as an example of interference of superior commands into the responsibilities of a subordinate, which were quite common in the Commonwealth ground forces at that time as a consequence of the order-oriented command and control principles.

35　See also Davin, pp.243-244.

36　New Zealand sources give as reasons the lack of ammunition for A and B Troops of 27th Battery, and the effects of the German air attacks. The battery from the Australian 2/3 Field Regiment, which also was to shell the airfield, had not yet been brought forward.

or seriously damaged Ju 52s. These were pushed to the edges of the airfield but still reduced the space for landings and take-offs. The management of the arrivals and departures was now smoothly executed by the airfield command under *Major* Snowadski, which successfully continued to remove crashing transport aircraft quickly from the runway.

GebPiBtl.95 was ordered to relieve the parts of *GebJgRgt.100* which were employed as a security screen toward the south and the west, and to reconnoiter with a company toward Kastelli, Deliana (about 12km south-west of Kolimbari), and Kandanos.

With the transfer by air of three battalions of combat troops, some independent units and elements for command and control, *Generalmajor* Conrad had achieved a remarkable organizational feat, all the more valuable, as this was accomplished by a quickly diminishing number of transport aircraft, some of which had to be diverted for re-supply flights to other air bridgeheads.

The command of *VIII.Flieger-Korps* also made use of the improving situation in the area around Maleme, as in the afternoon they dispatched an air control team. This considerably reduced the reaction times for the air support of *Gruppe West*.

In the early evening the commander of *5.Gebirgs-Division* and his battle HQ with its radio equipment arrived at the airfield on three Ju 52s. Subsequent to a briefing about the general situation from *Generalmajor* Schlemm and a briefing by *Oberst* Ramcke about the specific situation of *Gruppe West*, *Generalmajor* Ringel assumed command over *Gruppen West* and *Mitte*. He approved of the initiated envelopment movements, but ordered the attack of *Gruppe West* along the coastal strip, along the high ground close to the coast between Platanias and Ay Marina. Here the forces were to wait until the terrain in front of them was seized by troops from the *5.Gebirgs-Division*, advancing from the south.

In the extremely difficult and waterless terrain, the enveloping thrust of *I./GebJgRgt.85* had progressed just 11km to Hill 263, about 6km south-east of Maleme. At this time *I./ GebJgRgt.100* passed the line of sentries of *Gruppe West* to the south-east of its operational area. During the night an enemy force, approaching on trucks along the coastal road in front of Pirgos, was repelled by elements of *Kampfgruppe Gericke* and suffered heavy losses.[37]

Throughout 22 May *6./SturmRgt.* advanced in the direction of Kastelli. Throughout the course of the day it was reinforced with a motorcycle patrol from the mountain troops. Efficiently supported by fighters and bombers, the company was able to push back Cretan irregulars, resisting at Drapanias. During the further advance the strong occupation by the enemy of Kastelli and of a factory, located 2km to the east, was recognized. While the advance was stopped for the night, the company from *GebPiBtl.95* which was directed toward Kastelli, reached the height of the pass south-west of Kolimbari.

The inactivity of the enemy opposite *Gruppe Mitte* on 22 May was utilized by *Oberst* Heidrich to further solidify the air bridgehead, and to improve the situation for the link-up with *Gruppe West*. At 0600hrs and under their own initiative paratroopers from *7./ FschJgRgt.3* probed against Pink Hill but after initial successes they were hit by a counter-attack of Greek soldiers and armed civilians, and were thrown back in disorder with considerable losses.

---

37   It was the Australian 2/1 MG Coy which was sent forward as reinforcement for the counter-attack and which, through ignorance of the actual situation, had run into the Germans. It had lost all of its vehicles and equipment.

Support was provided for *I./FschJgRgt.3* when fighter-bombers attacked the heights south of Galatas between 0815 and 0915hrs. Re-supply from the air increased and most drops landed within the boundaries of the air bridgehead. A patrol from *FschPiBtl.7*, bypassing the heights at Galatas in the west, was able to get close to the coastal road near Ay Marina in the early morning without enemy contact. Upon its report, at 1600hrs *Major* Heilmann was ordered to advance with a combat group via Stalos to the coastal road, to block it from the enemy, and to seek contact with approaching forces of *Gruppe West*. The combat group was composed of the remainder of *III./FschJgRgt.3*, parts of *1./FschPiBtl.7* and a heavy machine-gun platoon from *2./FschMGBtl.7*, altogether 150 men and nine officers. The group departed a short time later, also bypassing the heights at Galatas in the west. Occasionally fired at by outposts of the enemy, by nightfall the advance party had reached the area west of Stalos. As the force became widely dispersed in the heavily broken and rugged terrain and some of the pack animals picked up in the drop zone had fallen into steep ravines, *Major* Heilmann decided to stop to reorganize and rest during the hours of darkness.

At about 1400hrs *Major* Derpa requested he take over the sector south of Hill 116, baptized 'Getreide-Höhe' by the Germans, with his *II./FschJgRgt.3*. *Oberst* Heidrich agreed but instructed *Major* Derpa to only reconnoiter against the hill and explicitly reserved the order for an attack for himself. But yet again faulty interpretation by a subordinate prevailed and *Major* Derpa ignored the instruction received; as such the point of his 6th Company (*Oberleutnant* Stangenberg) attacked Hill 116 at about 1745hrs. The attacking paratroopers initially gained the hill but were then beaten back in vigorous close-combat taking heavy losses. *Major* Derpa as well as the officer commanding the 5th Company, *Oberleutnant* Staab, were both mortally wounded in the action.[38] The 6th Company, which prior to the attack had been available in almost full strength, was now heavily depleted. *Oberleutnant* Stangenberg now assumed command of *II./FschJgRgt.3* for the execution of the original mission. The sector of *I./FschJgRgt.3*, except for occasional firefights between patrols and sentries, remained quiet throughout the day.

In the sector of *FschPiBtl.7* it was mainly its 2nd Company, in positions on the ridge south of Agia, which continually came under rifle fire from Greek soldiers and civilians. The attempt to silence the enemy by fire from an 8cm mortar from *2./FschMGBtl.7* failed and was answered by artillery fire from the area around Chania. Three of the anti-tank guns of the platoon that were assigned to the *FschPiBtl.7* were positioned at the water reservoir and north-west of it in the morning. From there they were able to engage targets at long range. In the course of the day the parachute engineer battalion succeeded in salvaging the wounded and supplies with two trucks, which had been left behind at its former command post.

Although the inconsiderate action by *Major* Derpa had resulted in an unnecessary weakening of the combat power of *Gruppe Mitte*, *Oberst* Heidrich, following the receipt of supplies, began the consolidation of the positions of *I./FschJgRgt.3* and *FschPiBtl.7* and the gains of terrain toward the north. Consequently by the evening of 22 May he could finally think about the planning and continuation of his mission.

---

38 *Major* Derpa died of his wounds on 28 May.

East of Rethymnon *Kampfgruppen* Kroh and Wiedemann, the latter now led by the commander of the parachute machine-gun battalion, remained separated. After the mission of the western group to seize Rethymnon during the evening of 20 May proved to be impracticable, it fought for its survival. Snipers on the high ground south of Perivolia and harassing artillery fire prevented the enlargement of the pocket and impeded physical contact with *9./FschJgRgt.2* on the *'Kapellenhöhe'*.

In the morning five Bren Gun Carriers, approaching along the coastal road from the east, turned off again before they came into the effective range of the recoilless guns of *2./FschArtAbt.7*, which were positioned along the eastern edge of Perivolia. An attack by dive bombers, which indicated targets by use of direction panels from the ground, provided some respite for the defenders for a short time. However the ability of the high command in Athens to obtain a clear picture of the situation in the area east of Rethymnon was unsuccessful. *Hauptmann* Kleye from the staff of *XI.Flieger-Korps*, who had taken off early in the morning in a Fieseler Storch from Athens to the operational area of *Gruppe Sturm*, was forced to conduct an emergency landing in enemy-occupied terrain and was taken prisoner. A German sea plane which landed close to the beach near the eastern part of Perivolia in the morning was so seriously damaged by machine-gun and artillery fire that it was unable to take off again. Its crew managed to get ashore in a rubber boat and carried with them the machine-guns from the plane. They were subsequently integrated into the ranks of the parachute battery. This unit was to face a particularly dreadful day. A shock troop which dispatched from it against the elevation south of its position was stopped by fire in the outlying terrain. In a counter-attack by Greek soldiers that skilfully made use of the ground and in which they feigned being friendly troops, created initial confusion, causing three machine-gun teams from the parachuteartillery, which remained forward of the positions of the battery, to be killed. Only one man survived. At nightfall the enemy continued his advance toward Perivolia, the battery-commander *Oberleutnant* Thorbecke, was wounded. Consequently an officer from the parachute infantry assumed command over the artillerymen and ordered them to make the guns unusable by removing their firing blocks and moved them back some distance into the village. After an attempt by the Greeks to break into the village at about 2300hrs was beaten back in close-combat the artillerymen prepared to reoccupy their former positions in the course of the night, and to make the guns ready for use again.

During the time *2./FschArtAbt.7* was under pressure, the enemy also attacked the adjoining positions of the 9th and 11th companies from *III./FschJgRgt.2* in Perivolia. By nightfall two thrusts by the Greeks had been repelled. However physical contact with parts of the 9th Company, defending the *'Kapellenhöhe'*, was lost.

Simultaneously with the attack against the south-eastern part of Perivolia, the enemy hit the now uncovered left flank of the paratroopers on the *'Kapellenhöhe'*. These were forced to fall back into the cemetery on top of the hill. While the combat was still raging in Perivolia, the commanding officer of *9./FschJgRgt.2*, *Oberleutnant* Begemann, appeared on the *'Kapellenhöhe'*. He was of the opinion that all of Perivolia had fallen into enemy hands and the defenders of the hill therefore had to fight through toward the west. With a group of his soldiers he now undertook a sortie. The group ended up in front of the positions of the 11th Company entirely unaware of the company's presence. During the 'blue-on-blue' engagement which developed in complete darkness, both sides took losses before the error was detected. The paratroopers from the 9th Company, who held on in the cemetery, commanded by *Leutnant* Kühl, in the meantime succeeded in beating off an attempted break-in by the enemy and cleared the *'Kapellenhöhe'* by a counter-attack, although they took severe losses due to these efforts.[39]

On 21 May *Kampfgruppe Kroh* had retired to the olive oil factory and the few buildings of Stavromenos, and on the morning of 22 May was under fire from Australian artillery from 0600hrs. An infantry attack building up at about 1000hrs did not come to fruition after the advancing Australian company suffered considerable losses from the fire of an 8cm mortar during the approach. Another thrust by about 40 Australian soldiers, conducted after preparatory artillery fire, was repelled at close quarters again, causing heavy losses for the attackers.[40]

Major Kroh was present in the olive oil factory and was particularly worried about the ever-increasing number of wounded and the lack of ammunition and food. However, up to now, the route toward the east was still open, as shock troops under *Oberleutnant* Rosenberg and *Leutnant* Fellner pushed from Stavromenos along the road for about 1.5km and occupied the area around a farm (nicknamed 'mortar-house' by the Australians). For the time being this action prevented the full encirclement of *Kampfgruppe Kroh*. However there was still no contact with the elements of the group, mainly from *2./FschJgRgt.2*, which still held out to the south-west.

In the area near Heraklion *Major* Schulz assembled his troops some distance away during the night 21/22 May, near the main dressing station of *2./FschSanAbt.7*. He also established contact with *II./FschJgRgt.2*, which now was subordinate to him. He intended to attack into Heraklion again on the following morning. For this operation he reinforced his *III./FschJgRgt.1* with two platoons from the 7th Company and a heavy machine-gun platoon from the 8th Company of *Hauptmann* Schirmer's battalion, as well as with the anti-tank platoon, which after the attack returned to the latter. Before the attack could be initiated an enemy officer with a flag of truce appeared in front of the German troops. He carried with him a request for surrender from the British sector commander. *Major* Schulz declined the request and sent the officer back with the reply that the German *Wehrmacht* had a mission to take Crete and that it was going to accomplish exactly this.

---

39   On the side of the enemy, the actions around Perivolia on 22 May were carried out by the Greek 5th Regiment, gendarmes from Perivolia and groups of irregulars, led by Greek officers, as stated in the original war diaries of the Australian 2/1 and 2/11 Infantry Battalions. *Australia in the War 1939-1945*, Series One, p.264, states that the Australian 2/11 Infantry Battalion had not been involved as a whole until 23 May.

40   This thrust had failed mainly because the c.200 Greek soldiers who were also assigned had not appeared at the decisive moment.

The attack against Heraklion commenced at 1000hrs. However it ceased after a short period.[41] The reinforcing sub-units returned to *II./FschJgRgt.2*, except the heavy machine-gun platoon, which remained positioned opposite the west gate of Heraklion. The reinforced *III./FschJgRgt.1* now provided protection against the town and toward the south-east.

Late in the afternoon two Matilda II tanks and four Bren Gun Carriers with infantry[42] suddenly appeared along the road from Timbakion in front of the positions of parts of *II./FschJgRgt.2*. While the 7th Company was able to force the Carriers to turn back and repel the dismounted infantry, the two heavily armored infantry tanks carried on and entered Heraklion but took no part in the fighting.[43]

The parts of *Kräftegruppe Bräuer* that were assembled east of the airfield set up defensive positions, as ordered by their commander, along the elevation east of the Karteros depression and up to the coast.

As earlier in other contested areas on Crete in the morning of 22 May the command of *Oberst* Bräuer saw itself confronted with the knowledge that the combat on the island had to be fought under conditions for which neither the commanders nor their troops had been prepared. A detachment was sent back to the area around Gournes to look after a number of paratroopers, who had been injured during the landing on 20 May and who had been left behind under the care of a medical soldier, when the troops had departed for the airfield. When the detachment arrived it found the corpses of 12 paratroopers, among them the medical soldier. Most of them had been cruelly mutilated. The injured men, armed only with their pistols, had been ambushed by Cretan civilians, who killed and mutilated them.[44]

The combat actions east of Heraklion airfield on this day were confined to firefights and occasional bombardments by enemy artillery. The last small groups of paratroopers who held out near the eastern edge of the airfield were pushed to the east by troops of the 2nd Black Watch. However these were prevented from following up by fire from the elevation east of the Karteros Valley.

Uninterrupted wireless communication with the command of the *XI.Flieger-Korps* warranted that the requested supplies and the replacements for lost heavy infantry weapons could be delivered by air to a drop zone, well outside of the range of the enemy's anti-aircraft guns, during the evening.

---

41   The available sources provide no information as to whether the attack had been stopped by orders of *Oberst* Bräuer or because of the strong resistance from Heraklion, which in the meantime had received parts of the British Yorks and Lancs as reinforcements.

42   It was the two Matildas, which shortly prior to the German attack, had been landed in the port of Timbakion. The Bren Gun Carriers and the infantry came from the 1st Argyll and Sutherland Highlanders, which was ordered to reinforce the defence at Heraklion.

43   On 23 May the two Matildas, together with six remaining operational light tanks of the Heraklion command sector and two 75mm guns, had been loaded on a lighter and had been brought to Souda. They were later employed in the withdrawal of CREFORCE. Therefore, no light tanks appeared against *Kräftegruppe Bräuer* from 23 May on.

44   The event has been confirmed by the only survivor of the massacre, who rested some distance away from his fellow-soldiers and was not detected. The man was saved by a Cretan farmer and after a long illness was returned to the German occupation force on Crete. Later, he had joined his parent unit. Back in Germany any statement regarding the fate of the 12 paratroopers as well as that of Lindenberg's platoon, was forbidden by *Major* Walther. The author is in possession of reports about the events by the former orderly officer of *I./FschJgRgt.1* on Crete and by a former member of *2./FschJgRgt.1* at that time.

23 May

In the early hours of 23 May and under the cover of darkness, two British destroyers[45] bombarded the area around Maleme, sinking the only motorised sailing boat of the *1.leichte Seetransportstaffel* which had almost made it into the Bight of Kissamo.[46] The Germans soon realized that the British Mediterranean Fleet, despite its losses the day before, was not willing to stay out of the waters north of Crete. The damage caused on the ground by the naval bombardment was negligible, but raised some unrest among the troops preparing for the attack and the receipt of further reinforcements.

The evening before *Generalmajor* Ringel had organized the troops available to him for the continuation of the attack into three groups:

- *Gruppe Oberst Utz*, with the three available mountain infantry battalions,[47] for the enveloping thrust in the south.
- *Gruppe Oberst Ramcke*, with the *SturmRgt.*, for the attack along the coastal strip
- *Gruppe Major Schätte*, with *GebPiBtl.95*, for the advance into the extreme west of Crete.

He had instructed Ramcke not to advance beyond the dominating range protruding toward the coast about one km west of Platanias, and there to wait out the effects of the enveloping thrust by *Gruppe Utz*. Ramcke divided his force into four parts:

- On the left, *Kampfgruppe Gericke*, with the majority of *IV./SturmRgt.*, into which the remainders of *5./* and *6./FschJgRgt.2* were integrated. It was supported by the guns of *1./FschArtAbt.7*.
- On the right, *Kampfgruppe Stentzler*, with *II./SturmRgt.*, less its 6th Company, but reinforced with Klein's company.
- A *Kampfgruppe*, mainly consisting of *1./* and *3./FschPzJgAbt.7*, commanded by *Hauptmann* Schmitz, was inserted between *Kampfgruppen Gericke* and *Stentzler* and was to move along the coastal road.
- A *Kampfgruppe* to the strength of 2 companies, formed by the remainder of *I./SturmRgt.* and from paratroopers who had been dropped as individuals together with *Oberst* Ramcke on 21 May. Commanded by *Oberleutnant* Stoltz[48] this was to follow behind *Kampfgruppe Stentzler* as reserve.

When *Hauptmann* Gericke received reports about the retrospective movements of the enemy in front of his sector he ordered his *Kampfgruppe* to attack after preparatory fire. *Kampfgruppen Schmitz* and *Stentzler* immediately joined the attack. Delayed only

---

45 The destroyers *Kelly* and *Kashmir* were summoned from Malta. Some hours later, during their withdrawal, they were sunk by 24 Ju 87s from *1./StG 2* south-west of Crete.

46 In *Die Gebirgstruppe* No. 4/1978, pp.21-15, Horbach reports that all of the passengers and the crew of the boat – a platoon each from *13./* and *14./GebJgRgt.100* and some shipwrecked soldiers who had been picked up on the way – were saved by air-sea rescue planes except four men. Before the boat had been sunk, a shock troop of 27 soldiers had already come ashore in rubber boats.

47 *7./* and *8./GebJgRgt.100* had been released from their security mission.

48 Stoltz was detached from the staff of *II./SturmRgt.* and had commanded one of the companies. The other one was taken over by *Oberleutnant* Jung. *Oberstabsarzt* Dr. Neumann and *Oberarzt* Dr. Weitzel had returned to their functions as medical officers.

for a short time by enemy rearguards, in the course of the late morning the three forward *Kampfgruppen* occupied the high ground west and south-west of the Platanias River.[49] From here the dressing stations of the New Zealand 21st and 23rd Battalions, with about 130 wounded and the medical and pastoral personnel for their care, fell into German hands. Though unusable, three field guns were captured south of Dhaskaliana and two more south of Kondomari, with which the enemy so effectively had shelled the airfield at Maleme.[50] Moreover a number of survivors from *III./SturmRgt.*, most of them wounded, were found on the way.

Against instructions from *Generalmajor* Ringel, to not advance beyond the spur west of Platanias, the forward parts of *Kampfgruppe Schmitz* and the leading elements of *Kampfgruppe Gericke* under *Oberleutnant* Trebes, moved on and against initially weak resistance, gained the area around the Platanias Bridge. An anti-tank gun was even pulled across the bridge.[51] All of a sudden heavy and precise artillery fire hit the area around this bridge.[52] The most advanced groups of German soldiers retreated some distance in disorder until they were halted, at gun point, by *Oberleutnant* Trebes. Behind the retreating paratroopers New Zealand infantrymen advanced toward the Platanias Bridge.[53] They took out the crew of the isolated anti-tank gun and captured a light anti-aircraft gun which had been left behind. Fired at by machine-guns and mortars the New Zealanders then retired to their original positions some distance away from the eastern bank of the Platanias. Quickly, parts of *Kampfgruppe Gericke* again occupied the ground which had been given up previously. During this action, contact was established with a group of paratroopers from *III./SturmRgt.* who had held out for two days in buildings at Gerani close to the beach. They had suffered some losses in engagements on this day with retiring soldiers of the New Zealand 28th Battalion, but were able to hold out.

In the afternoon *Kräftegruppe Ramcke* realized that the enveloping thrust by the mountain troops had not yet come to fruition.[54] Its *Kampfgruppen* were halted to rest and regroup and be re-supplied for the intended continuation of the attack on the coming morning. The high-angle weapons were relocated further forward and *Oberst* Ramcke moved his command post to the eastern edge of Modhion. Later in the afternoon, the

---

49   How weak the resistance opposite *II./SturmRgt.* on 23 May was is evident by its losses on this day: one KIA, four MIA and nine WIA.

50   The captured guns belonged to A and B Troops of the 27th Battery. They had to be left behind, as their towing-vehicles had not arrived in time.

51   Davin, pp. 257-258, reports 1015hrs as the time for this action. No time at all is mentioned in the war diary of the *SturmRgt.*

52   The observation post of this artillery was posted on the island Teodorhoi, 2km north-east of Platanias.

53   Davin, pp. 257-258, explains that the bridge had not been safeguarded at the time of the German thrust, as the two light tanks tasked with this mission had retired on their own and the two companies from the 21st and 28th Battalions which were to protect the bridge had not yet arrived. It had then been soldiers from the 28th Battalion on their way to their original defensive area, who had approached from the south.

54   Ringel, pp. 136-138, states that on 23 May at 0600hrs *I./GebJgRgt.85* had reported the seizure of Hill 259. When this report had turned out to be wrong and the enemy, assumed to be on Hill 259, were considered a threat to the left flank of *II./GebJgRgt.100*, approaching for the attack to the right of *I./GebJgRgt.85*, *Oberst* Utz in person interfered and forced the seizure of the height in the afternoon. After this action the exhausted men of *I./GebJgRgt.85* had been unable to continue the advance toward the north.

enemy artillery around Ay Marina[55] would be silenced by a mountain battery and by air attacks.

At dawn on 23 May, in the north-west of Crete, a shock troop of *6./SturmRgt.* advanced toward Kastelli and initially cleared the small settlement of Nopinia. Moving on into the extended terrain of a factory east of Kastelli, it came under heavy fire and was encircled by units of the enemy who defended the factory with about a battalion of Greek soldiers and a large number of irregulars. The encirclement caused the paratroopers two killed and five wounded, before they could be relieved, with difficulty, by approaching units of *GebPiBtl.95*. As previously near Kolimbari, the captured irregulars were shot on the spot at the end of the action.[56] The strong occupation of the factory and the eastern edge of Kastelli led *Major* Schätte, who was tasked with the attack against Kastelli, decide to postpone it to the next day after preceding air attacks.

3/GebPiBtl.95, which remained tasked with reconnaissance into the area around Kandanos, dispatched a combat patrol which consisted of mountain engineers and paratroopers from *16./SturmRgt.*[57] North of Kandanos, near the small settlement of Floria, in the evening the combat patrol fell into an ambush of Cretan armed civilians and was almost completely wiped out.[58]

Additional forces from the *5.Gebirgs-Division* also arrived on the airfield at Maleme on this day. These were *III./GebJgRgt.85*, *Oberst* Krakau, with more batteries from *GebArtRgt.95* under *Oberstleutnant* Wittmann and the first components of *GebPzJgAbt.95*. The delivery by air of the artillery guns and their ammunition was time-consuming and strenuous. Moreover it tied down considerable numbers of air transport aircraft.[59] The number of combat ready Ju 52s at the disposal of the *XI.Flieger-Korps* in the meantime dropped to 273 aircraft.

The R.A.F reappeared in the air space over Crete during the day. At about 1600 hrs, and again in the night, bombers of the R.A.F. from North Africa attacked the airfield

---

55 This was C Troop (four Italian 75mm guns) from the Australian 2/3 Field Regiment which was brought forward to support the counter-attack of the New Zealand Division, as well as two guns of C Troop of the NZ 27th Battery (one gun of the latter had been destroyed during the German counter-battery fire).

56 See also the after-action report of the *6./SturmRgt.*, enclosed in the war diary of the *Luftlande-Sturmregiment*.

57 This unit was placed subordinate to *GebPiBtl.95*.

58 The events around Kandanos during 23-26 May 1941 are based on two sources: the manuscript of *Hauptmann* (ret.) Manfred Rehm about the memorial for the *5.Gebirgs-Division* in Floria/Crete, planned for publication in the journal *Die Gebirgstruppe* No. 1/91, in which the after-action report of this division for 21, 22 and 24 May 1941 is reproduced. The description of the deployment of *Kradschützen-Btl.55* during the campaign in Greece 1941 is in Plato, pp. 135-135.

59 The ammunition at the required amount of 3,000 shells per gun had to be brought along from Wiener-Neustadt/Austria by rapidly-formed air transport formations from the *Luftwaffe* training organization, after it was discovered that the shells delivered in large amounts for the guns of the *22.(LL)Inf.Div.* during the preparation-phase for *Merkur* had been unsuitable for the more modern guns of the *5.Gebirgs-Division*, the stock of which the *12.Armee* had been used up during the campaign on the Greek mainland.

at Maleme. Utilizing surprise they were able to destroy some of the Ju 52s unloading during the afternoon attack.[60] Opposite the air bridgehead of *Gruppe Mitte*, the enemy again remained rather inactive during this day; the fighting was conducted on both sides mainly with artillery. Patrols of the parachute infantry and engineers that were probing forward met vigilant sentries. In the south armed civilians and small groups of Greek soldiers, occasionally infiltrating from the high ground in a northerly direction, engaged these troops in firefights. Late in the afternoon, advance elements of *II./GebJgRgt.100* took possession of the small settlement of Kufos after a short engagement with Greek soldiers and irregulars and were only 2km away from the southern edge of the air bridgehead of *Gruppe Mitte*. As ordered the battalion then turned north to Ay Marina. Only a patrol each from *II./FschJgRgt.3* and *II./GebJgRgt.100* met west of the air bridgehead for a short time. *Oberst* Heidrich still had to wait for a firm link with *Gruppe West*.

News about contact with *Gruppe West* also failed to arrive from *Kampfgruppe Heilmann*, from the area around Stalos. At 0545hrs the group reported that it had occupied Stalos without resistance. Shortly thereafter its parachute engineer platoon, positioned north-west of Stalos on outpost duty, was attacked from the direction of the coastal road. Soon the entire combat group was involved in the fighting. It was able to retain its positions until 0800hrs. Then the enemy, who had bypassed the engineer platoon and with the support of mortars, succeeded in entering Stalos. *Major* Heilmann now decided to retire in the direction of Maleme. An order by wireless combined with the information that the arrival of mountain troops from the south could be expected any moment, however requested Heilmann to remain in the occupied area. The *Kampfgruppe* now tenaciously held fast along the edge of Stalos and on the elevation north-west of it. At about 1630hrs the enemy discontinued his attack and retired toward the coastal road.[61] Around 1800hrs advance elements of *II./GebJgRgt.100*, approaching from the south, established contact with *Kampfgruppe Heilmann*. Here, *1./FschPiBtl.7* under *Oberleutnant* Griesinger, had suffered grievous losses in the preceding engagement.

East of Rethymnon *Kampfgruppen* Schulz and Kroh struggled to retain their positions. In the hedgehog defense at Perivolia *2./FschArtAbt.7* had reoccupied its original positions by dawn and rendered two of its guns ready to fire again with their lines of sight positioned toward the east. The groups of *9./FschJgRgt.2*, which on the previous night had retired from the 'Kapellenhöhe', returned. Here the defenders were under fire from a captured anti-tank gun which was manned by Australians. This fire forced the paratroopers to abandon the terrain around the chapel. In the afternoon fighter-bombers and a few dive bombers vigorously attacked Australian infantry to the strength of two companies, who appeared east of Perivolia near the beach. Taking advantage of the air attack, the parachute artillerymen moved forward against them. However the attack failed with considerable

---

60   Commonwealth sources differ in the number of attacking bombers. While *Australia in the War of 1939-1945*, Series One/ Army p.272 mentions only 4 Blenheims in the afternoon, Davin, p.254, speaks of 12 of these aircraft in the afternoon and "some Blenhein and Marylands" during the night and also mentions a report by the *5.Gebirgs-Division* to *XI.Flieger-Korps*, stating the loss of 6 Ju 52s in the afternoon and no losses during the night.

61   The attack against *Kampfgruppe Heilmann* had quite obviously been conducted to permit the forces retiring from the high ground south-east of Maleme an orderly passage toward the east along the coastal road.

losses due to the defensive fire of the Australians, who remained steadfast.[62] Led by their last combat-effective officer, the artillerymen now dug in about 300m east of Perivolia and the position was ordered to be defended to the last man. Only a sergeant with 13 other ranks could be spared for sentry duty toward the south. The firepower of *Kampfgruppe Schulz*, positioned next to them, was considerably strengthened with light mortars, machine-guns and a light anti-aircraft gun, which had been salvaged from the outlying terrain.

From 0600hrs *Kampfgruppe Kroh*, based in the olive oil factory, was again shelled by artillery.[63] At about 1000hrs, by mediation through medical officers of both sides, a ceasefire was arranged in order to remove the wounded in the contested area. About 70 paratroopers, most of them seriously wounded, and the medical personnel for their care, were moved from the captured German dressing station south-east of Stavromenos to the main dressing station of the Australians in the valley near the village of Adhele. From this location German and Australian medical officers and soldiers, as well as some Greek physicians, worked side by side.[64] However the German walking wounded were treated as prisoners of war and brought to a provisional camp north of Hill D, where they joined their already confined fellow-soldiers.

When a request for surrender from *Major* Kroh, delivered by *Oberleutnant* Rosenberg under a flag of truce to the Australian local commander, Lieutenant Colonel Campbell, was refused by the latter, the ceasefire ended at 1400hrs and the Australian artillery commenced firing on the olive oil factory. About the same time *Oberleutnant* von Roon, who remained with part of his company south of Stavromenos, was ordered by *Major* Kroh to rally the few paratroopers holding out since 20 May further to the south-west and to bring them forward to the area around Stavromenos. At nightfall the Australian artillery stopped shelling the factory; however, small arms fire lasted throughout the afternoon. Consequently the mostly exhausted defenders, who still had not received supplies from the air, had to remain vigilant.

In the contested area east of Heraklion the fighting was mainly restricted to *Kampfgruppe Schulz*. Here the British infantry, who had moved from Timbakion with four Bren Gun Carriers the day before, again advanced at 0600hrs against the positions of *II./FschJgRgt.2*. Its attempt to break through to Heraklion was repelled with the support of an anti-tank gun. Thereupon the British withdrew to the high ground to the south.

In the afternoon Heraklion was attacked heavily from the air. Taking advantage of the air attack *Major* Schulz sent an officer under a flag of truce to the Greek authorities with an ultimate request for surrender. The Greek troops in the town were to capitulate

---

62   *Australia in the War of 1939-1945*, Series One/ Army p.265 reports their losses from the air attack as 39 men.

63   The report that the factory was attacked by the Australians with the support of two Matilda II tanks on 23 May in KTB Korinth und Kreta des *FschJgRgt.2*, is not confirmed by Australian sources. It is stated in these sources that these tanks, which had been previously disabled, had been salvaged on 22 May and had been manned again by volunteers during the night 23/24 May, ready for employment.

64   KTB Kreta des *FschJgRgt.2*, and most of the German literature derived from it, place this event wrongly on 22 May.

immediately, saving the further destruction of Heraklion and further losses among its civilian population. The request was refused.[65]

The parts of *Kräftegruppe Bräuer* east of the airfield continued to occupy their positions along the Karteros depression. Here movements were possible only during the hours of darkness, as the enemy was able to survey the depression almost completely from the elevation east of the airfield. Probably upon instruction by Bräuer no attempt was undertaken to reconnoiter the terrain south of the main defensive positions or to block the roads leading from there toward the south. As a consequence the enemy was able to utilize this terrain for unhindered movements.

In the early afternoon the approach of several Hurricane fighters towards the airfield was seen from the observation post of *FschJgRgt.1*. After a massive German air attack, which also hit the airfield, the landing of fighters was repeated.[66]

Amongst the staff of *Generalmajor* Ringel it became increasingly apparent throughout the course of the afternoon that the enemy was planning a renewed defense line, stretching from the spur east of Ay Marina across the heights of Galatas to the high ground south of the road Chania-Alikianou. The heights around Galatas were regarded as the core of this line. Ringel now planned for *GebJgRgt.85* to bypass the air bridgehead of the reinforced *FschJgRgt.3* in the south. *GebJgRgt.100* was to be concentrated for the attack against the heights at Galatas between *Kräftegruppen Heidrich* and *Ramcke*. Accordingly he ordered the commander of *GebJgRgt.85* to have his recently landed *III./GebJgRgt.85* speedily follow up behind *I./GebJgRgt.85*. He also ceased the further advance of *II./GebJgRgt.100* toward the coastal road. *Kräftegruppe Ramcke* was to follow behind the retiring enemy along the coastal strip only until it came across his new defensive positions.

Throughout this day, the progress of the enveloping thrust of the *Gebirgsjäger* and its effects on the enemy were closely followed by the HQ of *XI.Flieger-Korps* in Athens. General Student fully approved of the intended course of action of *Gruppe West* and let things take their course there. His worries were mainly related to the two parachute infantry regiments which fought at Heraklion and Rethymnon. His instructions for this day were to ensure their most effective support and supply from the air and, if possible, their reinforcement. Probably in view of these aims he refused a request by *Oberst* Heidrich to provide two battalions by air and planned other missions for the paratroopers, who had been left behind on the Greek mainland and were now being assembled. The shock of the loss of a large

---

65   *Australia in the War of 1939-1945*, Series One/ Army, p.287, reports that Brigadier Chappel thereupon directed the evacuation of Heraklion and moved its c. two battalion-strong Greek garrison to the area around Arkhadia, about 10km south of the town. He had also sent two companies from the York and Lancaster Infantry Battalion into the town for its defence.

66   *Australia in the War of 1939-1945*, Series One/ Army, p.287, reports that of the six initially approaching Hurricanes, two had been shot down by friendly anti-aircraft guns, three had flown back to North Africa and only one had landed safely. Of the six fighters that were following up, four had been damaged during landing. Thus only three Hurricanes were combat-ready on the airfield on the evening of 23 May. After their first employment in the airspace over Heraklion, two were destroyed on the ground by German fighters on 24 May. The four damaged fighters had taken off again for North Africa, leaving one aircraft for further air-combat on the airfield.

portion of the *1.leichte Seetransportstaffel* had for the most part been overcome by now. Planning for the transfer of air transportable elements from the *leichte Seetransportstaffeln*, which returned to Piraeus, was in full swing. Despite the remarkable successes of *VIII. Flieger-Korps* against the British Mediterranean Fleet it was suspected that the latter would continue to block the nautical lines of communication to Crete and support the defenders on the island, as long as it was not decisively weakened. This was seen in the same regard by the *OKL*. Recognizing that the main efforts of the British naval squadron were in Alexandria and that the light naval units in Malta were now directed to the battle for Crete, the chief of staff of the *Luftwaffe*, *General der Flieger* Jeschonnek ordered the reinforcement of *VIII.Flieger-Korps* with the dive bombers of *III./StG 1*, *II./StG 2* and *StG 77*. *General der Flieger* Freiherr von Richthofen therefore provided the opportunity to transfer all of *StG 2* from the Peloponnese to Rhodes and thus reinforce the blockade of the Straits of Kaso, which constituted the sea approach to Crete from the east.[67]

During the evening of 23 May the command of CREFORCE could consider the situation in the sectors of Rethymnon and Heraklion with a degree of confidence, although no striking results had been achieved against the positions of the *Fallschirmtruppe* there. The order of the New Zealand Division for the retirement of its 5th Brigade arrived at the CREFORCE command on 23 May at about 0100hrs.[68] From 0530hrs onwards the movements of its units had been initiated after their commanders had coordinated them. It remained to some extent unclear how the battle was to be continued. It was planned that the 28th Battalion was to cover the retirement from its original positions around Platanias, that the 20th Battalion was to return to the area around Chania, now subordinate again to the 4th Brigade, and that the composite force of the New Zealand divisional engineers was to fall back to the area around Ay Marina.

By about 1000hrs the retirement of the 5th Brigade behind the Platanias River had been completed. When the enveloping movements of the German mountain troops were recognized a short time later and at 1310hrs paratroopers appeared in front of Platanias, Brigadier Hargest reported to the New Zealand Division that his forces, assessed by him at about 600 men, were forced to fall further back, which they did about an hour and 20 minutes later. Brigadier Puttick, whose staff still were involved in the coordination of the further course of action with the commands of Freyberg and Weston, approved this request 1515hrs but ordered the commencement of the retrograde movements no earlier than 2045hrs.

At 1700hrs the instructions for the further course of action were issued. The right flank of the new defensivee position, stretching from the spur close to the coast near Kolimvitra to the heights west of Galatas, was to be occupied by the 4th (New Zealand) Brigade, with the reinforced 18th Battalion. It was to relieve the exhausted New Zealand Composite Battalion, which was to be posted behind the 18th Battalion. The New Zealand Divisional Cavalry and the Petrol Company, now also subordinate to the 4th Brigade, were to remain in their positions immediately south of Galatas. The 19th Battalion from the 4th Brigade was to continue the defence around Daratsos. By these measures the 10th (New Zealand)

---

67 See also Gundelach, p.217.
68 The subsequent presentation of the events in the sectors of the New Zealand Division and Chania mostly stems from Davin, pp.250-269.

Brigade was in fact disbanded.[69] The 20th Battalion, which had been reassigned to the 4th Brigade, was to establish a defensive area north of Daratsos. The units of the 5th Brigade and subordinate New Zealand divisional engineers were to concentrate east of the 4th Brigade up to the mouth of the Kladiso river and to prepare there for new orders.

The sector command at Chania also ordered changes for the dispositions of its forces south of the road Chania-Alikianou. The 2/7 Infantry Battalion, which had been released from the reserve of the New Zealand Division, was to position itself north of the 2/8 Infantry Battalion up to the coastal road and establish contact with the New Zealand 28th Battalion there. The Greek 2nd Regiment was to expand its defensive area to Perivolia and to set up contact with the 2/8 Infantry Battalion.

These movements were completed shortly after midnight without interference by the Germans. The last unit, a company from the New Zealand 23rd Battalion, reinforced by two light tanks and some Bren Gun Carriers, had been deployed as a rearguard and also arrived safely in the assembly area of the 5th Brigade. Despite the short reaction time the units managed to settle down in their assigned areas. Only the Greek 2nd Regiment had not yet moved forward, as it was planned to first neutralize a position of the paratroopers that were blocking the route. During the relief of the Composite Battalion the 18th Battalion neglected to occupy the important Hill 116 '*Getreide-Höhe*'.

In his reports to Middle East Command Major General Freyberg expressed his concern about the effects on his troops of the continuous German air attacks. The commander-in-chief of the British Mediterranean Fleet, Admiral Cunningham, assessed the German air dominance over the waters around Crete as completely hindering the operations of his forces in daylight. Without suffering devastating losses they had become almost impossible. For this reason, and against instructions from the Admiralty in London, he discontinued the transfer to Timbakion of an infantry battalion, embarked since the morning of 23 May on the transport *Glenroy,* and together with its three escorting warships ordered it back to Alexandria. He regarded the sea transport of further reinforcements to Crete from now on practicable only by means of fast warships, which, in the course of one night would have to accomplish arrival and departure from Crete, in order to escape the German bombers.

24 May

At 0800hrs on the morning of 24 May *Kräftegruppe Ramcke* recognized the approach of mountain troops across the high ground about 4km south of Platanias. At 1000hrs *Kampfgruppe Stentzler* joined their advance on the left. In order to escape the threat of envelopment the rearguard of the enemy abandoned their positions at Platanias. *Kampfgruppe Gericke* immediately followed them, occupied Platanias late in the morning and in the afternoon advanced via Ay Marina to the heights south-east of Staliana Khania. Here it established contact with *1./FschPiBtl.7* from *Kampfgruppe Heilmann.* *Kampfgruppe Stentzler* needed more time in the rugged terrain against the more stubborn resistance of the enemy rearguard, but had gained the road leading from Ay Marina toward the south by the afternoon. By late afternoon the command post of the *SturmRgt.* was moved into a depression east of Ay Marina, where it was protected from observation by the enemy. From here *Oberst* Ramcke ordered his *Kampfgruppen* to set up defensive positions and be prepared for the continuation of the attack in the coming morning. Early in the evening the observation post of FschArtAbt 7, which was set up far forward, was detected

---

69   Colonel Kippenberger, however, was to command the troops immediately in front of and in Galatas.

by the enemy from the heights north-west of Galatas and consequently was bombarded by mortars, killing the commander of this unit, *Major* Bode, who happened to be present and his adjutant, *Oberleutnant* von Bühlingslöwen, who was seriously wounded.

In the north-west of Crete *GebPiBtl.95* (less its 3rd Company), which was reinforced with an anti-tank platoon from *GebPzJgAbt.95*, attacked the positions of the Greek 1st Regiment in front of and in Kastelli after a preceding air attack during the morning. The first objectives, the terrain around the factory and a fortress-like church in front of Kastelli, were seized after bitter fighting. In the afternoon the majority of Kastelli was in German hands. Throughout the course of the fighting 13 paratroopers from *Kampfgruppe Mürbe* were relieved. These men managed to escape from captivity during the air attack and had provided themselves with arms and set up positions in a building close to the shore with some prisoners, among them the head of the New Zealand advisory team with the Greek 1st Regiment. At the end of the fighting, in a valley outside of Kastelli, another eleven seriously wounded paratroopers from *Kampfgruppe Mürbe* were found by soldiers of *6./SturmRgt.* who followed up behind the mountain-engineers. Of the 48 men of this detachment who were believed killed, only 38 were found.[70] Some of the bodies had been mutilated.[71]

The area around Kastelli, particularly the shore at the Bight of Kissamo, which was planned for the landing of armored vehicles, was not yet completely cleared of the enemy. That the resistance in Kastelli had been a hard nut to crack was evident by the fact that the Greek 1st Regiment alone had lost more than 200 men.

The whereabouts of the patrol from *GebPiBtl.7* which had been dispatched the day before into the area of Kandanos remained unknown. Consequently a combat group formed by *3./GebPiBtl.95*, *16./SturmRgt.* and the recently-arrived company of *Kradschützen-Bataillon 55* advanced toward this settlement. Time and again attacked by irregulars, when the combat group reached the north of Kandanos, at the small village of Floria, they came across the location where the patrol had fallen into an ambush. Three of its seriously wounded soldiers were saved. All others, except two who were missing, were later found killed and mutilated. After the dead were buried the combat group retired to the area near Kolimbari, again under the fire of irregulars.

Along the front of the reinforced *FschJgRgt.3* opposite the heigths of Galatas, the enemy also remained quiet. From the south, however, Greek troops to the strength of about two companies attacked at dawn against the units of *I./FschJgRgt.3* that were positioned north

---

70   The statement about the liberation of the captured paratroopers from the town prison by *Gebirgs-Pioniere* in Ringel, pp.145-147, and repeated in some of the literature about *Merkur*, is incorrect. The narrative above is confirmed by the after-action report of *6./SturmRgt.* and by the report of the former head of the New Zealand advisory team, the-then Major Bedding. The latter also has stated that the captured paratroopers, including the seriously wounded, were protected by New Zealand advisers against excesses by Cretan irregulars and the inhabitants of Kastelli.

71   The mutilations are expressively mentioned in a response by Dr. Neumann, then *Oberstabsarzt*, in an article about the training status of the *Fallschirmtruppe* and *Gebirgsjäger* on Crete published in *DDF* May/June 1989.

of the ancient Turkish fort. The fighting lasted into the afternoon, before the attackers withdrew without success after suffering considerable losses.

During the morning, the thrust of *Kampfgruppe Heilmann*, together with *II./ GebJgRgt.100*, against the high ground north-west of Galatas became impracticable because the mountain battalion had moved into a staging area further to the south. Shortly prior to 0800hrs *Major* Heilmann dispatched *1./FschPiBtl.7* to the coastal road with the mission to block it from the enemy. The remaining troops were concentrated in a staging area east of Stalos, for the attack against the heights in front of the combat group. However the attack was not executed as *Kampfgruppe Stentzler* moved into the staging area of *Kampfgruppe Heilmann*. At about the same time *Major* Heilmann was ordered by *Oberst* Heidrich to support the attack of *GebJgRgt.100* against Galatas on the coming day and subsequently to return into the air bridgehead. Here, *Oberst* Utz, who had driven with a small entourage from his command post in Padhalari along the road to Agia through terrain still unoccupied by his troops, established contact with Heidrich in the prison. The commanders coordinated the interaction of their regiments for the attack against the high ground around Galatas. While *GebJgRgt.100* was to assault from the west, parts of *FschJgRgt.3* were to seize Cemetery Hill from the south and to assume the protection of the right flank of the mountain troops. After preceding air attacks the start of the attack by *GebJgRgt.100* was agreed upon for 25 May at 1220hrs. South of the air bridgehead of Heidrich's force, *GebJgRgt.85* was to take over protection in the area around Alikianou and the terrain east of it, and later was to attack into this region for the further envelopment of the enemy.

I./GebJgRgt.100 planned to attack on the right flank of *GebJgRgt.100* until nightfall of 24 May, and reached its staging area completely unhindered by the enemy. To the left of it, *II./GebJgRgt.100* had some losses to sniper and mortar fire during the move into its staging area. In the evening and throughout the night the enemy launched two counter-attacks against this battalion, with the aim of pushing back the mountain infantrymen, who came close to the heights north-west of Galatas. After hard fighting both thrusts were repelled by *6./GebJgRgt.100* on the left flank.

In the early morning of 24 May, in the area east of Rethymnon, British infantry attacked the position of *Kampfgruppe Schulz* from the west. Supported by the fire of *9./FschJgRgt.2* from the 'Kapellenhöhe' a shock troop from *11./FschJgRgt.2* under *Leutnant* Molsen surprised the attackers and beat them back inflicting heavy losses, 25 being killed.[72] The shock troop, too, lost three killed. Several air attacks flown in support of the defenders of Parivolia, mainly by fighter-bombers, prevented the enemy from launching further attacks for the remainder of the day.

At about 0500hrs a Matilda II tank advanced against *Kampfgruppe Kroh* in the olive oil factory, but then turned south, moving forward against the paratroopers from *3./*

---

72   The war diary of the Australian 2/1 Infantry Battalion mentions that it was a company from the 1st Rangers and and an anti-tank gun which had been brought along from Chania with the mission to clear the coastal road for supply traffic up to the airfield. After the attack had failed, the company returned to Chania.

FschJgRgt.2, who were engaged in fighting the Greek troops that were assembled for an attack against the factory. Cleverly the paratroopers retired where the tank made its appearance, but managed to keep the farmhouse 1.5km south-east of Stavromenos in their possession. When the tank made its way back to the airfield around noon it was fired at and damaged by the German anti-tank guns, positioned in Stavromenos. After the tank destroyed one of these guns, it moved on again.[73] The paratroopers south-west of Stavromenos now took the initiative and managed to beat the Greek troops back into the mountains from the hamlet of Kimeri, about 4km south-east of the olive oil factory. Now a drop zone was marked east of the factory by command of *Oberleutnant* von Roon. By means of letters written with stones, supply by air was requested. Throughout the day and well into the evening the defenders of the olive oil factory were under fire from artillery and snipers, which caused further losses. Around the terrain of the factory and in Stavromenos only about 250 men, among them six officers, remained combat effective. Moreover they had almost completely run out of ammunition and food.[74]

In the contested area around Heraklion, during the morning of 24 May the British brigade command realized that the superior German command had not written off its forces there. During the renewed attack of British infantry against the positions of *II./FschJgRgt.2*, which commenced at 0530hrs, a battalion of four provisional companies made up of paratroopers, who had been gathered around Athens, was dropped south-west of Heraklion at around 0735hrs.[75] It was commanded by *Hauptmann* Vogel, who had arrived in Greece as the adjutant of *Oberst* Ramcke, but had stayed behind when Ramcke had parachuted in near Tavronitis. Parts of the battalion immediately joined *II./FschJgRgt.2* in repelling the British infantry, which retired again into the mountains.[76]

On the orders of *Oberst* Bräuer the three parachute infantry battalions south-west of Heraklion were combined as *Gruppe Schulz*. *II./FschJgRgt.2* was now reinforced with parts of *12./FschJgRgt.2* who were dropped in the morning and by a company formed from the remnants of *10./* and *13./FschJgRgt.1* under *Oberleutnant* Egger. *Major* Schulz intended to seize Heraklion again, after the town had been the target of heavy air attacks throughout the day. At 1830hrs he tasked *II./FschJgRgt.2* with the attack of the town from the south on the coming morning at 0500hrs. To the left *Bataillon Vogel* was to join the attack.

---

73 The war diary of the Australian 2/1 Infantry Battalion notes that the commander of the tank was wounded by the anti-tank fire. Therefore the tank had not been available to support an attack by the 2/11 Infantry Battalion against the eastern part of Perivolia which had been planned for the afternoon. The attack was then postponed until the morning of 25 May.

74 This situation was evidently known by the local commander opposed to the defenders. In order to avoid unnecessary losses among his troops, he had already decided the day before to starve the Germans into surrender.

75 It has not been possible to find out exactly from which units the two heavy and two rifle companies of this battalion had been put together. Elements of *12./FschJgRgt.2* and probably also parts of *10./FschJgRgt.2* were included. Possibly *8./FschJgRgt.3*, which originally was planned for sea transport, was also part of this battalion.

76 The 1st Argyll and Sutherland Highlanders had refrained from attempting to get into Heraklion along the road from Timbakion. Two of its companies – a third was left back on the Messara-plain to safeguard the intended construction of an airfield– swinging toward the east, had managed to reach the British positions around the airfield in the course of 24 May. The losses of the battalion on 24 May were reported as two officers and 20 other ranks.

At Heraklion airfield the forces of *Oberst* Bräuer kept up their defensive position, though their actions were mainly restricted to fire from heavy weapons. The 8cm mortars, which had been dropped the day before as replacements for the ones lost, were able to bombard the airfield. Reconnaissance or offensive actions against the enemy's lines of communication in the south remained patchy.[77]

On 24 May the staff of *Generalmajor* Ringel was mainly occupied with planning for the thrust against the heights around Galatas. The signals detachment of the *5.Gebirgs-Division* had arrived with other troops on the airfield at Maleme, allowing for better command and control. A light anti-aircraft battery of the *5.Gebirgs-Division* was also deployed on the airfield for protection against renewed air attacks. Better security was expected by *Luftflotte 4* by the transfer of four Me 109 fighters from *JG 77* to the airfield.

During the course of the day the enemy was able to organize his forces with little pressure from the opposing German troops along a line stretching from the high ground around Galatas to the terrain south of Perivolia. The right flank of this line was occupied by the 4th (New Zealand) Brigade with the 18th and 19th Battalions and the New Zealand Divisional Cavalry in between. To the rear of them the New Zealand Composite Battalion and the remnants of the Greek 6th Regiment were positioned as quick reaction-forces.[78] The real reserve of the brigade, the 20th Battalion, occupied the area around the divide of the road toward Galatas from the coastal road south of the Apostoloi Peninsula.

The right flank of the defensive line was made up by the 19th (Australian) Brigade with the 2/7 and 2/8 Infantry Battalions and the Greek 2nd Regiment adjoining south of them. To the west the Greek 8th Regiment remained positioned in the area around and east of Alikianou; isolated but still full of fight.

Behind the defensive line, the depleted units of the 5th (New Zealand) Brigade reorganized in a small assembly area. Here they suffered considerably from constant air attacks.

The reports from Major General Freyberg to Middle East Command still sounded optimistic, although he was already convinced, in view of German air supremacy, that the battle for Crete could not be won.[79] He stated the losses of CREFORCE as 1,900 men, of which 75% had been suffered by the New Zealand Division. He assessed the German losses at more than 3,300 men, with about 1,000 killed.[80] From London and Cairo Freyberg received praise and encouragement for his struggle and the promise that everything possible would be done to allow for its continuation.[81] As a visible sign of this intent a contingent

---

77   Mößinger explicitly points out the negative effects on the morale of the troops caused by Bräuer's inactivity.
78   Davin speaks of about 350 men with a few officers. These had mainly been posted inside Galatas.
79   Davin, p.294, quotes from p.40 of the report by Freyberg to the New Zealand government after the battle. Freyberg states that he had been rather clear about the fact that the troops could not hold out much longer against the continual German air attacks. He continued that he had known with certainty by that time, that there were only two alternatives – to be beaten and captured on the battlefield or to commence the withdrawal.
80   This estimate shows that Freyberg was sceptical about the reports of his commanders related to the losses of the parachute forces at and immediately after their landing.
81   The high command in London had conveyed its belief to General Wavell that the perseverance of CREFORCE could lead to the discontinuation of the German attack, and requested him to send as many reinforcements to Crete as possible.

of 200 commandos from 'Layforce' arrived in the port of Souda on the minelayer *Abdiel* during the night of 24/25 May.[82]

CREFORCE command still anticipated German air and sea landings near Chania, on the Akrotiri Peninsula and along the coast of Souda Bay. Therefore the 1st Rangers and the Northumberland Hussars remained tied down as 'Akrotiri Force' on the peninsula. The 1st Welch continued to be the CREFORCE reserve south of Chania. For the protection of the entrance into Souda Bay the two Australian composite infantry battalions remained posted there.

25 May

While the first attacks of the *Luftwaffe* were flown against the heights around Galatas and the batteries of *GebArtRgt.95* commenced their preparatory fire against these targets, *General der Flieger* Student arrived on the airfield at Maleme. As he knew *Generalmajor* Ringel was fully occupied with the impending attack, he contented himself with a short situation report at the command post of the *5.Gebirgs-Division* and subsequently let himself be driven in a motorcycle sidecar to the *SturmRgt.* on the coastal strip, in order to observe its attack against the heights close to the coastal road north-west of Galatas.

The first assault by *GebJgRgt.100* against Galatas failed despite the preceding air attacks as the resistance of the defenders remained unbroken. Thereupon, *Generalmajor* Ringel requested air support and had the enemy positions shelled by his artillery. Following an air attack at 1625hrs an announced second one was not flown, so at 1700hrs Ringel ordered the start of the assault of his mountain infantry. After bitter fighting and with considerable losses *I./GebJgRgt.100* finally succeeded in entering Galatas from Cemetery Hill. *II./GebJgRgt.100*, which initially had been forced to ground in front of an elevation west of Galatas, was now able to advance into the town with supporting fire from *7./SturmRgt.* led by *Oberleutnant* Barmetler.

After savage streetfighting against an enemy who resisted stubbornly and skilfully, about half of Galatas was in the hands of the men from *II./GebJgRgt.100* by late in the evening. *I./GebJgRgt.100* joined the assault along the southern edge of the village across Cemetery Hill. Here contact was also established with parts of *FschJgRgt.3*.

At about 2300hrs the exhausted soldiers of *II./GebJgRgt.100* were hit by a determined counter-attack from the enemy – two to three fresh infantry companies, parts of the rallied defenders of the village and two light tanks. In fierce fighting at close quarters and in hand-to-hand combat lasting for several hours the mountain infantry were finally pushed back to the southern edge of Galatas. Here, they were able to set up for all-round defence.[83] There

---

82   The unit was named after its commander, Brigadier Laycock. Its two battalions had initially been designated for a landing near Kastelli. When this turned out to be of little value because of the changed situation there, the landing of the troops had been planned at Sfakia, on the southern coast of Crete. Stormy weather had prevented the execution of this landing. *Abdiel* had then steered to Souda and had left this port again in the early hours of 25 May with a number of wounded aboard.

83   The struggle for Galatas on 24 May is covered in great length in the literature about the battle for Crete on both sides. In the light of the subject of this book, it is, like other combat actions of the mountain troops, discussed only to the extent necessary for the understanding of the course of the battle on the German side.

was a stroke of luck at this time for the mountain troops as it turned out that both British tanks had been disabled during the fighting in the night.[84]

During this day the rest of the units of the *5.Gebirgs-Division* which could be transported by air were landed on the airfield at Maleme, among them *II/GebJgRgt.85* and medical troops. The former was ordered to follow immediately behind its regiment, which was in the process of enveloping the enemy from the south. For the coming day, the landing of *GebJgRgt.141* from *6.Gebirgs-Division* was also planned. The regiment was held available for commitment on Crete by the command of the *12.Armee*.

In the afternoon the airfield at Maleme was attacked again by Blenheim and Maryland bombers from Egypt. The damage caused was negligible, not the least due to the interference of Me109 fighters from *JG 77*.[85] A single Hurricane appeared over the airfield, and succeeded in destroying a Ju 52.[86]

GebPiBtl.95 cleared all of the area around Kastelli and Kissamo for good. Part of the battalion afterward moved out into the mountainous terrain to the south for security missions. Of the soldiers from the Greek 1st Regiment, only a few retreated into the mountains.[87] However, the irregulars found refuge in the south and made their appearance again around Kandanos.

The reinforced *FschJgRgt.3*, which had supported the attack of *I./GebJgRgt.100* into Galatas and had blocked any advance of enemy forces from the area around Daratsos, continued to hold its positions in the air bridgehead. It now prepared to attack along the road Alikianou-Chania. *Kampfgruppe Heilmann* maintained protective positions throughout the day toward the east, about 500m east of Stalos, where in the early morning the command post of the *SturmRgt.* was set up. During the night the combat group returned to its regiment. During its employment around Stalos, it had lost eight killed and 16 wounded.

South of the air bridgehead of *Kräftegruppe Heidrich GebJgRgt.85* gained the area around Episkopi with *I./GebJgRgt.85* and Kufos with *III./GebJgRgt.85*. The attack against Alikianou ordered by *Generalmajor* Ringel was not carried out, as the requested air support did not materialize. In the evening *Oberst* Krakau received the mission to continue the enveloping thrust toward Souda in the coming morning, bypassing the mountain slopes east of Alikianou that were still held by the enemy.

---

84   Two more light tanks of C Troop 3rd Hussars had not joined the fighting, as they had been kept back for a security mission in Daratsos.

85   For 25 May *Luftflotte 4* reported that four Blenheims and two Hurricanes had been shot down by them. The loss of the Hurricane was not confirmed by the British.

86   It may have been the last fighter, stationed on the airfield at Heraklion. British sources state that it was destroyed on the ground on this airfield on 25 May.

87   The majority of the Greek soldiers, who had formed the units in the west of Crete, were recruits, who had been brought to Crete from the Peloponnese shortly prior to the capitulation of the Greek troops on the mainland. For the most part, they were not Cretans and were unfamiliar with the conditions on the island. Therefore, they obviously preferred captivity over an uncertain fate in the mountains of the island. See also Mehtidis.

Early in the morning, east of Rethymnon Australian infantry with the support of a Matilda II tank, moved forward toward Perivolia from the east along the coastal road. When the tank became disabled during its approach, the infantry also discontinued its advance. This was to the advantage of *2./FschArtAbt.7*, which was almost out of ammunition for its two still-operational guns.

Opposite *Kampfgruppe Kroh* in the olive oil factory and in the buildings of Stavromenos, the enemy contented himself with artillery and mortar fire, which prevented any larger movement on the German side. Here there was almost no food left for the paratroopers. *3./ FschJgRgt.2* under *Oberleutnant* von Roon was entrenched in the farm 1.5km south-east of Stavromenos and in the hamlet of Kimari. From 0800hrs onwards they were shelled and shortly thereafter attacked by Greek troops, as a result Kimari was given up. The farm was also abandoned after some direct hits from mortar fire, which caused considerable losses. The paratroopers managed to establish themselves again on an elevation north-east of Kimari. From here, they turned back all further attacks by the Greeks.

In the afternoon, transport aircraft delivered supplies on the drop zone which had been set up by *Oberleutnant* von Roon by parachute. Together with the supplies an order from the command of *XI.Flieger-Korps* was dropped for *Kampfgruppe Kroh*. It was ordered to fight through to Heraklion and to join *Kräftegruppe Bräuer* there.[88] At about 2100hrs the order was in the hands of *Major* Kroh. He took immediate steps for the evacuation of the olive oil factory. However no thought was given to the integration of the troops at Perivolia during the move. The numerous prisoners and wounded in the hands of the enemy also had to be left to their fate.[89]

In the operational area of *Gruppe Schulz* opposite Heraklion, as ordered *Bataillon Schirmer* attacked at 0500hrs with two companies abreast and *12./FschJgRgt.1* in support against the southern perimeter of the town. *8./FschJgRgt.2* remained in the protective position of the battalion toward the south. At about 0630hrs the attacking companies advanced to the town wall of Heraklion in the south-west, but were stopped there by defensive fire. At 0800hrs *Major* Schulz ordered the attack discontinued, and conducted reconnaissance for the time being. The thrust of *Bataillon Vogel* against the western entrance into Heraklion failed in its initial stage in front of a newly-erected barricade across the street.[90] Until well into the afternoon the battalion was forced to repel artillery-supported counter-attacks by the enemy.

In the meantime the order by *FschJgRgt.1* to bypass Heraklion in the south with all available troops during the night and to establish contact with the forces of the regiment positioned east of the airfield, on Hill 182, about 4km south of the mouth of the Karteros,

---

88 In his memoirs in Götzel, p. 307, Student states that this order was given without his consent. Consequently it had probably been issued without knowledge of Student's intention to move *Gruppe Schulz* from the west of Heraklion to *Oberst* Bräuer's force for a renewed attack against the airfield. As the *Kampfgruppe* around Perivolia had evidently already been written off by the command of *XI.Flieger-Korps*, the movement ordered for *Kampfgruppe Kroh* would have brought it between two fire positions, probably resulting in its annihilation.

89 *Australia in the War of 1939-1945*, Series One/ Army, p.265, states that by 23 May 252 German wounded had been assembled in the main dressing station near Adhele.

90 *Australia in the War of 1939-1945*, Series One/ Army, p.287, reports that at the time of the German attack on 25 May Heraklion was defended by three reinforced infantry companies.

had arrived. This order was based on a directive from Student, who decided to let the reinforced *FschJgRgt.1* attack again after the concentration of its forces. Student anticipated that the enemy would fall back fighting from the west of Crete into its eastern part with the aim of retaining the latter. As he considered the timely relief of his *Fallschirmtruppe* at Rethymnon feasible only from the direction of Heraklion, the enemy there had to be neutralized as quickly as possible in order to muster troops from *Kräftegruppe Bräuer* for the relief operation, before the defence at Rethymnon could be crushed by the enemy forces approaching from the west.[91]

At about 2200hrs *Gruppe Schulz* commenced its flanking movement. The main dressing station of *2./FschSanAbt.7* under *Truppenarzt* Dr. Langemeyer with about 180 wounded was left behind, protected by a platoon from *7./FschJgRgt.2* and the anti-tank platoons of *14./FschJgRgt.1*.

In the area around Athens, the plans of the command of *Admiral Süd-Ost* for sea transports to Crete took shape again. For this purpose the larger ships that had been assembled were to be used, as they were able to make the passage into the Bight of Kissamo during daylight. The intention of conveying a floating bridge with the first sea transport, in order to have a 'gang-plank' constructed in the Bight of Kissamo by *GebPiBtl.95*, could not be carried out. Consequently, the landing of vehicles and supplies on a large scale in the Bight became questionable.

After the situation on Crete developed markedly in favour of the German troops on 25 May the high command of the *Wehrmacht* for the first time informed the German public on a somewhat broader scale about *Merkur*. Prior to this, only a short report about the parachute attack had been broadcast on the previous day.

On the morning of 25 May Major General Freyberg sent an optimistic report to Middle East Command, after the New Zealand Division had succeeded in moving its 5th Brigade behind the 4th Brigade. Moreover, it had been possible to set up for continued defence the area immediately west and south-west of Galatas with the fresh New Zealand 18th Battalion, reinforced with four anti-tank guns from the 106 RA, that is by a unit experienced in infantry combat. However throughout the course of the night, after he was informed by Brigadier Puttick about the critical situation at Galatas, he reported to General Wavell that the defensivee line of the New Zealand Division had broken down and expressed his fear that the troops in the sector Chania/Souda would now also be drawn into the battle. However, actions for the recapture of the important terrain for the defence of Chania were not initiated by him. Brigadier Puttick also showed no interest in this action. Instead he attempted to build up a new defensive line for his division, stretching from the Apostoloi Peninsula toward the south, to link up with the 19th (Australian) Brigade in the area around Platanos.

---

91   As noted in Student's memoirs (Götzel, pp.292 and 301), up to 27 May the general was convinced that the enemy would continue to fight for Crete and therefore would attempt to retain the eastern part of the island. This somewhat strange approach by Student toward the overall situation of the enemy and of the results of the actions by the mountain troops reflects his weakness as an operational-level commander and would have consequences later on.

26 May

In the morning of the 26 May, as the soldiers of *GebJgRgt.100* carefully felt their way back into battered Galatas, where the dead of both sides lay everywhere in the streets, they anticipated engaging the enemy at any moment. After a short time they became aware that the village must have been abandoned after the counter-attack and even the terrain adjoining to the east had only weak rearguards. Yet before the *Luftwaffe* commenced its attacks into the area west of Chania, and the town proper in the course of the morning, *Generalmajor* Ringel issued orders adapted to the new situation. He intended to strike out against Chania. As he anticipated a particularly strong defence immediately west of the town he first wanted the enveloping thrust of *GebJgRgt.85* to take its effect on the enemy.

The task organization for the frontal attack remained unchanged to that used two days before, but *Oberst* Heidrich was now also ordered to advance on the right flank of the attack front at 0730hrs, joining the attack of *GebJgRgt.100*. On the right of reinforced *FschJgRgt.3* Ringel placed the approaching *GebJgRgt.141*, to attack toward Souda bypassing Chania in the south. His artillery, which by now was available in adequate strength,[92] however still had to move forward for its supporting role. Almost all of its firing positions were located in the coastal strip, as the guns could only be moved there with the towing vehicles available.[93] The frontal attack against the new enemy defensive line was to commence late in the afternoon so that the setting sun would impede his observation.

Early in the morning the troops on the left flank of the attack front, taking advantage of the commencing air attacks and watched over by the heavy weapons, advanced through terrain which the enemy had given up. Parts of *GebJgRgt.100* quickly occupied Daratsos.[94] The attack on the right flank of reinforced *FschJgRgt.3* commenced after fire preparation at 0830hrs.[95] It hit the gap between the Australian 2/8 Infantry Battalion and the Greek 2nd Regiment around noon. After receiving very little fire from Greek positions, the paratroopers entered Perivolia. From here it was possible to engage enemy positions around Galaria with flanking fire. After renewed fire preparation, the paratroopers attacked on a broad front at 1400hrs. Skillfully coordinating fire and movement and utilizing the cover of olive groves, they managed to push back the opposing Australian infantry bit by bit. At nightfall, in the light of the limited numbers of attackers, their commanding officer decided to set up for defence. For the continuation of the attack in the coming morning, late in the evening *Oberst* Heidrich also ordered forward *FschPiBtl.7*, which was set free by the almost uncontested occupation of the area around Alikianou by *GebJgRgt.85*. Losses nevertheless had been suffered by the mountain regiment, despite only sporadic Greek resistance, when a Do 17 had dropped its bombs on the advancing infantrymen.

---

92 Two light detachments of *GebArtRgt.95* with three batteries of mountain guns each, the infantry gun batteries of *GebJgRgts.85* and *100* and *1./FschArtAbt.7*. The heavy 15cm infantry guns were dismantled for air transport.

93 In addition to captured trucks, these were mainly sidecar motorcycles, which had been brought to Crete in considerable numbers. A few of the new *Kettenkrad* had also arrived. During their first appearance in front of Galatas, they were initially regarded as light armored vehicles by the enemy, who placed anti-tank mines as defence against them.

94 New Zealand sources give 0930hrs for this event. At that time, however, only German patrols could have entered the village.

95 As no original German sources exist for this action, it has been described solely by reference to the war diaries of the Australian 2/7 and 2/8 Infantry Battalions.

As part of *Kräftegruppe Ramcke*, *Kampfgruppe Gericke* gained the entrance to the Apostoloi Peninsula at about 1100hrs. In the meantime the British tented hospital was vacated, under the care of the New Zealand medical personnel. A number of its litter cases, among them some paratroopers, were quartered safely in nearby caves. After an officer under a flag of truce achieved the agreement of the enemy to a ceasefire on the position of the hospital, the wounded from both sides were brought by captured medical personnel to the former Greek infirmary on the peninsula for further treatment under the guidance of the medical officer of *IV./SturmRgt.* There, as soon other captured medical installations of the enemy, it became evident that the parachute force was far better equipped with much superior medical gear compared to its opponent.

Kampfgruppe Gericke, under fire from the east and south, made no progress in the open terrain in front of Evthymi and suffered more losses. The wounded there were mostly brought back by captured medical personnel who volunteered for this task. *Kampfgruppe Stentzler*, after coordination with *GebJgRgt.100*, moved into the right part of the latter's sector, prior to the commencement of the attack because there were better prospects for its advance. It now followed close behind *Kräftegruppe Ramcke* and *GebJgRgt.100* and thereby provided for the protection of the inner flanks of both.

The circumvention of the area around Alikianou met almost no resistance from the opposing Greeks, who retired into the mountains to the south and disbanded there. However as the extremely difficult terrain ate up more time than calculated, Ringel was forced to postpone the attack against Chania until the next morning. Its start was set for 1000hrs and was to be launched with *Gruppe Ramcke* from the west, *Gruppe Utz* from the south-west and *Gruppe Heidrich* from the south.

For the moment *Oberst* Ramcke left the task-organization of his force unchanged. *Kampfgruppe Gericke* was to advance on either side of the coastal road aiming for the last heights in front of Chania. *Kampfgruppe Schmitz* was to protect it against tanks and was to keep its composite parachute company available as reinforcements behind its left flank. *Kampfgruppe Stentzler* was to advance together with *II./GebJgRgt.100* toward the settlement of Parigoria at the western perimeter of Chania. The two companies formed from *I./SturmRgt.*, were again to follow behind *Kampfgruppe Stentzler* as reserve.

A combat group, put together from the light companies of *Kradschützen-Btl.55*, parts of *GebPiBtl.95* and *GebPzJgAbt.95*, was sent on its way from the area around Tavronitis via Kandanos to the small port of Palaeochora on the south-western coast of Crete. Its advance party was involved in firefights with irregulars time and again, who always retreated into the nearly impassable mountains upon the approach of the German main force. Kandanos was occupied only after a short fight. Palaeochora was reached in the evening of 26 May. It turned out to be unoccupied by the enemy.

Around Kastelli *GebPiBtl.95* continued to clear the surroundings from last enemy stragglers. After burying the 38 killed from *Kampfgruppe Mürbe*, *6./SturmRgt.* moved off towards Kolimbari.[96]

---

96   The company was reassigned to its battalion in Chania on 28 May.

During the course of the day *III./GebJgRgt.141* and elements of the regimental-level units were landed on the airfield at Maleme.[97] The battle HQ of *XI.Flieger-Korps* also arrived, so that Student could now set up his own command post. Some time prior a liaison officer from the headquarters of the German *12.Armee* reported to the command post of *Generalmajor* Ringel.[98]

During this day, British bombers again attacked the airfield at Maleme. However they were unable to prevail against the now highly vigilant German fighter defence and lost four Blenheims. From then on no more bombing attacks were flown over Crete during the fighting for the island.

East of the airstrip at Rethymnon the still combat-effective paratroopers of *Kampfgruppe Kroh*, unnoticed by the enemy, abandoned their positions in the olive oil factory and in Stavromenos at 0200hrs and retired some distance to the east to the drop zone near the mouth of a dried-out small stream, which was safeguarded by parts of *3./FschJgRgt.2*. The litter-cases among the wounded and the prisoners of war were left behind, attended by a few men.[99] Two of the still operational light anti-aircraft guns were dropped into the sea. A third was dismantled and like one of the anti-tank guns, taken along. At 0400 hrs about 250 men arrived at the drop zone. Totally starved, they were first of all fed with the dropped food.

In the course of the morning B Company of the Australian 2/1 Infantry Battalion with the support of a tank, advanced against the olive oil factory but found it undefended. Those paratroopers that had been left behind were subsequently taken prisoner. However as a result of their pitiable condition, they were first fed on the spot. Australian soldiers protected them against the vindictive Greeks who now also appeared on the scene.

For the impending breakthrough to Heraklion, *Major* Kroh organized his force into five companies:

- 1st Company under *Oberleutnant* Schindler, consisting of the remnants of *1./* and *4./FschJgRgt.2*;
- 2nd Company under *Oberleutnant* Rosenberg, with the remnants of the signals platoon and *2./FschMGBtl.7*,
- 3rd Company under *Oberleutnant* von Roon, with his own company and the remainder from *13./FschJgRgt.2*;

---

97   The statement in Davin, that the reconnaissance unit of the *5.Gebirgs-Division* had also arrived on Crete on 26 May, cannot be verified in German sources.

98   Because of his career in the *Luftwaffe* Student was rather unfamiliar with the command and control procedures of the *Heer* at the operational level and obviously feared that *Generalfeldmarschall* List, as overall commander in Greece, could interfere in the operations on Crete. Up to this time he certainly had not spent much time considering the command arrangements for Crete after its conquest, which would come under the responsibility of List.

99   KTB 1 Korinth und Kreta for *FschJgRgt.2* reports 14 seriously wounded, a few medical soldiers and 11 prisoners of war. This differs from the war diary of the Australian 2/1 Infantry Battalion, which states 40 wounded and 40 unwounded Germans, who had been found in the olive oil factory.

- *Kompanie Hinz* (commander of *12./FschJgRgt.2*), with the remnants of *10./* and *12./FschJgRgt.2*;
- heavy weapons company under *Oberleutnant* Marr, with the remainder of *2./FschFlaMGBtl.7* and equipped with the light anti-aircraft gun, one anti-tank gun, one heavy machine-gun and three 8cm mortars.

The arms that were still available were distributed among the rifle companies, so that each of them had two light machine-guns, one 5cm mortar and 30 rifles. The soldiers who could not be armed were used as porters.

The start of the movement toward the east was scheduled for the evening of 27 May, after the delivery of additional rations by air. After some interruptions *Kampfgruppe Kroh* found time to rest during the daytime, despite Greek irregulars probing against the drop zone and having to be driven off several times.

In the evening the plans of *Major* Kroh suddenly became invalid when a new order from the command of *XI.Flieger-Korps* was dropped. It instructed the reinforced *FschJgRgt.2* to retain its present position and tie down the opposing enemy.[100] *Major* Kroh thereupon decided to stay in the area already occupied and to expand it on the morning of 27 May.

In the hedgehog position of *Kampfgruppe Schulz*, *2./FschArtAbt.7* succeeded in repelling Australian infantry who probed against its emplacements at the eastern perimeter of Perivolia. An attack of an Australian infantry company against the 'Kapellenhöhe', supported by a Matilda II tank, was discontinued after considerable losses when the main gun of the tank was disabled by fire from the anti-tank gun of the defenders.[101] For the rest of the day the Australian artillery repeatedly shelled the German positions around Perivolia. Losses were also suffered as a result of sniper fire from the remaining trenches in the outlying terrain. However further attacks failed to materialize, as the enemy obviously was discouraged by the ongoing presence of German fighter-bombers and dive bombers over the contested area.

Late on the evening of 25 May *Gruppe Schulz*, with *Bataillon Schirmer* as vanguard, commenced its movement from the area south-west of Heraklion in a direction toward the planned contact-point east of the airfield. Shortly prior to midnight the vanguard came across enemy infantry on Cemetery Hill south of Heraklion. In a surprise attack they were beaten back, leaving some prisoners in the hands of the paratroopers.[102] Incoming fire from artillery and machine-guns caused some losses among the paratroopers. Leaving

---

100 In his memoirs Student does not discuss the reasons for the new order by the Corps command, evidently in order not to disclose the lack of coordination between him and his staff in this matter. He points out, however, that the original order resulted in the re-organization of *Kampfgruppe Kroh* by its move away from the olive oil factory.

101 *Australia in the War of 1939-1945*, Series One/ Army, p.266, gives the losses of the attacking company as 4 killed and 26 wounded.

102 The war diary of the Australian 2/4 Infantry Battalion mentions that the men on Cemetery Hill belonged to the Argyll and Sutherland Highlanders. This battalion had been in the process of relieving the 2nd Leicesters.

the wounded of this engagement behind under the care of medical personnel,[103] *Gruppe Schulz* continued its march. In total darkness the column had to move in single file, causing much time to be lost. At 0440hrs, in the breaking dawn, the forward elements of the group reached the northern foot of Hill 296.5 (named Apex Hill by the enemy), about 2.5km south of the main positions of the enemy at the airfield. The height was occupied by an infantry platoon of the enemy in an outpost position. It now opened fire. The sub-units of *Bataillon Schirmer* that arrived at the foot of the hill – *7./* and *8./FschJgRgt.2* and *10./ FschJgRgt.1* led by *Oberleutnant* Paul – immediately assaulted and drove the enemy off after a short fight. Both sides took only few losses. However the majority of the defenders were able to escape toward the north in the rugged terrain.[104] In the course of the morning, the majority of *Gruppe Schulz* made its way into the area around Hill 296.5. The soldiers were exhausted to such a degree that all they wanted to do was to sleep. A few officers and men then took on sentry duty. *Oberleutnant* Graf von der Schulenburg reported the arrival of *Gruppe Schulz* to the adjutant of *Oberst* Bräuer, who came forward to Hill 296.5 in order to establish liaison.

In the afternoon, while most of Schulz's men still rested, measures for the re-organization of *Kräftegruppe Bräuer* were initiated. *Bataillon Schirmer* remained tasked with the defence of Hill 296.5. The move of the other two battalions of *Gruppe Schulz* to Hill 182 for the time being was cancelled as the men were still too exhausted and the enemy dominated the route to this point with covering fire.

Upon the initiative of the medical officer of *II./FschJgRgt.2* an agreement was achieved with the medical officer of the Australian 2/4 Infantry Battalion by the afternoon. This allowed the enemy wounded in the outlying terrain to be brought by German medical personnel to the village of Babali, north of Hill 296.5, where they were to be picked up by Australian ambulances. As the medical service of *Gruppe Schulz* was running out of supplies the construction of a landing site for transport aircraft commenced just north of Hill 296.5.

For the units of reinforced *FschJgRgt.1* that were entrenched in the Karteros depression the situation remained unchanged. During daylight the soldiers were under observed fire by the enemy and could be supplied only in the hours of darkness. Water became scarce, as the only available cistern, located near the bridge across the dried-out riverbed of the Karteros, was almost empty.

After the collapse of the front on either side of Galatas, Major General Freyberg lost hope of turning the battle for Crete in his favour. All that mattered now was to gain as much time as possible for the withdrawal of the majority of the troops of the New Zealand Division and the Chania/Souda command by means of successive delaying tactics. He planned to let these forces retire along the road that divided from the coastal road east of Souda and across the mountains to Sfakia on the southern coast of Crete. From there they were to be evacuated across the sea to Egypt. The troops still positioned at the southern entrance of Souda Bay and around Georgiopolis were also to use this road toward the south. He

---

103 See also Eiben, pp. 23-24.
104 A counter-attack by the enemy, mentioned in the war diary of *FschJgRgt.2*, is confirmed neither in the war diary of the Australian 2/4 Infantry Battalion nor in *Australia in the War of 1939-1945*, Series One/ Army.

assessed a continuation of the defence of Crete in its eastern part as unpromising. Therefore he arranged for the evacuation of the forces fighting at Heraklion and Rethymnon. The reports received about the poor state of his troops, particularly of the New Zealand Division, forced his conclusions. He therefore advised Middle East Command that he considered the situation on Crete as hopeless, as his forces had reached the limits of their endurance. He continued that if the decision was made to evacuate Crete, which he requested, he would be able to save the major part of his troops. However, in his reply, General Wavell did not agree to Freyberg's request, as he was aware of the fact that Churchill and the chiefs of staff in London wanted to retain Crete at all costs. He passed on Freyberg's request together with a justification for his now limited possibilities to send reinforcements to Crete. The reply from London underlined once more the importance of the continued defence of Crete and included the call to do the utmost for the reinforcement of CREFORCE.

In the morning Brigadier Puttick reported the withdrawal of his forces west and south-west of Chania as imperative. As at the time Major General Freyberg was determined to comply with the directives from Cairo and London, he ordered Major General Weston to take command of further operations in the area around Chania. By doing so, he hoped to overrule the pessimistic Puttick. As a measure to improve the situation in front of Chania a brigade, formed from the existing reserves – 1st Welch, 1st Rangers and Northumberland Hussars – was to relieve the 5th (New Zealand) Brigade. However in the meantime Brigadier Puttick, urged by the commanders of the 19th (Australian) Brigade and the 5th (New Zealand) Brigade, ordered the retreat of both brigades to a line along '42nd Street', stretching from the western end of Souda Bay to the mountain village of Tsikalaria in the south. The 19th Brigade, with the 2/8 and 2/7 Infantry Battalions was assigned the right flank and the 5th Brigade, with its partly mixed battalions – 21st, 28th, 19th and the remnants of the 22nd – on the left flank. The New Zealand 23rd Battalion was posted as reserve behind the left flank.[105] As Major General Weston remained ignorant about the decision by Brigadier Puttick, he ordered the three battalions of the former reserve, to occupy positions about 2km west of Chania during the night 26/ 7 May, which he coordinated with Major General Freyberg.

By the evening complete Greek formations were non-existent in the western and central parts of Crete, as the last of these, the Greek 2nd Regiment, was disbanded on the orders of its commander the previous evening.

The urgent and inevitable evacuation of Chania commenced after nightfall. The heavy coastal guns of the M.N.B.D.O. west of '42nd Street' used up as much as possible of their ammunition. Subsequently, they were, like the heavy AAA guns, rendered useless by their crews. The commanding officer and the rest of the Commandos, which during the night 26/27 May were landed by three warships in the port of Souda, were ordered by Major General Freyberg to prepare to become part of the rearguard during the retreat of CREFORCE toward Sfakia.

Also on this day the command of the British Mediterranean Fleet had undertaken an attempt to reduce the pressure applied by the *Luftwaffe* on the defenders of Crete. A task force, consisting of two battleships and nine destroyers, escorted the aircraft carrier *Formidable* into the waters near Scarpanto (today: Karpathos) for a raid with carrier aircraft against the base of *StG 2*. The attack, flown by only a few aircraft, had little effect. On the way back to Alexandria, the task force was attacked south of the Straits of Kaso by *II./StG*

---

105 Playfair, p.143, as well as Davin, describe the chaotic command arrangements around Chania on 26 May.

2. *Formidable* and a destroyer were seriously damaged before the force was able to make good its escape.

5

Onward to Victory

27 May

At dawn, as patrols probed ahead, the German forces moved into their jump-off positions for the thrust toward Chania and beyond on a broad front between the Apostoloi Peninsula and the area around Perivolia.

To the right of *Kräftegruppe Heidrich*, *GebJgRgt.141* was inserted into the front, and advanced with its two battalions in file along the northern slopes of the mountains, straight toward Souda. Its forward battalion had already reached the mountain village of Katsifariana around 0700hrs, about 2 km south-west of the docks of Souda. Further to the south, *GebJgRgt.85* continued its enveloping movement and reached the mountain path leading from Nerokomon to the east and advanced toward the village of Malaxa, located south of Souda.

The two patrols which reconnoitered ahead of *Kräftegruppe Ramcke* reported the high ground immediately west of the Kladiso stream as occupied by the enemy, as had been anticipated. Whereas the patrol from *Kampfgruppe Gericke* now stopped, the strong combat patrol from *II./SturmRgt.*, led by *Hauptfeldwebel* Barabas, succeeded in penetrating into the positions of the enemy south of the coastal road. Here they took out several strongpoints and remained in the occupied terrain even during air attacks by the *Luftwaffe*, retaining this breach for its battalion.

At 1000hrs the German attack on the coastal strip commenced on a broad front. With exemplary interaction between heavy weapons and assaulting troops, by noon *Kräftegruppe Ramcke* had seized the heights west of the Kladiso. Elements of the enemy were cut off from their routes of withdrawal and two companies of the 1st Welch, among them the battalion commander and numerous stragglers, were forced to capitulate. The remainder of three more battalions, which were positioned on either bank of the Kladiso, was pushed back partly in disorder, toward Souda and Akrotiri. In front of *Kampfgruppe Gericke*, only a small group of the enemy remained established near the coastal road.[1] With relatively low losses *II./SturmRgt.* suffered two killed throughout this day and made it evident how well fire and movement had been coordinated during the attack and how well advantage had been taken of the open left flank of the enemy by *Kräftegruppe Ramcke*.

As the order from *5.Gebirgs-Division* to bypass Chania in the south and to first surround the town had not reached *II./GebJgRgt.100*, and this unit had chosen the shortest route of advance toward it, *II./SturmRgt.* had to be taken out of the line, as there was no more space for its deployment between *Kampfgruppe Gericke* and *II./GebJgRgt.100*. It was now kept available, together with *I./SturmRgt.*, as reserve on the last heights west of Chania.

In the meantime, *Generalmajor* Ringel ordered the seizure of Chania in the light of the unexpectedly weak resistance in front of his attacking forces. Prior to the receipt of this order *II./GebJgRgt.100* (*Major* Schury), partly mounted on captured vehicles, penetrated into the town. Here the battalion found only a few enemy stragglers but did liberate more

---

1   It was forced to surrender on 28 May.

512

than 300 German soldiers from captivity, mainly from the parachute force and a number of Italian prisoners of war from the fighting in Albania and Northern Greece. The centre of Chania, particularly the port area, suffered considerably from German air attacks.

At about 1700hrs *Kampfgruppe Gericke* gained the north-eastern outskirts of Chania and took over the area toward the Akrotiri Peninsula. *Oberst* Utz, who arrived in Chania at about the same time, accepted the formal surrender of the town from its mayor.

A provisionally motorized advance party of *Kampfgruppe Schmitz* moved along the coastal road in the direction toward Souda together with *I./GebJgRgt.100*.

The reinforced *FschJgRgt.3*, which at the start of the overall attack had only occasionally been under fire, advanced along the road Alikianou-Chania, with *FschJgRgt.3* as point unit. On the way this unit occupied the enemy wireless station and dispatched a platoon, motorized with captured vehicles, toward Chania. When *Hauptmann* Freiherr von der Heydte realized that the town was already in the hands of mountain troops, he ordered his battalion to block the exit-streets along the western perimeter of the built-up area. On order of *Oberst* Heidrich, the units of his regiment following behind the point battalion, moved into a staging area near the south-western part of Chania.

Advancing toward Souda in the morning, *GebJgRgt.141* realized that the enemy had recovered from the actions of the day before and was ready to continue the combat in a most painful way. *I./GebJgRgt.141*, which shortly after 0700hrs seized the village of Katsifariana against little resistance, unexpectedly encountered the positions of the 19th (Australian) Brigade and the 5th (New Zealand) Brigade along '42nd Street', occupied by more than 2,000 soldiers. After a short firefight a large number of Australian and New Zealand soldiers charged the surprised mountain infantrymen with fixed bayonets and drove them back in disorder and with heavy losses.[2] It was only by an organised passage through the deployed *III./GebJgRgt.141* that a greater disaster was avoided. The hard-hit battalion was incapable of combat actions for the rest of the day. The parts of *GebJgRgt.100* that advanced along the coastal road toward Souda, delayed by occasional resistance and by roadblocks, could not close with the enemy along '42nd Street'.

In the evening, *Generalmajor* Ringel defined further tasks for his forces:

- to clear the southern coast of Souda Bay and to speedily repair the port installations of Souda for the conveyance of heavy vehicles and supplies
- to clear the Akrotiri Peninsula from parts of the enemy which have withdrawn that way
- to energetically pursue the retiring enemy
- to relieve without delay the forces holding out at Rethymnon and Heraklion
- to finally safeguard the west of Crete.

Oberst Ramcke received the mission to clear the Akrotiri Peninsula and firmly take possession of the western part of Crete. Therefore he was assigned the command of the

---

2   The figure of c.300 Germans killed in this engagement which Davin cites must be strongly doubted in the light of the overall losses of the *Gebirgsjäger* on Crete and at sea, as stated in the after-action report for *Merkur* of the *XI.Flieger-Korps* – 262 killed and 318 missing. The latter, mostly missing as a result of loss at sea, should also be counted as killed.

sector from Souda Bay to the western shore of the island. The majority of *GebPiBtl.95* and *Kradschützen-Btl.55* were withdrawn from this sector. Company-strength forces remained at Kissamo and in Palaeochora.

The pursuit of the enemy toward the east was taken over mainly by troops from the *5.Gebirgs-Division*. *General der Flieger* Student and *Generalmajor* Ringel made the assumption that the enemy would attempt to retain the eastern part of Crete.

For the speedy relief of the *Fallschirmtruppe* at Rethymnon and Heraklion, urged particularly by Student, *Generalmajor* Ringel ordered the formation of an advance detachment during the night. Led by the commander of *GebArtRgt.95*, *Oberstleutnant* Wittmann, the following units and sub-units were assigned to this force:

- *GebAufklAbt.95*, commanded by *Rittmeister* Graf zu Castell-Castell
- a company and command-elements from *Kradschützen-Btl.55*
- a provisionally motorized platoon from *GebPiBtl.95*
- the provisionally motorized heavy infantry gun platoon of *GebJgRgt.100*
- a battery from *GebArtRgt.95*[3]
- *1./FschArtAbt.7*
- an anti-tank platoon from *GebPzJgAbt.95*.

The advance detachment was to bypass the troops, moving along the coastal road and in cooperation with *Kampfgruppe Jais*, advancing to its right along the northern slopes of the mountains, was to fight through on the shortest route to the isolated paratroopers.

On the airfield at Maleme a few troops, but mainly supplies, were landed and the wounded were evacuated to the Greek mainland. Additionally, a barge, towed by the tug *Kentawros*, was on the way to the Bight of Kissamo after a short stop at the island of Kythira. The barge carried two Pz II from *PzRgt.31*. The transport was able to move no more than 5-6 sea miles per hour, to prevent the elderly barge from flooding.[4]

In the contested area east of Rethymnon, after artillery preparation the enemy, attacked again during the morning of 27 May with two Matilda II tanks and two companies of Australian infantry along the coastal road against the positions of *Kampfgruppe Schulz* at the eastern perimeter of Perivolia. At a distance of about 200m the tank, advancing immediately south of the road, was set ablaze by the hit of an armor piercing shell from one of the recoiless guns and was abandoned by its crew. The second tank, approaching on the coastal road, initially fired at its own infantry in front. Then it ran onto a mine and the explosion tore off one of its tracks. Rapidly fired at by mortars and recoilless guns its weapons were rendered useless. The enemy infantry, who suffered considerable losses, nevertheless came close to the German positions. However after both tanks had been put out of action they discontinued the attack and retired toward the east.[5] On the German

---

3   Personal photos of *Major* (ret.) Mößinger, who at that time had been the orderly officer in *FschJgRgt.1*, show that *Kettenkrad* had been flown to Crete as tows for mountain guns.

4   The transfer of these two tanks to Crete is described at some length by Visua.

5   For a description of this engagement see *Australia in the War of 1939-1945*, Series One/ Army p.267 and Mündel. The Matilda tanks had been those which were disabled on 21 May, but had been recovered on 22 May and after repair had been manned again by volunteers. The attacking infantry consisted of two companies from the Australian 2/11 Infantry Battalion.

side the last combat effective officer of *2./FschArtAbt.7* and a member of a gun-crew were killed in the engagement. *Kampfgruppe Kroh*, which had been satisfactorily fed with the rations dropped the day before, but short of small arms, commenced the expansion of its operational area in the morning. *3./FschJgRgt.2* seized Hill 157. The newly formed 1st Company occupied Hill 217. The 2nd Company advanced toward the village of Prinos, to the south, but met strong resistance from Greek troops and was forced to ground in front of the village, losing six wounded. However it captured about 20 Greek soldiers.

East of Heraklion *Oberst* Bräuer received orders from the command of *XI.Flieger-Korps* to seize in the coming morning the airfield of Heraklion using his now concentrated force, following preceding air attacks. However the preparations for this attack proceeded slowly. Moreover *Oberst* Bräuer reported to the corps command that he required artillery support for the attack. As neither recoilless guns for delivery by parachute nor gliders could be made available on the Greek mainland, only the landing of mountain guns and their ammunition by transport aircraft remained an option. Hastily the selected landing site, east of Hill 296.5 was now prepared.

Meanwhile *Hauptmann* Schirmer moved his paratroopers nearer to the front of the enemy positions. *Gruppe Schulz* also expanded its operational area toward the south-west. Here the area around Knossos was occupied by units of *Bataillon Vogel*. In the British hospital established in two country houses not far away from the ancient ruins of Knossos, British, German and Greek physicians and medical personnel had commonly cared for numerous wounded for several days, among them were about 250 paratroopers.[6]

Freyberg, whose headquarters was still established in the port area of Souda, hours had waited for a decision regarding his request for the evacuation of the island. During the morning Pressed General Wavell urged him to continue the defence of Crete in the east since the early morning. When Major General Freyberg accused him of being ignorant of the actual situation, Wavell finally agreed with the former's request. He reported his decision to the Chiefs of Staff in London and pointed out that a prolongation of operations on Crete would result only in a fruitless depreciation of the forces of all three services and negatively impact the overall defence of the Near East. The Chiefs of Staff replied without delay, and this time approved the evacuation of the island. Irrespective of material losses, as many soldiers as possible were to be saved.[7]

Within the command area of Major General Weston, who nominally was assigned the command over all troops of the former sectors of Maleme and Chania/Souda, the covering force operations and withdrawal movements of the 5th (New Zealand) Brigade, the 19th (Australian) Brigade and 'Layforce' were, for the greater part, conducted as planned by Freyberg throughout the day. The coordination was mainly done on the level of these formations, as Weston, lacking an adequate command organization, as well as experience as a tactical commander, did not involve himself in these matters, Major General Freyberg obviously not being aware of this problem. As the staff of CREFORCE saw no further

---

6   KTB 1 Korinth und Kreta des *FschJgRgt.2* dates the occupation of the hospital to 28 May. As the sources of the former enemy in this regard are considered more precise, their date has been used.

7   See also Playfair, p.142.

possibility to unite the troops at Rethymnon with the main force, they were advised to move on their own through the mountains to the Bight of Plaka on the southern coast of Crete for embarkation. As radio communication with them was no longer available an order was dropped by a supply aircraft, but as this failed to arrive and the chance was missed to send the order with a lighter which was sailing in the night from Souda to Rethymnon,[8] Lieutenant Colonel Campbell remained uninformed about the decision by the command of CREFORCE. At Heraklion, Brigadier Chappel[9] received the order to embark his troops in the night 28/29 May on warships that were entering the port of Heraklion. He therefore had sufficient time for planning and preparations for the evacuation of his sector.

While the British naval task force accompanied the heavily damaged aircraft carrier *Formidable* after the rather unsuccessful raid against Scarpanto, and sailed back to Alexandria, an Italian landing fleet set sail from Rhodes toward Crete. The preparations for the landing-operation evidently had not been detected by Middle East Command as the Italian landing fleet would have constituted a much more lucrative target for a naval task force a day or two after its departure than the airfield on Scarpanto.[10]

28 May

At 0300hrs Wittmann's advance detachment set out on the coastal road between Chanis and Souda with about 400 men for the relief of the *Fallschirmtruppe* at Rethymnon and Heraklion. Student, sitting in the sidecar of a motorcycle, worried about the soldiers of his force who stood isolated since their landing on 20 May. As in Rotterdam, one year previously, he decided to act without delay.[11] Ahead of *GebJgRgt.100* the advance detachment moved through Souda which had been abandoned by the enemy during the night 27/28 May, without being delayed by enemy stragglers, material left behind or occasional road obstructions. At about 0600hrs the point unit gained the area around Neo Chorion and Stilos. Here it supported the final phase of the combat of *GebJgRgt.85*, which pushed back and pursued an enemy rearguard along the coastal road.[12] As it was considered of overriding importance by the commander of the advance detachment to preserve his combat power for the actual relief operations, he decided to stop on the spot for the rest of the day and to advance toward Rethymnon again in the coming morning.

---

8   As the stocks of ammunition and food were running out in the Rethymnon sector, supplies had been dropped on 26 May by bombers from Egypt, and a lighter with rations for movement across the mountains had been sent in the night of 26/27 May.

9   The submarine cable from Chania to Alexandria via Heraklion, which had provided CREFORCE with unhindered telephone and teletype connections with the Middle East Command, had obviously been made unusable when Chania had been given up.

10 On 22 May Hitler, evidently in view of the difficulties on Crete, had accepted Mussolini's offer to participate in the conquest of the island.

11 Without any doubt, Student's attitude speaks for his courage. It may also indicate his striving for recognition. Contrary to many other senior commanders, he had little charisma and evidently looked for a way to be regarded as a superior who could always be found up front by both senior commanders as well as his paratroopers.

12 The events related to the retreat of the main force of the enemy toward Sfakia and its embarkation, as well as the German operations connected with it, will not be covered in this book, as they are not part of its subject.

The enemy in the contested area around Perivolia attacked the 'Kapellenhöhe' in the first hours of 28 May, but were beaten back. At 0320hrs, another attack was launched, this time against Perivolia proper.[13] While the thrust of about a company of Australian infantry along the coastal road from the east was repelled with heavy losses for the attacker at about 0430hrs, the enemy, to the strength of another company, penetrated into Perivolia through a gap between the *9./* and the *11./FschJgRgt.2* and managed to occupy some houses in the western part of the village. From here he harassed the defenders along the southern edge and caused considerable losses among them. Three shock troops of paratroopers failed to dislodge the Australians. The company commanders of the *9./* and *11./FschJgRgt.2*, *Oberleutnants* Begemann and Pabst, were killed at the head of counter-attacks, as well as *Leutnant* Molsen from *11./FschJgRgt.2*, who in previous days had distinguished himself several times as a commander of shock troops. Two more officers were wounded, among them the battalion-commander *Hauptmann* Wiedemann. At about 1400hrs only three officers of the entire combat group remained available for duty – *Hauptmann* Schulz, *Leutnant* Klitzing from the FschMGBtl and *Leutnant* Kühl from *III./FschJgRgt.2*. The latter now assumed command of the remnants of *III./FschJgRgt.2*. Supplies that were dropped around this time could not be salvaged until after nightfall, because of accurate fire from Australian infantry in and around Perivolia.

When the Australians, who had penetrated into the western part of Perivolia, could not be reinforced and were running out of ammunition, at about 2100hrs they attempted to break out along the shore toward the east. The breakout, however, was frustrated by the fire of a machine gun in a Ju 52, which had crashed on the beach.

Kampfgruppe Kroh was out of contact with the enemy. Nevertheless outposts toward the west were able to protect it against attack. Upon delivery by air of the urgently requested weapons, which was planned to happen during that day, after swinging out toward the south *Major* Kroh intended to move his force closer to the airstrip in order to at least tie down the enemy there. However *Kompanie Rosenberg* was still pinned down in front of Prinos, which Greek troops defended stubbornly. Despite urgent requests for support from *Kampfgruppe Schulz*, for the time being Kroh saw no possibility to intervene in its favour.

In the operational area of *Gruppe Ost*, *Oberst* Bräuer failed to complete preparations for the attack against the airfield at Heraklion, which was ordered by the command of *XI.Flieger-Korps*. The massive air attack which was flown to prepare the attack was wasted.

Early in the afternoon four more companies of paratroopers, formed by soldiers of *Fl.Div.7* which had to stay behind in the greater area around Athens on 20 May, was dropped near Gournes. They were commanded by *Hauptmann* Böhmler. As *Oberst* Bräuer had postponed the attack on the coming day, the new arrivals were inserted in the front. As an organizational matter, all members of *FschJgRgt.2*, who were dropped with the Vogel's and Böhmler's battalions were now concentrated in one company, which was assigned to *Bataillon Schirmer*. This returned Egger's company to *III./FschJgRgt.1*. Bräuer's attack order was ready at 1600hrs. By 1830hrs, the instructions were completed.

---

13 For this attack Lieutenant Colonel Campbell deployed the majority of the 2/11 Infantry Battalion with the aim of eliminating the German 'hedgehog' for good. By that time, he still had not received orders for the further operations of his force.

Around noon a Ju 52 with a mountain-gun,[14] its ammunition and crew aboard, touched down on the provisional landing site just north of Hill 296.5 after a masterpiece of flying by its pilot. After unloading the aircraft, which was overloaded with 20 wounded, he had managed to take off again from the 300m long cornfield and arrived safely at Megara.[15]

As the mountain infantry regiments relentlessly pursued the retreating enemy, whose intentions were still not clear to the German superior commands, the clearing and occupation operations in the new command area of *Oberst* Ramcke had commenced. *Major* Stentzler with his *II./SturmRgt.*, assumed the function of commandant of Chania. The heavily depleted *I./SturmRgt.* was tasked with the build-up of a collection point for the increasing numbers of prisoners of war and with the provision of guards for it. *Kampfgruppen Gericke* and *Schmitz* took over the protection of the northern coast of Crete between the eastern edge of Chania and the airfield at Maleme. *FschJgRgt.3* commenced with the clearing of the Akrotiri Peninsula. *FschPiBtl.7*, up until now subordinate, was drawn off and at 1300hrs arrived at Souda. After the clearing of the town and its port the battalion moved to a rest area south-west of Souda in the evening. The final pacification of the mountains around Kandanos remained incomplete for the time being, but was not forgotten.

The tug that was towing the barge with the two tanks from *5./PzRgt.31* aboard arrived at the shore of the Bight of Kissamo during the night 28/29 May. As there were no unloading installations, the barge was set aground on the beach. After its bow was blown off by explosives, the two tanks rolled ashore. They immediately set off to join Wittmann's advance detachment.

In the evening of 28 May about 2,500 Italian troops arrived by sea from Rhodes. Among them was a company of light tanks, which landed in the bay of Sitia without interference from the enemy.[16] The commanders of the German troops opposing the enemy knew nothing about the landing of the Italians. The information probably also remained unknown in the command post of *Generalmajor* Ringel and in the battle HQ of General Student until some time the next day.[17]

---

14 It had probably been from *3./FschArtAbt.7*. This unit, after the failed sea transport, was equipped with mountain guns from the stocks of the *6.Gebirgs-Division*.

15 See also the excerpt of the war diary of *Leutnant* Lankenau in Schaug, p. 92.

16 The force was made up of a battalion each from the 9th and 10th regiment of the *Regina* Infantry Division, a company of Blackshirt militia, two companies of marines, a company with 13 L 3/33 light tanks, a platoon of engineers, some trucks and numerous pack animals which had been brought along in six fishing trawlers, four steamers and two tugs and had been escorted by a destroyer, three torpedo boats and six submarine hunters. Three tankers were also part of the convoy. The landing force was commanded by Colonel Caffaro.

17 *Luftflotte 4* must have been informed in time, as its liaison officer was located on Rhodes. Moreover, reconnaissance and combat aircraft, patrolling over the eastern coast of Crete and the adjoining waters had probably reported the convoy.

During the night 28/29 May four British destroyers from Alexandria brought along rations to Sfakia and took back with them about 700 soldiers from CREFORCE, many of them wounded.

29 May

In the early morning Wittmann's advance detachment continued its march toward Rethymnon. It met no more resistance, but as far as Vrises the traces of the enemy's withdrawal were evident. Shortly before noon, the motorcycle infantry which formed the vanguard arrived in front of Rethymnon. The town had been abandoned by the enemy and undefended street obstructions were quickly circumvented. At the eastern exit of the town the motorcyclists received sporadic fire from machine-guns and mortars, from the heights south-east of the coastal road. When they advanced in this direction, almost a regiment of Greek troops ceased to fight and surrendered. Some of the Greek soldiers pointed out that German prisoners of war were still confined in Rethymnon.

The main force of the advance detachment now moved up behind the vanguard. Parts of it remained behind and occupied the town. About 300 paratroopers, who had been confined in the town prison, were liberated, among them *Oberst* Sturm.

At about 1300hrs the vanguard established contact with the defenders of the hedgehog at Perivolia. Less then one hundred combat-effective men had been unable to prevent the sortie of the Australian infantry company from the western part of Perivolia at dawn. From then on, except for occasional artillery fire, the enemy was no longer seen around village.

The relief for *Kampfgruppe Schulz* for the time being remained in Perivolia and Wittmann, advancing along the coastal road, came across well-entrenched Australian troops east of Platanes. After a spontaneous attack had collapsed due to heavy defensive fire, *Oberstleutnant* Wittmann decided to first bring his heavy weapons in position and to renew the attack in the coming morning.

General der Flieger Student remained in Rethymnon and summoned the last combat effective officer of *III./FschJgRgt.2*, *Leutnant* Kühl, for a report on the past events at Perivolia. He also found time to listen to the reports of liberated soldiers and to welcome back *Oberst* Sturm and *Hauptmann* Kleye.

During the day *Kampfgruppe Kroh* prepared for its evening attack. From several approaches transport aircraft dropped urgently required weapons, ammunition and rations. A patrol sought out the settlement of Panormos on the shore east of the staging area. Combat patrols were also dispatched toward the mountains in the south and Kimari[18] in the west, which was the objective of the attack in the evening. Circumventing Prinos, where the 2nd Company was to attack again in the evening, the 1st Company and *Kompanie Hinz*, followed by the 3rd Company as reserve, deployed at 1800hrs for the attack against Kimari. The assault, which commenced at 1930hrs, surprised the Greek garrison and resulted in the seizure of the settlement. At about the same time, the 2nd Company succeeded in seizing

---

18   This settlement, which is mentioned several times in German after-action reports, could not be located on maps. Therefore, it may well be that it was misprinted and should have read Kirianna, about 5 km south of the olive oil factory. It is also possible that the small settlement has disappeared because of restructuring after the war.

Prinos.[19] In the early morning of the next day, *Kampfgruppe Kroh* was to thrust forward from Kimari against the olive oil factory

To the west, in the afternoon *GebJgRgt.100* met the bicycle platoon of Wittmann's force at Vrises, which had been left behind as a reserve element. The mountain regiment then turned off as ordered onto the mountain road, leading to the plateau of Askifou and farther on to Sfakia. Its mission was to pursue and stop enemy units retreating there. Meanwhile *GebJgRgt.85* and *GebJgRgt.141* painstakingly advanced toward the east along the northern slopes of the mountains, as *Generalmajor* Ringel was still in the dark about enemy intentions.[20]

In the evening *FschPiBtl.7* was tasked with the repair of the port installations of Souda, as this port was now to be used without delay to unload larger ships, delivering vehicles, heavy material and bulk supplies.

In the contested area east of Heraklion, the reinforced *FschJgRgt.1* stood ready at dawn for the attack against the airfield. As the customary harassing fire failed to commence, and observation posts were unable to detect any movements in the enemy's field positions, patrols were immediately sent out, advancing against the airfield from the south and east. A short time later these reported that the enemy had vanished. Thereupon, the entire task force was set in motion toward the airfield and beyond to the coast. During the advance a number of straggling Greek soldiers, but very few of their Allied counterparts, were encountered and captured, mostly without resistance. In the morning Heraklion was occupied without a fight. *II./FschJgRgt.2* was now ordered to move out toward Rethymnon. At about 1600hrs the battalion reached the settlement of Gaji on the coastal road. The Ju 52s bringing along *3./FschArtAbt.7* were no longer required to touch down on the provisional landing site on Hill 296.5 but were directed for unloading on the airfield. As it was then found out that the airfield had been mined, a mine-clearing detachment from *PiBtl.659* was flown in on the same day.[21]

The evacuation of Heraklion and the embarkation of the British and Australian soldiers from there during the night 28/29 May had been accomplished undetected by *Kräftegruppe Bräuer*, mainly because it had shown in the previous days little of the aggressive spirit the *Fallschirmtruppe* was known for.[22] The *Luftwaffe* also failed to draw correct conclusions about the naval movements related to the evacuation.

---

19   In the evening of 29 May the Greek troops on the airstrip east of Rethymnon and in the area south-east of it had already begun to disintegrate and to move off into the mountains. This is confirmed by *Australia in the War of 1939-1945*, Series One/ Army p.272. This also mentions that in the evening of 29 May the Australian 2/11 Infantry Battalion had taken over the positions of the Greek 4th Regiment and had left only one company opposite Perivolia.

20   Ringel, p.192, notes that on 29 May the location of Freyberg's three divisions was still unclear to him.

21   In the course of several days this detachment had detected and neutralized 134 mines.

22   The evacuation operation and the events at sea are described in some detail in *Australia in the War of 1939-1945*, Series One/ Army pp.292-293 and in Playfair, pp.142-143.

On 28 May the evacuation fleet – cruisers *Orion*, *Ajax* and *Dido* and six destroyers – were attacked by German dive bombers from Scarpanto on their way from Alexandria. *Ajax* was damaged and forced to return to its home port. The other ships arrived north of Heraklion at about 2230hrs. While the two cruisers took up positions in the open sea the destroyers entered the port of Heraklion. The embarkation of the troops approached in packages at the correct times and transferred them to the waiting cruisers. Once these had been loaded the destroyers boarded the remaining troops. The embarkation was carried out to perfection. It was possible to clear the final rearguard positions around the port by midnight. At about 0200hrs on 29 May, the ships with more than 4,000 soldiers aboard, set sail back to Alexandria. The wounded in the hospital near Knossos were left behind, as it had come under the control of the Germans and a protective element at a roadblock about 16km south-east of Heraklion. The evacuation of Greek troops had not been considered. Therefore, they were not informed about the operation, as space on board of the ships was not sufficent and there had been little trust in the discipline and the state of training of the Greeks.

However the voyage back to Alexandria went off badly from the beginning. The destroyer *Imperial*, which had already been damaged by a bomb, was disabled for good half an hour after the departure of the convoy. Her passengers and the ship's company were shipped to the destroyer *Hotspur*, which, after sinking the *Imperial* with torpedoes, followed the main force. The latter, at about 0500hrs, entered the Strait of Kaso but by now the *Luftwaffe* was wide awake. The convoy was detected by dive bombers from Scarpanto and attacked almost ceaselessly with 400 sorties until 1300hrs. The destroyer *Hereward* was mortally hit, so that she had to be set aground on the eastern tip of Crete. Most of her passengers and ship's company survived, but were captured either on land or by Italian warships, coming to the aid of the shipwrecked. The cruisers *Dido* and *Orion* were also hit by bombs. On their crowded decks about 350 men, most of them evacuees from Heraklion, fell victims to the bombs. It was only after fighter cover from Egypt made its appearance that the German dive bombers desisted from further attacks, so that the remaining ships reached Alexandria at about 2000hrs. Of the more than 4,000 soldiers who had been evacuated from Heraklion, about 800 had perished at sea or had been wounded or captured.

The CREFORCE troops that were retiring toward Sfakia had been able to move along unhindered by German ground forces and were only occasionally annoyed by aircraft of the *Luftwaffe*. Major General Weston was able to maintain command over the still intact two brigades and one of the 'Layforce' battalions and to issue instructions for rearguard operations, which were planned by the method of leapfrogging. He still had a few light tanks, some field guns and a number of Bren Gun Carriers available.

While the communication between Freyberg and Middle East Command could be maintained continuously by means of a long-distance radio in the CREFORCE staff, which made it possible to coordinate the evacuation measures to some extent, there was again no wireless communication with the sector command at Rethymnon. A navy wireless station at Rethymnon still had communication with Cairo in the early hours of 29 May. From there, however, no instructions for the evacuation were passed on as the navy wireless in Rethymnon did not contain any encoding material.

30 May

While the main efforts in the areas which were already firmly in the hands of the *Gebirgsjäger* and *Fallschirmtruppe* were now directed toward the final clearing of the terrain of scattered enemy soldiers of irregulars, the collection and registration of prisoners of war, the sifting of the booty, the restoration of port installations and the repair of lines of communication, most of the mountain troops remained tasked with combat missions.

In pursuit of enemy forces withdrawing along the mountain route toward Sfakia and occasionally pushing back weak rearguards, *GebJgRgt.100* reached the undefended plateau of Askifou. *GebJgRgt.85* and *GebJgRgt.141*, advancing farther to the east along the mountain slopes south of the coastal road, made no further contact with the enemy.

From the area around Perivolia, after massive fire preparation, Wittmann attacked the blocking position of the Australians at the western edge of the airstrip east of Rethymnon. These defended stubbornly. However after about three hours of fighting two German tanks from Kastelli joined the engagement, and the thrust of the enveloping motorcyclists from the south took effect. Lieutenant Colonel Campbell capitulated at about 0900hrs.[23] Of the two infantry battalions 934 unwounded and about 190 wounded soldiers went into captivity. More than 100 combat support, command and logistic troops joined their fate. While the prisoners were rounded up and disarmed, elements of Wittmann's advance detachment moved into the olive oil factory. At Stavromenos they met with *Kampfgruppe Kroh*, deployed for the attack. The mutual greeting was joyous but remained short because of the pending tasks of the advance detachment.

When the responsibility for the operational area around Rethymnon was handed back to *FschJgRgt.2*, the advance detachment moved off toward Heraklion, 50km away. General Student again joined it. After a short firefight with Cretan irregulars in the pine woods near Prines, at 1215hrs the detachment met a motorized patrol from *II./FschJgRgt.2* about 35km west of Heraklion and some distance west of the town established contact with all of this battalion, which approached along the coastal road. On its arrival in Heraklion it was bid welcome by paratroopers, who had completely taken possession of the town. At his new command post in the control building of the airfield, *Oberst* Bräuer later reported to General Student the accomplishment of his mission. The latter now proudly and rightfully could state that the enemy on Crete had not been able to overcome any of the parachute task forces.[24]

In the meantime Wittmann had moved along the coastal road, near the sea port of Ierapetra and around midnight met troops and tanks of the Italian landing force, which had advanced there. It was through this encounter that all of the northern part of Crete could now be considered in Axis hands.

---

23 Shortly prior to the capitulation Lieutenant Colonel Campbell had left it to his soldiers to try their luck by escaping into the mountains. Most of the c.300 men were eventually captured within a few days of the fighting, as many Cretans had observed the German warning not to support the fugitives. Of the two Australian infantry battalions under the command of Campbell, only 68 men, among them 15 officers, reached Egypt after many weeks and under adventurous circumstances. See *Australia in the War of 1939-1945*, Series One/ Army, p.276.

24 The statement, as such, was correct. It had, however, never been followed up by a reminiscence of the errors which both Student and Bräuer had made in their appreciation of the situation at Heraklion during the planning and the conduct of the parachute assault there.

Imvros, as the bird flies, is only 6km away from the small port of Sfakia, but from where only a narrow mountain path winds down to the coast through a rocky defile, *GebJgRgt.100* was held, taking considerable losses from a strong rearguard of the enemy, supported by artillery and a few light tanks. It was only now that the German higher commands involved on Crete and on the Greek mainland finally realized that the enemy had extricated his main force from the grip of the mountain troops along an unexpected route. It had to be anticipated that the Middle East Command would do its utmost to bring back as many troops as possible by ships from Sfakia during the hours of darkness. Sea movements during daytime, as far as these could not be avoided, would probably be covered on their last stretch by fighters from Egypt and anti-aircraft cruisers.[25]

Additional mountain or parachute troops, particularly heavy weapons, were too far away to quickly support *GebJgRgt.100*. Therefore for the time being the unit had to act alone. In the light of enemy strength and his well-chosen positions, a frontal attack at Imvros was out of the question. As such the regimental commander decided to circumvent the rearguard across the cliffs, thereby gaining the beaches near Sfakia. This movement was to commence on 31 May at first light. Only massive interference by the *Luftwaffe* could offer any chance of preventing large parts of the enemy from making their escape across the sea to Egypt.

---

25   In fact, only the Australian cruiser *Perth* was hit by a bomb during the return passage. Of the anti-aircraft cruisers *Calcutta* and *Coventry*, which had been dispatched from Alexandria for additional protection of the final evacuation during the night 31 May/ June, the *Calcutta* had been sunk by two Ju 88s only 100 sea miles out.

6

The battle for Crete. Touchstone for the German *Fallschirmtruppe* and turning-point in its history

Whilst the 5,000 or more soldiers of CREFORCE, who had to be left behind in the area around Sfakia, surrendered to *GebJgRgt.100* on 1 June and *Generaloberst* Löhr reported to Göring that he had accomplished his mission, the last combat actions of the parachute force on the island had occurred two days previously. The time which followed was used to reorganize the combat-fatigued troops and care for their most pressing needs. Only gradually, however, did the picture concerning the events of the past days of fighting become clearer. Much of this information was ascertained only weeks after or at the end of the war. However, much of it would remain hidden forever.

There is no doubt that the decision to conquer Crete was made by Hitler. This decision had not been the result of long-lasting deliberations and staff work, but had been made as a result of the fast-moving situation on the Greek mainland. Hitler considered the taking of Crete as a possible objective in securing the eastern Mediterranean and providing a platform for further operations into North Africa and the Middle East. When the Italian navy had been hit hard and had found itself unable to guarantee protection of the sea lines of communication to Libya during the invasion of Greece, Hitler quickly realized the marginal significance of Crete for any offensive action in this area. In view of the campaign against the Soviet Union, which was to commence as soon as the weather would permit, he regarded the war in the Balkans as completed with the clearing of the Peloponnese of the British expeditionary corps.

However on 21 April 1941, Student, as commanding general of the parachute force with the support of the commander-in-chief of the *Luftwaffe* and the chief of its general staff, carried forward the idea to Hitler that Crete could, and should, be conquered from the air. The latter was of the opinion that a conquest of Crete was more preferable to an invasion of Malta. In justification for this decision Hitler emphasized the strategic advantages of the conquest of Crete for the protection of the Rumanian oil fields against British air attacks and the security of the sea lines of communication through the eastern Mediterranean and the Black Sea. Only the second advantage of Crete in German hands, however, had actually counted, which was the denial of its airfields to the enemy, in order to prevent him from providing fighter cover for air attacks against Axis shipping in the Aegean Sea and around the Peloponnese and to use Souda Bay for small warships with the same purpose. As for the threat of bombing attacks against the Rumanian oil fields, the problem for the British was that their most modern bomber, the Wellington, which could reach them easily from Egypt, could not be escorted by any fighters due to their limited range, even from Crete.

In the light of the concentration of the strongest possible combat power against the Soviet Union, the question of the retention of adequately strong and versatile German air assets in the eastern Mediterranean would soon become more important than the conquest of Crete.

Two other strategic options connected with the conquest of Crete had remained alien to Hitler's thinking, because of his total dedication toward the campaign against Russia. These were namely the chance to weaken the British Mediterranean Fleet during the battle for the island and to utilize it intensively for air attacks against the Suez Canal, the British lifeline to its Empire. His directive No. 28 therefore addressed Crete only in general terms as "a base for the conduct of the air war against England in the eastern Mediterranean," while it had gone into much detail about the reinforcement of the *Luftlande-Korps* by the *Heer* and about the provision of trucks for the transport of troops. Göring, probably for reasons of opportunism, made no use of his last chance in the conference on 21 April to convince Hitler of the idea of regarding Crete as a stepping stone toward the Near East in an extension of the war against Great Britain, and to thereby induce him to give up *Barbarossa* until a later time.

The motives of Student came into play again. He had not succeeded in obtaining an operational-level role for his parachute force in the planning for *Barbarossa*. Despite the merits of his troops in the campaign in the West, he had gained almost no influence on the *OKW*, and none at all on the *OKH*. Hitler, indifferent to the results of *Fall Gelb*, had not developed employment options of his own for the *Fallschirmtruppe*. In this situation only Göring could have helped Student find an operational-level mission in the impending campaign in the East. The former, however, for the reasons mentioned above, remained uninterested. Therefore Student according to his own statement, became uneasy about the morale of his soldiers, besides being driven by ambition, and thus used the chance which appeared given to him by Göring's deliberations about the war in the eastern Mediterranean.[26]

How strongly Hitler was impressed by Student's statement on 21 April, that his parachute force was impatiently waiting for a new chance to manifest its capabilities, cannot be known. It must be assumed, however, that Hitler, in his megalomania, expected this eagerness from all the soldiers of the *Wehrmacht*.

Notwithstanding the contemplated date of attack against Crete "around 15 May" and the caveat that the transport movements for *Merkur* should not lead to delays in the deployment for *Barbarossa*. Hitler made little haste in issuing the actual attack orders. *General der Flieger* Student, as can be read in his memoirs, obviously accepted the limited timeframe for the deployment of the majority of his forces over inconvenient lines of communications without objection. The timely arrival of his troops and the assigned air transport formations in the south of Greece had warranted his attitude. A number of the persistent deficiencies during the generation of the prerequisites for Operation *Merkur*, like the adequate provision of aviation fuel for the transport aircraft, the improvement of the conditions on the provisional airfields and the equipment of the troops with suitable clothing, which all would have negative effects on the course of the operations, could probably have been resolved or at least reduced with more preparation time.

It was only after the start of operations that the serious underestimation of the strength, combat power and fighting will of the Allied troops on Crete became apparent, and that the initial attack plan of Student and his staff to drop the first wave of parachute

---

26   That Student had known about Göring's deliberations becomes evident in his article 'Ein Angriff ohne Kenntnis der Lage'.

troops simultaneously at four main objectives was thus exposed. The plan has already been examined earlier in this book, but requires some more in-depth examination here to unearth its grave consequences, should it have been executed.

Measured by the number of Ju 52s which were available for parachuting during the morning of 20 May – about 410 aircraft, as those for towing the gliders and for dropping *Kampfgruppe Mürbe* have to be subtracted from the overall number – less than two battalions of parachute infantry could have been dropped at each of the four main objectives as a first wave, if at least some of the supporting weapons from the corps and divisional-level units were assigned to each of the three parachute infantry battalions. Only the *SturmRgt.* was somewhat better off by about half a battalion as it had been assigned the gliders for half of *I./SturmRgt.* and for *Sturmgruppe Braun*. Student and his planners had to assume that the enemy had carefully evaluated past German parachute assaults. Consequently they had to count on the strongest defense around the three airfields in the north of Crete and around the potential landing site for aircraft in Prison Valley. Even on the basis of the low initial appreciation of the strength of the Commonwealth troops on Crete, this would have meant that the enemy was capable of deploying up to two battalions of combat troops plus some combat support at each of these four locations. Incomprehensibly, Student, during the development of his original attack plan, assumed that the airfields at Maleme and Heraklion would be protected only by forces to the strength of one battalion, and the airstrip at Rethymnon by even weaker forces.[27] In the light of the actual attack plan for *Merkur*, the question as to what extent Student's initial plan would have required a completely new approach toward the missions for the regimental task forces and the operational plans of their commanders need not be followed up.

The most obvious weakness during the preparation of *Merkur* was the misjudgment of the numerical strength and the combat value of the forces mustered for the island's defense. The occupation of the island by the 14th British Brigade and some AAA units immediately after the start of Italy's attack against Greece had clearly been recognized by the Germans. Approximate figures for the forces of the British expeditionary corps which had been evacuated from the Greek mainland, also existed although it remained unclear how many of its troops were on Crete. It was also known that the soldiers of the expeditionary corps had left much of their heavy weapons behind on the Greek mainland. The transports, which in the first two weeks of May had entered Souda Bay and had departed again, had been estimated to be involved in the continuation of the evacuation process. In particular *Generaloberst* Löhr, the overall commander for *Merkur* and his chief of staff, *Generalmajor* Korten, had rated the strength of the Commonwealth troops on Crete as low. They had been strengthened in their perception by an appreciation of the situation by *Admiral* Canaris for the higher commands in Athens in early May, which stated that the majority of Commonwealth troops had already left Crete and that the Cretan authorities were awaiting the Germans, in order to disarm the remainder should these not have left the island by then.[28]

---

27   See Student's memoirs in Götzel, p. 207. Whether this assumption, which cannot be traced in the original documentation about *Merkur*, has been made up by Student after the war as justification for his initial plan of attack, remains unresolved.

28   See Student in ‚So sahen wir die Kreter'.

The essential reason for the erroneous estimate of the enemy situation on Crete has to be seen in the incapability of the German air reconnaissance to lift the veil on the dispositions of the defenders. During the preparation phase of the German attack, these had executed their movements almost exclusively in the hours of darkness, had masterly camouflaged their positions and had restricted the fire of AAA guns at the airfields to but a few guns. It was as a result of the air reconnaissance for all of the main initial objectives of the parachute force that an inaccurate picture of the enemy was generated there. Student seems to have relied on this information as he did not urge *Luftflotte 4* to intensified air reconnaissance efforts. For Heraklion and Rethymnon, despite his negative experience from the landings around Den Haag in the previous year, this incorrect picture evidently let him accept the direct parachute assault option against the airfields. The losses were therefore considered acceptable compared to the anticipated achievements. The situation was quite different for the drop zones south-east of Maleme and the heights at Galatas. Here air reconnaissance had almost completely failed to detect the extensive and densely occupied positions of the enemy, into which *III./SturmRgt.* and the majority of *III./FschJgRgt.3* were to be dropped with disastrous results.

At the end of this examination it is now clear that air reconnaissance may not always have been of the highest possible degree of accuracy. Serving as justification for this position are the facts that only four reconnaissance aircraft had been lost during the preparation for and execution of *Merkur* and that the movement of the main force of the enemy had remained undetected for almost three days.[29]

Almost all studies about the battle for Crete rightfully comment on the extraordinarily high losses of the German parachute force. It is now possible to state with a high degree of certainty that 3,162 soldiers of the German parachute force lost their lives in the battle for Crete. About 2-300 probably died of their wounds in medical installations after their evacuation to the Greek mainland.[30]

The number of these losses differs in the literature depending on the bias of the author, intentional or not.[31] Many include both paratroopers and other troops into their total, thus confusing the true numbers of parachute casualties.[32] Only an excessive underestimation of the enemy in every aspect can be seen as the explanation as to why about a third of the overall strength of *Kräftegruppen Bräuer* and *Sturm* were dropped directly over the airfields at Heraklion and Rethymnon, where the strongest firepower of the enemy lay. Moreover, only ignorance or disregard of the command principles for the attack, as laid down in directive 323 of the doctrinal *Heer* Field Manual 300/1 – Truppenführung,[33]

---

29   The author therefore disagrees with Student's perception about the "devoted" employment of the air reconnaissance arm, stated in Götzel, p. 331.

30   German accounts state that about 450 wounded soldiers of all three services of the *Wehrmacht* had died of their wounds in Greece and been buried at Lonkinia.

31   Student himself had belonged to the exponents of this way of thinking. *Brigadegeneral* (ret.) Dr. Günter Roth, in his article about Operation *Merkur*, quotes a remark by Student, which says that he had made a grave mistake with the proposal for the attack against Crete and thereby had caused the death of the German airborne arm, which he himself had created.

32   So, for example, by Uhle-Wettler, pp.230ff.

33   The content of this number had stated the following: Each attack requires unity of command. It must not split into solitary attacks. The main forces and the majority of the ammunition are to be used at the

which also applied for the use of parachute forces after landing, led to the dividing of the troops for the simultaneous seizure of two objectives at Heraklion and Rethymnon and the removal of almost one-third of the attacking force at Maleme from the direct influence of the task force commander. The disturbed order of arrival of *Kräftegruppen Bräuer* and *Sturm* over their objective areas and grave navigational mistakes during the last phase of the approach flight finally destroyed any chance of success for the operation plans, which were contrary to the regulations. The most appalling effect of the deficiencies and faults during the planning and execution of the initial parachute assaults, delineated before however, was the loss of between 1,200 and 1,400 soldiers of the parachute force on landing without any tactical achievement. These numbers alone constitute a marked difference to the overall losses of 1,133 men in the reinforced *5.Gebirgs-Division* – 321 killed, 324 missing (most of them at sea) and 488 wounded.

Student's decision to employ *Sturmgruppen Altmann* and *Genz* for the neutralization of enemy AAA positions outside the operational area of *Kräftegruppe Heidrich* proved to be rather pointless. As these groups had to come down in enemy-occupied terrain and, unlike *Sturmgruppen Braun* and *von Plessen*, were not backed up or relieved by paratroopers landing straight after them close by, they stood little chance of survival. Why these first-rate shock troops had not been used to initiate the assault against the heights at Galatas or to take out the AAA weapons around the airfield at Heraklion and thus fulfil the same role as *Sturmgruppen Braun* and *von Plessen* at the airfield at Maleme, remains a mystery which can only be seen in conjunction with Student's inappropriate 'oil drop tactics'. It cannot be completely excluded, however, that Student, with the employment of *Sturmgruppen Altmann* and *Genz*, had yielded to an explicit request from *VIII.Flieger-Korps*, which had been worried about the heavy anti-aircraft batteries around Souda Bay. The fact is that the use of 'oil drop tactics' in an area where almost nothing was known about the enemy and which led to the annihilation of *Kampfgruppe Mürbe*, was the fault of General Student.

General Student's decision to employ all *Fallschirmtruppe* that were still available in the area around Athens on 21 May, together with the *SturmRgt.*, for the seizure of the airfield at Maleme, was his only viable option in the light of his awareness of the general situation on Crete in the night 20/21 May. To rush all the paratroopers who had been left behind to Heraklion for the seizure of its airfield would have had little chances of success, as the division of the forces against two objectives and the disaster for the reinforced *II./ FschJgRgt.1* on 20 May had left *Kräftegruppe Bräuer* with but one parachute infantry battalion opposite the heavily-defended airfield.

However it was not Student's decision to place the main effort on Maleme which deserves to be accentuated, but rather the courage and the leadership qualities of subordinate commanders, particularly those of *Oberst* Ramcke and *Generalmajor* Conrad. The aggressive nature of the leaders and soldiers of the reinforced *SturmRgt.* were fundamental to the success of Student's decision. Despite heavy losses on 20 May the Regiment had wrested the western side of the airfield and the foot of Hill 107 from the enemy and had persistently continued to attack or to hold out in isolated positions. Nowhere on Crete

decisive point. If the decisive point cannot be detected beforehand, the main effort initially has to be generated into the unknown, to be changed later, if required. Adequate reserves must be available, if the main effort needs to be transferred or generated later.

was the determination of the men of the parachute force for independent action expressed stronger than during the fighting for Hill 107 and the airfield at Maleme. Nowhere was the superiority of the German command principle *"Führen mit Auftrag"* (mission-oriented command and control) over the command method of the defenders, which was based on the continuous communication of orders through the chain of command, more evident than at Maleme. Accustomed to hold fast on existing orders until the arrival of new ones, on 20 and 21 May the commanders of the 5th (NZ) Brigade between Maleme and Plataniason had waited to see whether their proposals for further actions would be transposed into orders by headquarters. Always one step behind actual events, neither Brigadier Puttick nor Major General Freyberg were able to act in time. The absence of a counterattack from all units of the 5th (NZ) Brigade in the early morning of 21 May, independent of its outcome, should be regarded as the decisive failure of the expeditionary force leaders in the battle for Crete, despite the gallantry of the troops.

Justification for the hesitant and insufficient reaction to the situation at Maleme from the commanders involved is comprehensible only so far as the entire length of the northern coast of Crete had to stay protected against German sea landings even after the situation at Maleme had become critical. During the preparation of the Germans for *Merkur* Middle East Command had been very well aware of the more than meager possibilities of the enemy to conduct a sea landing on Crete in the face of the presence of the British Mediterranean Fleet, all the more, as support by strong naval forces of the Italians could be discounted. The efforts of the command of *Admiral Süd-Ost* prior to the start of *Merkur* to put together sea transport forces from the few suitable Greek ships certainly had not escaped the Allied intelligence services. Admiral Cunningham could plan on the basis that the slow German sea transports would also have to sail in the hours of darkness. However during this time they could be attacked by his naval units without the threat of interference by the *Luftwaffe*. He directed his forces accordingly. Yet Freyberg had not totally relied on the capabilities of the British Mediterranean Fleet or had not been convinced of them in time.[34] As a consequence he ordered cover of the entire coastal strip between Maleme and the entrance into Souda Bay against sea landings. This order was strictly adhered to even after 20 May and after the attempt of a German seaborne-landing had already been repulsed. As is now understood, this attitude contributed to the failure of the last chance to turn the tables at Maleme. It should, however, not escape the reader's attention that Major General Freyberg's plans for defending Crete did include the British Mediterranean Fleet, as he had deployed no troops to the eastern area of the island as it was to be be protected by naval assets. It was here where Italian forces from Rhodes landed in considerable strength after they had skillfully utilized the protective umbrella of their own and German air forces.[35]

The active participation of Cretan civilians in the battle for Crete and the manner of their tactics, struck the German side completely unawares. Openly displayed passive resistance

---

34   On 3 May 1941 Churchill had informed the government of New Zealand that he thought a German seaborne attack against Crete unlikely to succeed. See Playfair, p. 126.

35   There had evidently been no coordination between the operations of the Italian sea-landing forces and the German commands on Crete, despite the fact that the latter had assumed the continuation of the defense of Crete by CREFORCE in the east of the island up to 29 May. The fault for it has to be credited to the command of *Luftflotte 4*, which had evidently left the necessary arrangements undone.

by parts of the population had been experienced in all previous campaigns and in rare cases in Norway and Holland they had even met with armed resistance by a few civilians. However in the light of the experiences on the Greek mainland even widespread passive resistance on Crete had been ruled out and the intelligence services had instructed the troops accordingly. In almost all of the contested areas on Crete civilians of every sex and age had taken to weapons of all kinds. This had been reason enough to plan their severe punishment. From the first day of the battle this had mostly been done by immediately shooting the non-combatants if they were caught armed. As it quickly became apparent that Cretan civilians had participated in the fighting in disregard of the rules of war yet they often could not be accounted for immediately, an appropriate response had to be found by the German command in order to maintain the morale of the affected troops and to deter the Cretans from the continuation of their actions. This response took the form of punitive measures. After Student, prior to his departure for Crete on 25 May and several times later, had received strict directives by Göring to exercise retaliation with the utmost rigor and disregarding any formalities[36] on 31 May he issued a directive which took into consideration Göring's demands, but also his own findings from the reports of the troops. In this he laid down as retaliatory measures shooting, levies, the burnings of settlements and the extermination of the male population of entire regions. As he had evidently been interested in preventing the retaliatory measures from becoming unconscionable, he reserved the permission for the two last named measures for himself and ordered that only older and therefore more mature officers be selected for this task.

Inspections and credible reports revealed that horrible mutilations had been committed on killed Germans and that defenseless soldiers were being murdered without mercy and in a cruel way by Cretan civilians.[37] Immediately after the capitulation of the remnants of CREFORCE investigations about the participation of armed Cretan civilians in the fighting and about their inhuman behavior against killed or wounded German soldiers commenced. In Alikianou and as expiation for the mutilated corpses of German soldiers which were found during the fighting, 38 able-bodied male Cretans were shot on 2 June and buildings were burnt down where the personal belongings of German and enemy soldiers had been found. *2./FschPiBtl.7*, to which most of the mutilated soldiers belonged, had taken part in this retaliatory act.[38] In Kondomari, a settlement in the drop zone of the reinforced *III./SturmRgt.* where many defenseless paratroopers had been murdered by Cretan non-combatants, 19 males had been shot in retaliation and dwellings been destroyed, likewise in Skines. The peak and also the end to the retaliatory measures was ordered by Student and occurred on 3 June in Kandanos and Floria. Both settlements were leveled to the ground and numerous inhabitants, who had not fled, were shot. It is verifiable that those officers who were tasked with the investigations had been willing to be just. One documented example in particular is a punishment action against Gournes where 11 injured soldiers and a medical orderly from *I./FschJgRgt.1* had been massacred by Cretan irregulars. The officer in charge, *Oberleutnant* Otto, who was an older and thoughtful man, had been

---

36   The roles of Göring and Student in the setting-up of retaliatory measures are described by the retired president of a superior provincial court, Dr. Franzki. Franzki had been tasked for many years with the jurisdiction of war crimes in the Second World War.

37   Later, Allied veterans from Crete also credibly reported about such events. Some of these reports can be found in Gavin.

38   See Austermann, p. 61.

detailed with a platoon from *2./FschJgRgt.1* for this action. During the interrogation of the inhabitants of Gournes he had gained the impression that these had been innocent of the crimes. He thereupon canceled the punitive action.[39] In this context it is noteworthy, that the number of Cretans shot dead during the retaliatory measures in early June 1941 did not exceed 200.[40] This number is less than that of the traceable cases of mutilated dead German soldiers during the fighting on Crete.

Yet resistance by the Cretans was not subdued, as from summer 1941 agents and commandos continued with local help to harass the Axis occupation forces.[41] Only from 1943 onwards, with the decline of German power in the Mediterranean, had action by partisans and gangs increased again on Crete – with the resultant punishments by the Germans – thus bringing this area of operations back into the focus of the Allies. After the war the Allies commenced prosecution of General Bruno Bräuer, who was handed over by the British to the Greeks because of his role in the commitment of German war crimes in his time as temporary commandant of *Festung Kreta*. In a trial, which was clearly more an act of revenge than a just investigation, Bräuer was found guilty and hanged.[42] Not forgotten by his fellow-soldiers, his remains were brought to the German war cemetery on Hill 107, where they now rest among the men who had been killed in the battle for Crete.

Hitler's decision to conquer Crete was made exclusively on the basis of his view about the importance of the island in conjunction with the impending campaign against the Soviet Union. Therefore the conquest of Malta, which at that time was more pressing and had been pursued by Jodl, the far-sighted chief of staff of the *Wehrmachtführungsamt*, found no place in his thinking. That the impulse for Operation *Merkur* had come from strategic the considerations of Göring, who was opposed to Hitler's plan for Russia, can be seen as a curiosity in the history of the Second World War.

For the British high command the retention of Crete as a base was unimportant. Gibraltar, Malta and Alexandria and to some degree also the coast of Syria, were the indispensable cornerstones for maintaining freedom of military action in the Mediterranean. Crete and Cyprus were seen primarily as connecting links in this strategic chain. After the loss of the Greek mainland, an intensive use of the port of Souda and of the efficient airfields in the north of Crete was estimated as impossible for the time being, in the light of the threat from the *Luftwaffe*. The British appreciation of the importance of Crete in the hands of the Axis powers was different. It was recognized that the air forces of the Axis, operating from Crete against the east-west sea and land lines of communications of the Commonwealth forces in the North African theatre of war, could significantly affect their most urgent task – the retention of Egypt, the Suez Canal and the oil fields of the Middle East. Alexandria, the vital anchorage and resupply installation for the Mediterranean Fleet, would also be well within the range of aircraft attacking from Crete and would receive only short warning times for its defense. Moreover a naval thrust against the sea lines of

39 The late *Major* (ret.), Mößinger, in his report about Heraklion, states he was a witness of this event.
40 This number was stated in 1963 after a year-long investigation by the office of the chief public prosecutor in Bochum, reference number 16/JS 30/57, dated 12 December 1963.
41 One of these was the commando raid against the airfield at Heraklion 8-11 June 1942, which resulted in the destruction of a number of Ju 87 dive bombers. See Cowles, pp. 179-183.
42 Franzki has described the violations of international law on Crete by the Germans as well as the proceedings against General Bräuer by a Greek court in an objective and professional manner.

communications of the Axis in the Aegean through the defile between Rhodes and Crete would become almost impossible after the loss of the latter. How ship movements in the eastern Mediterranean could be disturbed from Crete, became evident in the first half of 1942, when on 11 May 1942 three destroyers in the Bay of Sollum and between 12-15 June 1942 a cruiser, three destroyers and two transports in the convoy operation *Vigorous*, were sunk by air attacks launched from the island.[43]

From the very beginning of plans for a lasting retention of Crete it was recognized that a strong air force had to be made available for this task. Only by this precaution, was it deemed possible to protect the operations of the Mediterranean Fleet in the waters around Crete efficiently against air attacks and to challenge the *Luftwaffe* in the battle for the air space over Crete. However these conditions had not been met even at the time when the intelligence services had precisely reported the time and method of the German attack against Crete. Churchill, who explained his concept for the defense of Crete later in the war in the British House of Commons, clearly pointed out the effects of lacking adequate air support for the Mediterranean Fleet. Describing the foundation upon which the decision for the defence of Crete had been built, he stated that it was hoped to destroy the enemy who had landed on Crete with parachutes and gliders and to prevent him from utilizing the airfields and ports, with 25,000 to 30,000 good troops, including artillery and a number of tanks, and supported by Greek forces. He continued with the explanation that these actions were limited, as only a certain amount of losses of warships could be accepted before the surveillance of the sea region north of Crete had to be abandoned. If the ground forces on Crete were able to destroy the airborne invasion within the window of time for the presence of the Navy north of Crete, the enemy would have been forced to start his attack from scratch. Possibly, he may have been forced, at least temporarily, to give up the whole undertaking. In any case, much time would have passed prior to any new attempt.

The conquest of Crete after 13 days of fighting by the *Wehrmacht* demonstrates that this concept failed. Churchill's hopes for the destruction of the German parachute and glider forces did not come to pass. Freyberg's view – expressed to Churchill – was that he was not anxious about an attack solely conducted by airborne forces, but, without more artillery and transportation, considered an additional German seaborne-landing potentially dangerous.[44] Notwithstanding the question as to whether Major General Freyberg had grasped the fact that the British Mediterranean Fleet and their actions north of Crete had provided him with a window of opportunity within which he could have concentrated all of his forces between Maleme and Platanias for the night of 20/21 May for an all-out counter-attack against the reinforced *SturmRgt.* or whether he had listened too much to the pessimistic reports of Brigadiers Hargest and Puttick, the critical failure in delaying the planned counterattack on 21 May rests with him.[45]

---

43 See Gundelach, pp. 374-375.
44 See also Playfair, p. 126.
45 This critical fault is also reproached by British military historians of today, including Antony Beevor and Callum McDonald.

The decision to employ mountain troops in in *Merkur* in place of the *22.(LL)Inf.Div.* was the right one. Their combat experience and confidence after recent victories as well as their training for the terrain on Crete paid out from the very beginning of their appearance on the island. There is no doubt that the units of the mountain infantry, acting independently within the overall plans, took over the main burden of fighting in the western part of Crete soon after their arrival, and during the pursuit of the beaten enemy.

The employment of the aviation formations of the *Luftwaffe* was incontrovertible in its importance for the success of *Merkur*. Although air attacks in the preparatory phase caused few losses in personnel and almost none in material of enemy ground forces, they undermined Allied morale every day. The most efficient contribution of *VIII.Flieger-Korps* for the conquest of Crete, however, was that, it had worn out the British Mediterranean Fleet in several days of air-sea battles to such an extent, that it had to give up its blocking operations in the waters north of the island. Of value beyond all praise for the German troops on the ground was the close combat-support by fighter-bombers and dive bombers (once these had won a clear picture about friend and foe from the air). This had not always been easy to achieve, particularly as regards the *Fallschirmtruppe*, as clearly defined front lines were frequently non-existent, ground-to-air radio communications had still not been available and the enemy on several occasions had used captured communication equipment to its advantage.

The inability of *VIII.Flieger-Korps* – a fact which had already been observed in the end-phase of the campaign on the Greek mainland – to detect in time the start of the evacuation operation of the enemy, and the locations for the embarkation of his troops, was without great influence on the final victory on Crete. There had been some weighty reasons for this deficiency, such as the exhaustion of aircrews, restricted technical possibilities for reconnaissance and weapon employment during the hours of darkness and the shortage of bombs. Nevertheless, a last purposeful effort by *VIII.Flieger-Korps* seems to have been left out.[46] It would almost certainly have added to the overall enemy losses.[47]

The outstanding performance of the German air transport arm cannot remain unmentioned in any concluding reflections about *Merkur*. The war diary of *XI.Flieger-Korps* states the overall accomplishment of the air transport formations during the battle for Crete as follows:

- 23,484 soldiers, 353 guns, 711 motorcycles, 5,385 weapon and supply containers and almost 1,100 tons of supplies dropped or airlanded
- 3,173 German and enemy wounded flown out.

---

46   In his memoirs in Götzel, pp.332-333, Student even speaks of a failure by *General der Flieger* Freiherr von Richthofen.

47   Playfair, p.147, states the losses of the Commonwealth troops on Crete as 1,742 killed, 11,835 captured and 1,732 evacuated wounded. The additional losses of the Navy are stated as 1,838 killed and 183 wounded. The losses in material are stated as 3 cruisers and 6 destroyers sunk (the cruiser *York* in Souda Bay is not included), two battleships, one aircraft carrier, six cruisers and seven destroyers seriously damaged, as well as 23 fighters and bombers shot down in the airspace over Crete. The respective data in Davin differs only in the number of captured, which he gives as 12,254. He mentions additionally 260-300 soldiers of CREFORCE who perished at sea during the evacuation operations. Both authors state the losses in killed and wounded of the Greek troops on Crete as about 1,500. The war diary of the *XI.Flieger-Korps* mentions 177 officers and 5,078 other ranks of the Greek troops as captured.

The price paid for these achievements was more than 180 aircrew of the air transport formations killed, about 150 Ju 52s destroyed and another around 120 seriously damaged, corresponding with the losses in Holland the year before.

The performance of the German medical services on Crete was remarkable. In the German parachute force, this performance was achieved by the careful selection of the medical personnel in considerable strength, a generous staffing of the medical sub-units and units with medical officers, and with modern medical equipment and medicines. The companies of *FschSanAbt.7*, except the one for the field hospital, which had to be airlanded, were fully trained for parachuting. 3/FschSan Abt 7, which was dropped together with the *SturmRgt.* east of Maleme, and after its initial employment as combat troops, treated 531 German wounded, half of them during the first two days of the battle, 283 captured wounded enemy soldiers and 7 Italians. In the airborne hospital of *4./FschSanAbt.7*, which was landed on 23 May, 518 German wounded had been treated by 31 May. Most of these were flown out immediately after treatment.

Hitler had tasked Göring with overall command for *Merkur*, as he had seen the *Luftwaffe* as the principal service in the forthcoming battle. In his Directive No. 28, he had foreseen the reinforcement of the attack force by elements from *12.Armee* and requested the establishment of a sea line of communication, to be available ready for the initial phase of the attack. Therefore, procedures for the cooperation of all three services of the *Wehrmacht* had to be developed in the early phase of the planning process. Within the *Luftwaffe* the chain of command had been warranted by the subordination under *Luftflotte 4* of both *Flieger-Korps* which had been provided for *Merkur*. However, the majority of the ground organizations of *Luftflotte 4*, on which the *XI.Flieger-Korps* had to depend as it had almost no resources of this kind of its own, had already been drawn away to deploy for *Barbarossa*.

During the airborne attack against 'Fortress Holland' the air transport formations were subordinate to the *Luftflotte* in charge of the air operations. Upon the initiative of Student and his staff, who had found this command relation disadvantageous in their evaluation of the airborne operations in Holland, it had been changed, to the effect that the air transport formations would be placed under the command of the newly-created aviation commander of *XI.Flieger-Korps* shortly prior to their employment in *Merkur*. The possible problems of this solution, stemming from the remaining dependency of the air transport formations from superior *Luftwaffe* commands in the fields of command management and logistics, had obviously not been considered in depth. Some aspects allow for the supposition that the command of *Luftflotte 4* might well have been aware of the problems on hand for the *XI.Flieger-Korps*, but nevertheless had seen in the new regulations for the air transport formations a chance to commence the deployment for *Barbarossa* with the majority of its command-management and logistic assets, except those required for *VIII.Flieger-Korps*.

The assignment of the reinforced *5.Gebirgs-Division* as an air-landing force instead of the *22.(LL)Inf.Div.* had generated a new role for the *Heer* in the command organization for *Merkur*. As *Generaloberst* Löhr had not released Student and his battle HQ for transfer to

Crete on 21 May, the latter, in order to establish unity of command on the island, placed all troops already present there and those foreseen for transfer, under the command of *Generalmajor* Ringel.[48] The decision of *Generaloberst* Löhr prevented Student from assuming command of operations on Crete in person and appearing as force commander in the battle. It is highly probable that this had considerably reduced the latter's influence on Hitler and Göring immediately after Crete, and had contributed to the fact that the parachute force had not been engaged as a whole in tasks at the operational level in *Barbarossa*. After he was allowed to fly to Crete during the climax of the battle, the fact that Student had not assumed overall command of operations but had left them with *Generalmajor* Ringel, indicated good judgment.

The planning for the establishment of sea lines of communication reveals how unsatisfactory the willingness of the senior force commanders of *Merkur* must have been to jointly command and control the execution of Hitler's Directive No 28 or to propose ways for the best possible accomplishment of it under the existing conditions. Instead of combined and well-planned initiatives of this kind, sea transport squadrons of an *ad hoc* nature had been put together and set in motion at a time when efforts had not yet commenced to prevent the mighty British Mediterranean Fleet from operating in the waters north of Crete, at least during daytime. How insufficient the coordination between the commands of *Admiral Süd-Ost* and *XI.Flieger-Korps* was, was reflected in the continuation of the movement of *1.leichte Seetransportstaffel* during the night 21/22 May, with the area around the Bight of Kissamo still had not under German control and the situation in the extreme north-west of Crete unknown. As the risk of *1.leichte Seetransportstaffel* running into British naval units during the night was almost unavoidable, the attitude of *XI.Flieger-Korps* for the support of its movement was lax in the extreme.

Under the prevailing conditions Crete could be conquered only from the air. Contrary to previous campaigns of the *Wehrmacht*, in which parachute and air-landing forces had received specific missions in the overall plans, there was no alternative for Crete. The feats of the mountain troops and the combat formations of the *Luftwaffe* had played a decisive part in the outcome of the battle. Nevertheless, the operations could only successful through total dominance of air, land and sea. That this was not the case speaks highly of those troops, paratroopers and others who, after initial setbacks, fought to a successful conclusion, although at great cost.[49]

Hitler was indeed been convinced of the soldierly performance of the parachute forces, and in the weeks after Crete he decorated 24 of them, among them three non-commissioned officers, with the *Ritterkreuz*. However he had drawn a conclusion from the employment of the force on Crete, which signified the end of the further development of this arm in

---

48   See KTB Kreta der Führungsabteilung der *5.GebDiv*.

49   In June 1940 Churchill had requested the speedy build-up of an airborne force of at least 5,000 men. The realization of this request, however, had progressed slowly mainly because of the resistance by the R.A.F. Accelerated by the experiences from the battle for Crete, the first battalion of the British airborne force, to be designated The Parachute Regiment, was formed in September 1941, followed by the formation of a parachute and a glider brigade at the end of 1941.

the role which Student had foreseen for it. Nobody from the senior military commands attempted to counter Hitler and convince him of the foolishness of his perception. The man who probably would have been suited best for such an approach, the creator of the parachute force, had not received an opportunity for it, as he was ignored for an entire year by Hitler as well as by Göring. Generals of the *Luftwaffe* who had criticized Student for his faults in the planning and execution of *Merkur* and the training of the *Fallschirmtruppe*, however, had been able to gain the attention of Hitler and Göring.[50]

In the meantime, Student's force, despite the bitter losses, had returned from Crete unbroken in its spirit and attitude of mind and, in the light of its reputation, found no difficulty in closing the gaps in its ranks with volunteers. Mixed regimental *Kampfgruppen* participated in the bitter fighting in the East during the winter of 1941/42. It fought there as gallantly as always and maintained its reputation, although with no opportunity to develop the role Student envisaged for it.[51]

In the spring of 1942, when the opportunity offered itself to conquer the considerably ravaged island of Malta, the German parachute force stood ready for this task. However Hitler failed to recognize the strategic situation in the Mediterranean region and shifted the conquest of this island to a later date. As such, the parachute force, by default, received the role of crack infantry. Its men would eventually walk this route until the end of the war under the designation 'Green devils', given by their enemies in high esteem of their proficiency.

---

50   In his memoirs in Götzel, p. 337, Student mentions by name Generals von Richthofen and Korten.
51   Student, who had remained the commander and the inspector-general of the *Fallschirmtruppe*, continued to work on improvements energetically and with technical skill, such as radio devices for parachuting at night, the testing and introduction of giant gliders and the training of dispatchers. The benefits of these developments for airborne attacks, however, remained restricted to a few parachute operations at the tactical level.

General der Flieger Kurt Student.

Generalmajor Eugen Meindl.

Oberst Richard Heidrich.

Oberst Alfred Sturm.

Major Ludwig Heilmann.

Major Walter Koch.

Oberstabsarzt Dr. Heinrich Neumann.

Major Karl-Lothar Schulz.

Hauptmann Walter Gericke.

Hauptmann Gerhart Schirmer.

A group of *Fallschirmtruppe* shortly before boarding their flight to Crete. Despite the great heat, they had to wear the same uniforms as that used in Scandinavia and Holland, as tropical clothing had not arrived in time. Submachine-guns were carried on the jump. Not all are wearing life-jackets, and only one has knee protection. The jump smock pockets are filled with hand grenades.

The narrow coastal strip along the northern coast of Crete was intensively agricultural. Here one can see orchards between Maleme and Platanias. There were no easy areas for landing by parachute.

Maleme area – a view from the west, looking at the bridge across the River Tavronitis. A crashed glider from *Sturmgruppe Braun* lies nearby. The riverbed proved no obstacle to soldiers on foot.

The defenders of Crete had had sufficient time to prepare for an airborne assault and adopt counter-measures. This photo shows Hill 107, with its field of fire directed towards the airfield at Maleme.

The western part of the airfield at Maleme seen from the slope of Hill 107, to the south of it (a post-war image). The airfield could not be used as a drop zone or as a site for landing gliders by the *Sturm-Regiment* as it was heavily defended by infantry and anti-tank weapons positioned around its perimeter.

Maleme airfield after its capture. Those Ju 52s that had been destroyed or damaged during landing or by enemy fire were pushed to the edges of the airfield in order to keep it operational. Hill 107 lies in the background, to the right.

Oberstabsarzt Dr. Neumann, who had assumed command over the remnants
of I./SturmRgt. during the fighting at Hill 107 and Maleme airfield, leads
his men forwards along the coastal road west of the airfield. Small parties
of the enemy still occupied the area at the time this photo was taken.

A 3.7 cm anti-tank gun,
probably from *FschPzJgAbt.7,*
firing along the coastal road
east of Maleme. Due to
weight considerations, the
gun was frequently employed
without the protective shield.

The Maleme area – troops from the *Sturm-Regiment* on the slopes of Hill 107, observing in a westerly direction in expectation of enemy counter-attacks.

The drop-zone for parts of the reinforced *FschPiBtl.7* north of Alikianou. In the background, to the right, is the bridge across the River Jaroanos, which could not be crossed until 26 May. Soldiers from the Greek 8th Regiment engaged the *Fallschirmtruppe* as they landed from the slopes to the left.

A Ju 52 flying over Agia in a westerly direction. The aircraft are either returning from dropping elements of the reinforced *FschPiBtl.7* or are preparing to drop *Fallschirmtruppe* of *FschJgRgt.3* east of the prison. At the beginning of the assault Agia was held by troops from the Greek 8th Regiment. In the background are the northern slopes of the White Mountains.

Galatas area – a view from the area around the prison, looking towards the heights south of Galatas, one of the objectives of *FschJgRgt.3*. To the left is Hill 116. In the centre is the hill dubbed Pink Hill by the New Zealanders. The elevation on the right is Cemetery Hill, the village of Galatas lying immediately north of it.

Galatas area – a view from Cemetery Hill south of Galatas looking south-west into Prison Valley. The buildings of the prison can be seen to the left – *FschJgRgt.3* established its command post there, and *1./FschSanAbt.7* its main dressing station. In the background is Hill 259. (Courtesy of the Australian War Memorial collection databases)

Galatas area – the terrain along the Alikianou-Chania road, south of Daratsos. The hills in the centre ground were occupied by elements of *I./FschJgRgt.1*. (Courtesy of the Australian War Memorial collection databases)

Galatas area – Max Schmeling, world-famous boxing champion, was a Gefreiter with *FschJgRgt.3* and became injured during the landing. Here he can be seen being taken to the dressing station set up by *1./FschSanAbt.7*, located at Agia prison.

Galatas area – part of the village of Galatas seen from the north-east. Hill 116 lay behind it. Two battalions of *GebJgRgt.100* attacked the village from there, and from the area in the left-hand edge of the photo. (Courtesy of the Australian War Memorial collection databases)

Heraklion area – a view from the positions of the defenders east of
the airfield at Heraklion, looking into the Karteros depression, which
served as the drop-zone for *II./FschJgRgt.1* (less two companies).

Heraklion area – a view from Hill 296.5, looking north at the positions of the
Australian 2/4 Infantry Battalion, west of the twin hills, the 'Charlies'. The eastern
group of *II./FschJgRgt.1* was dropped on 20 May behind these hills, and cut up by
the defenders. (Courtesy of the Australian War Memorial collection databases)

Heraklion area – at the new command post of *FschJgRgt.1* shortly after the capture of the airfield. From left to right – *Oberleutnant* Zuber (probably detached from *FschJgRgt.2* to the HQ of *FschJgRgt.1*), Major Walther, an unknown *Oberfeldwebel*, *Hauptmann* Schirmer, *Oberst* Bräuer, *Oberleutnant* Graf von der Schulenberg (already in tropical clothing).

Heraklion area – *Major* Karl-Lothar Schulz, commander of *III./FschJgRgt.1* (back to camera, with scarf), negotiating the surrender of Heraklion with the mayor of the town, 21 May 1941. To the left of the mayor is *Oberleutnant* Kerfin, who had been awarded the *Ritterkreuz* for his actions during the capture and defence of the bridges at Rotterdam.

Rethymnon area – a view from Hill A looking east. The olive oil factory and village of Stavremnos were located where the coastal road on the left becomes invisible. The villages of Pangalokhori and Asteri are in the background, to the right. (Courtesy of the Australian War Memorial collection databases)

Rethymnon area – a view from the western part of Perivolia towards the hill which the *Fallschirmtruppe* christened 'Kapellenhöhe'. From 20 May 1941 until the arrival of relief troops, this hill was held by elements of *9./FschJgRgt.2*. The photo was taken a short time after the end of the war, and shows the serious damage caused to the village. (Courtesy of the Australian War Memorial collection databases)

Rethymnon area – soldiers from *FschJgRgt.2* pass a British Mark VI light tank abandoned by its crew. The hilly and densely-covered terrain generally favoured the defenders.

Rethymnon area – *Leutnant* Kühl, the last combat-effective officer belonging to those elements of *III./FschJgRgt.2* engaged at Perivolia, reports to Student.

Only the Ju 52 was used as a towing aircraft during the airborne assault
on Crete. Later on, He 111s were also used to tow gliders.

Recovering weapons from
an air-dropped container on
Crete. (Bundesarchiv, Bild 183-
L19105, photo: Grunewald)

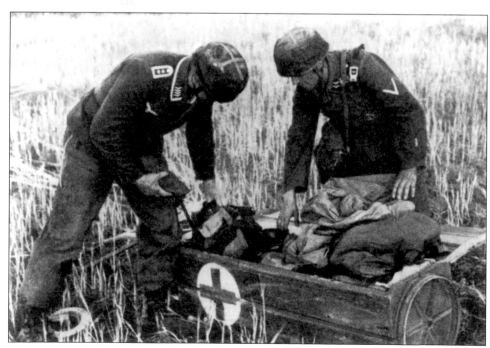

A *Fallschirmtruppe* radio team calling in shortly after landing. Wheels
have been attached to the container to facilitate landing.

Two parachute medical soldiers, an *Oberfeldwebel* and a *Gefreiter*, examine the
contents of a medical container. Neither yet wear Red Cross armbands.

A heavy machine-gun team. The tripod mounting allowed for an effective use of the MG 34 at up to 1,000m. Within its heavy weapons company, each parachute infantry battalion had two heavy machine-gun platoons, with a total of eight weapons.

A short pause in combat to take on water, *Fallschirmtruppe* on Crete. (Bundesarchiv, Bild 183-L19019, photo: Zeh)

Fallschirmtruppe moving through terrain typical of the area of operations on Crete. (Bundesarchiv, Bild 101I-166-0508-35, photo: Weixler)

The outflanking movements conducted by the *Gebirgsjäger* were, for the most part, made across difficult, dry and mountainous terrain devoid of trails. They were time-consuming, and demanded every ounce of energy from the heavily-laden troops.

Following his arrival on Crete on 25 May 1941, *General der Flieger* Student receives
a report from *Oberst* Ramcke, regarding the situation of the *Sturm Regiment*.

Fallschirmtruppe and *Gebirgsjäger* stand before the burial place of a
group of their comrades, Crete. (Bundesarchiv, Bild 141-0848)

Order of Battle of *Luftflotte 4* for Operation *Merkur*, Crete 1941

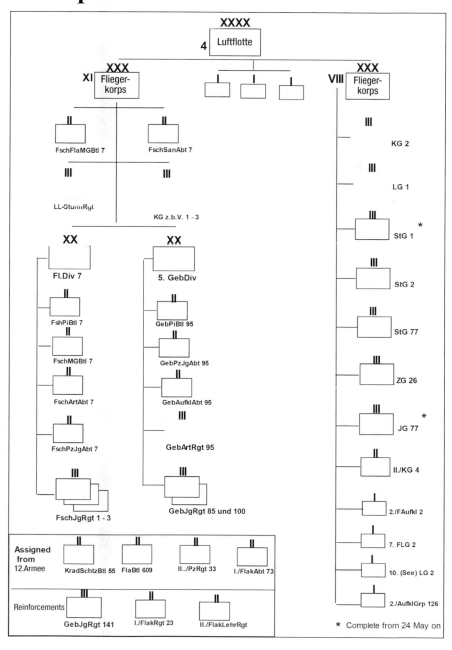

Bibliography

Original Sources at the Bundesarchiv, Freiburg (BA-MA)
Orders for Formation and Organization
Der Reichsminister der Luftfahrt und Oberbefehlshaber der Luftwaffe L.A. Nr. 5450/35
g. Kdos. L.A. II A vom 29. Oktober 1935
Der Reichsminister der Luftfahrt und Oberbefehlshaber der Luftwaffe L.A. Nr. 262/369
III, 1A vom 29. Januar 1936
Weisung des OKW Nr. 2676/38 g. Kdos. WFA/L v. 8.11.1938 Betr. "Luftlande- und
Fallschirmtruppe"
Der Reichsminister der Luftfahrt und Oberbefehlshaber der Luftwaffe
Generalquartiermeister, Generalstab 2. Abt, AZ. 11 b 12 Nr. 601/39 g. Kdos. (II A)
vom 7.3.1939

Directives and Orders for the Employment:
Operationsbefehl Nr. 1 der Gruppe XXI für die Besetzung Norwegens vom 5.3.1941
Operationsbefehl der Gruppe XXI für die Besetzung von Dänemark vom 20.3.1941
Operationsbefehl des X. FlgKorps für die Eröffnungsphase von *Weserübung*
Generalkommando X. Fl. K. I a. B. Nr. 100053/40 g. Kdos. vom 20.3.1940
Befehl zur Unterstellung des I./FschJgRgt.1 unter X. FlgKorps Der Oberbefehlshaber der
Luftwaffe Führungsstab I a Nr. 5681/40 g. Kdos. Vom 4.4.1940
Weisung OKW für den Kampf gegen die bei Åndalsnes gelandeten Kräfte des Gegners
OKW/WFA Nr. 88/40 g. K. vom 14.4.1940
Befehl für den Einsatz des LL-Korps im Fall "Festung" LL-Korps I a Nr. 2g. Kdos,
Chefsache vom 23.2.1940
Weisung des OKW für den Einsatz der Fallschirm- und Luftlandetruppen im
Westfeldzug vom 11. Januar 1940
Zuordnung der Lufttransportverbände Generalquartiermeister Genst. 4 Abt. (I) Nr.
595/41 g. Kdos. Vom 7.1.1941 Unternehmen *Merkur*
Befehl für das Heranführen der Fl.Div 7 und der Korpstruppen an die Flugplätze
Generalkommando d. XI. Fl. Korps Abt. I a Nr. 4000/41 geh. Vom 11.5.1941
Befehl für die Operation MERKUR, HQ XI. FlgKorps, OpAbt Nr. 47/41 g. Kdos., nur
für Kommandeure, vom 12.5. 1941
Lufttransportbefehl für Kreta XI. FlgKorps, OpAbt Nr. 5642/41, g. Kdos. Vom 15.5.
1941
Anweisung für die Vorbereitung des Unternehmens "Haifisch" ObdH/GenSt d H/
Op.Abt. II s/v/OQu 1 Nr. 718/41 g. Kdos. Chefs vom 24.4. 1941

War Diaries [KTB]
KTB Sturmabteilung Koch
KTB Gruppe XXI ("Weserübung") Bd. 1
KTB (Abschrift) der I./AufklRgt 9 für die Zeit 09.05.-15.05. 1940
KTB (Teile) des I./SchtzRgt 11 für den Einsatz in Holland

KTB Kreta des LL-Sturmregiments
KTB 1 Korinth und Kreta des FschJgRgt 2
KTB Kreta der Führungsabteilung der 5. GebDiv

After-Action Reports [Gefechtsberichte]

Gefechtsbericht des III./FschJgRgt.1 über das Gefecht am 14. und 15.9.1939 im Raum Suski Mlynek-Jasionna-Wtassyn-Branica-Stawinzyw
Gefechtsbericht des I./FschJgRgt 1 für den Einsatz bei *Weserübung*
Gefechtsbericht Einsatz Narvik der 1./FschJgRgt 1 (Abschrift, ohne Datum)
Gefechtsbericht Holland der 11./FschJgRgt.1 vom 16.5. 1940
Gefechtsbericht Holland des III. Zugs, 11./fschJgRgt 1 vom 18.5. 1940
Gefechtsbericht Holland der 2./FschJgRgt.1 vom 17.5. 1940
Gefechtsbericht Holland der 3./FschJgRgt.1, ohne Datum
Gefechtsbericht Holland des III. Zugs der 3./FschJgRgt 1, ohne Datum
Gefechtsbericht Holland der 4./FschJgRgt.1 vom 3.8. 1940
Gefechtsbericht Holland der 7./FschJgRgt.1 vom 19.5. 1940
Gefechtsbericht Holland des Gefechtsstabs des I./FschJgRgt 1 vom 18.5. 1940
Gefechtsbericht Holland des I./FschJgRgt.2 (ohne 3. Kp) vom 24.5.1940
Gefechtsbericht Holland des verst. InfRgt 16, Abt. I a, vom 26.5.1940
Gefechtsbericht Holland des I./FschJgRgt.1 vom 24.7. 1940
Bericht über den Einsatz von Panzern des Stabes I./PzRgt 33 gegen die Brücke südlich von Barendrecht niedergeschrieben 20.05 1940 durch Lt Grix
Gefechtsbericht Holland des I./InfRgt 72 vom 28.5. 1940 (Abschrift)
Einsatzbericht Narvik des I./FschJgRgt.1, erstellt Juni-Sept. 1940
Gefechtsbericht Korinth der Gruppe Sturm, Br. B. Nr. 97/41 g. Kdos. vom 5.5.1941
Gefechtsbericht Kreta des XI. FlgKorps (XI. Flieger-Korps Abt I a, Br. B. Nr. 2980/41 g. Kdos. Vom 11.6.1941)

Reports produced immediately after the end of the War

Aufbau der Fallschirmtruppe (BA-MA BW 57/164)
Bassenge, Wilhelm, Bericht über die Entstehung der deutschen Fallschirmtruppe (BA-MA ZA 3/69)
Einsätze der Fallschirm und Luftlandetruppe im Westfeldzug Teil I und II (BA-MA BW 57/311)
Einsatz des verst. InfRgt 16 bei Rotterdam (BA-MA BW 57/44)

Other materials from the Bundesarchiv

Käthler, Benno, Meine Erfahrungen als Leiter der Erprobung und Entwicklung bei der Deutschen Fallschirmtruppe (BA-MA ZA 3/69 13)
Bericht des Chefmeteorologen Dr. Brand über seine Erkenntnisse für die Sicherheit beim Fallschirmabsprung (BA-MA BW 57/26)
Erfahrungen aus dem Einsatz in Skandinavien
Fl.Div 7, I a Nr. 3144/40 geh. vom 23.4.1940 (BA-MA. BW 57/26)
Neumann, Heinrich, Entgegnung auf einen Bericht von GenStabsarzt a.D. Prof. Dr. Kittel über den Sanitätsdienst bei *Merkur*, BA-Ma BW 57/318

Grunau, Arthur, Bericht über den Einsatz der 12./FschJgRgt 2 bei *Merkur*, BA-MA BW 57/167

Verlustliste des FschJgRgt 3 für Kreta (BA-MA BW 57/111)

Vidua, Josef, Bericht von der Überführung zweier Panzer nach Kreta in *Kölner Stadtanzeiger*, Ausgaben 11-13.5. 1954, BA-MA BW 57/317

Other Primary Sources

Earl of Cork and Orrery's report to the British Admiralty regarding operations in North Norway from 17.7.1940 (published in *The London Gazette* 8.7.1947)

Feindnachrichtenblatt Kreta Nr. 3 und 4 des GenKdo XI. FlgKorps GenKdo XI. Flieger-Korps Abt I a, Br. B. Nr. 43/41 g. Kdos. Vom 17. und 18.5.1941

Franzki, Harald, Kreta 1941 bis 1945 – Partisanenkampf und deutsche Repressalien unter kriegsvölkerrechtlichen Aspekten, 2003 (manuscript)

Mössinger, Ernst , Die Geschichte des Luftbildes Iraklion Ost, Erinnerungen an den Kampf um Heraklion, mit zahlreichen Anlagen (in possession of the author)

Rehm, Martin, Die Gedenkstätte der 5. Gebirgsdivision in Floria/Kreta, 1990 (unpublished manuscript)

Simon, Ernst, Meine Kriegserlebnisse 1939-1945, written 1946/47, supplemented 1994

War diaries for Crete of Australian infantry battalions 2/1, 2/4, 2/7, 2/8 und 2/11 (from official Australian sources)

Books

Airborne Operations, A German Appraisal, CMH Publication 104-13 Washington D.C. 1989

Alman, Karl, *Sprung in die Hölle*, Rastatt 1965

Austermann, Heinz, *Von Eben Emael bis Edewechter Damm – Fallschirmjäger Fallschirmpioniere*, Holzminden 1971

Beekman, Frans S.A., *Sturmangriff aus der Luft : die erste Fallschirm- und Luftlandeoperation der Kriegsgeschichte in die Festung Holland*, Neckargemünd 1990

Bekker, Cajus, *The Luftwaffe War Diaries*, New York 1966

Boerger, Eberhard, *Erinnerungen eines alten Fallschirmjägers*, Rottach/Egern 2003

Böhmler, Rudolf, *Fallschirmjäger – Bildband und Chronik*, Bad Nauheim 1961

Boog, Horst, *Die Operationen der Luftwaffe gegen die Niederlande von 10. bis 15 Mai 1940*, Herford/Bonn 1993

Buchner, Alex, *Narvik: Die Kämpfe der Gruppe Dietl im Frühjahr 1940*, Neckargemünd 1958

Busch, Erich, *Die Fallschirmjäger-Chronik 1935-1945*, Friedberg 1983

Carell, Paul, *Verbrannte Erde*, Frankfurt-M./Berlin 1966

Cartier, Raymond, *Der Zweite Weltkrieg*, München 1967

Centre Liègois d'Histoire et d' Archeologie Militaire, *Construction du Fort d'Eben Emael*, Liège 2004

Churchill, Winston S., *Der zweite Weltkrieg*, Stuttgart 1954

Davin, Daniel M., *Official History of New Zealand in the Second World War 1939-45: Crete*, Wellington 1953

Derry, T. K., *United Kingdom Military Series, History of the Second World War, The Campaign in Norway*, London 1952

Edwards, Roger, *Deutsche Fallschirmjäger und Luftlandetruppen 1936-1945*, Hamburg 1976

Fest, Joachim C., *Hitler*, Stuttgart/Hamburg/München 1973

Frieser, Karl-Heinz (ed. MGFA), *Blitzkrieg-Legende, Der Westfeldzug 1940*, München 1995

Götzel, Hermann (ed.), *Generaloberst Kurt Student und seine Fallschirmjäger*, Friedberg 1980

Guhnfeldt, Cato, *Fornebu 9. April*, Oslo, 1990

Gundelach, Karl, "Der Kampf um Kreta 1941" in: *Entscheidungsschlachten des 2. Weltkriegs*, Frankfurt-M. 1960

Gundelach, Karl, *Die deutsche Luftwaffe im Mittelmeer 1940-1945* Band 1, Frankfurt-M. 1981

Halder, Franz, *Tägliche Aufzeichnungen des Chefs des Generalstabs des Heeres 1939-1942*, Stuttgart 1962-1964

Horne, Alistair, *Der Frankreichfeldzug 1940*, Wien/München/Zürich 1981

House, Jonathan M., *Towards Combined Arms Warfare*, Fort Leavenworth KS 1984

Hubatsch, Walther, *"Weserübung" Die deutsche Besetzung von Dänemark und Norwegen 1940*, Göttingen 1960 (2nd ed.)

Hubatsch, Walther, *Hitlers Weisungen für die Kriegführung 1939-1945*, Frankfurt-M. 1962

Irving, David, *Hitlers Krieg, Die Siege 1939-1942*, Herrsching 1988

Jacobsen, Hans-Adolf, *Der Fall Gelb. Der Kampf um die deutschen Operationspläne zur Westoffensive 1940*, Wiesbaden 1957

Kammann, Willi (eds. Werner Ewald & Arnold v. Roon), *Die Geschichte des Fallschirmjäger-Regiments 2 1939-1945*, Miesbach 1987

Kieser, Egbert, *Unternehmen Seelöwe, Die geplante Invasion in England 1940*, Esslingen/München 1987

Klee, Karl, *Das Unternehmen "Seelöwe"*, Band 4 b in the series *Studien und Dokumente Zur Geschichte des Zweiten Weltkriegs*, Göttingen 1954

Klitzing, G. (ed.Traditionsgemeinschaft Fsch.MG.Btl/Fsch.Gr.W.Btl1), *Geschichte des Fsch.MG.Btl und des Fsch.Gr.Werferbtl 1 1940-1945*, n.p., n.d.

Kühn, Volkmar, *Deutsche Fallschirmjäger im Zweiten Weltkrieg*, Stuttgart 1974

Kurowski, Franz, *Sprung in die Hölle Kreta*, Wölfersheim-Berstadt 2001

Kurowski. Franz, *Sturz in die Hölle*, München 1986

Liss, Ulrich, *Westfront 1939-1940, Erinnerungen des Feindbearbeiters im OKH*, Neckargemünd 1959

Long, Gavin, *Australia in the War of 1939-1945, Series One, Army, Volume II – Greece, Crete and Syria*, Canberra 1953

Manstein, Erich von, *Verlorene Siege*, Koblenz 1983

McClymont, W.G., *Official History of New Zealand in the Second World War 1939-45, Volume II – To Greece*, Wellington 1959

Mehner, Kurt, *Die geheimen Tagesberichte der deutschen Wehrmachtsführung im Zweiten Weltkrieg 1939 – 1945*, Band 2, Osnabrück

Melzer, Walther, *Albert-Kanal und Eben-Emael*, Heidelberg 1957

Merglen, Albert, *Geschichte und Zukunft der Luftlandetruppen*, Rombach 1977

Metzsch, F.-A., *Die Geschichte der 22. Infanterie-Division*, Kiel 1952

Meyer, Alfred, *Chronik der Fallschirm-Artillerie*, privately published 2002

Molenaar, F.J., *De Luchtverdediging Mei 1940*, Den Haag 1970

Morzik, Fritz (ed. Gerhard Hümmelchen), *Die deutschen Transportflieger im Zweiten Weltkrieg*, Frankfurt/M. 1966

Mühleisen, Hans Otto (ed. MGFA), *Kreta 1941*, Freiburg 1977

Nikunen, Heikki (GenLt), *Air Defence in Northern Europe*, Helsinki 1997

Ottmer, Hans Martin, *Weserübung*, München 1994

Plato, Detlef Anton von, *Die Geschichte der 5. Panzerdivision 1938-1945*, Regensburg 1978

Playfair, I.S.O., *The Second World War, Volume II The Mediterranean and Middle East*, London 1956

Richter, Heinz A., *Griechenland im Zweiten Weltkrieg*, Mannheim 1997

Ringel, Julius, *Hurra die Gams. Ein Gedenkbuch für die Soldaten der 5.Gebirgsdivision*, Graz /Stuttgart 1968

Rohwer, Jürgen with Gerhard Hümmelchen, *Chronik des Seekriegs 1939-1945*, Stuttgart 2000

Schaug, Georg (ed. Kameradschaft ehemaliger Transportflieger), *Geschichte einer Transportflieger-Gruppe im II. Weltkrieg*, Ronnenberg/Hannover 1989

Schenk, Peter, *Kampf um die Ägäis*, Hamburg 2000

Schenk, Peter, *Landung in England*, Berlin 1987

Schlicht, Adolf & Angolia, John, *Die deutsche Wehrmacht Band 1, Das Heer*, Stuttgart 1992

Schramm, Percy E. (ed.), *Kriegstagebuch des Oberkommandos der Wehrmacht*, München 1982

Schreiber, Gerhard, "Politik und Kriegführung 1941" in: *Das Deutsche Reich und der zweite Weltkrieg* Band 3, Stuttgart 1984

Simpkin, Richard, *Race to the Swift*, London 1986

Thompson, Leroy, *Unfullfilled Promise, The Soviet Airborne Forces 1928-1945*, Bennington VT 2012

Uhle-Wettler, Franz, *Höhe- und Wendepunkte Deutscher Militärgeschichte*, Hamburg/ Berlin/ Bonn 2000

Vogel, Detlef, "Die Eroberung Kretas" in: *Das Deutsche Reich und der Zweite Weltkrieg* Band 3, Stuttgart 1984

Winterstein, Ernst-Martin (ed.) (Suchdienstes des Bundes Deutscher Fallschirmjäger), *General Meindl und seine Fallschirmjäger*, Brunswick, n.d.

Ziemke, Earl F., *The German Northern Theater of War 1940*, Department of the Army Pamphlet 20-271, Washington D.C. 1959

Journal articles

DDF= *Der Deutsche Fallschirmjäger*; DGT= *Die Grünen Teufel*.

"Einsatz der FschPzJgAbt 7 in den Kämpfen der Gruppe West", DDF March/April 1986

"Gefechtsbericht Kreta FschJgRgt 3", excerpts, DDF May/June 1991

Baranck, Kurt, "Fallschirmjäger vom Ersten Regiment", DDF 4/1990

Börner, Hermann, "Fallschirm-Nebelwerfer auf Kreta", DDF May/June 1969

Brongers, H.E., "Het bombardement van Rotterdam – mei 1940", in *Armamentaria* 1989, Nr. 24

Dach, Hans v., "Der Luftlandeangriff auf Kreta", *Der Schweizer Soldat*, Sonderausgaben 8/71 und 11/71

Eiben, Wolfgang, "Als Arzt im Einsatz auf Kreta", DDF July/August 1965

Gericke, Walther, "Stoßtrupp übers Meer", DDF April 1953

Götzel, Hermann, "Wie es zur Luftlandung bei Korinth kam", DDF 4/1956

Götzel, Hermann, "Zur Geschichte unserer Panzerabwehr-Versuchskompanie 1939/40", DDF 2/1980

Heidrich, Richard, "Mein Soldatenleben", DGT November 1951

Horbach, J., "Schiffsstaffel Maleme", *Die Gebirgstruppe* Nr. 4/1978

Immans, F.-W., "Wie die Fallschirmtrupp Wirklichkeit wurde", DDF July 1954

Jacobsen, H.A., "Der deutsche Luftangriff auf Rotterdam", *Wehrwissenschaftliche Rundschau* VIII/1958

Kamphuis, P.H., "Der Kampf auf niederländischem Territorium im Mai 1940", *Österreichische Militär Zeitschrift* Heft 3/1990

Käther, Benno, "Vom RZ 1 zum RZ 36", DDF July 1954

Meier, W. "Gefechtsbereit nach dem Absprung" (aus dem Gefechtsbericht der Stabskompanie des SturmRgt), DDF May/June 1969

Melchior, Bruno, "Oslo-Einsatz 1940", DDF July/August 1997

Meyer-Wehner, Elimar, "Das Geheimnis von Eben-Emael", DGT November 1951 & January 1952

Mündel, "Der "Igel" von Rethymnon" (Einsatz 2./FschArtAbt 7), DDF April/May 1971

Nollen, Willi, "Der erste Sprung des Generals Meindl", DDF 9/1956

Renisch, Paul-Ernst, "Fallschirmjäger vom Ersten Regiment", DDF 2/1990

Roth, Günter, "Das Unternehmen *Merkur*", supplement to DDF 4/2001

Student, Kurt, "Angriff ohne Kenntnis der Lage, Grundsätzliche Betrachtungen zu Kreta", DDF May/June 1969

Student, Kurt, "So sahen wir die Kreter", DDF 1952

Thote, Werner, "Die Funkverbindung in der Luftlandung auf Kreta", DDF January/February 1996

Vanwelkenhuyzen, Jean, "Die Niederlande und der "Alarm" im Januar 1940", *Vierteljahreshefte für Zeitgeschichte*, 8. Jahrgang 1960, 1. Heft

Witzig, Rudolf, "Die Einnahme von Eben Emael", *Pioniere* Heft 2/1965

Miscellaneous materials including information from the internet

Berberich, Florian, Ausarbeitung eines Vortrags über den Kampf um Fort Eben-Emael vom September 1976

Goossens, Allert M.A., Zuidfront Holland mei 1940 (www.zuidfront-holland1940.nl/)

Goossens, Allert M.A., War over Holland (www.waroverholland.nl/)

Hummel, B., Vliegfeld Ockenburg (www.bhummel.dds.nl/gif/ockenburg.html)

Laursen, Gert, The German Occupation of Denmark, 1997-2005 (www.milhist.dk)

Jervaas, Bjoern, Norway in World War 2 (www.nuav.net)

Mehtidis, Alexis, Greek Ground Forces in Crete and their Small Arms November 1940-May 1941 (http://orbat.com/site/history/open4/GreekGroundForcesinCreteandTheirSmallArmsrev.pdf)

Peeters, Rogier, Royal Dutch Army Order of Battle May 10th 1940 (http://nubo.home.xs4all.nl/Rogier/)

Quast, Franz, Fliegerhorst Uetersen 1932-55 (www.luftfahrtspuren.de/uet.htm)

Simpson, H.W., Report upon operations carried out by force "Primrose" commanded by a Lieutenant Colonel H W Simpson, Royal Marines, during the period 13th to 30th April, 1940 (www. hmshood.org.uk/reference/official/adm202/adm202-422.htm)

Suntrop, Heribert & Müller, Werner, Geschichte der Kölner Luftfahrt, Teil: Der Angriff auf das belgische Fort Eben-Emael (http://www.koelner-luftfahrt.de/)

Vermeer, Wilco, Luchtlandingen in de Vestung Holland (www.go2war2.nl/artikel/818/Luchtlandingen-in-de-Vesting-Holland.htm)

Index

Index of People

N.B. – German ranks shown are highest achieved within the period covered by this book; Allied ranks shown are those contemporaneous with the events described.

Index of Belgian Military Units

Index of British & Commonwealth Military Units

Units are British unless noted otherwise.

Index of Dutch Military Units

Index of French Military Units

Index of German Military Units

Index of Greek Military Units

Related titles published by Helion & Company

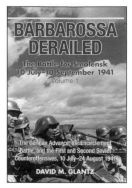

Demolishing the Myth. The Tank
Battle at Prokhorovka, Kursk, July
1943: An Operational Narrative
Valeriy Zamulin (edited &
translated by Stuart Britton)
672 pages   Hardback
ISBN 978-1-906033-89-7

Barbarossa Derailed: The Battle for Smolensk
10 July-10 September 1941 Volume 1: The
German Advance, The Encirclement Battle,
and the First and Second Soviet
Counteroffensives, 10 July-24 August 1941
David M. Glantz
624 pages   Hardback
ISBN 978-1-906033-72-9

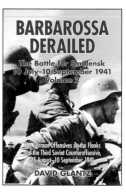

Barbarossa Derailed: The Battle for Smolensk 10
July-10 September 1941 Volume 2: The German
Offensives on the Flanks and the Third Soviet
Counteroffensive, 25 August-10 September 1941
David M. Glantz
624 pages   Hardback
ISBN 978-1-906033-90-3

Waffen-SS Armour in Normandy. The
Combat History of SS Panzer Regiment 12
and SS Panzerjäger Abteilung 12, Normandy
1944, based on their original war diaries
Norbert Számvéber
304 pages   Hardback
ISBN 978-1-907677-24-3

HELION & COMPANY
26 Willow Road, Solihull, West Midlands B91 1UE, England
Telephone 0121 705 3393   Fax 0121 711 4075
Website: http://www.helion.co.uk